The British Motorcycle Directory

The British Motorcycle Directory

Roy Bacon and Ken Hallworth

The Crowood Press

First published in 2004 by
The Crowood Press Ltd
Ramsbury, Marlborough
Wiltshire SN8 2HR

www.crowood.com

© Roy Bacon and Ken Hallworth 2004

All rights reserved. No part of this publication may be reproduced or transmitted in any form or by any means, electronic or mechanical, including photocopy, recording, or any information storage and retrieval system, without permission in writing from the publishers.

The information in this book is true and complete to the best of our knowledge. All information is given without any guarantee on the part of the authors or Publisher, who also disclaim any liability incurred in connection with the use of this data or specific details.

British Library Cataloguing-in-Publication Data
A catalogue record for this book is available from the British Library.

ISBN 1 86126 674 X

We recognize that some words, model names and designations, for example, mentioned herein are the property of the trademark holder. We use them for identification purposes only. This is not an official publication.

Typeset by Jean Cussons Typesetting, Diss, Norfolk

Printed and bound in Great Britain by CPI Bath

E&OE
This expression, which stands for Errors & Omissions Excepted, is a stock commercial term and has to apply to these pages. The authors may have researched diligently to uncover the most obscure British makes for this work, but know for sure that there will always be more. They hope not too many, but they will be there. In addition, there are obscure references to further makes but with no real evidence to support them.

Readers are encouraged to send any new material, either for fresh marques or to add to that we already have, to further the knowledge for all of us. Where possible, this will be added to any future reprint and we plan to leave a little room in the text for this purpose. More for the letter A than Z of course, while this note will remain in use for any further findings. No-one can ever say that a list such as this is complete for there is always something else out there.

ACKNOWLEDGEMENTS
Many people helped us with this book, not always while it was being prepared, but by conversations from the past. Material and details came from many sources, some of which would check out and others not, thus needing further investigation. In particular, Mike Worthington-Williams aided from his depth of knowledge of the obscure and unusual, which appear so often in his writings.

Every effort has been made to trace the ownership of all copyrighted material and to secure permission from copyright holders. In the event of any question arising as to the use of any material, we will be pleased to make necessary corrections in future printings.

Abbreviations that may be found in the text:
aiv – automatic inlet valve
cc – cubic centimetres
dohc – twin overhead camshaft
eoi – exhaust over inlet
ioe – inlet over exhaust
moiv – mechanically operated inlet valve
ohc – overhead camshaft
ohv – overhead valve
sv – side valve

British Motorcycle History

The British motorcycle industry was a late starter due to the restrictive legislation that kept its pioneers shackled. However, after the changes, such as they were, that came in 1896, they were able to benefit from the early work in Europe that had already investigated and discarded blind avenues such as steam or electric power.

At the close of the Victorian era there was no shortage of skilled cycle-makers in Britain and many looked to France or Belgium for an engine, or its parts, to import and bolt to their existing cycle. For the small cycle-dealer it was a good way of expanding their business by adding a more expensive line that required a good deal of service to keep it healthy. While small firms flourished, the larger held back, unsure of the long-term picture and wary of a downturn in trade that occurred around 1905. Some confidence returned, thanks to the appearance of more reliable models, the advent of the TT races in 1907 and the opening of Brooklands track to motorcycles in the following year.

For all that, the late-Edwardian machine lagged in its transmission as belt-drive remained prevalent and the means to vary the gearing while the machine was in motion was limited. Brakes were still minimal and engines, whether singles or V-twins, ran far too hot if called on for serious work. The move to the Mountain circuit for the 1911 TT emphasized the need for the countershaft gearbox and all-chain drive, but their implementation was delayed by the Great War. What that conflict did do was to force the pace of development of materials and lubrication to overcome the old technical problems while allowing a sharp increase in power output.

The 1920s seemed to be a golden era for the industry, with a frenetic order-book at the start when demand far outstripped supply and prices rocketed for a brief while. Many small producers entered the business, mostly assemblers who bought components from the factories around the Midlands, put these together and added a transfer. Prices differed little with most using much the same parts and by 1920 the boom was followed by a period of recession when prices dropped, and by 1925 many of these firms had either collapsed or turned to other products. During this time there came a wave of scooters, but most were too crude to succeed and their time was not to come for another three decades.

In the competition field Britain was dominant, winning every TT race in the decade, although there were a couple of close calls along the way. It was much the same in Europe at the major races, especially in the 350 and 500cc classes, and off-road in the ISDT where Britain took the coveted Trophy for each year from 1924 to 1929.

Steady technical progress was made through the 1920s with overhead valves becoming more common, followed by some engines with overhead camshafts. Total-loss lubrication was replaced by the recirculating dry-sump system with its separate oil tank

The Stockport Motor Cycle Club lined up in 1913, prior to a run out or some other form of social gathering – with families, so lots of sidecars present, as few could afford cars in those times.

and pump, while electric lighting took over from acetylene. Belt drive finally went, replaced by all-chain that was sometimes fully enclosed, but shaft drive remained rare. In most cases the gearbox was a separate assembly with hand change, but Velocette introduced the positive-stop foot-change in 1928 and this gradually became standard practice during the 1930s, although the hand type persisted for many years for lightweights. Unit construction was used, but mainly with the gearbox bolted to the back of the crankcase rather than having both assemblies within one pair of castings. Few machines had rear suspension at that time, while girder forks were the norm at the front.

A major change in style came towards the end of the decade when the saddle tank made its appearance. It marked the end of the flat-tank era and what became known as the 'First Golden Age of Motorcycling', reflecting a time when motorcycles had out-numbered cars on British roads. There was also a move to incline the engine in the frame, with the BSA Sloper of 1927 an early example, but it was not a style to last.

Then came the Depression, at a time when cheap cars were eating into motorcycle sales. Prices were cut and specifications tailored to allow the customer to choose the base machine and as many options as could be added under their personal

A view of the sidecar section of a dealer with solos as well, all crammed in to what is a limited space for the amount of stock being carried.

price limit. Despite this, there were two machines having four-cylinder, overhead camshaft engines at the 1930 Olympia show, but close by were some really cut-price lightweights at the other end of the scale.

Times and trade were hard and many firms failed, turned to other products, or amalgamated during the 1930s. However, British machines continued to do well in the major road races in Europe and at the TT, mainly thanks to Norton. Less so perhaps in the smaller classes, and by the close of the decade the German and Italian machines were ahead, both on the circuits and in the record tables.

As the decade progressed, a degree of prosperity returned and this was reflected in brighter finishes with more colour and chrome. Specifications altered little each year, although four speeds and foot-change became usual for larger models and the general style rounded out. Better brakes and improved electrics arrived, along with some fashions that came and went. Among these was the inclined engine and partial enclosure, neither of which had much lasting impact.

Sidecars continued in use, albeit in much smaller numbers than in the heyday of the mid-1920s due to the influx of small, cheap cars. Most were pulled along by side-valve engines, either singles or V-twins, with the

occasional ohv twin for those with a purse to suit.

The twin that would have the greatest and longest impact on the industry came late in 1937 when Edward Turner designed his famous Triumph Speed Twin. Smooth, fast, easy on the ear and light on the pocket, it set a format most other firms would have to follow.

Before that could happen there came the Second World War and again the call to arms. Some far-sighted firms had already badgered contracts from the government to produce tough machines for the services based on existing models but, at first, civilian and maker's stocks were commandeered for this use. This brought problems, so soon the major firms were hard at work, mainly building side-valve singles, a few with ohv and some small two-strokes.

Post-war, there was a massive demand for transport at home and a great need for exports to pay off the national debt. With most production going abroad, the home market had to settle for war surplus machines, hurriedly resprayed to hide the khaki. With the accent on numbers, there was little in the way of fresh design, so most models were really as they were in 1939 with the addition of telescopic front forks. Innovation did come from a handful of firms but their production was usually limited.

Early rally starting out from Rex Judd Motorcycles, a long-time dealer; the machines are from the era between the wars, the clothing ex-service for many riders.

The clip-on made its brief appearance, going back to the earliest of roots by adding an engine to a standard bicycle. Simple, sometimes crude, but adequate for short distances at that time, and above all economical in operation. More vertical twins appeared, all following the Triumph lead, and there were more new firms in the place of some of the many that had left the industry in 1939 or moved on to other war work, not to return. Most of the new began by installing a Villiers engine in simple cycle parts, some short lived but others to prosper for two decades or more.

On the road racing scene the British led the 350 and 500cc fields, but the Italians dominated the 250cc class, and the 125cc too when that emerged. Later, the well-developed big singles and twins from AJS, Norton and Velocette became outpaced by Gilera, Mondial and MV Agusta, while NSU had two good years and BMW took over the sidecar class for two decades.

Off-road, the British teams had several more years of success in the ISDT before the smaller European models began to outclass the large-capacity machines. The same trend was slower to affect trials and scrambles, so the big British four-strokes continued to succeed well into the 1950s.

That decade brought a scooter revival from Italy, led by Lambretta and Vespa, but few British firms made any real effort to compete in this class. They concentrated on their four-stroke singles and twins, the latter increasing in capacity to meet the demands from the USA for more 'cubes' and power. The lightweight end of the market became the province of many Villiers-powered models, plus the BSA Bantam and Royal Enfield RE, both copies of pre-war DKW designs.

Innovation came from Vincent with their fabulous V-twin, Sunbeam with their S7 and S8 in-line twins, Velocette with the super-quiet LE, and Ariel with the fully-enclosed Leader. Elsewhere progress was slow, with detail changes and new colours often the only revision from one year to the next. Rear suspension gradually became common and the late-1950s saw a move to some rear enclosure. Triumph led the way in this with their stylish 'bathtub' but few others could afford the good tooling needed for this. The result was often an attempt that was crude and bore a resemblance to a back-yard job.

Partial enclosure was a halfway step to the scooter, but the trend reversed in the 1960s to the stripped down café-racer style. One outcome was the bad publicity of the mods and

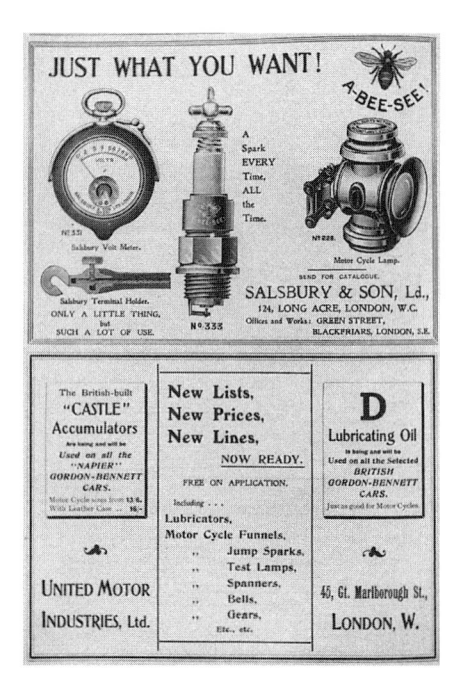

Spares, accessories, batteries, oil, plugs – there is no end to the list of items a dealer could sell to riders, the same now as here a century ago.

rockers groups, much hyped in the national press of the day and giving motor cycling the bad boy image in the public mind.

The last year of the 1950s proved to be the best ever for the sales of powered two-wheelers in Britain and the decade a second golden one. However, some of the gold was a little tarnished, for many sales were of imported scooters and mopeds and this was only the start of an invasion from Japan. Aimed at first at the bulk market for small machines, it soon took much of this over while British firms concentrated on big twins, mostly exported to the USA. Small-capacity British models continued to fit the now dated Villiers two-stroke engines, with their need to mix petrol with oil, while the new Japanese imports had oil-pump systems and a much improved performance. Inevitably, the British firms lost sales and gradually dropped from the market.

The Japanese moved on to offer larger models of considerable sophistication while the major British firms fell into disarray. One by one they went down, victims of market forces

Starting point for a North London club trial being held in the late-1940s period, when petrol rationing kept such events short and close by.

Nice line of flat-tank Norton singles lined up for a presentation day at Thruxton, with the AJS logo present to show the group affiliation.

and lack of investment and forward planning when times had been good. Tiny firms making specialist models survived and flourished by building what their customers wanted. In many cases they were run by men who rode their own product successfully and thus earned their orders.

The 1970s were the low years for the industry despite the boom caused by the explosion in fuel prices. This did little to create demand for large twins but brought a major one for mopeds, scooterettes and small machines for commuting and local runs. Most of this boom was filled by Japanese firms plus some from Europe. When that market faded, it was followed by another that did help the home industry, for it was for classic bikes, not new machines but those from the past. British makes led this wave of leisure activity and from it came a whole industry of small firms devoted to a new breed of customer.

In 1990 the remains of the once-great British industry was rejoined by the Triumph name, revived by industrialist, John Bloor. He created a new factory and a new range in the modern style to compete with the best in the world. He showed that Britain could still mass-produce a motorcycle while the rest of the industry continued to offer its specialist, well-made machines for the discerning. Classic bikes ran alongside this activity, playing their part in forming a coherent industry for the new century.

◆ A ◆

A&A AUTOCARRIER 1906–1907
This machine was seen at the late-1906 Stanley show and was a typical primitive of that era. As with so many, it came and then went just as quickly, the show model possibly the only one made.

ABBOTTSFORD 1920
This is best described as a three-wheeled scooter with 16in wire-wheels and a bicycle saddle supported on open framework with fuel tank beneath. It was built by the Abbottsford Motor Company of Kingston in Surrey with a 312cc two-stroke engine driving the rear axle through a clutch but with only a single speed. It was without wheel suspension, but had a useful carrier platform behind the saddle making it suitable for shopping trips and the like. It was said to be the only such three-wheeled device on the British market and was later given the name Abbottsford Supa Scooter; but it was quickly gone from public view.

ABC 1912–1923
The All British (Engine) Co. was based close to Brooklands at Weybridge, Surrey, where they built aero engines and in 1912 had their first involvement with motorcycles. Their designer was Granville Bradshaw, whose name was to become associated with many other projects over the years, and he was persuaded to produce some special parts for Les Bailey to fit to his 350cc Douglas. The parts included cylinders, ohv gear, pistons and connecting rods, the result running at Brooklands late in the year to set a new kilometre record for the class at over 72mph (116km/h).

At the same time ABC announced a new 494cc flat-twin ohv engine to be mounted in line with the frame and having the cylinders exactly in line. To achieve this, one piston had the usual connecting rod but the other had two that spanned the first. There was an outside flywheel and gear drive to the camshaft and magneto, while ball-and-roller bearings were used for both crankshaft and camshaft.

A few ABC machines were built for 1913 and two started in the Senior TT, both to retire. Early in 1914 Jack Emerson set new 500cc records at Brooklands using an ABC and shortly afterwards a two-model range was introduced. In both cases the flat-twin engine was used, but the TT version had ohv and the Touring an overhead exhaust and side inlet. Transmission was all-chain with a three-speed Armstrong gearbox, which was actually their hub gear normally fitted to the rear wheel but used by ABC as a countershaft box. The frame was conventional but both wheels were sprung using laminated leaf springs, a feature that Bradshaw would use elsewhere in later years.

The firm moved to Hersham, Walton-on-Thames, Surrey, where war work included engines for the services and a few motorcycles. For 1915 and 1916 these had an ABC four-speed gearbox with gate change and kept the spring frame.

In 1919 what became the definitive ABC appeared, built by Sopwith Aviation at Kingston-on-Thames, Surrey. Again designed by Bradshaw, it had a 398cc flat-twin engine set transversely across the frame and built in-unit with the four-speed gate-change gearbox. The engine had ohv, bevel gears turned the drive for the chain to the rear wheel and leaf springs continued to provide both front and rear suspension. It was a revolutionary design and orders poured in, but production problems delayed its appearance on the market, the valve gear gave trouble and it proved an expensive machine to make. By 1921 Sopwith were in liquidation

Famous ABC flat-twin engine, as first seen pre-Great War with 494cc ohv engine designed by Granville Bradshaw.

Post-war ABC flat-twin machine, as for 1920, with its unit construction and leaf-spring suspension utilized front and rear.

after making some 3,000 machines and the end for ABC in England came in 1923.

The design was also built under licence by the French firm Gnome & Rhone in the early 1920s. They listed a 494cc version as well as the 398cc, with an improved engine, and continued with them to 1925.

ABC C.1920–1924
This was a Birmingham make that had no link to the Bradshaw ABC, but was a simple lightweight powered by a 269cc Villiers engine, later replaced by the 247cc unit. The machine was of basic form with belt drive.

ABC SKOOTAMOTA 1919–1923
One of several scooters that appeared just after the Great War, the Skootamota was designed by Granville

Bradshaw and was one of the best of its time. It had a simple tubular frame with no suspension and 16in wire-wheels with external-contracting band brakes for each. The engine sat above the rear wheel and was derived from a wartime flat-twin that was reduced to a 124cc single with the cylinder pointing aft and the magneto clamped to the front of the crankcase in place of the forward cylinder. At first it had an eoi valve layout but late in 1920 this was changed to ohv, while transmission was by chain to the rear wheel. The fuel tank sat over the engine and a saddle was fixed to a pillar at the front of the engine so the rider was not forced to stand while in motion. Introduced by the ABC firm, it was later built and marketed by Gilbert Campling of Albermarle Street, Piccadilly, London.

ABERDALE 1947–1949
This firm was based in Edmonton, London, but their autocycle was made at the Bown factory in Tonypandy in Wales. The machine was typical of the type with a 98cc Villiers Junior de Luxe engine hung from its simple tubular frame. Petroil lubrication, direct lighting and blade girders were used, there was a carrier over the rear wheel and side panels extended down from the fuel tank to conceal the engine. It was built in this form up to 1949, after which it was revised and sold as the Bown.

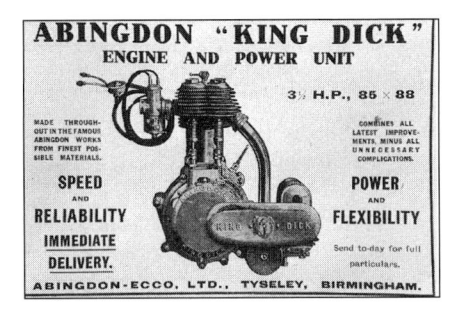

Abingdon became much better known for their engines and tools, hence the change of name, as here, and later to AKD.

ABINGDON 1905–1925
The Abingdon engineering firm was established in 1856 in King's Road, Tyseley, Birmingham, and became famous for their large range of tools sold under the 'King Dick' name. When they entered the motorcycle market in 1905, they used this name to promote their product and traded as Abingdon-Ecco up to the Great War. They listed machines that ranged from 2 to 3.5hp and were typical of the period, with solos and tricycles available, the latter with reduction gear and differential built into its rear axle.

From around 1907 they built the Kerry-Abingdon for that company, who bought and sold rather than manufactured, and, by 1910, they had a neat 3.5hp single, later joined by a 6hp V-twin. Both kept to belt drive and fitted a three-speed rear hub, the engines made by the firm itself, later to be supplied to other firms.

After the Great War they continued with the same two models, which were joined by a 4.25hp single in 1922 for the one year only. By then most had three speeds, but one single still retained direct-belt drive, while chain-cum-belt or all-chain was still listed.

By 1924 the range was down to two singles and a twin, one single still with belt final-drive, and this continued for their final year in 1925, as Abingdon King Dick. From then on they were known by their initials as AKD and continued as such to 1932.

The Aberdale firm was London based, but their autocycle was made by Bown in Wales and was soon replaced by that make.

ABJ 1949–1953
This was the firm that had built the pre-war Raynal autocycle and in 1949 was located in Pope Street, Birmingham. The new name came from the chairman, A.B. Jackson, and for 1950 they offered two machines, both using a 99cc Villiers engine. One was the Autocycle with the single-speed 2F unit, the other the Motor-cycle with the two-speed 1F. They shared common cycle parts with a rigid loop frame, simple telescopic forks and a single saddle on a pillar tube.

Both models were listed up to 1952 and in July that year were joined by the Auto Minor cyclemotor. This had a 50cc two-stroke engine mounted over the front wheel, which it drove by friction, the rest of the machine being pure bicycle. It alone ran on for 1953 but was then dropped.

ABJ contrived to offer two 99cc models from one set of cycle parts, by a simple change from one to two speeds in the Villiers engine.

ABJ took a look at the cyclemotor market in 1952 with this Auto Minor model, with 50cc engine driving the front wheel by friction.

ACCLES 1896
A tricycle built for Lawson's British Motor Syndicate, copied from the De Dion but having the engine ahead of the rear axle, which it drove by gears. The revised layout gave the machine

Built by one of Lawson's firms, this Accles tricycle with de Dion-type engine appeared in 1896.

better weight distribution; it utilized an open frame and so could be ridden by either sex.

ACKLAND c.1919–1924
One of the many that went into motorcycle production after the Great War, William Ackland adopted V-twin JAP engines rather than the more usual Villiers. He built a few machines using similar components to many other manufacturers.

ACME 1902–1922
Located in Coventry, Acme began by producing machines fitted with Minerva 2hp engines and then added the 2.75hp Auto-motor and 3hp Acme models they built themselves. For trailer use a 4.5hp Auto-motor engine was listed and by 1904 they were making the Auto engines themselves.

Two Acme twins ran in the 1908 TT but both retired, this being their sole Island appearance. No more was heard of them until after the Great War when they returned to the market in 1920 with a single 8hp model powered by a 976cc V-twin engine. This had chain drive to a three-speed gearbox and belt final-drive. For 1921 the twin was joined by a 2.75hp single of 292cc which had two speeds and chain-and-belt drive.

Both these machines bore a strong resemblance to the products of the nearby Rex factory in Earlsdon, Coventry, so it was little surprise to find that the two names had amalgamated prior to the Olympia show in December 1921, where the new name of Rex-Acme graced a more comprehensive range of models that was to continue through into the thirties.

ADDISON 1904–1905
A Liverpool firm that built forecars using 3.25hp engines having air or water cooling. They had chain drive and a clutch but only a single speed, this being rectified for 1905 when the engine was a 3.5hp Fafnir driving a two-speed gear. A 3hp solo appeared for 1905, again using a Fafnir engine but with belt drive.

ADVANCE 1902–1909
This Northampton firm was well known as a maker of adjustable belt pulleys before they moved on to complete machines. A few were built as early as 1902 but it was the late-1906 show before the name became reported. They then showed that they had a lower frame-line than most, but were otherwise typical of the period, using single and V-twin engines, belt drive and sprung forks. Engines ranged from 3hp single to 6hp twin, being joined by a larger twin for 1908.

AEB 1913–1914
A.E. Bradford was a schoolmaster keen on motorcycles and, prior to the Great War, built some machines at premises in Sweetman Street, Wolverhampton. These would have used proprietary engines and other parts, no doubt assembled to order. By 1916 he was using the name De Luxe, so the AEB marque was soon gone.

AEC 1914
In July of 1914, the Auto Engineering Co. of Coventry introduced a single model as their range. It was powered by a 211cc two-stroke engine that drove a two-speed, crossover gearbox by chain, final drive being by belt. The engine was held in the frame between steel strips that ran at the level of the top of the crankcase. The rest of the machine was similar to others of the time and was fitted with Saxon forks. As the Great War began in the following month, little more was heard of this marque.

AEL 1919–1924
As a retail spares and accessories dealer in Moor Street, Coventry, A.E. Lynes had the high-street premises necessary for selling machines badged under the company's own name, but not necessarily constructed by them. There were, though, numerous motorcycle factories around Coventry who could supply their needs and so models with 147 to 343cc two-stroke Villiers engines and JAP or Blackburne four-strokes were supplied and sold with the AEL transfer on their tanks, until demand fell below an economical level in the troubled mid-1920s.

AEOLUS 1903–1905
This machine was designed and built by E.H. Owen of The Motor Transport Co., Comeragh Road, London, and differed from most primitives in having shaft drive. Bevel gear pairs at engine and rear wheel turned the drive and the shaft incorporated a form of clutch. For the rest, the machine was much as others and soon vanished.

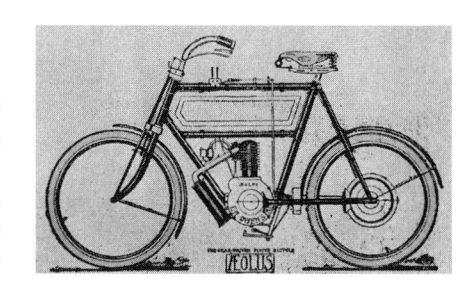

Unusual for such an early machine, this 1903 Aeolus had shaft drive, so the vibration was likely to have been severe.

AEOLUS 1914–1915
This name returned to the lists in 1914 when it appeared on a model powered by a 269cc two-stroke engine with petroil lubrication. This drove a two-speed gearbox by chain, final drive being by belt. The simple model weighed in at 146lb (66kg) and may have been associated with the Bown make from the same period, as this was similar in specification and was said to have been built at the Aeolus works. The marque remained

listed for 1915 before being dropped, no doubt in favour of war work.

AER 1937–1940

Albert Reynolds had produced special versions of the Scott in the early 1930s and in 1937 first showed his AER model, which had a 340cc twin-cylinder air-cooled all-alloy engine. It drove a four-speed Burman gearbox, had oil-pump lubrication and went into a conventional frame with Webb forks.

Production began in 1938 and in the next year the twin was joined by a single, powered by a 249cc Villiers engine. The war brought an end to this enterprise, but the last few machines remained in Reynolds' Liverpool shop long after its end.

A 1938 AER with twin-cylinder two-stroke 340cc engine and a nice stylish line, but the war brought the endeavour to an end.

AEROLITE 1922–1924

Also listed under the Zephyr name, this machine was a light motorized pedal-cycle of just 70lb (32kg) weight. It was built by the Small Engines Company of Coventry Road, Birmingham, with a 104cc Simplex two-stroke engine replacing the frame front-downtube of its special safety cycle frame. Drive from the overhung crankshaft was by chain to a countershaft in the bottom bracket location and thence by belt to the rear wheel. Braced forks were used and the fuel tank hung from the frame crossbar. With 15–20mph (24–32 km/h) available it provided transport at its most basic. A second version with a more conventional frame was also built.

AGA 1921

Very little is known of this marque but they were thought to have produced a 350cc model in 1921 using a JAP engine. If not, there were several other suppliers at that time or it could have been war surplus. Suffice to say, no more was heard of it.

AJAX 1923–1924

The newly introduced 147 and 247cc range of Villiers two-stroke engines allowed Ajax Motor Manufacturers of Birmingham to enter the market with a choice of ultra-lightweight motorcycles in early 1923. Chain-cum-belt transmission via a two-speed Albion gearbox was employed in either plain, or with clutch and kickstart versions. Single-blade link-action forks were fitted to conventional frame parts carried on 26in diameter wheels. There was also a model with the 348cc sv Blackburne engine, but the market was sluggish at the time of their introduction and the trade was reluctant to take on yet another assembled product, so public acceptance and knowledge of the Ajax never became sufficient to ensure the survival of the marque.

AJR 1925–1926

This was one of the few Scottish makes and was produced by A.J. Robertson of Queen Street, Edinburgh, who launched the name by riding in the 1925 TT races when nineteen. His machines all had a JAP engine and Sturmey-Archer gearbox, but in the Lightweight, Junior and Senior events the result was a retirement.

For 1926 he promoted a four-model range, all with ohv JAP engines, minimal primary chain cover, Sturmey-Archer three-speed gearbox and Druid forks. The Sports

Typical of the AJR models built in Edinburgh by A.J. Robertson with JAP engines, this is a 1926 model with 344cc twin-port engine.

models had 344 or 488cc engines and the Racing models 245 or 344cc. Single or twin-port forms were used but the machines were far more expensive than their better known and tested contemporaries.

A further 1926 TT effort brought a Senior retirement but a Junior finish in twenty-second place at 53mph (85km/h), but this hardly impressed potential customers when the winner exceeded 66mph (106km/h). Thus it came as no surprise that production of the AJR soon ceased.

AJS 1910–1945

The Stevens family of Wolverhampton were involved with motorcycles before the turn of the century and spent the Edwardian era supplying engines to other makers. They also produced frames and late in 1909 the four brothers founded AJS, using Albert John's initials.

First of the AJS models was this 2.5hp sv with direct-belt or two-speed transmission with chain. First seen 1910, this was for 1912.

Their first machines shared a 2.5hp sv engine of 292cc, with one model having direct-belt drive and the other a two-speed gearbox and chain drive. These models continued for 1911 and the engines were enlarged to 315cc for 1912, when they were joined by a 631cc V-twin. These engines introduced the AJS feature of securing the cylinder head to the crankcase top by a cross-bar secured by long studs. The machines were well made, popular and sold well, so for 1913 the belt-drive model was dropped, the single further stretched to 349cc and the twin to 697cc. Two or three speeds were the option for the single and three for the twin,

This 1931, AJS 498cc transverse V-twin model was smooth, neat, well equipped and quiet but failed to attract buyers.

which had a drum rear-brake and fully enclosed drive-chains. The twin proved a best seller for sidecar use and the firm was hard pressed to satisfy orders. The sidecars came from the Charles Hayward firm.

This pressure made them reluctant to run in the TT following the time and effort expended there in 1911 and 1913, but they were persuaded to enter the Junior. For the event the machines were fitted with twin primary chains to different ratios to give them four speeds in total. In the race the AJS machines gradually took command so that Eric Williams won, Cyril Williams, who was unrelated, was second and the marque also took fourth and sixth places. Eric was just twenty.

Inclined engines were popular in the early 1930s and this was the sv AJS format, in this case of 400cc and well fitted out.

Demand for AJS machines was boosted and the 1914 range included sporting and standard 349cc singles and the V-twin stretched out further to 748cc. Then came the war and munitions manufacture but the motorcycle range continued with four revised models for 1915. These had a new type of frame and comprised the two singles, the 748cc twin and a new 551cc V-twin listed as the Double-Purpose and suited to solo or sidecar use. That year there was also the Sociable, which had a much larger sidecar body in which both driver and passenger sat, the machine controls suitably extended, but few were made. Only one single was listed for 1916 and for the next two years just the big twin was built as a War Model for the services.

Post-war, for 1919, the V-twin was much altered with detachable heads for the engine, a massive cast-aluminium silencer and a saddle tank, but it kept the existing gearbox. It was built for sidecar use and ran on as such for 1920. That year the firm took over the Hayward business and returned to the TT. For this they prepared machines with an ohv engine that had the top-half secured directly to the crankcase by a steel strap secured by turnbuckles on each side. There were six speeds by use of the stock gearbox and double primary drive.

With six entries the works AJS were favourites for the Junior, but two went out after one lap and three more on lap three after leading. Fortunately Cyril Williams managed to take the lead and was fifteen minutes ahead when the gear-change gear failed 4 miles (6.5km) from the finish, but he managed to push home to win by over nine minutes.

There were many other sporting successes and for 1921 the road V-twin was enlarged to 799cc and joined once again by the 349cc single. The works racing machines were further improved for the TT that year with a new frame, Druid forks and revised engine, but just the conventional three-speed gearbox. The team went to the Island ready and tested, so

The AJS Big Port name continued on for a while. This is a 1932 example, with inclined 498cc overhead-valve engine, but still hand change.

had few problems and recorded a magnificent first, second, third, fourth and sixth with Eric Williams, Howard Davies and Tom Sheard at the front. This was not all, for two days later Howard Davies rode his 350 machine in the Senior TT, held second place for some laps and then took the lead to win by over two minutes.

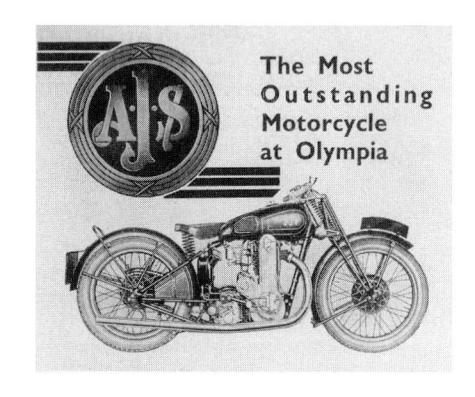

The overhead camshaft AJS engine dated back to 1928, but this was how it looked for 1934, with the cam chain-drive housed in an alloy case.

Buyers were disappointed that the 1922 list lacked an ohv 350, having to be content with a pair of sporting sv models. The firm returned to the Island where Tom Sheard won the Junior and it was that year that the term 'Big Port' was coined, referring to the large size of the exhaust valve and pipe.

An ohv 349cc TT replica was introduced for 1923, which was the year that the firm branched out into the new field of wireless, producing a line of receiving sets up to 1928. It was also the end of the TT glory days, as for the rest of the decade it was seconds and thirds only. However, they did begin to race in Europe and had a number of successes in major events in 1923.

The 1924 range extended to five 349cc models with two having ohv, one for road use and the Special Sports for competition. There were two versions of the 799cc V-twin, one de luxe and the other economy and lower priced. The same list continued for 1925, but the following year brought a racing Big Port and two

An upright 248cc AJS model with upswept exhaust pipe, displaying the forward mounting for the magneto in contrast to the Matchless.

499cc ohv singles for road and competition, built on the lines of the 349cc machines.

A 499cc sv model was added to this list for 1927, the year AJS won a contract to produce bodies for the Clyno Nine car, and decided to replace their racing engines with a new, ohc design. This was built in 349 and 499cc sizes and had the camshaft driven by a chain with a Weller tensioner to keep it under control. It was enclosed in an aluminium case that also extended forward to the magneto, while the rest of the engine followed AJS practice.

The new engines drove a four-speed gearbox and used the existing frame, Druid forks and drum brakes. They went to the TT but had problems, and their best was third in the Junior, thanks to Jimmy Simpson. Later that year he won several important European races but the design still required development.

However, camshaft models were listed in the 1928 range that extended to twelve machines and included a 249cc sv model for the first time. All had internal improvements and the old method of clamping the top half of the engine to the crankcase with a strap was abandoned. The camshaft engines had dry-sump lubrication and all models used the three-speed gearbox. That year was also the last one for the true Big Port models, although the name came to be used more generally by enthusiasts.

During 1928 the firm built an experimental machine with an in-line, four-cylinder, ohv engine that went into a duplex frame, but it was not taken any further. By then trading conditions were giving the firm problems and early in 1929 Clyno failed, bringing an end to the body-building contract. Undeterred, AJS then went into producing commercial vehicle chassis and late in 1930 added the AJS Nine car to their product line.

Before then the 1929 range took on a new look with saddle tanks and centre-spring forks, with two twin-port models added to the list. The V-twin was enlarged to 998cc and the machines had many detail improvements. There was an ohv model for speedway racing but it was short lived. Fewer models were listed for 1930 with just one V-twin, two 349 and a 499cc sv, a 349 and 499cc ohv, a 249cc model with a change to ohv and the two camshaft models with revised engine dimensions of 346 and 495cc. Some of these models were much as before but some adopted the fashionable inclined engine. The firm also built a 990cc ohc V-twin in an attempt to take the world speed record but this was not successful. They had better luck with a 248cc ohc machine that Jimmy Guthrie took to a 1930 Lightweight TT win.

The range increased for 1931, despite the hard times, with all the existing models continuing, the 499cc sv in light and heavy forms, and the smaller version stretched out to 400cc. Early in the year several more models were added with the weight cut to suit a tax limit or with a reduced specification to cut costs. One of these, a 349cc ohv, carried the Big Port name, the first and only official use of the famous nickname.

The V-twin continued to be listed by AJS right up to 1939, but used a 982cc Matchless engine from 1932.

There was one new model announced later that was a break with tradition as it had a 498cc transversely mounted, sv, V-twin engine. This drove back to a three-speed gearbox with chain final-drive and the frame was duplex. Smooth and quiet, it failed to sell well and was no help to AJS.

During 1931 the firm's financial problems came to a head and AJS was wound up, all creditors fully paid and the rights bought by Matchless. It was the end for the Wolverhampton firm, but not the Stevens, or of the AJS name.

The water-cooled, supercharged AJS 495cc V4, built for road racing. It was fast and competitive, set a lap record in the Ulster, but suffered from poor handling.

The new owners moved the firm to Plumstead and offered a restricted range without the camshaft singles or V-twins for 1932. This was rectified in the next year for the first, but only one, V-twin using the 982cc Matchless engine, and this range ran on for 1934. There were major changes for 1935 with the start of a move to Matchless-style vertical engines in 245, 348 and 497cc, the larger two in sv or ohv form. It was the start of common usage and badge engineering that would continue into the 1960s.

The camshaft singles ran on, and in 1936 were joined by another camshaft model, but with a 495cc V4 engine. Air-cooled, it had the camshafts driven by one long chain and was raced by the works that year and again in 1938 when it was supercharged. In this form it overheated, so was water-cooled for 1939 when it proved fast but very hard to handle.

The V4 never went into production so the firm kept to their singles and V-twin to the end of the decade. New versions of the singles appeared for competition and in super sports form when they were called the Silver Streak and had more chrome-plating. In this way the firm ran on to 1940 when they turned over to war work and AMC concentrated on the Matchless G3 and G3L until 1945. Few AJS machines were built in this period.

After the war the fortunes of AJS and Matchless became closely interwoven and that section of their history is covered under the one entry.

AJS & MATCHLESS 1945–1969
After the Second World War the AMC combine built AJS and Matchless machines at Plumstead in the same format with little to tell one from the other. For some years the magneto position was the main variation but even that went in time. The firm strove to keep marque loyalty high by running separate competition teams and this did work in the early post-war years when clubmen would declaim the merits of one over the other, even though it was well known that all were built on the same assembly line from common parts.

The post-war range comprised two singles for each marque, the 348cc model 16M and 497cc model 18 AJS, and the same size G3L and G80 Matchless. All were based on the pre-war and wartime Matchless with the ohv vertical engine, four speeds, telescopic forks and rigid frame. Differences amounted to the magneto mounting forward on the AJS and rear on the Matchless, the inscription on the timing cover, tank badges and the colour of the tank lining with gold for AJS and silver for Matchless to relieve the general black.

Early in 1946 a small batch of competition models were added with the letter 'C' included in the model code. Changes were minimal, with a 21in front wheel, alloy mudguards and suitable tyres. At that time production

Post-war AMC singles were much as pre-war, other than the adoption of the telescopic front forks first used on WD machines.

A competition version of the road model soon followed; this is the G3LC from 1955.

In 1948 the pre-war camshaft model returned as the 348cc 7R single, which had a wrap-round oil tank and enormous megaphone at first.

AMC joined the rush to vertical twins in 1949, using the cycle parts from the singles to offer the AJS model 20 and this Matchless G9.

Rear suspension came for the road models in 1949, this a later G80S model, the larger of the two singles.

was everything, so few changes were made to the listed models for a year or two, but AJS was active on the road-racing front and both marques off-road. In that period Hugh Viney won the Scottish Six Days Trial for three years in succession, from 1947 to 1949, on his AJS, it going to Artie Ratcliffe on a Matchless in 1950.

AJS had raced pre-war and were back on the scene in 1947 with a 497cc twin that became known as the Porcupine, thanks to its extensive fins. The engine and four-speed gearbox were built as a unit with the cylinders parallel to the ground. There were twin ohc driven by a train of gears and lubrication was dry sump. The Porcupine had a chequered race history but it all came good in 1949 when Les Graham won the 500cc world title and was the moral victor in the TT that year when the magneto drive let him down. It was only ever a works machine, but in 1948 was joined by a post-war version of the pre-war camshaft model, the 348cc 7R, soon known as the Boy Racer. This was a works and private-owner model.

For the 7R the firm retained the chain-driven ohc engine, but moved the magneto behind the cylinder to give a new line. It was well made and with fully-enclosed valve gear kept its oil inside. For the rest it was a four-speed gearbox, telescopics, pivoted-fork rear suspension and conical hubs with large drum brakes. On the grand prix circuit there were a few successes, including the 1954 Junior TT won by Rod Coleman with a special three-valve version, but the 7R won plenty of races in private hands.

The road range increased in 1949 with the addition of models with pivoted-fork rear suspension and identified by a letter 'S' in the code. Both sizes and makes were involved to produce the AJS 16MS and 18S plus the Matchless G3LS and G80S. It was also the year when AMC joined the trend to vertical twins with the 498cc AJS 20 and Matchless G9. The engines were in the British style, other than in having a third central main-bearing,

AJS & Matchless

The scrambles G80CS Matchless was fitted with GP carburettor and other suitable fittings including stand, but was still a hefty machine for off-road use.

while the cycle side was mainly as for the springer singles. The main marque variations were the dual seat and megaphone silencers that only went on the Matchless.

In 1950 the competition models had an all-alloy top half for the engines and springer versions were added the next year as the 16MCS, 18CS, G3LCS and G80CS. Aimed more at scrambles than trials, these springers had fatter AMC-made rear units that were called 'jampots', the earlier, slimmer ones being known as 'candlesticks'.

This set the range for some years with few real changes although the Matchless magneto finally moved ahead of the cylinder in 1952. In that year the Porcupine had its cylinders inclined at 45 degrees to become the E95 and the works 7R was fitted with an engine with three valves that became known as the 'triple-knocker'. At first this was done using a combination of the normal chain drive with shafts and bevel gears in the head, later by shaft and bevels up to the cambox, but the latter version was not raced. Of more lasting effect was the fact that late in the year AMC took over the Norton firm, although they remained in Birmingham for a decade.

With learner riders in the UK restricted to 250cc machines, AMC produced this semi-unit construction model under both marque names.

In 1953 the Matchless line added the G45 twin, which was a pure racing model that comprised a tuned G9 engine slotted into the 7R cycle parts. The prototype had won the 1952 Manx GP and the two machines made a good pair for a private runner, although the twin had few successes.

For 1956 the whole road range was amended, all the rigid models were dropped, the trials models in 348cc only had their own frame and the scramble models a short-stroke all-alloy engine. There was a new frame and cycle parts for the singles and twins, with the addition of a 593cc twin offering more power and listed as the model 30 and G11. Further versions of these were added in 1958, combining tuned engines and the scrambles frame to give the street scrambler 30CS and G11CS. By adding the standard fuel tank to these models the firm then had the desirable 30CSR and G11CSR models, which were soon known as 'Coffee Shop Racer' machines. That same year also brought alternator electrics to the road models.

CS versions of all the twins were listed for some years by both marques. This is the Matchless 646cc G12CS, parked by some export crates.

For the 1958 road racer there was the machine they had always wanted, the Matchless G50. This was simply the 7R stretched out to 496cc and no-one understood why it had taken so long for it to arrive. Less exciting that year was the arrival of the models 14 and G2, 248cc ohv singles that had the appearance of unit construction although this was an illusion. So was the lightweight tag, for this they were not.

Code numbers were changed for 1959, but only minor alterations for

New badges went onto the road singles for 1963; this the model 16 or 18 with brighter colours and a rear chainguard.

the machines although there were new models. These comprised CS versions of the 250 single and 500 twin, a CSR 500 twin, and a 646cc twin that replaced the 593cc twin as the 31 and G12. Both twins were listed in standard, CS and CSR form to increase options, but only the standard 500 model continued for 1960.

There were new duplex frames for the 1960 road models, along with a 348cc version of the lightweight, coded 8 and G5, with taller engines and better front forks. Changes then became fewer as sales fell, but a sports version of the 248cc model was added for 1961 when the 646cc CS twin was dropped. That year saw the final AJS success in the Scottish when Gordon Jackson famously dropped just one mark in the six days to take his fourth win in the event.

Jackson's success brought useful publicity and for 1962 the road 350 had its engine revised, while a 248cc CSR was added during the year. The 500 twin was dropped along with the de luxe 650, but there was a short run of two Matchless models for the USA. One was the G15/45 which had a 750cc twin engine installed in what were mainly CSR cycle parts

The AJS 31CSR had its own style of tank badge, but also used the Norton forks and hubs. Later still they used the 745cc Norton engine.

17

with some standard parts. The other was the G50CSR, which was built using a CSR frame and G50 engine with a dynamo clamped to it to enable lights to be fitted. Late in the year AMC moved Norton production from Bracebridge Street to Plumstead and in time this had many effects.

The range was thinned for 1963, when the 7R and G50 ceased to be built, and again for 1964 when the road models were fitted with Norton forks and hubs. In 1965, 745cc twins were added as the 33 and G15 in standard and CSR forms, but these had the Norton Atlas engine, so only the frame and tank remained real AMC parts.

The AMC days were approaching their end, for the firm was in financial trouble. Due to this, 1966 was their last year in their old form, after which the bulk of the range was dropped. There had been one new model for 1966, the Matchless G85CS scrambler with duplex frame and this did run on to 1969. The standard and CSR models of the AJS 33 ran to 1967 under new ownership, but the Matchless G15 in those forms was joined by a CS version and continued to 1969. Production then ceased and the old factory was demolished, but neither name vanished.

AJS TWO-STROKES 1967–1973

This name was revived late in 1967 by Norton Villiers for a couple of two-stroke competition machines powered by the 247cc Villiers Starmaker engine. For road racing there was the Double T Racer with six speeds and twin fuel-tanks, and for off-road the Alamos scrambler with four speeds. Neither really got off the ground, but for 1969 the scrambler became the Y4 Stormer and was joined by the 37A-T trials model of 246cc. Only the Stormer continued for 1970, along with a 368cc Y5 version, and two similar models for the USA, the Y40 and Y50.

Late in 1971 the Y5 was replaced by the 400cc Stormer 410 and by 1973 these were no longer offered in kit form as in the past. With the creation of NVT that year the small firm

The FB-AJS became AJS Two-Strokes in time, so the name continued, albeit on a small off-road model for the classic events.

From the start, AJW offered big motorcycles, such as this 1928 V-twin with 980cc overhead-valve JAP engine, the fuel tank with plated nose.

was sold on to Fluff Brown who created the FB-AJS range which later still reverted to the original AJS name.

AJS TWO-STROKES 1987–DATE

After producing the FB-AJS from 1974 to 1981, mainly in the image of the older AJS two-strokes, this firm returned to complete machines some years later. These were effectively the AJS Stormer models in 247, 368 and 400cc sizes. This suited the market of the time, which was as interested in the classic era as that of the present, so the firm rode forward on the nostalgia boom. From 1991 they also built replicas of the early-1960s Cotton models.

AJW 1926–1979

A firm on the edge of the industry in more senses than one, for Arthur John Wheaton, with a background in publishing, set up in Exeter, Devon, and his machines were assemblies of parts from many sources. However, they kept going longer than most, having commenced business late in 1926 with two ohv models, one with a 500cc MAG engine and the other with a 996cc V-twin British Vulpine. Both had bulbous saddle-tank styling, duplex frames and Druid forks, but

By 1967 AJS had become part of NVT and one result was this Double T Racer, fitted with the 247cc Villiers Starmaker engine.

Sensation of the late-1928 show was this AJW Super-Four, with a 985cc water-cooled engine, fully enclosed rear chain and massive frame.

only the twin went into production with a four-speed Jardine gearbox, with a light blue tank with a plated nose. By 1928 there were six models, some with 981cc JAPV-twin engines, and all had the option of a three-speed Sturmey-Archer gearbox in place of the Jardine.

At the late-1928 Olympia show the firm announced a radical new model, which had many unusual features, as the AJW Super Four. The engine was a 985cc water-cooled British Anzani that drove back through a cone clutch to a three-speed Sturmey-Archer gearbox. Bevel gears then turned the drive for the fully enclosed rear-chain. The engine and gearbox were carried in a frame comprising a channel-steel section beam along each side with tubular cross-members; the result, a car chassis in miniature. At the rear it was rigid, but at the front a vertical pin on each side carried a pivoted member. Each member had a further vertical pin on which the front axle supports slid under spring control. The whole was linked back to the handlebars to provide car-type steering. The Four carried its radiator ahead of the engine, and the fuel tank behind and under the saddle, but for the rest was fully enclosed with a dummy tank top. Massive 8in drum brakes were fitted, while the wire wheels carried 4in balloon tyres. The Super Four never did reach production. It was shown at the 1929 show but then dropped.

A model with a 994cc ohv Anzani V-twin engine was added for 1929 and then, for the next year, the range was extended to add JAP and Blackburne singles plus a range of two-strokes using Villiers engines from 172 to 343cc. They also had model names linked to foxes, of which Flying Fox and Silver Vixen were typical. Rudge Python engines were added for 1931 when some of the triangulated frames had no less than six tubes either bolted or brazed to the headstock. By the following year it was the Rudge plus the Villiers alone except for one JAPV-twin in its final year. They were down to three 499cc models by 1934 but then reverted to JAP engines in 1935, which, except for a Stevens engine for one year, were used until the end of the decade. In 1939 they added the Lynx model, a lightweight with a 249cc Villiers engine.

In 1939 AJW added this Lynx model, fitted with a 122cc Villiers engine, as used by many other firms around that time.

After the war the firm changed hands and moved first to Bournemouth in Hampshire and later to Wimborne in Dorset. Late in 1948 the post-war models appeared, two in number and both with JAP engines. They were totally different in purpose, for the Speed Fox was a speedway machine built in small numbers up to 1957 with the usual 498cc engine running on dope. The Grey Fox had the 494cc sv, vertical-twin engine in a plunger frame with telescopic forks and this road model was only listed to 1950.

From 1935, AJW made the Red Fox, fitted with a 488cc JAP overhead-valve engine, as the firm varied its suppliers.

AJW built a second prototype in 1952, copying the first, but used a 500cc ohv JAP engine hung in its spine frame with gearbox above the crankcase.

In 1952 the firm showed two prototypes with the engine set horizontal, one with the 125cc JAP two-stroke unit and the other with a 500cc engine from the same firm. Both had a spine frame, but although the smaller was listed for 1953 neither really got off the ground before the JAP road-engine supply dried up.

AJW returned to the road in 1958 with the Fox Cub which was really an imported light motorcycle with a 48cc Minarelli two-stroke engine. They continued with this up to 1964, during which time it was joined by three other versions, before leaving the market for a decade. They were back in 1974, again with imported mopeds, and this time continued to 1979.

AKD 1928–1932

After 1925 Abingdon King Dick were known by their initials but continued at the Tyseley, Birmingham, address. Production ceased for a year or two but they returned in 1928 with a six-model range, all using the same 172cc ohv engine driving a three-speed gearbox. Fixtures and fittings made the difference with some twin-port engines and a super-sports model.

The year 1928 was the first for the new AKD name of the old Abingdon firm, who continued to make their own engines, this of 172cc with ohv.

By 1930 AKD had more style for the fuel tank and this new 250cc ohv engine was listed in sports and super-sports forms.

An interesting 148cc model appeared for 1929 with the ohv engine built in-unit with the three-speed gearbox. It had gear primary drive, with this incorporated with the timing gears to the rear camshaft and magneto, and rockers that oscillated against a roller they held up against a fixed bridge. Four of the 172cc models continued and were joined by a 196cc ohv and 296cc sv, all in similar form and some with a saddle tank.

The 148cc machine was dropped for 1930 and a pair of 248cc ohv machines were added in the same form. For 1931 the model numbers were changed to astrological names and the 148cc ohv unit construction model returned, but with an inclined engine. Most of the others remained and were joined by a 349cc sv model, again with an inclined engine. The whole range ran on for 1932 but this was their final motorcycle year, after which they concentrated on producing hand tools.

AKKENS 1919–1921

The simplest format of a lightweight machine with direct-belt drive was chosen by the makers of the Akkens, who were Messrs Thomas & Gilbert of Smethwick, Birmingham. The engine, naturally, was a two-stroke rated at 2.75hp and it possessed both internal and external flywheels. Ignition was by Ericsson or EIC magneto, and fuel was supplied through an Amac carburettor. With Druid forks, a conventional frame and a weight of just 130lb (59kg) it was acceptable for short journeys and as basic transport, but those were its definite limitations.

ALECTO 1919–1925

Cashmore Brothers of Balham in London chose to make their own two-stroke engine for the motorcycle they introduced late in 1919. This displaced 345cc with chain drive to a Juckes two-speed gearbox, thence belt drive to the rear wheel. A CAV magneto was thoughtfully located behind the cylinder away from the weather and an Amac carburettor provided the mixture. With Druid or Brampton Biflex forks it was otherwise much like many other contenders and thus entered a very competitive marketplace. By 1920 a Burman gearbox replaced the Juckes and the following year production was interrupted when the original proprietors failed.

Production was resumed from the same premises under the auspices of Whitmee Engineering and a strengthened version of the model was introduced and listed in complete sidecar form. These two variants on a common theme were given the option of all-chain drive and were joined by a third in 1923, an all-electric model, having a CAV dynamo lighting set as part of its specification. Three speeds came in 1924, still with the final-drive options, but it was all-chain only the next year, when a two-speed sports model could be had, this being their final throw.

ALERT 1904–1906

Made by Smith & Molesworth of Coventry, the range comprised the 2.25hp Alert using a Belgian Sarolea engine and the 2.75 or 3.25hp Coventry Alert machines, plus the

This Alert is typical of the primitive period, with belt drive from its Belgian Sarolea engine hung from the frame.

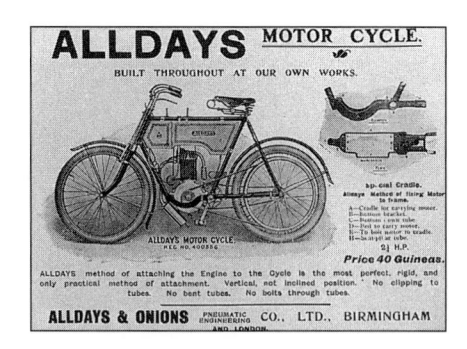

Late-1903 Alldays, with the engine mounted in a cradle in the lower frame, a system they were proud to promote.

Montgomery sidecar. They were also suppliers of fittings to the trade. The engine was hung from the downtube and construction was primitive.

ALLARD 1897–1902

A Coventry firm, whose origins lay in steel tubing and bicycles, that moved into power in 1899 with a car and a De Dion-style tricycle powered by their own 2.25hp engine, the tricycle first shown at the Crystal Palace show of 1898. A motorcycle followed in 1901, built entirely in their works, the engine of 1.75hp inclined to the line of the downtube. It was mounted in an aluminium cradle that fixed to the frame tubes.

The firm offered the machine as a kit of parts to the trade, making it easy for others to enter the market, and soon enlarged the engine to 2hp. By 1902 the inclined engine had been replaced by a vertical one, mounted in the new Werner style. During 1902 the machine was renamed the 'Rex', and from then on was sold as such.

ALLDAYS & ONIONS 1898–1915, 1923 AND 1927

This Fallows Road, Small Heath, Birmingham firm had its roots back in the seventeenth century, became bicycle makers in the nineteenth and in 1898 built a tricycle powered by a De Dion engine. In 1901 came a motorcycle that used a Minerva engine, as did many, but they then moved on to the new Werner layout.

By 1903 they had their own 2.25hp engine and fitted that into a cradle bolted in the loop frame. A

3.5hp forecar was also listed and the motorcycle became 2.5hp for 1904, joined by a 3.5hp version for 1905. There was a new 2.5hp model for 1909, but by 1911 only the larger machine was listed, still with belt drive and rigid forks.

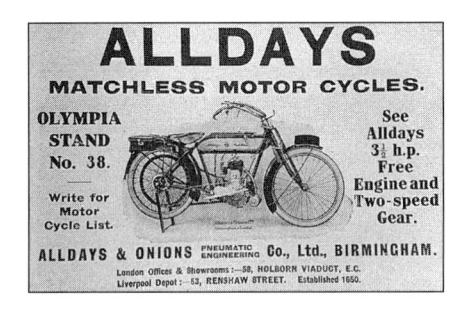

Later Alldays from 1912, showing the improvements common to many makes over the Edwardian period.

During 1911 the 3.5hp model was revised as 499cc with a two-speed gear, although the belt drive was kept. Druid forks were fitted and the result was well made and not too expensive. Late in 1911 the 6hp Alldays-Matchless twin with a three-speed gearbox and all-chain drive was added while 1913 brought a 3hp twin. By 1914 the range was down to the 3.5hp single and 6hp V-twin, plus a lightweight with a 269cc Villiers engine. From 1915 the firm produced their machines as the 'Allon' with two-stroke engines.

They did revert to using the 'Alldays' name once more, in 1923 when they listed the Alldays Sports which had a 348cc sv JAP engine, two-speed gearbox and either all-chain or chain-cum-belt transmission. Listed for just the one year, the name then returned once again in 1927, when they went back to four-stroke power and offered two models so fitted. One had a 349cc Bradshaw single engine, the other a 680cc V-twin, and both had three speeds and all-chain drive. They were only built for that one year as the New Alldays & Onions.

ALLEN 1990–DATE
Bernie Allen is based in Wiltshire and works closely with Summerfield to produce replicas of the 350 and 500cc Manx Norton in limited numbers and of the highest quality.

ALLON 1915–1926
This was the marque name adopted by Alldays & Onions of Birmingham in 1915 when they switched to producing a single two-stroke model. This used their own 292cc engine which had drip-feed lubrication and was unusual in having a horizontal crankcase joint with the top half in one with the cylinder. This engine drove a two-speed gearbox by chain, final drive was by belt; there was a single-speed option and either Druid or Saxon forks were fitted.

This model was listed for 1916 and was offered post-war when the make returned in 1919. It was little altered, but did add the option of a three-speed gearbox for 1922, to continue on in this form to the end of its days in 1926. For 1927 only, the firm went back to using the Alldays name and four-stroke engines.

ALL SPEED GEAR SYNDICATE 1907–1908
Late in 1907 this firm announced a model of bicycle construction, fitted with a 1.25hp Minerva engine under the downtube. Its main claim to fame was its transmission, which was by chain to a countershaft that carried a wheel that drove the inside of a dummy rim by friction. No more was heard of the make.

ALP 1914–1916
This was a branch factory of the Swiss Moto-Rêve firm based at Alperton in Middlesex. The single model had a 2hp 257cc four-stroke engine with an overhead inlet valve and an exhaust pipe that ran from the rear of the engine. Belt drive with an adjustable pulley was fitted, along with pedals and footrests with Druid front-forks. The make was no longer listed in 1915 but a brief 1916 note suggested that they were using a 3hp two-stroke engine. Production would have been limited.

The Alp was really a Swiss design, although built under licence in Middlesex to fill a need for transport in the early years of the Great War.

ALPHA 1907–1908
Johnson, Harley & Martin Ltd, of Gosford Street, Coventry, produced car engines around 1907–08. It is believed that they also built a few motorcycles around the same period, no doubt typical of that era.

One of the various Alpha engines, this one is the twin with central disc-valves fed by a single carburettor.

ALPHA 1965–1968
This firm, based at Dudley in Worcestershire, became involved with the competition scene when they extended their range of manufactured engine parts to add an improved crankshaft for tuned Villiers engines. From this came a complete bottom half and then managing director, Fred Cutler, went on to design an engine with the induction controlled by the flywheel flanges.

Later came a 247cc twin two-stroke with rotary disc valves. This differed from the usual layout in that the discs went between the flywheels in the middle and were fed by a single carburettor. Along with an Albion gearbox, the engine was fitted at first in an old DMW frame and later an Alpha frame with Ceriani forks.

In this form the machine was successful and showed development promise, but the controlling company brought it to a halt after eight engines had been built and components for more manufactured.

ALTA 1969–1970

Built in Wales and developed from work done to convert road Suzuki machines for use in trials, the Alta used the Suzuki 118cc two-stroke engine unit. This had the advantage of a dual-range gearbox to supplement the three-speed one to offer high and low sets of ratios. The unit went into a monocoque frame constructed of light-alloy sheet but this was changed to a tubular one in 1970. That year the cost of the engine to Alta rose significantly so production stopped to avoid too expensive a machine.

ALVIS 1920

This scooter was better known as the Stafford Mobile Pup and was a product of the Alvis car firm that had been formed in 1919. With its 142cc John engine hung to one side of the front wheel it was none too stable, while the frame construction was flimsy.

ALWIN 1920

It was standing room only on the Alwin scooter, simply because its makers didn't consider it necessary to fit a saddle! A 1.75hp two-stroke engine with crankshaft in-line drove directly by shaft to a bevel and crown pinion on the left side of the rear wheel. This transmission was hidden by a pressed steel platform, from which the rear wheel was suspended on leaf springs. The engine lay up front, immediately behind the short headstock, into which unsprung forks and a long handlebar stem were fitted. Solid tyres ran on pressed disc wheels and fuel was held in a tank clipped above the engine. Despite the relative sophistication of its shaft drive, the Alwin was otherwise a crude device and very similar in outline to a child's foot-propelled scooter; the company, unsurprisingly, also produced such devices.

Ambassador Popular model, as built for some years with various capacity Villiers engines and shown here with rigid frame.

AMBASSADOR 1946–1964

This Ascot, Berkshire firm was founded by Kaye Don, an ex-Brooklands driver, to expand his business post-war. He produced a range of lightweights and from around 1954 also imported Zundapp machines, but his first prototype was very different. It had the lines of a pre-war machine complete with girder forks, but the engine was a 494cc sv vertical-twin built by JAP and also used by AJW.

The first production model came in 1947 and was a simple lightweight with a 197cc Villiers 5E engine, three-speed gearbox, rigid loop frame and blade girder forks. It provided the basic transport then much in demand and for 1949 changed to the much improved and more modern 6E engine. The following year brought a version with telescopic forks called the Embassy and for 1952 the Supreme, which also had plunger rear suspension.

For 1953 the Self Starter model was added and this had a Lucas starter motor tucked under the front of the tank with belt drive to the engine.

Some Ambassador models were listed with plunger rear suspension from 1952, while the next year brought the Self-Starter version, as illustrated here.

There was also the Sidecar model which came as a complete outfit with Webb girder forks and must have severely taxed the engine. During the year the whole range changed to the 197cc 8E engine, little altered from the 6E, but for 1954 the Supreme was moved up to use the 224cc Villiers 1H unit with its four-speed gearbox and went into a new frame with pivoted-fork rear suspension.

The same type of frame was used for the 197cc Envoy of 1955 and for the next year this model, with 8E or later 9E engine, the Supreme and the Popular with a 147cc Villiers 30C engine comprised the range. There was some revision for 1957 with the 148cc 31C engine for the Popular, the Envoy only with the 9E and the Supreme with either the 246cc 2H single or 249cc 2T twin engine.

Ambassador followed the trend to partial enclosure for several models, including this 1961 Three Star Special.

A model with the 174cc 2L engine appeared in 1958 but 1959 brought replacements for the Supreme and a new style with some rear enclosure. These were the Three Star Special with 9E engine and the Super S with the 2T twin. These continued into the new decade to be joined by an electric-start twin and a 174cc scooter for 1961. A moped with a 50cc Villiers engine made a brief appearance in 1962, but late that year Kaye Don retired and the firm was sold to DMW. They revamped the range for 1963 but production ceased in the next year.

ANDREWS 1906

Described late in 1906 and seen at that year's Stanley show, this machine was built by Mr Andrews of Spalding, Lincs. It was powered by a vertical-twin engine that drove the rear wheel by a belt on either side, the pulleys arranged to give different ratios and thus two speeds. Leading-link front suspension was used, while there was rear suspension in the form of a fork, made from ash wood, that pivoted from the front of the frame to maintain belt tension. Nothing further was heard of the make, which was most likely a one-off.

ANGLIAN 1903–1912

Hailing from Beccles in Suffolk, this make made its debut at the Crystal Palace show held late in 1903. A typical primitive, it fitted a 2.75hp De Dion or MMC engine vertically in the frame, and had belt drive and strutted forks. For 1905 the engines were the De Dion, or a 2.5hp JAP for a lighter machine, and a twin-chain primary drive was added to give two speeds.

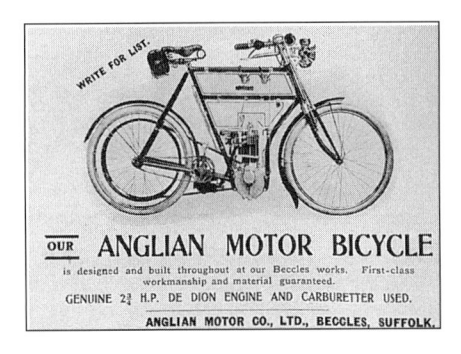

Early Anglian model from 1904, fitted with the De Dion engine in a typical primitive form, with cycle frame, braced forks and belt drive.

A forecar having a water-cooled engine, two-speed gear and chain drive was also listed, but by 1910 only models fitted with 2.75hp De Dion or JAP engines were available, which continued to 1912.

ANSEL c.1980s

Selwyn Perry started this firm to build frame kits for grass-track racing and then moved on to complete machines. Engines varied and ranged from the 250cc Maico to the 500cc JAP along with others.

ANTELOPE c.1902

A primitive product thought to have been made by the Lloyd firm of Birmingham, possibly simply a badge transfer change to give another name for the machine; a practice as common then as it still is now.

ANTIG 1966–DATE

A firm owned by Tig Perry and based in Gloucester, that built frame kits for grass-track racing. From this start came complete machines using engines ranging from the 250cc Bultaco to the 500cc JAP. He later took over the manufacture of Weslake engines and after this bought Alf Hagon's frame-building business.

ARAB-VILLIERS 1924–1925

Too small to merit an entry in the annual buyers' guides of the specialist press, the Arab factory on Bellbarn Road, Birmingham, nevertheless produced a number of ultra-lightweight machines for general sale. The 147cc Villiers two-stroke engine coupled to a two-speed gearbox with or without clutch and kickstart, and chain-cum-belt drive was the staple fare. One regular retail outlet for Arab was the large Birmingham business of Frank Whitworth, who also sold under their own Whitworth brand, probably no more than own-badged versions of the Arab product.

ARDEN 1912–1922

This firm was first known for its cyclecars and light cars, and was located at Berkswell, near Coventry. Post-Great War they developed and marketed a spring front-fork with side members from pressed steel and with links adjustable on cup-and-cone bearings. A 269cc two-stroke engine was also produced and both this and the fork were used by a number of smaller assemblers such as Endurance, Gaby, Norbreck and Priory. Production of complete machines would have been limited.

ARGSON 1921–c.1930

Although this company offered a scooter at the beginning, it was only for a short time and only alongside their principal product, which was a light tricycle specially designed and adapted for those without a leg or an arm. Such invalids were sadly all too prevalent in the years immediately following the Great War and the company found a ready market awaiting them. The tricycle had a single front-wheel, the other two fastened to a common axle at the rear and driven by a 170cc Beaufort two-stroke engine of the company's own manufacture. This engine also appeared in the Beaufort lightweight motorcycle built by Argson and, additionally, was sold out to other assemblers of lightweight motorcycles. There was a move from London's West End to Twickenham in Middlesex in 1922, and the option of an electric motor was offered on the tricycle the next year. A novel flat-twin engine in which but a single rocker served to operate both overhead valves on each cylinder was promoted by Argson in 1924. It was a development of a 175cc engine built to War Office requirements for a generating set and thought then to have a lightweight motorcycle application. Nothing more came of this, but the invalid tricycle continued to be produced for some further years.

ARGYLE PRE-GREAT WAR

A firm located in the street of that name in Birkenhead who built a few machines, no doubt a cycle dealer who based them on a heavy-duty cycle frame with an engine hung from it and with belt drive to the rear wheel; very basic and primitive.

ARGYLL c.1913

This name is better known for the cars that emerged from their factory in Glasgow, which first manufactured bicycles in Victorian times. In between they produced a few motorcycles from an address in Stoke, Coventry and were an early user of JAP engines. These were constructed much in the form of the time with Druid-style forks, upright engine installation and belt drive.

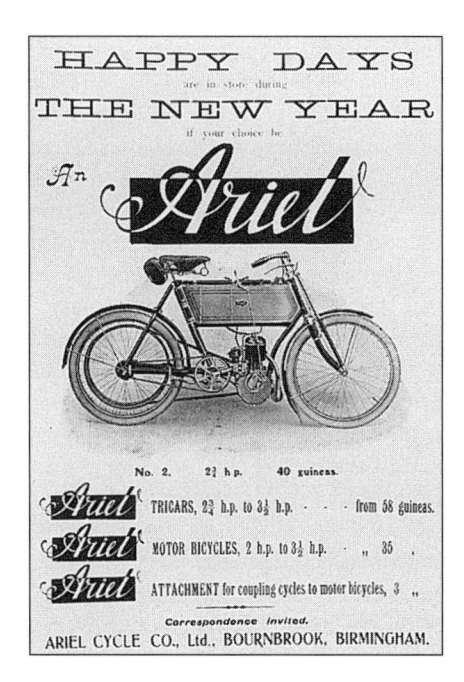

By 1904 Ariel had the engine in the low Werner position and had begun to build their own power units.

ARIEL 1898–1965, AND 1970

A major manufacturer based in Selly Oak, Birmingham, Ariel had its roots in the bicycle industry and the name was used as early as 1847 for a wheel design, and again in 1871 for a penny-farthing. The firm was bought by Cycle Components in 1897 and in 1898 built their first powered tricycle, based on the De Dion type, but with the engine ahead of the rear axle. This location improved the weight distribution and stability of the machine.

The engine was a 1.75hp single made under De Dion licence and drove the axle by fully enclosed gears. The original underpowered engine was soon replaced by one of 2.25hp that worked much better and was sold to other firms. By 1900 Ariel also offered a quadricycle, built by replacing the tricycle front end with two wheels with a forecar slung between them. For this application a larger 2.75hp engine with water-cooled cylinder head was used.

Late in 1901 the firm showed its first motorcycle, along with a car, using a 1.5hp Minerva engine hung from the frame downtube, the power rising to 2hp for 1902. In 1903 the first Ariel engine was built, of 2.25hp, and had a mechanically operated inlet valve, as did the Minerva by then. For 1904 they adopted the centre-engine position, using 2.25 and 3.5hp engines, although the Minerva-powered model continued. The 3.5hp engine had its valves at the back of the cylinder, worm drive for the camshaft and a detachable cylinder-head that screwed into place. Both tricycles and quads remained in the list, but were phased out that year, the forecar listed for one further season.

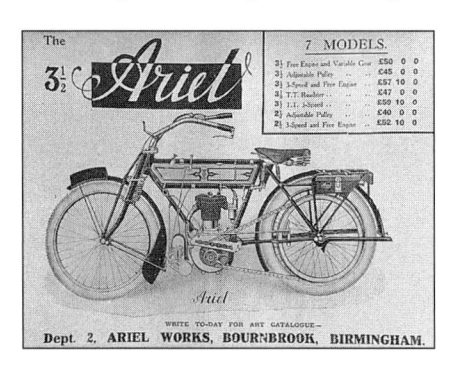

This 1912 advertisement might list seven Ariel models, but all used the same White & Poppe engine form that they would keep for over a decade.

By 1928 the Ariel single had adopted the rear magneto and a form that it would keep to the end of their four-stroke line.

The firm offered the Liberty cycle attachment as yet another form of transport, where a bicycle could be attached to the side of a motorcycle to form a quadricycle and avoid side-slip. In 1905 the smaller model was revised to 2.5hp and the two singles were joined by a 6hp V-twin, using a JAP engine, for 1906. The tricar went in 1908 when leading-link forks appeared and the models continued thus for 1909.

All were replaced by one basic model for 1910, this using a 3.5hp White & Poppe engine having its valves spaced far apart on one side of the cylinder and the Bosch magneto in front of the crankcase. Belt drive remained, either with an adjustable pulley or a variable gear, and Druid forks were fitted.

Late in 1910, a new and advanced model was announced as the 2.5hp Arielette. This had unit construction for its in-line 198cc ohv engine, three-speed epicyclic gearbox and bevel-drive gears. The magneto sat above the gearbox and chain final-drive was used. The cycle side was conventional with Druid forks, but the model failed to reach production.

By 1911 Ariel had bought the rights to the White & Poppe engine and began to make it themselves with the capacity increased to 498cc. They used it in a range of models for 1912 from tourer to TT racer with a variety of transmissions, but all with belt drive. This continued for 1913 when they were joined by a 7hp V-twin with chain drive, intended for sidecar work. It was replaced by a 5/6hp model with an Abingdon engine in 1914 when it and some singles adopted a three-speed gearbox and chain-cum-belt drive.

For 1915 the twin and two singles were to be joined by a 349cc two-

For 1931 Ariel followed the inclined engine trend to this extreme, but it had limited appeal and was soon dropped.

The major new model from Ariel for 1931 was the Square Four, with its geared crankshafts and overhead camshaft, the engine compact enough to fit the stock frame.

By 1933 the inclined engine had mainly gone, so the Ariel singles reverted to the 1928 arrangement which they would keep to the end.

stroke model, but this failed to reach production. After 1916 the firm supplied the War Office with 3.5hp singles and a few V-twins, and it was these models that comprised the 1919 post-war range, the twin enlarged to 6/7hp. They were joined by a 586cc single with an improved engine and chain drive for 1920; its capacity was increased to 665cc for 1922 when a V-twin with an 8hp MAG engine was added to the list.

A lightweight appeared in 1923 using a 249cc Blackburne engine, two-speed gearbox and all-chain drive. A sports version with ohv was added for the next year when they changed to a three-speed gearbox, but the other models were just three of 3.5hp and the V-twin. The range was now becoming dated and obsolete, for the engine had been in use for over a decade. For 1925 the range came down to four models, the two of 249cc and two with an improved version of the old engine with the dimensions changed to 81.5mm bore and 95mm stroke. These, and the resulting 499cc capacity, would be used by the firm for over thirty years.

During 1925 the firm recruited the brilliant Val Page to design new machines, and in the brief time available before the Olympia show he concentrated on the archaic engine. Using a simple construction he produced 499cc ohv and 557cc sv motors using the same stroke and many common parts. In both cases they drove a three-speed Burman gearbox and went into the old cycle parts but with 7in drum brakes. The next year saw the magneto moved to behind the cylinder, a new cradle frame and a stylish saddle tank that gave the machines a much improved line.

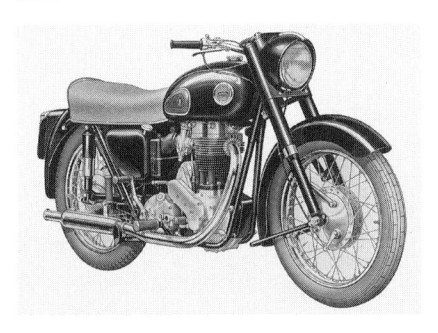

The tough, robust Ariel Red Hunter singles first appeared in 1932, this is a 1957–1959 type with improved suspension, but still with the 1927 engine lines.

This is an Ariel late model Square Four with four exhaust pipes, the model that kept the unusual link rear-suspension to the end.

In 1927 the firm won the prestigious Maudes Trophy and this highlighted the tough nature of the new design and was just one part of a determined promotion of the Ariel marque. They won the Maudes again in 1928 and for the next year added a 249cc model in sv and ohv forms, the latter called the Colt. This came from the horse motif they had adopted in their advertising and which would continue down the years. That year they gained further publicity by mounting a machine on twin floats and driving it across the English Channel. It was also the year when Edward Turner joined the firm to design a four-cylinder engine for them.

The existing range continued on for 1930, but 1931 brought inclined engines to suit the fashion of the time, most at 30 degrees, but with one at 60 degrees, while others remained vertical. Of far more impact was the debut of the Turner design with its four cylinders arranged in a square, the crankshafts geared together, an ohc and 498cc capacity. It was compact enough to fit into a stock frame and was listed as the Square Four but soon became known amongst enthusiasts as the Squariel. It was joined by a 601cc version for 1932.

That year saw the first of the sporting Red Hunter singles that had a tuned engine and red tank panels to set them off. Early in the year they learnt that they had again won the Maudes, in 1931, but despite this good publicity they were in financial trouble. They slimmed down with Val Page moving to Triumph, and settled for 248, 346, 498 and 557cc singles plus the 601cc four. All but the largest

Ariel joined the twin-cylinder fashion with their own 500cc model as shown here, and a second model which used a BSA A10 engine as its basis.

This is the competition version of the Ariel single, the HT5, which was so successful in trials when ridden by Sammy Miller.

singles had ohv and this took them on to 1936 when the sv model went up in size to 598cc and Turner also moved to Triumph, leaving behind a new four.

The revised four appeared for 1937 and was larger at 995cc with ohv in place of the camshaft. In 1939 a 599cc version was added and a link-plunger rear-suspension system made available for most of the range, which still comprised a line of sports and touring singles along with the fours.

During the war the firm built a military version of its 346cc ohv single and in 1944 Ariel were bought by BSA.

Post-war, they picked up with the 346cc model and a 499cc single with both in touring and Red Hunter forms, the 598cc sv for sidecar use, and the Square Four. It was 1947 before they all had telescopic front-forks and the option of the link-plunger rear-suspension that would remain for the Four to the end of its days.

In 1948 Ariel joined the general move to the vertical twin engine, having had a prototype running in 1944 and a development model seen two years later. Two versions were announced, a de luxe tourer and the sporting Red Hunter, and differed little. The 499cc ohv engine had a one-piece cast-iron block, a similar head, chain-driven camshafts fore and aft, and a forged crankshaft with bolted-on flywheel. The cycle side came from the singles with little change.

The Square Four had its heavy cast-iron head and block changed to light alloy for 1949 and the next year brought a 499cc competition single in rigid form only. In 1952 an all-alloy 499cc road model appeared as the various de luxe versions of both singles and twins were dropped. For 1953 the Square Four was introduced in a form having four separate exhaust pipes and just for that year there was an all-alloy twin.

There was considerable revision for 1954 when the ohv singles and twins adopted pivoted-fork rear suspension and four new models appeared. Smallest was the 198cc Colt, which was essentially a 249cc BSA single reduced in size. Largest was the 646cc Huntmaster twin and this too had BSA origins, for the engine was from the Golden Flash with minor changes. The other two models were singles for trials and scrambles, the first to later be developed by Sammy Miller who dominated the trials world up to 1964 using his much lightened machine.

Little more happened to this range from then on, for Ariel had dramatic plans for the future that burst on the world in July 1958. In a complete contrast to their past, they introduced the Leader, which had a 247cc twin-cylinder two-stroke engine built in-

The Leader was soon followed by the sports Arrow and this Super Sports, which used the basis of the Leader minus the outer panels.

Completely new and launched during 1958 by Ariel was the Leader, with its twin-cylinder two-stroke 250cc engine and pressed-steel chassis.

The Ariel Pixie shared its engine design with the BSA Beagle and had some style, but failed to sell.

The odd, three-wheeled, banking moped that cost Ariel so dear was a total flop and a major cause of the BSA group collapse.

unit with its four-speed gearbox. However, this was nothing compared with the rest of the machine specification, for the engine unit hung from a main-frame beam in pressed steel with trailing-link forks and the whole enclosed by panels.

The effect was scooter protection with motorcycle handling in a design built using modern mass-produced techniques and offering a long list of options to add to the basic, but well equipped, machine. It was the work of Val Page and once again demonstrated his brilliant design skills.

Once the Leader was established the whole of the four-stroke range was dropped, in August 1959, but 1960 brought the Arrow, which was based on the Leader but lacked the enclosure. For 1961 these two were joined by a Super Sports version that was immediately known as the Golden Arrow thanks to its finish.

In 1964 a 199cc Arrow was added to offer a machine in a lower insurance class and a new model appeared as the Pixie. This shared its 50cc ohv engine design with the BSA Beagle and had four speeds and a stylish spine frame. However, the two new models had a short life, for, in August 1965, the parent BSA firm brought Ariel production to a halt and they and the others were all dropped.

The Ariel name was briefly revived in 1970 for an odd three-wheeled moped that used a Dutch-built Anker two-stroke engine. It proved to be a costly disaster and one of the major causes of the BSA collapse.

ARION 1903
This model was believed to have been made by W.R. Heighton of Elton, near Peterborough, who also produced the Vinco. This had a similar early primitive format and a short life in the shops.

ARMIS 1919–1922
It isn't difficult to see where the origins of this marque name came from, the Great War having been over barely twelve months before its introduction. From premises in Heneage Street, Birmingham, the Armis Cycle Manufacturing Company first offered two models, both with Precision engines. The larger had the old 8hp sv V-twin in conjunction with a three-speed Sturmey-Archer gearbox, backed up by a medium-weight model with the new 349cc two-stroke Precision engine coupled to an Enfield two-chain, two-speed transmission. The business was founded by Messrs Harrison and Baker who were formally with the Calthorpe company, so had useful experience in the trade. The big twin soon went and the two-stroke had its transmission changed to a Burman two-speed chain-cum-belt; a complete sidecar outfit with this engine was also listed and a 292cc sv JAP model was added.

During 1921 a V-twin returned, with 654cc sv JAP engine, in solo or complete sidecar forms, this and the 292cc model going forward into 1922 to be joined by one with a 248cc ioe MAG engine and others with 346 and 548cc sv JAP engines. Both the latter were sold as outfits if required but, with this, the marque came to its end.

ARMSTRONG 1902–1905
A typical primitive that hung its small Minerva engine from the downtube of a heavy-duty bicycle frame fitted with rigid forks. The frame lugs came from Chater-Lea and much else was bought-in by this assembler.

ARMSTRONG 1913–1915
A make whose claim to fame was to offer a model powered by a four-stroke 2.75hp 349cc Villiers engine. This advanced design had unit-construction of its two-speed gearbox with chain primary-drive to the clutch. An overhead inlet valve was fitted and the train of timing gears ran up on the left of the engine to a rear-mounted magneto. For the rest, the machine was typical of the period with belt final-drive and sprung forks.

The four-stroke Villiers was short lived so, for 1914, the firm fitted the 269cc two-stroke Villiers as used by many others. It had petroil lubrication and drove a two-speed gearbox with belt final-drive, a single-speed version also being listed. These two ran on for 1915, after which production ceased.

ARMSTRONG 1981–1987
This large engineering group was interested in Triumph at one point but terms could not be agreed, so in 1980 they took over CCM. They immediately briefed CCM to build a road racer and this was soon on show as the CM35. It had a 247cc water-cooled tandem-twin two-stroke Rotax engine unit with six-speed gearbox from Austria. This went into a frame with rising-rate rear suspension, Marzocchi front forks and Brembo disc brakes.

The machine was immediately successful with a TT win and some grand prix placings in 1981. For 1982 it was joined by a 347cc version in the same format and the off-road CCM models became badged as Armstrong CCM, using Rotax engines from mid-1982. In 1983 Armstrong were supplying Can-Am with machines,

This is the larger of the two Armstrong race models with its tandem-twin Rotax engine, as used by other firms for similar projects.

badged to suit, and thus entered the North American market. One outcome of this in 1985 was a substantial contract to supply the British Army with trail machines to a military specification, for which the big four-valve Rotax single was detuned.

The road-racing twins continued to run but with less success as the years passed. Then, in 1987, Armstrong sold the military machine operation to Harley-Davidson and the rest of the business back to Alan Clews, the founder of CCM.

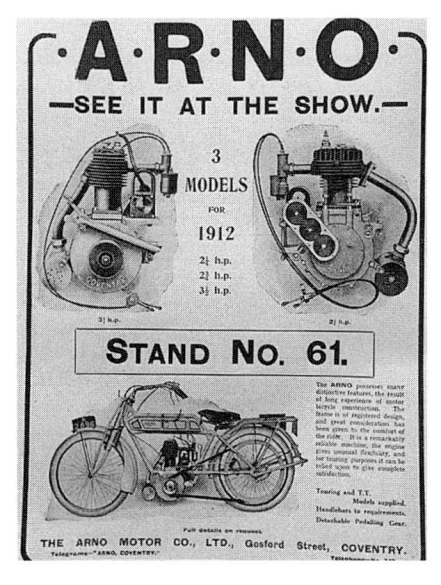

By 1912 the Arno had a dropped frame top-tube to lower the line, while this advertisement shows some of the engine features.

ARNO 1906–1915
A firm based in Gosford Street, Coventry, whose long and low singles joined their existing models at the late 1908 Stanley show. They were fitted with their own 3 or 3.5hp engines and had a rear-mounted chain-driven Bosch magneto and either an Amac or B&B carburettor. The cycle side offered sprung forks and detachable pedalling gear with footboards for the larger machine.

The two continued, to be joined in 1912 by a 2.25hp lightweight and a TT version of the 3.5hp model, this last a basic machine with direct-belt drive. In 1914 the TT model had a red finish and the marque took the name of Red Arno for a year or two with 3.5hp and 4.5hp models listed for 1915.

ARROW 1913–1917
Built by Kirk & Merifield of Bradford Street, Birmingham, who had begun making cycles in 1893, this was a typical lightweight powered by a 211cc two-stroke engine from Levis or Precision. A simple transmission and Chater-Lea cycle fittings completed this model, which was also sold under the Kirmer label from around 1915, mainly in Australia, and with a two-speed Burman gearbox.

ASCOT 1904–1906
A single cam mechanically opened both valves of this firm's 2.75hp engine, the machine being typical of the period but fitted with a band brake for the front wheel. The firm, based in Pentonville Road, London, listed a forecar as well as a solo.

The power rose to 3hp for 1905, when magneto ignition was an option. In addition, a 1hp French import was listed, its engine hung from the downtube, with belt drive and braced forks.

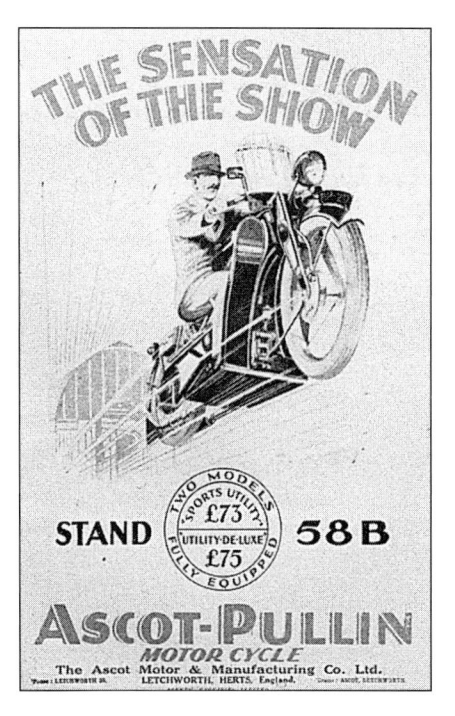

Late in 1928, Ascot Pullin ran this advertisement for their innovative new model, which had plenty of features but lacked handling.

The Ascot Pullin demonstrated Cyril Pullin's innovative thoughts, but also his lack of awareness of the rider's needs and desires.

ASCOT PULLIN 1928–1930
Cyril Pullin won the 1914 Senior TT and was involved with advanced designs, on and off, over the next forty years. His Ascot Pullin was announced late in 1928 as 'The New Wonder Motor Cycle', but was short lived as it suffered major development problems in 1929. By the end of the year the receiver was in and in 1930 the stock was being sold off by Rennos, a London dealer.

The machine itself bristled with innovation, starting with the 496cc ohv engine which was set horizontal with its three-speed gearbox built in-unit and located above the crankcase. Ignition was by gear-driven magneto and lubrication dry-sump.

This unit went into a frame built up from steel pressings with similar forks and the mechanics were hidden under pressed covers. Wire wheels with drum brakes were specified, but interconnected and with hydraulic actuation. There were fixtures and fittings as befitted a fully equipped tourer, down to a screen and wiper. Unfortunately it did not handle and the performance was sedate so few were sold.

Late in 1928 Pullin announced a sidecar to go with his motorcycle and, like that, it had pressed steel sides with these welded to the floor and ends to create a rigid shell. It was a monocoque structure and had a sprung sidecar wheel with hydraulic brake connected to the machine system. It was equally short-lived.

Thomas Ashburn chose to add front and rear suspension to his machine in 1904 and, a year later, went over to a JAP engine.

ASHBURN 1904–1905
Thomas Ashburn of Small Heath, Birmingham, modified his machine to a spring frame in 1904. At the front went long leading-links, supported by curved tubes that formed the front mudguard. For the rear, there was a pivoted fork controlled by a spring under the saddle – an early monoshock. For 1905 he fitted a 2.5hp JAP engine.

The forecar was quite popular in Edwardian days and this 1905 Ashford Greyhound was typical, but differed in having direct-chain drive.

ASHFORD 1904–1905
Based in Ashford, Middlesex, this firm produced a forecar called the Greyhound, which was powered by a 3hp engine from Fafnir or Minerva. Construction was typical of the type with a bucket seat for the rider and a wicker seat for the passenger, who sat over the front axle. Less usual was the direct drive by chain and the Bowden brakes. It was really only suitable for level districts as, without pedals or gears, hills would have been a problem. This was possibly the reason why the make was soon gone.

ASL 1909–1914
Associated Springs Ltd were based in Corporation Street, Stafford and differed from most others on two counts. Firstly, their machines had both front and rear suspension in an era of rigid frames and, secondly, they used air springs rather than the usual steel. At the front they fitted short leading-links and at the rear used short trailing-arms, in both cases controlled by a single air-spring. This could be pumped up as required to suit the rider's weight and a form of rolling seal was employed in the unit and claimed to be airtight.

Air Springs Limited models had front and rear suspension from the start, using air as the medium; this a 1910 example.

The rest of the machine was conventional with Peugeot single or V-twin engines and belt drive. For 1910 the single was a Fafnir, changing to a JAP or White & Poppe the next year, when the company name changed to Air Springs, and in 1912 Precision or Fafnir engines were used.

In 1913 a chain-driven two-speed gearbox appeared and the location of this was unusual for it was mounted ahead of the engine rather than behind. From this position it drove the rear wheel by a long belt, the pulleys being of much the same size. A conventional three-speed gearbox was a further option for the single and in this case a rigid frame was used although the front air-spring remained. For 1914, single and V-twin Precision engines were used along with a 5hp Fafnir V-twin and all models had the three-speed Sturmey-Archer gearbox and air suspension front and rear. This was the final year for this enterprising marque.

ASP 1997–1998
Andy Stevenson Performance, based in Nottinghamshire, produced this innovative, limited production machine which was first seen at the NEC late in 1997 where its price was given as £24,950. This reflected the advanced technology, hand-built construction, small numbers envisaged and the modern styling. The machine was designed around a Yamaha Thunderace engine unit that had both front and rear suspension systems bolted directly to it, each controlled by a single Maxton unit. There was hub-centre steering, cast-alloy wheels with disc brakes and carbon fibre bodywork to support the seat and enclose the fuel tank. It was expensive but light, slim and sleek with plenty of performance. However, by mid-1998 Andy had shelved the project as development costs looked to be too high, so only the prototype was built.

ASTER c.1910
Thought to have been made by a firm located in London but hardly a primitive at that date, by when cycle parts had moved on from the early cycle-frame layout and engines were much improved. Belt drive was still the norm and direct drive was usual, as was more than one speed.

Fine 1912 advertisement for Air Springs Limited machines, which were built with single or V-twin engines.

ASTON 1923–1925

This was the lightweight 148cc two-stroke built by the Aston Co. of Birmingham and first sold as the Atlas (see ATLAS 1921–1925). It had transmission options, rocking front fork and a simple construction, but was simply a replica with a new tank transfer. Like the Atlas it vanished when the trade slowed down.

ATLANTA DUO 1935–1936

One of the odd OEC designs of the 1930s, based on the Whitwood but without the car-type body. Its main feature was a 21in seat height that was achieved by lowering the engine and providing the rider with footboards that stretched forward beside the front wheel to form legshields. The low-slung frame had plunger rear-suspension and the OEC duplex steering, while there was a choice of 245 or 500cc ohv single or 750cc V-twin JAP engines. A dual seat with backrest provided the seating but even this luxury failed to impress buyers and, after a late-1935 announcement, there was no sign of it a year later.

ATLAS 1913–1914

A small and short-lived Coventry firm that only built TT machines using JAP or Blumfield 500cc engines assembled with other bought-in components under a new transfer and in a sporting style. They were finished in black and red with a torpedo tank held by plated bands, had Druid forks and fine looks, but failed to sell well.

ATLAS 1921–1925

Built by the Aston Co. of Witton Lane, Birmingham, this was another small lightweight first seen in the boom times of the early-1920s. It was typical of the time with a 143cc two-stroke engine with front Amac or Wex carburettor, rear-mounted CAV magneto and large external flywheel. This engine drove either a countershaft or a two-speed Albion gearbox by chain, final drive being by belt. A clutch was an option, while the frame was simple and fitted with rocking forks.

By 1924 the best model had three speeds and all-chain drive but it was back to the original models for 1925, their last year. Before then the firm tried badge engineering around 1923 by changing the marque name on the tank to their own Aston. This failed to help sales at all as the machines were otherwise the same.

AURORA 1902–1907

A small firm in Coventry that produced a 2.5hp machine whose engine they made themselves and mounted vertically in a loop frame. By 1904 it was joined by a forecar fitted with a 3.5hp engine, both engines still made by the firm, which soon dropped from the lists.

AURORA 1919–1920

This make was built in Ramsey, Isle of Man, by Graham Oates following construction of an initial machine in Douglas. It was an assembly job using parts bought in and had a 318cc Dalm two-stroke engine. Soon after it was finished it carried Graham and his father to the summit of Snaefell.

Two machines were prepared for the 1920 TT using a Juckes four-speed gearbox, but only one started and that retired. Only two or three more were built, one with a 4hp Blackburne engine, and that was the end of the project.

AUSTEN 1903–1905

A firm based in Lewisham, London, who entered the market offering a primitive powered by a 2.25hp Kelecom engine, vertically mounted in a loop frame. This was braced by an added upper chain-stay and extra top-tubes. Belt drive was standard but with chain and belt via a countershaft an option.

The Austen, a typical Edwardian model, used a purchased engine and strengthened loop frame with added brace.

Part of the 1920 boom, the Autoglider required the users to stand at first, although a seat did appear on later models.

AUTOGLIDER 1919–1921

One of several scooters of the post-Great War period. It had a 269cc Villiers or 292cc Union two-stroke engine mounted above the front wheel, together with its magneto and the silencer, and transmission was directly to this wheel by chain via a clutch. The rider had to stand on a platform and small disc wheels were fitted. The handlebars were carried by a long twin-tube extension and the cylindrical fuel tank sat between them. Later versions added a seat and lower bars with the tank set across them.

AUTOPED 1916–1921

An American scooter that began the post-Great War phase in Britain where it was built under licence by Imperial Motor Industries of London. It had a 162cc four-stroke engine that was fitted on the left of the disc front wheel, a pressed-steel platform frame, enclosed disc rear wheel and no seat. The lengthy steering column was the control for clutch and brake, it being pushed or pulled as required. A second version had an electric motor in place of the four-stroke, powered by batteries carried on the platform.

In 1919 one was on show in a Selfridge's store window and another in use in London by an MP, this acting as a catalyst for the short-lived scooter boom.

AUTOSCO 1920
One of the firms that turned to scooters after the Great War, Brown & Layfield of London adopted the complete Auto-Wheel unit as the rear wheel of their simple device. A tubular frame much along the lines of a ladies' pedal cycle, devoid of suspension either front or rear and with 20in spoked wheels, formed the remainder of the specification. It was single speed, of course, and light to handle, but otherwise a product of little merit.

AUTO SIDECAR 1914
This was a bicycle attachment with a difference, for the firm, based in Cubitt Town, London, offered a light wicker sidecar to clamp to your bicycle. The trick was the small two-stroke engine hung on the rear of the chair which drove the sidecar wheel and thus the whole outfit.

AUTO-TRICYCLE 1914
A short-lived three-wheeler built by Armstrong & Co. of Goldhawk Road, London, using a 2.5hp JAP engine. It had 20in wheels, the single at the front, and one bucket seat.

AUTO WHEEL 1910–1922
A.W. Wall first built a machine to his design in 1903 which became the Roc in 1904. Late in 1909 he had a new idea, the Wall Auto Wheel, which was an attachment that fixed to a bicycle on the right side of its rear wheel with a driven wheel of its own. It incorporated a 1.75hp two-stroke engine whose cylinder pointed to the rear, the Bosch magneto forward. Between them the crankcase and hub carried the crankshaft and the epicyclic reduction gear to the wheel. The mudguard was formed to act as the petrol and oil tanks, and two flexible clamps secured the wheel to the bicycle while allowing it to hinge to absorb road shocks.

The Auto Wheel unit attached to a stock bicycle, and was built from 1910 for some years and also used by other makers.

By 1911, the Auto Wheel had a 110cc flat-twin two-stroke engine with a vertical crankshaft and magneto above and flywheel below the crankcase. A spiral gear and then a bevel gear drove the road wheel. During 1912 the wheel changed to its final form with a vertically mounted 1hp 115cc four-stroke engine. This had a large external flywheel and its camshaft was geared at 4:1 so had two sets of cams fitted to it. This was done so that the chain drive to the wheel could be taken from it and the result gave the required reduction ratio.

The unit was said to be made by BSA for Wall, one was ridden by Prince George of Battenberg and in 1914 some were sold as the BSA auto wheel de luxe. One was fitted to a tricycle between the rear wheels and the attachment was sold up to 1914.

Post-war, in 1920, the unit was used by at least three firms as the motive power in the manner of the early Singer. Thus, it replaced an existing wheel, being the rear one for the Autosco and the Willow, and the front one for the Silva. Late in 1921 the Auto Wheel Motorette appeared with the rear wheel powered and this machine was retailed by Gamages store in London. The Auto Wheel continued in use to 1922.

AUTO WHEEL MOTORETTE 1921–1922
The major London spares and accessories retailers Gamages, who were nationally known through their advertising in the motorcycle press, regularly sold complete machines, often under their own name, but always manufactured for them by firms in the trade. This would certainly have been the case with this product, which took the form of a simple scooter with the motive power supplied by an Auto Wheel unit that replaced the normal rear wheel. The small aiv four-stroke engine gave 100mpg (2.8ltr/100km) and speeds of from 3 to 25mph (5–40km/h), but the device was unsprung and somewhat crude. In November 1921 Gamages were advertising it at £35, against a regular price of £42.50; exactly the kind of selling ploy they were good at exploiting.

AUXILIARY WHEEL SIDECAR 1905–1906
Located in Child's Place, Earls Court Road, London, at the late-1905 Stanley show, this firm introduced a sidecar attachment that fitted to the left side of a bicycle. It carried the engine, which drove the sidecar wheel by chain and belt, while the passenger sat above this in a wicker-work chair.

The Auxiliary Wheel Sidecar of 1905 was an attachment that carried the engine as well as the passenger, the drive going to the sidecar wheel.

AVON c.1919–1920
One of many firms that built a few machines in the early post-war years before lack of supplies halted them. They offered typical lightweights using the 269cc Villiers engine.

AVONDALE 1903
Built to the design of a Mr Price, a

cycle dealer of the High Street, Evesham, Worcestershire, this was a machine fitted with a 223cc Buchet four-stroke engine clipped above the downtube of its bicycle frame which had Chater-Lea fittings. A typical primitive, it had direct-belt drive and braced forks to complete the simple design. Production was limited.

AVONVALE 1903
This was thought to have been made in Worcester for a brief period, but not related to the Avondale made in Evesham. It must have been a primitive with an imported or bought-in engine and belt drive.

AYRES-HAYMAN 1920
One of a rash of machines at this date that were heavily promoted but came to nothing. This had the 689cc flat-twin sv Coventry-Victor engine, set in-line with a duplex tube-frame and leaf-spring rear-suspension. The maker's own gearbox was specified, but otherwise all the major components were to be bought in. It was envisaged as being most suitable for sidecar work and a price of 148 guineas was quoted in January 1920 for a complete outfit. But in March of the same year it was announced that Mr Harold Hayman had retired from the Viaduct Motor Company of Broadheath, Altrincham in Cheshire, the company behind the design, and that the project would henceforth be known as the Ayres-Layland.

AYRES-LAYLAND 1920
Successor to the Ayres-Hayman flat-twin and still a project of the Viaduct Motor Company, who now had Mr W.H. Layland advising and assisting in getting the 689cc sv flat-twin ready for production. By June 1920 a complete machine was shown for the first time, now with a three-speed Sturmey-Archer gearbox. It was described at some length in the technical press but, so far as is known, it never progressed beyond the prototype stage.

◆ B ◆

BAC 1951–1953
After manufacture of the original Bond motorcycle passed to Ellis of Leeds, the Bond Aircraft and Engineering Co., or BAC, introduced a more conventional machine. This was smaller than usual, but in proportion and called the Lilliput. It was powered by either a 99cc Villiers 1F engine with two-speed gearbox or a 125cc JAP two-stroke with three speeds.

They reached the market in 1951 but supplies of the JAP engine were not reliable, so only the smaller machine was listed for 1952. It was joined by the Gazelle scooter, which was of conventional form with small wheels and platform behind a frontal shield. At the rear it differed in the use of a grill of steel bars that ran around its 122cc Villiers 10D engine. For 1953 only the Gazelle was listed, but with the choice of the 99cc 1F engine as well as the 10D. After this, the model was taken over by Projects & Developments of Blackburn but no more was heard of it.

The BAC Gazelle scooter had its own ideas on style and line, but kept to a prosaic Villiers engine for its brief life.

BAINES 1901–1902
An advanced machine for its time, the Baines was built in Gainsborough, Lincolnshire using a De Dion engine located vertically in a bicycle-type frame with braced forks. Two versions were built, one with a clutch and direct chain-drive, the other with belt drive using similar size pulleys to a reduction gear at the rear wheel. In neither form were pedals fitted.

BAKER 1928–1930
Frank Baker was involved with the industry from its early days, working in America, then manufacturing the Precision engines and machines. He had a connection with Beardmore in the early-1920s, but in 1928 was located in Alvechurch Road, Northfield, Birmingham. From there he offered two lightweights using 172 and 247cc Villiers engines and three-speed Albion gearboxes.

For 1929 these two were joined by other versions of the same size plus 147 and 196cc models. The next year saw no 147cc but a 343cc in its place, along with two versions of the 172 and 196cc models. In addition to the two-strokes there was one further model with an inclined 249cc sv James engine offered from March 1930. However, late that year Baker sold out to the James firm who went on to use his frame for some of their models.

Only a manufacturer for a couple of years, Frank Baker listed lightweights such as this, but in 1930 sold out to James.

During 1930 a four-stroke Baker appeared, using a James side-valve engine thanks to the link established between the firms.

BAMBER 1903–1905
R. Bamber had a bicycle shop and cycle-making business in the Lancashire seaside resort of Southport. Around 1903 he extended his scope in trade by constructing a number of single and V-twin motorcycles of standard appearance and with direct-belt drive. One such example took part in the 1903 Speed Trials in the town, ridden by F.C. Barrow. The company's works were in Hall Street, where a team of forty mechanics were working soon after the turn of the century.

BANSHEE 1921–1924
A Banshee was a kind of female fairy who, it was said in Irish and Scottish folklore, attached herself to a particular house and foretold the death of an inhabitant by making an appearance. So, a very strange choice of name for a marque that emanated from the Worcestershire town of Bromsgrove. They began with a 269cc Villiers two-stroke and standard cycle parts with either a single speed or two speeds through an Albion gearbox, both of course having belt final-drive. These continued for 1922, plus a three-speed model for sidecar work, with a Barr & Stroud 349cc sleeve-valve-engined four-stroke model joining by the middle of the year.

They went unlisted in 1923, but must have remained in the trade, because by March 1924 they had expanded to encompass models with 147 and 247cc Villiers and 349, 499 and 998cc Barr & Stroud engines, the latter a mighty V-twin. A two-speed Burman gearbox appeared on the 247cc model and each of the B&S machines had all-chain drive. However, this huge effort must have exhausted the Banshee Manufacturing Company of Crown Close Works, who retired from the motorcycle business soon after.

BANTAMOTO 1951–1952
This was a cycle attachment produced by Cyc-Auto in their Acton, London works, that attached to the left side of the rear wheel of a bicycle. It had a 38cc two-stroke engine with vertical cylinder, flywheel magneto and petroil lubrication, the fuel carried in a tank mounted above the engine. Transmission was by three stages of spur gears, the last in mesh with an internally toothed gear-ring attached to the wheel. It was a neat design but must have been expensive to make, so Cyc-Auto soon went back to their own range.

BARBER 1966–DATE
A successful grass-track rider, Denny Barber turned to building machines carrying his name, working to his customer's specification. Another product was replicas of the old Rotrax speedway rolling chassis, all ready for the engine to slot into.

BARD 1898
A cycle firm in Birmingham who, among others, refused to pay Harry Lawson royalties on the patents he held for engines, and built them in the De Dion image in various sizes and powers, with most fitted to tricycles. The Bard tricycle was typical of the time and fitted a genuine 2.25hp De Dion engine hung out behind the rear axle in a heavy-duty frame with braced forks. The fuel tank went behind the saddle tube with the battery box under the top tube, which carried the control levers. An external-contracting band brake was fitted to the front wheel.

BARD-JAP 1919–1920
Less than a handful of V-twin JAP-powered sv machines, built for sidecar work by 'Wilkie' Wilkes of High Street, Walsall in Staffordshire, bore this name on their tanks. Three-speed Sturmey-Archer gearboxes were used, but other details are scarce. It is said that a well-known music hall artist of the day, Wilkie Bard, provided the spur for the marque name, given the similarity between his forename and the nickname of its constructor. At least one example survived into recent times.

BARNES 1904–1906
George A. Barnes of Lewisham, London entered the market using Stevens engines of 2.75, 3 or 3.5hp. He offered both a solo and a forecar, the latter having twin exhaust pipes that ran down to a single silencer.

For 1905 the forecar could have a 5hp water-cooled engine or a 4hp air-cooled one, the latter also available for the solo, lighter versions of which used a 2.25hp engine.

Barnes used Steven engines for both his solos and this forecar with its fine wicker passenger chair in period style.

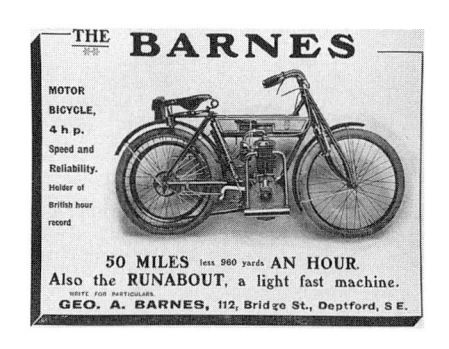

A Barnes Solo was advertised for 1905, with Stevens engine silenced by two exhaust pipes leading to a single silencer.

BARNSLEY 1898
It was claimed that William Barnsley of Bilston, near Wolverhampton, patented a motorcycle with the engine mounted within the frame. A dozen or so were said to have been built, no doubt with De Dion or Minerva engines, and that the patent was then sold to Humber. However, that firm was first involved with the Pennington and then produced machines using P&M patents in 1902, these using the engine as the frame downtube, rather than installing it within the frame.

BARNSON 1923
This was built by A.C. Barnes in his workshop at Barnes Garage, Wokingham, Berkshire and was a typical lightweight with two-stroke Villiers engine and either direct-belt drive, or chain drive to a countershaft gearbox and belt. Less than a dozen machines were constructed and exact specifications would have varied, depending on customer choice and the availability of components in such small quantities, but, so it was said, only first quality materials were used.

BARON 1921
A short-lived Birmingham marque, which offered lightweights of conventional outline fitted with 269cc Villiers or 292cc Union two-stroke engines and a medium-weight model with a 348cc sv Blackburne engine. Gearing options were Albion two-speed chain-cum-belt with or without clutch and kickstarter on all models, or single speed only on the lightweights. Senspray carburettors and Saxon spring forks were amongst the other bought-in fittings on these machines.

BARRON 1976–1981
This firm was based in Hornchurch, Essex and entered the market with the Barron 125, which featured an Italian Minarelli two-stroke engine unit with a five-speed gearbox. It was assembled in the UK and was soon joined by an imported moped and then a junior cross moped. Most of

Barron produced a range of small models assembled in the UK using Italian parts but, in reality, these were badged Fantics.

A mobile test-bed for Barr & Stroud sleeve-valve engines, created using 350cc AJS cycle parts and other proprietary components.

these were Fantic models with a change of badge and this arrangement continued for several years.

BARR AND STROUD 1921

In order to test out the capabilities of the single-sleeve-valve engine he had designed for motorcycle application, Douglas Barr installed his prototype in the frame and cycle parts of a 349cc AJS. Retaining most of the original machine's components, including its three-speed gearbox but of course excluding its engine, this test bed was run on the public road for several months in 1921 during which time his 348cc sleeve-valve four-stroke engine performed satisfactorily. It was made available to the manufacturing trade in November of that year and later joined by 499cc single and 998cc V-twin versions. Barr's mobile test bed survived, however, and was exhibited at motorcycle events in the 1990s.

BARRY 1904–1905, 1910

This was an unusual machine, built in the Glamorgan town of the same name, and had a flat-twin-cylinder rotary engine. It was first seen at the late-1904 Stanley show. Of around 200cc, the engine turned on its fixed crankshaft, the cylinders and heads bereft of fins, and was fed by a gas storage reservoir that balanced the silencer.

Enclosed in an aluminium case that had cooling air holes, the engine rotated between twin downtube sections of the frame. The drive to the rear wheel was lacking from the show model. Early in 1905 the engine was moved to just ahead of the pedals, the frame revised to suit and belt drive fitted, but after that there was no news for some years.

The engine came up again in 1910 as the subject of a patent in the names of W.A. Richards and C.R. Redrup, the latter to become known for a radial engine in later years. No more was heard of the rotary unit.

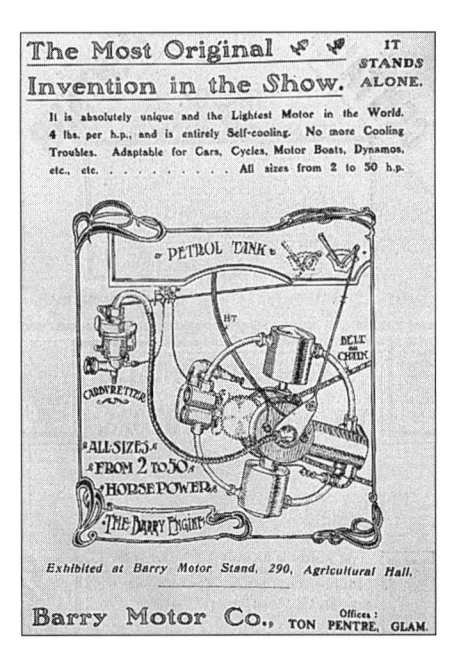

One of the strangest engines of the early days was this 1905 rotary Barry, with a flat-twin layout balanced by twin reservoirs.

BARTER 1902–1905

Joseph Barter of Aston Gate, Bristol, designed an engine that had its drive pulley mounted on the camshaft, thus allowing it to be larger than usual to reduce belt slip. The machine it went into was a primitive, the engine inclined above the frame downtube.

Few were built before Barter moved on to a flat-twin engine design, first called the Fée, then the Fairy, and the forerunner of the Douglas.

BARTON 1975–1982

Barry Hart had a background in developing Suzuki triples for road racing, trading as Barton Engineering, and in 1975 joined up with Spondon frames to produce the Sparton. While this was modelled on the Suzuki RG500, to the extent of using a square-four disc-valve two-stroke engine, it differed a great deal in its construction and details.

From this work came the Phoenix 500 and 750 fours which performed well and found fame as the Silver Dream Racer in the film of that name starring David Essex. The firm then became involved, along with CCM, with Armstrong Competition Motorcycles and worked on their engines. In time the Barton fours lost ground to Suzuki and Yamaha, who were constantly moving forward in research and design.

David Essex astride the Silver Dream Racer, actually a modified 500cc Barton, which he rode at Silverstone for the climax of the film.

BASIL 1911

These were built at the W.B. Payne Cycle Works in Harlesden, London using a JAP sv engine in the format of the period.

BAT 1901–1925

'Best After Test', so the slogan ran from 1903, but the name would seem to have come from the founder, Samuel Batson, while early advertisements showed a cricket bat and the mammal. Batson had been a cyclist for many years, but later became interested in motorcycles. This led to their study and, in 1901, to patents of some important improvements, the building of a complete machine to demonstrate them, and approaches to makers.

None took Batson up, so in 1902 he went into business at Kingswood Road, Penge, London to build machines and one, ridden by F.W. Chase, was soon setting records; hence the slogan. The machine used had a De Dion engine in typical primitive parts, but a sprung sub-frame was available as an option. For 1903 the engine was an MMC and no pedals were fitted, while the next year brought a forecar powered by a water-cooled engine and some machines with Minerva engines.

T.H. Tessier had joined the firm in 1903 and took many records riding BAT machines. In 1905 he bought the company and for 1906 switched to JAP, Stevens and Soncin engines. For road use there were singles and V-twins, either rigid or with the sprung frame, this actually a sub-frame that carried the saddle and footrests.

In a year or two Tessier moved over completely to JAP engines and competed in the first 1907 TT but retired. The next year saw Harry Bashall second in the twin-cylinder class on his BAT, but that was the best the make would do in the Island.

By 1908 the BAT was known for its comfort and speed, while it met with success at Brooklands where its build suited the track. For 1909 the range expanded to add a 2.5hp lightweight model alongside larger singles,

A 1903 BAT constructed with vertical engine, cylindrical tank and curious saddle support. A sprung sub-frame was an option.

The 1904 BAT had a De Dion engine, braced fork, direct-belt drive and sprung frame.

For 1910, BAT offered this single with JAP engine, magneto well out of harm's way, and sprung wheels front and rear.

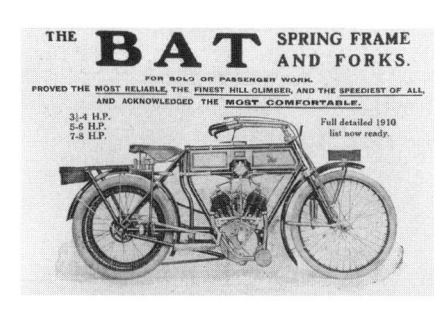

Two BAT twins were listed for 1910, now with the saddle mounted in the more usual manner but still with suspension and the high-level magneto.

all with mechanically operated inlet-valves, the twins still using the older aiv type. Racing versions were listed, while the firm also produced sidecars and a quadricycle in the form of a motorcycle with sidecar, but with two steering front wheels.

To alleviate production problems, the range was reduced to just three models for 1910, a 3.5hp single and two twins. A two-speed P&M gear was listed then but, by 1912, a countershaft gearbox with kickstarter had replaced it along with a clutch in the rear hub. The singles were dropped for 1913 when the TT model had ohv and the 8hp had all-chain drive. The last year before the Great War saw more models, all V-twins with ariations of transmission, while the marque continued to gain sporting successes.

During the war some machines were sold to Russia, but not all were paid for after October 1917 and motorcycle production gave way to shell cases.

The name was back in 1919 with 6 and 8hp V-twin models with three speeds and chain drive, but the machines were essentially built up from spares available on the store shelves. This continued from then on with a 4hp V-twin added for 1921, while in 1922 Tessier's sons took over the business. A 2.75hp single joined the twins for 1923 and in 1925 the make became Bat-Martinsyde when that firm was bought and its two V-twins added to the BAT range for what became their final year.

BAT-MARTINSYDE 1923–1925

Following the acquisition of the assets and designs of the Martinsyde firm in late 1923 by the Bat company of Penge in South London, the two ranges continued under the Bat-Martinsyde trading name. By 1924, 498 and 677cc eoi V-twins with three-speed gearboxes of Martinsyde origin, were listed alongside a Bat-evolved 976cc sv V-twin JAP model with Sturmey-Archer gearbox in the patent spring-frame and with Magdyno electric lighting. A 344cc sv JAP single completed the line-up for 1925, which was the final production year, although the company itself remained in the trade as repairers and suppliers of engine spares for some time.

BAUGHAN 1921 AND 1930–1936

H.P. Baughan had a business in Stroud, Gloucestershire and, in 1921, they tried out a light cyclecar with a single rear wheel driven by chain from a three-speed Sturmey-Archer gearbox, which in turn took its power from an 8hp sv Blackburne V-twin set across the frame. A dickey seat was built into the simple bodywork for an occasional second passenger, but it seems unlikely that the device progressed beyond the artist's impression published at the time of its announcement.

Much later Baughan turned to sidecar trials, driving in which he became very prominent and later became much involved with event organizing. His outfits had the sidecar wheel-driven, a useful advantage when event regulations allowed, and from 1930 he built machines, virtually to order. Solos as well as sidecars were built and the engines ranged from 250 to 500cc, had sv or ohv and came from Blackburne, Sturmey-Archer or JAP. Production was usually about one per month.

BEALE 1990–DATE

George Beale has been well known for his immaculate restorations of racing motorcycles and for the performance of his race entries for many years. From this work has come the production of Matchless G50 models in standard and lightweight form in small numbers, as well as foreign replicas in recent years. These last have culminated in multis from both Benelli, the fours, and Honda, the fabulous six as raced in the 1960s.

BEARDMORE PRECISION 1920–1925

During the Great War, F.E. Baker Ltd, of Moorsom Street and later Kings Norton in Birmingham, developed an advanced machine powered by a 349cc two-stroke in-unit with a two-speed gear. The company was well placed to produce such a motor, as its reputation came from the manufacture and supply of its own Precision

This was the unusual front suspension of the Beardmore Precision, with double leaf-springs and external-contracting drum brake.

engines to the trade in pre-war days. However, a complete machine was a different proposition and, though launched in 1919 under the Precision name, by early 1920 it had become the Beardmore Precision, following an association with the giant William Beardmore engineering group.

Frank Baker's engine was along conventional two-stroke lines, although the pumped lubrication system in which the magneto drive-chain doubled as an oil conveyor was novel. The gearing too was imaginative, in that sprockets at either end of the crankshaft connected through chains to differing sized sprockets mounted on a countershaft, selection being by means of expanding clutches from a handlebar control. The engine and gear were contained in aluminium casings as a complete unit.

The unit went into cycle parts that were a mixture of pressed steel and tubular construction, the petrol tank acting as frame top-tube and heavy deep-section mudguards doubling as stressed supports for both wheels. These were fully sprung, by a rocking action fork at the front and cantilevered arms at the rear, both controlled by multiple leaf springs. Large alloy footboards swept upwards at their front ends to become legshields, the whole presenting an unconventional yet practical package.

Unconventional also meant odd and this aspect of the machine did not find favour with the buying public, added to which the 349cc engine was somewhat lacking in power. A sports version without the rear springing was tried in 1921, then came a 598cc sv model with true three-speed gearbox in-unit, the shafts and pinions supplied by Sturmey-Archer. This went into the sprung frame and added the missing power, but didn't address the appearance problem.

A sleeve-valve 348cc engine from Barr & Stroud with three-speed gearbox and choice of chain-cum-belt or all-chain drive soon followed and then a team of three machines was entered in the 1922 Senior TT equipped with a new 496cc sv engine. These all retired, but later in the year a model with a 496cc sv engine was catalogued in the sprung or rigid frames but with a revised link-action girder fork. This was exhibited at the 1922 motorcycle show along with a 348cc sv having two-speed chain-cum-belt transmission. A sports version of the latter, with Ricardo aluminium piston, joined in 1923 and was followed by a 246cc sv machine, this time in a tubular triangulated frame, as the company began to address the appearance problems of the original concept.

Beardmore Precision repeated the odd suspension and brake at the rear of the machine, which involved extra pivots and links.

The 246, 348 and 596cc sv models went forward into 1924, when Frank Baker severed his connections with the firm, and experimental racing machines were entered for the TT: a 250cc ohv with leaf-spring controlled valves and an ohc 350 single with four valves, two carburettors and shaft-driven camshaft. Neither design brought success, but the ohv 250, with coil valve-springs, was added to the range for 1925, which together with its earlier sv equivalent, plus the 348 and 596cc machines, brought the marque to its close. Beardmore, however, remained involved with cars for several more years and Frank Baker was soon to announce a new marque under his own surname.

BEAUFORT 1922–1925

The Argson Engineering Company of Beaufort Works, Twickenham, Middlesex centred their main business around a three-wheeled carriage powered by a 170cc two-stroke engine in the years immediately following the Great War. For a short period they also produced their own complete lightweight motorcycle under the Beaufort name, utilizing the two-stroke engine with direct-belt drive in conventional cycle parts. A Villiers-engined version with crankshaft-mounted clutch was also available, but production was spasmodic, small and the machine typical of its time.

BEAU-IDEAL 1904–1907

This Wolverhampton make was seen at the late-1904 Stanley show, each machine fitted with a 3hp Fafnir engine and belt drive. They were typical primitives but short lived, soon fading from sight.

BEAUMONT 1920–1922 AND 1945–1947

Monty Beaumont and his brothers traded in Leeds and first produced machines using the 269cc Wall two-stroke and 348cc sv Blackburne engines, all with two-speed gearboxes. For 1922 they listed a 348cc two-stroke and 399cc four-stroke but that was their last year.

What was far more interesting was a 1920 prototype they built using a Redrup three-cylinder radial engine. The engine type became a fixation with Monty and he produced a number of paper designs for motorcycles using this engine type.

Much later, in 1945, leaflets and promotional mentions illustrated a new range of Beaumont motorcycles with telescopic forks and a twin-engine set across the rigid frame. At the same time he was involved with Mr Kendall, an MP, on the design of a People's Car that was to use the radial-three engine, but the few built actually fitted a French Grégoire flat-twin. A good deal of Beaumont's life was a mixture of fact and fantasy and he did step over the mark at least once, which resulted in imprisonment for false pretences.

BEESTON 1896–1901

One of Lawson's companies, this firm first produced a tricycle that mirrored the De Dion in having the 1.25hp engine mounted behind the rear axle, which it drove by gears. By 1898 they produced a quadricycle that was essentially the tricycle fitted with two front wheels, between which hung the passenger seat in forecar style. That same year brought a motorcycle whose engine went just ahead of the rear wheel, the frame being extended to accommodate it. Direct chain drive was employed. The company closed down in 1901.

BELVEDERE 1910–1911

This make appeared late in 1910, with the belt drive and spring forks that were typical of the times. Engines were either a 3.5hp Precision single or 6hp Sarolea or Precision V-twins, but the make was short lived.

BENTLEY 1904–1905

J.F. Bentley was based in New Bridge Street, London and showed a forecar constructed as a tradesman's sample cart at the late-1904 Stanley show. Powered by a 3.5hp Fafnir engine, it was of a light build and hardly up to the wear and tear of business life and the roads, tracks and cobblestones of the time.

BERNON-MORELLE 1923

While this machine had the lines of a light car, it was actually not one but two motorcycles held side by side and joined by a tubular structure. Each machine had a two-stroke Levis engine driving a three-speed gearbox and the rear wheel by chain, with sprung forks and a tubular frame. Seating for two went between the machines whose forks were linked, the two halves were easy to separate, and panelling, including a small door, enclosed the works to give the car appearance.

Beeston created this two-seater machine in 1898 by adding twin front wheels and forecar seat to a tricycle.

An extended frame was needed to accommodate the engine just ahead of the rear wheel, on this 1898 Beeston with direct-chain drive.

BERWICK 1929–1930

A curious lightweight that was built by the Berwick Motor Co. of Tweedmouth, Northumbria to show at Olympia. It used a Villiers engine, with 247 and 343cc sizes on offer, but turned round to put the flywheel magneto at the front. The crankshaft was extended aft to drive a three-speed gearbox bolted to the crankcase, and the box drove the rear

An unusual lightweight, the Berwick differed in having its Villiers engine turned to drive directly to the gearbox and had shaft drive.

wheel by shaft and underslung worm. The unit went into a duplex frame with Brampton girder forks, and 7in brakes were fitted front and rear. The company moved to Banbury, Oxfordshire; however, no more was heard of this marque.

BEWLEY 1962–C.1972
A grass-track model built by George Bewley in the format of the period. Later he went on to develop his own two-speed, quick-change gearbox.

B&H C.1923
This firm was an engine manufacturer in the main, offering 247, 349 and 498cc singles plus V-twins of 494, 698 and 995cc. They also built a few machines using the largest V-twin engine and proprietary parts, but this was a limited activity.

BIKOTOR 1951
This was a cycle attachment that sat its 47cc two-stroke engine over the rear wheel, which it drove by friction. It was an all-alloy unit to keep the weight down and had a flywheel magneto and petroil lubrication, the fuel contained in a tank strapped on top of the crankcase. Although neat and well made, it failed to catch on so soon went.

BINDY 1979–1980
George Harris was involved with racing Bantams for many years and in 1979 decided to use his knowledge of small two-strokes to create the Bindy, or 'Britain Is Not Dead Yet'. The 125cc engine came from Aubrey Upton of Leicester and was first designed for kart racing under the name Manx. George added water cooling, installed it in a Jack Machin frame and completed the machine using British parts except for the brakes. Ridden by Dick Hunter it proved to be competitive in Britain for a season or two.

BINKS 1903–1905
Later famous for carburettors, Charles Binks of Nottingham designed a machine powered by an advanced in-line four-cylinder engine in 1903. This fitted into a diamond frame to drive the rear wheel by an enclosed chain. Strutted front-forks were used, while the rider was offered a bucket seat mounted on coil springs.

For 1904 it was joined by a version having the engine mounted transversely but otherwise similar. Both models had a clutch, and an engine

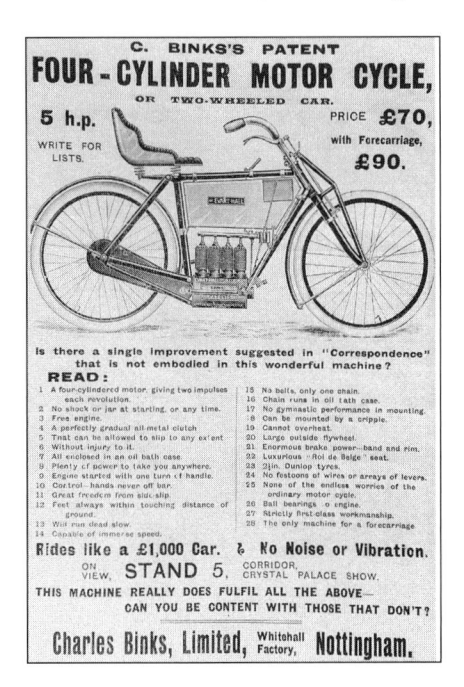

This 1904 advertisement shows the Binks four with the engine in-line, but they also built one with a transverse engine before they turned to carburettors.

speed of 2,000rpm was claimed, as was an output of 6hp. During 1904 the in-line machine was sold as the 5hp Evart-Hall.

Late in 1904 a demonstration was given at Coventry by two machines having in-line engines. The smaller had 2 × 2 inch (412cc) dimensions and weighed 145lb (66kg), the larger had 2.5 × 2.5 inch (804cc) and weighed 180lb (82kg). High costs soon sent Binks to design carburettors.

BIRCH 1902–1904
Designer J.J. Birch was one half of the Perks & Birch who produced the motor wheel later used by Singer. He also produced a primitive motorcycle that had the crankcase and bottom bracket as part of the main frame. Several engine sizes were built, of 2, 2.5, and 3.5hp, while the design was also built by Bradbury under licence.

BK 1904
Bransom, Kent & Co. of Goswell Road, London, having previously produced the Royal George make, exhibited their own machine at the 1904 Crystal Palace show, fitted with an upright 2.75hp Minerva engine. The marque went as quickly as it arrived.

BLACKBOROUGH 1919
Another short-lived post-Great War make that chose to use the 269cc Metro-Tyler two-stroke engine with chain drive to a two-speed gearbox from the same supplier. Belt final-drive and simple cycle parts completed the machine that was built in a garage in Reigate, Surrey by F. Douch.

BLACKBURNE 1913–1922
First known as the De Havilland, the Blackburne entered the market with a 3.5hp model early in 1913. Built by Burney & Blackburne at Berkhamsted, Hertfordshire its 499cc sv engine had a large outside flywheel and a one-piece forged crankshaft. These combined to make it one of the smoothest running engines of the

time. The machine had belt drive to a three-speed hub gear and was fitted with Saxon forks.

By late-1913 the firm had moved to Tongham in Surrey and changed their name from the original Blackburn without the 'e'. The model adopted a three-speed Sturmey-Archer gearbox, chain-cum-belt drive and Druid forks, while a single-speed TT model was also listed and both continued for 1915 and 1916.

Post-war, manufacture was in the hands of OEC at Gosport in Hampshire and there were three models for 1919, including the 3.5hp machine with three speeds from 1916 but with all-chain drive and rated at 4hp. The others were a 2.75hp two-speed single and an 8hp V-twin combination, but only this and the 4hp single ran on for 1921, and the twin alone for 1922.

Acknowledging the OEC involvement, from 1923 the two company names combined, until 1925, as OEC Blackburne. After this, Blackburne themselves concentrated on producing engines for other firms well into the 1930s.

BLACKFORD 1902–1904

This was a typical primitive with its Minerva engine hung from the downtube of a heavy-duty bicycle frame. No doubt one of the many cycle dealers who tried their luck with powered machines.

BLACK PRINCE 1919–1920

An advanced design by E.W. Cameron who had premises in Doncaster, Yorkshire, this machine was to use either a single-cylinder 292cc Union engine or a 396cc flat-twin, two-stroke engine having but a single sparking plug. This latter engine design was the patent of H. Singleton of Liverpool and the single-plug layout was achieved by connecting the two combustion chambers with a tube in which the plug went, along with an automatic poppet valve that controlled the passage of the mixture from the common crankcase to above the pistons.

The rest of the engine was more conventional, although the pistons had flat tops, which was unusual for the time. The big ends were offset to reduce the rocking couple, and they and the mains had plain bearings. The engine was installed along the frame and drove back to a clutch and two-speed gear that drove a bevel pair to turn the drive for a shaft to the rear wheel.

The rest of the machine was equally unusual, although it did not get past the drawing board. The frame, in pressed steel, was Cameron's work and comprised two sides that joined at the headstock and ran down and back to fully enclose the mechanics and then form the rear mudguard. The fuel tank was set in the top and the result was not unlike the Velocette LE of thirty years later. Suspension was by bottom-link forks at the front and pivoted-fork controlled by spring units at the rear.

All in, the Black Prince was a remarkable design and the engine at least was built and did run. However, it was too advanced for the times or any other than a well-financed firm, so it failed to make the market. In 1920 Cameron committed suicide at his home and with him went the future prospects of both the motorcycle and the Black Prince Runabout, a three-wheeler designed by A.G. Cocks and for which production arrangements were already in hand from a factory in Barnard Castle, County Durham.

BLENHEIM-JAP 1913–1914

A pre-Great War machine built for racing or fast road-work using an ohv JAP engine and belt drive. The rigid frame had Druid-pattern forks, while the minimal fittings would have allowed it to be ridden to an event, stripped, competed and then ridden home.

BLIZZARD EARLY 1900s

This marque was thought to hail from the East London area, possibly East Ham or Ilford, and was powered by Minerva or MMC engines fitted into a primitive frame assembly.

BLUEBIRD C.1920s

John Ireland, along with a Mr Johnston, patented a revised form of artillery wheel for cars using a weldless steel tube as the rim with hollow-cast aluminium spokes into which went wooden cores. Clever but not a commercial success, so in the early 1920s Ireland turned his hand to motorcycles and produced some machines under the Bluebird name using V-twin JAP engines for most.

BLUMFIELD 1903 AND 1910–1914

An early model with this name was known to have been running about Birmingham in 1903 powered by a Minerva engine. Later, the firm produced engines for the trade, while the marque reappeared in 1910 in its own right. In that year they were built in Lower Essex Street, Birmingham and ran in the TT; production models were listed late in the year. Two were available, using 5 or 7hp V-twin engines, belt drive and sprung forks typical of the period. For 1912 both singles and twins ranging from 3.5 to 9hp were offered, as well as a two-speed gearbox and frame fittings for the trade. They entered the TT again in 1913 but without any success, the firm dropping motorcycles in 1914.

BOND 1950–1953 AND 1958–1962

Best known for small three-wheeled cars, Lawrence Bond produced many other designs, including an odd motorcycle in 1950. This had an all-alloy frame, made from sheet rolled into a large tube, from which the

Sheet aluminium figured highly in the construction of the Bond Minibyke, with frame, mudguards and legshields so made.

Mrs Hulbert from Putney on her Booth, with its small engine hung from the ladies' cycle frame.

engine hung, and massive mudguards that enclosed most of each wheel.

The engine was the 99cc Villiers 1F with two speeds, there was no suspension other than the 4in tyres and the 16in wheels had split rims. Telescopic forks appeared during 1950 and a 125cc JAP two-stroke engine was offered in 1951, although supply problems held this back. During 1951, manufacture was taken over by Ellis of Leeds and Bond went on to design the BAC, but production of his original machine ceased in 1953.

In November 1955, Bond returned to two wheels with the Sherpa scooter, which used a 99cc Villiers 1F engine under glass-fibre bodywork. It was in the style of the time and was shown to the world in the Earls Court car park, but only the one prototype was built.

The name continued on the three-wheelers and the firm moved to Preston, Lancashire, where it returned to two wheels in 1958 to produce a scooter. This was typical of the type, although the body styling in glass-fibre was a trifle heavy, and the model was powered by a 148cc Villiers 31C engine with three speeds and a Siba electric start. It was soon joined by another model with a 197cc Villiers 9E and four speeds; both had a revised style for 1960 and ran on to 1962, after which Bond stuck to the cars.

BOOTH 1901–1903

A small maker, based at Putney in London, who produced models with De Dion and Minerva engines. Most were to specification and included a ladies' model for a Mrs Hulbert, this having an open bicycle-frame and the tanks revised to suit. Her husband, Frank Hulbert, rode a Booth in the 1903 ACU 1,000-mile trial, as did S. Bramley Moore, and at the end of 1903 they took over the firm and changed the name to Hulbert-Bramley, using the existing range before moving on to use a 2.75hp Minerva engine.

BORD 1902–1906

The Bord Motor Co., The Arcade, Finsbury Pavement, London, offered a clip-on 1.5hp engine to fit within the frame of a roadster bicycle. It came complete with tank and batteries, the drive to the rear wheel being by a belt that was tensioned by a jockey pulley positioned to improve the wrap on the engine pulley. The engine power went up to 1.75hp for 1904.

BORHAM 1902–1905

One of the many small firms that tried hanging a Minerva engine from the downtube of a heavy-duty bicycle frame. Most of these companies were cycle dealers who left the market when it turned down in the middle of the decade.

BOUNDS-JAP 1909–1912

A small firm, not even listed in con-

The Bord Motor firm sold an engine as part of a kit to convert a bicycle to powered transport.

Bowden from 1903, with the engine tucked in behind the bottom bracket just ahead of the rear wheel.

A 1904 advertisement for the Bowden control-cable system features that could be used by any owner; the machine illustrated is a Bowden.

temporary buyers' guides, that assembled machines using JAP single and V-twin engines. They would have bought-in all the other major parts, only producing a few brackets and other items themselves, as well as designing the transfer for the tank.

BOWDEN 1902–1905

Built by Frank Bowden at Gray's Inn Road, Holborn, London, the early model tucked its 2hp Simms engine with magneto in behind the seat tube and on top of the chainstays. From there, it drove the rear wheel by silent chain, with a clutch and shock-absorber being incorporated in the drive. The layout placed the pedals ahead of the crankcase. Later, in 1903, the engine support became a cradle and the ignition was by coil, while Bowden controls were fitted, as expected.

A further model fitted a Belgian FN engine in the same manner and the machines were also sold as the New Bowden in some cases. For 1904 the FN engine was retained and moved ahead of the pedals. Two tricycles and a quadricycle were also listed, the quad powered by a 4hp water-cooled Daws engine with magneto ignition.

After one more year the firm concentrated on the manufacture of control cables and levers, this activity being joined in due course by the production of carburettors. There was an apparent involvement with a lightweight motorcycle in the early 1920s, but this was short lived and could have been just a method of promoting their existing product line. Carbs, controls and levers all continued after the Second World War, but there were no more motorcycles.

The basic 1914 Bown with Villiers engine, direct-belt drive and front magneto; a format the firm would use for some years.

BOWN 1914–1923
This was a very basic machine built at Snow Hill, Birmingham and powered by a 269cc Villiers two-stroke engine. At that time ignition was by a front-mounted magneto, not the flywheel type to come later, and either single or two speeds were available, both with belt final-drive. Lubrication was by petroil, Druid forks were used and there was a further option of a 2hp Precision engine in place of the Villiers.

This model continued for 1915 but production then ceased until late-1921, when four models were offered. Two were four-strokes with one powered by a 348cc Blackburne engine driving a three-speed gear-

For 1951, Bown added a small motorcycle with a 99cc Villiers engine and also one of 122cc in 1952.

box, the other with a 293cc JAP engine and two speeds. The other models were two-strokes, one much as pre-war with the 269cc Villiers engine but with a flywheel magneto. The other was smaller, simpler and listed as the Bownian. Only the Villiers-powered models continued during late-1922 and for 1923 just one model with a 147cc Villiers engine was listed, this being Bown's last year.

BOWN 1950–1957
This firm was based in Tonypandy, Wales, where they built the Aberdale autocycle up to 1949. During that year they adopted the Bown name and revised the design to use the 99cc Villiers 2F engine with a cradle frame fitted with blade girder forks and enclosing side panels below the petroil tank.

For 1951 they added a small motorcycle using the 99cc two-speed 1F Villiers engine, which went into a neat frame with duplex downtubes and tubular girder forks. During 1952 these two were joined by their Tourist Trophy model using the 122cc Villiers 10D engine and this machine had telescopic forks.

Later Bown, as offered from 1956, although actually this was an imported German moped with Sachs engine.

In this form the range ran on to 1954 but then production stopped. The name returned in 1956 for an imported German moped powered by a 47cc Sachs engine, but this only lasted for two years.

BOYD 1923–1924
This was another small producer who took advantage of the ready availability of the 147cc Villiers two-stroke engine and other components from within the motorcycle trade to construct a few complete lightweight machines in the hope of greater success. Boyd Motors were based in Leicester, the difficulty in finding agents willing to stock their product outside their immediate locality proving insuperable to any prospects for expansion nationally.

This 1903 Bradbury was fitted with a Clement-Garrard engine driving a countershaft and thence to the rear wheel, all by chain.

BRADBURY 1901–1924
Located at the Wellington Works in Oldham, Lancashire, this firm began as others had with a Minerva engine hung from the frame downtube of a standard bicycle. Late in 1902 they began to offer machines built to the Birch design, where the crankcase was cast around two of the main frame tubes. In other respects they followed the lines of the new Werner and were typical primitives with direct-belt drive, pedals and braced forks. The main model with a 2.5hp engine was listed as the Peerless, but there was also a lightweight that had its Clement-Garrard engine fitted inclined above the frame downtube. From there it drove a countershaft mounted ahead of the bottom bracket and thence to the rear wheel,

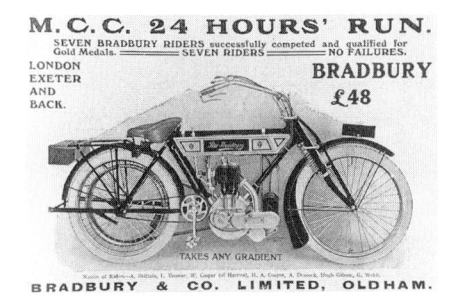

By 1911 the Bradbury offered just one 3.5hp model, still with cast-in frame tubes and with side-spring forks.

both drives being by chain. For the rest, it was little more than a heavy-duty bicycle.

Over the next few years the design of the main model ran on with the crankcase cast to the frame. Several power outputs were listed along with a tandem backseat frame, essentially a pillion seat with handlebars, and a forecar with a 4hp water-cooled engine, two speeds and chain drive.

In 1909 the firm standardized on a 3.5hp model, still of the same construction but now with sprung forks. Later came transmission options and in 1914 a 6hp V-twin was added, this having a three-speed gearbox, all-chain drive and a drum rear-brake.

Late in 1913 these two were joined by a 3.5hp flat-twin model whose engine had its magneto mounted on top of the crankcase, a chain-driven three-speed gearbox and the choice of chain or belt final-drive. This model also had the drum rear-brake and continued for 1915 along with the others, the single now rated at 4hp.

A 6hp V-twin engine was introduced by Bradbury in 1914, a type they built for a decade, although joined for a year by a flat-twin model.

Only the single, with various transmission options, and the V-twin ran on for 1916 and remained in production throughout the war for service use. This line continued for 1919 with the addition of a 2.75hp single having two speeds and chain-cum-belt drive, but for 1920 the 4hp single-speed model was dropped, leaving just three models, the 2.75 and 4hp singles and 6hp V-twin with three speeds and all-chain drive. In 1922 the smallest had transmission options, but by the next year it was only sold with three speeds and chain drive.

For 1924 there were just two models, both redesigned and enlarged, the single to 572cc and the V-twin to 872cc. There was also a racing model fitted with a 348cc ohv Blackburne engine. Early in the year the firm failed and production ceased, but the stock was bought by former employee Percy Platt who sold spares and new machines built from these for some years, still based in Oldham.

BRAITHWAITE PRE-GREAT WAR
Made by a gentleman of that name in some numbers at a location near Lake Windermere. For his own machine he fitted a Brough engine.

The Ducati Cucciolo engine unit was first sold as a bicycle attachment, but later as a moped using Royal Enfield cycle parts and assembled by Britax.

BRITAX 1949–1956 AND 1979–1985
This London-based accessory firm added motorcycles to their catalogue in 1949 by importing the 48cc Ducati Cucciolo bicycle attachment engine unit. This differed greatly from the rest, for it was a four-stroke with ohv opened by pull-rods and built in-unit with a two-speed gearbox with clutch and preselector control.

Very successful in its Italian homeland, it sold in Britain as a unit at first, but in 1953 Britax moved to a complete machine using Royal Enfield parts, the frame from a heavy-duty bicycle, but the blade girder forks from the 125cc motorcycle. In 1955 it was joined by a scooter and a racing model, known as the Hurricane and fitted with a full fairing, for the embryonic 50cc class. Neither had much success, the scooter world having already moved on, while the racer was soon outclassed by the Italian Itom.

Late in 1952 they imported the German Lohmann clip-on engine; this was different to the rest in that it was an 18cc compression-ignition two-stroke with variable compression ratio. This was designed to clamp under the bicycle bottom-bracket, so had a horizontal cylinder and very narrow crankcase. It was geared to a countershaft that drove the rear wheel by friction roller. First seen in 1949, it was only on the British market for a year or so.

After 1956 Britax went back to accessories as their main business but took over the Cyclemaster line for a while. The name made a further appearance in 1979 on an Italian 50cc fold-up moped sold as the Kari-Bike and this was listed up to 1985.

BRITISH ANZANI 1939
Best known for its engines, this Hampton Hill, Middlesex firm built a prototype in 1939 that foresaw the post-war clip-on trend. It was a simple 61cc two-stroke that sat alongside the left upper chainstay with its cylinder inclined along the frame tube. A friction-drive roller and its shaft was positioned above the engine to be moved down into contact with the tyre, and a chain connected crank and drive shafts. A flywheel magneto provided ignition and a petrol tank sat beside the drive roller. Other commitments prevented the firm taking the idea further.

BRITISH CHALLENGE c.1920
This was a short-lived firm based in Coventry who produced bicycles and carrier cycles before branching out into motorcycles using two- or four-stroke engines.

BRITISH RADIAL 1921–1922
Rights of production for the 2.75hp sv three-cylinder radial engine designed by C.B. Redrup were acquired by the British Radial Engine Company of Lacland Place, London SW10 in the spring of 1921, and they began to assemble a marketable machine shortly afterwards. The actual displacement of the engine was 309cc with valves placed either side of the cylinders, which themselves were spaced 120 degrees apart. This was mounted in-line with the frame, driving through a two-speed Sturmey-Archer gearbox with chain-cum-belt transmission. Both frame and forks were sourced from Chater-Lea, Senspray supplied the carburettor and Runbaken the magneto so, other than for the unusual engine configuration, the machine was of orthodox appearance and proven construction.

British Radial also offered the engine alone, for stationary applications. By 1922 they were specifying a Vici carburettor, but otherwise there would be little alteration in its short production life.

BRITISH ROADLESS 1920
An early experiment in tracked motorcycles, this machine propelled itself using a rubber V-belt that ran around front and rear wheels which were formed as pulleys with a series of miniature bogies on the lower run. Power came from a 348cc Douglas flat-twin engine mounted above the rear wheel and steering was by turning the front wheel a little. It lacked both grip and stability so no more was heard of it.

BRITISH STANDARD 1919–1925
A 269cc two-stroke single with direct-belt drive brought this marque to the marketplace in 1919 and carried them through 1920 too, with the simple addition of a two-speed model having the option of a clutch and kickstart. The following year they expanded a little and changed location from Aston to Newtown Row in Birmingham, from where the 269cc models were continued and supported by 348 and 545cc sv Blackburne four-strokes. There were sidecar versions of the two-stroke and the bigger Blackburne for 1922, when a 348cc ohv Blackburne engine was also tried.

This latter was replaced by a 349cc ohv Bradshaw oil-cooled engine with all-chain drive in 1923, when the two-stroke models became 147 or 247cc to choice, but both with two-speed gearboxes. These were retained for 1924 along with the 348cc sv Blackburne and 349cc ohv Bradshaw machines. Sales must have waned quickly though by year end, for early in 1925 an advertisement appeared offering no fewer than thirty 348cc sv Blackburne British Standards at clearance prices and the marque had slipped from the listings by the spring of that year.

BROCKHOUSE 1948–1955
This engineering firm in Southport, Lancashire, built the Corgi from 1948 to 1954. They became involved with the American Indian make and this led to them producing the 248cc model under that name from 1950 to 1955. During this period they also sold the engine unit with its three-speed gearbox to Dot and OEC.

BROLER 1920–1922
'You will never tire a Broler,' claimed Brooks, Tasler & Cox of Narborough, Leicestershire in promoting their particular 349cc two-stroke engine, which formed the basis of the motorcycle they offered for a short period at the beginning of the twenties. The engine was the usual three-port type but featured ball-and-roller bearings throughout for ease of running. The makers later changed their trading name to Broler Motors Ltd and sold the engine to other assemblers of machines, which kept the company going for longer than would otherwise have been the case.

BROOKLANDS 1983
After Norton stopped making the Manx, other firms took over the production of spares and even complete machines. In time, replicas in various forms appeared and the Brooklands Model 40 was one such. It was traditional in using the famed featherbed frame, forks in the Roadholder style and conical hubs for the drum brakes, the front a twin leading-shoe.

The difference was the 497cc Weslake engine which had chain-driven dohc opening four valves. An Amal Concentric supplied the mixture, ignition was electronic and lubrication was dry-sump from a massive oil tank. The primary drive ran in an alloy chaincase to a four-speed gearbox.

The Brough 1914 model was fitted with a flat-twin engine, having the magneto on top of the crankcase and gearbox on the underside.

BROUGH 1898–1925
William Brough was never to be as famous as his son George, but he began the Brough legend that later became Brough Superior. He built a small car in 1898 and followed this with a tricycle fitted with a 2.5hp De Dion engine that same year. In 1902 the first motorcycle appeared, having its engine hung from the downtube, belt drive and braced forks. Based at Vernon Road, Basford, Nottingham, he had greatly improved the design by 1906 and the 1908 model had a vertically mounted 3.5hp engine and sprung forks, soon joined by a 2.5hp and a 5hp V-twin, all made by the firm.

During 1910 Brough built an advanced experimental engine with a rotary valve above the cylinder, this driven by bevel gears, a shaft, and spur gears above the head and valve. The next year saw a flat-twin built and tried out, and a larger single. A larger 6hp V-twin appeared for 1912, available for touring or racing, while the 3.5hp single was enlarged and a two-speed countershaft gearbox added. There was also an 8hp V-twin engine for the Brough Monocar and a 3.5hp ladies' model with an open frame

George Brough was entered for the 1913 Senior TT on a model with a flat-twin engine, but for the race an ABC twin engine was used, as their own was not ready. However, he retired from the race. Later that year the firm announced their own 3.5hp, 497cc flat-twin model with ohv, the U.H. magneto clamped to the crankcase top and the two-speed gearbox to the crankcase underside. Chain drive was used from engine to gearbox while the final drive was from an adjustable pulley by belt. Druid forks were fitted.

By 1915 only the flat twin was listed but in two further forms, one with a three-speed gearbox and the other for racing. The standard models were joined by a larger 5hp version in 1916 and it was these that continued post-war up to 1923. They were then joined by a larger 810cc version and it was this that carried on for 1924 along with the 497cc model until production ceased in the next year.

BROUGH SUPERIOR
1919–1940

George Brough inherited his father's love of motorcycles and engineering skills, to which he added his own flair for publicity and an urge to build the best. His wish to produce a top-class machine resulted in him leaving the Brough works and setting up as Brough Superior in Nottingham during 1919.

From the start his motorcycles were special, built for the enthusiast

It was 1925 before the ohv Brough Superior SS100 reached the public, whose appetite had been well wetted by the earlier sv SS80, always with that tank.

The first of the Brough Superior Show Specials had this V4 side-valve engine, with clutch and gearbox built in-unit – a sensation.

and connoisseur who sought the best available at the time. He used the products of other firms, but persuaded them that what they supplied to him had to be that little bit better and special to the normal line.

So it was for the first Brough Superior, revealed through the press in December 1920 with its 986cc ohv JAP V-twin engine, three-speed Sturmey-Archer gearbox, Amac carburettor, ML magneto and so on. The frame was strong, the forks Montgomery and the tank the machine's crowning glory. A saddle type with bulbous nose, it was all curves and its form would characterize the marque throughout its history. The finish of the machine was of the finest quality.

An alternative 976cc JAP sv engine was available in 1922 but before then, in 1920, there was the option of the Swiss 733cc ioe MAG V-twin engine or the larger 993cc MAG. Yet another alternative was the 999cc Barr & Stroud V-twin sleeve-valve engine, but the model line was due for revision starting in 1923.

It was then that the SS80 made its debut with the 988cc sv JAP V-twin engine, which would power the machine to around 80mph (130km/h) and keep it there all day. The brakes remained the weak point, with a dummy rim still in the rear and the front a small drum, but this

The Brough Superior show model for late 1928 had an 817cc in-line four-cylinder MAG engine and the rear suspension already available.

Brough Superior Black Alpine 680 model for 1930, was complete with sprung frame and enclosed saddle springs.

changed for 1924 to drums in both hubs. Webb forks also appeared and by this time a reporter had dubbed the model 'The Rolls-Royce of Motor Cycles', an accolade that George Brough used from then on.

A superb publicist, George encouraged the use of his machines in competition and rode himself on a special SS80 known at first as 'Spit & Polish'. On this he won at Brooklands and, with it renamed 'Old Bill', he dominated sprints in 1923.

While the SS80 was fast it was still a sv model, so the next move was to add one fitted with the 981cc ohv JAP V-twin engine. Thus was born the fabulous SS100, first shown at the Olympia show late in 1924. It was simply more of the best; essentially the machine that George wanted for himself, regardless of costs, and he was able to attract enough buyers with deep purses to make it all viable.

With the JAP engine came the three-speed Sturmey-Archer gearbox with special strengthened internals, the rigid frame that handled so well, modified Harley-Davidson bottom-link forks and the stylish tank. A small drum front-brake was fitted, but had little effect, while an 8in rear-drum did most or all of the stopping. A real 100mph machine, it was the first superbike.

Before long, Castle forks replaced the Harley, effectively a copy, and for 1926 the SS80 was listed in three forms, but only one of these continued for the next year when two more

As the Austin Seven engine was water-cooled, the Special had to have a radiator and water temperature gauge.

The Brough Superior 1932 Show Special used an Austin Seven engine plus its transmission and, thus, had twin rear wheels to bypass the propeller shaft.

The SS100 Alpine Grand Sports model was another version of the well-tried Brough Superior theme, which performed so ably.

with ohv appeared. The smaller was the Overhead 680 with a 677cc JAP V-twin engine in the usual cycle parts of a reduced wheelbase. The larger was of more interest and was the Alpine Grand Sports, which was based on the SS100 but fitted with electric lighting, windscreen and panniers for high-speed touring in the grand manner. This suggested a change in George's personal tastes but competition riders were taken care of with the Pendine model, which had a tuned JAP engine and was for racing.

During 1927 a model with a 746cc sv engine appeared to offer good performance, quietness and minimal need for attention. It was also the year when George built the first of a whole series of show specials for the annual exhibitions at Olympia and Earls Court. The first had a transverse V4 994cc sv engine with the clutch and gearbox built in-unit but chain final-drive. It was shown off in a glass case with spotlights and a police guard.

The 1928 range saw a revised 995cc ohv engine for the SS100 and another show special that had an in-line four-cylinder 817cc engine built by MAG. This machine had a Bentley & Draper spring frame with the suspension spring under the saddle and this system became an option for other models in time. One such was the Black Alpine of 1930, which combined the frame with the 680 engine, a four-speed gearbox and an all-black finish. The 680, SS80 and SS100 were joined by the 500 for 1931; this had a 491cc ohv engine, but only nine were made so it was dropped for 1932.

Most photographs of the SS80 capture some element of its larger brother, the SS100, including the bulbous saddle tank with its fine finish.

The next special came in 1932 and for this George persuaded Herbert Austin to supply him with Austin Seven engines bored out to 800cc and fitted with an alloy head. With side valves and water cooling the noise level was low to suit the Grand Touring image while the Austin clutch, gearbox and propeller shaft had only one snag – that of arranging the drive to the rear wheel without offsetting the whole assembly. George solved this by simply fitting two rear-wheels, one on either side of the prop shaft, and listed the result as a sidecar model. Ten were built, some sold as solos, but it took some time to sell them all.

In 1933 the range was joined by two sv models, the 680 with an engine of that size and the 11.50 with a 1096cc JAP V-twin engine. The smaller was only built for one year but the 11.50 ran on to the end. There was no SS80 for 1934 but it returned for the next year in a new form when it was powered by a 982cc sv Matchless V-twin engine with the Brough Superior name engraved on it.

For the 1937 Show Special, George Brough used the SS80 engine set transversely to drive the Austin gearbox by chain to the rear wheel.

It was the same for the SS100 in 1936 when it adopted the ohv version of the 982cc Matchless engine complete with hairpin valve-springs. By then both SS models had four speeds, foot change and Castle forks as standard on the SS100 and an option for the SS80. The 680 was dropped at the year end to leave the two SS models and the 11.50 to run on.

Late in 1937 there was another show special, based on the SS80 but with the V-twin engine set across the frame. It drove back to a three-speed and reverse Austin Seven gearbox, but had chain final-drive, and went into a frame with plunger rear-suspension. Only one was built but the next year brought something far more special.

For the late-1938 show George Brough had his Golden Dream with a four-cylinder engine, but quite different from those of the past for the machine was in the Grand Tourer mould rather than the supersports of the first Broughs. Two machines were built, one with a golden finish from whence came the name. The engines differed internally and were of 988 and 998cc capacity with the four cylinders arranged as two flat-twins mounted on top of each other to produce the transverse four layout. In this way all four were well cooled without the need for water cooling.

In other respects the engine was conventional with ohv, wet-sump lubrication and twin carburettors. It drove a three-speed gearbox with shaft drive to an underslung worm drive at the rear wheel, the whole in a strong frame with Castle forks and plunger rear-suspension.

It took time to develop the Dream and then came the war, so it never went into production. Brough Superior motorcycles were built into 1940 but then came to an end as the firm was committed to high-precision war work – so high that they were entrusted to machine Merlin crankshafts for Rolls-Royce.

The final Brough Superior Show Special was perhaps the best, for it had a flat-four engine set across the frame with shaft drive. Its finish gave it the name 'Golden Dream'.

BROWN 1902–1915

Brown Brothers of Great Eastern Street, London were component suppliers to the trade who first produced their own motorcycle in 1902. They used Minerva engines of 2, 2.75 and 3.5hp, mounted vertically in typical primitive style with direct-belt drive and braced forks. Later came a 5hp V-twin and by 1908 the option of a two-speed gearbox and all-chain drive, although the braced unsprung forks remained to 1910.

Druid forks were adopted and the range offered a selection of powers in single and V-twin form plus a variety of transmission systems. By 1915, they used Precision and their own single cylinder engines only.

By 1904, the Brown had reached this form, with a Minerva engine hung in a primitive cycle frame with braced forks.

All-chain drive had come for the Brown by 1908, along with a two-speed gear and other improvements.

Production of Brown motorcycles then ceased and post-war they were sold as the Vindec, a name that they had also used and sold under from their earliest days, but not associated with the Vindec-Special or VS make.

BROWN-BICAR 1907–1913

This brand was unusual in having the engine enclosed, a feature that has run through motorcycle history but seldom found much support until the advent of modern supersports models. In Edwardian times this was not so, whether it was a single or a V-twin engine that was out of sight, and few of these were built or sold, even in the USA where it was built under licence.

BROWN & ROPER 1921

This was one of several attempts to produce a marketable single-track enclosed two-wheeler with something approaching the weather protection provided by an open car. Two engineers from Salisbury, Wiltshire, Messrs Brown and Roper revealed their device to the world in the summer of 1921. It was based around a 4hp sv flat-twin Douglas with the frame lengthened to permit the rider to sit low down in a space created between the existing saddle tube and the rear wheel. An auxiliary frame carried outrigger wheels, lowered or raised by a lever on the right of the machine, to keep things upright when at rest. Steering was by a wheel set immediately in front of the rider and connected to the fork top by long rods in tension. The Douglas three-speed chain-cum-belt gearbox and transmission were retained and quickly removable bodywork gave ease of access to the working parts. It is probable that only the prototype was built.

A good, solid, dependable motorcycle came from BSA and made their fortune for many years; this machine is a 1916 3.5hp TT model D.

BSA 1910–DATE

The initials stood for Birmingham Small Arms, for the firm was founded in 1861 to make guns using mass-production methods. In 1880 they added bicycles to their products and this led to them supplying parts to the motorcycle trade. By 1904 their line of parts was such that other firms could use them to build complete machines using Minerva engines.

It was not until October 1910 that BSA finally entered the market with a single model that reflected their standards for many a year. It was nothing radical, but combined the best practice of the day with good quality materials and sound design. While they kept to this they prospered well.

The first model had a 3.5hp engine mounted vertically in the frame with belt drive from an adjustable engine pulley, with a hub clutch an option. The chain-driven magneto sat ahead of the sv engine, there were sprung forks and the finish and detailing was excellent.

A two-speed rear-hub option and a TT model were soon added and in 1914 a 4.25hp sidecar machine appeared listed as the model H with a three-speed gearbox and all-chain drive. The H became the mainstay of

A new trend was to inclined engines and BSA responded with the 493cc 'Sloper' in 1927, this one from two years later.

A 1922 Light 6 BSA V-twin with sidecar attached, on show with a couple of BSA bicycles also just in view, an indication of the variety of the BSA empire.

The enterprising 1934 BSA model FF, had a 499cc engine driving a fluid flywheel and pre-selector gearbox, thanks to their Daimler links.

Top of the pre-war range was the BSA Gold Star, its engine derived from a series introduced for 1937 and to run on into the 1960s.

The 1940 Silver Star B29, from which the post-war B-series would be derived, adding suspension improvements and competition versions in time.

To back up the BSA single-cylinder range, there were V-twins with side or overhead valves; this the more sporting 748cc Y13 model of 1936.

By 1938 the 249cc side-valve BSA C10 had taken over the lower end of the range, a simple model that was also built in ohv form as the C11.

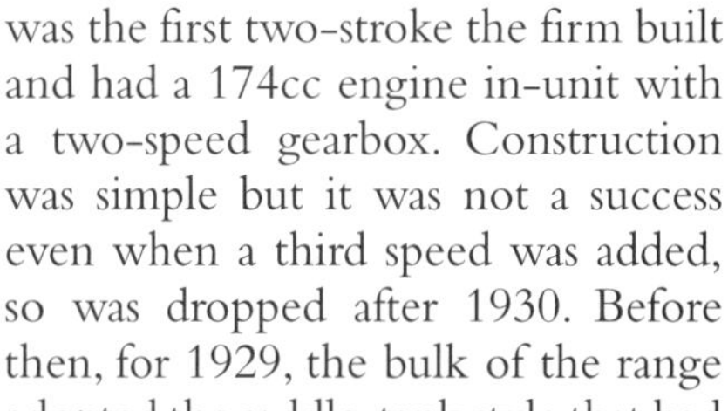

The bright new model for BSA in 1948 was the 123cc D1 Bantam, which soon added versions with plunger suspension and was enlarged to this 148cc D3.

the range when the Great War began and was joined by the model K, which had belt final-drive.

In 1920 the first BSA V-twin appeared as the model E with a 771cc engine, with the magneto at the front, a three-speed gearbox and all-chain drive with both chains enclosed in cases. This model would set a pattern that would last for two decades. For 1921 the 3.5hp model was finally dropped and the chaincases were changed to alloy, which gave the machines a nice style. The bad news for the firm that year was a disaster in the Senior TT where all their works entries retired, an event that kept them away from racing for a long time.

A larger V-twin was added for 1922 as the model F of 985cc, to become the model G for 1924, and two new singles appeared in 1923 as the 348cc model L and 493cc model S. Both were conventional sv models with chain drive, but the next year brought an ohv version of the model L, their first with the valves upstairs, and the model B. The latter was a low-cost model with a 249cc engine, two speeds, both brakes on the rear wheel and a cylindrical petrol tank, so was soon known as the Round Tank BSA and sold readily to those who sought basic and reliable transport.

This solid range served the firm well for the next two years, augmented by variations such as economy, de luxe or colonial. In 1927 they were joined by a new BSA legend, the Sloper, which had its 493cc ohv engine inclined in the frame. It performed well, was quiet, had a low saddle-height and proved to be popular and set the new trend for such a layout.

The next new model, the A of 1928, was much less of a success. It was the first two-stroke the firm built and had a 174cc engine in-unit with a two-speed gearbox. Construction was simple but it was not a success even when a third speed was added, so was dropped after 1930. Before then, for 1929, the bulk of the range adopted the saddle-tank style that had swept the industry and more had inclined engines. There was a short-lived speedway model, the Dirt Track, and tuned versions of the Sloper were listed and distinguished by a red star stencilled on the timing case. This was the first of the star line that would come later.

In the depressed early-1930s the inclined engines proved more expensive than the vertical and the fashion

Out on the highways, the men from the AA kept the nation running using their BSA M-series sidecar outfits while on patrol.

passed. The BSA range reflected the era with prosaic models, built right down in price but still offering reliable basic transport. As things improved they brought in the Blue Star ohv singles in 1932 with 499cc and then 348cc engines. There were also tuned Specials and the largest single was stretched out to 596cc with either valve type.

For 1934 there was a new ohv V-twin which had a 499cc ohv engine and was listed as the model J and developed for service use. With it came the model X, which had a 149cc ohv engine for the smallest class, and the model FF. This was a radical machine by BSA standards for its 499cc engine drove a fluid flywheel and preselector gearbox, but these reduced the performance so it had limited appeal and never reached the marketplace.

A larger ohv V-twin was added in 1936 as the 748cc model Y, much as the J, but at the year end there was a major change to the range with much revision to simplify the models, which had become too varied and diverse for economic production. The man behind this was the brilliant Val Page and his work would remain in production into the 1960s. From the past only the 748 and 985cc V-twins remained, the rest were new.

Page used just one engine design for his new range, split into the light B models and the heavier M range, both with much in common in their manner of construction. All had a vertical cylinder, gear-driven camshafts and rear magneto, dry-sump lubrication and were simple, robust and reliable. For the B-range there were 249 and 348cc engines with sv or ohv, with the sports versions listed as Empire Stars. The M-range had 349, 496 and 596cc engines, with the sports Empire Star again listed. These engines drove three- or four-speed gearboxes and went into tubular frames with girder forks and the fixtures and fittings of the times. It gave the firm a broad base of models with a similar styling theme that ran through the range and would serve them for a long time.

Two important new models were added for 1938 at either end of the scale. The smaller was the 249cc sv C10, which was reduced to the most simple form and had coil ignition. Often scorned for its basic format, it proved able to do its job over long periods with minimal attention. The larger machine was much more exciting, for it was based on the Empire Star, listed as the M24 but best known as the Gold Star. This arose from the performance of a tuned version at the Brooklands track and it featured an all-alloy bench-tested engine, sports fittings and was also available in competition and track-racing forms. Of further importance to the firm was a successful attempt to win the Maudes Trophy that year following a long and arduous test.

The Gold Star name returned in 1949 to compete in the Clubman's races held over the TT course and won the 350cc event they would dominate.

BSA soon joined the move to the vertical twin-cylinder engine post-war, their machine the A7 with plunger rear-suspension to come in 1949.

The pre-war BSA C-range came to its end with this C12, which combined the C11 engine with improved suspension.

In 1939 the ohv C11 model joined the range, identical to the C10 other than for the top half of the engine and a few other details. The Empire Star models changed their name to Silver Star in 348 and 496cc sizes, the 748cc V-twin was dropped, but the model G ran on still with some of its 1920s features.

During 1939 BSA built two prototypes to follow the vertical-twin success of the new Triumph Speed Twin, with one of 350cc with fully enclosed overhead valves and a touring line. The other was a 500cc machine with an overhead camshaft driven by shaft and bevels on the right and an alloy head with enclosed hairpin valve-springs. Aimed at the sports market, it was reputed to exceed 100mph (160km/h) so would have been a challenger to the Tiger 100.

There were to have been more new models for 1940: the C12 with a 348cc sv engine in the form of the C-range and the 348cc ohv model listed as the B29, but based on the M-range engine and with fully enclosed valve-springs. With the outbreak of war the first was dropped but the second led on to the WB30, which was built in small numbers and would lead to a post-war range. The bulk of wartime production was of the 496cc M20 sv model, with some C10s for training and C11s that went out to India.

Post-war, BSA announced a four-model range for 1946 with the C10, C11 and M20, much as for 1939, still with girder forks. The fourth model was the new B31, which was based on the B29 and so had the 348cc ohv engine, four speeds, rigid frame but new telescopic front-forks that would serve the firm well for many years.

Expansion soon came with the 591cc sv M21 added early in 1946 and followed by the competition B32 that was based on the B31 but had off-road tyres and much more chrome plating. During the year both C-range machines changed to telescopic forks, while late in the year the firm announced their first vertical twin, the A7.

Vertical twins were to become the mainstay of the British industry in the post-war years, following on the success of the Triumph Speed Twin first seen in 1937. All followed a similar concept and the A7 kept to this rather than adopt the 1939 forms, which were less conventional. Thus their new twin had a 495cc engine with ohv, gear-driven camshaft and rear magneto. The four-speed gearbox was bolted to the back of the crankcase to give a semi-unit form of construction and the cycle parts were much as the singles with telescopic forks for the rigid frame.

For 1947 the B33 was added to the range, a 499cc version of the B31, and later came the competition B34. For 1948 the M33 was created for the sidecar driver by fitting the ohv B33 engine into the M-range cycle parts, and during the year the M-range went over to telescopic forks. Of much more importance was the first appearance of one of BSA's most successful models, the Bantam, their first two-stroke since 1930.

Last and finest of the 650cc BSA twin series was the Rocket Gold Star, a supersports machine for road use or production racing.

For 1959 the 172cc BSA Bantam adopted a new frame, to become the D7 Bantam Supreme, and kept that engine size to the end.

The BSA Winged Wheel was a too-late attempt to enter the bicycle-attachment engine market, which was already on the wane.

52 BSA

The BSA Dandy had a 70cc two-stroke engine, with the ignition points most awkward to service and a two-speed pre-selector gearbox no-one liked.

The Bantam was actually based on a pre-war DKW and had a 123cc engine with the three-speed gearbox built in-unit with it. The cast-iron cylinder was inclined forward and topped by an alloy head. Carburation was by Amal and the electrics came from Wipac, while the exhaust pipe ran to a styled, flat silencer. Primary drive was by chain to the tough clutch and cross-over gearbox, which had rather wide ratios. The unit went into a loop frame with telescopic forks and was simple, cheap, worked well and, listed as the D1, it sold in thousands.

In 1949 plunger rear-suspension became an option for the A7 and the B-range, a sports twin listed as the A7 Star Twin was added and the Gold Star name was revived. This last was first offered as the 348cc B32GS, was soon joined by a 499cc version, and both were based on the B-models but with an all-alloy engine, plunger frame and a massive option list. It was offered in various builds to suit road, trial, scrambles or racing use and was a natural for the new Isle of Man Clubman's TT races, with the 350 winning that year.

There was a larger twin for 1950, the A10 Golden Flash, whose engine was based on the A7, but revised in the light of experience, and available with rigid or with plunger rear-suspension. The plunger option also appeared for the Bantam, C and M models with a competition version of the Bantam joining the lists. For the next year the two A7 twins had their engine revised along the lines of the A10 so that more parts became common.

During 1952 BSA made another successful attempt to win the Maudes Trophy by running three Star Twins around Europe and taking in the ISDT en route. Pivoted-fork rear-suspension appeared for the Gold Star models in 1953, listed as the BB type, and an export-only sports A10 was sold as the Super Flash but still used the plunger frame. At the bottom end of the scale the firm entered the cyclemotor market with their 35cc Winged Wheel that replaced the bicycle rear wheel. They also listed a complete machine with the Wheel, but the days of the type were near their end and it was dropped after three years.

The A-twins and B-singles were listed with the pivoted-fork frame for 1954, but mainly for export, so the original types remained for a year or two with the plunger A10 running on to 1957 for sidecar work. In the new frame the gearbox of the twins became separate as for the singles and the sports models became the A7 Shooting Star and A10 Road Rocket.

In the same year the competition B-range went into a duplex rigid frame with the pivoted rear fork an

For 1959 BSA introduced the new C-range unit-construction single as the 247cc C15, which was the start of a long series in several sizes.

option. The D3 Bantam was added with a 148cc engine and was listed in road and competition forms with rigid or plunger frame as for the D1. The C-range went over to alternator electrics with the sv model using some Bantam parts and a plunger frame to become the C10L, while the ohv model became the C11G in rigid or plunger forms. For the Gold Star there was a massive increase in engine fin-area and a swept-back exhaust pipe with the result listed as the CB type.

Little altered for 1955 and the range was slimmed down for the next year with the competition Bantam, Winged Wheel and M20 all being dropped and the C11G changed to the C12 with a pivoted-fork frame. At the same time the D3 adopted a similar frame, while the D1 was only listed in plunger form and there were fewer options through the range.

It was the time of the scooter, so BSA announced two models for this market although neither did too well. One was the 200cc Beeza with sv engine, and this failed to go into production at all, while the two-stroke 70cc Dandy with its awkward two-speed preselector gearbox did not reach the shops until 1957. There was

The final version of the BSA Gold Star ran on to 1963 in road, Clubman and Scrambles forms, this Clubman the most desired type.

further range contraction at the end of 1957 when the C10L, competition B-models and M33 were all dropped.

The Bantam was stretched further for 1958 to become the 172cc D5 and the sports A10 changed its name to the Super Rocket. With it came the export-only Rocket Scrambler, built for the US street-scrambler market with open pipes and off-road fittings, and sold as the Spitfire from 1960.

Late in 1958 BSA launched the first of a new range of unit construction singles as the 247cc C15. Based on the Triumph Cub design, it had a vertical cylinder and four speeds in the unit that went into conventional cycle parts. Early in 1959 it was joined by two competition versions, the C15S for scrambles and the C15T for trials, while the D5 became the D7 with a new frame. Another scooter appeared in 1959 with the choice of 172cc two-stroke or 249cc ohv twin engines. Sold as the BSA-Sunbeam and Triumph by badge changes, none sold too well, having come to the market too late.

By this time the Gold Star was only listed in Clubman or scrambles forms, the first the definitive sports single of its day, although the TT-series was long gone having been dominated by BSA in its later years. The long-serving B-range had gone by 1960, while the venerable M21 was to special order only and most went to the AA or the services. Expansion of the unit single range began in 1961 with the 343cc B40 and the 247cc supersports SS80. A year later the 343cc SS90 was added, but these high-compression singles proved to be somewhat fragile if abused.

A new range of twins made its debut in 1962 as the 499cc A50 and 654cc A65 models with unit construction and a new line but with the internals much as in the past. Alternator electrics were adopted along with coil ignition and the results were

From its start the C15 was offered by BSA in this C15T trials format with suitable changes, and also as the C15S scrambler, with a common frame.

By 1966 the BSA twin range had extended to off-road models, mainly for the US market, with this the A65H Hornet, with tuned engine and stripped cycle parts.

lighter but had a heavy look, so some of the appeal of the older models was lost. Based on the past there was one new supersports model, the Rocket Gold Star, which was first conceived as a Gold Star fitted with the sports twin engine. The result was only built for two years but became one of the most desirable BSA models of all time.

Most of the rest of the past had gone by 1963: the Gold Star, the older twins, the M21, the unloved Dandy and the most successful BSA of all time, the D1 Bantam. New that year was a trail version of the C15 for the USA, followed in 1964 by the B40E Enduro Star for the same market. As a replacement for the 123cc Bantam there came the 75cc Beagle, which had an ohv engine of the same basic design as the 50cc one used in the Ariel Pixie. The Beagle style was much more dated than its Ariel mate, along the lines of a 1950s moped, and it was not a success.

Sports export twins were added for 1964, named Lightning, Thunderbolt and Hornet in 654cc size and Cyclone with the 499cc engine. For home use there was the A65R Rocket in the same vein. Off-road the firm continued its long history of successes in trials and scrambles when Jeff Smith won the 500cc motocross world title in 1964 and 1965. From this came the 441cc B44GP Grand Prix motocross model based on the unit single and Smith's machine.

More twins were added for 1965 in sports and production racing sports forms and in both capacities, but the large and confusing array of twin models was simplified for 1966. For touring there were the A50R Royal Star and A65T Thunderbolt, while the sports versions were the A65L Lightning for the road and A65SS Spitfire for production racing. Off-road there were the A50W Wasp and A65H Hornet, while the capacities remained the same. Among the singles the range was the C15, C15 Sportsman, B44GP, B44VE Victor Enduro and two versions of the D7 Bantam. During the year the D7 was replaced by the D10 in four forms, with two of these fitted with a much needed four-speed gearbox. Of these, one was a sports model and the other built for trail use.

In 1967 the 247cc C25 Barracuda joined the unit single range with a new style and revised internals, becoming the B25 Starfire for the next year when it was joined by the 441cc B44VR Victor Roadster and the B44VS Victor Special trail machine. For 1968 the Bantams became D14 models in Supreme, Sports and trail Bushman forms, all with four speeds. The unit single range was reduced to the B25, B44SS Shooting Star road model and B44VS. Of the twins the A50W went and the Hornet became the A65FS Firebird Scrambler.

Of far more importance for 1968 was the debut of the A75 Rocket Three along with the similar Triumph Trident. Both had a 740cc three-cylinder engine built in-unit with a four-speed gearbox, but the BSA had its cylinders inclined forward while the Triumph was vertical. Their frames also differed, with the BSA based on that of the twins with duplex downtubes while the rest of the cycle parts were much as the twins. The result was an impressive machine with a fine performance, but it had to compete against the new Honda CB750 four for sales. However, it sold well and the works racing machines had many successes.

For 1969 the Bantam became the D175 in road and Bushman forms only and a low-cost single was added for the one year as the B25 Fleetstar. Otherwise the range ran on for 1970 with a major revamp announced at the end of the year.

BSA and Triumph staged a massive launch of their 1971 ranges which included many new models with considerable use of common parts such as forks and wheels. The Bantam was left alone but only listed in road form. There were five unit singles with two listed as the B25SS and B50SS Gold Star Street Scrambler and two as the B25T and B50T Victor Trail, plus one more as the B50MX Victor Moto-Cross, the engine sizes being 247 and 499cc. All carried their engine oil within the frame and had conical hubs and slimline forks. Only 654cc twins continued as the Thunderbolt, Lightning and Firebird Scrambler, again with oil-carrying frames, conical hubs and slimline forks. Even the Rocket 3 had the new forks and wheels and all were restyled with the frames finished in a light dove-grey that showed the dirt really well.

There was also a 349cc dohc twin-cylinder model shown that was never to go into production, and the Ariel 3-wheel moped. All this placed a great burden on the group, who were already in deep financial trouble, and none of this was helped by problems that arose with the new versions of the machines that remained in the lists. Inevitably the range had to shrink for 1972, with just three singles, two twins and the triple left, the last listed with five speeds that year, and the twins joined by a small batch listed as the A70L and stretched out to 751cc for the USA.

Then came the end, for BSA had lost its way and no longer built the type of machine that had brought them such success in the past. The motocross engine went on in the CCM but the great Small Heath factory was torn down and for BSA enthusiasts it was the end of the line.

However, the name survived and was seen again on a series of mopeds and small motorcycles, all assembled from imported components. This began in 1979 when the Easy Rider mopeds first seen under the NVT label became BSA models, still as the ER1 and ER2. At the same time two 50cc two-stroke machines came along as the Beaver for the road and the Brigand for trail use. Next there were the NVT Rambler models, which became the Tracker with BSA badges while keeping the same Yamaha 123 and 171cc engines. Late in 1979 the Boxer joined the list, being a derestricted model and in 1980 this became the GT50. The Beaver and Brigand soon went but the Boxer and mopeds continued up to 1987 and the Trackers to 1992.

In 1983 BSA had an involvement with Can-Am to assemble the Bombardier with its Rotax 250cc engine and five-speed gearbox for the

The most popular of the BSA sports 650 twins was this A65L Lightning, with its twin carburettors and ample performance for most owners.

This was to be the road version of the Fury 350, with its twin-cam engine and other features, but did not make it into production.

British Army. In this way the BSA name continued on machines built for third-world countries and the services using a variety of parts.

By 1994 the rights to the name had been acquired by MuZ for machines under 125cc and this led to an attempt to revive the Bantam. Styled by Seymour-Powell, the prototype used a Honda CG125 engine unit, but little came of this as MuZ were in financial trouble.

Next to use the name was Regal and by 1995 they had a 50cc child's motorcycle designed by John McLaren in production. Following this, in late-1996, came a much more

New, unit-construction twins of 499 and 654cc capacity were introduced by BSA in 1962 as the A50 and A65, to herald a new series.

In 1968 BSA and Triumph launched their triples as the Rocket 3 and the Trident, with some variation in engine and chassis layout. They proved to be quick and popular.

interesting project, the BSA SR models that revived the Gold Star name and style. Three versions were listed, all using a Yamaha 399cc single-cylinder ohc engine and five-speed gearbox. This went into cycle parts modelled on the Gold Star with a tubular frame, duplex downtubes, gaitered forks, separate headlamp and swept-back exhaust pipe.

The versions came from changing the tank, seat and exhaust system, with the Gold SR, Clubman SR and G40SR taking BSA, Norton and AJS lines respectively. Most were sold to Japan and there was a 500cc option suggested for other markets. Pure retro, but in the image of the original, although for BSA enthusiasts the end had come in 1972 and only machines built before then really counted.

BUCK 1910–1912
Buckman Engineering of Nottingham showed a 4hp 604cc model at the late-1910 Stanley show, with belt drive and an adjustable pulley. A two-speed gear was listed for 1912, along with a 6hp V-twin, but that was the firm's last year.

BUCKLEY 1903–1904
From Sheffield, this firm showed a motorcycle having a powered front-wheel at the late-1903 Crystal Palace show. The wheel had aluminium arms on one side only, the other being open for access, and the 2hp engine hung from the hub, driving it through gears. Magneto ignition was employed and the project short-lived.

The BSA C15 grew to the 343cc B40, both with sports variants, and then to the 441cc B44, also in several forms, this the Shooting Star.

BULLDOG 1920

H.H. Timbrell of Birmingham bought-in the 689cc sv flat-twin Coventry-Victor engine, and sent off to B&B for a suitable carburettor and to Thomson-Bennett for a magneto. Coupling them together, he fitted them into conventional cycle parts, added a three-speed Sturmey-Archer gearbox with belt final-drive and called the result the Bulldog. The frame had a stylishly sloping top-tube and red panels were applied to the black-painted tank and a complete sidecar outfit was said to be available.

All this happened in July 1920, a time when demand for new machines far outstripped supply, so the fact that immediate delivery was offered through selling agents, Central Garage, Olton, Birmingham ought to have ensured success. That it didn't was evidenced by the fact that Timbrell was forced to relinquish his interest in the Bulldog just three months later and the project then passed to Slaney Engineering, who tried to keep matters afloat by retailing the machine under their own Slaney name.

BURFORD 1914

A new make that appeared in June 1914, hardly the most auspicious time for such a venture, offering a machine powered by a 3.5hp sv engine. It had belt drive and a 3-speed Armstrong hub gear for transmission, Brampton forks and curved footboards, but was gone by 1915. Very short-lived!

BURNEY 1923–1927

Edward Alexander Burney was the designer of the original Blackburne engine before the Great War and, afterwards, was responsible for the design of the four-stroke Wrexham-built Powell machines. By the beginning of 1923, in partnership with Brooklands star Capt Oliver M. Baldwin, he had produced a new 495cc sv single cylinder engine with outside flywheel, typical of his line of thinking. This was coupled to a three-speed Sturmey-Archer gearbox and with all-chain drive went into a trim set of cycle parts that provided a solo with sporting appearance.

Burney motorcycles were initially built at the John Warwick works in Reading, Berkshire and later in nearby Twyford. The single model continued into 1924 with small alterations, centre-spring forks replaced the Druid pattern and a spring-top saddle gave greater comfort, but its small scale of manufacture and fine quality of finish meant that it had to carry a high price tag. At £75, the Burney was 26 per cent more expensive than a similar capacity BSA of the time and hence sales were never going to be big.

By 1925 production had ceased, but at the end of 1926 came an announcement of a stylish V-twin with 680cc sv JAP engine, from Burney Motor Cycles at Tillingbourne Works, Shalford, near Guildford in Surrey. Of sporting outline this new Burney had Brampton forks, a girder frame construction, 8in Enfield brakes front and rear, and twistgrip control for both ignition and the Binks carburettor. The frame was of registered design and gave a fashionable low riding position, but although listed in the spring buyers' guides of 1927, it evidently didn't establish itself sufficiently to enable the little company to continue beyond that time.

BUTLER 1884–1897

Edward Butler patented the world's first petrol-engined tricycle in 1884, a year ahead of Gottlieb Daimler in Germany. It had a single rear wheel, a single seat between the front wheels, and a horizontal twin-cylinder engine operating on the Clerk two-stroke cycle with pump compression. The cylinders went either side of the rear wheel, being directly coupled to it by curved connecting rods.

The original design was never built, but a revised version ran in 1888, this having a four-stroke engine and a reduction gear to allow it to run at 600rpm. This was called the Petrol-Cycle, was water-cooled and utilized coil ignition and a jet carburettor supplied by a float chamber. This was first used in 1889 and called 'Inspirator' by its designer. While the original machine only carried one person, the

The Brigand was one of many attempts to revive the BSA name in some way associated with motorcycles, but with limited success.

The Butler tricycle, as designed in 1884 but not built, was superseded by the Petrol-Cycle of 1888, which did run.

Butler produced glass-fibre items and then complete machines – the Star-rider with the 247cc Villiers Starmaker engine is illustrated here.

later version could accommodate two at the front between the twin front-wheels as well as the driver at the rear. It seems that this was actually a Bollée built by Humber and fitted with the Butler engine. Brilliant in its advanced features, the Butler fell foul of the restrictive British legislation of the period and its backers moved on to other fields.

The patents were bought by Lawson but never exploited, so the design languished, although the machine ran again in 1896 and its inventor lived on to 1940 and an age of ninety-three.

BUTLER 1963–1966

Chris Butler made a wide range of glass-fibre items for motorcycles from works in Dalston, London and in 1963 decided to build complete machines. His prototype had square-section tubing and a 246cc Villiers engine with a Parkinson top-half conversion, but the production models of 1964 were for scrambles and had round-tube frames. Three engines were listed, one as the prototype, one with a stock 246cc Villiers 36A and the third with the 247cc Villiers Starmaker.

Two trials models were soon added, sold in kit form and with square-section frame tubing. Engines were the 246cc Villiers 32A or the same with the top-half conversion. This line continued on to 1966 before production ceased.

CAESAR c.1922–1923

One of the many firms who assembled lightweight models in the early-1920s for a short time. They used the 269cc Villiers engine and a simple specification, but failed to survive.

CAIRN 1950

Built by a Mr Farrow of Reading, Berkshire, this was a prototype built in the style of the Corgi with small wheels and easy to transport. It used a 99cc Villiers 1F engine hung from a simple frame, had no suspension but rode on 4in tyres and disc wheels. Panels fully enclosed the works and the handlebars and saddle were adjustable for height. It was a neat effort but no more was seen of it.

CALCOTT 1910–1915

Calcott were a cycle and components firm in Coventry who entered the market with a machine powered by a 3.5hp White & Poppe engine. Belt drive and Druid forks were some of the fitments of a well-designed model. For 1911 they added a 1.5hp model that used an inclined engine mounted in a loop frame, with belt drive and sprung forks.

A 2.25hp 237cc lightweight comprised the range for 1912, but was later joined by a stretched 2.5hp 292cc model and both continued for 1913 when a 4.25hp machine was added. For 1914 the 2.25hp was listed along with a 2hp model fitted with a 170cc Precision engine that had ohv set horizontal to the cylinder, a two-speed gearbox built in-unit with the crankcase, belt final-drive and Druid forks. Only the 2.25hp was listed for 1915, the last year of production.

CALTHORPE 1909–1947

Built by the Minstrel & Rea Cycle Co. of Barn Street, Birmingham, this make made its motorcycle debut at the late-1909 Stanley Show when they were already well known for their cars. As with these, the motorcycles were fitted with a White & Poppe engine, of 3.5hp, and had a chain-driven Simms magneto, Amac carburettor, belt drive and Druid forks.

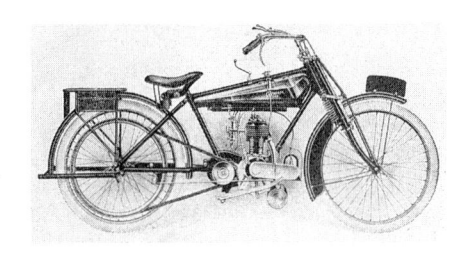

A 1920 Calthorpe, with a 2.75 JAP side-valve engine driving a two-speed Enfield gear with belt final-drive.

For 1911 they used Precision engines and began to add further models, including a lightweight. A later came with water cooling and for 1914 the Calthorpe Minor with a 1.25hp engine that had its two-speed gearbox in the crankcase. In 1915 there was also a two-stroke model and JAP engine in use, this continuing for 1916.

From then on a 2.75hp four-stroke and 2.5hp two-stroke, both with Enfield two-speed gears, were built and these two continued post-war until 1922 when the two-stroke was also available with a single speed and belt drive as an option. They were then joined by a 350cc two-stroke

Early Calcott Lightweight, as built for 1912, with their own 237cc four-stroke engine, rear magneto and Druid forks.

The Calcott range had added other models by 1914, with one having ohv, all improved, but still with belt drive and Druid forks.

with a three-speed Burman gearbox and chain-cum-belt transmission and for 1923 there was a version of this that came complete with a sidecar. At the same time the four-stroke changed to a 249cc sv Blackburne engine and adopted two-speeds and either belt or chain final-drive. There was a three-speed Burman gearbox for the 245cc two-stroke in 1924, the 350cc version was dropped and JAP engine used in sv and ohv forms along with a 147cc Villiers.

In the main these continued with gradual improvements, but all new for 1925 was the 348cc Sports model with their own design of engine, a three-speed Burman gearbox, light frame and Druid forks. A Super Sports version was added for 1926 when the 346cc JAP and 147 plus 247cc Villiers models continued. The important new model for 1927 was a 498cc ohc single of their own design.

The firm only used their own engines for 1928 with the 348cc in its two forms, but the camshaft model was then dropped and in 1929 there came the best known of their models, the Ivory Calthorpe. For this they took the 348cc ohv model, moved the magneto to behind the cylinder, revised the frame and cycle parts, added a saddle tank and finished the tank and mudguards in off-white. The older model stayed in the lists for one more year to hedge bets and clear stocks, but for 1930 it was a single-model range.

View of the timing side of the Calthorpe 1929 Ivory model, with its saddle tank, rear magneto and its own special colour.

The 1930 machine differed in having an inclined cylinder, this being the trend of the time, and was listed as Ivory the Second. It then became Ivory III, being joined by the 494cc Ivory IV for 1932 along with the 247cc two-stroke Ivory Minor for one year only. For 1933 only the 494cc model was listed, as the Major, but was joined by a 247cc version for the next year. Next came 348cc and competition versions, all running on through the decade.

In 1937 the marque was sold exclusively by Pride & Clarke of London and for this had a change of colour to become the Red Calthorpe. This failed to revive the sales; the firm went into liquidation and was bought by Bruce Douglas of the Bristol firm of that name. He moved the plant to Bristol and announced a three-model range in May 1939 using Matchless engines. Few were built before the premises were turned over to war work.

Post-war, the name reappeared in 1947 as the Calthorpe-DMW on a machine using a 122cc Villiers engine. This led in time to the DMW range in 1950.

CALVERT 1899–1904

Based in Stoke Newington, London this firm built basic, primitive machines using their own and Minerva engines. Simple and cheap, they lasted for a few years only, the 1903 model powered by a 2.75hp or 3.25hp engine. The forecar model had its single rear-wheel driven directly by chain. By 1904 the firm had turned more to the supply of engine castings for a variety of vehicles and so dropped out of the motorcycle lists.

The Calvert for 1903, fitted with a 2.75hp engine, belt drive and primitive design, but their adverts had fine slogans.

CAMBER 1908 AND 1920–1921

Bright & Hayles were motorcycle dealers with premises in Camberwell, London who, in 1908, offered a V-twin model that was built to order. The specification was thus as wide as the buyer's wallet was deep, which allowed for most engines, transmissions and cycle parts to be to suit and choice. The result would have been individual but expensive and most buyers soon turned their sights to a stock model.

The firm returned to the market in 1920 when they offered a model fitted with a 499cc Precision engine. This was possibly a venture to combat the shortage of new machines by using old or available stock and the same would have applied to the transmission, frame, forks and other parts. Inevitably, this was a short-term project that only lasted two years.

CAMBRO 1920–1921

Said to have been the cheapest three-wheeler available at the time of the 1920 Motorcycle Show, the Cambro was a primitive, by any standard. Its 20in wire-wheels, two at the front, one at the back, supported a skeletal frame and body with seating for one. Power came from a 154cc two-stroke flat-twin Johnson engine mounted over the back wheel, which it drove by chain.

This engine was of American origin, but had been taken up by Economic Motors of Eynsford, Kent who were then selling it as an auxiliary unit for pedal cycles. The Cambro, however, came from the Central Aircraft Company of Kilburn, London who were seeking means of filling their production capacity after the end of hostilities. This wasn't to be the answer and it soon vanished without trace.

Calthorpe produced the Ivory the Second model for the 1930 season, with an inclined engine that remained of 348cc, and the colour continued as before.

Campion provided many of these sidecar outfits in the Great War, where they acted as ambulances to ferry wounded men from the front.

CAMPION 1901–1925

A Nottingham firm, located in Robin Hood Street, that first appeared with a solo using a 2hp Minerva engine and a forecar powered by their own 3.75hp engine. By 1905 the solo was up to 2.75hp and the forecar had a water-cooled 4hp engine and a two-speed gear. The name was not seen much for a period from 1907 but returned in 1912.

JAP singles and V-twins with belt drive powered the new range, some with Roc gears, and soon with two speeds and chain drive. Later came models with Precision, water-cooled Green or Villiers engines alongside the JAP ones. There were three speeds by 1915 using Sturmey-Archer and Jardine gearboxes, but in 1916 there were four speeds for the twins.

They were back in the listings for 1920 with one model using the 770cc JAP V-twin engine and Sturmey-Archer transmission, this being joined by a 976cc version in 1921 along with 293 and 597cc sv JAP singles plus a 269cc Villiers model, all with two speeds. In 1923 the largest twin was listed with three speeds or a four-speed Jardine gearbox and in solo and sidecar forms. There was also a model using a Blackburne single engine, but the range then shrunk for 1924 to the 147cc Villiers, 293cc JAP and the 976cc V-twin. The next year saw them using Blackburne engines in 249 and 348cc sizes and touring sv or sports ohv. With this the firm bowed out in their own right, but remained in the trade building machines for New Gerrard for a couple more years.

CAP-'EM 1904–1905

A machine made in Edwardian days using a Kerry engine and one of the first P&M two-speed gears which was built by Charlie Drake of Bracken Road East, Brighouse, West Yorkshire. He arrived at the name for the machine by saying that he would 'Cap 'em', or show everyone that he could build a better machine than the 'professionals'. The type or model number shown in the 1921 registration document is 'Ancient'.

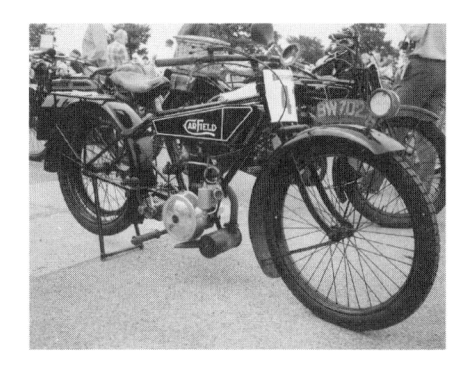

An early post-Great War marque, the Carfield was one of many that used the Villiers 269cc two-stroke engine with direct or two-speed drive, although few lasted.

CARFIELD 1919–1926

This make was produced at Windmill Lane, Smethwick, Birmingham and began by using the 269cc Villiers two-stroke engine in simple cycle parts. Transmission was either direct by belt or via a chain-driven Albion two-speed gearbox with belt final-drive. Druid forks were used and the fittings typical of the time. By 1921 a version with a spring frame and Brampton Biflex forks had been added along with models using 348cc sv Blackburne and 689cc sv Coventry-Victor flat-twin engines, the latter with three speeds. The twin soon went, but the other capacities continued for 1922, with the 247cc Villiers engine replacing the old 269cc capacity in 1923.

At the end of that year a 147cc Villiers engine was adopted for what would be their best remembered model, the Carfield Baby. This miniature performed well beyond expectations in prototype form in the 1923 Scottish Six Days Trial, and with two-speed Albion gearbox in chain-cum-belt or eventually all-chain forms remained in the range through to 1925. However, before that they had tried other models with the 249cc sv Blackburne and 349cc ohv Bradshaw engines, but by 1925 the firm went over entirely to Villiers engines, several versions of the Baby being backed by 172 and 247cc models. Only the two larger capacities went forwards into 1926, along with a new 292cc sv JAP-engined machine in two guises, both with all-chain drive and three speeds.

CARLTON 1922–40

This lightweight was powered by a 269cc two-stroke Villiers engine and was exhibited at the Scottish Motorcycle Show in February 1922. A choice of single or two speeds with clutch and kickstarter was noted, but no other details were provided and the marque then faded from sight with spasmodic appearances at times.

One at least appeared in 1930 when they offered a typical single of that time with a Sturmey-Archer overhead-valve engine driving a hand-change gearbox and all the features of the era. Little else was heard of them for some time but the name returned to motorcycles in 1937 through a new company based in Worksop, Nottinghamshire. They offered a neat lightweight using a 122cc Villiers engine unit with three speeds in a loop frame with blade forks, quite a utility model and one of several makes that adopted the small Villiers motor. It was built in this form to 1940 but post-war the firm stuck to bicycles.

The lightweight Carlton of 1937 with its 122cc Villiers engine as used by many firms in that period in a simple frame and forks.

CARTER c.1910

Carter was a cycle maker with his shop in the High Street, Grays, Essex and a garage in London Road. He dealt mainly in bicycles but also built at least two cars using parts he either bought or manufactured himself. No doubt he used the same technique for a few motorcycles, using his own cycle frames and a bought-in engine.

A primitive but well made Castell for 1903, with its engine held in a cradle, belt drive and braced forks.

CASSWELL 1904
A London firm, located in Great Eastern Street, that showed their machine at the 1904 Crystal Palace exhibition; it was powered by a 3.5hp Fafnir water-cooled engine mounted in a Chater-Lea frame. The radiator went flat beneath the fuel tank, while the transmission was by chain to a separate two-speed gearbox with clutch, and then by a further chain. Nothing else was heard of this enterprise.

CASTELL 1903–1904
This was a primitive built by a firm based in Kentish Town, London using a 2.75hp engine, designed by W.E. Fernhead and held in a cradle. Belt drive and braced forks completed the simple specification. For 1904 there was a ladies' tricycle having two front wheels, the engine mounted just behind their axle to drive the rear wheel by a lengthy chain.

CAYENNE 1913
Two 3.5hp Cayenne machines were entered for the 1913 TT by Hayes-Pankhurst of that company based in St Leonards-on-Sea, Sussex, but only one started, its rider J. Hayes to retire on the opening lap. The machine had a water-cooled engine with ohv, the rockers set across the cylinder head to run from the pushrods to the vertical valves. Each of these was mounted in a detachable manifold, the twin exhausts facing to the rear. The cylinder had a corrugated jacket and a cooling radiator of similar form was mounted ahead of it. A silent chain drove the forward magneto.

Castell built this tricycle in 1904 for the ladies, it having the twin front wheels, forward engine and long drive-chain thought to be suitable.

CC 1921–1924
The maker of the CC was Charles Chamberlain of Bispham on the Lancashire coast to the north of Blackpool. They listed various models having 147, 269 or 343cc Villiers two-stroke and 348, 499, 545 and 696cc sv Blackburne engines. Most were with chain-cum-belt transmission and some were single speed only. They were not widely known and appeared only rarely in trade publications or buying guides.

This is typical of the CCM off-road machines of modern times, some way on from their first days with modified, and fast, BSAs.

CCM 1971–1980 AND 1987–DATE
The initials stand for Clews Competition Machines and the firm was founded by Alan Clews at premises in Bolton, Lancashire. He had a background of success in scrambles and in 1971 bought a van load of parts from the BSA competition shop when this closed. These formed the basis of the first batch of machines, then called the Clews Stroka.

The Stroka worked well so there was soon a demand, and in May 1972 the first CCM machines were produced, based on the BSA B50 engine unit. These were either left at 499cc, or enlarged to 608cc, had a cylinder with the fins part-cut away and many other changes. These big four-strokes were successful right through the 1970s and late in the decade were joined by a 345cc trials model that used an engine based on and developed from the BSA B40. Later came two-stroke scramblers using Italian Hiro engine units of 125 and 250cc.

Financial pressures caused CCM to be taken over by Armstrong in 1980 and, while the machines kept the CCM name for 1981, by the next year they were labelled Armstrong CCM. During that year the engine unit was changed to the Austrian Rotax four-stroke single as Armstrong had other links with that firm, and the model continued in that form for some years.

However, in 1987 Alan Clews was able to buy his old firm back and over the next two years built it up by selling spares and Armstrong machines for outstanding orders. CCM returned to the competition field in 1989 with the range still based on Rotax engines. For trials there was a two-stroke engine but the motocross models used the big four-stroke single with a choice of 500, 560 or 590cc.

In this way they continued into the new decade and for 1997 added a super moto for use on the road. Based on the motocross machine, it used the 598cc Rotax four-valve engine in a modern package to offer an excellent, if expensive, model. At the same time the motocross model was available in Enduro or Rallye Raid trim, all with the 560cc Rotax, so all the CCM machines had a common base.

All this was fine until Rotax ceased production of the single, but CCM were able to conclude a deal with Suzuki to buy their 644cc XF650 engine unit, whose power output they improved by 10hp to 46hp. Among the plans for the future was to be a super trail model using a massive V-twin engine from Sweden, but nothing came out of this so CCM continued into the new century with the 664cc Suzuki plus a 400cc single.

CCR-JAP 1912
This was a Nottingham-built sidecar outfit with a 6hp JAP V-twin engine, three-speed Chater-Lea gearbox, engine clutch and chain transmission. Constructed by Smith Bros., the machine had Druid forks and a sidecar attached at five points. They also made a 4.5hp twin that had belt drive and an Armstrong three-speed hub gear.

CEDOS 1919–1929
This firm was located in Northampton and entered the market just after the Great War with ladies' and gents' lightweights powered by their own 211cc two-stroke engine. Both had a chain-driven, two-speed gearbox, belt final-drive and had to be push-started, while the ladies' model had an open frame.

Cedos came from the combination of the forenames of brothers Cedrick and Oscar Hanwell and they added a 247cc model in 1921, this also available in ladies' and gents' forms. Only the larger model was listed for the next two years and the company had to be restructured following liquidation. However, from 1924 they added models with a variety of engines and among these, at various times, were 348cc sv and ohv Blackburne, 349cc Bradshaw, 300cc sv JAP and a 976cc JAP V-twin for one year. Gearboxes became three-speed Sturmey-Archer with all-chain drive and for their last two years there were 147 and 172cc Villiers engines, but 1929 was their last year.

This was the ladies' model Cedos of 1926, with Villiers engine, modified frame and light build.

CELERIPEDE 1902–1903
John L. Thomas of Barnet, Hertfordshire, showed this make at the late-1902 Stanley Show. There was a choice of engine with either a 2hp Minerva or a 187cc 1.5hp Celerimobile being offered. There was also a motor-tandem on view, fitted with a 1.5hp Minerva engine and belt drive. Any model could be fitted with the firm's sprung front-fork, which was available from other makers under the Celeripede name.

Centaur for 1903, with its silencer forming the frame front-downtube and the inlet fed round the cylinder.

Drive side of the 1904 Centaur, showing the optional chain-drive with its two stages, along with other left-side features.

CENTAUR 1901–1914
A well made, Coventry-built primitive that, for 1904, used the silencer as the frame downtube between headstock and crankcase. The 3hp engine had its valves at the front of the cylinder, while the braced forks incorporated a rubber buffer to take some of the road shocks. Transmission was by belt or a two-stage chain-drive. A further model had an inclined engine, which replaced the downtube as in the Humber and P&M design, and a forecar was offered.

For 1905 the silencer reverted to being a separate item, no longer part of the frame, and the 3hp model was continued for 1906. Manufacture ceased for a while but the firm returned in 1910 with standard and TT models, both fitted with a 3.5hp engine that continued to have the valves at the front of the cylinder. The standard model had a Bosch magneto ahead of the crankcase and sprung forks, the TT version being rigid with a rear-mounted magneto. Two ran in the 1910 TT but with little success.

A free-engine clutch for the rear hub came in 1911 but of more interest was a 3.5hp vertical twin of 363cc, this having overhead inlet-valves. For 1912 there were 2hp and 3.5hp belt-drive singles, two speeds an option, plus a 2.75hp V-twin model that had direct-belt drive or a three-speed hub. There was also a 2hp ladies' model. These four continued for the next two years, after which the marque ceased.

CENTURY 1902–1905
This firm at Willesden Junction, London was best known for its Tandem model, a forecar design of some size and weight that was typical of the heavier kind. For 1904 they used a 5hp Aster engine driving a countershaft by chain, driving the rear axle by one of two chains to give high and low speeds. Steering was by a lever on the right moving to and fro, while there were some controls placed for the passenger to reach. A tradesman's carrier model was also listed. A steering wheel appeared in 1905 as car practice was adopted, but the make soon vanished as the cyclecar took over.

Century specialized in the forecar type, such as this Tandem, seen here in the Auto Club 1,000-mile trial.

CHANDLER 1921
A miniature machine based around a ladies' pattern safety-cycle but with sprung front-forks. The 1.5hp JES engine was fitted to the frame behind the steering head. The whole assembly weighed just 80lb (36kg) and was the brainchild of J.P. Chandler of St Botolph's Road, Shepherdswell.

CHARLTON 1904–1908
This make used the well-known French Buchet engine in machines that were typical of the Edwardian era, with belt drive and various transmission options. They appeared just before a sales downturn, so few can have been sold.

A 1904 Chase, which was offered with a choice of engines and a fine slogan, but failed to find many buyers.

CHASE 1903–1906
Based at Anerley, London, successful bicycle racing brothers A.A and F.W. Chase went into the motorcycle business in 1903, having had wide experience of powered machines of all types. Their machine was typical of the period and was the choice of Harry Tate, the music-hall artist.

Engines were vertically mounted and included 2.75 and 3.5hp MMC or 2.5 and 3hp Ariel, moving on to 4hp for 1904. That year they fitted magneto ignition to some machines and offered a forecar having air scoops to aid engine cooling. A 6hp racing model was listed for 1905, along with a 7hp twin-cylinder forecar with fan cooling, but they were only listed for one more year.

CHATER-LEA 1900–1936
Based in Golden Lane, London and later at Banner Street, a turning off it,

Early Chater-Lea from 1903, a time when they were a supplier to the trade, as well as building machines such as this, with its Minerva engine.

this firm was founded by William Chater-Lea in 1890 and began as a component supplier of lugs, castings and machined parts to the trade. Their first motorcycles appeared in 1900, essentially built to order using a variety of engines as required by customers, but in a few years they had one main model that was intended for sidecar use. Therefore it was of robust construction, powered by a 6hp JAP V-twin engine, had a two-speed gearbox, all-chain drive and leading-link front forks. There was also a 2.5hp solo with JAP engine and belt drive.

By 1909 they were using a three-speed gearbox and crankshaft-mounted clutch on the sidecar outfit; they then added alternative V-twin engines and further solos. For 1913 they reverted to one model, the 8hp twin sidecar model but added a 269cc two-stroke with two-speed gearbox and belt final-drive, with these two to continue for 1916.

They returned post-war in 1920 with just the 269cc two-stroke, but added a 976cc JAP V-twin for 1921 and a 488cc sv single of their own design for 1922. More models were added for the next year with 246cc

For 1909 Chater-Lea had this fine V-twin to offer with a variety of transmissions available to suit solo or sidecar use.

ohv and 346cc sv engines, while 1924 brought 348cc sv and ohv Blackburne engines, their own enlarged to 545cc, while the big V-twin entered its final year. It was also the year in which the firm began to fit saddle tanks to their models. During this period they made a name at Brooklands, where Dougal Marchant broke records and in 1924 became the first to exceed 100mph (160km/h) on a 350. For this he used a Blackburne engine modified to ohc.

A steady plodder in the Chater-Lea range was the 545cc Side Valve model they built for a decade, this one from 1928.

For 1925 only three singles were listed, but 1926 brought their new 348cc ohc model of the face-cam type. This had a vertical shaft driven by bevel gears from the crankshaft, the shaft with the camtracks mounted at its top, and rockers that followed the cams to lift the valves. The rest of the machine was typical of the period and there were also two other sports models of 348cc that used Blackburne or JAP engines. Finally there was the 545cc sv model.

Bottom of the 1928 Chater-Lea range was this lightweight model, which fitted a 247cc Villiers two-stroke engine.

Only the models using the Chater-Lea 348 and 545cc engines remained for 1927 and continued for the next year when the firm moved to Letchworth Garden City in Hertfordshire. A 247cc Villiers-powered lightweight was added for 1929 along with a Dirt Track machine, but only the three road models saw in the new decade. Then the two-stroke was dropped and for 1931 there were just the camshaft and sv models left to run on in a somewhat vintage style with few changes. The camshaft model ended in 1935 and the sv a year later, after which the firm returned to general engineering.

CHATFIELD 1903
One of many early primitives produced by a cycle dealer using a 2.25hp De Dion engine mounted in a heavy-duty cycle frame. The engine was supplied by a Longuemare carburettor, P&R accumulators were fitted and the machine rode on Clincher tyres.

CHEETAH 1967–1969
Built by Bob Gollner at Denmead, Hampshire, who put together an excellent frame and forks kit for trials riding, to which the buyer could add their own engine and wheels. A complete machine, in kit form, with a Villiers 37A engine was available, as were all the individual parts, all of high quality. Soon after this the supply of Villiers engine dried up and by

Chell was another firm that used the 122cc Villiers engine unit and simple cycle parts for a lightweight model around 1938–1939.

then the Spanish trials models were in the ascendants so the Cheetah came to an end.

CHELL 1938–1939
Based in Moorfield Road, Wolverhampton, this firm announced a pair of lightweights using Villiers engines for 1939. One was of 98cc with two speeds, the other of 122cc with three, and both went into a loop frame with pressed-steel forks. The brakes were 4in drums, the flywheel magneto provided ignition and lights, lubrication was by petroil and rear suspension was offered. The make was only produced for a few months.

CHENEY 1964–DATE
Eric Cheney was most successful in scrambles in the early post-war years and later moved on to machine preparation. This led to him designing a new frame which was one of the best made in the business and into which a variety of engines could go. AMC, BSA or Triumph units were usual, often modified, and both the frame kits and a few complete machines were very popular. This was as much due to the fine detailing, which came from long experience, as to the sheer excellence of workmanship. Such was the reputation of the machine that a trio of 504cc Cheney Triumphs ran as the British team in the ISDT in 1970 and 1971. Replicas were built later but a shortage of engines brought this stage to an end. Ken Heanes took over by an arrangement that resulted in the Heanes BSA Thumper, while Cheney moved on to making frame kits for Japanese and European engine units.

Also known as the JES, this 1913 City model was simple, basic and provided transport at the lowest cost.

CITY 1912–1913
This was another name for the JES ultra-lightweight and was listed as built at the City Motor Works, Gloucester. It had a 1hp engine with aiv, front-mounted magneto and outside flywheel fitted above the bottom bracket of a stock bicycle. Belt drive was used with a jockey pulley to set the tension and the front forks were braced. It was later sold as the Imp as well as the JES.

CLARENDON 1901–1904
Hannon & Smith of Dale Street, Coventry, built a sound motorcycle using their own or a proprietary engine in a loop frame. Their engine was rated at 3hp, with near equal

The Cheetah was one of several attempts to offer a quality trials model, prior to the Spanish models arriving on the British scene.

Clarendon either used a bought engine or their own, and mounted these in a fine loop frame. Note the extra, outboard main bearing.

bore and stroke, and featured an extra main bearing, outboard of the drive pulley. For 1904 there was a mechanical inlet valve, but the name soon vanished. They also built cars in the same brief period.

CLARK 1968
This was a moped built on the Isle of Wight by A.N. Clark of Binstead. It was based on a small-wheeled bicycle and had the 49cc two-stroke engine mounted to the left of the pressed-steel rear wheel. A clutch and direct gearing provided the transmission, brakes were drum front and calliper rear, while direct lighting was provided by the flywheel magneto. Sold as the Clark Scamp, the drive gears were prone to wear, so sales only amounted to some 200 units.

CLARK, NOBBY 1982–DATE
Based in Wiltshire, Nobby Clark builds scrambles machines based on the Rickman frame and usually fitted with a unit-construction Triumph twin engine, although others, such as Matchless and Jawa, have been used. All sizes are fitted and the machines normally built to customer specification.

CLEMENT 1922–1924
This was a miniature with open frame and four-stroke ohv engine fitted in front of the frame downtube and the pedalling bracket. The weight thus being carried low down made for good stability and the Clement was a workmanlike job. It was designed by a Belgian and manufactured originally in Germany, but by mid-1922 Mr A. Clement of Regent's Park in London had brought it to the British market. The tiny engine, quoted variously as displacing 43 and 63cc was in-unit with a reduction drive gear of 8 to 1, had an outside flywheel and carried its magneto upturned under the rear of the unit. A special butterfly-choke carburettor was employed and transmission was by chain.

The following year a sports model was listed and Clement entered a 63cc miniature for its class in the Grand Prix de l'Auto at the Parc de Princes track in Paris. It was said to have achieved a speed of 56mph (90km/h) in practice.

During 1924 there was a dispute over the British manufacture of the design, when it was announced that it would henceforth be known as the Wren and built under that name by Jennen Engineering of High Holborn, London. But this was contested by Mr Clement who seemingly retained his interest as it was as the Clement that the machine continued to be known.

Retailing was put in the hands of James Grose, the large retail outlet on Euston Road, London and the company began trading as The Clement Motor Company. There were some developments to the base model, a two-speed hub gear was introduced at option, the capacity was standardized on 63cc and there was talk of a sports model attacking world speed records in the 75, 100 and 175cc classes. On this optimistic note though, the marque slipped from the scene.

CLEMENT-GARRARD 1902–1905
Charles Garrard had premises in Birmingham and in 1902 imported the French Clément clip-on engine unit to fit to a standard bicycle. It was of 143cc with an overhead exhaust valve, small crankcase and large external flywheel. Thus it could be fitted inclined to the downtube, inside the frame, from where it drove the rear wheel by belt over a jockey pulley.

By 1904, Clement-Garrard had moved the single-cylinder engine to a much lower position, still with the weight well forward.

Frames for the new model were made by Norton who also dealt with spares and repairs for Garrard and used a 160cc Clément engine for his own first motorcycle. For 1903 a 3hp narrow-angle V-twin model joined the single, its engine mounted in the same position. It was intended for tandems but was used by Garrard in competition.

A new design was offered for 1904 with the engine vertically mounted just behind the front wheel, its weight hung from the downtube and braced to the bottom bracket. Most of the frame was occupied by the tank and its compartments, while belt drive and rigid forks continued. However, suspended forks of the leading-link type and a two-speed gear with chain drive were also advertised. The V-twin followed a similar format with the frame revised to suit the engine. Early in the year a new tandem was announced, actually a forecar with twin front-wheels, 4hp water-cooled engine, three-speed gearbox and shaft drive. This was sold as a Garrard and after this the name faded from sight.

From just before the Great War, the Cleveland was built in Yorkshire and offered a fine range of specifications to suit most tastes, this the 1913 machine.

CLEVELAND 1912–1914
Based in Middlesborough, Yorkshire, this firm offered 3.5 and 4.25hp models fitted with Precision engines, Druid forks, belt drive and options of a Villiers free-engine clutch or a Sturmey-Archer three-speed gear.

CLIFTON & DE GUERIN 1929
This was an obscure make built in Bath which fitted a 500cc overhead-valve JAP engine inclined forward in the current style with magneto ignition. Typical of the period it had hand change, a tubular frame, drum brakes and a saddle tank, but could hardly have chosen a worse time to enter the market.

An early Clyde from 1904, with a choice of engines and direct-belt drive as a solo or a forecar, with more power available and two speeds to choice.

CLYDE 1900–1926
George H. Wait built both cars and motorcycles at his Queens Street, Leicester works from the early days. The machines were typical primitives, but well made, with the engine mounted vertically in a loop frame with braced forks. By 1904 they offered two engine powers, magneto ignition and also a forecar with a water-cooled engine, and by 1906 had a V-twin and were using sprung forks.

For 1910, White & Poppe or JAP engines were fitted, but from the next year it was JAP power only, along with a variety of transmissions. This continued to 1915 and started up again in 1919 with a single and a V-twin, both having four speeds and chain drive. The two models reduced to three speeds for 1924 but ran on much as before up to 1926, their last

A 1912 Clyno V-twin, a model type they offered from their start. In this case the machine could have four speeds by combining a two-speed option with duplex primary chains. Note the chain enclosure front and rear.

year. The cars kept going a little longer, to 1930.

CLYNO 1909–1923
Frank and Ailwyn Smith were cousins who first made their name as a supplier of adjustable engine pulleys for motorcycles and sold these under the name of Clyno. They were based at Thrapston, Northamptonshire and used the same name when they moved on to complete machines which they first exhibited at the late-1909 Stanley Show. They had two models, a 3hp single and a 6hp V-twin, both fitted with Stevens engines, belt drive, their own adjustable pulley and sprung forks.

Late in 1910 Clyno production was moved to the Stevens' former Pelham Street factory in Wolverhampton for mutual benefit and for 1911 the twin had the option of two speeds and chain drive. This improved to four speeds in 1912 using twin sets of primary chains to double up on the ratios. The list stabilized in 1913 to just the V-twin with a three-speed gearbox and chain drive, joined by a lightweight with a 269cc two-stroke the next year. This had an inclined

First listed in 1914, Clyno kept this lightweight in the 1920 range, with its inclined engine and rear magneto.

cylinder and two speeds built-in with the engine.

A larger two-stroke made a brief appearance in 1915 when a second version of the V-twin was added, modified for use by the army as a combination to act as a platform to carry a heavy machine gun and its ammunition. This alone continued for 1916 and some were sent to Russia, followed by a later batch fitted with an 8hp JAP engine.

After the war they appeared at the 1919 Olympia show with the two-stroke and a new version of the V-twin with the engine of 925cc. For this model there was a frame fitted with rear suspension controlled by leaf springs, and it was intended for sidecar use rather than solo. However, a financial reorganization delayed its appearance until 1922, while the two-stroke was only built for a year or two. In 1923 it returned briefly to run alongside the V-twin, but at the end of the year motorcycle production came to an end to release space for the car production in which they had become immersed.

CMC c.1909–1911
The initials stood for the Cluett Manufacturing Co. of Tarporley, Cheshire who offered cycles and sidecars as well as motorcycles. They listed two versions of their 2.75 and 3.5hp models, one with direct-belt drive and the other with three speeds.

The engines were typical sv units fed by a B&B carburettor and ignited by a chain-driven magneto tucked away behind the cylinder. Druid forks and front rim plus rear belt-rim brakes completed a specification much as many others. Finished in black with the tank in aluminium with green panels, it was suggested to be the machine for colonial use. But the guarantee was only for three months!

CMM 1920
Offered by the Coventry Motor Mart of London Road, Coventry at the height of demand for personal transport after the Great War, the CMM

was of basic outline and specification. A 292cc Union two-stroke engine with direct-belt drive to the rear wheel gave the simplest model. For those with deeper pockets a two-speed Burman gearbox and belt final-drive could be specified or, for that little extra luxury, both a kickstarter and clutch were available at further cost. Of conventional outline, these lightweights would have been built for the Motor Mart by one of the city's many motorcycle manufacturers, then sold with the CMM transfer on the tanks.

COLCHAM 1962–1972
John Collins and Alan Chambers formed this partnership to build grass-track and a few speedway machines. They would fit any engine the customer required, but for his own racing John used Velocette units. They made their own front-fork dampers and fuel tanks, but bought-in most of the other parts.

COLONIAL 1911–1913
A short-lived make, but one that produced its own two-stroke engine that, at around 450cc, was a good deal larger than most singles of that type. This can hardly have helped sales as riders preferred a 3.5hp four-stroke, while the rest of the machine was much as others with bought-in parts.

COMERFORD 1930–1939
During 1930 the speedway machine frame designed by George Wallis was combined with the new JAP speedway engine and made a spectacular, winning debut. For some years they were marketed by Comerfords, the big dealers at Thames Ditton, Surrey and some 300 were built and sold. At first known as the Comerford Wallis, they were revised for the 1933 season to lengthen the wheelbase, steepen the fork angle, allow the rear frame to flex a little and place the engine, countershaft and rear wheel in line when viewed from the side. The first measures were made to suit the then current track conditions and the last to reduce the loads on the countershaft. Later they became the Comerford Special and then the Martin-Comerford or Martin-Rudge, the latter still fitted with the JAP engine, the name reflecting the Rudge speedway form of the frame.

COMERY 1923–1925
W. Comery had been Chief Engineer at Raleigh and responsible for the spring-frame flat-twin that brought the famous bicycle manufacturer back into the motorcycle business in 1919. By 1923 he had gone on his own and was trading as Comery Motors from premises on Vernon Road, Nottingham, from where a number of lightweight models issued forth in the hope of finding public acceptance. Villiers engines in 247 and 343cc capacities provided the motive power, with Sturmey-Archer three-speed gearboxes and chain-cum-belt drive. The bigger Villiers engine was considered capable of hauling a sidecar and thus a complete outfit was included in the range. During 1925, Comery disclosed details of a 439cc narrow-angle V two-stroke engine having a common combustion space – a split single. The engine was fully described in the specialist press and outline drawings of a complete machine were shown. However, this promising experiment did not proceed to the production stage.

COMET 1904–1905
Comet was based at Tanner's Hill, New Cross, London and used Minerva engines of 2.75 and 3.5hp fitted into BSA cycle parts. This was a typical primitive with braced forks, diamond frame and belt drive, and resulted in another firm that quickly disappeared.

COMET 1965–c.1975
This grass-track model followed the form of most others and was built in Yorkshire.

COMET-PRECISION 1912
This was the name under which two New Comet models were sold, a lightweight and a Colonial version of a standard machine, and were only used for the one season as an alternative to the marque name.

Only seen once, late in 1952, the Commander models had a spine frame and style but were never to reach the market with their Villiers engine.

COMMANDER 1952
The Commander appeared in dramatic style at the Earls Court show and was made by General Steel of Hayes, Middlesex. This make had a remarkable line with the engine hung from a spine frame and enclosed by a plated grill. Sadly, under the innovative lines was a prosaic Villiers engine of 99 or 122cc and no more was heard of this imaginative design.

COMPETITION CLASSICS
1991–DATE
This firm was formed by Clive Tomkinson to produce spares for the older Villiers engine units used in trials and scrambles. From the 34A and 37A motors, this spread to a much-improved ignition system, glass-fibre body parts, brake drums and then the Villiers Starmaker engine and Metal Profiles forks.

By this time Clive had found and restored a rare Starmaker Métisse

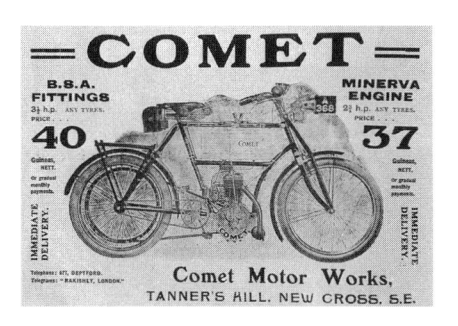

The Comet was a typical Edwardian machine, produced in London from BSA parts with a well-mounted Minerva engine.

and repeated requests for replicas brought him to the point of becoming a manufacturer. The result had a frame built from Renolds 531 tubing, nickel plated, and a much improved engine inside the copies of the original exterior. It was a fine replica available in scrambles and street-legal enduro or trail form.

CONDOR 1911–1914
The Condor was made by Broad Street Garage, Coventry, who built large singles. Little was recorded of the marque, but they had a 4.5hp single fitted with a 650cc engine and by 1912 there was also an 800cc single. In other respects they were no doubt typical of the time with belt drive, rigid frame and primitive forks, but built to suit their heavy-duty work.

CONNAUGHT 1912–1926
This make was built by the Bordesley Engineering Co. of New Bond Street, Birmingham and first seen at the late-1912 Olympia show. Their one model had a 293cc, petroil-lubricated two-stroke engine with an Amac carburettor at the rear of the cylinder, large external flywheel and front-mounted magneto. Inside the engine went a one-piece crankshaft, a connecting rod with split big-end, and a deflector piston. Belt drive, single speed and sprung forks completed a basic machine.

For 1914, variations of transmission were available to offer one, two or three speeds and belt or chain-cum-belt drive. There was also a lady's model but all kept to the same engine. A neat touch was an oil

Connaught built a variety of models over the years, this one from their first year in 1913, with a neat two-stroke engine, large external flywheel and belt drive.

This later Connaught from 1926, with 492cc side-valve engine, is hitched to a sidecar, this proved to be its final year.

receptacle held by bayonet joint to a tap on the oil tank to enable the rider to draw off a measured amount to mix with the petrol.

The range continued for 1915 and 1916 then production ceased, to return post-war in 1919 with single or two-speed variants plus a Miniature model, so named through its use of smaller, 24in wheels. The range continued mainly unchanged until 1922, when the Miniature was dropped and a 348cc two-stroke model appeared with a three-speed Burman gearbox and all-chain drive.

For 1923 the 348cc machine continued with the 293cc in various specifications that included a complete sidecar outfit using the larger engine. In the spring of 1924 the marque was bought up by the J.E.S. Motor Company and production moved across to Gloucestershire for a time, before eventually returning to Birmingham. Coupled with this change of ownership and move came a complete departure from previous practice with a four-stroke model using a 348cc sv Blackburne engine. If this was not enough, 1925 saw the addition of more four-strokes including one with a 349cc oil-cooled Bradshaw engine, a 348cc ohv Blackburne, and a newcomer with a long-stroke 348cc sv engine of their own make.

Such innovation was nothing new to the firm whose first engine had been an advanced unit and in 1915 had dabbled with a 340cc two-stroke flat-twin engine. Their last year was 1926, when they listed two models using their own sv engines, of 348cc and bored out to 490cc, and others with 298 and 346cc JAP engines, 348cc Blackburne and 349cc oil-cooled Bradshaw ohv engines. The solitary two-stroke remained to keep the memory alive of their early reliance on the type.

CONSUL 1922–1924
Johnson, Burton & Theobald Ltd, of Castle Street in Norwich tried for a short time to meet local demand by assembling conventional machines from parts bought-in, mostly from the Midlands-based motorcycle trade. Their first lightweights fitted the 269cc Villiers two-stroke engine with flywheel magneto ignition and a choice of 24in or 26in wheels, direct-belt drive, or two-speeds through a Sturmey-Archer gearbox. This policy was continued into 1923, except for standardizing on 26in wheels and the need to change to Villiers' new offering in the 247cc size, as the old 269cc motor was dropped. Then, in 1924, the single-speed model went and three speeds, again courtesy of Sturmey-Archer, became standard on the geared model with belt final-drive remaining until the end.

CONSULETTE 1922
This name was used by Johnson, Burton & Theobald of Norwich for one season on an ultra-lightweight version of their single-speed Villiers model. With 26in diameter wheels it weighed in at just 145lb (66kg) and sold for exactly £40.

CONTRAST-JAP 1912
A rare make not found in lists or seen at shows, but one ran in a 1912 trial organized by the Ilkley club. Maybe it was built by a local firm who used a 3.5hp JAP engine and cycle parts typical of the era.

COPE 1905
This was a Manchester firm that built forecars but added a 2hp light solo for 1905, basic but low in weight. It had the engine upright and well forward in a loop frame with braced forks and belt drive.

CORAH 1908–1914

This King's Norton, Worcestershire firm exhibited a 2.5hp model at the late-1908 Stanley Show, with a gear-driven Ruthardt magneto, Druid forks and low-built frame. Later came a 3.5hp single, and 3.5 and 6hp twins.

For 1910 there were three models, two using a 3.5hp JAP engine and either belt or two-speed P&M gear. The third used a 2.5hp JAP engine. In 1911 the singles were listed with 3.5 or 4.5hp Corah engines with a rotary valve and shaft drive, two speeds and both front and saddle suspension. The valve was drum-shaped and driven by a vertical shaft and bevels, sited next to the cylinder. The marque continued for 1912, the larger machine having two speeds and chain drive, the 3.5hp TT model with an ohv JAP engine.

JAP engines were adopted for 1913, either a 3.5hp single or 6hp twin offered with a two-speed gear, or a belt-drive 3hp twin. That year they had their sole entry in the TT and finished well down in the Junior due to a very slow first lap. They continued production for 1914 then stopped.

CORGI 1948–1954

This small, fold-up motorcycle was developed from the wartime Welbike that was made to fit in a container and dropped by parachute. The Welbike was made by Excelsior and used a Villiers engine, but the Corgi confusingly used a 98cc Excelsior Spryt engine and was made by Brockhouse of Southport, Lancashire, who also made the engine under licence.

First news of the Corgi came in 1946 but two years passed before it went on sale. Its two-stroke engine was much as the Villiers Junior, so had a horizontal cylinder and a countershaft for the clutch. It went into a low duplex frame with the petrol tank on top and rigid forks with fold-down handlebars. Small disc wheels and no kickstarter completed the crude but adequate transport for those days.

A kickstart and a sidecar platform soon appeared, while 1949 brought two speeds and telescopic forks as options, these becoming standard for 1952. It was built up to 1954 but by then standards were changing and its day was over.

CORONA 1901–1904

One of the many small firms, most being cycle dealers, who entered the market by adding an engine to a heavy-duty bicycle. A Minerva from Belgium or a French Clement were often used along with British copies and developments as they became available.

CORONA JUNIOR 1919–1922

Big things were promised by the Meteor Manufacturing Company for their Corona Junior on its announcement in 1919. Plans had been laid for the 448cc sv four-stroke single to be built in large quantities, with first deliveries promised early in the New Year. The engine had its cylinder and crankcase cast as one, with a detachable cylinder head and patented auto-lubrication system. Knock-out wheel spindles, drum brakes and enclosed front-fork springs all showed original and advanced thought. More individuality came from a striking tank finish in black and white stripes! Transmission options were single-speed belt, or two or three-speed chain-cum-belt.

Revisions later in 1920 saw mechanical-pump oiling replace the automatic system and the two-speed gear option withdrawn. Only the three-speed model with Sturmey-

The Corona Junior differed from others of the post-Great War era in using a four-stroke engine among its distinctive features.

Archer gearbox survived into 1922, after which no more was heard of a marque that had never remotely approached the expectations originally aroused.

CORYDON 1904–1908

Yet another firm that entered the market just as motorcycle sales slumped. Their machines were built by Bradbury Bros of Croydon, Surrey, and were of good quality and used both single and V-twin engines of various sizes in a frame and fittings typical of the times.

This early Cotton model is fitted with a 247cc Villiers engine, which had an external flywheel on the drive side to match the magneto.

COTTON 1919–DATE

Between the wars Cotton models were noted for their triangulated frame, which had been devised by Francis Willoughby Cotton as a straight-tube design first seen around 1913. As a trained lawyer, he was well able to deal with any attempts to copy the design that gave the machines their good handling.

The Cotton firm was located in Gloucester and the frame was based on four straight tubes running from headstock to rear wheel with others to act as downtube, saddle tube and chain stays. The layout enabled most

Basic early post-war transport was provided by the Corgi, which could be easily folded for storage, as was the Welbike on which it was based.

Typical road Cotton from the late-1920s, with its robust frame design that could accommodate such a variety of engines.

engines to be accommodated, which gave Cotton plenty of choice.

They began with the 269cc Villiers two-stroke driving a two-speed Albion gearbox by chain with belt to the rear wheel. In 1922 they added a 348cc four-stroke with similar transmission, but a Sturmey-Archer gearbox, and it was on one of these that Stanley Woods made his TT debut to finish fifth after many problems.

In 1923 the range expanded with a 247cc two-stroke and 249 and 348cc models with sv and ohv, the latter with inclined engines, all now with a Burman two or three-speed gearbox. Fame then came to the small firm, for Stanley Woods used the Cotton to win his first TT that year and the firm went on to record two seconds in 1924 and 1925 with the first three places in the 1926 Lightweight. All this established the marque name well above most others and by then the range had added a 545cc model that came in 1924.

By 1926 all models had three speeds and chain drive, being joined by a 500cc machine in 1927, the ohv machines still with inclined engines and from JAP or Blackburne. The two-stroke was dropped after 1925

New for 1932, this lightweight Cotton had a 148cc JAP side-valve engine driving a three-speed Burman gearbox.

but returned in 343cc form in 1928, reducing to the 247cc for the next year.

By 1930 the firm had added a saddle tank over the top frame rails for the ohv models but the others kept it between the rails. The range remained extensive, with engines from Villiers, Blackburne, JAP and Sturmey-Archer, these joined by the Rudge Python in 1931. All models had saddle tanks in 1932, when the firm added two models for the 150cc class, one with Villiers, the other with JAP power, and one with a 596cc Blackburne.

New firm owners in 1954 introduced new models with Villiers engines for post-war Cottons; this is a trials machine with a 197cc unit.

The Cotton Corsair was introduced for 1961, with a Villiers 246cc type 31A engine, some rear enclosure and leading-link forks.

This long list, with something for everyone, served them well right through the difficult times of the 1930s. By 1937 there was still one Villiers model but the rest, bar one, used JAP engines including a new high-camshaft type. These took the firm to the end of the decade along with a 122cc Villiers lightweight.

After the war the marque remained nominally available, retaining the famous frame and JAP engines. However, the models were largely

Later Cotton with Villiers engine was designed for trials use, with telescopic forks, more ground clearance and well tucked-in exhaust system.

unchanged from the 1930s, even showing girder front forks as late as 1952, when Dowty telescopics were an option. It is unlikely that many machines were built or sold in this period, which ended when ownership passed into the hands of Pat Onions and Monty Denley who redesigned and changed to two-stroke power from 1954.

The first of this new range was the Vulcan, powered by a 197cc Villiers 8E engine unit in a rigid frame. It was joined by a model with a 9E engine in 1955 along with the Cotanza that used the 242cc British Anzani twin engine and had a pivoted-fork rear suspension.

For 1956 a Trials model with 9E engine and a second 322cc Cotanza were added to the list, with a Vulcan Twin using a 249cc Villiers engine coming in 1957. This changed its name to Herald for 1959 when it gained a form of rear enclosure, a companion in the form of the Messenger with the 324cc Villiers-twin engine, and all models were fitted with Armstrong leading-link forks. The two Cotanza models were dropped, while 1960 brought a Scrambles model using the 246cc Villiers 33A engine, and the Double Gloucester, a sports version of the Herald.

The range expanded for 1961 with the 9E Vulcan Sports, a 246cc Trials with a 32A engine, a second Scrambler with a 34A, the road Corsair with a 31A and the Continental 249cc twin which had a new frame and a more sporting style. In 1962 the range was joined by the Cougar scrambler

Once Villiers ceased to provide engine units, Cotton, and others, turned to Minarelli engines and a lighter chassis construction.

with new frame and a modified 34A engine, while 1963 brought two new models using the 247cc Villiers Starmaker engine. One was the Cobra, a scrambler, and the other the Telstar, built for road racing.

There were fewer models for 1964 with the accent more on the sports and competition side, so the Continental Sports twin, Starmaker Trials and Cobra Special were introduced in an attempt to win customers in a declining market. Despite every effort, this decline continued so that each year saw fewer models until there were only three left for 1968 when Villiers ceased proprietary engine production with a major effect on many British firms.

Cotton then turned to the 170cc Minarelli engine, offering their trials machine in kit form until 1973, after when it was listed as the Cavalier. Late in 1975 it was replaced by the Meteor scrambler with a 125cc Minarelli but this went late the next year. Before then they were able to use a Villiers-type engine made by DMW for a trials model in 1976 and later still became involved with CCM and Armstrong. From this came the Cotton-EMC road racer of 1979 which used the 250cc tandem-twin two-stroke Rotax engine in a mono-shock frame with Marzocchi forks, Brembo brakes and Dymag wheels. With it came motocross models in 125, 250 and 400cc sizes, but these all quickly became Armstrong models to bring the Cotton name to an end until it was revived by Fluff Brown in 1991.

Since 1991, replicas of Cottons of the 1960s have been built by AJS Motorcycles of Andover, Hampshire, a firm formed from the FB-AJS that took over the old AJS two-stroke line back in 1974. The machines were the Cobra and Telstar with the Starmaker engine and the Trials Special with the same unit or the 37A. Strong demand for these continued, thanks to the nostalgia boom of the 1990s.

COULSON B 1919–1923

F. Aslett Coulson had been Managing Director of the Wooler company before starting out on his own and his new machine was introduced in November 1919 with full production promised in the near future.

Rear-wheel suspension by short swinging links under the control of laminated leaf springs was the special feature of the Coulson B. In other respects it mirrored contemporary practice, with a 349cc sv Blackburne engine, two-speed Jardine gearbox and chain-cum-belt transmission plus Druid front forks. However, the suspension system did improve the ride and it was neatly accommodated in the design, such that the machine in total was not in any way an oddity.

The one model soon expanded into a range, being joined by a 545cc sv Blackburne model and a two-stroke with the 292cc Union engine. The bigger Blackburne had a Sturmey-Archer gearbox and was also available in sports trim with single-speed belt drive.

During 1920 a number of improvements were deemed necessary, particularly to the stand, chain-case and gearbox attachment. In November, shortly before the motor-cycle show, competition rider Rex Mundy took a Coulson and sidecar on the London to Edinburgh run with an A-C.U. observer in a successful attempt to complete the distance without stopping the engine. Another publicity stunt at the same time proved the effectiveness of the spring frame, when 25 miles (40km) were covered riding on the rear wheel rim, the tyre and tube having been deliberately removed.

Sadly, none of this helped enough to maintain sales and the original company folded in 1921, but others had faith in the Coulson and later that year the marque was in the hands of A.W.Wall Limited of Birmingham. JAP engines now joined the Blackburnes and a Wall-built 269cc Liberty two-stroke attended to the lower end of the range. By 1923 H.R. Backhouse of Tyseley had acquired the rights from Wall and continued the 269cc Liberty model along with sv and ohv versions of the 349cc Blackburne. They also introduced a rigid-frame model with all-chain drive and by year end had changed the marque name to New Coulson.

COVENTRY 1910–1911

First seen late in 1910 and typical of that period, it had belt drive and sprung forks. The engine was of 3.5hp and the machine built by the Harris Cycle Co.

COVENTRY B&D 1923–1925

A wide range of capacity classes were covered by partners Barbury and Downes, who traded as Coventry Bicycles of Wellington Street, Coventry during their short existence, and in addition produced some models sold under the name styles of others. The little 170cc two-stroke Wee MacGregor was an example of the latter, whereas for their own models they went mainly for four-stroke power with JAP engines from 346 to 976cc. The 348cc Barr & Stroud sleeve-valve engine was also adopted and for a time this was sold under the Coventry-B&S brand name.

COVENTRY B&S 1923

This was a marque name used by Coventry Bicycles Limited of Wellington Street, Coventry. The B&S letters signified the fitting of a Barr & Stroud sleeve-valve engine, the 349cc single being adopted, driving through a three-speed Burman gearbox and chain to the rear wheel. There was also at least one machine with the so-called 'Octopus' B&S engine, which had two inlet and four exhaust stubs in an attempt to improve its breathing and exhausting.

Although only listed for 1923, the parent company continued with the B&S engine into 1924, but by then the models were badged with their regular Coventry B&D transfer.

COVENTRY-CHALLENGE 1903–1922

These were constructed by a cycle dealer who fitted various engines into his heavy-duty bicycle frames and completed the machines with bought-in parts. Engines were Minerva and Fafnir at first, with others such as JAP and Precision later. Although small, the firm kept going longer through the 1905 slump to run on to the end of the Edwardian era.

They then returned to bicycles only and traded as the British Challenge Cycle Co. Ltd before returning to powered machines around 1914. For these they used the 269cc Villiers two-stroke engine with the models sold as the Challenge-Villiers, but post-war went on to JAP single and V-twin engines. With supplies hard to obtain at first and then a surplus of machines, they no doubt went back to bicycles and carrier cycles as better business.

COVENTRY EAGLE 1899–1940

Based in Foleshill Road, Coventry, this firm had its roots in bicycles before turning to tricycles at the end of the Victorian era. Their products were usually an assembly of bought-in parts, but these were selected to go together well and the result given a

This model was produced in the very earliest days for Coventry Eagle, with a MMC-powered solo towing a trailer, an early attempt to add a passenger, who enjoyed the fumes and road dirt flung up from the machine until the tow bar snapped!

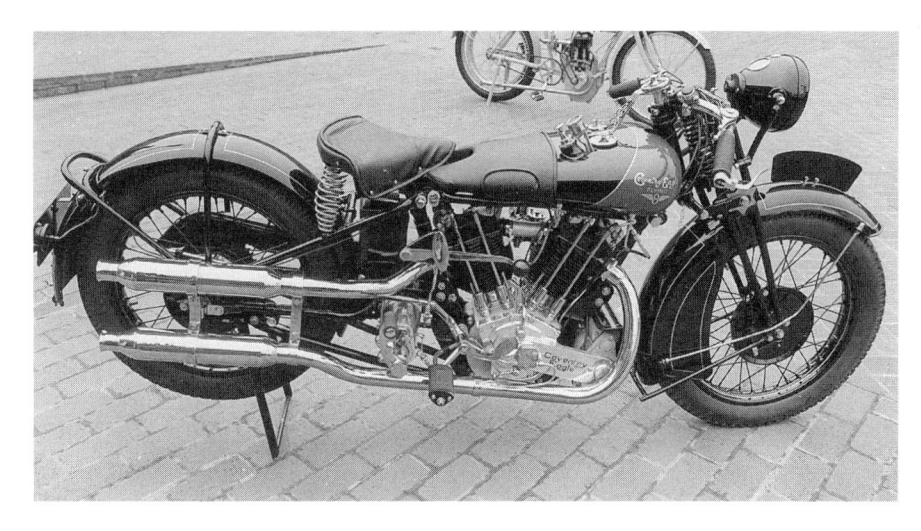

Around 1923, Coventry Eagle introduced their Flying Eight model with JAP V-twin engine, in this case with ohv and highly desirable.

The Coventry Eagle Pullman of 1937 featured enclosure, rear suspension, pressed-steel frame and a 249cc Villiers engine.

good finish. The product was mainly well received in the market and this enabled the firm to survive longer than most.

Their early range included a model with an MMC engine hung from the downtube and they also listed a trailer and a forecar before the sidecar came into use. For the Edwardian era there was a range of singles in loop frames with sprung forks and belt final-drive.

Little more was reported on the marque for some time, during which they continued to assemble from parts from outside sources, but by 1914 their range stretched to three models. Smallest was a lightweight powered by a 269cc Villiers engine driving a two-speed gearbox by chain and belt final-drive and with Druid forks. It was also available as a single-speed machine. Next came a 3.5hp single and 5–6hp V-twin, both with an Abingdon engine, three speeds and belt final-drive. For 1916 there was also a model with a 2.5hp JAP engine.

Post-war, there were only the singles until 1921, when the V-twin returned for one year, powered by a 680cc JAP engine. In 1922 it was singles only, using engines from Villiers, JAP and King Dick, and for 1923 there came a 147cc two-stroke claimed to be of their own design. This was enlarged to 170cc for the next year and then replaced by a 175cc Aza engine with Albion two-speed gearbox in 1925, before two-strokes were dropped altogether for a couple of seasons as the company cast its four-stroke net far and wide with a bewildering array of singles, twins and complete sidecar outfits throughout the mid-1920s.

In 1923 the 976cc JAP V-twin returned and a development of this model appeared as the 'Flying Eight'. In its various forms, this sporting twin would become one of the best

Coventry Eagle returned to four-stroke engines in 1937, using Matchless engines, in this case the 497cc single of 1938 with megaphone pipe.

The lightweight model Coventry Eagle for 1939 retained the 98cc Villiers engine, but had rear suspension and better equipment.

remembered motorcycles and by 1924 was available with sv or ohv JAP engines. With the latter and a Jardine gearbox it was the second most expensive machine on its market.

The four-stroke-only policy came to an end with the 1928 range when Villiers engines in 147, 172 and 172cc twin-port, supersports forms appeared in a set of pressed steel cycle parts, the result of twelve months of intensive development by the firm. Frames and forks pressed from sheet steel were not uncommon in Europe at that time, but Coventry Eagle were the first major producers in Britain to adopt this practice; one that they turned into a success and a range over the next decade.

Minor frame changes came for 1929 along with 196cc Villiers and 197cc JAP sv engines to give a five-model range of the type. Meanwhile, the Flying Eights continued their stately progress and a similar name style was conferred upon models using 344 and 490cc two-port ohv JAP engines which became the 'Flying 350' and 'Flying 500'. Both had a new cradle frame and the tubular Webb girder forks that had been fitted to all the four-strokes by 1929.

Most of the range continued on for 1930 when new models were added using dry-sump Sturmey-Archer inclined engines of 348 and 495cc in conventional tubular frames. After 1931 the twins were dropped to just leave the two-strokes for some years, although these were often distinctive. The Silent Superb series had a massive and stylish exhaust system; the most basic was the 98cc Marvel and other names were Wonder and Eclipse, most in the pressed-steel frame.

JAP-powered four-strokes returned for a season or two but the next sensation from the firm was the Pullman series of 1936. This had a new type of pressed-steel frame offering considerable enclosure of the mechanics and the rear wheel, while the rear suspension was controlled by leaf springs running along the frame sides. After this came a return to four-stroke singles in 1937 using Matchless engines in three sizes and these, plus the variety of two-strokes from an autocycle to the Pullman, ran on to the end of the decade. A curtailed range was listed for 1940 but few machines were built before production ceased, not to start again after the war.

In the late-1930s, Coventry Eagle added this Auto-Ette autocycle to its range, its line and details much as many others.

COVENTRY EMBLEM
c.1920
Another short-lived post-Great War hopeful that used a 269cc Villiers two-stroke engine and direct-belt drive fitted into basic cycle parts.

COVENTRY ENSIGN
c.1921–1923
A small, post-Great War make that had a short life and offered a model with a 292cc sv JAP engine and a similar specification to many others. Produced in Foleshill Road, Coventry, the firm had early roots with bicycles and continued with these for some years.

COVENTRY MASCOT
1922–1923
This was the first Coventry marque to utilize the Barr & Stroud sleeve-valve engine when it introduced a 349cc model in May 1922. The frame was given a bifurcated front downtube to clear the central exhaust stub on the B&S engine, Maplestone forks and Webb internal expanding brakes front and rear. Transmission was through a two-speed Burman gearbox with belt final-drive. There were options of three speeds and a Bentley & Draper spring frame with shock absorbers for 1923, plus a 349cc ohv Bradshaw model with all-chain drive. However, the makers from Stoke, a suburb of Coventry, withdrew from the market after this.

COVENTRY-MOTETTE
1899–1900
Another Lawson project, this involved a modified version of the Bollée tri-car that had its cylinder alongside the rear wheel, the crankshaft and reduction gear ahead of it, and belt drive. The driver sat aft of the passenger whose seat went between the front wheels.

The firm also built a ladies' motorcycle, the engine of which went just ahead of the rear wheel, which it drove by means of a wooden pulley pressed against the tyre. This layout placed the rider just above the petrol tank and hot-tube ignition burner but, despite this hazard, the machine was ridden from Coventry to London. It is said that Lawson presented the rider, a Mrs de Veulle, with a well-earned diamond ring for this feat.

This ladies' machine was a Coventry Motette from one of the Lawson factories and one of his most primitive.

COVENTRY-STAR c.1919–1921

This was one more short-lived assembler of lightweight machines who failed to survive the vagaries of the early post-war years. As with most, they used the 269cc Villiers engine.

A Coventry-Victor Super Six from the early 1920s, with its 689cc flat-twin engine and gearbox mounted under the rear cylinder.

COVENTRY-VICTOR 1919–1935

Like the more famous Douglas marque, this company kept faith with the horizontally opposed twin-cylinder engine throughout its existence. Built around a 689cc sv flat-twin, the first model from the Coventry-Victor Motor Company Limited appeared during 1921, but the engine had already been available from 1919 and sold to several assemblers – Ayres-Layland, Bulldog, McKechnie and Regent for example – for use in their own productions. The engine was produced by Messrs Morton & Weaver, who were associated with Coventry-Victor. Rated at 5/7hp the model, with the engine in-line with the frame, had its three-speed Sturmey-Archer gearbox mounted low down beneath the rear cylinder, all-chain drive and Brampton Biflex front forks. It was obtainable in standard or sports forms and one of the latter, somewhat modified, acquitted itself well in the Brooklands 500 Mile Race in 1921. A replica of the Brooklands machine was made available in 1922 as the Super Six and with bulbous-nosed saddle tank and high-level exhaust pipes gathered along the left side, it was an eyeable model.

A true racing version of the Super Six appeared the following year and a new 486cc ohv road model followed in time for the 1925 season. This, together with the 689cc sv in various forms, continued into 1926 and 1927 when, in the earlier year, a three-wheel runabout was introduced powered by the side-valve twin in either its existing 689cc capacity, or overbored to 749cc. A supercharged version of the 486cc machine was listed in 1927 and the sports 689cc sv model was guaranteed to achieve 80mph (128km/h).

The motorcycle involvement was scaled down a little for 1928, the 486cc ohv being named Super-Sports and the 689cc sv available in standard or now Silent-Six guise. However, a surprise came in 1929 in the shape of a 486cc ohv Dirt Track model, doubtless with the thoughts of emulating Douglas' success in that sphere. The 486cc ohv sports roadster continued and was joined by a sister model with bored-out cylinders, taking the capacity to 600cc, plus the 689cc sv twins as before.

At the end of the decade they just had the 486cc ohv and 689cc sv models and the 486cc ohv Dirt Track bike, which continued through to 1932, when a 600cc ohv version was introduced. The same engine format then appeared on the Super Six for 1933. By this date, with their unchanged vintage looks, the machines had become very dated indeed and with the day of the speedway twin having gone, the Dirt Track was dropped, followed by the 486cc ohv road bike in 1935. This left just the 689cc sv twin and that too went by year end to bring motorcycle manufacture to a close.

COXETER 1903

Located in Abingdon, Berkshire, this firm produced a machine in 1903 with a Minerva 2.5hp engine hung from the downtube, belt drive and typical primitive cycle parts. Sold with transfers as 'The Abingdon', it was built by Coxeter for a brief time. Later there would have been a clash with the Abingdon marque, so it is likely that Coxeter either built machines for others, as this was then a common practice, or just went on as a retail outlet.

The early model from 1903, built by Coxeter of Abingdon but named 'the Abingdon' and not to be confused with the marque of that name.

CRAIG 1896

The Craig was built by a gentleman of Putney, London, using a 1hp engine with a water-cooled cylinder head, aiv and massive flywheel. The cycle-frame tubes acted as the radiator and the engine drove the rear wheel by chain. Both wheels were smaller than usual which gave the machine a tall appearance, and Craig rode it on the road on Emancipation Day in November that year before selling it.

CRAVEN 1913–1914

Craven was a London firm who sold a combination powered by an 8hp JAP V-twin engine in a lengthy frame having leaf-spring suspension. At the front went leading-link forks while transmission was by chain and

A 1929 Coventry Victor Silent Six with 689cc flat-twin, as presented for that season, with the accent on the smooth engine.

gearbox. This was yet another short-lived make.

CRESCENT 1915
This was reputed to be a utilitarian model produced by Rudge-Whitworth. Powered by the 269cc Villiers two-stroke engine with separate magneto for its ignition, it had belt drive, basic specification and was well removed from the up-market Rudge image. It was most likely built as a batch for war service.

CREST 1922–1923
Crest were another of the hopeful firms who adopted the sleeve-valve 349cc Barr & Stroud engine, coupled to a two-speed gearbox with chain-cum-belt transmission. The Crest Motor Company occupied Blackdown Mills in Leamington Spa, Warwickshire for a few months in 1922 and 1923, but was soon gone from the scene.

CROFT CAMERON 1923–1926
Big twins with bulbous saddle tanks along the lines pioneered by Brough-Superior were the staple fare from this enthuiast company with works on St Michael's Road, Stoke, Coventry. V-twin ohv engines were supplied by Anzani and fitted into capable frames. The Super Eight was possibly their best known model, but production was always on a small scale.

CROWNFIELD 1903–1904
Made by James Perkins of Leyton, London, these machines were designed for the ladies, so had open frames. The 2.25hp Kerry engine was inclined within the frame loop and the top belt run was guarded to keep it clear of the dress of the day. Short-lived.

Crownfield-built machines were designed to suit the ladies, but only for two years.

This is just one of the Chris Tattersall racing machines built over two decades for the TT and other events, where they always performed well.

CROYDON 1904
Made by the Bradbury Bros of Croydon, Surrey, the Croydon appeared at the 1904 Crystal Palace show with a 4hp twin-cylinder engine mounted in a loop frame with duplex forks. It vanished as quickly as it came.

CRYPTO 1902–1909
Makers of motorcycles and forecars, they used Peugeot and MMC engines of various powers, and early on offered a two-speed gear for some models. Their light model for 1904 fitted a 2.5hp Peugeot engine to a modified frame, better braced than many, while the heavier model used the 3.5hp MMC engine and flat-belt drive.

The firm also offered a range of electrical equipment, more for the home and garage than a powered vehicle. During 1905 they took over the agency for the Belgian Kelecom range, offering both singles and twins for 1906, plus a 5hp four. They continued in this manner to 1909.

CTS 1931–1953
Chris Tattersall came from St Annes, Lancashire, hence CTS, and built a long series of 250cc racing machines that were used in most TT races from 1931 to 1953. Two ran in the 1931 Lightweight TT with G.L. Boudin from the Channel Isles finishing twelfth, although Chris himself retired.

A JAP engine was used that year and in 1932 when Chris finished fifth, his best position. Rudge engines were also used in the CTS as well as the JAP and the rest of the machine was built up from proprietary parts. Two machines ran in 1937 and three in 1939 when Les Graham was up to fourth before gearbox trouble forced him out.

Post-war saw three entries in the 1947, 1949 and 1950 TTs; by then the Italian machines were dominant but a CTS or two finished each year. The final entry came in 1953 when Chris retired, having ridden in TT races since 1928.

CURRY 1913
Little reported in the lists of the time, this was most likely a simple lightweight built and sold for local use. A 292cc sv JAP engine went into a diamond frame with belt drive.

CURTIS 1922
Taylor & Hayter of Park Street near St Albans were the people behind the Hagg Tandem and H.T. marques, who for a short time also promoted this machine, fitted with the 349cc Barr & Stroud sleeve-valve engine.

Before the autocycle came on the scene, the 98cc Cyc-Auto appeared for 1935, with its main engine components set in-line.

CYC-AUTO 1934–1958
The forerunner of the autocycle, the Cyc-Auto was designed by Wallington Butt in the early-1930s and first appeared in 1934, with the firm based at Park Royal, London. It had a 98cc two-stroke engine with vertical cylinder and the crankshaft running along the axis of the machine. The magneto went on the crankcase front and the drive came back to a worm and wheel built into the bottom bracket of the bicycle frame with chain drive to the rear wheel. Lubrication was by petroil.

In 1953 this small motorcycle, based on the Cyc-Auto, went on show carrying the Scott name, as they had been making the engines since 1938, but failed in the marketplace.

Different versions were offered for the next two years and for 1937 there were others using a 98cc Villiers engine. In 1938 Butt sold the firm to Scott who built the engines at their Yorkshire works while assembly moved to East Acton, London. The line continued in this way to 1940 and was revived post-war to run to 1958.

A motorcycle using the same engine, two-speed gearbox and shaft drive was shown at Earls Court late in 1953. It had a loop frame, telescopic forks and plunger rear suspension, but nothing came of this venture.

CYCLAID 1950–1955
Built by British Salmson at Raynes Park, London, this was a 31cc two-stroke clip-on engine that sat over the rear wheel of a bicycle, which it drove by belt. It was an all-alloy unit with horizontal cylinder, flywheel magneto and had the petroil tank fitted above it. The engine drove a countershaft carrying the belt pulley and the whole unit was spring loaded to maintain belt tension. It worked well and stayed on the market as long as most.

CYCLE COMPONENTS 1898
The company that was formed in 1894 to amalgamate various others in

One of the bicycle attachments to appear after the Second World War, to fit over the rear wheel and drive it by belt in this case.

One of a variety of attachments produced by Cyclemaster that converted a bicycle to powered transport, in this case by changing the complete rear wheel.

one combine acquired the Ariel firm in 1897 and built that company's first tricycle the following year, the engine a De Dion made under licence. From then on the Ariel marque name was used.

CYCLEMASTER 1950–1960
This cycle attachment was sold as a complete rear wheel to be exchanged for the normal bicycle one. It was made by EMI at Hayes in Middlesex to a Dutch design and comprised a large hub with the whole assembly within this. The engine was a 25cc two-stroke that had a disc inlet valve, and it drove a countershaft carrying a clutch by chain with a further chain drive to the hub. The petroil tank went above and behind the engine and it amounted to a neat and successful package.

For 1952 the capacity was increased to 32cc and in the next year the firm offered a complete machine and a version called the Roundsman which was built as a delivery bicycle with a large carrier hung over a small front wheel. In 1955 they moved to Chertsey, Surrey and later manufacture passed to Britax. On the road in 1955 the Cyclemate was created in the moped image by mounting the engine ahead of the bottom bracket of a bicycle made by Norman. Despite becoming dated, the engine unit was sold up to 1958 and the Cyclemate to 1960.

Before then, in 1956, the firm introduced the Piatti scooter. This had a 124cc two-stroke engine and three speeds, built as a unit with the rear wheel, with the whole assembly pivoted to provide the rear suspension. The frame was in pressed-steel and of inverted-bath form so the works were completely concealed within it. For maintenance the machine was simply laid on its side, but its small and low build was not to all tastes so it was only listed up to 1958.

CYGNET 1923

This was a prototype machine of the all-weather type, built by two enthusiasts who were translating their thoughts into an 'ideal' design. Few details were given of the engine or transmission arrangements, possibly because several options could readily be accommodated. The frame, though, was built up from a number of formed steel plates and a single malleable casting which served as the steering head. The plates were fashioned to enclose the working parts, to provide legshielding and semi-enclosure of the rear wheel. Channel section steel was used to support the plates where necessary and for the rear wheel stand. A completed machine was shown, but that was all. The designers' names were not divulged, but it was noted that the machine was reminiscent of the pre-

The later 133cc Cykelaid two-stroke unit, fitted to a standard bicycle as a complete front wheel, in this case a ladies' machine.

1914 Swan motorcycle and that the choice of the Cygnet name may have had within it an undeclared connection.

CYGNUS 1912–1913

This was the name of the company that built the Swan semi-enclosed machines using JAP and Precision engines at works in Frodsham, Warrington. The machines were normally known as Swan but sometimes referred to as Cygnus.

CYKELAID 1919–1926

This make hailed from York and began as a powered wheel designed to replace the rear wheel of a bicycle and drive it by friction. In production it went at the front with the 104cc two-stroke engine on the left with its mainshaft run through the wheel spindle to a flywheel. Ignition was by a chain-driven magneto bolted to the crankcase base, while transmission was by chain up to a countershaft carrying a clutch and then back to the wheel by a second chain.

The firm offered a package of wheel, engine unit and front fork, or a complete machine in ladies' or gents' bicycle form, but none of these found much favour with buyers. This led to some modifications, first seen late in 1922 when the machine was called the New Cykelaid. In this form a flywheel magneto went on the right to simplify the ignition and petroil replaced a pump system, while the capacity was increased to 133cc. Girder forks were added and for 1925 a dummy-rim rear brake was adopted, but 1926 was the last year.

CYMOTA 1950–1951

A cycle-motor attachment, made at Erdington, Birmingham that sat above the front wheel, driving it by friction. The 45cc two-stroke engine was unsophisticated, but enclosed in a nicely styled cowling that carried the headlight. Sold by Blue Star Garages in London, it came and went in two short seasons.

◆ D ◆

DALESMAN 1968–1974
This firm was formed by Peter Edmondson in 1968 and based at Otley, Yorkshire, where it built off-road competition machines using the 125cc Puch engine made in Austria. The results were machines for trials, scrambles and enduros with many common parts. The engine with its four-speed gearbox in-unit went into a duplex frame, with the Puch forks used at first soon replaced by REH ones. The make had some successes and in 1971 their US importer injected finance, so effectively took the firm over. Edmondson was joined by Bill Brooker from Greeves and the marque continued up to 1974.

DALM 1914–1915
Another very short-lived make that did not come on to the market until late in 1914. The machine was built by J.C. Dalman of Birmingham and powered by a two-stroke engine. A typical lightweight model of the period, it soon vanished, although the Dalm engine remained available as a proprietary unit until well into the twenties.

DALTON 1920–1922
This marque announced itself with an advertising flourish in 1920, but it is unlikely that many machines were actually built. The Dalton Motor Co. Ltd took its name from its address on John Dalton Street in Manchester's business district. It is therefore probable that manufacture took place elsewhere. Models with 348 and 499cc sv Blackburne and 689cc sv flat-twin Coventry-Victor engines were listed and illustrated.

This early Dalton 2.75hp model with countershaft and belt final-drive, is as seen during 1920.

DANE 1920
Utilizing the 348cc two-stroke Precision engine, coupled to a two-speed gearbox, the Dane cost £75 and was produced by Dane Works, of 131A Uxbridge Road, West Ealing in Middlesex. There was also talk of an 8hp twin fitted with a three-speed Sturmey-Archer gearbox, but it is unlikely that any such models were built.

DART 1901
F.E. Barker of Dern Gate, Northampton, produced a basic motorcycle using a heavy-duty bicycle fitted with a 1.5hp Minerva engine mounted inclined above the downtube. It drove the rear wheel by belt and had standard bicycle forks. Typical of the very early days, few would have been made.

DART 1923–1924
The Dart had a 349cc ohc engine designed by A.A. Sidney, who had worked previously for the Beardmore company. It was with the engine that the Dart Engineering Company of Coventry were principally concerned, for they hoped to find sufficient takers from within the trade not to concern themselves with manufacture of complete motorcycles. However, to generate interest they offered a Dart machine priced at £85 in April 1923, which showed the engine to have its overhead camshaft driven by three long cranks spaced at 120 degrees and driven by eccentrics on a timing pinion in mesh with the crankshaft pinion. The firm also adopted its own carburettor, which had a flat slide. In May 1923, one of these Darts was entered at Brooklands in the 'Century' races for W.H. Sinnett to ride, but failed to make its mark. Later the same year the business was operating from an address in Bristol and in early 1924 the first example of a Dart-engined model by an established manufacturer was seen in the New Scale from Manchester. However, the engine now had the camshaft driven by roller chain, concealed in an aluminium case on the right of the cylinder barrel, somewhat similar to the later AJS pattern. New Scale were soon to be gone from the trade and evidently Dart found no other outlets for there was no further news of the company nor its engine.

DAVIS 1911
The Davis Double was a motorcycle attached to a wide-bodied sidecar in which both driver and passenger sat. Normally fitted with an 8hp JAP V-twin engine, it had options of Chater-Lea sprung forks or a 4hp single-cylinder engine. The controls went in the body which had a screen, hood and dash.

DAVISON 1902–1904
A Coventry-made primitive that used 2 and 2.75hp Simms or 2hp Minerva engines. Both petrol and oil gauges were fitted on the 1904 models.

DAW 1902
The Coventry firm of Dalton & Wade made engines under licence from Minerva in a range of sizes. They also offered their own motorcycle for a short period.

DAY-LEEDS 1912–1914
This was a Leeds firm that built motorcycles and cyclecars, the first typical 3.75hp singles with direct-belt drive, free engine or two speeds, and Druid forks. They only differed from many others in having an overhead inlet-valve, while for 1914 there was all-chain drive and a P&M two-speed gear. Motorcycle production ceased

Best known for their engines, Dalton & Wade also produced a few complete machines under their Daw name.

The Dayton name returned to the market in 1939, for this typical autocycle with 98cc Villiers engine.

The marque reappeared in 1920 using the 269cc Villiers engine in a simple lightweight that had a cylindrical and tapered fuel-tank hung from the top tube. Late in the year there was also a mention of a 161cc motorized bath-chair that had been first seen in 1919. This had a two-stroke engine that drove the nearside front wheel, while the single rear wheel did the steering with tiller control. At the late-1921 show at Olympia the firm showed the lightweight as before and a three-wheeled single-seat machine with a 4hp Blackburne engine, three speeds and wheel steering.

when the Great War began but the car side continued to 1925.

DAYTON 1913–1922

This lightweight was produced by Chas. Day of Shoreditch, London, and had a 1.5hp 162cc two-stroke engine fed by an Amac carburettor. The magneto was chain driven and sat ahead of the cylinder, lubrication was by petroil, and transmission was by a chain-driven two-speed gearbox and belt final-drive. Either Druid or Saxon forks were fitted and a single-speed model was also offered. The range continued for 1915, when a ladies' model was added, but then manufacture ceased.

The 1914 Dayton was a simple model with small two-stroke engine, but came on the market at just the wrong time.

DAYTON 1939 AND 1955–1960

The Dayton name was well established for bicycles and returned to motorcycles from their base in North Acton, London, with an autocycle powered by a 98cc Villiers engine. Typical of the type, it was only listed for 1939.

Post-war, they made bicycles for some years but in 1955 entered the scooter market with a model called the Albatross and powered by a 224cc Villiers 1H engine unit. This made it larger and heavier than the popular Italian machines, while its frontal line and name did not help sales. In time it was joined by versions using the 249cc Villiers 2T twin engine, the 246cc 2H single and finally by the 174cc 2L single, this being the Flamenco model, but production ceased after 1960.

Dayton attempted the scooter market, but their machine had a heavy style and was not helped by its 'Albatross' name.

DEFY-ALL 1921–1923

Leaf springs controlled both the front fork and triangulated rear fork suspensions in this machine, designed by a Mr Craddick. It first utilized the 269cc two-stroke Villiers Mk IV engine with two-speed Sturmey-Archer gearbox and chain-cum-belt transmission. Blackburne 348 and 549cc sv-engined models followed from the works in Stalybridge, Cheshire but, despite the proud name, there was little such a small company could do to defy the might of the major firms and thus it soon succumbed.

DE HAVILLAND 1911–1913

This make of machine was built privately at Warwick Row, Coventry for some years before public sales were contemplated in 1911. The engine had an overhead inlet-valve whose pushrod ran through a tube set in the inlet tract and which was closed by a leaf spring. An outside flywheel and belt drive were used. In 1913 it became the Blackburn.

DELTA 1997–DATE

A modern clip-on, this 35cc two-stroke has a horizontal cylinder, electronic ignition and an automatic clutch. It can be fitted under the bottom bracket of a standard bicycle which requires one new pedal crank to clear it, with the fuel tank clipped to the frame. Drive is by friction to the rear tyre, giving fuel consumption around 200mpg (1.4ltr/100km) and the unit is sold as the Dart.

DE LUXE 1920–1924

These machines were the product of the small and spasmodic production by A.E. Bradford of Wolverhampton who operated as Motorities from premises on Sweetman Street. The company specialized in buying up remaindered stock for sale and many such items would have been utilized in the assembly of De Luxe machines, which would therefore have been to varying specifications. However, in 1922, when they were trading as the De Luxe Motor Company of Corporation Street, Birmingham, they were offering a firm specification for a 349cc Barr & Stroud sleeve-valve-engined model, with Brampton forks, ML magneto and Amac carburettor.

DENE 1903–1924

After managing the Jesmond company, J.R. Moore left to form Dene in Haymarket, Newcastle-on-Tyne and launched that make in 1903 with a

One of the 1913 Dene range was this fine V-twin; they continued post-war while sales held up.

machine using a 3.5hp Fafnir engine, Chater-Lea spring forks and direct-belt drive. From this he soon advanced to use all-chain drive in 1906 with a Dene two-speed countershaft gear working on the epicyclic principle and with a clutch. It was progressive, but perhaps too far, as two years on saw a two-speed hub gear patented.

He moved on to use Precision engines by 1910 and the machines became typical of the period with belt drive, sprung forks and a gradual move from a three-speed rear hub to a two-speed gearbox. Singles and V-twins were built, joined by a two-stroke in 1914, with some production in 1915. Post-war, they were listed in 1922 with one model with an 8hp JAP V-twin engine, three-speed Sturmey-Archer gearbox and all-chain drive. However, this was short lived with production coming to an end by 1924.

DENNELL 1906–1908

Herbert Dennell, of the West Leeds Motor Co., built a machine for J.W. Fawcett in 1906 that had an 8hp three-cylinder in-line sv JAP engine with the cylinders mounted on a round crankcase. Skew gears turned the drive to across the machine frame and from this two belts ran to the rear wheel, one on each side. Rigid forks were fitted.

In 1908 Dennell built a rather more conventional machine for a Mr Bates. This had a 4.5hp V-twin Minerva engine in a Dennell frame with belt drive, Roc two-speed gear and braced forks. A feature of the frame was its low build and the use of straight tubes. This seems to have been the extent of production.

DENNIS 1898

This Guildford firm became famous for its fire engines but did build a few tricycles in the De Dion mould. They had a single front-wheel, twin rears and a rear axle driven directly from the engine, which went behind the rider. Located in Surrey, they were one of the few companies of the time not based in the Midlands.

DERBY 1901–1902

A typical primitive in that it had an imported 1hp aiv engine mounted in a heavy-duty bicycle frame, but not typical in that the engine sat inclined above the downtube and drove a countershaft by chain. This was fitted behind the seat tube from where it drove the rear wheel by belt. The batteries and ignition coil were hung behind the saddle and the make was handled by Edw. De Poorter & Co. of Great Tower Street, London, but was short lived. Later they fitted an MMC engine and also supplied engines to other firms.

DESPATCH-RIDER 1915–1917

Built by Dreng & Co. of Fern Road, Erdington, Birmingham to serve the army in France and on other fronts where the motorcycle was an essential link in the communication chain. These were simple machines with the 210cc Peco or 269cc Villiers two-stroke engines and direct-belt drive, but ladies' and gents' versions were built and Druid, Saxon or Brampton forks fitted as available. Thus, they could be used and then disposed of to suit the needs of war.

DETACHABLE 1904

Based in Westminster, London this firm offered an ancillary engine that was carried in a light frame and attached to the rear of a roadster bicycle. The frame had its own small caster-wheel to support it and drove the bicycle wheel by chain. First examples used a Minerva engine.

This Detachable, an early idea, also pursued by others, provided the motive power in its own assembly and then was attached to the rest of the cycle.

DIAMOND 1908–1933

The Diamond bicycle was built by D.H. & S. Engineering at works in Sedgley Street, Wolverhampton, but when they announced a four-model motorcycle range in mid-1908 they became Dorsett, Ford & Mee, or D.F. & M., with sales handled by the Victoria Trading Co. of Lamb's Conduit Street, London. All four motorcycles were powered by Belgian FN engines, but did not have the shaft drive normally associated with that firm. There were two singles, of 2.5 and 3.5hp, and 3.5 and 5hp V-twins that had the rear cylinder positioned vertical, and all had a Bosch magneto and FN carburettor. The models were long and low for the time and all except the smallest had sprung forks. Direct-belt drive was employed and the finish was in French grey. Typical primitives, production was limited.

Late in 1912 they announced a far more advanced and interesting 2.75hp model. Both the valve gear and the transmission differed markedly from the norm and the first had an overhead inlet above a side exhaust, both at the front of the engine. Their camshaft ran forward along the right engine side and was driven by a bevel gear on the end of the crankshaft. It extended on to the magneto at the front of the crankcase and was fully enclosed.

The crankshaft bevel also drove a second shaft that ran back via a cone clutch to a housing, in which went two sets of bevel-gear pairs to provide both a two-speed gearbox and a means of turning the drive. Final drive was by an enclosed chain. The cycle side was more conventional, although the rear chainstays ran straight forward to pass either side of the crankcase just below the cylinder and thence to the downtube. Druid forks were fitted.

This 1914 Diamond shows its advanced, clever and unusual features that combined engine and transmission in one.

The 1919 Diamond was much more conventional, with two-stroke engine and belt final-drive in simple cycle parts.

Early in 1913 the magneto was turned to fit across the frame and this introduced a further bevel pair. Otherwise the model ran on to 1915 when it was joined by one fitted with the 269cc Villiers two-stroke engine with two-speed gearbox. This had belt final-drive and in 1916 was joined by a model using a 2.5hp JAP engine.

Post-war, the firm moved to Vane Street, still in Wolverhampton, and continued with these two models, entering the TT for several years, although without success. The range expanded with further Villiers, Blackburne and JAP engines, plus a Barr & Stroud and then an oil-cooled Bradshaw. By 1927 they were back to two-strokes only and after 1928 production stopped for a period.

The make returned in 1930, located in St James' Square, with a single

The early 1903 Dickinson was advertised in this manner to show the friction drive to the front wheel.

247cc two-stroke soon joined by others including two with overhead-valve JAP engines. This continued for a couple of years, but in 1933 there was just one model with a 148cc Villiers engine and after that the firm turned to making trailers and milk-floats.

DIAMOND 1968–1969

Based in Birmingham, this was a name from the past that was used once more for a series of off-road competition machines aimed mainly at the American trials market. For this they took on a trail format, but there were also trials and scrambles machines in small numbers. All had a 125cc Sachs engine with five speeds, a duplex frame and REH forks, and were sold in kit form at home. They were well made but soon gone from the market.

DICKINSON 1902–1905

Built at the Dickinson (sometimes spelt Dickenson) Toledo works in Aston Brook Street, Birmingham, this machine was of the bath-chair form, having a single front-wheel. This carried, and was driven by, the engine, which was at first a two-stroke with friction drive to the front tyre. Later came the Morette version, which was powered by a 2.5hp four-stroke that lay to the left of the wheel. Transmission was a mixture of friction from the flywheel and then chain to the hub. Pull starting by cord from the seat was used. There was also a 4hp twin-cylinder version shown in 1902 and this was of a heavier build and had a variant of the transmission system.

DKR 1957–1966

A scooter built in Wolverhampton that was launched in July 1957 as the Dove. It used a 147cc Villiers 30C engine with fan cooling and three-speed gearbox and was nicely styled, although with a rather heavy line to the front end.

The Dove was joined by the Pegasus with a 148cc 31C engine and the Defiant with a 197cc 9E engine for 1958, all using the same body and chassis. The Manx with 249cc 2T twin engine came in 1959, while 1960 saw the Dove II with 148cc engine and the Pegasus II with the 174cc 2L engine.

The DKR scooter was offered in several capacities and names, but all shared a common chassis and body, this is the 1958 Pegasus.

Most of these models were replaced in 1961 by a new range called Capella, with a new style and bodywork. Engines continued to be from Villiers with the 148cc 31C, 174cc 2L and 197cc 9E, while standard and de luxe models were offered. This range then ran on to 1966 when production ceased.

DMB c.1927

This make was built in Birmingham by the cycle company of that name. Typical lightweights were offered using 247 and 343cc Villiers engines set in a diamond frame and with chain-cum-belt drive. These were similar to many others and soon gone from the market.

A 1950s DMW for the road, with usual Villiers engine provided adequate performance for its ride-to-work job.

DMW 1950–1967

Dawson's Motors of Wolverhampton were in the motorcycle business pre-war and briefly linked to the Calthorpe name post-war, but their motorcycle production did not start until 1950 when their Valley Road Works was located in Sedgley, Worcestershire. They used Villiers engines for nearly all their machines over the years and their first range had the choice of 99cc 1F, 122cc 10D or 197cc 6E units. All had MP telescopic forks, another product of the firm, and the larger pair had the option of plunger rear-suspension.

In 1951 two De Luxe models with frames made from square-section tubing were added, while the 99cc model was dropped after that year and a 197cc Competition model was added for 1952. From then on they would use both round and square tubing for their frames, along with some sheet steel in later years.

DMW sprang a surprise in 1953 when they introduced models using 125 and 170cc ohv engines from AMC, this being the French Ateliers

In 1957 DMW tried the light scooter route with this Bambi with 100cc Villiers engine, but it was not a success, so was dropped in 1961.

de Mécanique du Centre, not the British firm at Plumstead. This link brought two further models, one with a 249cc ohc engine and the other a 125cc dohc racing machine called the Hornet.

This liaison did not last long and DMW were soon back with a range of two-strokes that included trials and scrambles models as well as the road ones. To these was added the Leda with 147cc 29C engine and the Cortina with the 224cc 1H, while the competition models became more built-for-purpose and less related to the road bikes.

The real DMW strength lay in competition, with this a 1961 trials model, with 32A Villiers engine and leading-link forks.

In 1957 the Bambi scooter appeared fitted with the 99cc 4F engine under a monocoque frame that was also the body. The Dolomite joined the road models and used the 249cc 2T twin engine, this unit also going into a scrambles model for 1958. More sensible was the 1959 use of the 246cc 32A engine for trials and the 33A for scrambles, while a 324cc 3T version of the Dolomite was also added.

In the 1960s the Bambi was soon dropped but 1961 saw a new concept, the Deemster. This combined the merits of scooter and motorcycle to offer weather protection and good handling, powered by the 249cc 2T engine. The rest of the range continued with improvements and late in 1962 DMW took over Ambassador, which resulted in some rationalization. The next year brought a new competition model, the Hornet road racer with a 247cc Starmaker engine

More brutal scrambles DMW, fitted with the Starmaker engine that they also used in their Hornet road racer.

in a form popular at that time. Later on, the firm built a 500cc twin using two of these engines but that was strictly for themselves to run.

The range shrank in 1966 when the Deemster was built using a 247cc Velocette flat-twin two-stroke engine as well as the usual 2T, but only the Hornet racer and the Highland Trials model, using a Cotton frame and a 37A engine, ran on to 1967. Then the firm effectively ceased making motorcycles, although they continued to make parts and the occasional trials machine. In the late-1970s they did produce some Villiers-type 246cc engines that they supplied to Cotton and Dot, but this did not last long.

This 1923 Dot was powered by a 350cc oil-cooled Bradshaw engine, but was otherwise much as most other singles of the early 1920s.

DOT 1907–1978

This firm was founded by Harry Reed and located in Hulme, Manchester, and was still there some ninety years later, albeit no longer producing motorcycles. The first Dot, the name said to mean 'Devoid Of Trouble', had a 3.5hp V-twin Peugeot engine and belt drive. Its fuel tank was of torpedo shape and helped to give a low line to the machine.

Reed took part in competitive events around the country to promote the firm with considerable success. The highlight of those early years came in 1908 when he won the twin-cylinder class of the TT. He was to continue to race for many years and as late as 1924 was placed second in the Sidecar TT.

The road range was typical of the period with a variety of engines from Peugeot, JAP and Precision, singles and V-twins, and gradual improvements to the transmission. By 1915 this had settled down to JAP engines only and Albion or Jardine gearboxes with two, three or four speeds.

A small range reappeared post-war comprising a single and two twins, but this expanded for 1923 when the JAP-powered models were joined by one using the 348cc oil-cooled ohv Bradshaw engine. This, along with the same size of Blackburne engine, expanded the 1924 range which also introduced a model with an ohv JAP V-twin engine and another with a similar Anzani.

The range then shrank to three 350s for 1925 and little more for the next year when Harry Reed left the firm, which passed to new hands. The new owners extended the range again and included a 172cc two-stroke, adding 147 and 247cc models the next year. These ran alongside the various 350cc four-strokes, but then came the depression and the range quickly shrank with manufacture ending after 1932, the company again changing hands.

Dot left the motorcycle market in 1932, its range by then a few two-strokes, with this 247cc Villiers model typical and from 1931.

However, this was not the end of the Dot motorcycle, for just after the Second World War the firm began to produce a three-wheeled motorcycle truck powered by a 122cc Villiers engine. In 1949 this led to a single road-model with a 197cc Villiers engine unit and from this sprang a new series of mainly competition machines. Further road models did appear and one such came in 1951 and differed in using the 248cc

Post-war, Dot began with road models, which were basic but good enough for the times, this one with a 197cc Villiers engine and girder forks.

By 1963 Dot had a good range of competition models; this trials bike has square-section tubes, leading-link forks and a Villiers 32A engine.

Famous Douglas flat-twin engine in 1910, with the magneto placed on top of the crankcase and interesting exhaust pushrod and rocker valve gear.

Brockhouse sv engine. The Mancunian in 1956 utilized Villiers 9E power and yet another, for 1959, used the 349cc RCA twin two-stroke, but these were soon dropped.

The range became trials and scrambles machines with various combinations of front suspension, lights and exhaust systems. At first the 197cc Villiers engine was used alone, but this was joined in 1953 by the 246cc Villiers in its various forms and finally by the Villiers Starmaker unit.

To augment their range, the firm added the Dot-Vivi mopeds from 1957, but these were all imports using Victoria engines. From 1959, there were the Dot-Guazzoni two-stroke machines from Italy in 98, 125 and 175cc sizes, but all were dropped by 1962. The line shrank in the 1960s as trading conditions worsened and, after 1968, machines were only available in kit form to suit a tax loophole. In addition, the supply of Villiers engines dried up, so they had to turn elsewhere and used the Italian 170cc Minarelli for their closing years. This combination was built in small numbers up to 1977 and in the next year they used a Villiers-type 246cc engine built by DMW, but this effort came to nothing in the face of the Spanish trials machines then available. After this the firm continued in business producing shock absorbers for cars and motorcycles.

DOUGLAS 1907–1957

This major British firm was located at Kingswood, Bristol, well away from the industry centre in the Midlands. They became famous for motorcycles with a flat-twin engine, seldom using any other form. The Douglas brothers, William and Edward, founded the firm in 1882 making quality castings and by Edwardian times were supplying parts to Joseph Barter for his Fairy engine. This led to them taking Barter into the firm and designing the Douglas motorcycle that was based on the Fairy.

Their first model was introduced at the 1907 Stanley Show and had its 2.75hp flat-twin engine mounted high in the frame, with direct-belt drive and braced forks. At the same time the firm showed a 6hp V4 engine that was compact and had a 90-degree angle, horizontally-split crankcase and outside flywheel. The V4 went into cycle parts that differed from any other Douglas, and drove a countershaft by chain with two final-drive belts, one on each side and giving different ratios, to the rear wheel. Only two or three were made, for it was far too early for such a design.

Little was altered for 1908, but the next year brought a magneto mounted on top of the crankcase and a lower build thanks to a new frame design. During 1910 a two-speed gearbox became available and this went beneath the engine where it was driven by chain, final drive remaining by belt. The gearbox soon moved further aft to be just ahead of the rear wheel and in 1912 a ladies' model with open frame and some enclosure of the rear cylinder and gearbox appeared.

In that same year Douglas began supplying Williamson with 8hp flat-twin engines for their machines, and the firm had their first TT success when Harry Bashall won the Junior.

An early Douglas from 1909, when the flat-twin engine still sat rather high, with direct-belt drive.

The 1912 Douglas flat-twin, had a chain-driven two-speed gearbox under the rear cylinder, while belt final-drive remained.

86 Douglas

Close up of the Douglas engine showing the angled valves, top magneto and details of the carburettor and inlet pipes.

They managed a second in the following year.

The one model, in various forms, took them on up to 1914, when a three-speed gearbox was on trial and a larger 3.5hp model was added, mainly for sidecar work. The engine was much as the existing one, but with improvements, and the two-speed gearbox bolted to a slanted mounting on the back of the crankcase to allow for chain adjustment.

With the outbreak of war the 2.75hp model was quickly taken up for service use along with the 3.5hp machine, which was joined by one of 4hp in 1915. Some 25,000 machines went to the forces during the war and served their riders well. After the war, surplus machines were the first to reach the civilian market and it was 1920 before matters improved. During this time Douglas had their three twins, but 1921 brought changes.

The 3.5hp model was dropped and rear suspension made a brief appearance. This was of the pivoted-fork type and had first been seen in 1916 when laminated springs were used, but these were later revised to a form of monoshock. However, this system and others never went into quantity production, nor did they take up the Edmund type they tried.

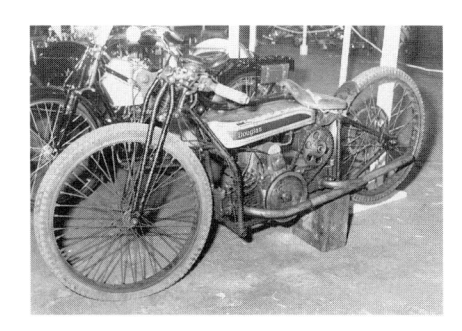

Late in the year came the more important introduction of two models with ohv engines. First built in 348 and 494cc capacities, when they reached the market as 1922 models they were of 494 and 736cc. Both had their three-speed gearbox tucked under the rear cylinder and all-chain drive. Chain-cum-belt drive remained for the older models and stayed with the two-speed 2.75hp model to 1926.

The 1932 Douglas Terrier, with 350cc engine in the well-established flat-twin form that served them well, but failed to avoid finance problems.

It was a Douglas year at the TT in 1923, for they had revised machines of 347, 494 and 596cc with the engines lower in the frame, the gearboxes above the rear cylinder and a form of disc brake. The outcome was that Tom Sheard won the Senior, run in poor conditions, a Douglas was third in the Junior, and Freddie Dixon won the Sidecar race using a machine with a banking sidecar controlled by the passenger. The firm followed this up in 1924 with a third in the Senior and a further Sidecar win in 1925 when Len Parker was the driver.

On the road the 1923 range comprised 348 and 593cc sv plus 348 and 736cc ohv models, all with various specifications. This continued on for 1924, when the ohv models adopted the layout with the engine much lower in the frame and the gearbox above the rear cylinder, while the rest of the range was little changed for that year or the next. It

The Dirt Track Douglas that proved so successful in that branch of the sport from 1928, until superseded by machines with JAP engines.

In 1935 Douglas tried the transverse flat-twin layout and shaft drive for the Endeavour model, but found that this layout needed experience.

was during this time that Cyril Pullin became Chief Designer for Douglas, having had a long association with the firm.

A new 348cc sv model was launched for 1926 as the EW and kept to the existing concept, but was greatly improved in all areas. It was aimed at buyers who required an acceptable performance without the expense of a more powerful model and was effectively all new. Among the changes were the brakes, which became 8in drums housing a Dixon-designed servo-operation, these being used on all models in time. Unfortunately, the basically good design was lightened in various ways to get below the 200lb (90kg) tax limit and this caused too many problems. Eventually they were dealt with, but the episode did nothing to enhance the model's reputation.

By 1927 there were five versions of the EW in 348 and 596cc capacities in the list, plus the ohv version of the larger. A bad fire at the works that year failed to disrupt production and that year saw a Douglas successful in dirt-track racing in Australia. It was the first sign of the suitability of the low-

Speed Special Douglas of 1935, with 596cc engine, overhead valves, and gearbox mounted above the rear cylinder.

slung twin for such work. Early in 1928 Cyril Pullin left the firm and Freddie Dixon returned to produce a racing TT model, while the rest of the range ran on. At the end of the year it was joined by the dirt-track model built specifically for the new speedway sport and saddle tanks appeared on some models.

There were new models for 1930, designed by Dixon, with the usual flat-twin engines but revised to dry-sump lubrication. Capacities were 348, 499 and 596cc with sv engines, plus the larger two in ohv form for competition, in all cases driving a three-speed gearbox. A hand start-lever was an option in place of the usual kick starter and all models were fitted with a centre stand.

Tartan borders ran around the petrol tank panels for 1931 when ohv road models were again listed, but near the end of the year the family sold the firm, which became a public company. Three new models were added for 1932, these being a 750cc sv, and 350 and 500cc models with short-stroke ohv engines. At the same time all models were given names of dog breeds, but the revamped firm was soon in financial trouble.

The final true Douglas was the Dragonfly, with improved engine, Earles forks and some styling for the headlamp. However, slow sales turned the firm to building Vespa scooters under licence.

Post-war brought a new transverse flat-twin engine design for Douglas with advanced long-travel suspension.

Little was built in 1933 other than from spares. There was to have been a complete break with tradition by listing the Bantam, which had a 148cc Villiers engine mounted horizontally within enclosing panels. For 1934 it had a Douglas-Villiers two-stroke engine and was joined by a 245cc flat-twin model with the remainder much as before although four-speed gearboxes were used for some. Old William Douglas bought back the ailing business and for 1935 Douglas added the 494cc Endeavour, which had a transverse engine and shaft drive, but during the year the firm was reformed yet again. This resulted in a smaller 1936 range of sv models only, reducing to three for 1937, two for 1938 and just one, of 585cc for 1939.

During the war Douglas turned to other products, but post-war saw them launch a new model in 1947 using a 348cc flat-twin engine set transversely across the frame. It had ohv, unit construction of its four-speed gearbox and chain final-drive. This all went into a duplex frame with leading-link front and pivoted-fork rear suspension. Both had torsion bars acting as springs, but for production the front was changed to compression springs. A Sports version was added for 1948 and both improved in 1950 when a rigid Competition model and two more sports models listed as the 80 Plus and 90 Plus were added, these being finished in maroon and gold respectively.

The stock model became the MkV for 1951 but of much more importance was an agreement for the firm to build the Italian Vespa scooter under licence. This was the start of a trend in Britain and Vespa was one of the major players, offering a lively performance from its 125cc two-stroke engine. It and the MkV, 80 Plus and 90 Plus flat-twins, ran on until 1955, when the Vespa was revised and joined by a 145cc Gran Sport model.

At the same time the flat-twin line became a single model, the Dragonfly, which had the engine improved and was given a better line. The frame adopted conventional rear units and Earles front forks, while the headlamp mounting was an extension of the petrol tank. However, sales of the twin were slow and late in 1956 the firm was taken over with production ending early in 1957. The Vespa continued to be imported but the Douglas motorcycle was no more.

Later, still trading under the Douglas name, the company imported Gilera mopeds and lightweight motorcycles, so continued its involvement with two-wheelers for many years.

DOWNER-GROVES 1920–1922

Cecil Downer-Groves, a compulsive inventor, designed and built two motorcycles for the use of himself and his family, both of individual appearance and both constructed in his home workshop in Croydon, Surrey. The first of these was a motorized cycle with 1.75hp two-stroke engine located inside the frame diamond of a gents' safety-cycle frame. Next came a motorized tandem, this more substantial and along the lines of later Autocycles, but of course with extended frame and seating for two. Both machines survived to be used in vintage events in later years.

DREADNOUGHT 1902
The Dreadnought name was used by Harold Karslake for a special he built around 1902 with a 402cc De Dion engine with twin exhaust pipes from its single valve. It varied over the years and still exists, now owned by the Vintage Motor Cycle Club.

DREADNOUGHT 1915–1922
A product of William Lloyd's Cycles of Freeman Street, Birmingham, where they also built the LMC, this was one of the many firms that adopted the 269cc Villiers two-stroke engine. It had a simple specification and continued post-war with its Albion two-speed gearbox and belt final-drive. A version with single speed came in 1921 but the make went a year later.

DRENG 1915
Located in Fern Road, Erdington, Birmingham, this firm listed a lightweight motorcycle in 1915 under the name of Despatch Rider. The Dreng had a 211cc two-stroke engine with Amac or B&B carburettor, Dixie or Ericson magneto, Saxon, Brampton or Druid forks and direct-belt drive. It was finished in service khaki and soon adopted the Despatch Rider name, which it kept up to 1917.

Not all Dresda machines used the Norton Featherbed frame, although most did, but this one still had the Dave Degens touch.

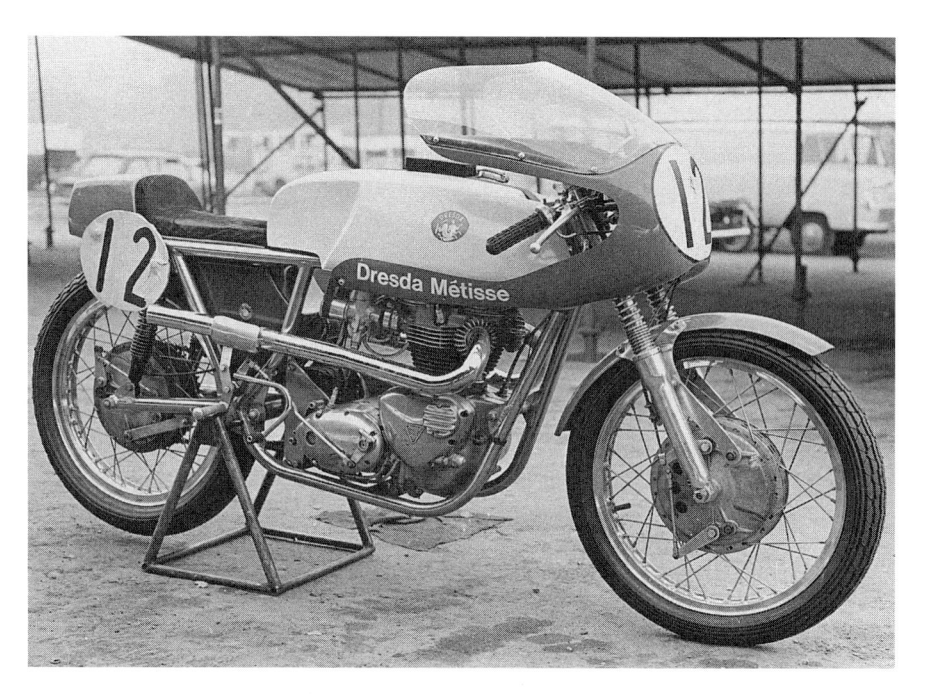

A link between Degens and the Rickman brothers resulted in this fine Dresda Métisse race tool, just itching for the start.

DRESDA 1961–DATE
Run by Dave Degens in the early 1960s, Dresda Autos was in at the start of the Triton cult, and if not the originator, Dave did more than most to make the idea popular. The machines were an immediate hit and in 1965 were given a real boost when Degens and Rex Butcher used one to win the tough 24-hour endurance race at Barcelona. Degens would repeat this win again in 1970.

Around 1967 there was also a link with the Rickmans to produce the Dresda Métisse using the brothers' frame and a tuned Triumph engine for road racing. Tuning and custom parts were also made and sold from the shop.

Degens then rode an Aermacchi for Syd Lawton, and from this developed the Dresda frame and built many more Tritons. During the 1970s he went on to other projects, but the classic revival of the 1980s saw a return of the demand for the Triton. So, Dresda came back and Degens went racing again in classic events, proving to be as quick as ever. The Dresda frame was used for most of the later Tritons, as featherbed frames became harder to find, but they also made replicas of these on demand.

DULA c.1970s
A firm involved with grass-track racing but only in so far as to produce frame kits. These would take most of the usual engines found in that branch of motorcycle sport, ranging from 250cc to the 500cc ohv single JAP or Jawa.

DUNEDIN 1906–1910
A cycle maker based from 1902 in Dunedin Street, Edinburgh, George E. Rutherford later moved to new premises to produce a small number of motorcycles. These were assembled from bought-in parts using Chater-Lea frame lugs, Druid forks and various engines, and were most likely built to order.

DUNELT 1919–1935 AND 1957
This firm was an offshoot of Dunford & Elliott, a steel producer in Sheffield, but was based in Bath Street, Birmingham. They were first seen at the Olympia show late in 1919 but production did not really get underway for another year. Their engine differed from others, not only in being a 499cc two-stroke single when side valves were the norm for such a capacity, but in having a double-diameter piston and cylinder. This

For 1920, Dunelt offered a two-stroke engine with double-diameter piston fitted into conventional cycle parts.

improved the crankcase compression at the expense of increasing the length and weight of the piston, while assembly was tricky unless the compression ring supplied in the tool kit was used.

The rest of the engine followed standard practice with a one-piece crankshaft, to which the bob-weights were bolted, and roller big-end, the rollers retained by plates riveted to the connecting rod. The engine was inclined in the frame and drove a three-speed Sturmey-Archer gearbox by chain with belt final-drive. Thanks to the engine design and a massive external flywheel, the Dunelt would pull like a steam engine from very low speeds, but acceleration was a gradual process. Thus they were ideal for sidecar work and were offered as a complete outfit in various guises.

All-chain drive and light-alloy pistons arrived for 1923, when the sole model was joined by three other versions, and there were no less than eight for 1924 including outfits of commercial van, truck and box carrier types. For that year only they used a three-speed Burman gearbox, but then reverted to the Sturmey-Archer for 1925 when all models had chain drive and mechanical lubrication via a Pilgrim pump. That year brought fire engine and milk truck variants, and there appeared to be a saddle tank for some, but this was actually two tanks with a centre join, two caps and an oil tank built into one.

The special Dunelt engine and its piston was still in use late in the 1920s, but with much improved cycle parts.

By 1930, Dunelt had this model T in their lists, with a 250cc Sturmey-Archer engine with face cams at the top of the vertical shaft.

Naming this Dunelt with its 348cc Sturmey-Archer engine the Vulture was hardly the best marketing ploy in 1931.

Neat Dunelt lightweight for 1933, with 148cc Villiers engine, similar to others of that time, but the range was soon all gone.

This long list of 499cc models was joined by one of 249cc for 1926 that followed the same lines for its engine. It kept the three-speed gearbox but had a diamond frame in place of the loop, and a wedge tank. However, its performance matched that of the larger model and a sports version was added for 1927. A de luxe 250 model was added the next year, which was the last year for the 499cc model, while for 1929 there were just three versions of the 249cc two-stroke. However, there was now the first Dunelt four-stroke with a 348cc Sturmey-Archer ohv engine inclined as usual in the frame.

It was 1929 when the firm first won the prestigious Maudes Trophy and for this they used the ohv 350. They repeated this success for the next year using one of two new models with a 495cc ohv engine from the same supplier. The start of the new decade saw the end for the 249cc two-stroke, but in that year they listed a model with a 249cc ohc engine of the face-cam type.

The ohc engine proved too noisy to be a success, especially in the depression, so the 1931 range comprised machines with 297 and 598cc sv, plus 348 and 495cc ohv Sturmey-Archer engines, along with one using a 346cc Villiers. All were given bird names such as Cygnet, Drake or Heron, but Vulture was hardly one to tempt buyers. Late in 1931 manufacture was transferred from Birmingham to Sheffield and the machines given the name of Sheffield-Dunelt to highlight this. They kept this new name for a year or two but then went back to plain Dunelt.

It was back to model codes for 1932, with much the same range plus a 148cc Villiers lightweight. For 1933, 249cc Villiers and 248cc ohv Python models were added, while for 1934 it was 148 and 249cc Villiers, plus 248 and 495cc ohv Python engines. Time was running out for the Dunelt motorcycle as the 1935 range was down to the two Villiers models plus 245 and 490cc ohv JAP machines, and that was their final year.

The Dunelt name re-appeared in 1957 for this 50cc moped with two speeds and good lines, but it failed to make an impact.

The name did appear briefly in 1957 when it was revived for a 50cc moped. This had a two-stroke engine built in-unit with a two-speed gearbox, spine frame and suspension for both wheels. It was a neat and tidy design but soon left the market.

DUNKLEY 1914–1916

Dunkley, a Birmingham firm located in Jamaica Row, offered a range of models using Precision 2, 3.5 and 4.25hp single engines, or 4 and 6hp V-twins. The smallest had the horizontal ohv usual with the engine make, a two-speed gear in the crankcase and belt final-drive. Druid forks were used.

They also listed a similar model with a 349cc two-stroke engine having drip-feed lubrication. This had three speeds for 1915 when the others ran on, but for 1916 JAP four-stroke engines were used for all models.

DUNKLEY 1957–1959

A short-lived marque made at Hounslow, near West London, that first appeared early in 1957 with the Whippet 60 Scooterette, which was powered by a 61cc ohv engine. Later that year it was joined by the 64cc Super Sports 65, which had a spine frame and Continental style.

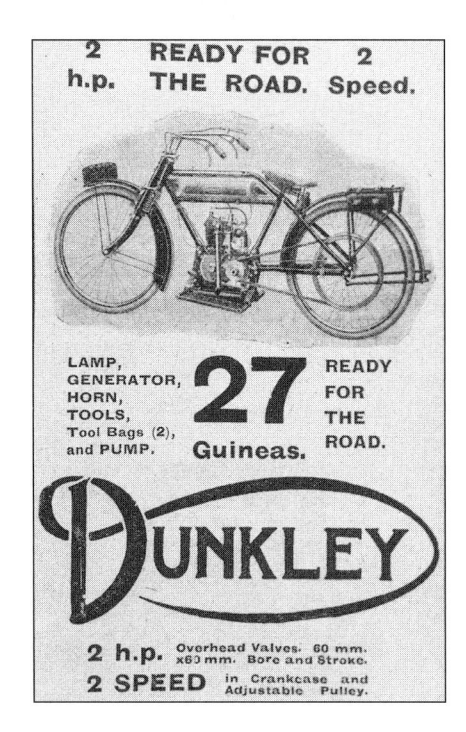

For 1958 these two were joined by the S65 Scooter, which had new cycle parts, and 1959 brought two models with no rear suspension, the 49cc Popular Scooter and a larger 64cc version of this. At the end of the year the marque vanished.

DUNSTALL 1967–1982

Paul Dunstall made his name racing Norton twins and from his preparation work first came tuning items and eventually fully modified Nortons in the café racer style. By 1967 he was registered as a manufacturer and his machines had many successes in production racing, including the 1968 TT 750cc class.

After 1970 he was more involved in producing tuning kits and custom parts, at first for the Norton Commando, but later for the Japanese machines. He collaborated with Suzuki to produce modified fours and these combined new exhaust systems with all the items needed to make a café racer.

All these parts were well designed and made, something that always characterized his work, but around 1982 Paul moved on to other fields.

DURSLEY PEDERSON 1903

This is a name best associated with bicycles based on a special design of frame using many tubes in a triangulated pattern. While these were the firm's main line, they did build a motor-cycle in the same form by fitting a single-cylinder engine designed by W.J. Barter. Described under his name, few were sold and Barter soon went on to design a flat-twin engine from which came the Douglas make in time.

Dunstall had links with both Degens and Rickman, which resulted in some very choice machines, such as this Rickman-Métisse with its Norton engine.

A range of scooterettes were made by Dunkley, but too many models and a variety of engines was not the way to go; so Dunkley went.

It was not a good time for Dunkley to enter the motorcycle market with a range of models and it was all very short-lived.

DUX 1904–1905

This was a Coventry firm that built machines using a Rex frame and a variety of engines to produce basic primitives. They launched with a two-page advertisement for their 3.25hp model prices at 35 guineas, but were short-lived in the market.

DUZMO 1919–1924

Designed by John Wallace and built initially by the Portable Tool & Engineering Company of Enfield Highway, Middlesex, the Duzmo was an uncompromising sportsman's machine. Wallace designed a 492cc ohv single-cylinder engine with a detachable head, aluminium piston, outside flywheel and pressure lubrication. It was advanced for its date, but relied upon direct-belt drive and was fitted into conventional cycle parts. A prototype 8hp ohv 50-degree V-twin in competition trim was built in 1920, being virtually a double-up of the single.

Interest in the design from the public soon overwhelmed the original company and Wallace bought them out to continue alone, although

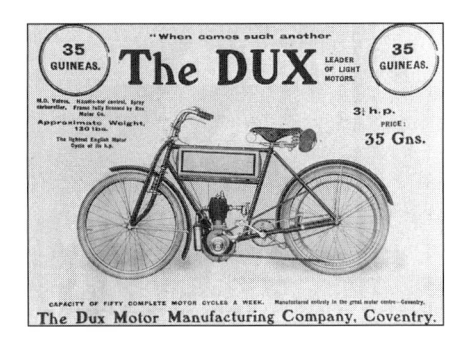

Dux was an Edwardian marque for a couple of years, with primitive form but neatly constructed for its time, but the market dropped badly in their second year.

he was assisted in development and competition work by an old friend, the famous rider/tuner Bert Le Vack. There were design changes to the engine by 1921 and the production V-twin arrived in the September of that year. It had all-chain drive and a three-speed Sturmey-Archer gearbox but, amazingly, a single-speed belt-drive option was available on this too. Le Vack and T.W. Dickinson campaigned Duzmos in the Senior TTs of 1920 and 1921 respectively, but retirements came on both occasions.

With Le Vack gone, eventually to greater things at JAP, Duzmo (the name was said to be a corruption of 'Does More', as in miles per hour) began to fade; only the single went forward for 1923 and into 1924, now with the engine sloped slightly forward in a revised frame, which had a dropped top tube, and with the three-speed Sturmey-Archer all-chain set-up as standard. Sadly, Wallace was then forced to liquidate the business, but the marque name ran on for a while under D.J. Shepherd & Company, who became sole manufacturers from February 1924 at the Enfield Highway address.

DYSON-MOTORETTE
c.1920–1922

This was one of the early attempts to offer the scooter form that came and went so quickly in the early 1920s. This one put the weight around the rear wheel with the engine to one side and the fuel tank above – just as Vespa would in the real scooter boom years ahead.

◆ E ◆

EADIE 1898–1900
Eadie formed the Enfield firm in 1893, with its roots in sewing needles, bicycles and rifle parts. When that name, as Royal Enfield, planned to build a quadricycle, Albert Eadie adapted the design to build a tricycle in 1898. It was powered by a 2.25hp De Dion engine and followed the pattern of that make. It was sold in some numbers but dropped out of sight as Royal Enfield moved forward. In 1907 BSA took over the Eadie assets, including its Redditch factory, but not Royal Enfield, and Eadie joined the BSA board, becoming managing director.

EAGLE 1912
This London firm announced a range of models early in 1912, the first a 2hp lightweight whose engine had an overhead inlet-valve. Druid forks and belt drive were typical, 3.5, 4 and 8hp twins were promised, the last with the option of chain drive. There were also to be 2hp single and 4hp twin models for the ladies.

In April 1912 they added a 10hp V-twin that had a curious double exhaust, the tops of the heads being connected by pipe in addition to the twin exhaust pipes, while overhead inlet-valves were fitted.

This ambitious programme soon collapsed under its own weight.

The Eagle-Tandem was a heavy-duty forecar, usually powered by a water-cooled engine and photographed here in 1903.

EAGLE-TANDEM 1903–1905
This was a heavy forecar designed and built in Altrincham, Cheshire, that used a De Dion engine in a format more akin to the cyclecar than the motorcycle. For 1904, water-cooled engines of 4.5, 6 or 9hp were listed, driving through chains and countershaft to provide two speeds. A further 1904 model fitted a 4.5hp Fafnir engine, but production was limited.

EAGRE 1920
This machine had a 348cc Precision two-stroke engine, two-speed Sturmey-Archer gearbox and chain-cum-belt drive and was typical of that post-war era and soon gone.

EBO 1911–1914
Ebo was listed late in 1911 with two models, one using a 3.5hp Precision engine and belt drive, the other a 4.25hp Precision and P&M two-speed gear. A short-lived make that was not mentioned again after it was announced.

The 1904 Eclipse, fitted with a V-twin engine and conventional belt-drive in place of an earlier, complex, rod system.

ECLIPSE 1903–1905
The Eclipse was made in John Bright Street, Birmingham and was exhibited at the late-1903 Stanley Show. Their machine had a novel variable-speed gear, the engine driving the rear wheel through two reciprocating rods and free-wheel clutches. The rods were coupled to a variable-throw crank mounted on the engine crankshaft and a mechanism moved this to adjust the ratio. A forecar was also offered.

This must have been a little too clever as, later in 1904, a wide-angle V-twin was added, this fitting into a loop frame having braced forks and conventional belt drive.

ECLIPSE 1912
This was designed by H.A. Smith and built by Job Day & Sons of Leeds, who made their own 499cc engine that had an overhead inlet-valve and a special lubricating system. It was fitted with a gear-driven Bosch magneto and a half-compression device for easy starting. The frame was made by Edlin, and the machine had Druid forks and belt drive.

ECONOMIC 1921–1923
This make used an interesting flat-twin two-stroke engine, which originated in the USA to power a Great War generator. Of a modest 165cc, the crankcase split on the centre line with each half cast in one with a cylinder. Post-war, surplus engines were available and installed by Economic at first in-line and then across the frame. Transmission by means of a friction drive was involved. Although a cheap machine, it soon left the market, either because the engine was unreliable or simply when supplies dried up.

EDDINGTON 1904
This firm built tandem tricycles, offering two models for 1904. The first was essentially a 3hp motor-cycle having twin rear-wheels, the drive to their axle by chain through a Dupont two-speed gear. The passenger seat went between the rear wheels, behind the driver.

The second model had a 4hp, water-cooled engine mounted aft of the rear axle, again driving a two-speed gear, the driver perched on the bicycle front-end, the passenger seat behind. Seating for one or two extra passengers could be fitted by those optimistic as to the available power. The make was also known as the Hillsdon.

EDLIN 1911–1912
The Edlin company from Birmingham, showed a 2.75hp model at the late-1911 Olympia show. Its engine and one of 3.75hp were made by Illston & Son, also of Birmingham, while the machine was fitted with Druid forks. However, this model was short-lived.

EDMOND c.1900s
W. Edmond had his business in Station Road, Chingford, from where he built cycles, motorcycles and tri-cars as well as selling as an agent. He offered single or V-twin engines for the motorcycles, which had direct-belt drive and braced front-forks in a primitive format. The 6hp Tri-Car had two wheels at the front, a passenger seat hung between them and chain final-drive.

EDMONTON 1903–1910
This was a small firm that assembled motorcycles using Minerva or Fafnir engines fitted into a heavy-duty bicycle frame. Transmission was by belt with options of engine-shaft clutch and gears, or hub gears. This was only limited production from, no doubt, a cycle dealer.

EDMUND 1910–1926
A firm based in Crane Bank, and later Milton Street, Chester, who introduced their 1911 conventional belt-drive single, with a 3.5hp JAP engine, with less usual suspension front and rear. The front had the fork legs able to pivot about the bottom crown under the control of a leaf spring attached to the underside of the crown and linked to the fork ends by stays. For the rear, the saddle, footrests and fuel tank were suspended rather than the wheel, involving extra tubes and laminated leaf-springs to achieve this.

A V-twin was added for 1913, along with Fafnir singles, and 1914 brought Villiers and MAG engines, but by 1916 they were down to two models. One used the 2.5hp JAP engine, the other a 2.75hp two-stroke Peco, and both had two speeds, chain drive and sprung forks.

Post-war, the marque reappeared with two models for 1920, one with a 293cc sv JAP engine, two-speed Burman gearbox and chain-cum-belt drive, the other with a 293cc Union two-stroke engine and Enfield two-speed all-chain transmission, both still using the patent spring frame. The two-stroke was dropped for 1921 when the JAP was joined by a 348cc sv Blackburne, while the next year saw these two with models using 545cc Blackburne and 348cc sleeve-valve Barr & Stroud engines. The larger was only built that year, but the others had an ohv 348cc Blackburne with them for 1923.

During 1923 the firm suffered a financial collapse and was quickly reformed to run on for the next two years using the same JAP, Blackburne and Barr & Stroud engines. By 1926 only the 348cc sv and ohv Blackburne engines were in use and this proved to be their last year.

ELAND 1908–1910
A make listed in 1908 as fitting a 3.25hp Minerva engine and typical of its time, not listed for 1909, but back for 1910. In that year a choice of JAP engines was offered, either a 4hp single or a 6hp V-twin, the machine having belt drive and sprung forks.

ELF c.1913
Said to hail from Blackpool in Lancashire, this marque was a lightweight powered by a 149cc ioe engine and built by the Nestor Motor Co. Basic, simple and built for local sales in small numbers.

ELF-KING 1908–1909
A short-lived Edwardian make listed early in 1908 with a 3.5hp single of primitive form. There was also a model using a Minerva V-twin engine and this had a crank handle for starting the engine in the manner of a car.

ELFSON 1923–1925
Built by Wilson & Elford of Aston, Birmingham, this was a typical lightweight with 293cc two-stroke engine, Amac carburettor, Fellows magneto and Maplestone front forks. A three-speed Albion gearbox gave it more ratios than most of its competitors and a choice of belt or chain final-drive was generous too, but single-speed and belt was also offered to those watching every penny. A Burman gearbox replaced the Albion for 1924, a two-speed option was added and a complete sidecar outfit could be ordered, the maker's own engine, rated at 3hp, evidently thought to be sufficient for the job. This pattern was repeated for 1925, after which the marque dropped from the lists.

ELGIN 1908–1909
Shown at the late-1908 Stanley Show, this make had a 1.75hp lightweight built in ladies' and gents' styles. The engine was a 143cc two-stroke that had a drip feed for its lubricating oil and drove the rear wheel by belt.

ELI 1911–1912
A make built by Eli Clarke at Station Road, Bristol and first seen at the late-1911 Olympia show. He used a 3.5hp Precision engine at first, but later listed Precision engines of 2.5, 3.75 and 4.25hp, the largest employing chain-and-belt drive, the others using the simple belt. Another short-lived make, but one that featured excellent mudguards and additional shields for weather protection.

ELK 1908
Only listed as a 1908 model using a 3hp engine and of typical primitive form, with belt drive and a high frame. Few can have been built.

ELLEMAN 1908

A make that had a brief life and used a 2.75hp JAP engine as its basis. The specification was much as others of the period so, with no special features, it soon went from the market.

ELLISON c.1911

A name that came and went all in one year, perhaps over-ambitious in specification for the depth of their purse. Supposedly with a choice of home-grown JAP or imported Peugeot engines, it also specified a sprung frame at a time when such was thought to be too much extra expense for most owners.

ELMDON 1915–1921

Built by Joseph Bourne & Sons of Bath Street, Birmingham, this machine had a 269cc Villiers two-stroke engine and the option of single- or two-speed transmission, both with belt final-drive. Druid forks and a Senspray carburettor completed a basic specification that was produced in small numbers for a few years. A 6hp model was also built in the later years.

Built in Birmingham by Alf Ellis, the Elstar used a BSA unit single or speedway JAP engines, among others, installed in the strong frame.

ELSTAR 1965–1971

This was a Birmingham firm whose name was the combination of the founder, Alf Ellis, and the BSA Star model whose engines his early grass-track frames were built for. There was also a version for speedway where a JAP engine was used and later came trials models in kit form. These were of a simple construction with an engine cradle that could be varied to suit that chosen. British or foreign engines were used along with a variety of forks and wheels, but the firm came to an end when, sadly, Ellis was killed in a car crash.

Elswick V-twin for 1914, shows the conventional form for engine, frame, side-spring forks and cycle details.

ELSWICK 1903–1915

This was a bicycle firm based at Barton-on-Humber, Yorkshire, that in 1903 listed machines with either a 2hp single or 4hp V-twin engine. One or both cylinders of the latter could be used as needed but little more was heard of the make for some time.

They returned in 1912 with models using 2.5 and 3.75hp Precision engines in a conventional format. Later came 4.25hp and V-twins, plus a model using a 269cc Villiers engine or a 2hp Precision. This continued into 1915 but then production ceased. There were plans for post-war production but these came to naught so, after 1920, Elswick concentrated on bicycles.

EMC 1939–1953 AND 1983–1990

Josef Ehrlich came to Britain in 1937 and by 1939 was testing a machine with his 240cc twin-piston split-single two-stroke engine. Post-war, he built a 345cc machine of this type from 1947 using Dowty Oleomatic front forks and a rigid frame.

In 1951 Ehrlich built a 125cc road-racing model using an Austrian Puch engine as the basis, while the following year saw a road model with a 125cc JAP two-stroke engine on show at Earls Court. The firm was wound up in 1953, but Joe went on to new fields while remaining involved with racing for many years.

The 240cc EMC, first seen in 1939, with the split-single engine type Josef Ehrlich was so fond of at that time.

In 1982 he became involved with the Waddon project and soon had the machine on form. In 1983 it became an EMC, still with the Rotax tandem-twin two-stroke engine unit

Ehrlich produced this model, with a 350cc split-single two-stroke engine, in the early post-war era and claimed excellent mpg figures for it.

Shown in 1952, an EMC fitted with a 125cc JAP engine unit hung with its transmission from the spine frame, the whole assembly controlled by a spring unit that was also the front downtube.

and won the Junior 250cc TT that year. It repeated this in 1984 and 1987, but then gradually slipped back as the Honda and Yamaha models moved ahead.

EMERALD c.1903
Many cycle dealers added a motorcycle to their shop-window stock in the early days by fitting an engine to a sturdy cycle frame. This name appeared on one such, which used a loop frame and was powered by a 1.75 or 2.75hp engine but differed in incorporating a two-speed gear in the simple transmission.

EMPIRE 1912
Empire was a foundry firm in London who built an experimental 1hp engine having a slide valve in 1912. The valve was moved by a slipper that ran in eccentric grooves cut in the overhung crankshaft. The intention was to offer 2.25 and 3.5hp machines, but no more was heard of the enterprise.

EMPRESS 1900
An Empress tricycle ridden by H. Ashby took part in the 1900 Thousand Mile Trial. Little is known of this early make, which no doubt was powered by a De Dion engine, or a copy, driving the rear axle.

EMPRESS 1926
After Harry Reed left the Dot company he had founded, he moved to the Empress Brewery site in Manchester. There, he sought to produce the 'Harry Reed Empress', which was similar in style to the NUT, but this was a very short-lived project and soon gone.

ENDRICK 1913–1915
Based in Olton, near Birmingham, this firm offered touring and TT models using 3.5hp Fafnir or Peugeot engines. Construction was basic, so they had belt drive, but they were fitted with Druid forks. JAP and Precision engines were also listed as alternatives.

For 1914 a model with a 2.75hp Peco two-stroke engine was added, while the four-stroke alternative was a 3.5hp Precision. Both models continued into 1915 before becoming war casualties.

ENDURANCE 1915–1925
Built by C.B. Harrison of Birmingham, this was a single model listed for 1915 and fitted with a 269cc Villiers engine. As usual with such, it was a basic machine with belt drive and petroil lubrication.

Post-war, their address was in Sheepcote Street, Birmingham and they first used a 269cc Arden two-stroke engine late in 1919, then their own 259cc two-stroke in 1920, before returning to the 269cc Villiers unit for 1921. All these models had the choice of single speed with belt drive or two speeds and chain-cum-belt.

The range remained the same for 1922, but for that year the 269cc Villiers engine adopted a flywheel magneto and a pressure-fed oiling system. By adding 343cc Villiers-powered versions, the range was doubled for 1923 and continued in this way to its final 1925 year.

ENERGETTE 1902–1903 AND 1907–1908
This was the name under which the early Norton machines were advertised, these being powered by 160cc French Clement engines. Either direct-belt drive or chain to a two-speed gearbox and final belt-drive was offered.

The name was revived in 1907 for another model, this time powered by a V-twin 274cc Moto Rêve engine. The engine was small and neat, the complete machine weighing in at a mere 76lb (34.5kg). In 1908 it was joined by the Nortonette, a model fitted with a 2hp single-cylinder engine, but this was soon dropped and the Energette took the Nortonette name before itself vanishing from the Norton range.

ERSKINE JAP 1955–c.1960
This was a typical speedway machine built in small numbers by Mike Erskine. It had the usual JAP engine, countershaft, rigid frame and short-travel forks, and provided a contrast to the usual Jackson-Rotrax.

ETA 1921
G.E. Halliday of Halifax, Yorkshire, had been successful in a magazine competition to design the 'Ideal Motorcycle' shortly after the Great War. Putting his ideas into practice, he built a 7hp machine powered by a three-cylinder sv radial engine mounted across the frame and displacing 1007cc. This was built in-unit with a three-speed gearbox and had shaft drive to the rear wheel. The fuel tank of pressed steel construction doubled as the frame backbone and leaf springs provided suspension for the frame and front forks. Deserving of more development, the ETA unfortunately never progressed into full scale manufacture.

ETNA 1902
The Etna was a mighty tandem tricycle built at the Brixton Motor Works by Hubert Fawconer Harding for his own use. It featured a 1750cc water-cooled V-twin engine that went well to the rear between the back wheels and beneath the passenger. The engine had overhead inlet and side exhaust-valves, and the crankshaft extended across the frame to a detachable starting-handle.

The two radiators went between the rider's knees with a pump to keep the water on the move, ignition was by trembler coil to start and then magneto for running, while the fuel tank went alongside and above the engine. Two crown wheels, two pinions and an epicyclic gearbox gave a total of four speeds and a complex selection process.

A substantial frame carried the mechanics and, in time, the original front forks were changed to Chater-Lea. The brakes were hardly up to the performance, for the Etna could reach 70mph (112km/h), really quick for the days when the limit was first 12 and then 20mph (19 and 32km/h). The machine still exists and usually takes part in the Pioneer Run.

EVART-HALL 1904–1905
This was the name applied to the tank of the Binks motorcycle fitted with the in-line four-cylinder 5hp engine. This went into a diamond frame having braced forks and drove the rear wheel by enclosed chain. It was also offered as a forecar, but its £70 price as a solo model made it a luxury model.

EVER UPRIGHT 1910–1911
Listed late in 1910, this machine had a 2hp Minerva engine fitted with an FN carburettor. It drove the rear wheel by belt and had rigid forks, becoming another short-lived model the next year.

EXACTWELD 1984–1987
Guy Pearson and John Baldwin were running a competitive 250cc Yamaha, but sought something better for the grand prix circuit. The result was highly innovative in both engine and chassis, for most of the machine was built in their workshop at East Grinstead, Sussex.

The 250cc engine was a water-cooled tandem-twin two-stroke but, unlike the Rotax or Kawasaki, had the cylinders inclined forward at 45 degrees. It had disc valves on one or both sides of the crankcase, electronic ignition and, along with its six-speed gearbox, was a compact unit.

The chassis was quite novel, for the team used the engine assembly to connect the front and rear suspension systems. The telescopic forks pivoted

A 1904 Excelsior forecar tandem, with the lady nearest the accident – not for the faint-hearted.

in a sheet-alloy fabrication that bolted to the cylinder heads and carried the radiator. At the rear the fork pivoted in a casting bolted to the back of the gearbox and was controlled by a single horizontal unit.

It took much hard work to produce the machine, which ran well and produced plenty of power. However, development was harder to carry out and each year saw the Japanese relentlessly move the goal posts further away.

EXCELSIOR 1896–1965
The firm of Bayliss, Thomas & Co. of Coventry was one of the earliest to produce penny-farthing bicycles and moved into the powered field in 1896. That year they demonstrated their motorcycle, fitted with a 1.25hp Minerva engine, in the Crystal Palace grounds during an exhibition. Some 250 people had a ride on the machine and none fell off!

In 1900 the firm adopted the MMC engine to propel a typical primitive machine with the engine hung from the downtube and with belt drive. Their rider, Harry Martin,

By 1912, Excelsior were producing both V-twins and singles, such as here, but still with belt final-drive and rim brakes.

began his track career by record breaking at Canning Town cycle track and won many events. During that part of the Edwardian era they built sound machines that gained a good reputation. By 1904 they offered 2.75, 3 and 3.25hp models and a forecar with some water cooling, the engines made by the firm under licence from De Dion. In time they settled for a 3.5hp model, typical of the time with belt drive and Druid forks, but left the motorcycle field around 1905 when trade was poor.

In April 1909 they returned to the market with a single model having a 3.5hp Excelsior engine with gear-driven Bosch magneto ahead of the crankcase. The machine had belt drive and Druid forks, while there were twin fuel-tanks that fitted to the frame to conceal the top tube as with the saddle type.

The 1920 Excelsior V-twin, which had all-chain drive, well protected thanks to front and rear cases.

Part of the extensive 1930 Excelsior list was this lightweight, with a 196cc Villiers engine and complete with legshields.

Two V-twins were added for 1911, one of 2.75hp and the other 5hp with overhead inlet valves, and both had a two-speed gear and Druid forks. The next year a 4.5hp single for sidecar work was added, but the twins were dropped, and 1913 brought an even larger 5–6hp single of 811cc for really heavy-duty work. Chain drive and gearboxes arrived for 1914 offering two or three speeds, while the older

Excelsior also produced a lightweight with 149cc four-stroke ohv engine for 1933.

transmission remained available. In 1915 the three singles were joined by a V-twin with an 8hp JAP engine and two small two-strokes of 210 and 349cc, the larger with two speeds and chain drive, and this range ran on for 1916.

After the war they moved to Tyseley, Birmingham, where they introduced a 1920 range of 269cc two-strokes, 348cc single, and 771 and 976cc V-twins. The singles had two speeds and chain-cum-belt drive, but it was three and all-chain for the twins. The 651cc single, the old 4.5hp model, returned in mid-1920. Around 1921 the firm began to trade as the Excelsior Motor Company and dropped the original Bayliss, Thomas & Co. after a couple of years.

An attempt by Excelsior to cover all needs in 1933 resulted in this model with its 249cc water-cooled Villiers engine, a neat machine.

For 1923 there were 147 and 247cc two-strokes in place of the 269cc models alongside the 348cc Blackburne and the twins. Two models with a 545cc Blackburne engine were added for 1924, one for sidecar work and the other a TT model, while 1925 saw 172cc Villiers, 249cc Blackburne and 349cc Bradshaw engines join the list, but the twins were dropped

The range was smaller in 1926, but included a 346cc ohv JAP model with a 490cc model added for the next year, when engines were Villiers or JAP. This continued for 1928 with just one two-stroke of 247cc, but others were added for 1929. That year saw the firm's efforts in the TT since 1923 rewarded when Syd Crabtree won the Lightweight race. With this encouragement they had an extensive list for 1930 ranging from a 147cc Villiers machine to a 490cc JAP. In 1931 there was more, including the Universal powered by a 98cc Villiers engine and priced at 14 guineas, the lowest of all. At the other end of the scale came a model with a 600cc sv JAP. More variations with Villiers or JAP engines came in 1932 and in 1933 there was a model with a 249cc water-cooled Villiers engine and another using a 149cc long-stroke ohv Excelsior engine.

The Excelsior Autobyke was introduced for 1938 and followed the general pattern for the type with the 98cc Villiers engine.

The firm was still supporting the TT and for the 1933 Lightweight used a special Blackburne engine, the machine known as the Mechanical Marvel. This was due to the four radial valves opened by twin high-

The Universal Excelsior model listed from 1937 used the 122cc Villiers engine unit, as did many others at that time, but did include legshields.

camshafts using pushrods and rockers, twin carburettors and dry-sump lubrication. The complication enabled Syd Gleave to win the race but the engine often lost its tune so had little other success, although the model was listed for 1934.

In its place came the 246 and 349cc Manxman for 1935, with a strong engine with ohc driven by shaft and bevels. It was listed in sports and racing forms along with a series of ohv models and the range of two-strokes, all with names as well as model codes. A 496cc Manxman was added for 1937, but a better indication of the firm's future was a new Universal

The basic Excelsior M1 of 1949 was a small machine, with a choice of 100 or 125cc engines to offer the simplest transport, right for the times.

Top of the 1935 Excelsior range was the famous Manxman, which was built in three capacities and proved successful on road and race-track.

with a 122cc Villiers engine. The next year brought the Autobyk, a 98cc autocycle, and this took the firm to the end of the decade.

During the war the firm built the Welbike, which became the post-war Corgi, but they themselves returned with just the Autobyk and the 122cc Universal whose main feature was that the gear lever worked in a slot in the petroil tank. They also offered a JAP Speedway model for several seasons. In 1947 two more autocycles were added using one- and two-speed 98cc Excelsior engines and 1949 brought the Goblin, a miniature motorcycle using the 98cc two-speed unit or a 123cc version. That year also saw the Universal with the Villiers 10D engine, plus the similar Roadmaster using the 197cc 6E engine.

The 1957 Excelsior Skutabyke was based on the Consort, but had the addition of large panels to keep the weather at bay.

A twin-cylinder, two-stroke 243cc engine joined the Excelsior range for 1950 as the Talisman Twin and had its own form of plunger rear-suspension.

A twin was added to the range for 1950, the Talisman Twin with a 243cc Excelsior two-stroke engine, in a plunger frame also used by the other models. A Sports version was added for 1952, while 1953 saw the Universal replaced by the Courier with a 147cc Excelsior engine. New was the Consort with a 99cc Villiers 4F engine in basic cycle parts, and 1954 saw the Roadmaster with an 8E engine and pivoted-fork rear suspension which also went on the twins.

This established the range for much of the decade with only minor changes and model variations. The autocycles went after 1956, while 1957 brought the Skutabyk, which was a Consort with side panels to fully enclose the engine unit. A 328cc Super Talisman was added for 1958 and the next year saw the firm with a scooter that had a 147cc Excelsior engine and body parts shared with DKR and called the Monarch.

The range continued into the new decade, but sales began to drop off.

Excelsior built this simple 125cc Condor model in 1954 for the ride to work, albeit without the benefit of rear suspension.

In 1959 Excelsior introduced this Monarch scooter with their own 147cc engine, but used the DKR frame and bodywork.

The scooter had new bodywork for 1961, a year when more variants were tried, but this had little effect so the 1962 range was reduced, but did include a model in kit form to exempt it from purchase tax. Sadly this failed to help, so the 1963 range was down to just two models with 98 and 148cc Villiers engines. Both had gone by 1965 to bring the marque to its end, and the name passed to the Britax organization.

EYME 1912

This was another make that made a brief appearance in the lists, ambition seeming to override practicality. A full range was promised, the singles including machines having 2.5, 3.5 and 4.25 Precision engines, plus a 3.5hp TDC or a 5hp Buck, all having direct-belt drive. In addition there were to be twins using either a 6hp Precision or 7hp Blumfield engines, again with belt drive. It was hardly surprising that nothing further was heard of this enterprise.

The Universal Excelsior could be bought in kit form for 1962, to avoid tax, and had a 148cc Villiers engine, but failed to save the firm.

◆ F ◆

FACELER 1903–1904
Faceler offered a 2hp engine designed to fit to a heavy roadster bicycle. This was done by cutting out part of the seat tube and replacing this with the engine. Chain drive was employed but few could have cared to have their bicycle frame cut up, so little more was heard of this effort.

This shows the odd engine location used on the Faceler, where it replaced the saddle tube of the bicycle frame; direct-chain drive was also unusual.

FAGAN 1935–1936
An obscure make, built in Dublin, Ireland, that was assembled from British parts to avoid tariff charges. They only had one model, powered by a 148cc Villiers engine housed in a loop frame made by Diamond and fitted with Webb forks. Typical of the type, it soon went.

FAIRFIELD 1914–1915
This make came from Alfred Forster of Warrington, who used a 269cc Villiers two-stroke engine to power his machine. Direct-belt drive or an Armstrong three-speed hub were offered and the machine had Druid forks. For 1915 only the direct belt and rigid forks were offered, but the make was soon a war casualty.

Assembled in Dublin to avoid tariff costs, the Fagan fitted the usual 148cc Villiers engine into a frame made by Diamond.

FAIRY 1906–1907
This was the Anglicized name of the Fée, the machine built by Joseph Barter of Bristol in 1905 following an earlier single carrying his own name. The 2.5hp flat-twin engine went high in a stock bicycle frame and transmission was by chain to a countershaft and clutch, and thence by belt to the rear wheel.

In 1907 the design was taken up by Douglas, whom Barter joined.

FARNELL 1900–1901
Built by Albert Farnell of Bradford, who had been a racing cyclist of the 1890s, this early primitive had a Minerva engine fitted to a bicycle frame. It was much as others of that time and only the one was made, it being too highly geared at first for the local hills until revised pulleys were fitted.

FB 1913–1922
Late in 1913, Fowler & Bingham of Coventry Road, Hay Mills, Birmingham introduced their 411cc two-stroke engine. The design included a one-piece crankshaft and thus a connecting rod with a split plain big-end, a deflector piston and one-piece cylinder and head. The lubrication system was stated to be pressure-fed, but on test petroil was used.

This new engine was not taken much further for, by 1914, the model was fitted with a 269cc Villiers engine, belt final-drive and Druid forks. In this form it was sold as the Wizard and both single- and two-speed versions were listed, but for that year only. The FB name did appear post-war, still on the small two-stroke, and was available up to around 1922.

The Fairy was really the English name for the Fée, with its flat-twin engine set high in the lengthy frame.

FB-AJS 1974–1981
One outcome of the turmoil of the British industry in the early 1970s was that 'Fluff' Brown was able to buy the remains of the AJS two-stroke exercise that had begun in 1967. From 1974, he was in business from premises near Andover, Hampshire and at first concentrated on spares and the machines that existed. The aim was to supply trail, motocross and enduro machines that were easy for the average clubman to ride, with a good spares backup they could afford. The results handled well and were tough enough to stand plenty of use and abuse.

Engine sizes were 247 and 368cc, based on a common stroke, driving a four-speed gearbox, and installed in a chassis having plenty of suspension travel.

This activity continued to 1981 with some of the last machines fitted with Rotax engines. The firm then concentrated on supplying spares but later returned to complete machines under both the AJS and Cotton names.

FEATHERSTONE 1903
Made by a firm in Bethnal Green, London, this was a typical primitive having a vertically mounted engine and curved frame downtube. Belt drive, rigid forks and pedals completed a machine that was typical of the era.

Featherstone offered a typical primitive for the 1903 season only, and had a link with the Thorough marque.

FEDERAL 1921–1929
This was the name used by the Co-operative Wholesale Society for the lightweight versions of its Federation brand. First seen in 1921 with a 269cc Villiers two-stroke engine, the Federal was a conventional machine for its day. Later, 172cc Villiers engines were adopted along with three-speed all-chain transmission and Sturmey-Archer gearboxes. After 1929 the name was dropped.

FEDERATION 1921–1937
Built at the C.W.S. cycle factory in Tyseley, Birmingham, the models offered were primarily concerned with providing reliable transport to and from work for those thousands of people who regularly shopped at the Co-op. Indeed, the machines could be ordered through any one of the numerous Societies throughout the United Kingdom. They began with a 292cc sv JAP single in 1921, driving a belt to the rear wheel through a two-speed Sturmey-Archer gearbox. Brampton Biflex forks were fitted, together with a choice of touring or TT type handlebars.

Aimed at Co-op customers, the Federation was sold between the wars and offered a good range to cover most needs, this one with 148cc Villiers engine.

There were few sporting pretensions but, nevertheless, Federations did distinguish themselves in competition, winning no less than fourteen class awards in their first season. A 677cc sv V-twin JAP model was added the next year and a motorized cycle was tried in 1923 with a 147cc Villiers engine. The same year saw a short-lived three-wheeler, but it was the motorcycles that continued on, with JAP engines, and later Burman gearboxes, always being favoured. Side valves were the staple diet until a 346cc ohv model arrived for 1929 along with saddle-tank styling.

A sv 500 was added for 1930, followed by one of 677cc and an ohv 500 in 1931. This alone of the four-strokes ran on for 1933, but was joined by a 245cc ohv model with the line completed by a couple of 150s with Villiers engines. This line took them through to 1937 when the Co-op dropped motorcycles.

The Fée was the flat-twin machine that later had its name changed to Fairy and, in time, led to the Douglas range.

FÉE 1905
Joseph Barter of Bristol began his motorcycle career with a single-cylinder machine offered under his own name, but in 1905 turned to a flat-twin engine. This was later known as the Fairy and was the forerunner of the Douglas.

The Fée engine gave 2.5hp and was mounted high in the frame of a stock bicycle with braced forks. A large flywheel went on the left, the transmission being by chain to a countershaft carrying a clutch, and thence by belt to the rear wheel. Within a year the name was anglicized to Fairy.

FELIX 1924
This machine was a special, based on a 350cc Raleigh, which was modified by Bill Bradley to have two-wheeled drive. It achieved this using a series of chains to take the power to the front wheel with suitable shafts and couplings to allow for the steering to take place. The rear-wheel drive was conventional and the concept of the added traction did give it an advantage when run in an early scramble.

There was talk, even at that time, of the concept being taken up by the army for further development but nothing came of this. However, the machine deserves its place in history as the idea was taken up in America in the 1960s by Rokon, who produced a machine with two-wheeled drive, the wheels being of massive section to give aid as floats. It could run most places and climb most places so, in its way, proved that Felix was a sound concept from Britain!

Back in the early days of films there was a cartoon character called 'Felix' – who kept on walking – hence the name for the machine.

FEW 1920 AND 1926–1928
F.E. Waller had already exploited a niche market by 1920 with his patent valve-spring attachments for most side-valve engines, which kept road dirt away from exposed stems and springs and thus increased their operational life. These enclosures were sold under his own initials as the FEW. It was only natural that he should use this established trading title for his ventures into motorcycle manufacture, which began with a 6hp sv V-twin JAP engine in a low and sporting frame equipped with Saxon spring forks. Drive from the engine was direct by belt to the wheel, but there was talk of a novel type of friction gear, details of which were not disclosed. A prototype was constructed and shown to the public and trade in September 1920 with a view to interesting a company to undertake its manufacture, but evidently none came forward and the idea lapsed.

Moving forward to 1926, Waller was back in the news with an unorthodox machine of the car-on-two-wheels kind. The rider sat low down in a bucket seat with the engine and transmission fully enclosed by sheet metal panelling. The motive power in the new FEW was provided by 600cc sv single or 976cc sv V-twin JAP engines driving through three-speed Sturmey-Archer or Burman gearboxes and all-chain transmission. There was a choice of models from the Popular (600cc) and Special (976cc) to the Paramount Duo (976cc), the latter being fitted out to accommodate two persons, both sitting within the wheelbase on bucket seats.

The multi-tube frame of the FEW lay at wheel-spindle height or below, until, from a point there, a triangulated maze of tubes rose upwards to a normal steering-head and link-action girder forks of conventional outline. The panels over this elevated forward structure were carefully arranged to act as legshields, whilst panelling over the rear wheel provided a clean area for the carrying of luggage. An instrument panel was formed behind the steering head and a small screen in Triplex glass gave further rider protection. Cast-alloy footboards kept more road dirt at bay and, of course, the engines were equipped with FEW valve attachments.

After presentation at the Olympia Show in late 1926, there was a period of inactivity as far as manufacture was concerned but, by the 1927 Show in October, news was confirmed that the models would be available in 1928 together with a slightly lighter variant in which a 499cc sv Blackburne engine would be used. Three models were subsequently displayed by Selfridges in their London store and the marque was listed in buyers' guides for 1928 but, afterwards, this enterprising machine was lost from sight.

FHW 1924
Based in Hitchin, Hertfordshire, F.H. Wells built just two machines using the 680cc JAP V-twin engine. One was a sports model and, sadly, a friend was killed while riding it so Wells built no more.

FIELD 1914
This was a steam-powered motorcycle that had a single-acting two-cylinder engine. While this type of engine removed the need for clutch or gearbox, its many ancillary fittings and the time taken to fire up the boiler and start away meant that it was always a minority choice. The time of the debut was no help to the Field either.

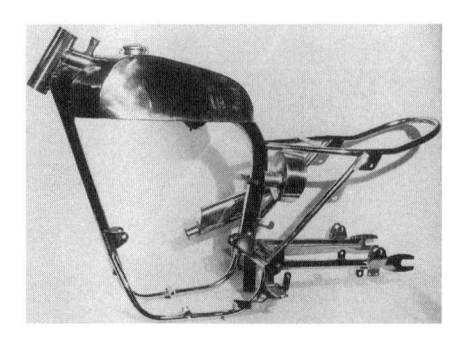

The Firefly was a frame kit for trials machines which was able to take a variety of engine units, but tax changes brought it to an end.

FIREFLY 1965–1970
This was a light and well-made trials frame-kit originally built to take the BSA C15 engine but later adapted for others. Made in Lowestoft, Suffolk, production was very limited, virtually made to order, for few knew of its existence or how good it was. Later, this improved to some extent, but the arrival of the Bultaco and the change in taxation that removed the advantage of supplying in kit form ended the enterprise.

Frank Leach produced this FLM lightweight, using the 125cc JAP engine in a channel-section frame, with the rear suspension under the engine in tension.

FIRTH c.1910
Arthur Firth of Cleckheaton, Yorkshire offered a series of engines ranging from 2hp with moiv up to 6hp V-twin. He also supplied many other components, which suggests that he could have built a few complete machines for favoured friends.

FLEET 1905
This was a name used by Components Ltd of Birmingham who manufactured bicycles in the main but did produce a few motorcycles in Edwardian times. Both names were later more involved with Ariel, and the Fleet models were essentially that marque using 2.75 and 3.5hp engines mounted vertically in the frame – badge engineering from an early time. One other model they offered used a 2hp engine hung from the frame downtube in the fashion then common.

FLEETWING 1906
A very short-lived make that was only listed in 1906 and fitted a 2.5hp NSU engine from Germany, this driving the rear wheel by belt. A spring frame was said to be used, but nothing more was to be heard of the machine.

FLM 1951–1953
Built by Frank Leach Manufacturing of Leeds, this was a lightweight powered by a 125cc JAP two-stroke engine. The frame was unusual in being built from channel-section steel, while the pivoted rear fork was suspended by springs fitted under the engine. It had telescopic forks and there was talk of other models, but nothing came of this and once supplies of the JAP engine dried up the FLM left the market.

FLY c.1903
The Fly used an engine supplied by the Carlton Motor Co. of London, who were specialists in component sales. It took the form of a very basic, typical primitive with the engine hung from the downtube of the bicycle frame, direct-belt drive and braced forks.

FORFIELD c.1920

This small firm was based in Leamington Spa and run by H.J. Stretton-Ward who had previously been involved with Triumph and Premier Cycles. He held several motorcycle agencies and manufactured the Forfield from offices and works at numbers 11 and 13 Forfield Place, so the machines must have been very basic and produced from bought-in parts. Quantities would have been small and he soon found it easier to sell others' products.

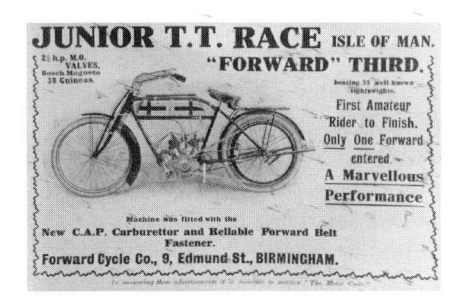

A 1911 Forward illustrated with V-twin engine and belt drive; the marque had some success in the early TT races, as advertised.

FORWARD 1911–1915

Based in Edmund Street, Birmingham, this was a bicycle firm who moved into motorcycles with a 2.75hp model powered by a V-twin engine of 345cc capacity. The specification was basic with belt drive and Druid forks, so typical of the era. However, they did have some success in the Junior TT with Harold Cox finishing third in 1911 when he was the first private owner home. He repeated his third place in 1912, when P.W. Owen rode a second Forward into fifth place, but their luck was out in 1913 when they were joined by George Hill but all three men retired.

In the standard range a ladies' model was offered for 1912 and a larger, 3.5hp V-twin added in 1914, this range continuing for the next year, after which they ceased production.

FRANCIS-BARNETT 1920–1966

Gordon Francis and Arthur Barnett formed this firm at Lower Ford Street, Coventry in 1919 and offered their first model in 1920. It had a 292cc JAP engine driving a two-speed gearbox by a chain within an aluminium case, belt final-drive, footboards with toe guards and sprung

This 1921 Francis-Barnett was an early model with JAP engine, two speeds, and chain-cum-belt drive, also listed with a Villiers engine.

In 1923, Francis-Barnett adopted a bolt-up tubular frame concept, which worked well, this one from 1928.

Enclosure arrived for Francis-Barnett in 1933, with this Cruiser model that cleaned up appearance no end.

Francis-Barnett normally used two-stroke engines, but this Stag of 1936 had a 247cc Blackburne four-stroke for its three years.

Francis-Barnett enclosure continued post-war, once the basic range was established, with this 1956 Plover showing the way.

forks. For the next year it was joined by another using the 269cc Villiers engine and 1922 brought a model with a 346cc JAP engine and all-chain drive.

In early 1923 the firm introduced their famous 'built-like-a-bridge' frame concept. Devised by Gordon Francis, it comprised seven pairs of tubes, all but one pair straight, that bolted up to form a triangulated frame that was cheap to make and easy to assemble. Into it went a 147cc Villiers engine and the result sold well at a rock-bottom price.

This one model plus the 346cc machine in Sports and Touring forms formed the 1924 range, but during the year the 147 was joined by a 172cc model with all-chain drive. The 346cc JAP engine came back for 1926 along with a 175cc JAP-powered model, its engine sold as the Aza. It was two-strokes only for 1927 in 147 and 172cc sizes, plus the Pullman model that had a 344cc vertical-twin engine made by Villiers for the firm. Unusually, the cylinders and crankshaft were set along the frame to drive a three-speed gearbox built in-unit, with a worm drive to a shaft carrying the final-drive sprocket. The straight-tube frame housed the engine unit but production was limited.

The range was the same for 1928, but for the next year the Pullman had gone; however, 196 and 247cc models were added, to be joined by one of

343cc for the new decade. Model names such as Merlin, Kestrel, Lapwing and Plover were used and in 1933 these, and others, were joined by the Cruiser. This was a major change, for it had a new frame using channel-section members and enclosure of the 249cc engine, gearbox and rear chain using panels that just left the cylinder in view.

For the rest of the decade the firm built a range of two-strokes using Villiers engines from 98 to 249cc. The smallest did not appear until 1938, but before then, in 1935, they did offer a four-stroke using a 247cc Blackburne engine that had crossed pushrods. It was listed for three years as the Stag. Frame design moved away from the 1924 bolted-tube construction in time, but remained a little different from the norm in using channel sections in various places.

Falcon was always the Francis-Barnett name for its 200cc models and this is the 1960 version with some enclosure to clean the line.

A new style arrived in 1962 for Francis-Barnett with this Fulmar model, while production was moved to the James factory.

This took the firm up to 1940 and post-war they began with just two models, the Powerbike, an autocycle with a 98cc engine, and the Merlin with a 122cc Villiers 9D engine unit. In 1947 they became part of the AMC group, but it was some time before this had any real effect.

The range expanded for 1949 with a revised Powerbike using the 99cc 2F engine, the Merlin with a 10D engine, and the Falcon fitted with a 197cc 6E unit. The motorcycles all went over to telescopic forks with pivoted-fork rear suspension appearing in 1952 along with competition models. For 1954 the Cruiser name was revived for a 224cc model which had a frame incorporating pressed members, as in the past, but without the enclosure. This range took them on for some years but in 1957 they, along with James, were forced by the group to fit the new 249cc AMC engine into the Cruiser.

The AMC design was never to be too successful, as it gave trouble and lacked the reliability of the Villiers. Despite this, a whole range appeared in due course, of 149, 171 and 199cc, to gradually replace the Villiers for all the Francis-Barnett models. Among these, there came a second Cruiser for 1959 that had the entire rear-end fully enclosed, even the pillion rests folding flush, and legshields as standard.

This AMC-powered range took the firm into the 1960s, but in 1962 they had to turn to Villiers for their Cruiser Twin, which used the 249cc 2T unit. A year later they changed back to 246cc Villiers singles for the competition models, a 32A for trials and a 36A for scrambles, the latter joined by and then replaced by the 247cc Starmaker in time.

In 1962 production was moved to the James factory at Greet. At the same time they added the Fulmar model, which had a new style thanks

The 1963 trials model 92 Francis-Barnett fitted with a 246cc Villiers 32A engine, with well tucked-in exhaust system.

The final Francis-Barnett road model was this Plover model 95 with 149cc AMC engine, spine frame and its own styling.

to a spine frame, leading-link forks and pressed-steel bodywork, but had to make do with the 149cc AMC engine. For 1964 the same engine went into a single-tube spine frame to produce a restyled Plover, but by 1966 this was replaced by a simple, basic model.

Sadly, this was the last year for Francis-Barnett who ended production in October 1966, brought down by the troubles of their parent group along with James. So ended a firm regarded as one that built a better machine than most in the lightweight class.

FRANK 1925

Rear suspension of any kind was uncommon on 1920s motorcycles, but to consider a system of interconnected front and rear spring was, well, futuristic. Messrs Kerslake's Ltd, of West Derby, Liverpool, projected just such a design in 1925, powered by a 349cc ohv Bradshaw oil-cooled single-cylinder engine. The suspension was achieved by a common pair of leaf springs suitably connected to the relevant parts of the machine. They decided upon the marque name of the Frank for their prototype and announced that production would begin shortly after it had been revealed to the press in March of that year. Afterwards, all was silent.

FRAYS 1910–1911

This make was listed as offering two models late in 1910. They were typical of the era, using a 2.5 or 3.5hp single-cylinder JAP engine fitted with an Amac carburettor, and having direct-belt drive, Bates tyres and sprung forks. However, the make went as quickly as it came.

FROST 1920S

This name was applied to an unusual engine built by Romney Frost of Wolverhampton. It was a flat-twin tandem, so had the normal opposed cylinders plus a further cylinder added to the end of each. This complex unit was to be offered to other firms, but only one was made and fitted into a machine. On test, Frost fell off and broke a leg, after which no more was heard of the design, possible due to its high projected cost.

FRUIN 1957–1963

Bert Fruin was a keen supporter of the 125cc road-racing class in the 1950s and for this he built a single-cylinder ohc engine. Later, he built a 125cc twin and was a regular rider in UK events and in four TT races.

In the late-1950s, Bert became interested in the new 50cc racing class, and from this went into limited production of machines for this class and a similar one for sports road use. Both used Demm engines from Italy and used tubular frames with conventional suspension. Sold as the Dart, they were well built and Bert rode one in the early 50cc TT races. There was also a proposed 200cc engine to be sold in kit form and this comprised four Demm engines built up in-line, but this came to nothing so Bert went back to the daytime job.

FULLER 1904

Exhibited in 1904, the Fuller machine was fitted with their own 2.75hp engine, whose exhaust noise was kept down by a six-chamber silencer. The firm's main business was in the supply of ignition and other electrical equipment and nothing else was heard about their motorcycle. No doubt they found that supplying components was better business for them.

◆ G ◆

GAB 1919
This was a crude attempt to join the post-Great War scooter boom, with a pressed-steel platform frame for the rider to stand on. A New Hudson engine drove the rear wheel via a countershaft, with a small fuel tank between it and the headstock. The forks had small leading-links, a long extension carried the bars and disc wheels were used.

GABY 1914–1920
It was not until late in 1914, well after the outbreak of the Great War, that this make was listed as producing a single model. Their address was the County Buildings in Corporation Street, Birmingham, but assembly would have taken place elsewhere. The machine was powered by a 269cc Metro two-stroke engine that drove a Roc two-speed gear by chain and the rear wheel by belt. It was basic in construction and perhaps the builders really believed that the war would be over by Christmas.

As early as 1903, Gamage stocked and sold a wide range of motorcycle equipment, as well as machines carrying their name, although made by another firm.

After the war, in 1920, the Gaby was listed with a 269cc Arden engine, two-speed Albion gearbox and chain-cum-belt drive from John Burns & Co. in Holloway Road, London, but no more was heard of them.

GADABOUT 1947–1951
This was the name used by the Swallow sidecar firm for its simple scooter introduced in the early post-war years. At first fitted with the pre-war 122cc Villiers 9D engine and later the 10D, it lacked the style of the Italian makes but provided basic transport. Its last year brought a version with the 197cc 6E engine which was listed as the Major.

GAINSBOROUGH 1903–1906
Production was by C.E. Hammond of Ipswich, Suffolk, who had similarly built pedal cycles from the turn of the century. They were typical primitives of their day, with proprietary engines in strengthened bicycle frames.

GAMAGE 1903–1923
The famous store, based in Holborn, London, sold machines built by various factories but by 1903 had a model with their own name on it. The machine had a 2hp engine mounted vertically well back, so the bicycle pedals went ahead of the crankcase, and the seat tube bolted to the top of the crankcase. Belt drive and rigid forks were used and the result had several competition successes that year.

For 1904 the engine was moved forward and went into a loop frame fitted with braced forks, and a forecar powered by a 3.5hp Hubbard engine was added. The firm then took to selling the German Dürkopp machines for some time, along with the 2.5hp Arno with their own transfer, but by 1911 had their name on a model with a White & Poppe engine, three-speed rear hub and Druid forks. By 1913

By 1913 Gamage listed just one model, still with direct-belt drive and well supported by accessory sales.

they listed just one 2.75hp model with single-speed or three-speed hub, belt drive and Druid forks, that was sold from stock for the next two years.

Post-war, there were only two-strokes, with a 269cc model fitted with a Burman two-speed gearbox and chain-cum-belt transmission for 1919. This had to be push started but in 1921 was joined by a kickstart version and a single-speed belt-drive model. For 1922 these three were enlarged to 348cc and joined by a four-stroke of the same capacity, while for 1923 the kickstart machine was given three speeds and all-chain drive. However, this was their last year, for the firm then concentrated on its many other lines.

GANAREW 1903
With premises in Monmouth, the Ganarew Cycle Company of Priory Street were offering a motorcycle with a two-speed gear and, possibly, a Clement-Garrard engine, assembled into strengthened cycle parts principally to meet local demand. They claimed to have supplied a machine to no less a personality than Lord Llangattock, the father of the Hon. C.S. Rolls of Rolls-Royce fame.

GARRARD 1904
After his association with the Clement machines, Charles Garrard went on to show a forecar tandem early in 1904 at his Birmingham

The 1904 Garrard forecar tandem performed but showed the trend from motorcycles to more wheels and weight.

works. It had a water-cooled 4hp engine driving back to a clutch, three-speed gearbox and thence by shaft to the single rear-wheel. Leaf-spring front and pivoted-fork rear suspension was used, along with a saddle for the rider aft of the passenger seat. It was a practical design that proved itself at a hill climb later in the year, but was more car than motorcycle and was not taken further.

GAUNT 1969–1970

Peter Gaunt had been the force behind the Alta, but when Suzuki would not supply him with engine units for replicas he switched to an 89cc Jawa two-stroke engine with five-speed gearbox. This was hung from a spine frame, with downtubes to protect the engine, and the whole machine was light and easy to handle. It was only built for two years.

GB 1905–1908

The GB Motor Co. was run by F. Claassen & Co., based in Sydenham, London, and made its debut at the late-1905 Stanley Show. They listed a 3hp single plus 3.5 and 5.5hp V-twins, all fitted with a gear-driven magneto. Both spring forks and a free-engine clutch were options, along with a sidecar with coach or wicker body. A tricycle with passenger seat installed behind the rider's saddle and carried between the twin rear wheels was also listed.

All the models were low in build with a lengthy 58in wheelbase, so were advanced in this respect from most of their contemporaries. They continued to 1908 when they used either a 4.5hp Minerva single engine or a 5.5hp Zedel V-twin, but then left the market.

GENN 1904

W.W. Genn of Wimbledon, London built a light machine powered by a Clément-Garrard engine fitted into a frame built up from Chater-Lea parts. The engine hung vertically under the downtube, braced forks were fitted and the machine weighed 76lb (34.5kg).

GEORGE ELIOT c.1904

The pseudonym of author Mary Ann Evans was used by John Birch for machines built to his design with the crankcase cast around the frame tubes. In other respects it was a typical primitive, while the cast design was also licensed to Bradbury.

The GB was offered with single- or twin-cylinder engine for 1906, mounted in a lengthy frame.

GERRARD 1914–1915

This was another short-lived make that fell as a wartime casualty. Built in Hagley Road, Birmingham, it used a 269cc Villiers two-stroke engine that drove a two-speed gearbox. Transmission was by chain or chain and belt, while Druid forks were fitted.

GIBSON 1898

An advanced design for its year, this machine, constructed by George Gibson of Birkenhead, had a 1.75hp engine built into the frame. The crankcase formed the bottom bracket, the seat tube attached to it and the downtube bolted on the top of the inclined engine. The pedals fitted to the ends of the crankshaft, which drove the rear wheel directly by chain. Only the one machine seems to have been built.

Peter Gaunt with one of his trials machines fitted with the Jawa engine unit, to produce a most workmanlike model.

Triangulation is always a good way of designing strength into any structure and the Gibson of 1898 demonstrated this well.

GIVAUDAN 1908–1914

Givaudan was one of the many assembly firms of the early days who combined engines from sources such as Blumfield, Precision or Villiers with frames built up using BSA or Chater-Lea lugs. With the addition of a gear set and various fittings plus a transfer, yet another make was born. Givaudan kept going longer than many as, being an assembler, they could avoid over stocking or over production while keeping up with developments and trends.

GLANFIELD RUDGE 1928

A machine that was built for the then new sport of speedway or dirt-track racing by Stanley Glanfield. He used a 499cc Rudge engine fitted into a duplex frame with strutted tubes, while the front forks and wheels were Rudge. This venture was short lived as Rudge themselves introduced their own speedway model later that year, it being very successful for several seasons.

GLENCAIRN 1902

Very few examples of this make ever saw the light of day, as production was minimal. The machine was assembled from bought-in parts and no doubt based on a standard heavy-duty gents' bicycle with an engine of the most basic form and either imported or bought from a Midlands firm. It was said to be built for export, but whether this was into Europe or elsewhere is not clear.

GLENDALE 1921–1922

The Glendale Works of Messrs Luke Atkinson & Son, in Wooler, Northumberland bestowed their name upon this minor marque, which assembled models from bought-in components. The 545cc sv Blackburne engine was used, together with a three-speed Sturmey-Archer gearbox and belt final-drive. Brampton Biflex forks and 6in-wide mudguards with 3in valances attended to the comfort and protection of the rider. The wild spaces of northern England were largely unpopulated, so a petrol tank capacity of 1.75 gallons (6.6ltr) must have been barely sufficient, yet the maker's provided a larger than usual oil tank – holding 6 pints (2.8ltr) – so, they said, that lubricant of a preferred brand might by bought in quantity.

The Globe company built forecars and trailers for a short while, but their weight and awkward nature told against the type.

GLOBE 1901–1905

A typical primitive, also offered with the Trimo forecar or a trailer for 1904, despite such fittings nearing the end of their time. The forecar had a 3.5hp engine with a water-cooled cylinder head inclined and hung from the downtube, the water circulated by a chain-driven pump. A clutch was fitted to the crankshaft and the drive to the rear wheel was by belt.

Globe did venture into the solo motorcycle field with this 1904 machine, but it had no more success than the ones with three wheels.

GLORIA c.1924–1925

Emile Train was a French constructor for many years and as well as building machines he also sold his engines, from 100 to 1,000cc, to other firms. Gloria was one such who used the Train 175cc two-stroke for their short-lived lightweight, which made a change from the usual Villiers.

This 1932 Triumph with its 98cc Villiers engine was sold at a rock-bottom price, so it was given the Gloria name, which was also used for a nice car.

GLORIA 1932–1933

This was actually a Triumph model built for the absolute bottom of their range at a cut price. The name had been used on their bicycles, their sidecars, and even for one of their nice cars, but the motorcycle was very basic with a 98cc Villiers engine, two-speed Albion gearbox, open diamond frame and girder forks. For 1933 they added a model with a 147cc Villiers engine, but that was the last Gloria year, as Triumph then sold their own brand of lightweights for that section of the market, but soon left it altogether.

For 1933 the Gloria range was increased with the addition of this model with 147cc Villiers engine, soon replaced by proper Triumphs.

GMCC 1902–1903

Introduced by the General Motor Manufacturing Company late in 1902, this machine had chain drive, a clutch for starting and magneto ignition. The engine was mounted vertically ahead of the pedals in a typical primitive frame with rigid forks and a contracting-band front brake. The left pedal was used for starting the engine, after which the clutch was engaged to drive away.

GODDEN 1962–DATE
Don Godden was one of the most successful in grass-track racing, so it was no surprise that he should produce frame kits and then complete machines. Later still, came his own engines.

GODIVA c.1900
Payne & Bates of Coventry built cars of various types early on under their own name and also as the Stonebow. They also produced a few motorcycles using an aiv engine in typical primitive cycle parts during the same period. With four wheels or two, they were soon gone.

GOODWIN 1901–1902
An early primitive based on a heavy-duty bicycle fitted with a small Minerva engine hung from the downtube to drive the rear wheel by belt. Built by Goodwin Brothers Engineers of London, they produced enough for their engines to have their name cast on the crankcase, but any small order would give this. They were soon gone from the market.

GORDON-SIMPLEX 1920–1921
The 689cc sv flat-twin Coventry-Victor engine fitted in-line with the frame was the standard motive power in the design offered by the Gordon-Simplex Engineering Company of Aylesbury in Buckinghamshire and Bournemouth in Hampshire. A Lamplugh mechanical pump was attached to the engine to provide lubrication for it, the gearbox and the entire transmission, all components being enclosed. The engine itself went under a steel bonnet, there were deep section mudguards and the wire-spoke wheels were covered by fashionable spun-alloy discs. It was a machine of ultra-clean outline, but only an artist's illustration appeared in the press. It is therefore doubtful whether production models ever left the works.

GOUGH 1920–1921
Arthur Gough had been a motorcycle journalist before going into production with his own design of lightweight motorcycle from premises in Broad Street, Birmingham. He chose the 269cc Villiers two-stroke engine and Brampton Biflex forks as being good and reliable components, adding a frame and ancillary items all of proven form. A single-speed model was the lowest priced, with a two-speed Burman gearbox available for those with a little more to spend, belt drive to the rear wheel being standard in both instances.

Sturmey-Archer gearboxes were favoured for 1921, when a pair of four-stroke models made their appearance. One of these had the 292cc sv JAP engine, the other taking the 499cc sv Blackburne. There were three speeds for the bigger model only and the smaller had a single-speed option, which of course was also continued on the two-strokes, as was belt final-drive for all. As public demand waned, the marque was gone by that year end.

GOVERNER-VILLIERS 1914
Little is known of these lightweights with 269cc two-stroke Villiers and direct-belt drive, built by one of the larger Birmingham firms – possibly R. Walker & Sons or W.A. Lloyds – especially for the New Zealand market.

GOVERNMENT 1914
It is not clear whether this marque name was chosen to benefit from the patriotic furore of the year or because the firm had won orders to supply machines to the forces. Either way, they had a 292cc sv JAP engine, a variable-ratio belt pulley on the crankshaft and thus direct-belt drive. Basic cycle parts would have completed a very simple motorcycle.

GRADIOR 1912
First listed for 1912, this machine was built by Gradior Machine of Stafford and used a 3.5hp JAP single-cylinder engine. This drove a two-speed countershaft gearbox, the transmission being all by chain and the machine fitted with leading-link forks. The firm also offered a larger engine for sidecar work, but the make soon vanished.

GRAHAM 1903–1904
This firm was based in Enfield and showed their flexible sidecar attachment at the late-1903 Stanley Show. One was fitted to a Humber, the other to their own machine, which was powered by a De Dion engine.

GRANDEX 1910–1916
This firm was based in Gray's Inn Road, London and, in 1910, offered a neat model with 2.5hp JAP engine, belt drive and Druid forks. This was soon joined by other models using JAP and Precision engines, but by 1913 only the latter were fitted, along with a Green water-cooled engine for a short time. This continued up to 1915, when they added a 225cc Peco two-stroke model with two speeds. During these years they were listed as Grandex-Precision and ran on for 1916 in this form.

This was one of the 1914 range of Grandex models, which offered a wide choice of specifications including two speeds.

May 1914 was hardly the time to enter the market but Graves, and others, did, this being the smart result.

GRAPHIC 1903–1906

Graphic was a small firm who built typical primitives with a De Dion, Minerva or MMC engine fitted into a heavy-duty bicycle frame with belt-drive transmission. No doubt a cycle dealer who felt the effects of the 1905 downturn and wisely left the market once he had cleared his stock.

GRAVES 1914–1915

Another firm that sought to sell at the wrong time, they were a Sheffield store who had their machine built for them. It was listed as the 'Speed King' and powered by a 2.5hp JAP engine that drove a two-speed gearbox by chain, final drive being by belt. Druid forks were fitted, but it was soon gone from the market.

GREAT 1995–1998

This firm was based in Cullompton, Devon, where they built small motorcycles called the Bushboy for children, using parts from home and abroad. The engine unit was a Morini with an automatic gearbox, and the front forks Paioli, but the frame was made in Britain along with other components. Three seat-heights were offered and, while most machines were built in an off-road form with tyres to suit, a road style was also available. Wire wheels were usual, but a smaller cast-alloy type was fitted in some cases.

GREEN 1903

Patented by F.H. Green of Cheltenham, this machine differed from most primitives by carrying its fuel within the frame tubes, which were larger than usual. The rear mudguard was hollow and carried the engine oil, while the motor itself, a Minerva, was hung from the downtube. The idea of using the frame tubes as tanks was also used by the American Pierce make.

With the petrol carried in the frame tubes and lubricating oil in an enlarged rear mudguard, the Green was certainly different.

GREEN 1909 AND 1921

Gustavus Green of Berners Street, London was a strong advocate for water-cooled engines and built these as early as 1905, with them in use by Rex the next year. For 1909 only, he offered complete machines fitted with his special cylinder that had ohv and a copper radiator on each side, which made the system very direct in action. The complete machine had a frame in which the tank formed the top member, being divided into two so the front section carried excess water. For the rest it was belt drive and Druid forks.

By 1912 Gustavus and his son Charles were associated with the Regal-Green make who fitted their water-cooled engine up to the war, keeping the ohv and 499cc capacity. However, Gustavus became involved in engine design for aircraft and motor gunboats during the Great War and afterwards retired to concentrate on advanced ideas in horology and photography.

The Green motorcycle made one more appearance for 1921 as a 3.5hp water-cooled machine in its pre-war form, but this was no doubt a stock-clearing exercise.

GREEVES 1954–1978 AND 1999–DATE

Bert Greeves came into the motorcycle business after building up Invacar after the war to meet the need for an invalid carriage. This work gave him the suspension units with rubber bushes in torsion for the motorcycles and these were tried out in scrambles as well as on the road.

Built for young riders by Great motorcycles and named Bushboy, these machines came in off-road form with adjustments to suit various ages.

This early Greeves model has a 8E Villiers engine and unusual suspension, front and rear, with inbuilt dampers.

Their first machines appeared for 1954 and all four used the 197cc Villiers 8E engine, common to many makes, but what made the Greeves unique was both the frame and suspension. The frame was tubular with a cast-alloy beam in place of a downtube moulded around the tubing, while the suspension was controlled by rubber bushes in torsion with inbuilt dampers, the front being leading-link. The four models comprised two road machines, one with three speeds and the other with four, and a trials and a scrambles model. These were joined by the roadster Fleetwing during the year and this was powered by the 242cc British Anzani twin two-stroke engine.

In 1956 models using a conventional tubular frame appeared, along with a twin using the 322cc British Anzani. At the same time the original rear suspension system was replaced by conventional rear units and the 9E engine took over from the 8E. In 1957, hydraulic dampers went into the front forks and the twins began to change to the 249cc Villiers 2T twin engine.

This early Greeves scrambles model of 1956 shows the cast-alloy frame member that was so much a trade-mark of the firm for so long.

The 1958 competition models moved further away from the road ones and took the names of Scottish for the trials and Hawkstone for the scrambler, in recognition of the places they had performed at. By then Brian Stonebridge had sorted out the Greeves suspension and was joined by Dave Bickers to compete in the European 250cc series. Sadly, Stonebridge died in a car crash in 1959 when well placed to take the European title, but Bickers took the task over and went on to win the 1960 and 1961 titles. At the same time the Greeves became the favourite trials model for the clubman and the make sold well.

In 1959 the 197cc machines were joined by 246cc versions for road or competition use with the A-series Villiers engine. This continued for 1960, when a road twin with the 324cc Villiers 3T engine was added and this range would run on for much of the decade. However, as early as 1961, the 246cc scrambler had the option of a Greeves top-half for its Villiers engine and this practice would continue.

On a couple of years to 1958 and the Greeves trials model had changes to the run of the exhaust system, but retained much that was familiar.

For 1963 they branched out into road racing, a new area for them, following the success of a modified scrambler. Known as the Silverstone, the 246cc racer was built up to 1968 for club racing, where it performed well. At first it had a Villiers engine with Greeves alloy top-half, but for 1964 they fitted the Challenger engine and sat this on a Greeves crankcase containing an Alpha crankshaft. Just as quickly, this engine went into the scrambler.

The trials machine became the Anglian for 1966 with revised forks and late that year the road models were all dropped. Telescopic forks became an option for the next year when a 362cc scrambler with Greeves engine appeared, while 1968 brought the 344cc Oulton road racer.

By then Villiers were in trouble, but Greeves were able to continue with

Greeves concentrated on competition models but did include road ones, such as this from 1957, with the early front-suspension system.

just the 246 and a 380cc scrambler sold as the Griffon and in a new, tubular frame. A trials model with a 169cc Puch engine was introduced in 1970 but had little success, while a link with Queen's University, Belfast brought the 380QUB. However, motorcycle production effectively stopped in 1972, although the company trickled on to 1978.

In 1999 the Greeves name returned to the market with an Anglian replica trials model, the 24TJSB, with traditional Villiers bottom half and Challenger head and barrel for the 246cc engine. The frame continued with the cast-alloy front beam, twin rear-shocks, MP telescopic forks and conical hubs, all updated using modern materials and techniques. Built in Essex close to their original home, the machines were aimed to sell for classic trials use and to enthusiasts of the marque.

GREYHOUND 1904–1906
Based in Ashford, Middlesex, this firm offered a forecar in 1904, listing it as the Greyhound. It was powered by a 3hp Fafnir engine and fitted with a two-speed gear, chain drive and Bowden brakes to offer a modest performance at a modest price. A second model was fitted with a 3.5hp Antoine engine, this having a separate three-speed gearbox.

In 1963 Greeves went road racing and this was the result; the 24RAS Silverstone model with 246cc engine developed from the scrambler.

Their motorcycles used the same engines or a 2.75hp Bowden and the make was listed up to 1906.

GRI 1920–1922
Distributed by Macrae & Dick of Inverness, the focal point of this make was the engine designed by G.R. Inshaw, who first promoted the machine himself in April 1920. Produced in 350 and 500cc sizes, this had one overhead valve opened by a

Late days for Greeves involved a link with Queen's University in Belfast with this result, and changes to engine, frame and suspension.

chain-driven ohc and rocker, plus a rotary valve.

The engine went into a conventional frame with Brampton forks to drive a two-speed Sturmey-Archer gearbox with belt final-drive. As was common with rotary valves, it was not totally satisfactory, was viewed with suspicion by the public and this ensured an early demise for the make.

GRIGG 1920–1925
This firm, based in Twickenham, Middlesex, entered the market with a basic scooter that had its 145cc two-stroke engine mounted to the right of the rear wheel. Ignition was by magneto, lubrication by petroil and the fuel tank sat over the engine with a

Trials Greeves type 24TGS, showing the banana forks and box-section rear fork among the features brought in to improve the model.

seat on it. Transmission was by chain-cum-belt with a single speed and no clutch. The tubular open frame had bicycle forks, wire wheels and a calliper front brake, but no weather protection.

For 1921 the engine, enlarged to 162cc, was used with a two-speed gearbox for a light motorcycle with a duplex tubular frame, not unlike the triangulated Cotton design. This led to a three-speed version in 1922, a good move as the scooter boom died, and a larger range for the next year. Models with 247 and 343cc Villiers, 195cc ohv Shaw, and Blackburne four-strokes in various capacities including a 696cc V-twin then became available.

During 1923 the company began offering machines with B&H engines (Bacher & Hellow patents), which comprised a suite of single and V-twin sv designs from 249 to 998cc, all with detachable heads and some with water cooling. These, however, made little impact on the established trade in proprietary engines and, although they were continued for 1924, the company's ultimate demise was by then becoming evident.

A move had been made to premises in South Croydon, Surrey at the end of 1923 and an arrangement to build Wooler motorcycles was entered into for a short while, plus general machining facilities were offered in an attempt to keep going. By 1925, however, they had succumbed, leaving few survivors today to mark their endeavours.

GRINDLAY-PEERLESS 1923–1934

Located in Shakleton Road, Coventry, this firm was at first known for its excellent sidecars prior to entering the motorcycle lists in 1923. With their background, it was hardly surprising that they scorned the usual lightweights that most started with, instead offering a model powered by the massive 999cc sleeve-valve Barr & Stroud V-twin engine. This drove a three-speed Sturmey-Archer gearbox with chain final-drive and was well

Although Grindlay-Peerless began with a big V-twin, they soon added others, with this lightweight for 1928 with 172cc Villiers engine.

finished, so a fine sight, especially when coupled to one of their own sports sidecars.

The V-twin was joined by a single with a 488cc ohv JAP engine for 1924, but the next year saw this replaced by a 499cc sleeve-valve Barr & Stroud. These two were joined by three smaller singles, one with a 348cc sleeve-valve engine and the other two with 344 and 346cc ohv JAP engines. The 488cc JAP returned for 1926 and it was that year when the marque began to become noticed at Brooklands.

This was thanks to Bill Lacey, who became famous for his tuning and riding abilities, and also for the immaculate, clean appearance of all his machines. He began to win using a 344cc JAP-powered Grindlay-Peerless in 1926 and two years later set the 500cc one-hour record at 103.3 miles (165.25km), increasing this to 105.25 miles (168.4km) in 1929.

The sleeve-valve models were dropped for 1927 to leave the 344, 346 and 488cc JAP engines. The larger was revised to 490cc for the next year when the range was extended to add models with 677cc sv JAP V-twin and 172cc Villiers two-stroke engines. All went forward for 1929 with a 490cc ohv single, and 674cc ohv and 750cc sv JAP V-twins

This 1930 Grindlay-Peerless was fitted with a 680 or 750cc JAP V-twin engine to offer style and performance.

for the close of the decade and 1930. The new decade added 196 and 247cc Villiers two-strokes, a 245cc ohv JAP, and more versions of the 490cc ohv JAP.

For 1931, the firm dropped the Villiers and JAP V-twin engines, kept some JAP singles for that year alone, and turned to the Rudge Python engine. They used this in 348 and 499cc sizes, including the Ulster, but cut the range to three models for 1932, all with Python engines. Smallest was the 248cc ohv Tiger Cub and the others the 499cc ohv Tiger and Tiger Chief. More variants were added for the next year, but the good days were over and after 1934 the firm turned to other products.

By 1933 only Rudge Python engines were used by Grindlay-Peerless, this model the Speed Chief, with the 499cc Ulster the largest.

GRINDLEY 1922–1939

Bill Grindley was a sporting motorcyclist who built a number of specials over a long period of time, all of them to his own taste and on which he was very successful in local competitions. A 249cc sv JAP-engined sports model with two-speed Burman gearbox and all-chain drive provided him with a promising beginning in the 1922 Six Days Trial and afterwards replicas were listed at £75 each. From then through to the Second World War he and his machines were well known amongst serious enthusiasts; the few that were built for sale came from the Grindley Motor Company of Prees in Shropshire.

GROSE-SPUR 1916

During the Great War, motorcycles for private use were still sold to the public well into 1916 with most of simple construction to minimize material use and machine cost. They were then sold by firms such as dealer

James Grose of London who bought them in from one of several manufacturers and applied their own label to them. In this case the machine had a 318cc two-stroke Dalm engine and belt final-drive.

GROSESPUR 1938–1940

Built by the Carlton firm for George Grose, a large dealer in Ludgate Circus, London, this machine used a 122cc Villiers engine with three-speed gearbox. It was typical of the type with petroil lubrication, direct lighting, simple frame and blade girder forks. Built for three years, it was not revived post-war.

Built by Carlton, using the 122cc Villiers engine, and sold by George Grose, a large London dealer, the GroseSpur filled a gap in the market.

GSC 1920

This was built in April 1920 by J.W. Clarke of Kenilworth, Warwickshire, to the design of Capt Smith-Clarke and very much along the lines of the latter's earlier Kenilworth machine. The GSC had an ohv four-stroke John engine driving by Whittle belt to a countershaft and then chain to the rear. Spoked wheels of 18in diameter maintained the scooter style of the Kenilworth and by June it was announced that preparations were rapidly being completed for production in small numbers, but in fact nothing further was heard of the project

GSD 1922–1923

This make was first seen at the 1922 Olympia show where it created much interest. It was designed by R.E.D. Grant, who had set up in Coventry, and the initials stood for Grant Shaft Drive, this being just one of its features. In addition to the shaft to the underslung worm at the rear wheel, it took the drive from a four-speed car-type gearbox built in-unit with the 350cc two-stroke engine built by White & Poppe and set across the frame. The clutch between engine and gearbox had the choice of hand or foot control and the assembly went into a duplex frame with Brampton Biflex forks and footboards for the rider.

A further odd feature was the location of the magneto behind the gearbox and alongside the output shaft. In this position it must have been driven by a long quill shaft that ran straight through the clutch and gearbox mainshaft. Comfort and weather protection were advertised features and a cowling to enclose the engine was said to be available.

A 976cc sv JAP V-twin engine was proposed as an alternative for the machine, as was a 494cc flat-twin Bradshaw, and the latter was built as a machine in 1923. However, little more was heard of these ideas for it was an unusual and expensive design, so there were few prospective buyers from the conservative motorcycle public and the make soon dropped from sight.

G&W 1902–1905

An assembler in South John Street, Liverpool, Guy & Wheeler used a variety of engines and in 1903 offered machines fitted with a Johnson two-speed hub gear. The engine was set well back and the basic bicycle frame extended to provide a 62in wheelbase, the saddle fitting back over the rear wheel.

G&W set the engine well back in the extended wheelbase frame of this 1903 model; the saddle also moved aft.

GYROSCOPIC 1912

No doubt a one-off, this machine had a rotary engine, a form then common in aviation. The motorcycle also had shaft drive but the cycle parts were more basic, being a heavy-duty bicycle frame and forks simply pressed into service to carry the mechanics.

The GYS was a typical post-Second World War cycle attachment engine, also known under two other names for its brief life.

GYS 1949–1955

An all-alloy cyclemotor attachment that fitted above the front wheel, which it drove by friction roller. The 50cc unit was made in Bournemouth and had an upright cylinder that was cast in one with the crankcase. The silencer bolted directly to the cylinder and both it and the petrol tank were aluminium castings. The whole unit was carried in a frame that could be raised or lowered for contact with the tyre.

Distribution was by the Cairns Cycle firm and in 1951 a kit was offered by Cobli of London to mount the engine under the saddle for it to drive the rear wheel. In the same year the GYS name was changed to Motomite, but then altered again to Mocyc for 1952, retaining this up to 1955.

H

HACK 1921–1923
Located in Hendon, North London, this firm offered a simple scooter during the early-1920s boom. It had an open, tubular frame with unsprung forks, 20in wheels and an alloy platform for the feet. The 104cc Simplex two-stroke engine sat low down on the right of the rear wheel, had a clutch, and drove the wheel by chain. With the engine mounted low and tucked away with the petroil tank over the rear wheel, it made an improvement on many of its contemporaries.

HADEN 1920–1923
Constructed on conventional lines around the 349cc Precision two-stroke engine, this marque was the product of A.H. Haden, Princip Street, Birmingham, who also produced the New Comet machines. Either two-speed chain-cum-belt or single-speed direct-belt transmission was available initially, the engine breathing through any carburettor that the purchaser cared to specify. By 1922, however, the single-speed option had been dropped, the carb had become an Amac without choice and the previously unspecified gearbox was now proclaimed as an Albion. It is unlikely that Hadens were built in any sizeable quantities.

HAGG TANDEM 1920–1922
Introduced in April 1920 and seen at the 1921 Olympia show, Arthur Hagg's Tandem offered more than usual for two people and everyday travel thanks to its enclosure. This extended from the downtube to include the rear mudguard and from footboards up to the fuel tank with legshields at the front.

Beneath this went a 349cc Precision two-stroke engine driving a two-speed Burman gearbox by chain with belt final-drive. Starting was by a long hand-lever, in the manner of the LE Velocette to come some thirty years later, and seating was a Lycett pan-saddle for the rider and a bucket seat for the passenger. Comfort was enhanced by Brampton Biflex front-forks and rear suspension using a laminated leaf-spring. An option was a 250cc Union two-stroke engine and the whole machine a real advance.

The Hagg was built in Park Street village near St Albans, Hertfordshire, but Arthur soon found that innovation seldom resulted in sales. For 1922 he tried fitting the 349cc Barr & Stroud sleeve-valve engine, giving more power and less noise, but this failed to improve matters, so for 1923 he added a conventional machine using the same engine and sold both machines as the HT. This change was really too late and production ceased after 1924.

HAGON 1956–c.1990
Alf Hagon was one of the best known riders in grass-track racing, dominating the sport for many years. He produced frame kits and complete machines for others using 350 and 500cc JAP engines, always well built and one of the best tools for the job. While anyone could buy the machine, they could not purchase his skill, so he kept on winning. He also built some speedway machines in a similar format

Later, Alf was offered a ride on a sprint machine, recorded a fast time and soon had his own, which reflected his astute ideas. He was just as successful in that branch of the sport. After retiring from active competition he built up a business specializing in wheels and shock absorbers for classic and modern machines.

HAL 1911
Offered by Holborn Autochange of London, a large motorcycle dealer of the time, this model had a 3.5hp engine, belt drive and Druid forks. Thus it was much as many others and essentially a new machine created by a transfer on the tank. It left the market as quickly as it came.

HALESON 1903
A completely different special, for this was a steam-powered motorcycle built by William Hale of Hanham, Bristol and an engineer at a brickyard. Equipped with a flash boiler for moderately quick starting, it ran on paraffin and the steam drove a 200cc single-cylinder engine having side valves rather than the more usual slide valve of the type. Boiler and engine were housed in a tubular frame with braced forks, the drive being by belt with no need for clutch or gearbox.

HAMILTON 1901–1907
Another Coventry firm and one that made its own engines as well as the cycle parts, selling the power units to other manufacturers. Singles of 2.25, 3.25 and 4hp were listed along with a 4.5hp V-twin on which either cylinder could be cut out at will. Typical primitives, the machines ran for a few Edwardian years only.

HAMMOND 1903
Operating from an address in Croydon, Surrey, Mr Hammond used the small advertisements in magazines to sell his 2hp motorcycles. He gave no other details and they were no doubt typical primitives and he an established cycle dealer.

The HAL was sold by a London dealer, who created it mainly with a new tank transfer on an existing model.

Hamilton built both engines and the cycle parts of their machines, and offered singles plus this 1903 V-twin, which could be run on one or both cylinders.

HAMPTON 1912–1914
Made by a firm based at King's Norton, Worcestershire, the single-cylinder model had a 3.5hp Hampton engine, Saxon forks and belt drive. For 1913 a 2.5hp model was added, this having a fixed or free gear, or a three-speed hub, while for 1914 the make fitted 3.5hp TDC engines.

HANSAN c.1920–1922
This company was typical of the short-lived small firms that sprang up after the war and soon disappeared. Dalm and Arden two-stroke plus 346cc sv Blackburne engines were used, along with a two-speed gearbox and belt drive – simple and basic.

HARPER 1954–1956
This was a scooter prototype built by Harper Aircraft at Exeter Airport and intended to use a 122 or 197cc Villiers three-speed engine unit with fan cooling and a starter motor. The body was in glass-fibre with the front much as a full fairing and carrying twin headlights. Development work continued for a year or two but few machines were built.

HARPER RUNABOUT 1921–1924
Designed by R.O. Harper of Salford, the city adjoining Manchester, and built in the nearby A.V. Roe aircraft works, this very practical runabout was best described as a three-wheeled scooter. A single front-wheel was steered by long bars, the rider sitting on an upholstered seat above and between the two rear wheels, one of which was chain driven by a 269cc two-stroke Villiers engine through a three-speed gear. Shapely enclosure panels gave considerable protection all round and additionally it was a very capable device, as the inventor and another showed by riding successfully through a Scottish Six Days Trial.

However, the public could be fickle and although the Harper ought to have provided all that could be asked of a design, from those seeking everyday transport, it was unconventional in that it had something of the appearance of a motorized bath-chair, which could have led to ridicule in the eyes of mischievous small boys. This and the loss of spending power after the post-Great War boom, may have been enough to ensure its premature demise.

Hampton used their own engine, as seen in this advertisement for the 1912 single, which came with full equipment, ready for use.

HARRIS PERFORMANCE c.1978–DATE
This firm has a great range of experience in building machines to specification for road or track use. Japanese engine units are commonly used but British ones can be accommodated just as easily with frame kits and rolling chassis available as well as complete machines. Based in Hertfordshire and founded by two brothers, the Harris name stands for quality and is highly respected.

HARWOOD 1920–1921
Available either as a motor attachment or as a complete motorized bicycle, the Harwood utilized a 110cc two-stroke engine with integral mountings for fitting into the frame diamond of a safety cycle. Weight of the engine was under 21lb (9.5kg) and its single speed drove the rear wheel by chain, with a shock absorbing device provided in the sprocket. An Amac carburettor and gear-driven magneto completed the unit. Makers were the Harwood Motor Company of Bexleyheath in Kent.

HASKARD 1903–1907
S.B. Haskard & Son were a small-scale manufacture of motorcycles and tri-cars, built in premises on Curzon Street, in Derby.

HAWKER 1920–1924
Harry Hawker and Tom Sopwith are best remembered for their work in aviation, but were involved with motorcycles with the ABC, built in the Sopwith factory at Kingston-upon-Thames, Surrey. When that began to falter they turned to building the Hawker which was powered by a 292cc two-stroke engine driving with twin-chain primary drive and belt final-drive.

Announced right at the end of December 1920 and sold by Jarvis, the big car firm in Wimbledon, this first model was joined by three with Blackburne engines late in 1921.

This was the Harper scooter prototype of 1954, with its glass-fibre body, twin headlamps and a 122 or 197cc Villiers engine.

These were 348 and 545cc sv plus a 348cc ohv, all driving a three-speed Burman gearbox with chain drive. The 1923 range was the same, plus a model with a 249cc ohv engine, but this reduced to the 1922 four-strokes only for the next and final year. After that the Hawker firm stuck to aircraft right up to today's Harrier.

HAXEL-JAP 1911–1913

Few machines were produced by this small firm, which assembled bought-in parts. The engine used was the 292cc sv JAP seen in many other makes, as were most of the other components. With little to distinguish it from the competition, it soon left the market.

HAYDEN 1904

F. Hayden of Cheltenham had the idea that a motorcycle could use the frame as a fuel tank and had one such built for him by Kynochs of Birmingham in 1904. The tubes were of a larger diameter than usual, while the oil was carried in a reservoir by the bottom bracket. In addition, the frame had a simple form of plunger rear-suspension and braced forks were fitted. Power was provided by a vertically mounted Simms 2.75hp engine with magneto and FN carburettor, and the drive to the rear wheel was by belt. At least two examples of this innovative design were built.

The Hayden was built in 1904, to an order which required that the frame acted as the fuel tank, and had a form of plunger rear-suspension.

HAZEL 1910–1912

Made by the Cripps Cycle & Motor Co. of Forest Gate, London, this machine used a 2.5hp JAP engine and weighed in at under 100lb (45.5kg).

A neat lightweight for 1912, the Hazlewood used a JAP engine installed in a trim and tidy machine.

It was quite basic, having belt drive and braced forks. For 1911 it was joined by 3 and 4.5hp JAP-powered models, with the option of sprung forks. There were also models fitted with V-twin JAP engines of 5, 6 or 7hp, while for 1912 the firm used both JAP and Precision engines of 2.5 and 3.5hp.

Hazlewood also offered a V-twin model for 1913, still with JAP power but with chain-cum-belt transmission.

HAZLEWOOD 1911–1924

The Hazlewood was introduced late in 1911 and built at West Orchard, Coventry by a firm established in 1876. The one model used a 2.75hp JAP engine and had belt drive to a three-speed Armstrong rear hub. Druid forks were fitted, the brake gear was well executed and the pedals retained, mounted to an eccentric bottom bracket.

By 1912 they had a Colonial model for South Africa and for 1913 added a twin, powered by a 3.5 or 5hp JAP engine. The smaller twin kept to the hub gear of the single, but the larger fitted the hub as a countershaft gearbox driven by chain while keeping the belt final-drive. This line continued for 1914, but the next year saw the single with a 3.5hp JAP engine driving the countershaft gearbox; all ran on for 1916.

Post-war, they returned to the listings for 1920 with just the 5–6hp 654cc V-twin fitted with their own three-speed gearbox with chain-cum-belt drive, but the following year the range extended to add a larger 976cc V-twin and the option of all-chain drive for both. Only chain drive was used in 1922, when the twins were joined by 292 and 488cc sv singles with JAP engines.

The range was down to the 292cc single and 654cc twin for 1923, the latter with the choice of transmissions, and just a 678cc V-twin for the final 1924 year, still with the final-drive choice.

HB 1910–1923

This Walsall Street, Wolverhampton make was first listed late in 1910 when the initials, standing for Hill Brothers, appeared on a 1.25hp 136cc engine. Possibly intended as a bicycle attachment with belt drive to the rear wheel, no more was heard of the firm for some time.

Post-war, they had a 348cc single listed in 1920, this conventional with a two-speed Burman gearbox and chain-cum-belt drive. This was joined by a 499cc, three-speed version in 1921, and a 550cc model plus one fitted with a 348cc ohv Blackburne engine for the next year. This must have stretched the firm too far for there were just the two 348cc models for 1923, albeit with all-chain drive.

Hill Brothers offered this model in their 1921 HB range, a neat machine for that time but the firm only had a couple of years more to go.

HCL 1922

HCL machines were made at Railway Road by Hezekiah Close of Leigh, using the initials of name and town, in the post-Great War years. The engines used were either a 269cc Villiers two-stroke or V-twin four-stroke JAP driving a Burman or Sturmey-Archer two-speed gearbox. The simple frame used Saxon forks at the front, but only six machines were actually made before Close gave up and turned to being a professional musician. Later he ran the Spring View Inn in Leigh up to his death in 1950.

HE c.1935

George Hanstock used the initials of his firm, Hanstock Engineering of Maltby, near Rotherham in Yorkshire, when he built frames to carry a range of Villiers two-stroke engines. Not in the lists, so most must have been sold locally with two at least going to Maltby residents.

HEALEY 1971–1976

Long after Ariel ceased producing the Square Four, the Healey brothers found themselves hunting for spares, then making them and then in business supplying others. This led to a plan to build a complete machine and for this an adaptation of an Egli spine frame was chosen, this bringing pivoted-fork rear suspension in place of the Ariel link system. The frame spine also carried the engine oil, there was a front tie-bar to support the engine, and Metal Profile forks were fitted. Wire wheels with Italian hubs and alloy rims were used and the result combined the Squariel line of old in a modern form.

By 1973 there was a disc front-brake and the next year brought an alternator. For 1976 it was cast-alloy wheels and a rear disc-brake along with styling changes. However, it became too expensive for its limited market so no more were made.

HEANES 1971–1973

Ken Heanes, a most successful off-road rider in scrambles and the ISDT, made an arrangement with BSA and Eric Cheney to combine the unit single engine from one and a frame kit from the other. The result was the Heanes BSA Thumper, which did its off-road job well.

HEC 1923–1924

A lightweight machine built much like many others in 1923, with the 247cc two-stroke Villiers engine, chain drive to a two-speed countershaft gearbox and thence by belt to the rear wheel. The next year a three-speed Sturmey-Archer gearbox was standardized, but the belt remained, although a special competition model with all-chain drive, internal expanding brakes and a 54mph (86km/h) speed potential could be obtained, before production ended.

The 1938 HEC was of autocycle form, but used an 80cc engine made by Levis in rather dated cycle parts.

HEC 1938–1940

This was an autocycle first seen late in 1938 at the Earls Court show and made by the Hepburn Engineering Co. of King's Cross, London. It differed from the rest in using an 80cc two-stroke engine of their own design that was made for them by Levis. This engine drove a clutch mounted on a countershaft with chain drive from the unit to the rear wheel. The whole unit was mounted above the bottom bracket of the heavy-duty bicycle it drove. Well thought out, it failed to survive the war, during which HEC merged with Levis.

HEIGHTON 1904–1905

This was a forecar powered by a 4hp Rex water-cooled engine driving a two-speed gear. It was made at Elton, near Peterborough in Cambridgeshire by the firm of that name and also sold as the Vinco.

HEJIRA 1981–1986

Hejira was another small firm that produced racing machines in the 1980s using a Rotax engine, in their case the 250cc two-stroke single at first. Based at Stony Stratford, Buckinghamshire, they developed a twin-spar frame that linked headstock and rear-fork pivot directly. From this hung the engine unit and, by 1986, versions were available for singles and twins in various sizes. Along the way

Based on the Ariel Square Four, the Healey brought that model's specification up to date, creating a desirable machine.

One of the range of Heldun models, all of 50cc; this 1966 model was built for trials use and fitted with an overhead-valve engine.

there had been a machine with the fuel tank under the engine and another with a prototype hub-centre design. As with so many of these enterprises, they were long in good ideas but short on the finance to develop them fully.

HELDUN 1965–1968
This Shropshire firm only made 50cc machines, offering both complete models and kits. They had an ambitious list, using German and Italian two- and four-stroke engines, and offered models for road, road racing and trials in a variety of forms. By 1967 they had added a scrambler, and supplied in kit form only, while only one trials model from this long list was mentioned for 1968, after which the name had gone.

HEMMINGS c.1995–DATE
Based in Northamptonshire, Mick Hemmings specializes in the sale of Norton and Norvil spares, so most machines he builds are based on these models. However, G50, 7R and Manx racing singles plus Triumph twins are also listed and built to customer specification.

HENLEY 1920–1926
Starting out in premises on Spring Hill, Birmingham, the Henley Engineering Co. Ltd first offered a 269cc two-stroke model powered by the ubiquitous Villiers engine and available in two forms, single-speed or with two speeds through a Sturmey-Archer gearbox, but both with belt drive. Machines with 293 and 677cc sv JAP engines, also with belt final-drive, soon joined the lightweight duo, but by mid-1922 they were concentrating on a single model range, utilizing a 348cc sv Blackburne engine. Demand was such that a move was made to new workshops on Doe Street, where they remained for the next four years. In the autumn of 1922 the 350 moved on to ohv power, courtesy of the oil-cooled Bradshaw engine, a three-speed gearbox, all-chain drive, internal expanding brakes and a sporting frame layout with sloping top-tube, all adding up to an appealing presentation.

Competition successes and an Isle of Man TT race entry with this model enhanced the prestige of the small firm. 249/348 ohv and 545cc sv Blackburne-powered models quickly followed; some in De Luxe or Super Sports forms, others as complete sidecar outfits. However, during 1926, the original company was acquired by new owners and the trading name was changed to New Henley as it ran on to 1931.

This was one of the Henley models for 1924 with sv, others being offered with ohv.

HERCULES 1912–1914
Hercules was a Birmingham firm that offered 3.5 and 4.5hp models using Precision and Sarolea engines. Saxon forks and a two-speed gear option completed a machine that was typical of the time. For 1914, both JAP and Precision engines were used, the model with the 6hp JAP unit having a three-speed Sturmey-Archer gearbox.

HERCULES 1956–1961
Built by a large bicycle firm, this was a moped fitted with a 49cc JAP two-stroke engine and sold as the Grey Wolf at first, although this was soon

A 1957 Hercules fitted with a JAP-built engine with two-speed gears, based on the Cyc-Auto design but only available for two years.

changed to Her-cu-motor. The engine had the crankshaft set along the machine to drive back to a two-speed gearbox and bevel box with chain final-drive. The unit hung from a spine frame with leading-link front forks and the machine had a good line.

Production came to an end in 1958 after supplies of the JAP engine dried up, but the firm introduced a new model for 1960. This was the Corvette and used a 49cc French Lavalette engine in a simple, rigid frame with telescopic forks. It only lasted to the next year.

HERNER 1923
A vogue for all-weather machines, providing the rider with protection from the elements, came during the mid-1920s and attracted attention from manufacturers large and small.

Once the JAP engine unit was no longer available after 1958, Hercules changed to this Corvette model, actually using a French Lavalette moped engine.

Falling firmly into the latter category were Herner Engineering of Coventry, who issued a 147cc two-stroke Villiers-engined model with extensive weather shielding and including a windshield in its standard specification. The frame was built up from straight tubes, the two-speed Albion gearbox was held within steel plates and belt final-drive was used. Handlebars were attached to a long column projecting rearwards from the steering head and passing through the windshield. The considerable front area must have taken its toll on the tiny engine and forward progress would have been painfully slow.

HERWIN 1905–1906

An exhibitor at the late-1905 Stanley Show, the firm of Herwin, Canny & Co. offered a low-built model fitted with a 5hp twin-cylinder engine. Springing for the machine was effected by the Simplex anti-vibration and brake mechanism, which comprised a spring fork on the front wheel carrying an arm that held the brake band in position. A similar arrangement was fitted to the rear wheel so that the machine was well sprung and claimed to give a most comfortable ride.

HESKETH 1980–DATE

Lord Alexander Hesketh ran his own car in Formula 1 with James Hunt as the driver, moving on to motorcycles with a launch in 1980. His machine was intended to be a high-class high-speed tourer with modern features combined to give the best of quality in all areas. Sadly it did not work out that way.

The machine had a 992cc 90-degree V-twin engine with the front cylinder close to horizontal. Inside went a massive crankshaft with gear-and-chain drive to the dohc, opening four valves per cylinder. Two Amal carburettors, soon changed to Dell'Orto units, supplied the mixture that was fired by a Lucas RITA electronic system, while starting was electric only, no kickstart being fitted. Primary transmission was by gears to

Close up of the 992cc V-twin engine, showing its gear-plus-chain drive to the camshafts, gear-driven gearbox but chain final-drive.

The hefty Hesketh, which was intended to be a high-speed tourer with its massive V-twin engine, came out too complex and with faults.

Port side of the Hesketh, parked outside the ancestral home near Towcester, which gave the machine a magnificent backdrop but, sadly, it needed rather more.

a five-speed gearbox with chain final-drive in place of the shaft originally intended.

This massive, over complex and weighty unit went into a tubular frame to act as a stressed member. It was fitted with Marzocchi front forks and Girling, soon changed to Marzocchi, units controlled the pivoted rear-fork, while the wheels were Astralite alloy and brakes by Brembo. The whole was fully equipped and the result large and impressive with a fine finish.

Unfortunately, it turned out to be far from fully developed, with a noisy engine that leaked oil and a poor gear change that drowned the engine clatter. There were hosts of minor troubles as well, so it was 1981 before the machine went on public view. It still suffered in a way that was not acceptable in a high-class and now most expensive machine, so it was not until 1982 that the first machines reached their customers as the V1000. It still had far too many problems for a machine with no really special technical features and the people who had placed their orders immediately compared it with memories of the Vincent and more recent experience with Ducati.

By this time the firm was in deep financial trouble and, in June 1982, the official receiver was in charge. In time the firm was reformed and, in 1983, the touring Vampire version with fairing was added but to no avail, as production dried up by the year end.

Development continued under Mick Broom and the company name became Hesleydon. Construction passed to dealers Mocheck in London where Mick Broom continued with the machine to the end of 1986. After then the development continued with machines built to special order back at Towcester, Northants, where they had begun.

HEWETSON 1902
This was a Laurin & Klément by another name and all the way from Austria. Thus its 1.75hp engine had

With the crankcase a stressed member of the frame structure and an oscillating magneto drive, the Hillman differed from most in 1902.

aiv, a fuel tank that acted as a surface carburettor and the magneto bolted to the underside of the crankcase and driven by an eccentric from the crankshaft. The resulting extended engine height did not have the benefit of the usual L&K frame with its deep loop, so the engine was mounted high. From there it drove the rear wheel by twisted-hide belt over a jockey pulley. A contracting band brake was fitted to the front wheel and a rear brake was an option, as was a flat raw-hide drive belt.

HILLMAN 1902
William Hillman was prominent in the bicycle trade and later founded the Premier and Sparkbrook firms, among others. In 1902 he produced a motorcycle with a number of interesting features, including all-chain drive.

He mounted the 1.5hp engine high up, just behind the headstock, where its crankcase became a stressed member in the downtube. Its magneto was driven by a crank and rod, so oscillated, and the chain drive was in two stages, via the bottom bracket. A crude spray-carburettor provided the mixture, so the model had advanced features for 1902, but perhaps too advanced as no more were built.

HILLSDON 1904
A motor tandem, also called the Eddington, powered by a 4.5hp water-cooled engine driving the rear axle through a Dupont two-speed gear. The machine had a long wheelbase and was well built, but showed its motorcycle origin for the front half, the passenger seat being located behind the rider.

HJ 1920–1921
A very short-lived marque that was introduced by Messrs Howard & Johnson of Birmingham. The sole model was a lightweight with the 269cc two-stroke Wall engine and a Roc two-speed gearbox with chain-cum-belt transmission, or single speed at optional lower cost. An Amac carburettor, Runbaken magneto and Best & Lloyd drip-feed lubrication were all industry-standard items for the time, but the spring front-fork was H&J's own patent, in which two curled leaf-springs replaced the normal solid-steel top links of a Druid-pattern fork.

This 1904 Hillsdon tricar tandem was heavily built, with ample support for the passenger, and was also being known as the Eddington.

HJH 1954–1956
Based in Neath, Glamorgan, this Welsh firm was run by H.J. Hulsman, who began with a conventional lightweight with a 197cc Villiers 8E engine. It was joined for 1955 by models using the 147cc 30C and 224cc 1H engines, all with the name of Dragon in some form. This variety was extended for 1956, but the firm then ran into financial troubles and closed in October that year.

HOBART 1901–1924
This marque was produced by Hobart Bird of Coventry, who were also suppliers to many other firms. They began with a primitive using an inclined engine but, by 1903, had added a model with a vertical engine in a loop frame fitted with braced

HJH produced a small range of models, using Villiers engines much as others, but had too many financial troubles to survive.

forks. This continued up to 1906, but they were then just suppliers until 1910, when they returned to complete machines.

The new Hobart was a lightweight, having its 2.5hp engine inclined in the frame over the downtube. A gear-driven Bosch magneto was used along with an adjustable pulley for the belt drive and Druid forks. For the next year it was joined by a 3.5hp twin and a ladies' model. This had a revised open frame and the engine mounted lower with the cylinder horizontal, all the works being fully enclosed.

By 1913 they were using JAP engines as well as their own and added a 225cc two-stroke the next year. This went over to a 269cc Villiers for 1915 along with a 6hp V-twin with a JAP engine and three speeds. Post-war, the two-stroke, including a spring-frame model was listed, plus a 292cc JAP four-stroke for 1920. More versions of both were listed for the next year, including the spring frame for both sizes, but this feature was not continued with after that year.

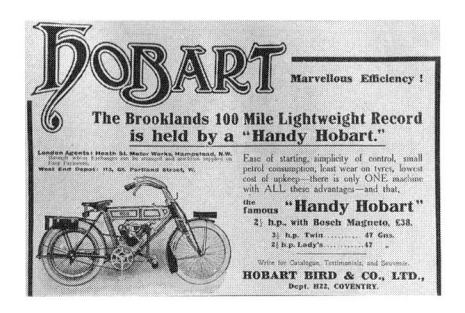

A 1911 advertisement for the Hobart, offering single, V-twin and ladies' models and proclaiming some success at Brooklands.

For 1922 there were new machines with 348cc Blackburne and 346cc JAP sv engines, both listed in solo and sidecar forms, while the next year saw the 269cc Villiers replaced by a 170cc Hobart two-stroke engine driving a two-speed gearbox and the 292cc JAP by a 249cc sv Blackburne. All the four-strokes had a good range of transmission options, with two or three speeds and final drive by belt or chain. The range went down to the 170cc two-stroke and 346cc JAP for 1924, plus the 292cc JAP once again, but after this the marque was no longer listed, although Hobart engines continued to be supplied to other firms for some years.

Part of the 1911 Hobart advert, showing the general layout and the open frame plus enclosure offered for the ladies.

HOCKLEY 1914–1916
A Barr Street, Birmingham firm that chose December 1914 to announce their new motorcycle intended for colonial use. It was powered by a 269cc two-stroke engine that either drove the rear wheel directly by belt, or by chain to a two-speed gearbox and then by belt. The engine had a Senspray carburettor and M&L magneto, while the frame had twin downtubes.

HOLDEN 1897–1902
This was the world's first four-cylinder motorcycle, patented in 1894 and first produced in air-cooled form in

Line drawing of the Holden, the first motorcycle to have four cylinders, had direct drive to the rear wheel, and was water-cooled after 1899.

1897. Designed by Col. Holden, the horizontal cylinders drove the rear wheel directly and the camshaft was driven from this by chain and worm gear. There was coil ignition, a surface carburettor and geared pedals for the front wheel.

The 1899 version had water cooling and went into production, but the result was heavy and expensive. By 1902 it was no more, already an obsolete relic of the earliest days.

HOLLOWAY c.1905
This was built by the family of that name who were located in Shoreham-by-Sea, Sussex, and was a machine typical of the Edwardian era.

HOLROYD 1922–1924
John Spear Holroyd had been a notable competition rider in the pre-Great War days, closely associated for a time with the Motosacoche marque. Later he rode Blackburne, Massey-Arran and Edmund machines and opened a retail motorcycle business in the London area. By 1922 he had become a manufacturer in his own right, offering models with a sporting style. These were powered by JAP engines in 248 and 346cc capacities, and racing versions appeared with some modest success at Brooklands track.

By 1924 just a 346cc sv JAP model was listed, this with a three-speed Burman gearbox, all-chain drive, internal expanding brakes and a leather toolbox mounted atop the fuel tank. It was every inch the sportsman's ideal middleweight, but sales would have been confined to

HOLT 1957–1958
The Sherpa was a scooter offered by Harry Holt of Ilford, Essex, but with no relation to the Bond model of that name. It was available with 49 or 98cc engines and various specifications as a moped, as well as a scooter. Built of prefabricated parts bolted together, it had a limited style and soon vanished from the market.

The Hopper was unusual for a 1904 model, in having a water-cooled engine of only 317cc capacity, most such being larger.

HOOPER 1921
Yet another lightweight designed and intended for large-scale production in the heady days after the Armistice. W.F. Hooper had been involved with the Superb Four, but now turned his attention to this machine, which was to have a 125cc four-stroke engine fed by a Willis carburettor, set into a duplex frame with short leading-link front forks. The cylinder of the engine was horizontal and faced forward and an output of 2hp at 5,000rpm was claimed. The machine was reviewed and illustrated in July of 1921 and, although Hooper's name was attached to it, it was said that the actual marque name had still to be decided. It was also reported that arrangements had been made for a large production in a London works, but nothing further was subsequently heard of the project.

HOPPER 1904
A water-cooled machine, shown at the Farman Automobile depot in Long Acre, London, that had its engine mounted vertically in a loop frame. The capacity was 317cc, while the machine weighed 108lb (49kg) and was priced at £45.

HORLEY c.1902
This marque was named after the town in Surrey where it was located and offered a basic primitive for a year or two before moving onto building cars, these also named 'No-Name'.

HOSKISON 1919–1922
Introduced at the height of the post-Great War demand for personal transport, the Hoskison lightweight had the 292cc Union two-stroke engine driving a two-speed Burman gearbox by chain, then by belt to the rear wheel. The remainder of the machine followed accepted lines, as it was meant for quick and ready assembly, with the works set out to meet an expected annual production target of 2,000 machines. The first examples were due off the line in December 1919 and the Hoskison Manufacturing Company of Digbeth, Birmingham kept to their one-model strategy through 1920.

By 1921, however, they had changed direction and their name, becoming Hoskison Motors of Lozell's Road, Birmingham, and dropped the two-stroke altogether; in its place came two models with Blackburne side-valve engines. Both the 348 and 499cc machines had two-speed Burman gearboxes and both retained belt final-drive, each had a B&B carburettor and a sidecar equivalent of the solo version, so a wide range of possible purchasers was covered by a minimum of models. The high hopes of 1919 had soon evaporated though and the marque was no longer listed by the spring of 1922.

HOSSACK 1984–1988
Norman Hossack was a chassis man and designed a new form of frame with a novel front fork. While it looked somewhat like a girder fork, it was actually a twin-wishbone system not unlike that of a car front suspension. It worked well and several were built, housing a variety of engines. At first these were Honda, Rotax and Yamaha two-strokes, but later came a front-fork conversion for a K100RS BMW.

HOULDSWORTH 1895
This Liverpool firm exhibited a steam motorcycle at the 1895 Crystal Palace Cycle Show, but there is some doubt as to whether this was a serious endeavour. It could have been based on the French Dalifol that existed at that time.

What looked like a blade-girder fork on the Hossack was actually a wishbone system, as on a car.

HOWARD 1905–1907

A small number of machines bearing this name were made by the Howard engineering business in Coalville, Leicestershire. A horizontal engine was located above the pedalling bracket and below the lower fuel-tank frame rail, which, it was alleged, had fuel injection rather than a carburettor for its fuel supply. However, this was most likely a form of controlled and adjustable drip feed, just one of many different arrangements then in use to mix air and fuel for an engine.

HOWARTH 1931

A three-cylinder water-cooled two-stroke engine is not a common type, either now or in the 1930s, but when coupled with a supercharger and desmodromic inlet-valves it becomes really rare. However, this was what was proposed by Whittaker Howarth, a Scott enthusiast and one-time manager of the Scott Liverpool depot and producer of the excellent Howarth silencer for the Scott.

The 499cc engine was of simple construction as far as most aspects were concerned. The cylinder block had exhaust ports along both sides, while the inlet was by poppet valves in the head, these opened and closed by positive cams without springs. This was necessary, as the chain-driven camshaft had to run at engine speed to suit the two-stroke cycle. In place of the normal crankcase compression there was a vane-type Foxwell supercharger, mounted behind the cylinder block and also chain driven.

This engine drove back to a four-speed gearbox with chain final-drive.

A typical HRD machine, the Super 90 was fitted with a 500cc ohv engine in a well designed and constructed set of cycle parts.

The whole unit was intended to be mounted in a conventional frame with girder forks and the usual fittings, but it is unlikely that this was ever built. However, the engine was, and did run up to 5,000rpm, although it was not the best of times to launch such an innovative design. It was hardly surprising that no more was heard of it.

H&R 1923

The initials sheltered the full name of this company, who were Messrs Hailstone & Ravenhall, of Clay Lane in Coventry. Their product was a 147cc Villiers-engined two-stroke of simple form and equipped with a two-speed Albion gearbox. Unusually, they also sold the machine under the R&H brand name involving a mere reversal of their trading style shown above.

Howard Davies after his winning ride in the 1925 Senior TT. His HRD machines were built using the best, so were expensive.

HRD 1924–1928

Howard Davies was a famous rider well before he used his initials for his own make of motorcycle. He rode a Sunbeam in the 1914 Senior TT when he tied for second place and flew in the Great War. During 1917 he was shot down and mistakenly reported killed.

He rode for AJS in the early 1920s and in 1921 was second in the Junior TT and then went on to win the Senior on the same 350cc machine. However, he had no success in the next two years, or in 1924 with an OEC.

In 1924, Davies decided to build motorcycles using his racing and trade experience to produce a quality, medium-weight machine. He sought one that handled well, thanks to good frame design, and had good brakes as well as fittings and the best components. From this came the choice of JAP engine, Burman gearbox, Webb forks and items from AMAC, Renold, BTH and KLG, all reflecting experience. The design was by E.J. Massey and hard work saw a range on show at Olympia for the 1925 season.

The firm was based in Wolverhampton and the models with ohv were the 344cc D70 and D80, and 488cc D90. There was also the D70S, a 488cc sv model listed with or without a sports sidecar. All had three speeds and all had a saddle tank, fine lines and did their job well.

Davies promoted his machine as 'Produced by a Rider' and supported his claims by entering the 1925 TT races, where he repeated his 1921 successes by finishing second in the Junior and winning the Senior. It is quite remarkable that he only finished four times in the Island to take two wins and two seconds. For 1926 the D70 was dropped, the D70S made available with a choice of 490 or 597cc engine, and there was a new Super 90 with a two-port ohv engine. There was no TT success that year, but in 1927 Freddie Dixon won the Junior on his HRD.

The 1927 range had several new models including the Super 600 with a 597cc ohv engine. At the other end of the scale were 346cc models in sv and ohv form and most of these ran on into 1928. However, by then the firm was in financial trouble and early in the year was bought by Ernie Humphries of OK Supreme. He in turn soon sold on to Philip Vincent who went on to produce his own Vincent-HRD machines, but never met Howard Davies personally until 1969.

HSM 1913–1915

Advertised late in 1913 by Turner, Marr & Co. of New Bond Street,

London, this was one of those odd cyclecars that comprised most of a motorcycle and sidecar, but with the controls, including a steering wheel, all in a large wicker sidecar body. Known as the Sociable, the machine was powered by a V-twin engine and substantial leading-link Chater-Lea forks were fitted.

The 1904 Hubbard was a forecar with water-cooled engine, two speeds and the choice of belt or chain drive.

The 1914 HSM was an odd cyclecar where the controls went into the sidecar body for better weather protection for all.

HT 1922–1924
The Hagg Tandem was an advanced, well-enclosed machine that was innovative but failed to sell too well. By 1922, it was powered by a 349cc Barr & Stroud sleeve-valve engine driving a two-speed Burman gearbox and for 1923 Arthur Hagg changed the name to the HT.

He also added a conventional model sold as the HT Sports, using the same engine and gearbox in quality cycle parts. Sadly this failed to raise sales enough, so that 1924 was the last season for this small firm from Park Street village in Hertfordshire.

HUBBARD 1904–1905
Based in Much Park Street, Coventry, Hubbard was the producer of a forecar fitted with an inclined 4.5hp water-cooled engine, separate two-speed gearbox and flat-belt drives. Chain drive was an option, as was a carrier basket that went in place of the normal passenger seat for trade use.

HUDLASS 1920
This prototype scooter was designed by F. Hudlass, who was engineer to the RAC. He adapted the popular Auto-Wheel unit to take the place of the normal rear wheel and arranged for it to be sprung from the main frame. Front forks were also sprung by a combination of compression and rebound springs, but otherwise it was an intrinsically simple device. Mr Hudlass put out feelers to seek a manufacturer for his baby, but seemingly none were forthcoming. However, the Autosco and the Witall scooters, which appeared during 1920, also used the Auto-Wheel unit in a similar way and may therefore owe something to the Hudlass design.

HULBERT-BRAMLEY 1904–1906
Frank Hulbert and S. Bramley Moore both rode Booth machines in the 1903 ACU 1,000-mile trial and later took over the make and changed its name, continuing at the Putney, London works. The range comprised a 2hp ladies' model, 2.75 and 3.5hp solos, and a forecar powered by a 3.5hp engine, Minerva engines being used. Only solos were listed for 1905 and the partnership soon ceased building machines.

HUMBER 1896–1905 AND 1909–1930
This bicycle firm was founded by Thomas Humber and came into the powered transport field by building Leon-Bollée tricars under licence from H.J. Lawson. It was in their works that the eccentric Pennington machines were built and in 1898 they constructed a tandem driven by an electric motor powered by batteries. This was used for cycle pacing on racing tracks, for which its speed was useful and short life unimportant.

As early as 1898, Humber built this 'Olympia Tandem', based on the Pennington, hence the engine set right at the rear.

At this time the firm listed a Ladies Motor Safety, which was a ladies' bicycle modified to carry an engine behind the seat tube. There was also a forecar known as the Olympia Tandem, based on the Pennington design with the engine hung out behind the rear wheel. None of these early efforts ran on past 1899.

This odd-looking Humber tandem had an electric motor to add power to the rider's efforts for cycle-pacing work, where it had speed but a short life.

It was 1902 when Humber really began producing motorcycles, offering two models, both to prove successful. The smaller used a 1.5hp engine hung from the downtube with belt drive, the larger was made under licence from Phelon & Rayner, so had the engine fitted as the frame downtube. From there it drove the rear wheel by chain in two stages.

By 1902, Humber were using Phelon & Rayner patents under licence, hence the engine layout that would remain with Panther to their end.

The 1902 models proved themselves at shows and in trials, which led to the development of new machines for 1903. All had chain drive and comprised 1.75 and 2.75hp solos, a 2.75hp tricar with single front-wheel, and the Olympia Tandem forecar. All were listed in two forms, the Beeston or the cheaper Coventry, as was Humber's bicycle practice. The tricycle was dropped for 1904, the smaller model became 2hp and the Olympia was fitted with a 3.5hp water-cooled engine. However, by 1905, the firm was concentrating on its car business so the motorcycles were dropped for a while.

The name returned in 1909 with just one 3.5hp model of conventional form with belt drive and the option of a two-speed rear hub. Less usual was the silencer that formed part of the frame downtube and the sprung front-forks whose blades pivoted on a bearing in the lower crown against springs. For 1910 these were replaced by a normal silencer and Druid forks, the firm entered the TT and added a 2hp lightweight model during the year, with this also offered in ladies' form.

The TT races moved to the Mountain course in 1911 and Humber built a new 2.75hp V-twin model to run in the Junior event. Of 339cc, the engine was unusual in having a master connecting-rod to which the second rod hinged. The Bosch magneto was gear driven and clamped to the rear of the crankcase, the carburettor a B&B, and Druid forks used. The new model made a remarkably good debut in the TT with all six entries finishing and P.J. Evans winning.

For 1924, Humber listed models such as this, with conventional form and build in several sizes.

The 1929 Humber with the 349cc overhead-valve engine shared many cycle parts with the sv model but adopted a saddle tank.

For 1912 the 3.5hp model was revised and a 2.75hp V-twin introduced, while the 2hp machine ran on as it was. All continued much as they were for the next two years, and they were joined by a water-cooled version of the 3.5hp model for 1914, this intended for sidecar work.

However, late in 1913, Humber announced a new model with a horizontally opposed three-cylinder engine. This unusual layout was achieved by having one 373cc cylinder facing forward and two 185cc cylinders with a common combustion-chamber facing aft. The crankshaft was formed to take the two

For 1903 there was this 2.75hp Humber, with improvements in design and construction to benefit all aspects.

This fine Humber ohc 349 joined the sv and ohv models for 1928 and all three then ran on to 1930.

rear-rods either side of the front one, there was a large external flywheel and the magneto sat on top of the crankcase. This extraordinary engine drove a three-speed car-type gearbox by chain with chain final-drive. Only one small batch of this model was made.

By 1915 only the 3.5hp single remained in production, while the three was replaced by a conventional 6hp water-cooled flat-twin driving a three-speed gearbox with chain final-drive. In 1916 only flat-twins were built, with the 6hp model joined by an air-cooled 3.5hp model, also with three speeds and chain drive, but few of these were actually produced.

The 349cc ohc Humber model ran on to 1930 along with the ohv and sv machines. They were well made, but perhaps too well made for the Depression.

Post-war, the 6hp twin was dropped, while the 3.5hp flat-twin was first joined and then replaced by a 4.5hp version of 601cc. A sports model was added for 1921 and, in 1923, the twins were joined by a 349cc sv single and then dropped. The one single, in two forms, was joined by an ohv model of the same capacity for 1927 and the next year brought a neat ohc version with shaft

Years later and a fine overhead camshaft Humber from their last days is shown at a modern rally.

and bevel drive, rear magneto and the oil pump driven from the camshaft end. These three 349cc models continued as the motorcycle range to 1930, after which the firm concentrated on its cars.

HUNTER 1904
Hunter produced a typical primitive, but one having chain drive and the novelty of a crankshaft-mounted shock absorber. In this, the loads were taken by a clock spring, but no mention was made of the limitations of such a system. If the spring was able to respond to light loads then power would wind it up and hold it so, while fitting a stiffer spring would reduce the effect overall.

HYDE 1921
Hyde was a small assembler of machines from bought-in parts and soon gone from the scene. The 348cc sv Blackburne engine was used together with a two-speed countershaft gearbox with kickstarter and clutch.

HYDE 1980–DATE
Norman Hyde was a long serving Triumph man who became a Trident specialist supplying parts and improvements for both the triples and the twins. Much of this was the result of his time at Triumph combined with a great deal of successful drag racing. In time this led to new frames, disc brakes, tuning parts and custom items. The eventual result was a complete machine that was called the Hyde Harrier, built in the café racer style and supplied with twin or triple engine as required. Into each could go as much or as little as the customer desired, working from a large catalogue of goodies for either engine type. Less known but just as good was a similar range for the BSA A65 unit twin.

In the 1990s a new model joined the Harrier, but differed in being based on modern components. Named the Hyde Hornet, it used a 636cc Rotax four-valve engine and Harris Performance frame with Yamaha forks, wheels and many detail parts. The result had a fine modern style and it came about from Hyde's interest in single-cylinder racing and was first built for that, the road model following in 1996.

I

IDEAL 1902
This was made by W. Bravery of Tunbridge Wells, Kent and had its 2hp engine mounted vertically in a loop frame. A Simms-Bosch magneto went behind the cylinder and a choice of surface or spray carburettor was offered. The frame downtube was curved to allow the engine to be well forward and low down. Transmission was by belt to a rim held to the wheel rim by eight arms.

IMP 1913–1914
This was a simple ultra-lightweight based on the JES, as was the City, and sharing the same small 1hp engine made by J.E. Smith of Gloucester. As with the others, construction was very basic, the engine with aiv and outside flywheel. It mounted above the bottom bracket of a stock bicycle and drove the rear wheel by belt over a jockey pulley used to set the tension. Braced forks were fitted.

IMPERIAL 1901–1903
This was the name used by Norman Downs when he founded his company and before he added the 'New' in front of it. Based in Birmingham and an established bicycle firm, they entered the powered market in 1901 at the Stanley Show where they offered a 3.5hp model that had the engine mounted above the front wheel which it drove by belt. Only one of these was sold, the rest being used by the staff. At the 1902 show they had a 2hp model, but soon afterwards left the market.

IMPERIAL 1914–1915
Based at Saltley, Birmingham, this was another make that set up too late to do much before the Great War. They used the 269cc two-stroke Metro engine and offered a single- or two-speed transmission using either direct-belt drive or a combination of chain and belt. Either Druid or Brampton Biflex forks were fitted and the model continued into 1915.

IMPERIAL METRO 1914–1915
The name under which the Birmingham Metro machine was known in their early days, it having a 269cc two-stroke engine, one or two speeds and a choice of transmission and front forks.

IMPERIAL SWIFT 1904
This was a Walsall firm that built a forecar fitted with a water-cooled engine and Garrard two-speed gear and clutch. It was moderately priced and typical of the type and period, but short lived.

INDIAN 1950–1955
This American make had several links with British firms but the first came with Brockhouse. This Southport, Lancashire, firm had produced the Corgi and in 1950 introduced the 248cc Indian Brave. This had conventional lines for its rigid frame and telescopic forks, but the sv engine had the three-speed gearbox built in-unit, an alternator, and the gear and kick-start pedals on the left, all unusual for a British machine at that time.

Indian – a name introduced from the USA but for a British-built machine, which was sold as the Brave in both countries but with limited success.

Unfortunately, the Brave failed to make much impact in the USA or even when released to the UK, and the addition of a version with rear suspension in 1954 did little to help this. Thus, both models were dropped after the next year. There had also been a 125cc two-stroke prototype whose engine was based on the 250 bottom-half, but this never came to anything.

INDIAN PRINCE 1920–1924
Better known as the Silver Prince, this model had the usual 269cc two-stroke Villiers or 292cc sv JAP engines with single speed or two-speed Sturmey-Archer or Albion gearbox and chain-cum-belt transmission. For 1924 there were 147 or 247cc Villiers engines with the same transmission options, but then both went from the lists.

INGLESENT c.1900
Charles Inglesent, a Manchester man, was in the cycle trade, so it was natural that he should build a motorcycle in the early days. No doubt this was a primitive using a heavy-duty bicycle frame with a Minerva engine hung from the downtube.

INVICTA 1902–1906 AND 1913–1925
This name first appeared on a primitive assembled using Minerva and Kelecom engines from Belgium and basic cycle parts. Short lived, the name returned to the market in 1913 with a small range of lightweights designed by Arthur Barnett, who later joined up with Gordon Francis to form the famous Francis-Barnett company in 1919. Prior to then he built the Invicta at his firm, A. Barnett & Co. of West Orchard, Coventry.

The machines used the 269cc two-stroke Villiers engine, with petroil lubrication and a chain-driven magneto, and there were two models on offer, both with Druid forks, one with belt drive, the other with a two-speed Jardine gear and chain-cum-belt drive. In this form they continued up to 1916 and, in effect, after the Great War when the new Francis-Barnett model was much as the old Invicta aside from the tank transfer. This continued until Barnett adopted their bolted-tube frame design to continue on their own path.

This left the Invicta to continue with the 269cc two-stroke Villiers engine, which was joined by 346 and 678cc sv JAP plus 499cc sv Abingdon engines. Chain drive appeared for the largest and by 1923 the range had reduced to 247cc Villiers and 292 and 346cc four-stroke engines. The next year saw four-strokes only, but these were joined by a 147cc Aza two stroke for 1925, which was their last year.

IRELAND 1912–1913

This marque was built by Ireland's Garage, Wolverhampton, who offered 3.5hp single cylinder and 4 or 5hp V-twin Blumfield engines in their models. They fitted Bosch magnetos, Saxon forks and belt drive, so were of the period. All three models were listed for 1913 and nothing after then.

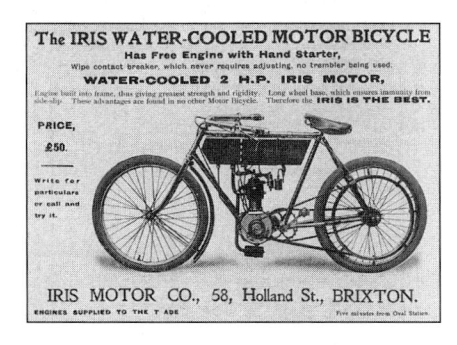

From the start, Iris produced singles and V-twins with water-cooled engines, a feature not common in that Edwardian period.

IRIS 1902–1904

Based in Brixton, London, this make had a water-cooled 2.5hp engine of their own manufacture fitted into a diamond bicycle frame. The belt drive included a free-engine pulley to act as a clutch and there was a hand starter. The radiator for the cooling system was formed as the front section of the tank, air tubes running from the front to exit some way along each side.

By 1903 they were offering a 5hp, water-cooled V-twin as well, but fitted into a loop frame while retaining

The timing side of the single-cylinder Iris of 1903 shows the abbreviated front and no rear mudguards just part of the basic construction.

The water-cooled V-twin Iris engine went into a loop frame, but its other features were much as for the single; later came air-cooled engines.

the other features. Both models continued and shed the loop frame for 1904, while an improved radiator was adopted and air-cooled models also listed.

IVEL 1901–1903

Made by Dan Albone, a bicycle and pioneer petrol-tractor builder of Biggleswade in Bedfordshire, this was

The Ivel followed common early practice, with Minerva engine, heavy-duty bicycle frame and solo or tricycle layout.

one of the many motorcycles that comprised a Minerva engine fitted to a strengthened bicycle. He also built a car, but was best known for farm tractors. For 1903 he offered a tricycle, again powered by a Minerva engine, the frame being further strengthened to suit.

IVY 1910–1931

This make was built by S.A. Newman of Aston Cross, Birmingham and was first listed late in 1910 with a model having a 3.5hp Precision engine, belt drive and sprung forks. This was soon joined by other singles, V-twins and, in 1914, by a 225cc Peco two-stroke. For 1915 the four-strokes had JAP V-twin engines and this continued for 1916. During this time Newman rode several times in the TT, gaining third place in the 1913 Junior.

The Ivy two-stroke for 1920 was fitted with disc wheels, a popular feature of that era, but the marque disappeared in the Depression.

Post-war, they began with 225 and 349cc two-stroke models and gradually gave these more speeds and all-chain drive. In 1923 they added a 198cc two-stroke and 348cc four-stroke and by 1925 had switched mainly to this type, with one model having ohv while the 225cc two-stroke ran on. This may have over-extended the firm, for 1928 saw them back with a two-model range of the Popular with a 247cc two-stroke engine and the Model X with a 292cc JAP. With these two they ran on to 1931.

IXION 1902–04

Produced by the Primus Motor Works, Loughborough Junction, London, the name first appeared on a

The Ixion name appeared more than once, in 1902 and then in 1904, by when the engine was in the central position.

machine with a 1hp two-stroke engine attached to a bicycle to drive its front wheel by friction. By 1903 they had a complete machine to sell with its 1.5hp engine hung from the frame top-tube to drive the rear wheel by belt. For 1904 the engine was up to 3hp and vertically mounted ahead of the bottom bracket, still with direct-belt drive and in a frame essentially from a heavy-duty bicycle with unbraced forks.

IXION 1910–1923

The Ixion name returned late in 1910, the firm Whittal Engineering of Whittall Street, Birmingham using it on a pair of singles with 2.5hp JAP and 3.5hp Precision engines, belt drive and spring forks. By 1912 they were using 3.5 and water-cooled 4.25hp Precision engines and a 3.5hp JAP for the TT model, the machines fitted with two-speed Bowden gear, Saxon forks, oil tank mounted on the saddle tube, and fully enclosed chain final-drive. The range added a 269cc Villiers two-stroke for 1914, again typical of the type, with two speeds, belt drive and Druid forks. This was joined by a similar model with a 349cc Peco engine for 1915, plus a model with a four-stroke Villiers engine and one with a V-twin King Dick.

After the war they moved to Smethwick, Staffordshire, but with just one model using the 269cc Villiers engine, either with direct-belt drive or two speeds and chain-cum-belt drive. Only the second was offered in 1922 and late in 1923 production ceased.

IXION 1930

The Ixion name was re-used by New Hudson when they failed to sell a large batch of 249cc sv models built to capitalize on the public interest in that type. It had begun thanks to the success of the BSA Round Tank model but, by 1929, there were too many on the market, some lacking

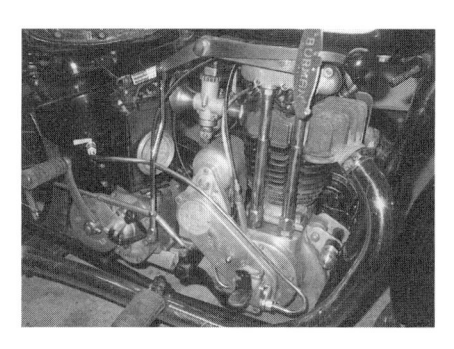

The Swedish Rex model used the ohv Ixion engine built by New Hudson; due to the declining market segment, these engines were then sold off to others.

the stamina of the BSA. The Ixion name enabled New Hudson to cut the price drastically to clear stocks and they also used it for engines sold to other firms at home and abroad, one such being the Swedish Rex.

Close up of timing cover of the 500cc ohv Ixion engine showing typical engine-number stamping of the type.

◆ J ◆

JACKSON 1902–c.1905
The established cycle firm of Jacksons of Horsham, Sussex, turned to power in Edwardian days using Minerva and Fafnir engines. Typical primitives of that era, they were built in fair numbers with most sold locally.

JACKSON 1919–1920
R.L. Jackson had been involved with the motor industry since 1896 and after the Great War he quickly foresaw the interest in machines with enclosure and small wheels, which could carry two people in some comfort. This early scooter boom didn't last long, but Jackson's design for a model with tandem seating on a sprung platform, a duplex tube frame and a 292cc Union two-stroke engine with two-speed gear and sprung forks proved quite successful. Made initially by his company in Pangbourne, Berkshire, it was later developed further and built by A.W. Wall in Birmingham and sold then as the Reynolds Runabout.

JACKSON-ROTRAX 1946–c.1976
A post-war speedway machine that followed the established format, using the 500cc JAP engine running on alcohol fuel and a countershaft carrying the clutch mounted in a rigid frame with forks having little movement. Very well made and finished, it was most successful in its task for many years.

This two-stroke James shows the staggered cylinder fins which were introduced in 1914 and continued post-Great War with the name 'Pineapple'.

The 1909 Safety James model had all the frame on the left of the wheels and other unusual features, which included staggered fins for the cylinder.

The Jackson-Rotrax speedway machine was well developed by 1946, having had various engines, but JAP dominated for many years.

JAMES 1902–1966
Harry James set up to build penny-farthing bicycles in 1880, took Charles Hyde on as works manager in 1890 and retired in 1897 to leave Charles as managing director. It was 1902 before the firm turned to power, by which time Harry was dead and Charles had moved on to leave Fred Kimberley in charge. He was still there half-a-century later, while the firm was still at Greet, near Birmingham, to where they had moved in 1908.

The first James motorcycles were much as other primitives, two models being offered. The first had a Minerva engine hung from the downtube and direct-belt drive. The second used a Derby engine, mounted within the frame, with a short chain-drive back to a spring loaded friction roller, in contact with the rear tyre. A lever allowed the drive roller to be lifted clear and both frame and forks were simple bicycle.

For 1903, only the Minerva style was listed, 2 and 2.5hp versions being offered, but for 1904 the design changed to a loop frame and an FN engine with a cast-iron crankcase. They dropped out for a while, but for 1909 James announced their radical

By 1928 James were fitting Villiers two-stroke engines, this 172cc model typical of their move toward the lightweight end of the market.

'Safety' model, a product of the brain of inventor P.L. Renouf.

Advertised as the 'one-track car', the design had all the frame tubes to the left of the wheels, which ran on live axles, the front with hub-centre steering. Laminated springs provided the front suspension, while the saddle was supported by flat and coil springs. Both hubs had internal-expanding metal-to-metal brakes, while the wheels were easy to remove and interchangeable. The petrol tank went in front of the headstock and acted as a front mudguard.

The 523cc engine was initially inclined back to the headstock angle but soon adopted a vertical position. It had variable lift of the inlet as a control, ball bearings for all shafts except the gudgeon pin, cylinder cooling-fins that were square in plan but alternately staggered around the casting, chain-driven rear-mounted magneto and a free-engine pulley design. Transmission was by belt, a handle was provided for starting, while footboards aided rider comfort.

A 499cc Rudge Python engine was used for this 1931 James model, but they then returned to using their own James twin.

The fine James V-twin continued to the mid-1930s, this a 1931 Flying Ace model, but by then the bulk of the range had two-stroke engines.

The machine was modified for 1910, when the engine was enlarged to 558cc and adopted conventional sv and gear drive to the magneto. The front tank became the oil tank and toolbox, while the petrol tank fitted over the frame top-tube, an early form of saddle tank. For 1911 the front suspension was revised to a parallel-link form while retaining the hub-centre steering.

As others found, before and after, the British motorcyclist was ever conservative and advanced designs seldom won many customers. So it was for James; so, for 1911, they added more conventional machines to augment their range. They used the existing engine with a modified magneto drive in a diamond frame with simple forks and belt drive to produce two models, Tourist and TT.

The Safety was dropped for 1912 when they introduced a 3.5hp model with all-chain drive, two-speed gearbox, kickstarter and clutch, to move from the unconventional to modern in a stroke, although the belt-drive machines continued to be listed. For 1913 a model with a three-speed gearbox was added to supplement the others.

In August 1913 James announced their first model with a V-twin engine. This had the cylinders set at 50 degrees, a 495cc capacity and side valves, the chain-driven magneto set high up behind the rear cylinder. Transmission was all by chain with a three-speed gearbox. The single was enlarged to 598cc for 1914 and intended as a sidecar model, so had taper-roller bearings fitted to the front hub. It was joined by a small two-stroke, powered by their own 225cc engine, driving a two-speed

By 1938, James had this lightweight fitted with a 122cc Villiers engine. It served in the war, known as the 'Clockwork Mouse', and proved very useful.

gearbox by chain with belt final-drive and Druid forks. These three models continued with the staggered cylinder fins, generally known as 'pineapple', and ran on for the next two years, while the big single was built throughout the Great War.

Post-war, the two-stroke ran on as it was with two V-twins, one the original of 495cc and the other of 662cc, both with three speeds and all-chain drive. By 1920 the big single was back and for the next year the two-stroke was enlarged to 239cc and the big twin to 749cc.

For riding to work, James produced this 1951 Cadet model, fitted with the 122cc Villiers 10D engine, while the Captain had the 197cc version of the engine.

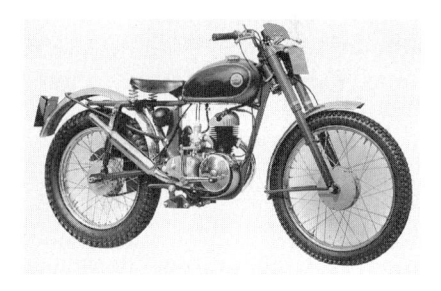

By 1957, this trials James had pivoted-fork rear suspension, but kept to the same 197cc Villiers 7E engine.

The two-stroke adopted chain final-drive for 1923, when the big single was reduced to 349cc and the same engine dimensions as the larger V-twin. To this range was added a 249cc single for 1924, when the 598cc returned but only for one year. In 1925 the two-stroke had gone, the largest single was of 550cc, but a 349cc ohv single was added to the list.

For 1928 the range of four-strokes had redesigned frames and saddle tanks, and was reduced to the 349cc single in sv or ohv form, the 550cc

James listed a line of twin-cylinder road models using the Villiers engine, to offer Superswift models in standard and Sports forms.

single and the 495cc V-twin. To this was added a lightweight with a 172cc Villiers engine. The big single was dropped for 1929, but the V-twin was joined by an ohv version with four speeds, this also an option for the sv model. This ohv twin was also listed in speedway form, when it had a single gear. A second two-stroke of 196cc appeared to suit that end of the market. In 1930 the V-twins reverted to three speeds with four an option, the 249cc single returned and was joined by a 247cc Villiers-powered model. At the year end the firm bought Baker and began to use that marque's frame design.

The depression years pointed the way James were to go, moving away from their well-built singles and twins to utility models, mainly powered by Villiers two-stroke engines. They did use a Rudge engine for one model in 1931 and, for a while, claimed to be building some of the two-stroke engines themselves.

The V-twins lasted up to 1935, along with four-stroke singles in the three usual sizes, but by then they were outnumbered by 148, 172, 196, 247 and 249cc two-strokes. In 1936 these were joined by a 122cc model that was to do sterling service in the war and 1938 brought a 98cc autocycle. This list carried the firm to 1940 and they then built the 122cc Military Lightweight for the services, who named it the 'Clockwork Mouse'.

Some enclosure and style reached the Comet, which continued to use the 99cc Villiers with just two speeds in the gearbox.

After the war they began with just the Superlux autocycle and 122cc ML, which was their wartime model with a change to maroon paint. This kept them going until 1949 when the range was revised and extended, other than the autocycle that had to wait one more year. There were three road motorcycles and two for competition, the former the 99cc Comet, 122cc Cadet and 197cc Captain, names that would continue to the last days of the firm. The engines were the Villiers 1F, 10D and 6E respectively and the two larger formed the basis of the competition versions, while all still had girder forks. This changed for 1950 when Dunlop telescopic forks using rubber cushions as springs were adopted, except for the autocycle, which was revised to use the 99cc 2F engine, and plunger rear suspension became an option for the Captain.

In 1951 the firm became part of the AMC group and this would have its effect in due course. For the machines there was just enclosure of the engine unit for the Comet to produce the Commodore, and for 1952 the 197cc competition model became the Colonel. This set the style of the range which moved on to mechanical-spring telescopic forks and a road Colonel with a 224cc 1H engine in 1954, with this and the Captain in a pivoted-fork frame. The 122cc engine was replaced by one of 147cc, the autocycle was dropped and this took the firm on to 1957.

There was a new Commodore for 1957 and this used the 249cc AMC two-stroke engine forced upon them by their group master, to be followed by a similar series in various sizes and also used by fellow group member Francis-Barnett. Unfortunately they were to prove troublesome and less reliable than the Villiers.

However, this was in the future, so James continued with its Comet, Cadet and Captain for 1958 when they were joined by the Cavalier, which used a 171cc AMC engine. The next year brought the 149cc Flying Cadet and 249cc trials Commando and scrambles Cotswold models, all with AMC power. For 1960 the Captain turned to the 199cc AMC engine, so only the Comet was left with the Villiers. In May that year the James Scooter was added, using a variant of the 149cc AMC engine and in the style of the type with enclosure and leading-link forks.

This continued into the new decade with a Sports Captain added in 1961 and the Superswift in 1962, this fitted with a 249cc Villiers 2T twin engine. It was joined by the Sports Superswift in the next year, when the competition models switched back to 246cc Villiers engines, the 32A for trials and the 36A with a Parkinson top-end conversion for scrambles. A second version with the 247cc Villiers Starmaker engine followed in 1963 and all benefited from having Norton forks fitted to them.

The 249cc AMC engines were dropped for 1963 when a new Cadet, still with the 149cc AMC unit, replaced the older model and was a carbon copy of the Francis-Barnett Plover, apart from the badges and colour finish. As with the other firm, it was replaced by a simpler model in 1965 and a reduced range offered for the next year. However, the problems of the group brought production to an end in October 1966, a sad end to a long and successful history.

JAP 1903–1908

Based in Tottenham, London, and best known as a supplier of engines to other firms, J.A. Prestwich was earlier involved in the cine-camera field. He built his first engine in 1901 and displayed complete machines at the Stanley Show held late in 1903.

The JAP motorcycle used a BSA frame and sprung forks, while the vertically mounted 3.5hp engine had ohv, an early use of this type. Both valves were opened by a single pushrod that moved a rocker arm which spanned both, the cam having track to

JAP were famous for their engines for many years, but did make a complete motorcycle for a short while, this one from 1904.

pull and push as required. A second machine used a 2.25hp inclined engine to offer a lightweight model.

The motorcycles continued for 1905 as 2.5 and 3.5hp, along with a car-like three-wheeler. In 1906 there was a 3.5hp single, a 6hp V-twin and a forecar having an 8hp three-cylinder in-line engine. By 1908 the firm was concentrating on engine manufacture, so the motorcycles were dropped.

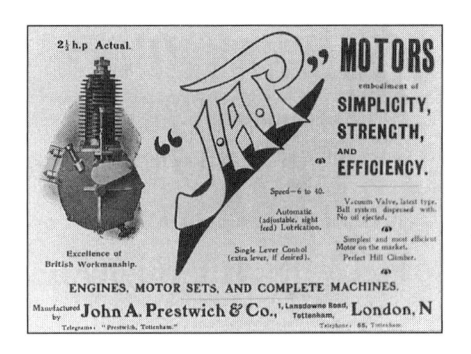

A 1903 JAP engine, from which simple beginnings came so many record breakers all over the world and, in particular, at Brooklands.

JD 1922–1926

This miniature machine was marketed by the Bowden Wire Company and had a 116cc two-stroke engine clipped to the inside of the front downtube of a safety-cycle pattern frame. Ignition was by magneto and the drive was taken by chain to a friction pulley working on the inside flange of the rear-wheel rim. A long slim fuel-tank clipped beneath the frame top-tube, braced but unsprung forks were standard and in every respect it was a motorized bicycle. A further model with an open ladies' style frame was added for 1923, after which there was little change until the final year, 1926, when only the gents' model was listed.

JEHU 1901–1905

Jehu was an early maker of primitives located in Brooke Street, Holborn, London using Minerva, MMC and their own engines. The 2hp model of 1903 was offered with belt or chain drive and with or without a free-engine facility. There were also 2.5,

The Jehu of 1903 was a typical primitive but did mount the engine in a good position, so the firm survived for a few years.

2.75 and 3hp models, mainly built as solos, but the largest also as a tandem forecar. For 1904 the chain-drive transmission added a countershaft and clutch.

JENNER-MINERVA 1904

These were primitives built with the Belgian Minerva engines, by A & C Jenner of Mitcham in Surrey.

JEPSON c.1920s

This was a range of machines sold by A. & W.N. Jepson from premises in Penny Street, Lancaster under their own label. The models with two- or four-stroke engines and a variety of transmissions would have been produced for them by one of the many factories in the Midlands, so would have been nothing remarkable, but possibly cheap.

JES 1909–1924

J.E. Smith of Gloucester offered this auxiliary motor set to fit within a bicycle frame and drive the rear wheel by belt. The engine was a 1hp 116cc four-stroke with a front-mounted gear-driven Fischer magneto.

First seen in 1909, it continued in this form as a bicycle with braced forks and the fuel tank hung from the top tube, and was also built and listed as the City and then as the Imp. For 1920 the engine was enlarged to 142cc and inclined in the frame, but the original simple concept remained. In 1921, a 170cc two-stroke miniature motorcycle with two speeds was added with a vertical engine, and was joined by a single-speed version for the next year.

A JES auxiliary engine unit installed in one of its early simple applications, although the range expanded post-Great War.

For 1923, the four-stroke was dropped, while the single-speed two-stroke ran on with a three-speed version. These were joined by a lightweight motorcycle with four-speed chain-transmission and the choice of 247cc two-stroke or 249cc ohv Blackburne engines. This was part of a move to more conventional machines, which took place along with the acquisition of the Connaught marque of Birmingham during 1924. The JES range for that year was just the two lightweight models, one still with the 247cc two-stroke but the other with a 348cc sv engine, both with three-speed Burman gearbox and chain-cum-belt transmission. During the year an auxiliary motor set was reintroduced, with a 123cc two-stroke engine, chain drive and in either a gents' or ladies' pattern bicycle-frame. It was also available as a conversion set, but the make went at the end of that year.

JESMO 1910–1915
This machine was built by Motordom of Spring Bank, Hull by a Mr Capes, who had been an agent for the JES engine unit. Aiming to improve on this, he used a Chater-Lea frame for his machine, so the result was a motorcycle rather than a cycle plus engine for its few short years.

JESMOND 1899–1904
Jesmond were one of the pioneers who fitted imported engines into strengthened bicycle frames. They were based in Newcastle-upon-Tyne and it was 1902 before they had a catalogue model, but prototypes would have been built earlier. They used a loop frame with solid forks having twin blades on each side. Into this went a Fafnir engine with direct-belt drive. By 1903 they had progressed to a 2.5hp water-cooled engine mounted in the loop frame that was formed to carry the water tank ahead of the top of the vertical downtube, with this further braced to the headstock. Control was by varying the exhaust-valve lift, but that year saw the manager, Mr J.R. Moore, leave to form the Dene company.

JH 1914–1916
James Howarth, who had worked for the Bradbury concern, offered his new range in October 1914, some months after the Great War had begun, thus showing some degree of optimism. He was based in Castle Mill Street, Mumps, Oldham and bottom of his range was a model fitted with a 269cc Villiers two-stroke engine, transmission being by direct-belt drive.

He also offered a machine fitted with a 2.75hp 349cc four-stroke Villiers engine, this model having a two-speed gear and chain-cum-belt drive. Larger models were listed using 6 or 8hp JAP or 6hp MAG engines, the last with a three-speed gearbox. In November 1914 a racing model fitted with a 3.5hp MAG engine was added, for some racing did take place at Brooklands during 1915.

For 1915, JH offered the two Villiers-powered machines plus models using 3.5 and 6hp MAG V-twin engines, the latter with a three- or

JES supplied a number of other firms with their engine unit, but this did not stop them offering their own machine, as seen here for 1914.

Water-cooled in 1903, the Jesmond was a pioneer in more than one sense, with its loop frame and braced headstock.

four-speed gearbox. For 1916 the engines were the 269cc two-stroke Villiers, a 3.5hp JAP and V-twins of 3.5, 6 or 8hp from MAG, or 6 or 8hp from JAP.

JNU 1921–1922

This marque was a product of John Nickson of Bamber Bridge, Preston, who also built the Nickson B machines at the same time. The first JNU had a 318cc two-stroke Dalm engine, an Albion two-speed gearbox and chain-cum-belt transmission; a kickstarter was an optional extra. Further specifications are uncertain and may well have been influenced by whatever residue of components remained from building the Nickson B, the firm's premier brand.

JOHNSON 1902

This make hailed from Scunthorpe, Lincolnshire and was a typical primitive, with a Minerva engine hung from the downtube of a heavy-duty bicycle frame. Cycle forks and brakes, belt drive and pedals completed the machine.

JOHNSON c.1921–1924

This was a flat twin-cylinder, two-stroke, single-speed, chain-drive cycle attachment; it originated in the USA, from where the engine had come to power generators in the trenches of the First World War. Post-war it was used over a bicycle rear wheel and was better known as the Economic, which see, but it had an equally short life in either case once supplies dried up.

JONES 1904

A primitive model powered by a Coronet engine mounted vertically in a diamond frame. Belt drive, pedals and braced forks completed the basic specification.

JONES 1936

A prototype autocycle built by G.H. Jones in conjunction with Villiers, and from which came their 98cc engine and the machine-type built by many firms. The engine differed from what followed, in that the pedal shaft ran through the clutch shaft, which made for a neat unit but would have given trouble if bent in a fall. Otherwise, it was the father of the autocycle and the engine became the Villiers Junior.

The 1936 Jones that was the prototype of the autocycle with Villiers engine, the only real change being the moved position of the pedal shaft.

JOYBIKE 1958–1960

The Joybike was produced by H.V. Powell (Cycles) Ltd of Birchfield Road, Birmingham as a moped or a scooterette powered by either a 50cc Trojan or 79cc JAP two-stroke engine. The scooterette had a two-speed gearbox in-unit with the engine, telescopic forks and 4in drum brakes, while the moped had a single speed, no suspension and smaller brakes. Both had 23in wheels and a limited market, while, for 1960 only, the single-speed 79cc JAP engine was listed with telescopic forks, but in this form failed to qualify as a moped.

JP 1913–1914

Offered early in 1913 by John Piggott of Cheapside, London, this machine had a 2.75hp engine, belt drive and sprung forks. A hub gear was an option and the machine was still listed in the middle of the next year, soon to become a war casualty.

The 1904 Jones was a primitive with a Coronet engine in a diamond frame and few could have been built.

John Piggott offered his JP for just two years, but his machine then became a war casualty and maybe he, too, fell in the conflict.

JUCKES 1902–1925

This make was built by the Efficient Motor & Engineering Co., East End Works, Bilston Road, Wolverhampton, who produced road engines, marine engines and gearboxes among their products, and built their first motorcycle in 1902. Machines were built in a very small way until the 1920s when they went into proper production of a range powered by their own two-stroke engines.

The most basic model had direct-belt drive, but was also offered with four-speed gearbox and chain-cum-belt drive. A slightly larger engine was an option and a machine could be lightened and tuned. They were well made and finished.

In 1924 a model fitted with a 349cc ohv engine appeared, with all-chain drive and a four-speed gearbox. There were two-strokes, one of 277cc with belt drive, the other bored out to 293cc with chain drive. Both could have two, three or four speeds, and all models were well finished in black and gold.

For 1925 they offered the four-stroke in sv or ohv form and the 277cc two-stroke, all having chain drive and the four-speed gearbox. Bracing tubes were added on each side of the frame to run from the headstock to the rear wheel, but by then the firm was in financial difficulties. So ended an underrated marque.

JUNO 1905–1924

This name was used by the Metropolitan Machinists' Co. Bishopsgate, London, who sold machines and parts, often built to order. They began with a 3hp solo and 3.5hp forecar using Fafnir engines, but later turned to Precision, JAP and the 269cc Villiers. Belt drive, one or two speeds and Druid forks were typical of the era, but this was a small firm and production limited.

Having stopped in 1915, they resumed post-war in a modest way, building much to order using the major items their customers requested. This continued to at least 1924 when, as the Juno Cycle Company, Bishopsgate, they were advertising a 147cc Villiers-powered lightweight with two-speed gearbox and electric lighting.

JUPP 1921–1925

One of the numerous scooters on the market at this date, it was introduced by L. Jupp of Tunbridge Wells in Kent, who later formed the Jupp Motor Company to produce the machine. An open frame with good weather shielding, 18in wire-wheels, Brampton spring forks and a 269cc Villiers two-stroke engine placed well forward and low down, formed the basis of the Jupp. A hand starter brought the engine to life and transmission was arranged through a two-speed Sturmey-Archer gearbox with all-chain drive. It was considered one of the best machines of its type by the press. A 269cc two-stroke Liberty engine replaced the Villiers for 1922 and a model suitable for carrying a passenger was evolved.

As the scooter craze went and sales fell, Jupp redesigned and brought out a miniature motorcycle with a 147cc Villiers engine, two-speed Albion gearbox and chain-cum-belt transmission. This, like its predecessor, was enclosed by panelling and must be considered as an all-weather machine, its semi-open frame layout making it suitable for either sex. The design deserved to thrive, but the uncertain years of the mid-1920s caused the company to fail.

K

KD 1908–1909
A bicycle attachment, offered by Leo Ripault of Poland Street, Oxford Street, London, that fitted within the main frame to drive the rear wheel by belt, tensioned by a jockey-pulley. Two engine powers, of 1.75 and 2hp, were available and the make remained in the lists for two years.

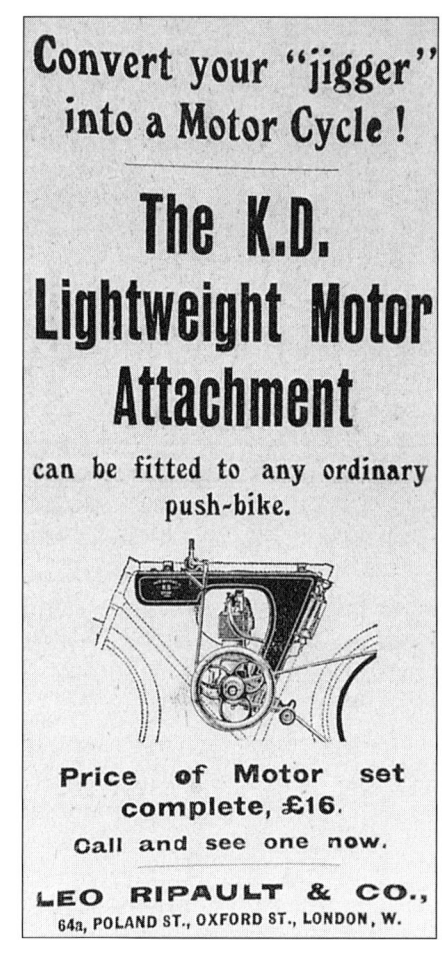

Convert your "jigger" into a Motor Cycle!

The K.D. Lightweight Motor Attachment

can be fitted to any ordinary push-bike.

Price of Motor set complete, £16.
Call and see one now.

LEO RIPAULT & CO.,
64a, POLAND ST., OXFORD ST., LONDON, W.

The KD was a late-Edwardian attachment suitable for fitting to a standard bicycle, to take the work out of riding it.

KELLY 1921
This was an unconventional open-frame machine of very primitive design. A 318cc two-stroke Dalm engine and two-speed Sturmey-Archer gearbox were both sprung by means of a leaf spring together with the rider's saddle and a rear carrier; this provided insulation from the main frame and forks and thus from road shocks. However, when under test by a specialist magazine, the reporter discovered that uncoordinated movement between the gearbox output and rear wheel caused the drive to become deranged and the test had to be curtailed. Modifications were said to be in hand, but nothing further was heard of this effort from Kelly Patent Cycles, of Black Lion Street, Brighton, in Sussex.

KEMPTON 1921–1922
An ultra-lightweight machine, of the type known at the time as a Miniature, the Kempton adopted the 124cc ohv ABC engine previously used in the Skootamota. This, with its horizontal cylinder facing forwards, was coupled to a two-speed gearbox by chain, with belt final-drive. A Willis carburettor provided the mixture and 26in diameter wheels were used. The frame layout gave a very low seating position, as the top tube sloped steeply down from the steering head, thus providing a feeling of security for those timid riders at which the machine was aimed.

KENILWORTH 1919–1924
This machine, built by Captain Smith-Clarke for his wife, was more of a small motorcycle than a scooter with central engine and 18in wire-wheels. It had front and rear suspension plus some panelling to enclose the rear wheel, but without saddle and still with the scooter open-frame. The 142cc Norman four-stroke engine drove by Whittle belt to a countershaft with chain final-drive and was put into production by Booth Bros of Coventry.

Customers did not have to stand for too long, for a saddle was soon added, this linked by a subframe to footboards and all sprung together for comfort. A clutch was incorporated by 1922 and a handle starter followed the next year, when the transmission changed to friction with variable ratios and a three-wheeled box carrier model was devised. This had twin front-wheels after the fashion of the early forecars. By this date the makers had become Kenilworth Utility Motors of Much Park Street, in Coventry and the machine became the sporting Miniature motorcycle with the Norman engine enlarged to 170cc, although the friction transmission remained. However, the general concept had already run its course and production ended during 1924. Nevertheless, the Kenilworth had outlasted most of its kind, a tribute to the sound thinking behind its original conception.

KENTISH WHEEL c.1908
This model was a copy of the early Triumph single with its sv engine, belt drive, diamond frame and rocking front fork. Such copying is never too popular in any sphere, so the Wheel soon rolled on out of sight.

KERRY 1902–1915 AND 1960–1967
Sold by the East London Rubber Co. of Shoreditch, these machines used Belgian Kelecom and FN engines in their early days. A loop frame with curved downtube was used, along with belt drive and braced forks in typical high-built primitive form.

The 1903 Kerry with an imported engine installed in the loop frame with braced forks.

Kerry offered a Ladies model in 1904, this having a special loop-frame to accommodate the engine with skirt clearance.

There were various engine powers and a ladies' model and, in 1906, they were linked to Abingdon to add V-twins to their range. In time they were sold as the Kerry-Abingdon, (*see also* Abingdon) using their engines, and continued with a 3.5hp single and 6hp V-twin to 1915. Production then ceased but the name did appear once again, from 1960 to 1967, on a range of imported mopeds sold as the Kerry Capitano.

KESTREL 1903
A typical primitive combining a heavy-duty bicycle frame with a Minerva or MMC engine, usually hung from the downtube. Direct-belt drive, some fittings and a new transfer added another make, no doubt built by a cycle dealer.

KESTREL 1980
Based in Southampton, this firm produced mopeds using Italian Minarelli engine units hung from a spine frame. These were listed as the KRM50 in three forms: an automatic, four speeds, and with the addition of a fairing. The bodywork was stylish with a dummy tank, seat fairing and side panels in glass-fibre, and the machine

By 1910 the marque name was Kerry-Abingdon, with the design quite conventional for that period.

A short-lived British-based moped, the Kestrel was assembled from mainly Italian components but was soon gone from the market.

was on view at the late-1980 Earls Court show. However, no more was heard of this venture.

KIEFT 1955–1957
This range of moped and scooter models came from the German Hercules firm, but were assembled in Wolverhampton by Kieft. Typical of the decade, the moped had a Sachs two-stroke two-speed engine unit hung from a pressed-steel, spine frame. There was no rear suspension, but rubber in torsion gave some movement to the front wheel. The scooter had a 191cc Sachs engine, four speeds and electric start under typical bodywork.

For 1957 the range was extended and added two scooters fitted with Villiers engines of 147 or 197cc. The original moped was joined by one with rear suspension and a further model was the Hercules motorcycle with a 200cc Ilo engine. During the year a further moped, the Sport model, was added and this was more a motorcycle and had three speeds.

However, in September 1957, distribution of the Hercules moved on from Kieft to BP Scooters of Wolverhampton and were then sold under the Prior name.

KING 1901–1905
King was a firm based in Cambridge which began with tricycles but later moved to motorcycles. Their 1903 model was a typical primitive, having its 2.75hp MMC engine mounted vertically, driving the rear wheel by belt. They offered 3.5 or 4hp, water-cooled engines as options in 1903, but for 1904 settled for 2.75 to 3.5hp engines from Daw or MMC. Direct-belt drive or two speeds and chain were available, and a forecar was listed.

Tricycles first and then solos, such as this 1903 model with 2.75hp MMC, were built by King during the firm's short life.

KINGSBURY 1919–1923
Kingsbury were an aircraft firm based in Croydon, Surrey, who entered the scooter market after the Great War with a model that put the 2hp two-stroke engine at the front of the

platform frame. It drove the rear wheel by chain via a countershaft, had disc wheels with brakes and front suspension by plungers. Riders were expected to stand, although a seat did become an option in time.

During 1920, a true lightweight motorcycle joined the scooter; it was powered by the same 254cc two-stroke engine, but with two-speed transmission by chain and belt through the maker's own gearbox. In all respects it was conventional for its date and thus carried the company forward into 1921 as the scooter boom quickly faded taking the original Kingsbury product with it. Respite was short lived however, for the lightweight too failed to be listed for the next year, bringing to an end the brief existence of the marque sold by London & Midland Motors of London W1.

KINGSLAND 1902
This firm was based in North London and offered a typical primitive with vertical aiv engine, single-speed belt drive and rigid forks. Both down- and seat-tubes were curved to follow the line of the wheels and the lower frame-tube ran along from the crankcase front at crankshaft level past the pedal shaft to the rear wheel in a straight line. It was short-lived.

KING'S OWN 1910
A machine that ran at Brooklands in April 1910, ridden by E.B. Ware, powered by an 8hp JAP V-twin engine, and with a P&M two-speed gear and all-chain drive.

KINGSWAY 1920
A lightweight machine with the 269cc two-stroke Arden engine, CAV magneto, B&B carburettor, Best & Lloyd lubricator, Lycetts leather pan saddle and either direct-belt drive or two-speed countershaft gearbox with chain-cum-belt. It was therefore much as many other contenders with little to distinguish it, except that the makers, the Kingsway Motor Cycle Company of Stoke, Coventry, chose to fit the 'Y' spring fork in place of a

Kingsbury was a post-Great War marque that began with a scooter and then used the same engine for this lightweight.

better known proprietary item. Neither the fork nor the Kingsway would establish themselves in the long term.

KIRMER 1915–1917
This name came from Kirk & Merifield of Bradford Street, Birmingham, who began making cycles in 1893 and entered the motorcycle market in 1913 with the Arrow machines. These were simple lightweights with 211cc two-stroke engines from Levis and Precision, basic transmission and usual fittings. The Kirmer name seems to have been used for machines sold in Australia, where they fitted the Precision engine and a Burman two-speed gearbox.

KNIGHT 1894, 1914
J.H. Knight of Farnham built a steam tricar around 1894 and twenty years later produced one powered by a water-cooled four-stroke engine. A two-speed gear was provided and the tricycle had a single front-wheel with tiller steering.

KRM 1973
Early in 1973 Kingston Racing Motors from Hull showed a 348cc racing four at a London show. It was in the style of that time with the cylinders inclined forward, dohc, four carburettors, four exhaust pipes with megaphones, and Lumenition electronic ignition. The crankcase split horizontally, the crankshaft ran on six plain bearings and there were plain big-ends. A centre gear drove a countershaft from which there was chain drive to the camshafts, the ignition rotor and a distributor mounted on their ends.

The engine and six-speed gearbox was hung from a tubular spine frame with conventional suspension, wire wheels and disc brakes front and rear. A fairing was fitted and the machine advertised as the Silver Streak.

It was an enterprising effort but bulky when compared to the MV Agusta at the same show, highlighting the years of experience needed to achieve a really tucked-in design. No more was heard of the KRM.

KUHN 1968–1972
Gus Kuhn raced in the TT, at Brooklands and on the cinders in pre-war days and afterwards built up a business in Stockwell, London. In 1968, the firm changed its emphasis from cars to motorcycles and began customizing Norton models, supporting this with an extensive racing programme. They used the Commando for production machine events and a pair of Seeley singles for the open race classes.

From this came the Gus Kuhn Norton, a café racer that was available in a variety of specifications using the custom list. Later they moved on to BMW flat twins, so the Norton side faded.

KUMFURT 1914–1916
Based at Cookham Rise, Berkshire this was another firm that optimistically entered the market late in 1914, the German ring to the name hardly one to enthuse the customers. Their smallest model used the 269cc Villiers two-stroke engine, which drove the Roc two-speed gearbox by chain, final drive being by belt. A larger single had a 499cc Precision sv engine, Sturmey-Archer gearbox and belt final-drive, while there was also a model fitted with a 655cc JAP V-twin engine.

The range was little altered for 1915, although a 2hp model with Precision engine, two-speed gearbox

Transport side by side was provided by the 1904 Kyma Light Car, which carried two and had the option of one- or two-cylinder engines.

and chain-cum-belt transmission was added. They continued to be listed for 1916 but then ceased production.

KYMA 1903–1904

This firm, based in Peckham Rye in London, produced a Sociable tricycle in 1903, the front section being basically motorcycle and the rear a wickerwork body offering two seats, side by side. Two engine sizes were listed, one of 2.75hp and air-cooled, the other of 4hp and water-cooled. The transmission was by chain to a countershaft and thence by belt on each side to the rear wheels. A two-speed gear was included and steering was by wheel. By 1904 the power was by the 4hp engine or by a 5hp V-twin.

KYNOCH 1904–1913

A firm in Witton, Birmingham, that began with a model having a 2.75hp engine and chain drive. At that time they also built a couple of machines for Hayden Green with the fuel carried in the frame tubes, that were larger than normal to suit. The machine also had rear suspension and was powered by a Simms engine.

As sometimes happened, there was no mention of Kynoch for several years, but they surfaced once more in 1912 with a model fitted with a

Basic specification for the 1904 Kynoch included chain drive and an external-contracting front brake.

By 1912, Kynoch were back in the market with a conventional machine, which was offered with a range of specifications.

3.5hp JAP or Precision engine. The machine had a BSA two-speed gear or free-engine option, and was fitted with Druid forks. For 1913 only JAP engines were used, either a 4hp single or a 6hp twin, driving a Sturmey-Archer three-speed hub gear, the machine having belt final-drive. The single was also listed with direct-belt drive.

KYRLE 1903

Unlike most of their kind, G & W Butcher of Brookend Street, Ross-on-Wye claimed to make the engine as well as the cycle parts of their Kyrle models. As they were but a country town cycle business, this seems unlikely, but they may have had access to foundry and machining capacity locally that permitted them to translate their own ideas into metal, for a short time.

◆ L ◆

LADIES PACER 1914–1915
First seen in 1914 and also known as the Pacer, this machine was designed for ladies by K. Millard & Co. of Guernsey. It had an open frame, Druid forks, and was driven by a small 1hp JES engine that had an overhead inlet-valve. Transmission was by a round belt that ran over a tension pulley to the rear wheel. It was listed for 1915 but no later.

This primitive 1903 Lagonda had their own engine hung from the frame, with belt drive to the rear wheel.

LAGONDA 1902–1907
Later to become a famous car producer, this Staines, Middlesex-based firm began with tricycles but then built motorcycles. Their 1903 solo used their own 2.75hp engine hung from the frame downtube and was of conventional design.

For 1904 they offered a forecar fitted with a 5hp engine, inclined in the frame, driving the rear wheel through clutch, two-speed gear and chains. The solo model's power went up to 3.5hp, while a 4.5hp was also listed. By 1906 the 3.5hp model had an inclined engine and leading-link forks, but retained direct-belt drive, continuing in this form for 1907. Then Wilbur Gunn, the factory owner and an American of Scots descent, turned to cars.

LAKE & ELLIOT c.1904–1905
This company was well known for its general engineering products for car and motorcycle repair work, sold under the Millennium label in the early days. They are said to have built a 3hp motorcycle in Edwardian times, no doubt using proprietary parts, but became more famous for the products such as hydraulic car jacks that came from their Braintree, Essex, works.

LANCER 1904
Built in Coventry using an upright Minerva engine set in a diamond frame, this machine had belt drive and braced forks. Powers of 2, 2.75 and 3.5hp were listed, along with a free-engine option during the make's brief life.

LARGE 1909
A rather dated outline was presented by the only known example of this marque, which fitted the heavy early design of the De Dion aiv four-stroke engine. Unsprung and unbraced front forks and direct-belt drive were also features soon to be out of their time. Makers were Large & Company, of Chorlton-cum-Hardy, a suburb of the city of Manchester. This was to be a very short-lived model.

LAWSON 1900–1901
As well as promoting his companies, Lawson did produce, or had made, machines bearing his own name. One was on the lines of the Pennington, having the engine hung out behind the rear wheel, which it drove by belt. Another, shown in 1901, had its engine on one side of the front fork and the flywheel on the other. It was

By 1905 Lagonda had this fine forecar on offer, which had more car aspects than motorcycle, including suspension all round.

built by the Crypto Works but was not a success.

LAWSON 1948
This was a special based on a Ner-a-Car of the 1920s and built by Alec Lawson of the Sackville firm in Sparkhill, Birmingham, who supplied accessories to the trade. It differed from than the usual Ner-a-Car, while retaining the feet-first posture with the low seat set between the wheels, for the frame was extended some 5in (12cm). In addition there was an extensive body in aluminium, outrigger wheels, twin headlamps, a windscreen, facia for the instruments and an exhaust system that used the main frame members as silencers with some of the hot gases piped into the handlebars for warmth when needed.

If this was not enough, the engine used, designed and built by a Mr Haythorn, was a 288cc air-cooled in-line ohc four. This drove a three-speed gearbox bolted directly to it with a bevel drive for the rear chain. It was quite an achievement by both men, but there was never any intention to market it.

L&C was a new name for the Leonard firm of the previous year and lasted no longer, while still having its French connections.

L&C 1904
Lurquin & Coudert was the new, 1904, name for the Leonard firm located in Long Acre, London and they offered 2.75 and 3.5hp models using MMC engines. Typical primitives, they had braced forks and belt drive but were short-lived.

LEADER 1903–1908

A runner and award winner in the 1904 1,000-mile trial, this machine was built by Eli Clarke of Bristol, using a 2hp Minerva engine hung from the downtube. It had Preston Weir wheels, each built in two parts to absorb road shocks.

The make was listed in 1906 and by 1908 used mainly JAP engines, the singles being of 2.5, 3.5 and 4.5hp and the V-twins of 6, 7 or 9hp. A 3.5hp Fafnir single was also offered, but little more was heard of the make.

LEA-FRANCIS 1912–1924

Richard Lea and Graham Francis were bicycle makers from 1895 and dabbled briefly with cars around 1904 before they turned to motorcycles in 1912. Based in Lower Ford Street, Coventry, their one model introduced in August that year had a 3.25hp JAP V-twin engine with chain-driven Bosch magneto, a two-speed gearbox, plate clutch and fully-enclosed chain final-drive. The forks were Druid and dummy-rim brakes went on both wheels. The aim was to offer a sound tourer with comfort and reliability the keynotes, and the model continued by itself until joined in 1914 by a prototype combination using a 6hp V-twin MAG engine. This was shelved due to the outbreak of war, while the 3.25hp model was up-rated to a 3.5hp JAP V-twin engine and ran on alone to 1916 with a three-speed gearbox from the year before.

The same model, but with only two speeds, reappeared for 1919 to be joined by one with a 3.5hp MAG engine the next year. This, plus a 5hp version, were the 1921 models and had three speeds, the engine capacities being 495cc and 592cc. The two ran on, along with a stripped sports version of the 3.5hp model for 1922 only. There was a Burman gearbox for the 592cc machine in 1923, this alone being offered for 1924, after which motorcycle production ceased, although the cars that had been built from 1920 were to run on to 1953, with revival attempts in 1960 and 1978.

LEECHAM 1914

Douglas Leecham unveiled his frame design in June 1914, it being of the loop type with braced headstock. This meant that the petrol tank had to be of the saddle type, long before it became the fashion, while the machine had sprung forks, a sv engine and direct belt drive. It was not the best of times for a small firm to launch its new design and no more was heard of it.

LEONARD 1903–1904

This was a small firm located in Long Acre, London, run by J.J. Leonard, whose machines used Minerva, MMC or Fafnir engines fitted into a conventional loop frame. Braced forks and belt drive were used, as was then the norm. For 1904, the engine became the 3.5hp MMC but a 2.75hp was also listed. During the year, the make changed its name to L&C, or Lurquin & Coudert.

Leonard was the predecessor of L&C, which offered more of an engine range but was otherwise similar.

LETHBRIDGE 1923

Two-stroke engines of the vintage years were invariably distinguished by a huge outside flywheel; the designer of the Lethbridge, however, chose an internal pair for his 293cc engine. It was thus unusual and also had a special scavenging device claimed to cool the sparking plug points, the device appearing as a well-finned external passageway connecting crankcase to cylinder head. In other respects the model was standard, with a two-speed Burman gearbox having both clutch and kickstart and all-chain drive.

Attempting to ensure ready public acceptance for the marque, a further model with the 348cc sv Blackburne engine was also offered. This had a three-speed Burman gearbox, all-chain drive, internal expanding Webb brakes to both wheels and Maplestone centre-spring forks. A BTH Sparklight electric lighting set was listed as an option for either model, but, notwithstanding all this, Lethbridge Motors of Birmingham were unable to secure a permanent place for themselves in the market.

LE VACK 1923

Although fully employed at the time by the famous JAP engine factory and a record breaking rider of other manufacturers' machines fitted with the Tottenham-built engine, ace tuner and rider Bert Le Vack also lent his name to a sporting motorcycle. The sole model had a 344cc ohv JAP engine, with three-speed Burman gearbox and all-chain drive and was available only during 1923.

LEVIS 1911–1940

Early in 1911, Howard Newey, designer of the Levis, was seen riding a small two-stroke model that was well able to carry a passenger despite not having pedals. The firm had their works in Stechford, Birmingham, which was run by the Butterfield brothers.

The machine was soon on the market, to be sold first as the Baby but then as the Popular, which became abbreviated to Levis Pop. It was indeed popular, especially for new riders, for it was such a simple

Although listed as the 'Baby' for 1912, the 211cc Levis two-stroke was soon known as the Levis Pop, and was simple and easy to ride.

The 247cc engine went into this model Z Levis of 1931, which gained foot-change for its three speeds plus the option of four.

machine, just a 211cc two-stroke engine with magneto ignition and direct-belt drive. Inside the engine went a one-piece crankshaft, but lubrication was by drip feed from a separate oil tank, which avoided the problems of mixing petrol with oil. There was also a ladies' model with open frame and a heavier 269cc version, both similar and with Druid forks.

The larger model grew to 293cc for 1914, a two-speed version of this appeared and 1915 saw a 349cc model as well. However, it was the Pop that remained popular and, post-war, the only model for 1919 and 1920. Then came a 247cc TT model in 1921, for the firm had taken the first three places in the 1920 Junior 250cc TT, were to be second in 1921 and won again in 1922, also winning the French and Belgium that year.

The simple Pop ran on to 1924 but other versions were more complex, added a gearbox and needed an alternative engine stretched to 247cc to keep the performance. In this they lost the basic simplicity of the original. By 1926 the 247cc was the only capacity, listed in two forms, increased to three and joined by a 346cc ohv

One of the four-stroke Levis singles of the period was this 1935 D Special, with its ohv pushrods in a single tube suggesting ohc.

four-stroke for 1927. This was joined by a 247cc six-port two-stroke in 1929, while the new decade brought a move to four-stroke power. The 247cc two-stroke did continue through the years, joined by a four-stroke range of 247, 346 and 498cc models, most with ohv, plus one of 591cc from 1937.

There was also a 247cc ohc model for 1934 that had chain drive to the camshaft but kept the total-loss lubrication system the firm used for its four-strokes. During the decade the models followed the general trends and the machines were always well made, albeit not in large numbers. Those who knew them were sorry to see production come to an end in 1940.

The real ohc Levis was this 247cc CB of 1935, with chain camshaft-drive and Weller blade-tensioner in the alloy housing.

By 1939, the Levis 346 and 498cc singles were available in a new frame with plunger rear-suspension units linked hydraulically.

LGC 1928–1931 AND 1949
The Leonard Gundle Motor Co. was based in Hockley, Birmingham and made butchers' cycles and ice-cream trikes. Len added motorcycles in 1928 with three JAP-powered models using a 300cc sv and a 346cc ohv engine, the latter in single or twin-port form. All drove a three-speed

Len Gundle built ice-cream trikes but, in 1928, added LGC motorcycles with JAP engines, either a 300cc sv or this 346ohv, for a few years.

gearbox, either from Albion or Burman, and had a diamond frame, girder forks and the style of the vintage period. A model with a 247cc Villiers engine was added for 1929 and this small range continued on to 1931, after which Len went back to his bicycles.

The name returned post-war on a tricycle powered by a 197cc Villiers engine with three-speed gearbox. The rear half was a conventional motorcycle but at the front end went two wheels, of the same size as the rear, with a seat mounted between them. A tube ran behind this for steering and to carry the controls, while the result was just as a forecar from the early days. A commercial body was also to be offered but no more was heard of the project.

L&H 1923–1925
Better known for its holiday beaches, the Devon coastal town of Ilfracombe was also home for a short time to the L&H big twin, made by Messrs Luxmore & Hubbard. A 976cc sv V-twin JAP engine provided the power and, to cope with the hilly terrain thereabouts, a four-speed Jardine gearbox was wisely chosen. Being so far from the centre of industry a small local need would have existed at the time, but once that had been filled, demand for the L&H evaporated.

LIGHTNING 1900
Arthur Burgess operated the Lightning Cycle & Motor Works in Malvern, Worcestershire and, from premises at Barnards Green, offered a range of vehicles extending from pedal

cycles to motor cars. In between came a motorized Quadricycle, which was of De Dion form, but with twin front-wheels and an upholstered seat between them. It was a popular layout for its day and although the device carried the Lightning marque name, indications are that it was probably built for them by Components Limited of Selly Oak, Birmingham, who themselves sold under the famous Ariel name.

LILY 1914–1915
Lily were another hopeful firm that first appeared late in 1914 to offer a small range of models. One used the 269cc Villiers two-stroke engine, or a Peco of the same size, to drive a two-speed Albion gearbox with belt final-drive. Others used 2.75 or 3.5hp TDC sv engines and a similar transmission, but the make only lasted for a few months.

LINCOLN ELK 1902–1925
This name was first seen on bicycles and the marque was built at Broadgate, Lincoln by James Kirby with his partner Edwards. By 1902, when Kirby was in his sixties and minus partner, the first powered model appeared, a heavy-duty bicycle fitted with an engine.

By 1905, the model had a 2.25hp engine fitted to a loop frame with braced forks and belt drive, and in time came 3 and 3.5hp engines made by the firm. There were also Druid forks and, for 1912, an ingenious two-speed gear where a chain-driven countershaft had two clutches to engage either a belt drive to the rear wheel or a chain, these being on either side of the machine and giving the two ratios. A 6hp V-twin was added for 1914 to join 2.25 and 4.25 hp singles, all to run on to 1916.

Post-war, there were three sv models, singles of 349 and 597cc, and a 771cc V-twin, that ran on to 1925, with the option of a direct-belt drive version of the smallest in 1922 and all-chain drive on all three from 1924. Production came to an end with James Kirby then well into his eighties.

LINDSAY 1904–1905
This Clerkenwell, London firm showed a forecar at the late-1904 Stanley Show, the machine having a form of variable gearing in its transmission, achieved by moving the V-belt pulley flanges.

Making your debut early in 1914 proved to be a mistake for the Little Giant, who offered this neat model for their customers.

LITTLE GIANT 1914
Based in Uxbridge, Middlesex, this firm offered a single model powered by a 2hp Precision engine that drove a two-speed gearbox incorporated in the crankcase. Either belt or chain final-drive was available, while Druid forks were fitted and a ladies' model offered. This turned out to be another short-lived effort.

LIVINGSTONE 1912
Assembled in Newport, South Wales, by Ashton & Sons, this model, possibly a one-off, was built to order using a 2.75hp Arno engine. It had 24in wheels to achieve a low saddle height, with rigid forks and belt drive.

LLOYD 1902–1903
One of several Lloyd firms, this was the earliest and founded by W.A. Lloyd as Cycle Fittings Ltd in Birmingham, using their own 2hp engine and primitive fittings. W.A. had earlier been involved with W.J. Lloyd at Quadrant, the latter moving on to form LMC in 1903 while W.A.

A Lincoln Elk of pre-First World War days with two speeds and two final drives: the belt on the left for high speed and the chain on the right for low.

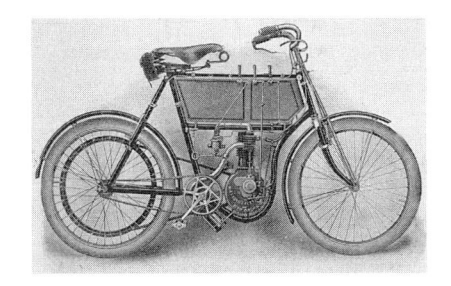

The earliest of the Lloyd marque names was used by W.A. Lloyd and resulted in this model for 1905; he had been involved earlier with W.J. Lloyd at Quadrant.

produced the Dreadnought from 1915 to 1922.

LLOYD THOMAS c.1905–1910

Hailing from Wales, this Edwardian marque used imported power and direct-belt drive with a single speed. Early models fitted a 3hp aiv Antoine engine but later ones had the 2hp sv Minerva. All were typical of the period, while production was limited.

LMC 1903–1922

The Lloyd Motor Engineering Co. of Monument Road, Birmingham began building machines in 1903 under the owner's name. He was W.J. Lloyd, a component maker, involved with Quadrant at one time, and his first machines were built up using stock parts from his stores.

Stevens engines were used at first and the machines were typical of the time, being sold as the LMC by 1908, when the 3.5hp single was joined by a 2.75hp vertical twin which was devoid of cooling fins. The cylinders were separate, to allow air to flow between them; the firm claimed no overheating problems, but it was not seen again. A larger single was added for 1912 and gained a two-speed gear for 1914, with a V-twin model in 1915, along with other transmission options including a countershaft gearbox for 1916.

They returned in 1919 with a 597cc single and a 842cc V-twin, both with three-speed gearbox. There was only the twin for 1920, it being also available in overseas form with a larger tank and different suspension. In 1921 a 960cc V-twin joined the smaller and these two ran on for one more year with all-chain drive, the belt remaining an option for the 842cc model.

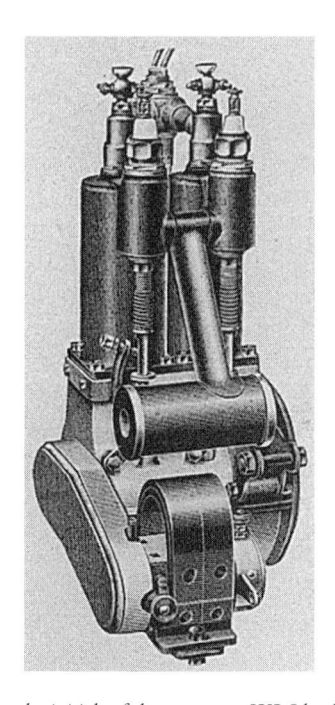

One of several LMC models listed for 1912, with interesting features. The marque was to survive to the post-Great War era using V-twins.

Using the initials of the name saw W.J. Lloyd in his own works, no longer with W.A. or Quadrant. Shown is the vertical twin, which lacked fins and was not seen again.

LOMBARD c.1914

Little is known of this marque, which must have had the briefest of time in the marketplace. It was most likely very basic with the usual 269cc Villiers two-stroke engine and direct-belt drive.

Available for just one year, the London machine used their own engine made under licence from Rex.

LONDON 1904

London was a small business, located in Clapham, London, that offered a 3.5hp model in 1904, the machine having the diamond frame, braced forks and belt drive of the typical primitive of the period. It was short-lived and not heard of again.

LONDON AUTO COMPANY 1896–1906

Claiming to have been established as early as 1896, the London Auto Company specialized in assembling models from a wide range of component parts. They would build a machine to individual specification, which doubtless appealed to those who wished to convert their fantasy designs into metal. Engines from JAP, Peugeot, Minerva, Zedelm, Brown, Stevens and others were fitted into frames of various outlines. They were suppliers to the colonies and to the trade, so doubtless constructed many own-badged machines for mail-order houses and the like. A one-year guarantee on all machines showed confidence in their standards of workmanship.

LOW 1922

Professor Archibald Montgomery Low was a major figure in the first fifty years of the British motorcycle, his agile and inventive mind and aptitude for all matters administrative inevitably ensured his involvement with the trade and the sport. Early in 1922, he demonstrated an 'ideal' design of machine with a pressed-steel frame, enclosure of the working parts, shaft drive and a four-cylinder two-stroke engine. This was a three-port design displacing 493cc, with its air-cooled cylinders in a monobloc casting and set in-line with the frame. Coil ignition was through a skew-gear-driven distributor and a single Binks carburettor attended to mixture needs. A Rotax dynamo, gear-driven from the one-piece crankshaft, provided battery charging with an electric lighting set included in the specification. A three-speed gearbox was in-unit with the engine.

The experimental machine had covered at least 1,500 miles (2,415km) by February 1922 and a number of modifications were said to be in hand, although the likely selling price for a production model was admitted to be too much for it to be a viable proposition. It was claimed to be the first ever four-cylinder two-stroke motorcycle and in its external appearance somewhat resembled the Pullin motorcycle. The Low did not proceed beyond the stage of an interesting exercise.

LUCAS 1952–1965
Charlie Lucas began by building speedway machines in Watford using JAP engines. Later came similar style grass-track models, with the addition of gearbox and brakes, and later still some for road racing.

Lugton had a brief life in London, producing a machine typical of the time and era, before they folded when the war came.

LUCKHUST 1965–c.1978
Reg Luckhust built both grass track and speedway machines down in Kent, both conforming to the format of the times. He used JAP and other makes of engine.

LUGTON 1913–1914
Based in Old Street, London, Lugton offered a 3.5hp model with belt drive and sprung forks. The engines were most likely from Precision or JAP and output must have been minimal, as no more was heard of the firm.

LYLE PRECISION 1912–1913
This model was built in Portsmouth using a 600cc Precision engine and standard components including Druid forks, but was short lived.

◆ M ◆

MAB 1909–1910
Built by A.G. Fenn of London and shown at the late-1909 Stanley show, this machine had a 2.75hp JAP engine and belt drive. It was also listed with a 3.5hp Peugeot V-twin engine but little more was heard of the make.

MABON 1903–1908
A small producer, based in Clerkenwell Road, London, who built a primitive using their own 3.25hp engine. They sold the Phoenix Trimo as a forecar as well at first, but for 1905 kept to their belt-driven solo. Sprung forks, magneto ignition and a free-engine clutch were added for 1906. For 1908 they listed engines as their own 3.5hp single or a 6hp V-twin Sarolea, but were not mentioned any more.

MACBETH 1904–1913
This Birmingham firm used the Minerva engine fitted to a typical frame of the period for their early model, but soon ceased manufacture and returned to the retail trade and bicycles.

They were back at the late-1911 Olympia show with Macbeth machines using their own or a Precision 3.5hp engine. A two-speed Roc gear option, belt drive and Druid forks completed a conventional design. The make was listed for 1913 as a 3.5hp model with an Armstrong three-speed hub gear, but still with the belt drive.

MACKLUM 1920
Simple scooter-style machine with 16in wire-wheels, but showing originality in that the foot platform was a one-piece steel stamping that doubled as the frame. The two-stroke 292cc Union engine was sited over the front wheel, which it drove by chain. Designed by F. McCallum, it was built in the works of Alfred Wiseman Ltd, makers of Verus and Sirrah motorcycles.

MADISON 1903
This was a 2hp attachment made in Derby to fit any standard roadster bicycle. They also produced machined castings and soon returned to this business, nothing more being heard of the attachment.

MAJESTIC 1904–1907
Conventional machines with the engine located in the new Werner position. JAP sv engines with automatic inlet-valves were amongst those used and although the location of the factory is not certain it was probably in the Sheffield area of south Yorkshire.

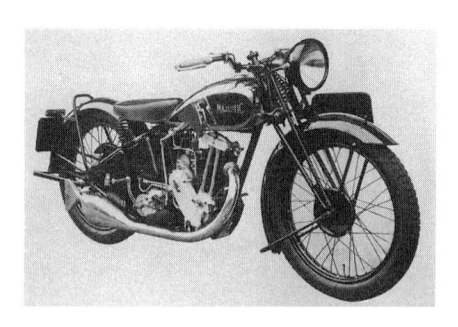

Only listed for 1933, the Majestic used the Stevens engines and was sold by OK Supreme as an up-market line.

MAJESTIC 1933
This was an attempt by Ernie Humphries of OK Supreme to offer up-market models under another name. The inclined engines came from Stevens, all had ohv, and were of 249, 348 and 499cc. A four-speed gearbox was specified, the machines had a nice, if conventional, line, but after the announcement in January, no more was heard of them.

MANXMAN 1980
This machine featured in the *Tomorrow's World* TV programme and was notable for its monocoque frame made from two plates of aluminium bolted together. It was built by Tony Dawson for road racing and was successful in the 125cc class, while Dawson also produced the Astralite wheels made in the same manner. It was suggested that a series of Sachs engines from 125 to 250cc would be used, but the finance was lacking, so little more was heard of the machine although the wheels rolled on. In 1981 it became known as the Scitsu.

MANXMAN 1989–1993
This was a further attempt to produce a motorcycle in the mould of the Manx Norton, but in this case using the ohc engine as found in the Inter. The result first appeared in 1989, built by Neville Evans who had many years of experience of the type.

It was a close approximation to the original with the famed featherbed frame, Roadholder forks and Armstrong rear units. The front wheel had a Grimeca hub housing a four-leading-shoe drum brake, while a Triumph conical hub went at the rear.

The 499cc engine was in the earlier Norton style, all alloy with many internal improvements using modern materials. The camshaft drive was by bevel gears and vertical shaft as always, but the valve rockers were enclosed, as were the coil springs adopted after early use of hairpins. Belt primary-drive was specified and drove an AMC-type gearbox with four, five or six speeds available.

This Manxman has the optional high-level exhaust pipe fitted, but is otherwise in the same format as usual, although other options were also available.

The machine was built at Port Talbot in west Glamorgan, performed well on the road but had limited production.

MAORI 1914–1919
Although this marque name was clearly inspired by its intended market in New Zealand, the actual machines were constructed in England by Zealandia Motor Works in London NW. The machines were built to the design of New Zealander A.R. Bannister specifically to cope with road conditions in his home country. A 292cc sv JAP engine was used, but with a novel and infinitely variable gear mechanism built onto the drive-side crankcase. Belt final-drive and Saxon spring-forks were adopted, the frame layout being conventional but sturdily constructed. Footboards and thorough shielding of the rider from mud were notable features.

The first shipment by sea met with disaster and then the Great War interrupted production, but an example was still receiving press coverage as late as June 1919 in England. It is thought that only one example actually reached the distributors, Johns, Bannister & Co. Ltd, of Gisborne, New Zealand.

MARCH 1996–1998
This firm, with works at Bicester, Oxon, found fame building Formula 1 racing cars in the 1970s but in later years also aimed to produce an exclusive high-quality motorcycle to rival the best. They were in the news in 1996 with plans for a 750cc V-four engine, to be followed by a much more exciting 1500cc V8. Both were to be very advanced with the latest of modern technology and were designed by MCD of Rochdale with finance from the USA.

Although production by October 1996 was forecast, it was late-1997 when the March name was once more in the news. This time it was coupled with that of Norton in a deal to use that company's badges on the March range that now included a 600cc single-cylinder sports model as well as the four and eight, the latter now known as the Nemesis.

Early in 1998 it was reported that March had bought a racing car factory in Norfolk, but further talks with the owners of the Norton name failed to come to completion, so that that was the end of the project.

MARLOE 1920–1921
The Marloe Motor Company of Bordesley, Birmingham, at first adopted the 348cc Precision two-stroke engine in their machines, with Burman two-speed chain-cum-belt transmission. Later, models with Blackburne sv engines of 348 and 499cc, three speeds and a choice of all-chain drive were added; the maker's own front fork with movement controlled by leaf spring was only specifically unusual feature.

MARLOW 1921–1922
No connection existed between the similarly named Marloe and Marlow marques. The Warwick-built Marlow had 269cc Villiers two-stroke and 292cc JAP sv engines with single or two-speed belt drive during the brief period of manufacture.

MARS 1904
The Mars Motor Co. of Finchley, London, launched a forecar in 1904, this being powered by a 4hp water-cooled White & Poppe engine. It had chain transmission and two speeds, but made no impact as nothing further was heard of it.

MARS 1922–1924
All the popular single-cylinder proprietary engines were utilized by the

The Mars of 1904, called the 'Carette', was really a forecar with the passenger carried ahead of the rider, who sat above the water-cooled engine.

makers of the Mars and in various capacities too, including Villiers 147, 269 and 342cc, JAP 292 and 597cc, Blackburne 348cc, Bradshaw 348cc, plus the sleeve-valve Barr & Stroud of 349 and 499cc. The premises of Mars Ltd were located on White Friars Lane, Coventry.

MARSEEL 1920
A small-wheeled scooter, devoid of suspension and with a 232cc two-stroke engine located horizontally beneath the foot platform. A bicycle saddle supported on open tubular framework was the sole concession to rider comfort. The Marseel Engineering Company of Coventry announced production to begin in February 1920, but few were made.

MARSH 1904–1905
A 3.5hp Marsh was shown at the late-1904 Stanley show by W.P. Brough of Kettering, Northants. A typical primitive, it had a flat belt for its transmission, which was tensioned by a jockey pulley, while a tandem was also shown. Neither was heard of again.

MARSHALL c.1905
Built in Eldon Street, Clay Cross, Derbyshire, this was a typical primitive with its 2hp Minerva engine hung from the downtube of a bicycle frame. Braced forks and direct-belt drive completed the basic layout.

MARTIN 1911–1915 AND 1920–1921
Harry Martin had his works at Croydon, Surrey and was an early competitor at the Brooklands track. Late in 1910 he listed two machines using JAP engines, one a tourer, the other for racing. This range grew and by 1914 was listed as Car & Motor Sundries of Shaftesbury Avenue, London, with a line stretching from a 2hp ohv single to an 8hp V-twin, the smallest with a Precision engine and listed as the Martin Junior. This in sv form and a 2.5hp JAP were the only 1915 models.

Post-war, Martin was not on the market for long but offered a range of models, including this lightweight for 1921.

In July 1920 it was announced that production was about to recommence with a range concentrating on twin-cylinder speed models powered by MAG engines. Production was based at the works of A.G. Millier in Willesden and entries were made in Junior and Senior 1921 TT races but with limited success. For that year they listed models with 293cc sv single and 498cc V-twin JAP engines fitted with Claudel Hobson carburettors, an unusual choice, and driving Albion and Burman gearboxes respectively. Production then appeared to fade away and the marque disappeared once more.

MARTIN 1932–1939

During 1932 the JAP firm arranged for sales of their speedway engines to be handled by Victor Martin Ltd, of Cheshunt, Herts, he being an employee who had been involved with the development of the engine. He set up to build complete machines using the engine and fitting it to a frame made to the Rudge speedway form. He also sold the Comerford Wallis machine that became the Comerford Special for 1933 with some changes. Later this became the Martin-Comerford, while the original with the Rudge-type frame became the Martin-Rudge, but both kept to the faithful JAP engine.

MARTINSHAW 1923–1925

Never destined to be more than a minor marque, the Martinshaw from Twickenham, Middlesex never-the-less cast its net wide, beginning with an all-Blackburne-engined range stretching from the 348cc sv single to the 998cc V-twin. By 1924 they were down to just the 348cc sv model and the similar 545cc sv, both with three-speed Sturmey-Archer gearboxes and all-chain drive. These continued for 1925, when Moss gearboxes were standardized and additionally a couple of ohv models were tried, one with the 348cc Blackburne, the other with the 349cc oil-cooled Bradshaw, but it was to be their last year.

Victor Martin was involved with the development of the speedway machine and, by 1939, it had reached this familiar form with JAP engine.

This view of a Martinsyde V-twin machine includes the eoi valve arrangement, cylindrical tank and rim front-brake.

MARTINSYDE 1919–1923

Martin & Handasyde had been major producers of aircraft during the Great War, but with the Armistice came a need to diversify and they turned to motorcycle manufacture. Utilizing their undoubted production capacity and reputation for quality, they chose to manufacture most of the component parts in-house, including the V-twin engines with unusual eoi valve layout. Badged first as the Martinsyde-Newman, thus acknowledging that the engine design was down to H.C. Newman, a member of the family involved with the Ivy marque, the 677cc V-twins quickly gained a reputation for reliability through extensive trials work. All-chain drive was standard with a three-speed gearbox made under licence from AJS. Complete sidecar outfits were offered, including one with a special body for commercial applications.

A 498cc model with similar engine layout followed in 1920, but trading difficulties the next year caused large-scale lay-offs at the works. There was a sports version of the 498cc model and, in 1922, a 738cc sports developed by H.H. Bowen and named the Quick Six. Experiments were conducted with valve gear controlled by leaf springs, and then a vertical single model of 347cc was tried, but towards the end of 1923 the business failed. The stock of parts and rights to manufacture were acquired by the old established Bat Motor Company and during 1924 the twins continued briefly under the Bat-Martinsyde trading name to 1925.

MARVEL-JAP 1909–1912

A little-known make that had a short life fitting JAP engines into stock cycle parts in small numbers. The design was typical of the era and both single and V-twin engines were used.

MASON & BROWN 1904–1906

This make appeared at the late-1904 Stanley show and their machines differed from others in that the engine went well above the bottom bracket with the cylinder laid down to point forward. Inside went a one-piece crankshaft with adjustable ball bearings, and there was no carburettor as the action of the inlet valve was said to do away with the need for this. The engine was controlled by a single lever and had ducts around it to guide the cooling air draught.

Two sizes of 2 or 3hp were listed and both had direct-belt drive, rigid forks and cycle-rim front brake. The machine weights were 75lb (34kg) for the 2hp and 95lb (43kg) for the 3hp.

MASSEY 1923–1929

Having severed his connections with the Massey-Arran company in 1922, E.J. Massey proceeded to launch a new marque under his own surname. From premises on Belgrave Road in Birmingham, the Massey motorcycle was available from January of 1923 with a 545cc sv Blackburne engine for solo or sidecar use and featured internal expanding brakes to both wheels. By the early spring further models had been added with an ohv version of the 348cc Blackburne, plus 292cc and 346cc sv JAP engines. A cheaper 292cc sv JAP model with two-speed chain-cum-belt transmission and V-rim brakes followed soon after, but before the year end production had ceased.

However, in early 1924, the rights to manufacture and the name were acquired by R.L. Jepson of Blackburn, and Massey machines continued to be available with Blackburne and 172cc two-stroke Villiers engines until the end of the decade, after which the Massey Motor Company remained in the trade for many more years specializing in frame and fork repairs.

MASSEY-ARRAN 1920–1924

Few marques can have had so many manufacturing addresses in such a short lifespan as this Birmingham make. They opened up in the middle of 1920 with a 292cc sv JAP-powered design in either touring or sports trim, regarded as well made. The machines had Arden or Brampton forks, CAV magnetos, Amac carburettors, two-speed Sturmey-Archer chain-cum-belt transmission and a straight-through exhaust pipe on the sports. A 677cc sv V-twin JAP model arrived in 1921 with a distinctive saddle-style toolbox in place of the usual rear carrier. Then, in 1922, it was 350s only again, with either Blackburne or JAP engines. However, the departure of E.J. Massey in that year unsettled matters and by mid-1923 it was gloomily advised that spare parts would in future be obtainable through Messrs Hobbis Bros, makers

This 1925 Matador was fitted with the 349cc oil-cooled Bradshaw engine with ohv, an alternative being a JAP of the same size and type.

of the Triplette machines. During 1924 there was an attempt to resurrect production of complete machines, through a reorganized company from premises in Smethwick, but this did not prove successful.

MATADOR 1923–1927

Designed as a sporting middleweight, the Preston-built Matador adopted the 349cc oil-cooled ohv Bradshaw engine from the outset and remained faithful to it throughout the lifespan of the marque. All-chain drive and a three-speed gearbox were standard items too, though the stopping arrangements, with both brakes acting independently on the rear wheel, were unusual in this class of machine. Webb centre-spring forks were fitted for 1924 and an alternative model with the 348cc Blackburne engine in either sv or ohv forms expanded the range somewhat. Patent adjustable handlebars and a patent silencer featured for the first time, all, together with the original design of the machine, coming from the fertile brain of rider/manufacturer Bert Houlding. Houlding left the company during 1924, but the marque continued on into 1925, adding a model with the two-port 344cc ohv JAP motor, whilst Brampton forks were now specified and one brake per wheel became normal practice. It was back to Bradshaw engines only in 1926, the standard model being joined by a TT replica, this having a roller-bearing engine, Webb forks, Brampton close-ratio gearbox and three brakes – one on the front and two on the rear wheel. However, with Houlding having gone to involve himself with the Toreador marque, the Matador design stagnated and 1927 was to be their last year, when the two Bradshaw-engined machines offered were the standard and Super Sports.

MATCHLESS 1899–1945

One of the most important British motorcycle firms, founded by brothers Harry and Charlie Collier, that had its roots in bicycles and first experimented with power in 1899. This first machine had the engine mounted above the front wheel and was followed by other experiments, including one of 1901 where the engine was crammed into the space between the seat tube and rear wheel, but this overheated in use.

The first Matchless motorcycle had the engine above the front wheel but, for the 1901 machine, they moved it into this cramped position.

For their first production machine the Colliers, who were based in Plumstead, London, adopted a 2.75hp MMC engine that was hung from the frame downtube. Within a year they were involved in competition, both the brothers competing at Canning Town cycle track with success, and by 1904 had a more powerful solo fitted with a 3.5hp MMC engine. They also offered a forecar, with De Dion or MMC engine, and a pillion attachment for the solo.

During 1905, suspension was added, by short leading-link forks at the front and pivoted fork at the rear. Later that year a model fitted with a 6hp V-twin JAP engine was added, this using the spring frame, and it was joined by a rigid model having a 5hp Antoine V-twin engine for 1906 when the forecar was dropped. Other

By late 1903 the Matchless engine had moved again, to hang from the downtube, an improvement, but later it took the better central position.

1906 models used a 3.5hp White & Poppe engine in the spring frame and a 3.5hp Antoine in the rigid one, a third single being a ladies' model that had a 2.5hp JAP, again in a spring frame.

The Collier brothers continued to be active in competition, both being selected for the British team for the 1906 International Cup Race. It was the problems there that led to the Isle of Man TT, where the brothers were to race with success; meanwhile they continued to set records at Canning Town and elsewhere. At the first 1907 TT Charlie Collier led from start to finish, while Harry lay second until late in the race when a valve broke.

The production range for 1907 saw the 3.5hp Antoine engine replaced by a JAP, while 1908 brought further revisions, a two-speed gear and a TT model having an ohv engine similar to the TT-winning one. The Colliers went back to the TT but were unable to repeat the 1907 success, Charlie finishing second and Harry running out of petrol. However, Charlie broke the world one-hour record riding at Brooklands.

Around 1907 Matchless offered this ladies' model, with suitable frame changes and low-set engine.

For 1909 the road models used JAP engines, 2.5 and 3.5hp singles and a 6hp V-twin. Rigid or spring frames, two-speed gears and ignition options were offered, while the 3.5hp White & Poppe engine remained available. Early in the year Harry set a twenty-four-hour record at Canning Town, averaging over 32mph (51km/h) despite problems and delays that added up to several hours. Brooklands began to run motorcycle races, in which the Colliers had their share of

A V-twin engine soon joined the Matchless singles and both had other improvements to the engine, transmission and cycle parts.

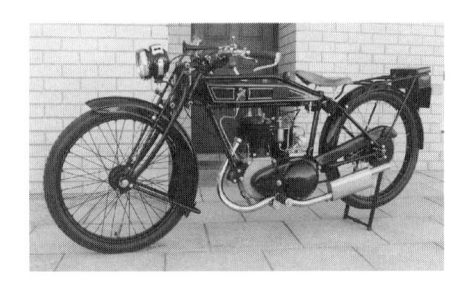

This fine 1925 Matchless 350cc single had side valves, three-speed gearbox and small drum-brakes.

successes, while the 1909 TT saw Harry the winner and Charlie retiring. The range expanded for 1910, having JAP engines in the main, along with some V-twin Peugeots, but remained with belt drive. Competition successes continued and in the 1910 TT Charlie won with Harry second, the brothers thus having taken three of the first four TT races.

For 1911 it was JAP engines for all models, including the TT, which had a 5hp V-twin ohv engine. In the first TT held on the Mountain circuit Harry was second in the Junior race or class that was held for the first time, but in the Senior Charlie finished a

The Matchless 246cc utility model of 1926 had good lines and all the features such a model would have around that period.

close second only to be disqualified. It was an end to the TT glory days of the firm, although they placed third and fourth in 1912.

It was mainly twins for the 1912 model range and for a good few years after that, with some fitted with a modified version of the Zenith Gradua gear to vary the ratio. The singles went for 1913, when the V-twins ran from 3.5 to 8hp and one of the largest finally had all-chain drive. For 1914 the range came down to a 3.5hp model with three-speed hub gear and chain-cum-belt drive, and two 8hp machines with chain drive. One, with a JAP engine, had two speeds, but the other had a 993cc MAG engine and a three-speed gearbox.

Only the model with the 8hp MAG engine continued for 1915 and 1916, with some machines using the JAP engine built for service use in 1917. It was in that year that the firm released news of a proposed model with a 731cc flat-twin engine, three speeds and chain drive. This was to have a frame with rear suspension, but no more was heard of it.

Post-war, the firm continued with the model they had supplied to the

Matchless offered a big V-twin model for many years, this the 982cc X/2 of 1930 with side valves and well suited to sidecar work.

152 Matchless

For 1930, Matchless introduced the Silver Arrow, with a narrow-angle V-twin engine and rear suspension, aimed at the touring market.

Late in 1921, the model J was added with a rigid frame and either JAP or MAG V-twin engine. These twins took the firm on for the next two years, but for 1923 they added a single fitted with a 348cc sv Blackburne engine. Work also began on an ohc 350 single and there was a brief foray into the car market with a light tourer using a flat-twin engine, but this was short lived.

In 1931 the Matchless Silver Hawk was added to the Arrow, but with a V4 engine and an overhead camshaft to create a de luxe sports model.

services, listing this as the Victory. It used the 976cc sv V-twin JAP engine, three-speed gearbox and chain drive, and was sold in solo or sidecar form. It was soon joined by their model H, which was based on the 1914 springframe sidecar outfit, but with the Victory engine. It was also available with the MAG engine and in either form was destined for a long run.

Less exciting in the 1930 range was this prosaic Matchless single, with its 497cc sv engine set upright in the frame.

For 1924 the single was fitted with their own Matchless engine and was joined by the camshaft model. The engine of this had the vertical drive shaft at the rear of the cylinder so the camshaft was set along the machine and the ports were on each side. Another newcomer was a 591cc single with a Matchless ohv engine and 1925 saw a Matchless V-twin engine starting to replace the JAP and MAG. A 245cc sv model appeared for 1926, together with a 498cc single. To round out the range in sv and ohv forms with their own engines for most models, a 495cc ohv single provided the missing link in 1927.

The model H was dropped after 1928, but a 245cc ohv model was added and so the firm ran to the end of the decade. They had models for all classes, with various options available to suit needs and purposes, and set a fashion for brighter finishes with white-panelled tanks from 1928. This continued into 1930, but with one innovative addition, the Silver Arrow which had a 394cc in-line narrow-angle sv V-twin engine.

The new twin was designed as a quiet, smooth tourer and among its features were an oil tank attached to the front of the crankcase, enclosed valve gear, three-speed gearbox, pivoted-fork rear suspension and interconnected brakes. However, it retained chain drive and was never to offer the performance buyers wanted.

This changed for 1931 when Matchless, despite the depression, launched the Silver Hawk. This was something different, for it had a 592cc narrow-angle V4 engine with a shaft-driven ohc. As with the Arrow, the oil

This close up shows the Matchless Silver Hawk V4 engine with shaft drive up to the camshaft and back to the magneto, and the oil tank bolted to the crankcase.

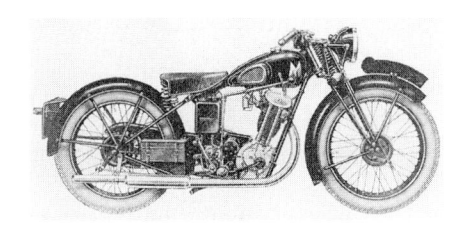

Inclined engines went into the 1931 Matchless range in several sizes, this a 1934 example with ohv, coil ignition and the big plated M on the tank.

tank attached to the crankcase front and there was a similar spring frame and coupled brakes. Built as a de luxe sports model, it remained in the lists to 1935 but was too expensive for the times to sell in quantity.

There were changes to the singles for 1931, when inclined engines were adopted, and this took the firm on for the early part of the decade, with steady improvements such as the saddle tanks of the 1920s taking on a more rounded form, more speeds in gearboxes and foot-change.

The famous 348cc G3 Clubman Matchless model was to set the standard for the range in 1935, also for AJS for many years.

In April 1935, Matchless announced the G3 Clubman which was to be a most significant machine for them. Its 348cc ohv engine had a vertical cylinder, the chain-driven magneto tucked in behind this, and the dynamo underneath the magneto being chain-driven from the crankshaft. There was a four-speed Burman gearbox and the mechanics went into a cradle frame with duplex downtubes. It was the start of a long-running line.

There was a major revision for 1936 with the 245cc G2 and 497cc G80 singles on the lines of the G3 replacing most of the inclined engines. These ended for the next year when vertical sv models appeared and the G-series was built in standard and competition forms with various specifications.

The 1937 Matchless G80 Clubman model had the 497cc engine, raised exhaust-system and electrics out of sight and hard to service.

Even the old V-twin was refreshed for 1937, but still continued to do its sidecar duty, while the firm also sold the engine to at least five other manufacturers and also for the Morgan three-wheeler. That year saw Matchless purchase the Sunbeam firm and form the AMC group, for they had acquired AJS back in 1931. They sold Sunbeam on to BSA in 1943, but the AMC name remained.

By 1939 there were twelve models in the Matchless range and all, other than the twin, were of the one G-series family. Fewer were listed for 1940, as by then they were building for the services and for them settled on just one model, the G3. In 1941 this became the G3L, a favourite with the forces for it had telescopic front-forks in place of the girders and also changed to a frame with a single downtube. Light and handy, its performance made duties easier to carry out.

After the war, the fortunes of AJS and Matchless became closely interwoven and that section of their history is covered under the one entry.

MATCHLESS 1987–1993

Years after AMC had failed, the Matchless name returned to the market. It had passed into the hands of Les

The Matchless name reappeared in 1987, for a machine fitted with a Rotax engine unit and other European components.

Harris, who also built the Triumph Bonneville under licence after the close of Meriden and, once that was underway, he sought to add a single.

The new Matchless was listed as the G80 and used a 494cc ohc four-valve Austrian Rotax engine. The frame was British but the forks, front disc-brake, rear units, exhaust system and carburettor came from Italy. The style was in the classic image, but sales were slow and, from 1990, to special order only up to 1993.

MAX 1907–1909

Late in 1907, Johnson & Phillips of Charlton, Kent, produced a 2hp motorcycle of the early scooter style. Thus, it had small-diameter wheels but no seat, the rider having to stand on footboards to control the machine. The engine pulley was geared down to allow the use of larger belt-pulleys. It appeared at the Stanley show on the Louis Burn stand and by then had gained a folding seat, but failed to make any lasting impact.

MAXIM 1912–1913 AND 1920–1922

Late in 1912 this firm listed one model fitted with a 3.5hp TDC engine, a three-speed Sturmey-Archer gear and belt drive. It failed to catch on so had a short life in the market.

The name returned briefly post-war, with lightweight models utilizing bought-in components. They had two-stroke engines from Dalm and JES, magnetos from EIC and Runbaken, Amac carburettors, Albion two-speed gearboxes and so on, so were therefore much as many others and not sufficiently individual to ensure survival in a competitive market.

MAY BROS 1903–1906
Most likely a family cycle business that went into power using a heavy-duty bicycle frame to carry a Minerva, MMC or Sarolea engine. Direct-belt drive with some transmission options was offered, as the machines were built to order.

MCC 1903–1910
A firm that produced machines in typical primitive form using De Dion and Minerva engines, belt drive, transmission options and bought-in parts. They also produced engines in the Minerva form.

McEVOY 1924–1929
Michael McEvoy specialized in fast road and racing motorcycles, built to exacting standards at high cost. V-twins with 996cc Anzani or 980cc JAP ohv engines formed the basis of the range, which with bulbous saddle tanks and large diameter drum brakes took on much of the appearance successfully pioneered by Brough-Superior. Smaller capacity engines were offered too, including 348cc ohv Blackburne, 344 and 490cc ohv JAP and even the 172cc two-stroke Villiers Super Sports. Then, in late 1928, models with 346cc ohc single and 600cc ohc four-cylinder own-design engines were exhibited at the motorcycle show. These were catalogued for the 1929 season, but it is doubtful if any were produced and the marque from Derby ceased trading in that year.

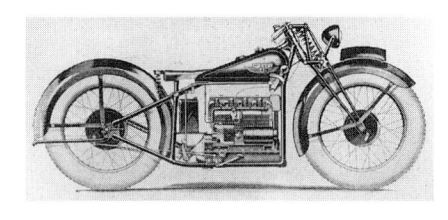

The straight-four 594cc ohc McEvoy model stood out from the more prosaic machines of the 1929 range.

McKECHNIE 1922
An intriguing spring frame, in which engine, gearbox, tank, footboards, saddle and so on, were all suspended as a unit by means of a leaf spring, marked the McKechnie out from the crowd. This sprung assembly lay between straight duplex tubes connecting steering head to rear-wheel spindle, with a Montgomery leaf-spring fork attending to the steering. The 698cc sv Coventry-Victor flat-twin engine provided the power, driving through a four-speed Jardine gearbox and all-chain transmission. A novel design, quite suited to sidecar usage, but sadly McKechnie Motors of Coventry failed to impress themselves upon a fickle market.

McKENZIE 1921–1925
A genuine attempt to provide a machine suitable for everyday transport, the McKenzie was an ultra-lightweight, or miniature as it was then termed, with open frame, unsprung forks, direct-belt drive and a 170cc two-stroke engine of Hobart manufacture. Sizeable numbers were sold in the first year of production, such that the basic model continued for 1923 and a new two-speed lightweight motorcycle was added with Druid forks. This machine was uprated in new design for 1924 and received a new 147c Aza two-stroke engine, plus Albion two-speed chain-cum-belt drive, clutch and kick-starter, the open-frame miniature also benefiting from a two-speed gear. However, the business faltered during the year and was reconstructed with George McKenzie securing the goodwill to continue into 1925, their final season, with the same two-model range but with a larger 175cc Aza two-stroke engine on the lightweight motorcycle and gear options from single-speed to three-speed chain-cum-belt.

MEAD 1911–1915 AND 1922–1924
This make used a 3.5hp Precision engine and was thought to have been made by Premier of Coventry for the Mead Cycle firm of Paradise Street, Liverpool. It was not seen at any of the early shows, nor did it appear in any of the lists, so must have been one of the smallest producers over the next two years.

However, the name did appear in 1914 with a larger range using various Precision engines, these being 2.5, 3.75 and 4.25hp singles, plus 6 and 8hp V-twins. All had a variety of transmission options ranging from direct-belt drive to gearbox and chain-cum-belt. During the year a lightweight was added using a 2hp, 170cc Precision engine and this had a two-speed gear built into the engine unit, belt drive and Druid forks. The whole range continued for 1915 but production then ceased.

Post-war, they had an address in Birmingham as well as the Liverpool premises and from 1922 to 1924 the name returned as an assembler using 1.75, 2.75 and 3.75hp engines from Precision, Wall and Villiers, the last the usual 269cc two-stroke single. The machines were typical products of their time.

MELEN 1912–1913 AND 1922–1926
Shown at the late-1912 Olympia show by F&H Melen of Cheapside, Birmingham, this machine was a combination fitted with a 6hp JAP V-twin engine, Roc two-speed gear and belt drive. The sidecar was in wicker and its chassis had a four-point attachment, but the enterprise was short-lived at the time.

The name returned in 1922, for a tradesman's motor carrier tricycle, this taking the form of a conventional motorcycle from the handlebars rearwards, but with two wheels to the front and a closed top delivery box set between them. Thus, it resembled the forecars of the veteran years and was powered by a 292cc two-stroke Union engine driving a three-speed Burman gearbox with chain final-drive. By 1924 a 343cc Villiers engine had replaced the smaller Union, but otherwise the design continued largely unchanged until 1926.

The Mercury name lasted for only three years but, in that time, quite a number of models came and went, this Pippin scooter among them.

MERCURY 1933–1959
This was a very limited production of machines built by a group of enthusiasts in Croydon, Surrey. All had Scott twin-cylinder engines mounted in a frame constructed from I-section light-alloy extrusions. At the front went a form of duplex steering similar to that used by OEC with a type of telescopic fork, while the rear suspension was devised to maintain constant chain tension. Alloy hubs with 8in brakes were used, the machine sides fully enclosed and a stepped dual seat fitted. A prototype with tubular frame and five machines were built and all survived into the 1980s.

MERCURY 1956–1958
From Dudley, Worcestershire, this bicycle firm made its motorcycle debut in 1956 and listed two models. One was the Mercette moped which had a 48cc ohv engine built in-unit with a two-speed gearbox and installed in a rigid frame with telescopic forks. The other was the Hermes scooter and that used a two-speed 49cc ILO two-stroke engine.

These two were joined by others for 1957: the Dolphin scooter with a 99cc Villiers 4F engine; the Whippet 60, an enlarged Mercette; and the Grey Streak motorcycle with a 99cc Villiers 6F engine. Only this and the Mercette ran on for 1958, joined by the Pippin scooter with 4F engine, but production then ceased.

Mercury might have been a short-lived marque in the 1950s but did list many models, this the Grey Streak with a Villiers engine.

Mercury was the name given to a few machines built by enthusiasts between 1933 and 1959, using Scott engines, light-alloy frame and many novel features, including full suspension.

Another Mercury model was this Mercette moped-type, with the ohv engine and neat lines, seen here in 1957.

MÉTISSE 1961–1976
The name used by the Rickman brothers for their scrambles machines to indicate the variety of parts used in their construction. Thus, there was a Triumph twin engine, BSA gearbox, BSA Gold Star frame, Manx Norton forks and a high standard of finish. From this start came a whole series of machines using a variety of engines in Rickman frames, all prepared to the same standards and for road racing as well as off-road work. The Métisse name is French for a mongrel and the feminine of the word was used as it had a more attractive ring to it.

METRO 1914–1916
Based in Adderley Road, Saltley, Birmingham and sometimes listed as Imperial Metro in its early days, this firm offered one model fitted with a 269cc two-stroke engine with chain-driven Ruthardt magneto. One or two speeds and belt or chain-cum-belt transmission were available and the forks were either Druid or Brampton Biflex.

It continued in these forms for the next year, but only as a single-speed model for 1916. Post-war, the name was bought by Tyler of London in 1919.

METROPOLITAN 1928
Whether or not any Metropolitans were actually built is uncertain, but an advance specification notice for such a marque was issued during 1928.

This is a typical Metisse scrambler as built by the Rickman brothers; their road-racing machines were to the same high standards.

This detailed the intention to produce a lightweight motorcycle with 172cc Villiers two-stroke engine lubricated on the Auto-Lube system and driving through an Albion three-speed gearbox and clutch. Brampton Biflex forks steered a Brampton frame set, over which was to be fitted a black-enamelled fuel tank with blue side-panels. Internal expanding brakes, all-chain drive, semi-TT handlebars and a Villiers direct lighting set were all said to be standard equipment.

METRO-TYLER 1919–1924

Tyler of London took over the Birmingham Metro firm and began post-war production in 1919 by continuing the 269cc two-stroke in either single-speed belt drive, or two-speed chain-cum-belt forms. For 1920 there was just a two-speed model, this completely redesigned with their own neat two-speed gear and enclosed primary transmission in a welded frame. In 1921 a three-speed version was added, the model then remaining in the range with various gearbox options, including Albion, until 1924. Two four-stroke machines were added in 1922, a 348cc single and 698cc V-twin, both with Blackburne sv engines. In 1923 a new 147cc two-stroke miniature known as the All Black Baby, from its all-weather finish, was added and had single or two-speed belt drive. At the same time an all-chain version of the 348cc Blackburne together with a similar size ohv machine were listed while the V-twin ran on as before. However, this was to prove the high point for, in 1924, just the 269cc two-stroke and a new 247cc Villiers model, both with Albion two-speed box and chain-cum-belt, were listed, upon which note the name disappeared from sight.

MIDGET BICAR 1905–1912

This machine was exhibited at the late-1905 Stanley show and built by J.T. Brown of Oxford Road, Reading. It differed from most of that time in that the frame and tank were constructed of sheet steel so the only tubing used was for the braced front-forks, handlebars and headstock. All the frame joints were riveted and the result gave the outline of a normal frame but with enclosed sides, other than for the engine, which was a 3hp Fafnir.

The machine was long and low with footboards and a prop stand on each side. There were no pedals and this allowed for the drive belt to be tensioned by moving the rear wheel, as became common for chains in due course, a useful feature. Some versions had a foot-controlled free-engine clutch, while the frame construction allowed for the battery tray to hinge out from its compartment for servicing.

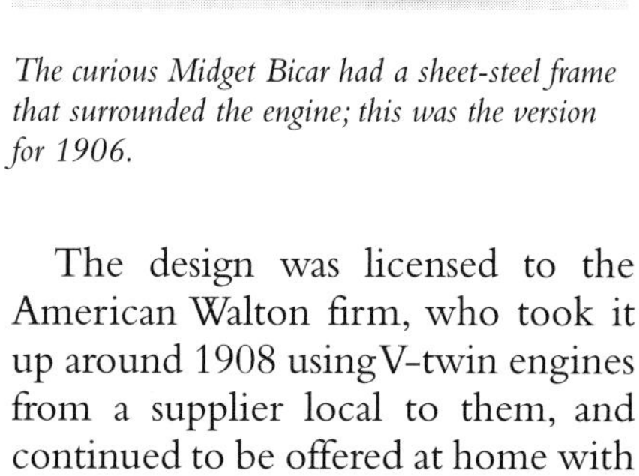

The Metro-Tyler name arrived in 1919 on this two-stroke model, which had a choice of transmissions and the option of wheel discs.

The curious Midget Bicar had a sheet-steel frame that surrounded the engine; this was the version for 1906.

The design was licensed to the American Walton firm, who took it up around 1908 using V-twin engines from a supplier local to them, and continued to be offered at home with a choice of a 3.5hp single or 5hp V-twin engine. A two-speed option was added for 1909 and in 1910 Druid forks and 3.5 or 4.25hp Fafnir engines were fitted. For 1911 they used a 3.5hp Precision engine with a

The Midget Bicar shown in its 1911 form, by when some of the sharp edges had been smoothed out and the front forks improved.

4.5hp listed for sidecar work. The smaller of these was used for the 1912 ladies' model and that year brought a 2.5hp lightweight machine to the list, after which the name vanished.

MILLER 1968–1969

Sammy Miller excelled at all branches of motorcycle sport that he turned to – road racing with works rides and then trials where he dominated the scene for so many years. An off-shoot of this was a host of improved parts and accessories for competition use sold from his shop in New Milton, Hampshire, including the High Boy frame.

In 1968 he began to produce a complete trials machine using his own frame, many detail parts from his list and a Villiers 37A engine. It was a quality product that worked well but, sadly, the engine supply dried up to bring the project to an end. Since those days, Sam has built up a museum, with the accent on both the unusual and competition, now world renowned.

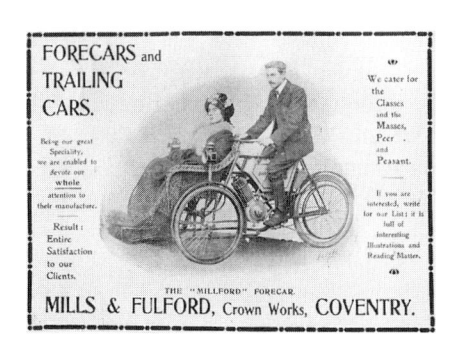

Mills & Fulford produced trailers and sidecars, so were tempted to offer complete forecars for a short while, this the 1903 model.

MILLFORD 1903–1904

The firm of Mills & Fulford of Coventry was best known for trailers and sidecars, but did briefly produce motorcycles. For them the frame was easy, as they had that expertise, but for the engine they turned to Hamilton Motors, who supplied 2.25 and 3.25hp types. These were either hung from the downtube or fitted vertically in the frame, in either case with belt drive to the rear wheel.

The firm also offered the machine in kit form and later added Fafnir or Whitley engines as options. However, as the trade slumped in 1905, they must have found it better to keep to the sidecar business they knew, so the motorcycles were dropped. There was a suggestion that the machines were much as another Coventry make, possibly Excelsior or James, so there could have been some association in frame manufacture.

One way of selling two Millford attachments at once, provided that the machine could cope with the load and the ladies remained friends.

MILLIONMOBILE 1902

A grandiose name for a typical primitive that comprised a heavy-duty bicycle fitted with a small engine, most likely a Minerva. It was built by Strettons Ltd, of The Million Garage, Wellington Street, Cheltenham, who also made a trailing car a little later.

The Mini-Motor was one of the best-selling bicycle attachments during the period when these were so popular – simple, easy to use and reliable.

MINI-MOTOR 1949–1955

Perhaps the best known of the British clip-on engines, although of Italian origin. Built in Croydon, Surrey, it appeared in 1949 and sat above the bicycle rear wheel, driving it by a friction roller. The 50cc two-stroke engine was basic, having a horizontal cylinder, Wipac flywheel magneto for ignition and the drive roller mounted on one end of the crankshaft. The petrol tank sat over the engine, there was a means of lifting it to disconnect and re-engage the drive, and it had enough power to propel a tandem nearly as well as a bicycle so could help two people along. Production ceased in 1955 as the moped began to take over at the bottom end of the market.

M&M 1914

A very short-lived make that took up the 269cc Villiers two-stroke engine and fitted it into bought-in parts. Many firms did this that year; some to supplement an existing range, others making their appearance, but most were swept away by the war.

Copied from the De Dion tricycle and retaining the rear mounting for the engine, MMC was one of the Lawson firms of the early days.

MMC 1898–1904
Lawson's companies were reconstructed as the Motor Manufacturing Company in 1898 to make MMC tricycles and copies of the De Dion engines. The tricycle was a virtual copy of the De Dion and was used by the British Army in the Boer war. They also advertised the Motocyclette, which was a machine in the original Werner style with the engine over the front wheel, which it drove by belt. This was said to be made at the Motor Mills, Coventry and an 1898 testimonial said that it handled better than a standard bicycle. However, this was from an inspector of a mutual assurance company.

Machine production did not last long but engine manufacture continued into the new century.

MOCYC 1952–1955
Name used by the all-alloy GYS cyclemotor from 1952, it having been GYS for 1949–50 and Motomite for 1951.

MOHAWK 1903–1904 AND 1922–1925
A firm based at Chalk Farm, London, who produced a primitive design in 1903 using a 2.25 or 3hp engine fitted with a Longuemare carburettor. The engine was mounted vertically in the diamond frame with flat or V-belt drive to the rear wheel and braced forks.

After a time away from the market they returned in 1922, based at Hornsey, London, to offer a six-model range using a 269cc Villiers two-stroke, or 292, 346 and 680cc JAP and 499cc King Dick engines. It was single-speed for the simplest model, but a Sturmey-Archer gearbox and chain-cum-belt transmission for the others. All were finished in the firm's distinctive green and yellow, with gold lining. All-chain drive was standard on the 680 and an option on the 346 in the next year, before drastic pruning to the range in 1924 left just the 292 and 346cc JAP models, with a sports specification offered on the larger. These two continued into 1925, their final year.

MOLNAR 1997–DATE
The Stainless Engineering Company was set up by Andy and Kim Molnar in the 1970s to produce spares for classic machines, especially Manx Nortons. With the rights to the Manx name acquired in 1994, plus original factory drawings, they began building complete machines in 1997. Externally they look original, but inside they are much further developed to produce around 59hp at 7,500rpm while the weight has been reduced to 260lb (118kg).

MONARCH 1912 AND 1919–1921
Even in the press of 1912 the Monarch was referred to as a comparatively unknown make and so it was, for it went unlisted up to the war years. The machine was typical of the times with a single engine, most likely from Precision, belt drive, maybe a hub gear option and braced spring-forks – much as many others.

They were reputed to have been built as cheaper versions of Excelsior models post-war from 1919 to 1921 using 269cc Villiers and 293cc JAP engines.

MONARD 1964–1965
Geoff Monty and Allen Dudley-Ward were business partners for many years and both were successful road racers. They built two Monards for racing, using 500 and 650cc pre-unit Triumph engines and Norton gearboxes, each in a frame much as that used for Geoff's successful 250cc specials. It comprised a single large-diameter tube running from headstock to curve behind the gearbox, twin downtubes, a rear sub-frame and alloy mounting-plates for the rear fork.

Geoff had the knack of picking out riders with real potential and so Bill Ivy rode the Monards in 1964, but moved on early the next year. For this and other reasons only the two machines were built, but they made their mark.

MONOPOLE 1902–1903, 1912–1924 AND 1927
This name first appeared late in 1902 when the Monopole Cycle Co. exhibited their machine at the Stanley show. It had a 2.25hp engine and was in the form of most primitives of that era, other than in having single-lever control. It failed to appear the next year so was short lived, although the name did return late in 1912 at Olympia as the Monopole Cycle & Carriage Co. of Foleshill, Coventry.

For that show they exhibited two models of similar type with 2.5 and 3.5hp Precision engines, the smaller with direct-belt drive and the larger the same to a Sturmey-Archer three-speed hub gear. Saxon forks were fitted and, while the specification was quite conventional, the detail design and finish was of a high quality. The firm continued with these models to 1914, were not listed in 1915, but did list one model with a 269cc Villiers engine for 1916. This had a Jardine two-speed gearbox and belt final-drive, a single-speed version also being available.

Post-war, the two-stroke ran on, to be joined by four-stroke models with JAP and Abingdon engines, having transmission choices from single-speed to three-speed Sturmey-Archer gearbox, but all with belt final-drive. All-chain drive was standard on some sports variants. By 1924 just 292 and 346cc JAP models remained, to bring the venture to a close, except for a brief resurgence in 1927 when a 147cc lightweight with

Montgomery were involved with sidecars from their start, so it was no surprise that, when they added motorcycles, these had big V-twin engines. They continued for years in this way; this a 1925 model.

Aza two-stroke engine came and went in one season.

MONTGOMERY 1905–1940

An early maker of sidecars from 1904 who, while concentrating on these, added motorcycles to offer complete outfits for some years. They were built in Bury St Edmund's, Suffolk at first and the 1905 model had a 5hp V-twin engine and a wicker-work sidecar body. The sidecar could be detached in two minutes, it was claimed, while the connections to the machine were flexible on some models to allow them to bank for corners. In one advertisement that year they showed a machine with a sidecar fitted on each side of the motorcycle, one for the wife and the other for her sister, as Millford.

For some years they continued to list machines to suit their sidecars, while concentrating on these, and by 1911 had moved to Coventry where they would stay. In general, the machines were bought in or built up using bought-in parts in the firm's frame.

Late in 1913 they introduced a motorcycle fitted with a Coventry

At one time Montgomery gave their models the names of dog breeds, so this is a 1931 Greyhound, with a 680cc ohv JAP V-twin engine.

Victor 689cc flat-twin engine and intended for sidecar use. Its transmission was unusual, for it was by direct belt to a three-speed rear hub but taken from a large pulley mounted on the camshaft. For the rest, the frame had duplex members around the engine and was fitted with Biflex forks. For 1915, the engine had grown to 708cc but the other features remained.

Post-war, the firm changed direction and began to build up a range of models from a 147cc two-stroke to a 996cc V-twin in various forms, some aimed at the sidecar market and most with three speeds and chain drive. They also built a useful proprietary front-fork with leaf springing that they used on their own big twins and sold to others such as Brough-Superior and Coventry-Eagle. Following modest entries in the TT, ohv engines began to be used but were always bought in from firms such as JAP or Anzani.

The Terrier model joined the Montgomery range at the bottom end of the market in 1936, with a 122cc Villiers engine in simple cycle parts, later to be joined by a 98cc version.

This 1939 Greyhound Montgomery model had a JAP 499cc engine, with fins all the way up the head and barrel, and plunger rear-suspension.

Late in 1925 their works went up in flames, which disrupted production for some time, but they kept going on the same lines into the next decade. The engines came from Villiers or JAP and the range size

From Morris's bicycle shop in Oxford, via this 1902 motorcycle, the mighty Nuffield empire and millions of cars grew.

varied, many models having canine names such as Greyhound, Terrier, Retriever or Bulldog. The four-strokes ran from 247 to 994cc with sv or ohv and the machines progressed through saddle tanks and foot-change along with the industry. The two-strokes ran from 98 to 247cc, were simpler and fulfilled a need, but the outbreak of war brought the 1940 range to an end, not to restart.

MOONBEAM 1920

A 100lb (45kg) lightweight with roller-bearing 269cc two-stroke engine, direct-belt drive or optional two-speed chain-cum-belt transmission. Briefly appeared in mid-season, promoted by the M.R.P. Trading Company of Pall Mall, London, and waned with the moon!

MORRIS 1902–1905

William Morris, later Lord Nuffield, began his career as a cycle agent in Oxford and had premises in George Street. In time, bicycles led to motorcycles, before he turned to cars, and he began using 2.75hp De Dion and MMC engines of a primitive type with belt drive. He set the engine upright in the frame that was formed to run under and round the crankcase. Later he turned to chain drive and a clutch, listed a forecar, and used MMC engines only.

MORRIS 1913–1922

Having no connection with William Morris or Morris-Warne, the business of John Morris of Knowle in Warwickshire manufactured a two-stroke engine of 247cc with CAV magneto, Amac carburettor and Best

& Lloyd lubrication. They fitted it into conventional lightweight cycle parts of the time with a choice of single speed, two-speed or three-speed chain-cum-belt drive. The engine was also offered to other small assemblers, but few responded to this with orders, although Triple-H of Coventry were one to adopt it.

MORRISON 1913
This firm was located in Leicester, where they built sidecars, and in 1913 they announced a motorcycle fitted with a 6hp V-twin JAP engine. No doubt intended for sidecar work, it would have been built to suit that, but few can have been sold as no more was heard of it.

MORRIS-WARNE 1922
Based in Acton, London, this firm built a pair of models fitted with a 247cc two-stroke engine in two different ways. In the first the cylinder was horizontal and drove the rear wheel directly by belt, so there was no clutch and push-starting was needed. The second had the cylinder vertical, chain drive to a three-speed gearbox and belt final-drive. Production was limited and for the one year only

MORTON-ADAM 1923–1925
This Coventry firm began with a 246cc two-stroke lightweight, using their own engine which had an overhung crank, outside flywheel and one-piece barrel with crankcase casting and detachable head. The frame had provision for a two-speed gearbox, although single-speed belt drive was standard, as were Webb forks. During 1924, a simple overhead-camshaft engine also of 246cc was designed and constructed along similar lines but with chain drive to the single camshaft, this being built into a machine with three-speed Burman gearbox and all-chain drive. The two models went into their final year, 1925, with transmission options.

MOTOFRIP 1911–1912
A three-wheel scooter designed by Mrs Olive Kent and seen at the 1911 Olympia show on the Moto-Rêve stand. It had a 1.25hp M-R engine with belt drive to the rear axle but only one of the 10in wheels was driven. It had a loop frame, cycle forks and calliper front-brake, while the rider stood on a platform between the rear wheels.

MOTO-MERIDEN 1976–1977
In the dark days of Triumph at Meriden the workforce had to turn their hands to anything that would bring in some money. One result was a job of assembling Moto Guzzi machines with a 121cc two-stroke engine and five speeds. Marketed as the Co-Uno, it failed to sell well due to poor quality control and unreliable electrics, and despite a lively performance and keen price. It was soon gone from the lists.

MOTOMITE 1951
Name used by the all-alloy GYS cyclemotor for 1951, it being changed to Mocyc for 1952–55.

Motomite was one of the three names this cycle attachment was sold under, the others being GYS and Mocyc, and all were able to be fitted over front or rear wheel.

MOTORPED 1919–1922
A strengthened bicycle propelled by a two-stroke auxiliary engine mounted above the rear wheel and available in either ladies' or gents' pattern frames. Its 104cc engine had a horizontal cylinder with fuel tank above, magneto ignition, Amac carburettor and drove the road wheel by chain; a plate clutch was optional. The makers, Patrick Engineering of Birmingham, also offered the power unit separately as the Simplex, for attachment to any machine.

MOUNTAINEER 1902–1904
This firm offered a typical primitive using a heavy-duty bicycle with the engine securely clamped within the main frame and driving the rear wheel by belt. They were based in Baker Street, London and claimed to have works in Coventry as well as abilities that would stretch modern publicity advertising, much less that of 1902. They were truly built in Coventry, but by Rex, so they were well made although Rex themselves soon moved on to a new design and the Mountaineer was no more.

MOUNTAINEER 1920–1924
Having no connection with the earlier name, the new marque was based in Marsden, Yorkshire, and built by Richard Wylde, a small producer who did not appear at the big London shows or in the lists of the time.

He entered the market with one basic model powered by his own 269cc two-stroke engine and offered in two forms. One had direct-belt drive and the other a two-speed Albion gearbox and chain-cum-belt drive. This range kept them going to 1921 when a Sturmey-Archer gearbox was an option and a special two-speed racing model could be had. These variations only lasted the one year however, after which it was as before, until the option of a three-speed Albion gearbox in 1924, which proved to be their last year.

The Mountaineer of the 1920s was a simple lightweight with a small two-stroke engine and a choice of transmissions.

MOVEO 1910–1911
Moveo was listed late in 1910 as a make with a range of five models, all having belt drive and sprung forks. Engines were 2.5 or 3.5hp JAP singles, a 3.5hp Precision single or 4 and 8hp JAP V-twins – another short-lived enterprise.

MPH 1921–1922
Commencing in March 1921 with a lightweight of conventional appearance powered by a 269cc Wall two-stroke engine and choice of single- or two-speed transmission, the latter having a Roc gearbox, the firm of Peter Hay, based in Tyseley, Birmingham, only persisted in the trade for one further year. By 1922 they had embraced the Broler 349cc two-stroke motor which gave more performance and, accordingly, the transmission options changed to two or three speed, this time through Albion gearboxes, though the belt final-drive remained.

MRD 1983–1989
This was Model Replica & Design that was run by Pat French and started out making models, but in time this changed to producing full-sized replicas of the Rickman Metisse. In the main, this entailed frames and rolling chassis for a variety of engines and to customer requirements. There were some complete machines, some in small batches, and later came many replicas of the Rickman frame. Produced at Kingswood, Bristol, all were as well made and finished as the original Rickman.

Later came a chassis developed for hill climbs and, during the 1990s, a flat track design to run alongside the street scrambler and café racer types. The 750cc Triumph twin was the usual engine fitted but the 650cc T120 unit and other makes could be accommodated. Well made, they were in demand.

MUNROE 1909
Hub-centre steering is one of the old ideas and was used by G. Munroe for a machine built for him by James Fryer, Borough Motor Works, Leominster. The result had a lengthy 63in (160cm) wheelbase and low build. It was powered by an old 2.75hp De Dion engine. The idea failed to catch on.

MURPHY 1913–1914
This was built by 'Billy' Murphy at works in Deritend, Birmingham, where he produced both the two-stroke engines and the frames. Typical of the period, and the name went when Billy was killed in an accident while driving a combination in the city.

N

NEAL 1910–1922
A firm located in Sparkbrook, Birmingham run by S.G. Neal, which assembled machines from bought-in parts using Precision engines of various sizes. Typical of the times, they were not seen at the London shows or listed in guides, but did return to the market post-war. They then used a 318cc Dalm two-stroke engine, but production continued small and soon ceased, their main line of business being in the bicycle trade. They were generally listed post-war as Neal-Dalm.

NEOFOLD 1905–1906
Late in 1903, a Mr Clark of Battersea Rise, London designed a tricycle whose front wheels could be collapsed into each other to enable it to be wheeled through a narrow gateway. At the late-1905 Stanley show he exhibited a powered version, the 2.5hp engine being fitted just behind the front axle. Ingenious, but not taken up by the public.

NER-A-CAR 1921–1927
This was an American design built at Syracuse, New York and licensed to Sheffield Simplex in Kingston-on-Thames, Surrey. The name was a play on the designer Carl Neracher and the style of the machine, for it had a monocoque frame, so that the rider sat low behind a generous front mudguard and had footboards to keep the weather at bay.

A strange design in just about all areas, the Ner-A-Car had its origins in the USA and sold well in Britain for most of the 1920s.

The frame was made from pressed-steel channel-section members that ran from the rear wheel, splaying out to carry leading links for the hub-centre steering pivot. Panels went on the frame to conceal most of the mechanics, with just the cylinder on view, and ran on to the front mudguard. The cylindrical fuel-tank went under the saddle and both drum brakes were in the rear hub.

The American model had a 211cc two-stroke engine with the crankshaft set along the frame. Its flywheel was placed at the rear to drive a friction wheel at right angles to it, with this able to move across its face. This movement varied the ratio between them and was controlled by a lever that at first was fully variable but later had a choice of five positions. From this a chain drove the rear wheel.

Front-end detail of the Ner-A-Car, showing the support springs and their attachments for the hub-centre steering pivot that turned the wheel.

The Ner-A-Car was an innovative design, but the day of the motorcycle in the USA was already on the wane, courtesy of Henry Ford and others. However, the machine found a market in Britain, at first with the 211cc engine and for 1923 one of 285cc. The Ner-A-Car was aimed at the market outside the normal motorcycle one and had some success, being easy to mount and ride.

To augment the limited power, the next move was to change to a 348cc sv Blackburne engine driving a three-speed gearbox, this version appearing for 1925. For the next year an ohv Blackburne model was added to produce even more performance but sales of the machine were never too great, while Sheffield Simplex were in trouble, so 1927 was the last year.

NESTOR 1913–1914
A small firm from Blackpool, Lancashire, that built in limited numbers using bought-in parts. Engines were the 269cc Villiers two-stroke and Precision 296 and 347cc sv driving a variety of transmission options. They ended as a casualty of the war.

NEW BOWDEN 1902
Name used at first for the Bowden, built from 1902 to 1905 using Simms and FN engines, usually located aft of the seat pillar with silent chain-drive including a clutch to the rear wheel. The prefix to the name was soon dropped and the firm later became much better known for its carburettors and control cables.

NEW CENTURY c.1901–c.1909
Someone had to use this name around the time and it was this firm in St Albans, Hertfordshire, who built typical primitive machines using 2.75hp Gavandau engines imported from France. They were raced in early events by D.R. Clarke, C. Reid and A. Cummins up to around 1908, and a 344cc machine ran at Brooklands in 1910.

The New Comet originated in Edwardian times and, by 1914, listed this neat two-stroke with a choice of transmissions, here seen from the drive side.

NEW COMET 1905–1931

A.H. Haden of Princip Street, Birmingham designed and built his machines from the Edwardian era up to the start of the Depression years. Starting with a primitive, he was soon offering singles and V-twins using Zedel and Peugeot engines among others. By 1910 it was Sarolea or JAP power, along with the Peugeot V-twin, and the next year saw the addition of Precision singles. For 1912 it was all Precision power, including both a lightweight and a Colonial model; these also sold as the Comet-Precision.

For 1913 there was also a model with a JAP V-twin, and late that year Haden took over the Regal-Green business and began to use the water-cooled Green engines along with the others. In 1914 a 210cc two-stroke joined the range, it having direct-belt drive or a chain-driven two-speed gearbox, and Druid forks. There was also a 349cc version and all these models continued to 1916.

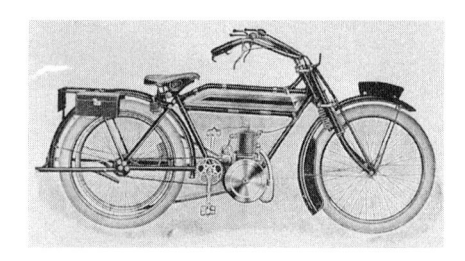

The timing side of the 1914 New Comet, with magneto tucked up behind the cylinder with a short lead to the plug.

Post-war, they listed a 292cc two-stroke and a 499cc four-stroke, but from 1920 restricted themselves to two-strokes only. Two or three versions of the 292cc model were listed for each year, being joined for 1924 by one with a 147cc Aza engine. More versions of this were added for the next year, but reduced to one for 1926 with this also listed for the next year. In 1928 there was just a 172cc Super Sports model with three speeds and being one of the few they built with all-chain drive. There was a break for 1929, but 1930 saw the 172cc machine return, while for 1931 it became the 196cc Super Sports. However, that was the last year of motorcycle production and from then on they were component suppliers to the trade.

NEW COULSON 1923–1924

This was the successor marque to the Coulson B, with H.R. Backhouse & Co. Ltd, of Tyseley, Birmingham becoming sole manufacturers after the failure of the original company. Production of models with 348 and 545cc sv Blackburne engines and the Coulson spring frame continued, together with a 269cc two-stroke having a Liberty engine, also of Blackhouse manufacture, but devoid of rear suspension. A similarly unsprung sports model with the 349cc ohv Bradshaw oil-cooled engine arrived in the spring of 1924; this had Druid forks and Burman three-speed all-chain drive. It wasn't enough to secure the future of the business.

NEW COURIER 1899 AND 1919–1923

Originally a Wolverhampton bicycle maker who dallied briefly with primitive motorized tricycles at the end of the nineteenth century, the New Courier name was resurrected after the Great War by the manufacturers of the Olympic motorcycle as a low-priced alternative to their principal marque. Medium-weight models with a variety of engine and gearbox combinations could be obtained, as the frame layout was specifically designed to encourage such choice of specifications.

NEW CRESCENT 1912

A rare marque, of which only one survives, fitted with a 5hp Precision engine mounted in a conventional frame with Druid forks. It had belt drive to a three-speed Armstrong gear in the rear hub that also contained the multi-plate clutch. It was typical of the period.

NEW CYKELAID 1922–1926

The name adopted by the firm in York for its revised powered-wheel

New Era offered this tricar in 1908, which could carry two people, albeit in something with the looks of an invalid carriage.

model. It had a 133cc two-stroke engine fitted to the left of the front wheel, chain drive via a countershaft, and a flywheel magneto on the right driven by the mainshaft running through the wheel spindle. An adequate performer, its day just passed.

NEW ERA 1908–1911

The New Era Motor Co. of Lonsdale Road, West Kilburn, London launched their Phenomobile tricar late in 1908, with a 7hp V-twin engine mounted over the front wheel, which it drove by chain. The handlebars stretched back to the driver, who sat beside the passenger in a seat located between the rear wheels and fitted out as a car body with luggage space under the seat.

A curious device, not unlike an invalid carriage, it appeared once more, late in 1911, fitted with a vertical-twin engine whose exhaust-valve caps had extended radiators attached to them. In this form the machine was called the Cyclonette.

NEW ERA 1920–1922

Built by the Era Motor Co. of Liverpool, who listed a 318cc two-stroke with an Albion two-speed gearbox and chain-cum-belt drive in two forms, with or without a clutch. They also listed a 499cc four-stroke with either a fixed-belt drive or with a three-speed Burman gearbox and chain-cum-belt drive.

These models continued up to 1922 when production ended.

NEW GERRARD 1922–1940

This Edinburgh firm was a one-man show run by Jock Porter, who

Jock Porter built his New Gerrard machines using various engines, such as this Blackburne, and, in his early days, won two TT races using his machines.

designed, built and raced the machines. He retired from the 1922 Junior TT, but made his and the marque's name in the next three years when he won the 1923 250cc and 1924 175cc races, with a third in the 1925 175cc TT.

His premises were Porter's Motor Mart but his road models were, for a time, built by Campion of Nottingham and for 1924 used a 348cc Blackburne or Barr & Stroud engines of 348 or 499cc, three-speed gearbox and chain drive. Only Blackburne engines were used for 1925 and were of 249 or 348cc with sv or ohv, while 1926 saw the 348cc models only, but joined by one of 549cc.

It was just the 348cc ohv model for 1929, listed in road and racing forms, and for 1930 the engine became a 346cc JAP. This one model continued to be listed right through to 1940, no doubt built up from spares in stock, with parts bought-in as needed.

NEW HENLEY 1926–1931

This was the successor marque to Henley, when production was continued from the same Doe Street, Birmingham works by New Henley Motors Ltd, from late in 1926. There

The last year for New Henley was 1931, when they still listed this model with 346 or 490cc JAP engine and other options.

was an immediate change from Blackburne to JAP and MAG engines in various models spanning the 346, 490 and 747cc capacity classes when the 1927 range was announced.

During 1928, when engines were exclusively from JAP, a move was made to Warstone Lane in Birmingham and, the following year, all the ohv models had two-port heads and cradle frames were adopted through the range, except for the lightweight 300cc sv JAP-powered machine known as the Pup. Direction of the company was by Arthur Greenwood and Johnnie Crump, both being Lancashire based, so that yet a further move to the old Bradbury works in Oldham in 1929 was no great surprise. A well-known sporting rider, Greenwood piloted one of his own machines in that year's Lightweight TT race, but without success.

By 1930 Crump was going it alone and introduced 172, 196 and 247cc Villiers two-stroke models to bolster the JAP range of 346, 490 and 747cc machines. The 172 was dropped for 1931, all the others continuing, including sv and ohv versions in 346 and 490cc capacities. But, before the end of the year, 'Mad' Jack Crump had run out of money and the marque name was gone, this time for good.

NEW HOTSPUR 1913–1914

This make was built in Tottenham, London, by Strutter & Abrey, so it was hardly surprising that they chose a JAP single-cylinder engine for their machine. It was typical of the period with direct-belt drive, hub gears, Druid forks and footboards. Little is known and few were sold.

NEW HUDSON 1903–1933 AND 1940–1958

This Birmingham bicycle firm, based in Icknield Street, began its motorcycle line with an early primitive using a De Dion engine, but soon left the powered market to return late in 1910 in Summer Hill Street. They then listed two models of conventional design using 2.5 or 3.5hp JAP

The 1912 New Hudson had the hub gears and belt drive of the time, as well as Druid forks and flat tank.

engines, belt drive, Druid forks and various transmission options. The next year saw them add their own 3.5hp engine, while for 1913 they dropped the JAP motors and added their own of 2.75hp. A 6hp V-twin appeared for 1914 and during that year they added a 211cc two-stroke lightweight. This and the 3.5hp single ran on to 1916 but, post-war, only the two-stroke was listed at first.

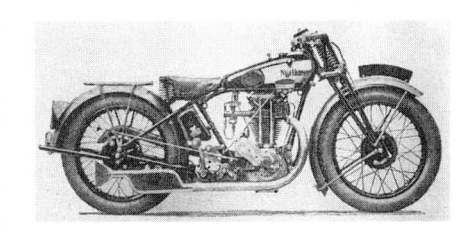

Timing side of a 1929 New Hudson fitted with the 496cc ohv engine; the model was also available with a 346cc engine in the same style and cycle parts.

By 1922 there was also a 594cc four-stroke single and the next year saw the end of the two-stroke and brought 346 and 496cc models. In 1924 a 346cc ohv model appeared, to be joined by ones of 490 and 594cc in 1926, all with suitable sporting names. The largest was short lived but they heralded New Hudson's best year in 1927 when Jimmy Guthrie finished second in the Senior TT, while Bert le Vack set records at Brooklands.

This took them to the end of the decade, by when there was also a 249cc sv that was sold as the Ixion at a reduced price to clear stocks. However, they revamped the range for 1931 with inclined engines and partial enclosure. Unfortunately, the first,

This is the BSA version of the pre-war New Hudson autocycle as for 1950; it was restyled in 1956.

as a style, was on its way out, enclosure did not catch on and the new engines had problems, all of which dragged the firm down at the worst of times. They kept going to 1933 but then turned to making Girling brakes.

The New Hudson name reappeared in 1940 on an autocycle powered by a 98cc Villiers engine and by the time the war ended the firm was part of the BSA group. The autocycle continued as it was until 1949, when it was revised to use the Villiers 99cc 2F unit. It continued with this, was completely restyled during 1956 and ran on in this form to 1958.

NEW IMPERIAL 1912–1940
After the abortive entry into the powered market under the Imperial name in 1901, Norman Downs returned to the fray with a revised name to indicate a better machine. They were based in Loveday Street, Birmingham and their range had 2.5, 3.5 and 4.25hp models, all with JAP engines, belt drive and sprung forks, the largest model intended for sidecar use. These were joined by a 6hp V-twin for 1913, when the firm first raced in the TT, and this range continued to 1916.

An early New Imperial shown as listed for 1914, with a good specification, with 293cc JAP engine and two speeds.

After the war they finally settled in Hall Green, Birmingham and listed a 292cc single and 998cc V-twin for 1921, both having JAP engines and a three-speed gearbox. That same year they had their first success in the TT, when Doug Prentice won the 250cc class of the Junior race. With this to advertise the make, the range extended and they had further TT successes in 1924, when Kenneth Tremlow won the Junior and his brother Eddie the Lightweight. Eddie repeated his win the next year when Ken was third and this really put the firm on the map.

This is the Blue Prince New Imperial for 1931, with 499cc twin-port engine and their own three-speed gearbox.

During the 1930s, New Imperial built machines with the gearbox bolted to the back of the engine and gear primary-drive enclosed in a cast-alloy case, this a 1933 machine of 247cc.

By the middle of the decade the firm was well on the way to making their own engines, so the JAP motors became an option before being dropped. The extensive range was pruned in time, so by 1930 there were six single-cylinder models, which continued for 1931. However, 1932 brought a major step forward, with the first of the firm's unit-construction models that not only built the engine and gearbox as one unit, but also had wet-sump lubrication and pivoted-fork rear suspension with the springs up under the seat in modern

The 1939 New Imperial Grand Prix model of 346cc, which took a conventional form of engine and cycle parts.

monoshock style. Later came gear primary-drive and a whole range of sizes that all ran alongside more conventional models.

They did not neglect the sporting side either, with another Lightweight TT win by Leo Davenport in 1932, a second in 1933 and another win in 1936 by Bob Foster to bring their total to six. These, plus other sporting successes, kept the firm well to the fore through the 1930s. The range ran from 148 to 496cc with ohv and unit-construction plus a few sv models, some of the range with a separate gearbox. Among them were 245 and 344cc Grand Prix machines, based on the works racers and for fast road or racing use. The smaller was also the basis of a 491cc V-twin the factory used to become the first British multi to cover 100 miles in the hour on British soil.

Sadly, Norman Downs died in 1936 and this led to financial problems and the sale of the firm to Jack Sangster in 1939. He planned to move them to the Triumph factory in Coventry but production continued at Hall Green until the end of the decade. The move did take place, as the abbreviated 1940 list was based on the same Dale Street address as Triumph, which meant that the make perished when that plant was bombed late in the year. Plans to use the name post-war for an economy range failed to mature, as production capacity was fully employed building the Triumph twins.

NEW KNIGHT 1923–1929
Holloway & Knight of Bedford tried their hand at first with a range of

lightweights having 147cc, 247cc and 349cc two-stroke Villiers engines, plus a solitary 293cc sv four-stroke from JAP. This latter didn't last long, however, as the marque itself soon faltered, leading to its re-introduction with 147cc and 247cc Villiers-engined models in the summer of 1924; these machines featured saddle tanks and drum brakes to both wheels. The 147 continued for 1925, plus a new 172cc model, and these then formed the basis of the range for several years; Albion two or three-speed gearboxes and all-chain drive were standard. Only the 172 appeared in 1928, but the next year this was joined by a supersports version of the same capacity and a 247cc model appeared again, both the new machines having Sturmey-Archer three-speed gearboxes, but with the onset of the Depression years, the company turned away from the market

NEWMAN 1905

A motor factor based in Tabernacle Street, London EC who offered a primitive with the engine set vertically in the loop frame. Rigid forks, single-speed belt drive and a rim front brake completed a simple specification, no doubt contrived from stock proprietary parts.

NEWMOUNT 1929–1933

This make was really a German Zundapp with a change of tank badge, assembled in Coventry with a tubular frame in place of the pressed-steel one favoured in Europe. The engine was a 198cc two-stroke that drove a three-speed gearbox, and in 1931 the range expanded. One new model had a 300cc Zundapp engine, but others had 348 or 499cc ohv Rudge Python engines. This range continued to 1933 and then left the market.

NEW PARAGON 1921–1922

Originally sold as the Paragon from 1914 to 1921, the marque added 'New' to its name during that year with just one model. This continued with the 358cc two-stroke engine, but this now drove a separate two-speed Albion gearbox by chain, with belt final-drive. Ignition was by means of a CAV magneto bolted directly to the offside crankcase, and by casting mounting-lugs integrally with the crankcase the use of engine plates was avoided. This modified Paragon was produced by The Motor Works, Cressing Road, Braintree, Essex, who added a single-speed option for 1922, their final season.

NEW PROGRESS 1930–1932

This was the final form of the strange Seal three-wheeler that had a central front wheel. For 1932 there was a carrier version that had the 680cc JAPV-twin engine mounted above the front wheel. It drove this via a three-speed-and-reverse gearbox, but only the prototype of this odd design was seen and the Manchester firm then closed.

NEW RAPID 1902–1903

A cycle firm that adopted the 2.25hp Kelecom engine as its motive power, while the cycle fittings included an indicator petrol gauge. Other bicycle features were used along with Bowden wire for some controls, while the finish was excellent, as was usual at that time.

NEW REVOLUTION 1903

This firm, sometimes known as Revolution, offered a primitive, powered by a 2.5hp engine fitted with a special carburettor. This was claimed to run on an equal mixture of petrol and paraffin without loss of power, but nothing further was heard of either the machine or the carburettor.

NEW RYDER 1914–1919

Built at works first in Corporation Street and later at Belmont Row, Birmingham, this firm's range was typical of early two-stroke machines in using a 269cc Villiers engine. This had a choice of Amac or Senspray carburettor. Transmission options were fixed-belt drive, two-speed counter-shaft with chain-cum-belt, or a three-speed Armstrong hub, and the fork choice was Druid or Saxon. Other models were a Semi-TT and a ladies'.

The range continued little altered up to 1916 and appeared briefly in 1919 with the choice of single or two-speed models.

NEW SCALE 1920–1925

Early in 1920, the Manchester-based Scale motorcycle company was reformed as New Scale. Without outside backing and from fresh premises in nearby Droylsden, various models followed with Precision two-stroke, Blackburne and oil-cooled Bradshaw singles, these being finished in cerise colour. TT entries were made in various classes from 1921, a fourth in the Sidecar race of 1924 was their best reward. A 147cc Villiers lightweight with two-speed chain-cum-belt transmission was tried in 1924, when they also listed a machine fitted with the 349cc ohc Dart engine, but towards the end of the year Harry Scale left the company, which soldiered on for one more season with just 349cc Bradshaw and 348cc ohv Blackburne models on offer.

NEWTON-VILLIERS 1920–1921

A simple lightweight with single-

The Newmarket was really a 1930 German Zundapp with a 198cc two-stroke engine, three speeds and typical external flywheel, but was not sold in Britain after 1933.

Newton-Villiers was one of the many who set up in business just after the Great War, using a Villiers engine and simple specification. Not too many such marques survived past 1925.

speed belt drive, Brampton Biflex forks and the Mk IV 269cc Villiers two-stroke engine with flywheel magneto. In appearance much the same as many other hopefuls, but luck wasn't with Newton Brothers of Levenshulme, Manchester, whose stay in the trade was therefore pitifully short.

NEW TRACK c.1970s
This firm produced grass-track-racing frame kits for use with 250cc two-stroke engine units. By keeping to this size they could be lighter than if designed to carry a 500cc ohv engine as an alternative, and this gave them an edge in races.

NICHOLAS PRE-GREAT WAR
Lost in the mists of time, this was a small early producer, most probably a small-time cycle dealer, who used proprietary engines, most likely a 1.5hp MMC, in typical cycle parts of the period.

NICKSON-B 1921–1927
Powered initially by Blackburne engines, hence the B appendage, John Nickson from Bamber Bridge in Lancashire also fitted Brampton forks and Burman gearboxes to the machines that carried his name. First came 348 and 499cc sv models, but in 1922 a Villiers two-stroke was added and was joined in 1924 by a 349cc Bradshaw oil boiler, by which time the larger Blackburne model had gone. Production continued spasmodically thereafter, with the Bradshaw model listed into 1927. The JNU motorcycle originated from the same works.

NLG 1908–1915
North London Garage have a place in history as the marque to win the first official motorcycle race at Brooklands. The rider was Will Cook, the year 1908 and his machine, the NLG, fitted with a 944cc V-twin Peugeot engine. It pulled a high gear and weighed under 120lb (54.5kg). Cook had further successes in 1909, also attempting world records using an NLG fitted with a vast 20hp 90-degree V-twin JAP engine of 2,700cc, but without success.

For general use the firm offered more prosaic models, using a 3.75hp Peugeot engine unless the buyer specified otherwise. By 1910, sprung forks were standard, but the rigid remained an option and 3.5 or 4.5hp JAP engines were listed, also the 5 and 7hp Peugeot V-twins, plus an 8hp JAP V-twin. For 1911 there was a 4hp racer and another fitted with an Anzani V-twin engine.

Only JAP engines were used from 1912, normally either a 4hp single or a 6hp twin, the range reducing to the single for 1915, after which production ceased.

NOBLE 1901–1909
Noble were one of the first to adopt the central engine location, using De Dion, Minerva or MMC engines. By 1903 they produced their own 2.5hp engine at their Blackfriars, London works and hung this from the frame downtube in Minerva style. A mechanical inlet-valve was a feature, along with belt drive and braced forks.

Both valves, the inlet in the head and the exhaust in the cylinder and facing it, were opened by a single cam. This moved a vertical rod both up and down so that arms clamped to it opened the valves in turn, springs closing them as usual. For 1904 the engine was rated at 2.75hp, located vertically in the frame, and adopted the conventional twin-cam method of opening side valves. A larger 4.5hp version was available for racing, but could be adapted to 3.5hp for touring, while the earlier model stayed in the list.

The range continued using both their own and Peugeot engines for the next few years, but failed to survive out of the Edwardian era.

NOBLE-PRECISION 1912
Alfred Noble had his premises at Stoneleigh Works, Hill Street, Coventry and built a typical machine using a 3.5hp Precision engine. Belt drive and Druid forks were employed but the make was only listed for the one year, despite the good detail work and smart appearance.

NOMAD EARLY-1920s
This small two-stroke differed in having its exhaust pipe emerging from the side of the cylinder, which cannot have done much for the cooling. Believed to hail from Coventry, it had few other redeeming features, so few were made or sold.

NORBRECK 1920–1922
Arden pressed-steel spring forks and an Arden 269cc two-stroke engine were utilized in the Norbreck, which was built in Wellingborough, Northants. Transmission was either single speed or two-speed Burman, with belt final-drive in both cases. Later a three-speed box of the maker's own design could be specified and a medium-weight model with 348cc sv Blackburne was mentioned, although not listed. In 1922, their final season, a Moss two-speed box was the option to single-speed, and a Ladies' Model, with open frame, was available.

NORCROFT 1998
This firm, based in Hove, Sussex, launched its V-twin RE Interceptor Series V in April 1998 at the Classic Bike show. Hand built to customer specification, its engine was based on the use of two Royal Enfield 500cc Bullet top-halves, imported from India, where that model was still in production, mounted onto a common crankcase.

Two 28mm Mikuni carburettors supplied the mixture, which was fired

Noble produced their machines throughout the Edwardian era, with some advanced and often unusual features appearing from time to time.

by electronic ignition; there was electric start and the result was around 60hp on tap. A four-speed Enfield gearbox was used and a whole host of options existed on the cycle side. The frame used was a modified Enfield India but others, including the Norton Featherbed, were equally feasible. Norton Roadholder forks and a 9in Grimeca drum brake went at the front, along with a 7in drum at the rear.

In most areas of the machine the customer could do as little or as much of the work as they wished, using new, modified or existing parts. This opened up the prospect of reducing costs and incorporating one's own ideas on detail fixtures and fittings, much as with the café racer format. The production models kept much to the style of the old Royal Enfield parallel-twin Interceptor model, thus keeping the link from past to present.

Norman usually offered a competition machine in their range and this is the trials model for 1956, with a 197cc Villiers 9E engine.

An interesting attempt by Norcroft to build a 1000cc V-twin engine, using two 500cc Royal Enfield Bullet top-halves from the Indian plant, combined with other desirable components.

NORFOLK 1902

Stanley Norfolk was an early racer at Catford in London, who built his machine in typical primitive form. Thus, the 2.75hp MMC engine hung from the downtube of a heavy-duty bicycle frame and had direct-belt drive. The frame headstock was strengthened, rim brakes were fitted and a top speed of 40mph (64km/h) claimed on the flat. Built at Lee in SE London, only one or two were made.

NORMAN 1939–1962

A bicycle firm at Ashford, Kent, who entered the powered field in 1939 with two models, one the Motobyke, an autocycle, the other, the Lightweight, a 122cc motorcycle, both powered by Villiers engines. The autocycle had rigid forks, but was joined by the De Luxe with Webb girders for 1940, plus a lower-geared Carrier model and a 98cc version of the Lightweight. Norman also made autocycles for Rudge that year, but then production ceased until 1946.

They picked up the threads after the war, still with Villiers power, the range comprising the 98cc Autocycle and the 122cc Motorcycle. For 1949, these became the model C with 99cc Villiers 2F, and model B1 with 122cc Villiers 10D engines. They were joined by the B2, this using the 197cc Villiers 6E engine, both B models listed in standard or de luxe forms.

When Norman entered the autocycle market in 1939, they chose to call their machine the Motobyke, but used the same 98cc Villiers as others.

By 1954, the Norman 122 and 197cc road models were available with rear suspension having laid-down units; this is the smaller machine.

They were joined by the model D for 1951, powered by the 99cc Villiers 1F unit, and, for 1953, rear suspension was added to create the B1S and B2S, while the B1 became the model E and a competition model, the 197cc B2C was added to the range.

The models E and B2 went after 1954, the year the 8E replaced the 6E, and the D and B2C after 1955, the year the B1S changed its engine to the 147cc Villiers 30C and a twin, the model TS, was introduced using the 242cc British Anzani engine. That year saw the first use of Armstrong leading-link front forks, which became standard wear for all models the following year. For 1956, the B2S was listed with the 197cc Villiers 9E engine, the 8E remaining available to 1958, and the B2C/S, a sprung version of the B2C using the

9E engine, appeared. The B1S was listed with the alternative of the 148cc Villiers 31C engine for 1957, both continuing to 1959, 1957 also seeing the adoption of rear enclosure by most models.

The twin changed its engine to the 249cc Villiers 2T for 1958 to create the model B3, and was joined by the B3 Sports for 1959, a B2S Sports model of 197cc also appearing, using the same sporting cycle parts. For 1961, the twins were modified and became the B4 models, while the competition machines changed to the B4C Trials with either the 9E or the 246cc Villiers 32A engine, and the B4C Scrambles with the Villiers 34A engine. Only the twins survived into 1962, the year that motorcycle production ceased.

New for 1956 was the 48cc Nippy moped, Sachs powered and based on a Continental design. For 1959, it was joined by a version powered by a 50cc Villiers 3K engine and the Lido model, which had a styled enclosure for the power unit. These models were followed by improved versions, but during 1961 the firm moved to Smethwick, having been taken over by Raleigh Industries. During the final 1962 year mopeds based on Raleigh models were built, but then production ceased, bringing the Norman name to an end.

NORTHUMBRIAN 1920–1921

An obscure post-Great War marque that used a 3.5hp engine and was built in small numbers in the north east.

NORTON 1902–DATE

Founded in Edwardian times by James Lansdowne Norton, this marque became one of the most respected of all in the British industry. Norton himself was a deeply religious man who brought his high standards to all he did, using his toolmaker apprenticeship skills to achieve perfection in his trade. He began supplying fittings to the two-wheeled trades in 1898 and in 1902 built his first motorcycle using an imported 160cc

Even as early as 1908, Norton were using their 'Unapproachable' slogan and noting their TT victory of the previous year.

Typical Norton model of the 1922 period, in this case with the drive chains enclosed, but braking limited to the belt and cycle rims.

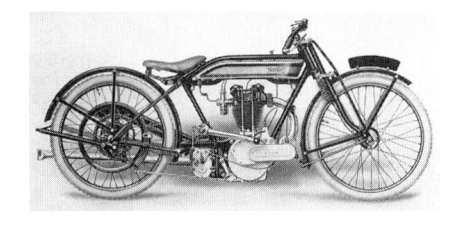

The Norton ohv engine used the common cycle parts to create the model 18, which had a drum front-brake from its 1923 debut.

By 1928, Norton had an overhead-camshaft racing engine and, for that year, created the CS1 model by installing it in the ES2 cradle frame.

The original Moore ohc engine was replaced in 1930 by the Carroll unit that served Norton so well for many years, to win many races.

Clement engine to power it. Hung from the bicycle frame downtube it was typical of the time, but its transmission was either direct belt or by chain to a two-speed gearbox and then by belt. This showed advanced thinking, and the machine was advertised as the Energette.

More machines were offered in 1903 and for some time Norton concentrated on parts supply, with complete machines built to customer order, mainly using Peugeot engines, so by 1906 a range could be said to exist. It was the next year when Norton achieved his breakthrough, for Rem Fowler won the Multi-cylinder race at the first TT, his machine powered by a 690cc Peugeot V-twin engine. This success was highlighted in advertising, while Norton himself went back to his Birmingham works and the design of his first engine.

The engine was a sv 475cc and had a line that would run down the years for over four decades. Simple, basic and well built, it would prove reliable, and easy to maintain and to tune. There was also a V-twin, much like the Peugeot, and another model which used a 274cc Moto Rêve V-twin engine, but neither stayed in the range for long. Both the Energette and Nortonette names were used in 1908, when the famous slogan 'Unapproachable Norton' first appeared in advertisements.

Norton remained intent on the technical side and his opinions were highly regarded, but his neglect of the finances brought trouble and the result was a buy out by R.T. Shelley, who became joint managing director with Norton. This put the firm on a much better footing and they ran forward at their own steady pace. Change was not to happen too often, with major alterations few and far between over the decades. The single was the centre of the firm for many years and the range became just two models of 496 and 634cc, the larger known as the Big Four and intended for sidecar work. There were a few options, including a three-speed rear

The 16H Norton served during the Second World War, but this is a 1954 version, by when it had a modern gearbox and telescopic forks.

hub, but direct-belt drive remained the norm.

In 1912 the smaller engine was revised to 79×100mm dimensions and 490cc, a format that would remain with the firm for a long time and become nearly as famous as the name itself. That year they began to make their mark at Brooklands, even if there was no further success in the TT, and the next year brought tuned models listed as the Brooklands Special and Brooklands Road Special. These BS and BRS machines had engines that had performed to required standards at the track in a slave frame and proved popular.

The firm had little involvement in the Great War but, during 1915, a three-speed gearbox and all-chain drive appeared, although belt drive remained usual. This led to the model 16 in the next year; one that would run for a long time, with its sv 490cc engine, three-speeds and chain drive. Later came a Colonial version listed

The Norton model 18 with overhead valves for 1932 took the same route forward as the sv model 16H, including the revised front-forks.

as the model 17C, so the first version became the 16H for home.

The range was listed by model numbers, a practice that the firm used for most of its life and which seemed random at times but did have some form of logic. Variations using alternative transmissions meant for more numbers, but the basic machines remained the 16H and the 634cc Big Four plus the tuned BS and BRS machines with direct-belt drive.

After the war, in 1920, Norton moved to Bracebridge Street, where they would stay until 1963 – an address that was known over the world. Little was altered until 1922, when the first ohv Norton appeared at Brooklands with the familiar 79×100mm dimensions. It was raced that year and was in the range for 1923 as the model 18. That became the final year for belt drive and some better success at the TT with second places, while the firm won the

prestigious Maudes Trophy for the first time it was to be had.

It was better still in 1924, when the firm won two TT races, several European races and retained the Maudes Trophy. Sadly, James Norton died in the following year, having kept going through two painful years thanks to his will-power. His name continued on machines that reflected his nature with their upright cylinders.

Little really altered on the Norton models through the second half of that decade, but 1926 brought the model 19 of 588cc with ohv and the option of four speeds in place of the standard three. The firm won the Maudes yet again, so, including their 1925 win, it was four in a row. In addition, Stanley Woods won the Senior TT using a model 18, even though this was now really in need of replacement.

While the stock range continued by combining parts in various ways, there was a new engine on its way for racing and this was designed by Walter Moore. The result appeared in 1927 and was the first ohc engine from the firm. Based on the familiar dimensions, its camshaft was driven by shaft and bevels, and the magneto went behind the engine rather than in front as was usual. The new unit went into a new cradle frame and the result won the 1927 Senior TT.

The cradle frame was then used for the ES2, which had the 490cc ohv engine but with the magneto at the rear, and this was first listed for 1928 along with the ohc model as the CS1, both with saddle fuel-tanks in place of the flat tanks still used by the rest of the range. They also had a strange double-barrelled silencer, while 1929

Norton gave their sv and ohv models a new line for 1932, with a revised engine and other changes that would continue to be added in time.

The post-war ES2 always had rear suspension but, at first, of the plunger type, as here for 1951, while up front went the Roadholder forks.

The racing Norton returned in 1947 as the Manx, in 348cc Model 40 and 498cc Model 30 sizes, with plunger rear-suspension and Roadholder front-forks. It was destined for a long life.

saw the saddle tanks on the rest of the range, which was extended with 348cc models. There were two of these and, as with the new 500s, they had a cradle frame with the JE using the ohv and the CJ the ohc engine.

Little racing success came in 1929, so Walter Moore moved on to NSU in Germany and Joe Craig took over as race manager, having been racing and winning on Nortons for some years. He would become famous as the firm's race director and for his ability to pick the best riders and keep the machines at the front. His first move was to design a new racing engine in conjunction with Arthur Carroll. The result was first seen late that year and took much of the next to come true, but was one of the truly great designs of all time. The line of the crankcase, square-bottom bevel box, vertical shaft and rear magneto would remain much the same for over thirty years and post-war found fame as the Manx.

Before then, the firm was on the threshold of a great period in their racing history, but it was late in 1930

The model 7 Dominator twin followed the trend and was added to Norton's range for 1949, using the ES2 cycle parts at first, but its engine was always good.

A fine example of an International Norton with plunger suspension parked outside a London dealer offering spares and alternative items for sale.

Norton created this 500T model for trials use by using a short frame and alloy engine, the result proving much better than their attempts pre-war.

In 1952 Norton created the model 88 by installing the twin engine in the famous Featherbed frame, which was renowned for its roadholding.

before the new design won a classic event. All changed in 1931, when the firm began their domination of the racing scene, winning Junior and Senior TT races and setting a new hour-record. It was also all change for the sv and ohv engine, with the magneto moved to behind the engine, the dynamo strapped to the magneto and dry-sump lubrication with a gear pump in the timing case. In this form they would run to the end of their days, still retaining the line first seen in 1909. Both the ohc models went over to the new style of engine, always known from then on as the Carroll type to distinguish them from the earlier Moore type. The frames were revised to be shorter and lower, and this set the firm off for another decade or so.

Norton dominated classic racing for much of the decade with riders such as Tim Hunt, Stanley Woods, Jimmy Guthrie, Freddie Frith and Harold Daniell among their many stars. Near the end, the 350cc Velocette gave them trouble in that class and the German BMW and Italian Gilera with supercharged multis took over in the Senior class, while Norton dropped out of racing for 1939, to concentrate on WD work.

During the decade the road machines were gradually improved and 1932 brought International versions of the ohc models, with these built in racing trim but available for road use as well. In 1933 a 348cc ohv model was listed, the next year

The 490cc ES2 and 348cc Model 50 both changed to the Featherbed frame for 1959, the smaller often destined to finish up as a Triton basis.

The Manx had long since adopted the Featherbed frame and remained in production to 1962, and was later to perform well in classic racing.

brought an oil-bath primary chaincase and for 1935 there was the Norton four-speed gearbox that would serve the firm well to their final days. Plunger rear-suspension came as an option for the Inters, as the Internationals were known, in 1938 and was extended to other cradle-frame machines in the next year. That year saw the Inter listed in Manx Grand Prix form as a pure racing model – to become the Manx post-war.

During the war the firm concentrated on building large numbers of the 16H for the services, along with a number of Big Four outfits that had sidecar wheel drive. Many would be sold off post-war to a population desperate for transport. The range for 1946 was just the 16H and 18, still with girder forks but both in the cradle frame. Late in the year a few Manx Nortons were built; these had the plunger frame and new Roadholder telescopic forks developed from a pre-war type to which had been added hydraulic damping. By 1947 the Manx was listed in 348 and 498cc capacities, along with the International in two sizes and the Big Four and ES2, this last also in the plunger frame. There were also two trials models, but both were far too heavy for their purpose and so were soon dropped.

In 1949 the firm introduced their first twin for a long time as the 497cc model 7 Dominator. It was a conventional ohv vertical-twin that had its one camshaft at the front driven by gears and chain. It was designed by Bert Hopwood and had an excellent combustion-chamber form that would stand it in good stead down the years. Construction was typical of the era and the cycle parts came from the ES2 with four speeds, plunger frame and telescopic forks. Also new that year was the 500T, which was purpose built for trials with an alloy engine and most successful.

The firm had returned to road racing after the war with some good results, but the plunger frame had become very dated. This did not stop Eric Oliver winning the first sidecar world title in 1949 or Geoff Duke from success in the Clubman's and then the Manx GP that year. The outcome was history, for in 1950 the famous featherbed frame designed by Rex McCandless made its debut with Geoff Duke as one of its works riders. At the same time the standard Manx was fitted with a dohc cylinder head and in 1951 it went into the featherbed frame. By then Duke had begun his domination of the racing scene, with both 350 and 500 world titles going to him in 1951.

Reacting to customer demand, the firm introduced the model 88 Dominator for 1952 by fitting the twin engine in the featherbed frame. At first an export-only model, it was an immediate success and would run for years. The next year saw the ES2 and model 7 in a frame with pivoted-fork rear suspension, the twin in this form intended for sidecar work as the featherbed was not then thought suitable. That year also saw the International with an all-alloy engine and the featherbed frame, and there was a one-off sv twin, based on the Dominator but in a rigid frame and intended for service use. It was also the year when Norton was taken over by AMC although this had no immediate effect.

For 1961, the Jubilee was stretched to 349cc to create the Navigator, which benefited from the addition of Roadholder forks and the front brake from the big twins.

The Norton model 88 was, in time, enlarged to the 600cc model 99 and then to a full 650, with all models available in this form using the Jubilee enclosure.

There were short-stroke engines for the Manx models in 1954, by when the works racing successes were declining, although Ray Amm won the Junior and Senior TTs, Eric Oliver won his fourth sidecar title and there had been innovation in the form of a fully-streamlined kneeler that was raced once and took many world records late in 1953.

Around 1965, Norton built this 800cc twin prototype with overhead camshafts driven by a chain in the tubes, but it went no further.

Some of the older road singles were dropped after 1954 but others of 597cc appeared, to be joined by 348cc models in 1956, by when Joe Craig had retired after many years of service to the firm and his much-developed Manx singles. The International models were only available to special order by then, but for the road there came the model 99, a 596cc version of the featherbed twin. The Manx Norton now had little effect on the world scene, but the standard versions continued to fill the bulk of the grids at most race meetings.

For 1957 the model 77 joined the range for sidecar work, being an

The big Norton twin engine fitted well into a Matchless G85S scrambles frame to create this off-road P11.

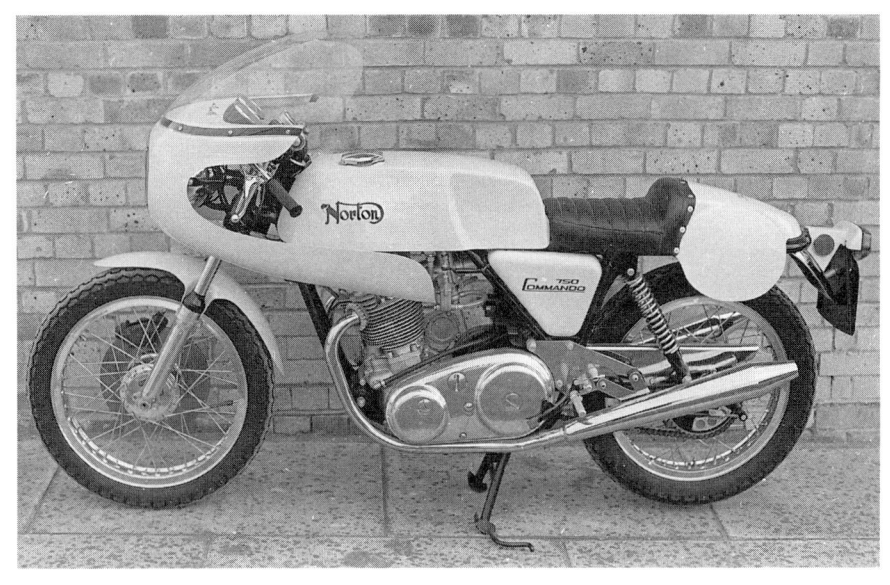

A Production Racing version of the Commando was a useful addition to the line up, but the added power did bring some problems to the engine.

amalgamation of the ES2 frame and the 596cc twin engine. The next year brought the off-road Nomad, which was built for the USA and comprised the 77 frame with a tuned 99 engine having twin carburettors, magneto ignition and an alternator for the lights. The stock twin-models also changed to alternator electrics that year and a twin-carburettor option became available.

In 1958 Eric Oliver came out of retirement and drove a featherbed sidecar-outfit in the TT, finishing tenth to prove that the frame was suitable for such work. From this came a sidecar kit, while the models 77 and the 597cc single were dropped.

For 1959 there was a new twin, the 249cc Jubilee named to celebrate sixty years in business. It had a conventional ohv engine built in-unit with a four-speed gearbox and this went into a composite frame based on a Francis-Barnett design. In the trend of the times the rear of the machine was enclosed, so most of the rear wheel was hidden. That year brought radical changes to the 50 and ES2 singles, which went into the featherbed frame and adopted alternator electrics and coil ignition. For the Manx there was a change to the camshaft drive, so

that the bottom bevel-box disappeared.

The Jubilee rear enclosure went on to the 88 and 99 for 1960 and in this form they were listed as de luxe machines. To enable this to be done, the main frame tubes were pulled in around the dual-seat nose and this type was soon known as the 'slimline'; thus the earlier type became the 'wideline'. An 88 Nomad joined the 99 version, but both were soon dropped from the range.

The Commando came in several forms, this the Roadster with smaller side panels and standard dualseat.

In 1961 the ES2 and 50 changed to the slimline frame while the smaller-twin range was extended by the 349cc Navigator and by offering both small twins in a standard form without the rear enclosure. Of more interest to the sports rider was the

This was the Wulf 500cc two-stroke cross-flow engine, another experiment, but hardly in the Norton image of lusty four-strokes.

announcement of the 646cc, twin-carburettor Manxman-twin which was first sold only in the USA. Later that year it was available in Europe in the same finish as the other twins and was listed just as the 650. Equally interesting was the appearance of two sports twins as the 88SS and 99SS, fitted with twin carburettors and other sports features. It was also the year when Mike Hailwood won the Senior TT, with Tom Phillis finishing third on a Domiracer-twin tuned by the factory.

Production of the Manx was reduced to building from spares in 1962, when the range was extended with a 650 de luxe with rear enclosure, 650SS and a further extension of the original engine for the 745cc Atlas. This only had one carburettor and was intended to give performance from capacity, allied to torque for acceleration.

The range was reduced for 1963, with the 88 and 650 in standard and SS builds only, plus the Atlas. The small twins were joined by the 383cc Electra, which was based on the Navigator but had electric start. Of more concern to enthusiasts for the marque was the closing of Bracebridge Street, with production moved to the AMC factory at Plumstead. One result was the first hybrid, the Atlas scrambler which used the 745cc Norton engine in an AMC frame fitted with Norton forks and wheels.

After 1963 the Manx was no more and the two road singles were dropped, along with the de luxe versions of the small twins and the standard ones of the larger twins. The hybrid model became the N15CS'N' but was little altered. In 1965 the ES2 and Model 50 returned to the range, but were really AMC models fitted with Norton badges and so annoyed Norton, AJS and Matchless fans alike during their brief life. At the year-end the Navigator and Electra were dropped, with the Jubilee going a year later along with the 88SS. A new idea was about to come from the firm under new ownership, but the older machines continued to the end of the decade, with the 650SS becoming the Mercury in 1969 and the off-road model joined by the P11 in 1967. This had the 745cc Norton engine in a Matchless G85S scrambles frame, had its code changed but was soon dropped.

The new idea was released as the Commando and went on sale in 1968. It combined the existing 745cc twin engine and AMC gearbox in a frame with insulating mountings for these two components and the rear fork. Known as Isolastic, this kept vibration away from the rider and, in this design, the engine was inclined forward a little. The new model had its own style, with the seat extended forward to form knee grips and a glass-fibre tank and seat moulding that included a tail section.

Introduced as the Model 20, it soon changed its name to Fastback and was joined early in 1969 by the R and S version built for the US street-scrambler market. Both lacked the tail unit, while the S had style thanks to having the twin exhausts run along the left of the machine. In 1970 there came the Roadster, which was an S with low pipes, and later other versions. One of the most significant was the Production Racer which was built for that purpose and was successful. In contrast there was the Hi-Rider for the custom market and a police version known as the Interpol.

There were problems in 1972, when the Interstate model was added and a performance engine known as the Combat appeared. This was simply asking too much from what was essentially a twenty-five-year-old design and it was 1973 before all the troubles were sorted out. Early that year the engine was stretched yet again to 829cc and this took over from the 745cc engine by the year end. Roadster, Interstate and Hi-Rider models were built, to be joined in 1974 by the John Player Norton which came with a fairing as standard. It reflected the sponsorship the firm had received for their road racing over the previous two years.

In 1975 the twins added electric start and moved the gear lever to the left side to suit the US market, but by then had been drawn into the general crisis affecting the British motorcycle industry, so production struggled on to 1977 and then ceased.

Norton tried the rotary engine path in the 1980s, with this an early example, which relied on air cooling for the three-chamber body.

However, this was not the end for Norton. In the 1970s they had dabbled with other twins, one the Wulf two-stroke with just the prototype built, and the Cosworth which was meant for road and racing use. Neither came to anything but, during that time, the firm inherited a rotary, or Wankel, project that reached them from Triumph via BSA.

First customers for the rotary were the police, who could give service feed-back, and in 1983 a second version appeared as the Interpol 2. A production model finally came in 1987 as a limited Classic edition and the 100 built had air cooling. Promotion was by road racing and, in 1988, a water-cooled model was launched as the Commander. The next year saw John Player sponsorship once again and a successful season in the UK, followed by the introduction of the sports F1 model for 1990 with this finished in the JPS livery.

This should have been the start of a revival, but the recession and Norton's own financial troubles stopped this. The F1 Sports replaced the F1 for 1992, when the Commander continued with a second version complete with panniers and Steve Hislop won the Senior TT for the firm. This high note could not continue with the money morass they fell into through some dubious financial dealings and production ceased in 1993. A sad end to a glorious history.

However, the name refused to die and late in 1997 a new Norton appeared at the NEC motorcycle show as the result of the trading of the famous name. The machine had the 652cc engine from the BMW F650, actually a Rotax from Austria, with four valves for its single cylinder, and water cooling. This went into a modern chassis with a retro line and was to be built in Britain, but could not be sold there as a Norton due to a name rights problem.

This was rather swept aside early in 1998 when a link with March was established, whereby their range would carry Norton badges; this was launched in April. It was nothing if not extensive, radical and complex, for the top model was the Nemesis with its 1,497cc 60-degree 32-valve V8 engine. This was to be built in two forms, one with three plugs per cylinder, electronic management and fuel injection systems and barrel throttles to produce 280hp at 14,000rpm. The second had a less complex ignition system, but was to produce 235hp at 12,500rpm.

The specification then went on to include a six-speed gearbox with push-button gear changing and clutch operation, so the clutch lever was only used for starts and stops. There was an aluminium or magnesium-alloy twin-spar frame cast as one item, telescopic forks with the sliders cast to include the brake callipers and half the front mudguard, rear fork cast with brake calliper, alloy wheels and rim-mounted disc brakes for the front wheel. A single disc brake went at the rear and active suspension control was to be included to modify the settings as required.

Along with the V8 came a slant-block 748cc four that shared much from the eight and was also to be built in two forms as the 750 Manx. Next came another V8, the 1,497cc Commando cruiser model with different engine dimensions, ohv and only two valves per cylinder, simpler fuel injection and only four speeds. This would go into a tubular frame, but would share the Nemesis suspension system and brakes.

Finally, there was the intention to produce a 600cc single in several forms. With desmodromic valve operation it would be the International and built in race replica and super moto forms. Lower powered road and trail singles with ohc were also to come. All in all it was a most ambitious programme and whether the team would fulfil the aim to start production late in 1998 remained to be seen. It all added up to a highly over-ambitious plan with little chance of success and little more was heard of it making any progress.

In 1999 a far more realistic machine made its appearance, built to the design of Kenny Dreer whose Vintage Rebuilds firm did much

A sporting version of the Commander was added in 1990 as the F1, replaced the next year by the F1 Sports.

Norton Commando work. It was the VR880 Commando Sprint Special, which retained much of the Commando line with some useful improvements. The engine was stretched to 872cc, but retained its classic Norton lines along with the four-speed gearbox and diaphragm clutch, albeit with belt primary-drive. The Isolastic frame was used with twin front and single rear disc brakes, and modern suspension units and improved electrics. The style had much of the lines of the old Roadster but with a well-shaped seat with rear hump.

In all there were forty-seven VR880s built, but then Dreer moved on to a revised twin with 952cc engine and fuel injection. Scheduled for 2004, it looked set to keep the famous Norton name at the front of the classic movement, taking its place just at the Big Four had done back in Edwardian days and quite as significant.

NORVIL 1989–DATE
This name was first used by Norton-Villiers when they opened a performance shop to build special versions of the Commando and to sell racing and custom parts. Years later the name passed to Les Emery, who continued to produce the parts and, from 1989, complete machines. All were of the Commando type, some much as the original but plus improvements, others with more of the Norvil performance parts.

NUT 1911–1933
Based at South Benwell, Newcastle-upon-Tyne, this make took its name from the initials of its home town. It

A fine NUT V-twin model was introduced for 1920, which used their own engine and kept their well-known cylindrical tank, changing to flat tank for 1927.

Close up of the NUT cylindrical tank and its transfer, which spelled out the firm and where it was located.

Even in their last year, 1933, NUT continued to build fine motorcycles with the 692cc V-twin engine.

was backed by the Angus Sanderson firm and their manager, Hugh Mason, promoted the name in competition along with his friend Robert Ellis, who finished sixth in the 1912 Junior TT using a 344cc Moto-Rêve V-twin engine.

Their 1913 range only used JAP engines, with a 3.5hp single plus 2.75 and 3.25hp V-twins, and it was the smaller 345cc twin that both men used in the Junior TT that year. Mason had a serious accident in practice, but rode well enough to win by less than a minute, with Ellis eighth. Sensibly, they concentrated on V-twins for their production machines and built up a range extending from 2.75 to 8hp by 1916.

Post-war, they moved to Derwenthaugh, Swalwell, near Newcastle and continued with V-twins using their own engines and three-speed Sturmey-Archer gearboxes. However, the financial backing was lost and for a time the firm traded as Hugh Mason & Co. Ltd, before a further upheaval finally steadied them for a while as the NUT Engine & Cycle Company by 1923.

Production was naturally affected by all this and the range shrank to one sv V-twin of 700cc, but available in several specifications to meet most requirements including colonial. The big London dealers, Maudes Motor Mart, were sole concessionaires by 1924 and for a time promoted them heavily. The marque's familiar cylindrically shaped fuel tank in nut-brown finish was replaced by a plated flat-tank for 1927 and then a saddle tank the following year, as the trade as a whole switched to this styling.

The NVT Easy Rider used imported engines but made little impact on the moped market, so became just another chapter in a sorry story.

A 172cc Villiers two-stroke model was added for 1928 only, as was a sports 747cc sv twin with specially tuned engine. Then in 1929 came further singles with 248cc ohv, 346cc sv and ohv, and a 496cc ohv V-twin, the latter also being offered in 692cc form, with its own sv equivalent, to see them through the decade. Their cycle side was conventional and the machines were fully equipped and well made. Unfortunately, this made them too expensive for those times, so they struggled on to 1933 but then the minimal production came to a halt.

NVT 1976–1979

Norton Villiers Triumph was one short-lived result of the cataclysmic days of the British industry in the 1970s. Formed by various amalgamations, its first machines appeared in 1976 and were a series of moped called the Easy Rider. All used imported Morini engines from Italy and there were models with one or two speeds, one styled to motorcycle form with a dummy tank, and two with four speeds.

The mopeds had limited success in a field dominated by Puch and the Japanese, but an off-road junior Easy Rider was added. In 1978 they were joined by the 123 and 171cc Rambler trail models, but both used Yamaha engine and gearbox units and other imported components. All were withdrawn in 1979 when the Ramblers became BSA Trackers.

NVT also tried the trail-model route with this Rambler, which used Yamaha engine units, failed to sell and then became the BSA Tracker.

NYE 1910–1912

R.G. Nye & Co. of Leather Lane, London, were agents for several makes, but late in 1910 showed machines under their own name at the Olympia show. There were touring, TT and Colonial models having a 3.5hp Precision engine with Bosch magneto, Druid forks, belt drive and the option of a two-speed rear hub. They also showed a 2.5hp lightweight.

For 1912 they only listed a single machine, with a 4hp JAP engine, two-speed Albion gearbox and belt drive, but then reverted to acting as agents. As such, their name was linked to the Stuart two-stroke, tandem twin model announced late in 1912, and also to PV, but the NYE name left the lists.

◆ O ◆

OAKLEIGH 1910–1914
A make that used a 3.75hp single or 5hp V-twin Peugeot engine, direct-belt drive and a spring frame having sprung forks. This specification changed for 1911 to the use of a 4.5hp JAP engine in a rigid frame, alternative engine options being JAP V-twins of 6, 7 or 8hp. By 1914 they were down to a 3.5hp JAP single and then became another war casualty.

OEC 1901–1954
Originally the Osborne Motor Manufacturing Co. of Lincoln, the name later became Osborn Engineering Company, or OEC. Due to some of their designs the initials were sometimes read as 'odd engineering contraptions' and not without reason. The founder was Frederick J. Osborn, who built his first machine in 1901 using a 4hp engine hung from the frame downtube and driving the rear wheel by a flat belt. He already had experience of assembling machines for others and went on to produce four-speed engine pulleys for general use.

Their 1909 single had a 3.5hp engine, fitted with their own pulley, and a means of sliding the rear wheel to adjust belt tension after changing the pulley speed. There was also a form of trailing-link front fork, so the unusual designs were already appearing. Production then concentrated on the pulleys for some years.

An unusual OEC, built in 1928 for War Office testing to see how twin rear-wheels would aid traction, these being fatter but on smaller wheel-rims.

The combination of the OEC duplex steering and the Tinkler combined engine and gearbox unit resulted in this machine, on show late in 1928.

Post-war, they built a 499cc sv single and 998cc V-twin with Blackburne engines for Messrs Burney & Blackburne and didn't appear as manufacturers under their own name until late 1922. Then the transfer on the tanks of these machines was changed from plain Blackburne to OEC-Blackburne, as Blackburne concentrated solely on the supply of engines to the trade. However, the appearance in 1921 of a combination for taxi work, with peculiar wheel-steering in place of handlebars, possessed all the hallmarks of an OEC production, so their presence behind the scenes could easily have been detected.

Typical OEC, this is a 1931 Flying Squad model with their unusual front and rear suspension systems, and a 980cc JAP V-twin engine in this example.

Models having 348cc Blackburne engines with sv or ohv were added for 1923, a 147cc two-stroke joined in 1924 and in 1925 they launched an ohc model with 348cc engine. This carried the OEC-Atlanta name, which was extended to encompass a range of JAP-powered models the next year, when even more diversity was seen with the appearance of OEC-Temple sports motorcycles. This developed from a close involvement with the record-breaking exploits of rider Claude Temple, for whom OEC built the frames and assembled the right cycle parts.

At Arpajon in France during October 1926, Temple captured the World's Motorcycle Speed Record at 121mph (194km/h) riding an OEC-Temple-Anzani and, naturally, for 1927 this led to an extended choice of models featuring the famous man's name. Sturdy duplex tube frames with Druid forks were fitted with a wide choice of engine sizes from Blackburne, British Vulpine and own-brand Atlanta – these in 348 and 497cc ohc form.

Even the lightweight OEC had rear suspension in 1934, but kept to conventional girder-forks and a 148cc Villiers engine.

At the end of the year, after practical testing in the TT races, came a new OEC novelty in a patent duplex steering system, in which the bottom frame rails extended forwards almost to the front-wheel centres where they bowed outwards to provide turning clearance on full lock. The front end of each rail was joined to a tube that ran up and back at an angle, in the manner of an extended steering head, the two tubes being united across their top ends by a cross member that was part of the main frame. Into each tube went bearing races and a spindle, which had links attached top and bottom; these links pointed ahead, their forward ends joined by two more spindles. Two further tubes pivoted on

OEC offered this Atlanta Duo in 1936 with a choice of engines, but feet-forward failed to catch on, any more than their duplex steering.

these, thus lying parallel to and ahead of the first fixed pair and with the wheel held between them and able to move in tune with road irregularities, checked by springs. The total effect was what is known to engineers as a four-bar chain and, viewed from above, was much as Ackermann car steering but turned around. Models with this unique feature were naturally, in OEC parlance, christened OEC-Duplex, a name that was to be used right through to 1940.

A 994cc ohv Atlanta V-twin Duplex model appeared for 1928, when the model range as a whole reached almost unmanageable proportions, with JAP, Blackburne, Villiers, MAG, Bradshaw and Atlanta engines offered in numerous permutations of frames and forms, further extended by the introduction of a sprung version of the duplex frame and a complete machine with Tinkler engine-in-a-box, both of which were on view at the Olympia show in November. The Tinkler had its water-cooled ohv engine with horizontal cylinder, three-speed gearbox and ancillaries all enclosed within an aluminium box fronted by a radiator; the complete unit nestled comfortably in OEC's widely spaced frame, but it was not a commercial success. Not unexpectedly, 1929 brought a reduced choice from a 172cc Villiers two-stroke to a 747cc sv JAP V-twin but, with Blackburne engines and the Duplex steering as options, still creating great variety.

The fine series of records was besmirched in 1930 when Joe Wright set the world maximum to over 150mph (240km/h) on, it was claimed, an OEC, which was shown at the Earls Court show instead of the Zenith he actually used for the record runs.

Despite this, the firm continued with its long range of models, using engines from Blackburne, Sturmey-Archer and JAP, from 350cc singles to 750cc V-twins. They moved across the harbour to Portsmouth in 1932 but continued to offer their duplex steering and spring frame either as standard or an option, this to vary from year to year. In practice, this meant that what any customer asked for would be provided. A 250 was added for 1933, by when only JAP engines were used, but 1934 saw a change to Matchless four-stroke engines and Villiers two-strokes of 148, 249 and 346cc, plus a second, water-cooled, 249cc.

It was conventional lightweights for OEC after the Second World War, with this 122cc model at the bottom of the 1953 range, first seen in 1949.

During 1934 OEC announced their novel two-wheeled car, listed as the Whitwood, and this design led them on to the Atlanta Duo of 1936 to revive a name of the 1920s. This was a foot-forward design with a very low seat height and footboards extending beside the front wheel, available with a choice of engines, but the design was not to catch on.

From 1937 the firm used AJS engines instead of Matchless, plus a JAP V-twin that year only, and adopted a revised form of their pivoted-fork rear suspension. By 1938 they were down to three models, all using AJS single engines, and 1939 brought Girling brakes and two simple lightweights using 98 and 122cc Villiers engines.

OEC did not start building motorcycles again until 1949, when they

OEC used pivoted-fork rear suspension for their post-war lightweights, with no sign of the complex pre-war systems; this is a 1953 model with a 197cc Villiers engine.

listed two conventional lightweights using the Villiers 122cc 10D and 197cc 6E engines. Rear suspension appeared in 1951, while 1952 brought the Apollo that fitted the 248cc sv Brockhouse engine, also used by Indian. The next year saw a trials model with a two-stage rear chain-drive, for constant chain tension, but this odd idea found little favour. A small range ran on for 1954, but came to an end late that year to conclude an interesting and innovative marque.

OGSTON 1914

The name of the Acton, London firm that produced the Wilkinson-TMC machines for a brief period. At that time they had an 848cc, in-line, four-cylinder engine, three-speed gearbox, shaft drive, rear bevel-box and bucket seat. They were advanced and expensive.

OK 1899–1926

Humphries & Dawes were partners based in Hall Green, Birmingham, where they made cycle parts and built their first motorcycle in 1899. They expanded the business to include motorcycle parts, but built few machines during the next decade, using Minerva, Precision and Green engines.

For 1912, when located in Lancaster Street, they introduced a new range using 2.5, 3.75 and 4.25hp Precision engines with belt drive and hub gears. The next year saw the largest replaced by a model with a 6hp JAP V-twin engine, two speeds and chain drive.

The OK Junior was introduced for 1914 and its 2hp engine had an overhead inlet valve and drove a two-speed gearbox by chain. Final drive was by belt and the fittings included an Amac carburettor, Ruthardt magneto and Druid forks. Other models were the 3.5hp single and 3hp V-twin, both with OK engines. A 269cc two-stroke model and a 2.5hp JAP were added for 1915, when the V-twin was dropped, and only the Junior and the 2.5hp were built in 1916.

In 1919, appreciating the overwhelming need for cheap personal transport, they decided to concentrate on a one-model only policy and that of the simplest form. This was the OK-Junior with 293cc Union two-stroke engine and direct-belt drive, which was claimed to be the 'Ford' of the motorcycle world. Arrangements were made to build up production to over 20,000 Juniors per annum by 1921. By the middle of 1920, 200 per week were leaving the works when the option of a 269cc Villiers engine was available, but afterwards demand fell as the post-Great War buyers' market faded. To increase appeal a two-speed Albion chain-cum-belt version was listed in 1921 and a three-speed Moss geared model the next year.

For 1923 the range really began to expand, with two four-stroke models having 249cc sv or ohv Blackburne engines joining the 293cc two-stroke, and for the following year came 349cc oil-cooled ohv Bradshaw and 348cc ohv Blackburne machines with three speeds and all-chain drive. With small changes, these models were again seen in 1925, when Burman gearboxes were standardized with the Moss an option. For 1926 a three-speed, all-chain version of the Junior with dummy belt-rim brakes to both wheels was announced but, early in the year, the partnership between Humphries and Dawes was ended. Veloce Ltd moved into the Hall Green works and Dawes rented a section of them to concentrate on bicycle manufacture under his own name, but Humphries moved to new premises and began afresh with motorcycles under the OK Supreme marque name.

OK-Supreme's famous 'Lighthouse' model was easy to spot, with the camshaft drive chamber running up the side of the 248cc engine as in this 1932 example.

OK-SUPREME 1926–1940

Formed by Ernie Humphries from the split of the OK partners, the existing range continued with a 293cc two-stroke and four-strokes using 300cc JAP, 349cc Bradshaw or 249 and 348cc Blackburne engines, all with three speeds. Still in Birmingham, this kept the firm going until 1927, when only JAP engines were used, and they went back to the TT to take third place in the Lightweight.

They improved to a win in 1928, when Frank Longman led from start to finish. For this he used a JAP engine with a new cylinder head designed by G.H. Jones which had twin exhaust ports and a downdraught inlet. Longman was third in the 1929 TT but had other successes, all of which encouraged the firm to offer a much extended range for those two years, most with JAP engines, some still with Blackburne. For these, an advanced cellulose finish was introduced on the tanks, handlebars and wheel hubs for 1929.

This expansion continued into the new decade, when they first raced an

A 1935 Flying Cloud OK-Supreme fitted with the 245cc engine, with some enclosure of both engine and gearbox to clean up the lines.

ohc model that became a production model in 1931. Known as the Lighthouse, its engine had the camshaft drive in a tunnel on the right with the cams at its top end to move tappets and rockers. A small glass window at the top of the tunnel gave the model its name, but it was the older models with JAP engines that were placed in the 1930 TT.

In the early-1930s the firm began to give its models names and the best known were the Flying Clouds, some of which had a conventional ohc engine in 248 and 346cc capacities. The cycle side developed as for the era, with girder forks, saddle tank, hand change replaced by foot, and some enclosure of the engine and gearbox when this was in fashion. Engines developed, most from JAP, but with Matchless appearing in 1939. Before then there had been a high-camshaft JAP, with ohc lines, but this was short lived.

The range continued to be extensive to the end of the decade and most of it was listed for 1940. However, the firm was soon engaged on vital war work, so motorcycle production ceased. It was rumoured that, post-war, a small batch of their competition grass-track special models were assembled using JAP engines.

The timing side view of the OK-Supreme 300cc sv model shows its JAP engine set in the neat cycle parts, along with hand-change gearbox, lights and other fittings.

This 1938 OK-Supreme had a 245cc high-camshaft JAP engine, but this was only used for that one year.

OLIVOS c.1920–1921

Another short-lived post-war marque, but one that differed from most in fitting a 499cc Blackburne engine, rather than the usual Villiers, and in providing a spring frame. Production would have been limited by the supply of the engine and other parts.

OLYMPIC 1902–1905 AND 1919–1923

F.H. Parkyn, a cycle maker in Wolverhampton, used this name for his early conventional motorcycles of 1903, which were powered by 2.75hp MMC engines. Few were made and production soon ceased.

The name returned in 1919, based at Granville Street, for a quality light- and medium-weight range of models that used a selection of engines from Villiers, Blackburne, Verus or Orbit. These went into a straight tube frame that was designed to suit these and other engines and had a patent swinging gearbox mounting, which allowed for simple adjustment of the transmission. The firm also produced the New Courier marque for the lower end of the market, but both went after 1923 as trade slumped.

The OMC was built by the brother of the maker of the SOS and fitted with a 172cc Villiers engine, but only for the one year.

OMC 1930

This lightweight was built at the SOS works run by Len Vale-Onslow and marketed by his brother. It used a 172cc Villiers engine and three-speed Burman gearbox, with these fitted into a pin-jointed frame with Webb girder forks. It was a neat and well finished machine with its own style, but few were built and the name was soon gone.

The first Omega was a bicycle with a small engine mounted at the bottom bracket with a clever transmission, but it failed to catch on.

OMEGA 1909–1910

Based in Wolverhampton and first seen at the late-1909 Stanley show, this firm built a machine designed by B.S. Roberts and S. Dorsett, who was later with Diamond and Orbit. It was, in essence, a bicycle with a 1.5hp 203cc engine fitted at the bottom bracket.

The engine had a horizontal cylinder and a crankshaft formed as a large-diameter eccentric, so that the pedal shaft could pass through its centre. An epicyclic reduction gear went in a chamber next to the crankcase with chain drive to the rear wheel and gear drive to the Simms magneto mounted above and behind the crankcase. It was clever and well made in ladies' and gents' form, but short lived.

OMEGA 1914–1927

This Omega was built at the works of W.J. Green & Co. at Croft Road, Coventry and appeared during 1914 as a 3hp 336cc two-stroke model. It had a two-speed Toroga gearbox and chain-cum-belt drive, chain-driven U.H. magneto, petroil lubrication and Druid forks.

Post-war, this model was soon joined by others but concentrated on a 292cc sv JAP-engined lightweight in three forms, these determined by transmission choice. A 545cc sv Blackburne version was added to these for 1921, after a move to larger premises enabled production to be increased. For 1922, an innovative 348cc two-stroke with widely splayed duplex tube frame and new spring forks of low unsprung weight, built throughout by the company, was offered as an all-weather mount. The engine from this was also available in a model of more conventional outline, as were other lightweights with 248 and 292cc sv single and 677cc sv V-twin JAP engines, and single speed or Sturmey-Archer geared drives.

Only the 293cc JAP was continued for 1923, along with the 348cc two-stroke, both in various forms, to be joined by a 170cc two-stroke miniature with forward-sloping engine in a loop frame and with two speeds. Next season the range expanded, with 249cc Blackburne and 348cc Barr & Stroud sports models, plus a Ladies' Model variant of the 170cc miniature. Only the 248cc Blackburne failed to go ahead into 1925, when 346cc sv and 344cc ohv JAP models were added, with a 490cc sv JAP finding favour too in 1926, as the 348cc two-stroke and Barr & Stroud models were dropped.

Back came the 677cc sv V-twin for 1927, which was to be the final year, plus all the JAP-engined singles and the 170cc miniature, the four-strokes presenting a cobby appearance in short-wheelbase frames and with internal expanding-drum brakes. A neat three-wheeler with two front and a single rear wheel in two-seater sports or family versions was introduced in 1926 and heavily promoted, but possibly over extended the firm financially, thus leading to their withdrawal from the market in total.

ONAWAY 1905–1908

This firm was located in St Alban's Road, Watford, Hertfordshire and introduced their interesting new

Long and low was not the usual form in 1905 and perhaps this was why the Onaway failed to catch on, despite its comfort and easy controls.

model at the late-1905 Stanley show. It differed from others in having a frame constructed solely from straight tubes for strength and lightness, the engine being carried in a cradle between the down and saddle tubes. The twin top-tubes ran directly from the headstock top to the rear axle, so the large seat was mounted well above it on coil springs but still gave a low riding height. Rider comfort was further enhanced by large sprung footboards.

The engine was a 5hp Kelecom V-twin, but a single was also available, and drive was by belt from an Osborne free-engine pulley, either direct or with four-speed gear. Braced forks were fitted and there were two petrol tanks. However, the lines failed to attract the buyers so the make did not last too long.

ORBIT 1913–1924

This firm was founded by S. Dorsett of the Diamond company using their old works in Vane Street, Wolverhampton. Their first experimental machine was seen in June 1913 and showed much promise, with unit construction, enclosed rear-drive chain and an internal-expanding rear brake.

The engine was a typical sv type, 2.75 and 3.5hp sizes being proposed, as far as the top half was concerned, but it was in the crankcase that the innovation was to be found. Thus, the primary drive was by gears to the camshaft and thence by a second gear-pair to a clutch on the countershaft of the two-speed gearbox. The magneto sat ahead of the crankcase, all the mechanism was fully enclosed and the exhaust pipe forked to connect to footboards that also acted as silencers. Little more was heard of the Orbit pre-war, for enterprising designs often found the going hard in the market.

It was the 1921 season before the first post-Great War models appeared, powered by the company's own 261cc two-stroke engine and with belt drive and either single-, two- or three-speed transmissions. By late 1922, further models were shown, with 348cc Barr & Stroud sleeve-valve, 349cc oil-cooled ohv Bradshaw and 348cc ohv Blackburne engines, three-speed Burman gearboxes as standard and an overall sporting appearance. This expansion was short lived, however, and only the Bradshaw model and their own two-stroke made it through into 1924, when they were one of the few firms to actually fit the twelve-speed Phillipson variable pulley drive on one version of the 261cc machine.

ORLESTONE c.1902

J. Caffyn & Son of the village of Ham Street in Kent had fingers in many pies, being bakers, merchants and agents as well as making Orlestone cycles and motorcycles. These last were basic primitives, with the engine hung vertically in the frame ahead of the pedals, a transverse fuel tank and braced forks. Only limited numbers were made.

This was an advertisement for the early Ormonde, suggesting all manner of fine features, including singles or tandems with a fore-carriage option.

For 1904, Ormond moved the engine to the better central position, continuing with a new Kelecom engine offering all of 3hp.

ORMONDE 1900–1904

A primitive fitted with a Belgian Kelecom engine that was tucked into the space between the seat tube and the rear mudguard. This reduced the belt centres to a minimum, enhanced belt-slip and placed the top of the sparking plug close enough to the left thigh to keep the rider alert.

During 1904, Ormond continued to include this forecar with fan-cooled 3.5hp Kelecom engine, but a merger with that firm failed.

They persisted with this layout, even for a special Paris-Madrid model that ran at 60mph (96km/h) during speed trials held in Phoenix Park, Dublin. Engines of 2.25 or 2.75hp were offered by 1903, along with solos, tandems and a forecar.

For 1904 they adopted the conventional upright, central position within the main frame loop for the 3 or 3.5hp Kelecom engine. They also introduced a drive belt fitted with cross pins, these to engage with grooves cut in the engine pulley, the rear left plain to enable shocks to be absorbed by slippage. Tandems, forecars, sidecars and trailers were all listed along with the solos, some of which had fan-cooling for the engine.

During 1904 Ormonde and Kelecom merged, but the firm failed before the year was out, with the assets bought by Taylor Gue who had been making their frames. A year later they built their own machine and, in time, became Velocette.

ORTONA 1905–1906

Based in Egham, Surrey, this firm offered a well-equipped machine of typical primitive form. The upright 3.5hp engine went in a diamond frame with braced forks and transmission was by belt. An external flywheel on the right was concealed by an aluminium cover, the crankshaft was a one-piece forging, and the valves went at the front of the cylinder.

The Ortona was well made, conventional in design and had some neat features, so deserved better, but arrived at the wrong time.

ORWELL 1919
The name possibly used by Ransome Sims & Jefferies of East Anglia for their battery-powered sidecar machine. Only a prototype was thought to have been built, but the Orwell name was used for other products.

OSBORNE 1901–1909
The name first used by Frederick Osborn for his early motorcycles that became OEC after the Great War. He began with a primitive, with its 4hp engine hung from the downtube and with a flat drive belt. He also produced a four-speed engine pulley and his 1909 single had one fitted, plus a means of moving the rear wheel to adjust the belt tension. When the firm came back to motorcycles it was as OEC.

F.J. Osborn built this early primitive around 1901, with flat-belt drive and four-speed engine pulley. Using his initials, he later founded OEC.

OSCAR 1953–1954
This scooter was shown late in 1953 and had a bulbous body made in glass-fibre by the firm in Blackburn. The format was typical of the type and the engine was to be a choice of 122 or 197cc Villiers unit, with rubber mountings to conceal any vibration. Later on it was used by Siba for test work, but never reached production.

OSMOND 1902–1925
In November 1902, Osmonds Ltd, of The Tower, Birmingham, advertised their Slip-Not motor bicycle, and compared it with their standard Manumotive cycle. They were to show their machine at the Stanley show that month but, while the sales pitch was long and wordy, machine details were short, with no indication of engine or its position. Most likely it was a Minerva, but no more was heard of the firm's motorcycle for a decade.

The name returned at the late-1911 Olympia show, by when they were based at Sparkbrook, Birmingham. They exhibited two models using 3.5hp Precision engines with Bosch magnetos, either direct-belt drive or a Villiers hub gear, and Druid forks. Little more was heard of the marque until post-war when, for 1923, they introduced a miniature with open frame and braced unsprung forks, propelled by a 104cc two-stroke Simplex engine, with chain drive to a countershaft and then belt to the rear wheel.

In 1924 this single-speed machine, with its frame suitable for use by either sex, gained the model name of 'Junior', probably to distinguish it from a new introduction, the Osmond Royal, which was a true lightweight motorcycle with 249cc two-stroke engine, Druid sprung forks and two-speed chain-cum-belt drive. Both engines were claimed to be of Osmond manufacture by this time, but only the 240cc Royal model reached the lists in 1925, after which the company withdrew entirely from the market.

The Oscar went on show late in 1953, its body in glass-fibre but, underneath, there was a prosaic Villiers engine of 122 or 197cc.

OVERDALE 1921–1922
Lightweight machines built in Scotland, with 269cc Villiers two-stroke engines, two-speed Burman chain-cum-belt transmission and Gosport spring forks. Exhibited at the Scottish motorcycle show in early 1922, but production would have been very limited.

OVER-SEAS 1914–1916
A Birmingham firm that was floated to build machines to go abroad. Designed by W.J. Lloyd, the original designer of the Quadrant, the Over-Seas model had a 3.5hp engine mounted in a robust frame. Belt drive was specified, there being the option of a three-speed, Sturmey-Archer rear hub, while Druid forks and pannier frames were all part of the equipment.

For 1915 there was the choice of the 3.5hp single or a 7hp V-twin engine, this continuing for 1916, after which production ceased.

◆ P ◆

PACER 1914–1915
Also known as the Ladies Pacer, this machine first appeared in May 1914. It was designed by K. Millard & Co. of Guernsey specifically for ladies, so had an open frame that was fitted with Druid forks. The engine was a small 1hp JES, which had an overhead inlet-valve, and this drove the rear wheel by a round belt that ran over a tension pulley. It was still listed for 1915 but no later.

PALLION 1905–1914
A small firm that went into the motorcycle business when it was in a slump, but survived that period to become a war casualty. They assembled machines from bought-in parts, possibly to order, as part of a bicycle dealer business and used engines from Fafnir, Minerva, JAP and Villiers.

PANTHER (P&M) 1904–1968
The famous Yorkshire firm, based in Cleckheaton, was known at first as P&M from the names of the partners, Joah Carver Phelon and Richard Moore. They came together late in 1903 to develop the P&R that Phelon had originated with Harry Rayner in 1901 and that Humber were building under licence.

They kept the main distinguishing feature of the P&R, where the inclined engine replaced the frame downtube, to the end of their days. The all-chain drive of the P&R was replaced by a simple two-speed gear using twin primary chains of different ratios. They were selected by clutches and the assembly mounted in the bottom bracket with chain retained for the final drive.

A forecar was first offered with the two speeds, but few were sold and the partners soon moved on to motorcycles. Their first models were of 2.75 and 3.5hp, typical of the era in respect of the cycle parts but with the inclined engine built into the frame and the two-speed gear. They soon made a name for themselves in trials and hill climbs and, by 1907, only the larger model was listed, to be the mainstay of the firm into the 1920s. A 2.5hp lightweight was added for 1910 but only listed for three years.

During the Great War the 3.5hp model was adopted by the air force for despatch riding but plans for a 90-degree V-twin were shelved when war broke out. Post-war it was still just the one model with its two speeds at first, but in 1922 a 4.5hp

A P&M machine on duty with the RAC during the 1920s and in the traffic of those times.

The P&M for 1912, with two speeds controlled by a lever fixed at the rear of the tank and magneto located just under that same tank.

From the start, Phelon & Moore used the engine as the frame downtube and would continue to do this with at least one model all their days.

Drive side of the 1914 P&M that would serve its time in the Great War, where it was used by dispatch riders, the chaincases proving a benefit.

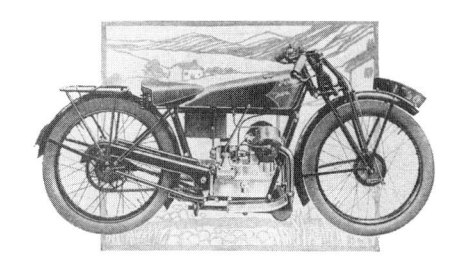

The 1927 Panther line had the Panthette added to it, with V-twin 242cc ohv engine, unit construction, four speeds, a high price and low sales.

model was added and was essentially a new design, although it retained the inclined engine as of old, the actual capacity being 555cc. It had four speeds, contrived by combining the existing two speeds with a two-speed layshaft. In sports-model form it introduced the Panther name to the firm, which would in time become its accepted title.

A 1928 P&M, by which time it also carried the Panther name, which it had done since 1922 if in sports form. It was now provided with electric lighting.

Only the 4.5hp model was listed for 1923 but the next year brought the first ohv engine, of 499cc, designed by Granville Bradshaw of ABC fame. At first it used a conventional four-speed gearbox, but 1927 brought a Sturmey-Archer three-speed gearbox with the four-speed box optional, and much-needed drum brakes in place of the dummy rims. Changes to the lubrication system had introduced the forward extension to the crankcase for the oil, another feature to remain to the end. The sv model was dropped at the end of 1925, the year when Tommy Bullus was fourth in the Senior TT, their best result. This left just three versions of the ohv machine for 1926.

Late in 1926 the firm stole the Olympia show with their 242cc V-twin Panthette. This was another Bradshaw design, with unit construction of the transverse engine, four-speed gearbox and bevel final-drive gears, all housed in a horizontally split crankcase-casting. The overhead valves had leaf springs and the magneto sat behind the cylinders. The frame had a forged-steel backbone from which the engine unit was hung with bracing tubes and the forks were Brampton. Too advanced for many, and expensive, it failed to sell in any numbers, but was listed to 1929.

A Panther with 247cc Villiers engine joined the range in 1931, a sign of those tough times for sales at any level.

A speedway model was listed for 1928, along with a 247cc Villiers two-stroke in Panthette cycle parts that sold much better than the V-twin. It was also the year when the 594cc single made its appearance, to go on to serve for many a year. The two-stroke line was extended for 1929 with 147c and 196cc models, and the big singles became available with a tuned engine when they were listed as Redwing models.

A 1931 feature was twin headlights for the 600s, with the right one for main beam and the left able to swing

By 1931 the Panther had a saddle tank, twin headlamps, roll-on rear stand and foot-change for the gearbox, but still the inclined engine.

By 1931, the Panther two-stroke model was listed as the 25 and continued to use the 247cc Villiers engine with left-side outside flywheel.

The big Panther Redwing 90 of 1932 had a 490cc sloping engine and a form to stay for so many years to come.

This is the famous Red Panther, introduced in 1932 and sold by Pride & Clarke at a rock-bottom price. It was tough enough to win the Maudes.

to its side under twistgrip control. Much more important was the introduction of a 249cc model in 1932. The engine had the cylinder inclined and oil tank formed in the crankcase, but went into a conventional frame with downtube. For 1933 it was joined by a 348cc version, but the good commercial news was a link with London dealers, Pride & Clarke. They took large numbers of the 250, which was given a red-panelled tank, plus mudguards in 1939, and sold at a cut price as the Red Panther. It had some scorn poured on it, but proved an excellent basic machine for local work and won the prestigious Maudes Trophy in 1934.

That year brought a 348cc Red Panther and Stroud trials models in

While the Panther big single ran on to the end at 645cc, it was joined by a series of machines with Villiers twin-cylinder two-stroke engines.

Post-war, the 249cc Panther 65 single had an upright engine, and telescopic front forks, but retained the rigid rear end.

The big Panther had been built with a 594cc engine pre-war and continued with this alone in early post-war years, this example from 1951.

both capacities. Meanwhile the big singles just ran on, improving each year and cementing their reputation for sidecar work, and this list of models took the firm right up to the outbreak of war. The range was joined by a 498cc version of the smaller inclined-engine models in 1938, this the Model 95. There was to have been a spring frame using leaf springs, vertical engines, one with sv, and a vertical twin for 1940. The last had a tandem-twin, in-line ohv engine layout with the crankshafts coupled at first with chains and then helical gears. Only the prototype was built and none of the other new ideas came to pass, as the firm turned to war contracts.

After the war they picked up with just three singles of 249, 348 and 594cc, all very much as pre-war. Dowty Oleomatic telescopic forks appeared for 1947 and for 1949 the two smaller singles adopted vertical cylinders and were joined by a trials version with the Stroud name. The smaller road models changed to conventional telescopics and added pivoted-fork rear suspension for 1953 and the 594cc followed for the next year, by when the Stroud machines were dropped.

In 1956 the three singles were joined by two lightweights with 197cc Villiers 8E or 9E engines. The next year brought versions with the Villiers 246cc 2H single and 249cc

Post-war saw Panther add a range of lightweights to the big singles, this one with a 197cc Villiers engine and leading-link front forks.

2T twin engines, but the single soon went. For 1959 the two-stroke line was joined by one with the 324cc 3T engine, but the real Panther news was a larger, 645cc, version of their big single.

Late in 1959 the firm added the Princess scooter, which was powered by a Villiers 174cc 2L engine and shared body panels with Dayton and Sun. This line took them into the new decade but a contracting market, especially for sidecars, thanks to the advent of the Mini. Panther had to call in the Official Receiver late in 1962, the range was thinned to five models for 1963, and three for the next year.

This left the 249 and 324cc two-stroke twins and the big 645cc single. From 1965 it was just a twin and the single, these to trickle on to 1968 when production ceased. However, from first to last they never stopped using the engine as part of the frame for at least one model.

Panther entered the scooter market late in 1959, using a 174cc Villiers engine and body panels shared with Dayton and Sun, and sold as the Princess.

PARAGON 1914–1921

This marque was produced by Portway-Cooper of Brantham, Manningtree, Essex, with a single model for 1914. This had a 2.25hp 225cc two-stroke engine with petroil lubrication, chain-driven U.H. magneto and Amac carburettor. A two-speed Paragon gearbox was driven by an enclosed chain with belt final-drive. The machine had Radco forks and a distinctive fuel tank of torpedo shape. For 1915 this model was joined by others of 346 and 511cc, which had hand-pump lubrication but kept the other features.

After the war, as the Paragon Motor Manufacturing Company, they returned with a 358cc two-stroke engine in-unit with a chain-driven two-speed gear and belt final-drive. This went into a spring frame in which compression and rebound coil springs were contained within tubes positioned vertically either side of the rear forks ends and also doubled as supports for the rear carrier. Lugs projecting through slots in these tubes accommodated the wheel spindle ends, a system giving some 2in (5cm) of wheel movement.

It was an imaginative attempt, but by early 1921 the makers had ceased production. However, moves were soon afoot to re-enter the market with a revised design that retained the frame features. In this form they became the New Paragon to continue on for one more season.

PARAMOUNT-DUO 1927–1928
A model produced by FEW of unusual form, with two bucket seats and a degree of enclosure on the lines of the OEC Atlanta-Duo of the 1930s. Engines were either the 499cc Blackburne or 981cc JAP V-twin driving a Burman or Sturmey-Archer gearbox. As with others of the type, it found few buyers and soon left the market, a fate to meet most such designs.

PASHLEY 1949–1953
Located in Chester Street in Aston, Birmingham, this firm introduced a three-wheeled commercial vehicle late in 1949, using a 197cc Villiers engine with three speeds to power it. The rear part was based on motorcycle practice, but at the front went twin independently sprung 8in wheels with the open truck body between them. Steering was by wheel and all three drum brakes interconnected, while the whole of the rear section and engine was enclosed by a steel bonnet on which went a pad for the driver. Four body types were listed and production continued to 1953, by when such vehicles had become dated and overtaken by other forms. The firm then turned its eyes to a light three-wheeled car on the lines of the Bond, but this failed to get into production.

PAX 1921–1922
Pax Engineering of Acocks Green, Birmingham offered medium-weight machines of conventional appearance during 1921, with 348 or 499cc sv Blackburne engines, two or three-speed Sturmey-Archer gearboxes and Druid front forks. For 1922 the bigger model was dropped and an ohv 348cc Blackburne model offered, with all-chain transmission. However, the marque disappeared soon afterwards.

PB 1903
Late in 1903, Pitcher & Barlett of London built a motor tandem, the 2.75hp Chapelle engine fitted in-between the two riders. Drive to the rear wheel was by crossed flat belt, while the frame was for a gentleman at the front and a lady at the rear. The crossed belt ensured that it was not heard of again.

PDC 1903–1905
This short-lived marque was sold by the Imperial Motor Co. of Brixton Hill, London and in 1903 offered a range of solos plus a forecar attachment. Engines of 2, 2.5, 2.75 and 3hp were listed and the design was typically primitive, but did include an external-contracting band front brake.

PDM-ILLSTON 1914
Another short-lived war-time casualty whose range comprised just three models. Two fitted 2.75 or 3hp single-cylinder engines having overhead inlet valves, while the other used a 5hp V-twin. The smallest had belt drive, but the larger single offered three speeds. All the engines were made by G.H. Illston of Gooch Street, Birmingham, who was no doubt diverted to war work during the year.

PEARSON 1904
Brothers who built machines at Southsea, Hampshire using a 4hp Aster engine from Paris, mounted in a special frame that combined the merits of the loop and diamond types. The result was a serviceable tourer for one short season.

PEARSON-COX 1912
Well known for their steam-powered cars, this Kent-based firm showed a motorcycle using the same form of power in 1912. The result of two years of experiments, the machine had its 3hp single-acting engine tucked in-between the seat tube and rear wheel, which it drove by chain. A paraffin burner was employed for the flash-steam boiler, while the machine was fitted with Druid forks and footboards.

PEARSON & SOPWITH 1920–1922
Another name for the P&S marque involving aircraft pioneer Tommy Sopwith, whose machines were reputedly produced by the Monarch firm. Conventional in form, they used a 318cc Dalm or 269cc Villiers two-stroke engine or the 293cc sv JAP. A 499cc sv Blackburne model joined the two-strokes for 1921, while transmission became all-chain with two or

One of a series of machines sold by PDC for a short while, all were typical primitives and with the option of a forecar attachment.

three speeds, courtesy of Sturmey-Archer.

PEBOK 1903–1906
A firm that built their own engines to fit into typical primitives. They began with a 3.5hp engine for their first machines and always used mechanical inlet-valves from 1904, when powers of 2.25, 2.75 and 3.5hp were listed.

PECO 1914
Best known for their engines, the firm of Pearson & Cole of Birmingham also built a few machines. They used their own 2.75hp two-stroke which was conventional apart from its oiling, which was by a drip feed. The machine itself was conventional.

PEERLESS 1902–1905
The name under which some of the early Bradbury machines were sold, they being identical and built in the same factory at Oldham, Lancashire. They featured the same Birch design with the crankcase cast around the two main frame tubes.

PEERLESS 1913–1914
This was an assembled make that used Veloce 293cc ioe and 499cc sv engines for their machines. They were built by the International Manufacturing Co., who may have been a branch of Veloce before that firm became Velocette. Construction was typical of that era and the make a war casualty.

PELLO 1914
Pell & Parker of Peterborough, Cambridgeshire were cycle makers who bought six 3.5hp Arno engines in 1914 with the idea of fitting them into their own locally-made frames with Druid forks and direct-belt drive. At least one machine was completed and sold in June that year to a local farmer, who fell off first time out and never rode it again. Over fifty years later it surfaced and was finally run-in!

PENNINGTON 1897
An American businessman who had two machines built to his design by the Humber firm in Coventry. Much advertising and some extravagant claims enabled him to sell the designs to Lawson for a reputed £100,000, but the massive production that would recoup this never happened.

A motorcycle and a tandem were built, the engines having two cylinders, horizontal and aft of the rear wheel. Drive was direct, the cylinders were devoid of fins, and the only control a needle valve that adjusted the drip of petrol into the air intake. Low-tension ignition provided a claimed 'long-mingling spark', just one of the many Pennington tales.

Just one of the extravagant claims made by Pennington, while he sold the designs for massive sums to men with no mechanical knowledge.

The Pennington tandem used much of the design of the solo machine, including the large section tyres in white.

One of the Pennington machines, which had the engine bulk behind the rear wheel, no cooling fins and a drip feed of fuel into the inlet.

One of the men involved in the construction did much of the riding and reported its speed range as 8 to 30mph (13–48km/h). On most trips the ignition would soon fail but, if it held up, the machine would run for 10 miles (16km), despite the poor cooling.

Pennington also offered the three-wheeled Torpedo Autocar in 1896 with two cylinders and a duplex frame. From this, other tubes supported no less than four seats in a line, the front one between the two front wheels, the centre ones facing right and left, while the rear rider had the handlebars. There was also the 1898 Raft Victoria with front-wheel drive, rear-wheel steering and rope transmission, but both projects were as farcical as the motorcycles.

PENN NIB 1925
These were made by H.W. Boulton, who owned the Penn Garage on Lloyd Hill in the Penn district of Wolverhampton. He built a small number of machines using two-stroke and four-stroke engines, proprietary gearbox and Druid forks. The feature that distinguished them from others and gave them their name was the tank. This was formed and painted to resemble a pen-nib, which made a neat touch.

PENTON 1970–1975
The name under which Wassell machines were sold in the USA, these at first with the 172cc BSA Bantam engine unit, later with a 125cc Sachs with six speeds.

PERFECT 1913–1914
The Perfect and Runwell Cycle Companies were linked and had their main offices and works in Lawson Street, Birmingham. The Perfect was offered in two sizes with 2.75 or 3.5hp engine, listed as a TDC when carrying the Runwell label on the tank, and was much as others of the time. Thus, it had a Bosch magneto, B&B carburettor, direct-belt drive with the option of an Albion free-engine clutch or an Armstrong three-speed hub, rim brakes and Saxon forks. Both were soon gone.

PERKS & BIRCH 1900–1901
These were the originators of the idea of building the complete engine unit within the wheel it was to drive. The single-cylinder engine was fitted between the spokes of an aluminium wheel, there being eight or ten spokes on each side, looking much as the cast-alloy wheels of eighty years later. A low-tension magneto provided the spark and the assembly could be fitted in place of the rear wheel of a bicycle or the front one of a tricycle. In 1901 the design was taken up by Singer.

PERRET 1962–1969
Alan Perret built grass-track machines in the style of the period, but used BSA engines for most, although there were some with the JAP unit. He also made his own fuel injector and his machines won at least one national championship.

PETERS 1920–1925
Although this firm had an address in the Isle of Man, it was made on the mainland. First described late in 1920, the first machine was introduced at the late-1921 Olympia show and was a good deal different from the normal run of assembled lightweights. In place of the usual bought-in components was a Peters engine and frame with rear suspension by pivoted-fork controlled by springs in monoshock manner. The engine was a two-stroke of 296cc, soon increased to 346cc, with the cylinder inclined forward and a large flywheel incorporating a variable-gear pulley for the belt drive. This was controlled by a lever and further mechanism moved the rear wheel to maintain belt tension.

The frame was effectively a spine type with a large welded sheet-steel assembly that included petrol and oil tanks, steering head, support from where the engine hung and saddle tube running down to the crankcase. The rear fork pivoted from this point and the rear springs were anchored to the back of the frame assembly. At the front the fork pivoted at the lower crown under the control of a leaf spring mounted inside the steering head.

Little more was heard of the Peters and output must have been small. However, it was listed for some years in its early form. By 1924 production was in the hands of C.L. Brock & Co. of Teddington, Middlesex and a version with a three-speed Burman gearbox and chain-cum-belt drive appeared. In 1925 all-chain drive was an option for all and a new model with a 348cc sv Blackburne engine coupled to a three-speed Jardine gearbox was an addition. Sadly, this worthy effort then slipped from sight.

PHELON 1903
After the sad death of Harry Rayner, Joah Phelon continued with his original business and also produced a few machines under his own name. These included a forecar as well as a solo and both were in the form of the P&R. This activity only lasted for a short while until Phelon met up with Richard Moore and they formed P&M, later to become Panther.

The Phillips P39 Gadabout moped was built with various engines and forms over a decade, under a variety of model names and codes.

PHILLIPS 1954–1964
This cycle firm, based at Smethwick, Birmingham, entered the powered world late in 1954 with a complete machine derived from a bicycle. The 49cc two-stroke engine was mounted above the bottom bracket and drove the rear wheel by chain, with the petrol tank on the top tube and braced forks.

This model was listed up to 1957, but a year earlier was joined by the Gadabout moped with a 49cc Rex engine, two speeds, spine frame and telescopic forks. In 1959 this was joined by the single-speed Panda, a three-speed Gadabout and another of these with a 50cc Villiers engine.

A Panda Plus was added in 1960, but by 1962 they were down to the Gadabout with either Rex or Villiers engine. That year two new models were added and these were based on Raleigh mopeds, so actually made under licence from Motobécane of France. They alone were built for the last two years of the make, after which their owners, Raleigh, dropped the name.

The Phoenix rose from the ashes, but this one appeared at the turn of the century with its Minerva engine hung from the frame.

PHOENIX 1900–1908
One of a number of firms who took advantage of a chance to buy some Belgian Minerva engines to attach to its bicycles. Run by J. Van Hooydonk from premises first in Holloway Road and later in Caledonian Road, London, in 1902 he offered a forecar attachment that replaced the single front wheel by two, carrying a seat between them. Removal was said to take five minutes if a quarrel with the passenger arose. The attachment was sold as the 'Trimo' and could be fitted to most other makes, so proved popular.

The Phoenix Trimo added a forecar to the motorcycle and was one of the first of its type, but these and trailers were all replaced by the sidecar.

During 1903, a Trimo was adapted to use a Singer motor-wheel in place of both its engine and the usual rear wheel, an interesting device. During that year they built a model fitted with a new 3hp Minerva engine having a cam-operated inlet valve, but the motorcycle remained as before, the engine hung from the frame, remaining so for 1904 with variations of transmission available.

During 1904 a ladies' version of the Trimo model was added with a drop frame and upright engine. The range of solos continued for 1905, offering belt or chain drive, either with one or two speeds, plus the forecars. A solo ladies' model was added during the year, the 2hp engine being fitted to an open frame to drive a two-speed gear by chain.

For 1906 the open frame became available for general use, fitted with a 2 or 2.75hp engine and two-speed gear, while the Trimo moved more to the car format. By 1908 the solo, sold as the Cob, had a 3.5hp Fafnir engine. Phoenix was only ever a small firm and, despite producing a well made and much advertised product, it was unable to stay in the motorcycle business.

PHOENIX PRE-GREAT WAR
This marque hailed from Worcester in small numbers and had nothing to do with the London firm of the same name.

PHOENIX 1956–1964
This was a scooter range built by Ernie Barrett in Tottenham, London, always with Villiers engines. The first was seen in 1956 and was typical of the type, although rather heavy in style, and fitted with the 147cc 30C engine. In 1958 the rear body was changed to a much improved glass-fibre moulding and the 148cc 31C, 197cc 9E and 249cc 2T engines joined the original. De luxe and standard versions were offered for most and these were joined in 1960 by the 174cc 2L and 324cc 3T engines.

This continued into the decade with the addition of a model with the

The 1958 Phoenix scooter, the year the rear body was revised and much improved, while still being available with several engine choices.

The Phoenix scooter viewed from its other side: the model was available with a choice of 147, 148, 174, 197, 249 and 324cc engines, all from Villiers.

99cc 6F engine in 1963, but in a declining market the firm sensibly stopped production in the following year.

PIATTI 1956–1958
A scooter designed by Vincenzo Piatti, with a 124cc two-stroke engine and three-speed gearbox in-unit with the rear wheel. This whole assembly pivoted to provide the rear suspension and went under the pressed-steel frame of inverted-bath form. This concealed the works, so it was laid on its side for maintenance. Built and sold by Cyclemaster in Britain, it was short lived.

A curious small scooter, the Piatti hid its mechanics under the body, these being serviced with the machine laid on its side.

PICK 1905
An Edwardian machine, possibly from the Stamford cyclecar firm of that name, that consisted a 6.5hp

V-twin using one make of cylinders on another make of crankcase. Later in its life it was fitted with Dalm cylinders, but remained typical of the early era with sprung braced forks and direct-belt drive. Some of its features suggested a one-off special, maybe a prototype or simply made for a Pick staff member.

PILOT 1904–1915
Based in Farm Street, Birmingham, this firm was involved with cycles by 1884 and with motorcycles at the turn of the century, when they offered frames, forks and many other parts to the trade. They could supply the machine all ready to take the engine, designed to take the Minerva and Excelsior vertical pattern, and by 1904 there was also a complete motorcycle listed for £32.

It would seem that they dealt mainly with components during the Edwardian era and only returned to complete machines late in 1910, with a range having belt drive and sprung forks. Engines were a 4hp JAP or 4.25hp Fafnir single, or 6 or 8hp JAP V-twins for 1911, but the next year changed to 3.5 and 4.25hp Precision singles and just the 8hp JAP. The JAP single was back again for 1913, while 1914 saw only Precision engines being used, the singles of 2.75 or 3.75hp and the V-twin of 6hp.

The 1914 four-strokes were joined by a model fitted with a 318cc two-stroke engine, this keeping to the belt drive, while for 1915 the range was reduced to models having Precision singles of 199 and 597cc, plus a 499cc V-twin, all with sv, and the two-stroke.

PIONEER 1912–1914
Said to have been the first machine to be built in Wales, although there could be other contenders, the Pioneer was assembled by J. Parsons of Car Distributors (Cardiff) Ltd and included in its specification a 3.5hp White & Poppe sv engine and Chater-Lea-style spring front forks. There was direct-belt drive and a conventional appearance, although one notable difference lay with the exhaust silencer, which was fixed close up to the engine's exhaust port.

PLANET c.1919–1920
One more small and short-lived marque that sought to exploit the postwar boom but had no more luck with supplies than most others. They used the 269cc Villiers engine plus various sizes from Union and Blackburne. The rest of the machines were typical of the time, no doubt built from whatever could be obtained from the usual sources.

P&M 1904–c.1925
The initials of Joah Phelon and Richard Moore came together in 1904 following the earlier association of P&R and the Humber company. They continued to sell their motorcycles as the P&M before adopting the Panther name that was first used after the Great War for a particular model. In time they became better known as Panther, so all machines thereafter from the Cleckheaton factory bore that name.

PMC 1908–1911
The Premier Motor Co. of Aston Road, Birmingham was a major dealer, but had no connection with the Premier Cycle Co. of Coventry. This led to some confusion, especially in 1909 when they used the name Premo for what was the Rex Valveless two-stroke engine. An injunction from the other firm late in 1909 brought all this to an end, after which they used the PMC name.

They listed the two-stroke for 1910 and 1911 under the PMC name but, for 1912, turned to selling the Rex-JAP models made for them by Rex with V-twin JAP engines and sold only through their own retail outlet.

PORTLAND 1910–1913 AND 1920
Listed late in 1910, by dealers Maudes Motor Mart of Great Portland Street, London and Halifax, this machine had a 4hp JAP engine, belt drive and

Portland was a marque name used by Maudes' Motor Mart; this machine dated from 1911 with JAP or Peugeot engine, and they kept to this practice.

Druid forks. A Peugeot engine was an option, while for 1913 they were using a 4hp JAP or 3.5 and 4.25hp Precision engines, still with belt drive.

Post-Great War they continued to sell their own brand of machine, built by a trade supplier, using components such as 269cc Arden two-stroke engine, Amac carburettor, two-speed Albion gearbox and Saxon forks. The result was a typical lightweight of the period but they soon dropped from the market once business turned down.

The Pouncy Cob appeared in 1931, fitted with a 346cc Villiers engine, so was larger than most small two-strokes, although others followed.

POUNCY 1931–1936
Built at Dorchester in Dorset, this make appeared in 1931 with a single model called the Cob and powered by a 346cc Villiers engine. Typical of the type and the times, it was joined by a competition version and a 148cc model for 1932, while 1933 saw no Cob but a 249cc model listed as the Pal. During the year the firm moved to Hampshire, but the range reduced to a new version of the Pal for 1935. This had a duplex frame and a form

of pivoted-fork rear suspension for its Villiers engine, and in this way it ran on for one more year.

POWELL 1920–1925

Having engaged engineer E.A. Burney to design their initial model, Powell Brothers of Wrexham not unexpectedly entered the market with a most capable middleweight, having a side-valve engine of 548cc with outside flywheel and a distinct resemblance to Blackburne (Burney & Blackburne) practice. Sloping 30 degrees forwards in its frame, the engine was readily removable for maintenance and drove back through a three-speed Sturmey-Archer gearbox and belt drive to the rear wheel. Announced in 1920, it was the following year before worthwhile numbers became available, after which small improvements were made annually.

In 1922 a new range of miniatures was launched, with choice of 147cc Villiers, 170cc Beaufort or 193cc Powell engines, all two-strokes, and with various two- and three-speed transmission options. One of these models featured a sheet-steel enclosure, enveloping all the mechanicals and providing legshields, yet readily removable for engine adjustment. By 1925 only the miniatures, led by the All-Weather, as the enclosed model was known, were offered before the brothers returned their Cambrian Foundry premises to more mundane but profitable products.

POWERFUL 1903–1905

Built by H.W. Clark of Coventry, this make first appeared fitted with a 2.25hp Buchet engine, others being available to demand. The engine was inclined and mounted above the downtube, within the frame, but the make was short lived.

POWER PAK 1950–1956

One of several clip-on units offered in the early-1950s to power a standard bicycle, this 49cc two-stroke hung over the rear wheel with its cylinder inverted. It drove the wheel by friction roller, and had a flywheel magneto and petroil lubrication, while the layout enabled the fuel tank to fit neatly over the crankcase. In 1956 the firm tried to adapt the engine to fit under the bottom bracket to produce

The Power Pak attachment, which fitted over the bicycle rear-wheel and drove it by friction. A neat design that served owners well.

Close-up of the Power Pak engine unit installed over a rear wheel, neatly arranged for the weight to hang low and to keep the heat away from clothing.

a moped, but this was always a non-starter.

POWERWHEEL 1951

A clever design from Cyril Pullin, intended to be built and sold by Tube Investments, this was a cycle attachment that replaced the bicycle rear wheel. What made it unusual was that it was powered by a 40cc two-stroke rotary engine in which the crankshaft stayed still and the rest revolved around it. This introduced a good deal of complication to arrange the porting, balance the complete assembly and devise a drive to the wheel to give the reduction ratio. All this made it a complex solution to a simple task best done by a two-stroke engine and friction roller onto a tyre.

P&P 1922–1930

Born out of a desire to build a sophisticated and quiet motorcycle, partners Packman & Poppe adopted the whispering sleeve-valve Barr & Stroud engine and added enclosure panels to their Silent Three model, which appeared in 1922. P&P frames sloped in a straight line from headstock to rear wheel spindle, thus giving a low and reassuring saddle height; an unusual feature was the use of a live

Power Pak attempted to create a moped by fitting their attachment engine to the bottom bracket of a special frame with sprung front forks.

P&P produced a variety of models in their decade but, by 1930, were down to four models, this 500 Silent the largest.

rear-wheel spindle, self-aligning bearings being housed in the frame fork ends. By mid-1923 they were adding 293cc sv and 344cc ohv JAP-engined models with sporting lines and then came the Special Eight, powered by a 976cc sv V-twin JAP motor, all of these going into the Silent Three frame to good effect. Novelties such as tank-top instrument panels and combined prop-cum-centre stand began to appear from the innovative duo, but in June 1925 Gilmour Packman was killed in tragic circumstances.

The firm could have folded and a break in production did follow, but by 1926 it had resumed with Rexine covered tanks and further engine variety from MAG and Blackburne, although the big twin had gone for a time, to be revived the next season when it was joined by another of 677cc, again with JAP engine, and the range switched to saddle tanks. During this period the firm became linked with the Wooler firm and, for 1929, they introduced an option of plunger rear-suspension to his design for all four models, this also available for other machines. There were just four road models for that year, with 346 single and 677cc V-twin sv JAP, plus 348 and 499cc ohv Blackburne engines, these two last also used for Dirt Track models.

In 1930, their final year, there were only four models, the 500 Silent, the 90 with an ohv 500cc engine, the 80 with a 245cc ohv JAP engine and the 60 with a 199cc two-stroke. During 1930 the firm folded, but many years later Poppe designed the Sunbeam S7.

P&R 1901–1903
This fore-runner of the P&M, or Panther, firm, was based in Yorkshire and combined the talents of Joah Phelon and his nephew, Harry Rayner. By 1896 they were in business in Cleckheaton, where they built a quadricycle whose single run on the road provided much information.

In 1901 their first motorcycle appeared, using a format that was to last for over sixty years, the De Dion-type engine replacing the downtube of the heavy-duty bicycle frame. Unlike its contemporaries, the machine had all-chain drive, this being in two stages, the first to a countershaft fitted to the bottom bracket, the second from there to the rear wheel. The usual bicycle pedals and chain were still fitted.

The design worked well, so was offered around the firms in Coventry, but only Harry Lawson expressed any interest. The upshot was that Humber began to make machines to the P&R design, although their origin was not publicized.

Few P&R machines were built, most being sold locally, and in 1903 tragedy struck when Rayner was killed in a car accident. Phelon then concentrated on his original business and built a few machines under his own name until the end of the year when he met Richard Moore. This resulted in the formation in 1904 of P&M, later Panther.

PRECISION 1902–1906
A typical primitive, built in small numbers and powered by a Minerva engine.

PRECISION 1912–1919
Based in Moorsom Street, Birmingham, Frank Baker produced Precision-brand engines in a range of sizes for the motorcycle industry. In 1912 he began to manufacture complete machines, but soon found that this was less than popular with his existing engine customers. Therefore he chose to export complete machines far from his home shores, Australia being a favourite destination. This activity did

Premier began with a single, this the 1913 version, using quality components that were bought-in, although common with other marques.

not last long, however, but in 1919 he again offered a complete Precision motorcycle on the home market; this was the 348cc two-stroke of revolutionary appearance, which was to be manufactured and sold under the Beardmore-Precision name from 1920 onwards.

PREMIER 1908–1920
The Premier Cycle Co. of Coventry had no connection with Premier of Birmingham who used the name Premo until an injunction against this was obtained late in 1909, after which they became PMC. Meanwhile, Premier in Coventry put together a sound model using a 3.5hp White & Poppe engine, Brown & Barlow carburettor, Bosch magneto and belt drive. Inside a year they were building their own version of the engine and the original Chater-Lea forks had been replaced by a new type of their design. The single was joined by a 3.75hp V-twin for 1910; this was distinguished externally by horizontal cooling fins and internally by a crankshaft that allowed both pistons to move together despite the 90-degree V-angle. Otherwise the two models were similar.

For 1910 Premier introduced this V-twin, with engine fins level with the ground and pistons that moved as one.

A completely new 3.75hp V-twin engine was announced late in 1910 with the cylinders set at 45 degrees, but still firing evenly with the pistons rising and falling as one. This was done by means of a special rear connecting-rod that was forked and ran on a very large big-end bearing. So large that the front-rod bearing could be inside it and thus offset. There were overhead inlet-valves and a rear-mounted magneto for this new design which kept the horizontal cooling fins. A two-speed gear was available and the cycle parts as before, as was the single.

During 1911 a 2hp lightweight model joined the range and this had its engine mounted inclined in a loop frame above the pedals. The Bosch magneto went at the rear and it had direct-belt drive and Druid forks. Later in the year a 2.5hp single was added to the range, much as the larger one, with rear magneto, belt drive and Druid forks. For 1912 the range was joined by a 3.5hp ladies' model with open frame, while the next year brought a two-speed gearbox and Druid forks for the 3.5hp single. The V-twin was new and increased to 7–9hp with a 50-degree engine driving the two-speed gearbox, but the 2hp model was dropped.

Late in 1914 a new model was announced, but few were built. It had a 2.75hp in-line twin-cylinder two-stroke engine of 322cc with 64×50mm dimensions, so was well over-square. This had the magneto mounted at the front and drove a three-speed gearbox, the whole unit mounted in a duplex frame. The range was listed to 1916 but after the war they concentrated on a three-wheel Runabout until, in September 1920, the company was bought out by the Singer car firm.

PREMO 1909
The name used by the Premier Motor Co. of Birmingham for the two-stroke Rex model they sold until the use of the name was stopped by an injunction from the Premier Cycle Co. of Coventry.

Pride & Clarke sold this lightweight with 122cc Villiers engine as the Cub and with their own name on the tank.

PRIDE & CLARKE 1939
Major London dealers with premises along both sides of much of Stockwell Road in Brixton, London, this firm was best known for its special deals with manufacturers. These enabled them to offer machines at really low prices and, pre-war, this was best known with the Red Panther, but also for AJW and Calthorpe. Many others followed post-war.

In 1939 they added their own lightweight model, which they called the Cub. It was much as many others, with a 122cc Villiers engine with three-speed gearbox built in-unit, a simple loop frame and blade girder forks – neat and tidy but only listed for the one year.

PRIEST-JAP 1910
Built by Priest & Co. of Bishops Street, Birmingham, this machine had a 3.5hp JAP engine, direct-belt drive via an Albion clutch on the crankshaft, and braced sprung forks. Typical of the period and soon gone.

PRIM 1906
Built by A. Money & Co. of High Wycombe, this make had a large-diameter frame top-tube that doubled as the fuel tank. The engine was a 5hp V-twin Sarolea and the machine was fitted with sprung forks.

PRIMUS 1902–1903
The Ixion motorcycle issued from the Primus Motor Works at Loughborough Junction, London and the same company also built machines using the Primus label. It was just as much a primitive and equally short lived.

PRINCE GEORGE PRE-GREAT WAR
This is a rare make with little known of it. It was made by G.A. Davies of Dalston and Battersea, London, who was no doubt a cycle dealer and the machine a typical primitive based on a bicycle frame with an imported engine hung in it.

PRINCEPS 1903–1905
A Northampton make produced by J.E. Hutton that offered customers the choice of belt or chain drive. For 1904 their range comprised a 2.25hp single and 4hp V-twin, plus a forecar. Their advertisement mentioned a five-speed gear and free-engine, metal-to-metal clutch.

The Princeps was a typical primitive, had some good features, offered the customer a choice of specification, but went in the 1905 slump.

PRINGLE 1908–1909
Shown at the late-1908 Stanley show, this machine had a Sinclair frame, suitable for either sex, fitted with a 3.5hp Minerva engine and Osborne four-speed pulley. Another make that was short lived.

PRIOR 1936–1937
The name under which the German Hercules machines were sold in Britain. First shown at Olympia late in 1936, the four-model range comprised a Velomoteur, two lightweights and a larger single. The first had a 98cc Sachs engine and two-speed gearbox hung in a loop frame with pressed-steel girders. It came with pedalling gear, so was similar to British autocycles and a popular class in its own country.

One of the other lightweights fitted a Sachs engine, while the other used the 122cc Villiers unit with its unit construction and three-speed gearbox, its twin exhaust pipes running straight back from the ports. The final model had a 248cc ohv JAP engine, four speeds, foot change and a Bosch dynamo but Miller points.

The make was not sold in Britain for long and was an absentee from 1937, but the name returned in 1957 to replace that of Kieft for the Hercules imports and ran on to 1961.

PRIOR 1957–1961

The marque name adopted for the German Hercules machines after they were taken over by BP Scooters from Kieft, both of Wolverhampton. The range of three mopeds, two scooters and a 173cc motorcycle was mainly imported with some British parts, but the scooters using Villiers engines were dropped. By 1959 the British content was minimal and for 1960 the Prior was a German import, but only for one more year.

PRIORY 1920–1924

Lightweights of conventional design, often enhanced by Ace wheel discs and with Arden pressed-steel front forks. The Priory Engineering Company of Kenilworth also chose the 269cc Arden two-stroke engine in preference to others, linking it to an Albion two-speed gearbox and chain-cum-belt drive. Later, they also used 147 and 269cc Villiers and 292cc Union two-strokes, plus the 292cc sv JAP engine on occasion during their short period of manufacture.

PROGRESS 1900–1905

The Progress Cycle Co. was based in Foleshill, Coventry and was one of several who purchased some of the first Minerva engines to come to England from Belgium to hang from the downtube of an existing heavy-duty bicycle. First seen at Cordingley's Motor-Car Exhibition in the Agricultural Hall, London, in 1900, from this they progressed to a tricycle and then a quadricycle, either complete or as conversion kits. Other engines followed, but trading conditions worsened in the middle Edwardian period and the marque vanished.

PROGRESS 1930

Name used for the strange Seal three-wheeler for a few months, after a revision and the appearance of a commercial model. With this the driver sat on the machine rather than in the sidecar, to increase the load capacity.

PROGRESS 1957–1958

An imported German scooter first seen in Britain in 1956 and, for 1957, listed with Villiers engines. All three models had the same chassis and glass-fibre body, while they ran on 16in wire-wheels. Models were the Anglian with 147cc 30C engine, Briton with 197cc 8E and Britannier with the 9E. After two years they were discontinued.

The Progress was a scooter imported from Germany, fitted with a choice of three capacities of Villiers engines.

P&S 1920–1921

The initials stood for Pearson & Sopwith, whose London showrooms were backed by works in Worthing, Sussex, although reputedly the machines were built for P&S by the Monarch firm. For 1920 a conventional set of cycle parts could be fitted equally with 318cc Dalm or 269cc Villiers two-stroke engines, or the 293cc sv JAP. A Dalm-engined sidecar outfit was also listed, which was supplied complete with two bodies, one for touring and the other for commercial use. In 1921 a 499cc sv Blackburne model was added and Sturmey-Archer all-chain transmissions, either two or three speed, became standard throughout.

A conventional lightweight was the P&S offering in the early post-Great War years, so was much as many others who tried their luck at that time.

PULLIN 1920–1925, 1928–1930, 1951 AND 1955

After he had won the 1914 Senior TT, Cyril Pullin was involved with unusual designs for the next four decades, on and off. The first was the Pullin-Groom, produced in conjunction with S.L. Groom, which had an open frame built up from steel pressings welded together. A similar form of construction was used for the front fork, which pivoted about the bottom crown against its spring unit, while pivoted-fork rear suspension was employed.

The engine was their own 200cc two-stroke with horizontal cylinder, flywheel magneto and a combined mixing valve controlling both fuel and lubrication. It was fully enclosed by the frame, with access doors for servicing, and drove their own two-speed epicyclic gearbox, the transmission being all-chain drive. Both brakes went into the rear wheel and, while the rider had a sprung saddle, any passenger would have had to sit on the rear mudguard which moved with the wheel.

It was an ingenious design with a pleasing and ultra-modern line that was much praised in the press, but too advanced for riders of the times. The company failed to bring it to full production and it dropped from view until 1923 when it was revived by The Pullin Motor Cycle Company run by W.M. Brooks. By then the engine capacity was up to 310cc and had a Villiers flywheel magneto fitted, while a floatless carburettor supplied the mixture. The transmission was by a conventional two-speed gearbox with all-chain drive, but the external appearance was unchanged.

Deliveries began early in 1924 and the marque was listed into 1925 with engine capacities of 348 and 368cc before this imaginative machine disappeared.

By 1928 Pullin was involved with a new project, the Ascot Pullin, which again featured full enclosure of the working parts, a horizontal 496cc ohv engine built in-unit with the three-speed gearbox, and pressed-steel frame. It was no more successful, so was gone by 1930.

The Pullin name returned to the scene post-war in 1951 when he designed the Powerwheel which was intended to replace the normal bicycle wheel. Thus, it mirrored the Cyclemaster, Winged Wheel and early Singer, but in a complex way. In place of the usual simple two-stroke engine there was a 40cc rotary two-stroke, in which the crankshaft stayed still and the rest of the engine rotated. This introduced all manner of technical complications plus a gear train and, while it ran smoothly, it was an involved alternative to a clip-on with friction-roller drive.

After this exercise, Pullin turned to scooters and, in 1955, produced a prototype that he offered to manufacturers. It had a 197cc fan-cooled Villiers engine with Siba electric start, monocoque chassis and a nice style, but no-one took it up.

A spring frame from the start was a real innovation for the PV in 1911, which used single or V-twin engines and lasted into the 1920s.

PV 1911–1924

Built in Perry Vale, Forest Hill, London by Elliston & Fell, later P.V. Motor Cycles Ltd, and first seen late in 1911, this make featured a spring frame for their earliest models, which were powered by single and V-twin JAP engines. Druid or Chater-Lea forks went at the front while the rear wheel was carried in stays that pivoted at a point ahead of the wheel spindle. The forward end of the stays acted against springs around the curved seat tube, the result a form of pivoted fork.

After 1912 the firm concentrated on using V-twin engines, moving in time to a countershaft gearbox, and for 1914 considered the use of the ABC flat-twin engine. In 1915 they added a lightweight using a 269cc Villiers engine and only that was listed for 1916.

The small two-stroke was the only post-war model but, in December 1919, a model was shown with the new Stanger V-twin two-stroke engine, Brampton forks, three speed Sturmey-Archer chain-cum-belt transmission and a 56mph (90km/h) speed potential. The basic spring frame design then continued to house a multiplicity of proprietary engines from Villiers, JAP and Barr & Stroud, including the 998cc V-twin B&S sleeve-valve motor in 1924, their last season in the trade.

◆ Q ◆

QUADRANT 1900–1927

A cycle firm run by W.J. Lloyd and based in Sheepcote Street, Birmingham, who took the common route to the motorcycle by fitting a Minerva engine to the downtube of a heavy-duty bicycle. They soon moved on to add a forecar and, by 1903, had their own design of engine mounted in a loop frame. A special feature was a single lever that controlled the throttle, ignition switch, spark advance and valve lifter to ease the problems of riding the machine. This helped to increase sales that were further improved when Tom Silver set a new Land's End to John O' Groats record in June 1903 riding a 3hp model. For 1904 they added a forecar that had twin 2.5hp engines, mounted side-by-side with a clutch between them so one or both could be used. That year also introduced a short leading-link front fork for the solo models that ran on for a while.

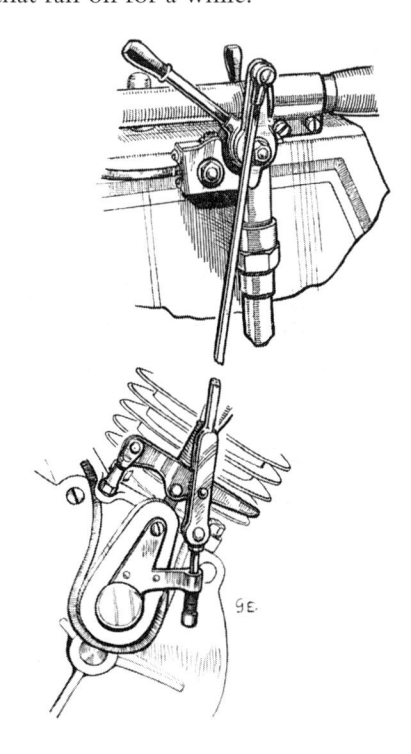

The 1904 Quadrant had an inclined engine in a loop frame plus leading-link front suspension, but was essentially a primitive.

The firm was revised and moved to Earlsdon, Coventry in 1908, when they introduced a new 550cc engine with its valves at front and rear of the cylinder in T-head style, and thus had a camshaft for each, the gear drive to these extending back to the magneto. It also had the crankcase cast as one major part, with a door on the right which was the inner timing case as well. This engine kept to belt drive, with the option of a Roc two-speed gear, and had leading-link forks. By 1910 the exhaust valve had moved to the more usual position to one side of the cylinder, but the inlet would stay at the rear for some years.

By 1906, Quadrant had adopted vertical mounting for the engine and had other improvements, but was otherwise much as before.

A 2hp lightweight was added for 1911 and a 4hp model for sidecar work during the year. A more suitable V-twin appeared for 1913 with a 7hp engine, with overhead inlet valves, a two-speed gear, all-chain drive and a new centre-spring fork. There was a 4.5hp belt-drive single for 1914 and, late that year, a 2.5hp two-stroke model with two speeds. These two, plus the V-twin, were listed for 1915, but only the big single for 1916.

Post-war, they kept to singles, with a 565cc model with a three-speed Sturmey-Archer gearbox and the choice of chain-cum-belt or all-chain drive. This was joined by a 654cc version in late 1920 and it was this which ran on, to be joined a year later by a 490cc model with a new side-by-side valve engine design and all-chain drive. In the spring of 1923 a similar 624cc version was added, and thus the old Quadrant idea of placing the inlet valve around the back of the cylinder had gone for good. These machines carried through to late 1924 when a 490cc ohv model, based on the sv engine but with vertically positioned valves, joined the range.

By 1911 the Quadrant had advanced, but kept its inlet valve behind the cylinder, although the exhaust had moved to the side.

This sports machine failed to last more than a year, but they had another go at the concept in 1926 with a redesigned ohv engine of 499cc with twin exhaust ports, 7in coupled drum brakes and a three-speed Burman gearbox, this by then common to all Quadrant models. This, together with the 490 and 624cc sv dual-purpose machines went forward into 1927, which proved to be the last full season for the company that had advertised itself as the manufacturer of 'Britain's Oldest Motor Cycle'.

The famous Quadrant single lever had four functions to serve the rider in the early Edwardian years: throttle, spark, switch and valve lifter.

Malcolm Newell seen with passenger in one of his Quasar machines, which was not the first or last of his advanced and clever concept-projects.

QUASAR 1976–1981

Malcolm Newell was unconventional and his various specials all reflected this. The one he is best remembered for, and which generated a cult following of feet-first machines, was the Quasar which advanced the concept of the enclosed motorcycle far beyond previous efforts.

It was a startling machine of some length, for the occupants sat between the wheels under a roof and behind a windscreen fitted with wipers. Behind them, over the wheel, was a luggage compartment with an enormous rear lamp system mounted to it. At the front were twin headlights under the lower part of the windscreen.

Under all the glass-fibre went a strong frame, which also acted as a safety roll cage, with leading-link front suspension, and cast-alloy wheels with twin front and single rear disc brakes. Power came from a four-cylinder all-alloy 848cc Reliant engine driving a four-speed gearbox with shaft final-drive. The fittings were as for a car, with heater, demister, turn signals built in and full instruments.

Production of the Quasar was always small and passed to other hands, while Malcolm moved on to other projects, one the Phasar, which used a Kawasaki Z1300 six-cylinder engine but lacked a roof. The Quasar lived on as a memorial to a clever and innovative man.

QUB 1970–1975

Dr Gordon Blair carried out research into two-stroke engines at Queens University, Belfast, and one result was the 250cc QUB road-racing machine. This was raced with some success in Ireland and later there came a 500cc single. After that, Blair concentrated more on research work for companies in many countries.

From the Quasar came this Phasar, which was powered by a massive Kawasaki Z1300 six-cylinder engine with handy shaft drive.

◆ R ◆

RADCO 1913–1933, 1954 AND 1966
Built by E.A. Radnall & Co. of Dartmouth Street, Birmingham, this marque was first seen at the late-1913 Olympia show. It was a simple design with a vertically mounted 2.5 hp two-stroke engine of 211cc, with rear magneto, petroil lubrication and external flywheel. A chain-driven two-speed Albion gearbox and belt final-drive or a single speed with direct belt were offered, and Radco forks used.

This is a ladies' model Radco of 1926, with open frame and neat two-stroke engine, rear magneto and chain drive to the rear wheel.

Post-war, the 211cc model continued, to be joined in 1920 by a 247cc version with a change to Burman gearboxes with two or three speeds. The smaller engine was dropped the next year when a ladies' model was added and with this, plus a complete sidecar outfit and various transmission choices, the 247cc single comprised the range through to 1926. They then built their first four-stroke using a 300cc sv JAP engine.

From 1927 Radco listed four-strokes, this the 1930 model K with a 490cc JAP ohv engine.

The Radco name returned in 1954 on this prototype lightweight, fitted with a 99cc Villiers engine and short leading-link front forks.

A 248cc ohv JAP model joined for 1927, with two 490cc models further swelling the four-stroke involvement by 1928. Both were JAP powered, one a sv and the other a sports model with a choice of single- or twin-port engines and called the Radco Ace. All were retained for the last year of the decade, but the 247cc two-stroke changed to a Villiers engine and an Albion three-speed gearbox.

In 1930 they added models using 147 and 196cc Villiers engines, kept their own 247cc Radco two-stroke and reduced the JAP models to the 245cc and two of 490cc. By 1932 they were back to just the two-strokes and continued with these for 1933, after which they dropped motorcycles and just produced components.

However, this was not the end of the name, which returned in 1954 on a lightweight that revived the Ace name. This had a 99cc Villiers 4F, two-speed engine unit and leading-link forks, but no more was heard of this after the news of the prototype.

Late in 1966, the name was back once more for the Radcomuter, which was a very basic mini-bike powered by a 75cc sv Villiers lawn-mower engine. It was typical of the type but came to nothing.

RADMILL 1912–1914
A small firm that assembled machines using bought-in parts for local sale and not one seen at the major London shows. Engines were the 269cc Villiers and 346cc Precision two-strokes, with others available to order.

RAGLAN 1903
A Coventry firm that exhibited at the late-1903 Stanley show, claiming a stout frame and excellent 2.75hp engine. They also showed a forecar fitted with a 3.75hp engine that had a water-cooled cylinder head. As with so many, it was short lived.

RAGLAN 1909–1913
This name reappeared on machines built in Birmingham by M. Adler Ltd. They used Precision engines of 292, 347 and 496cc, while construction was on familiar lines with belt drive, hub gears and Druid forks. In addition, they also used the 490cc water-cooled Green-Precision engine and a 3.5hp one of their own. Production would have been limited and the name soon vanished once again.

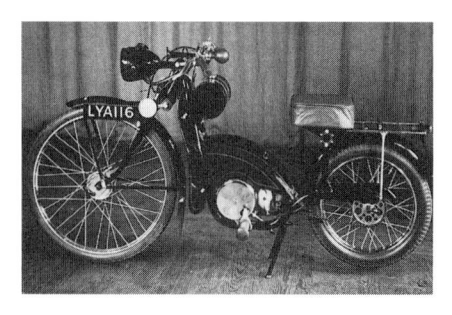

The Rainbow was a prototype seen in 1950 and built with a 99cc Villiers engine, in a form that would come again as the scooterette.

RAINBOW 1950
This was a prototype built in 1950, by a gentleman of that name, as a form of step-through. He used a 99cc Villiers two-speed engine unit that went under a cover, a tubular frame and light girder forks. To keep the saddle height down there was a 20in rear wheel, while the front was a 26in bicycle-type, both with small drum brakes. Legshields were fitted and the

For 1904 Raleigh offered this solo, with central engine position and two-stage all-chain transmission via a countershaft with clutch.

machine was well made with a hint of what would come with the C50 Honda. Sadly, the Rainbow failed to go into production.

RALEIGH 1901–1906, 1920–1933 AND 1958–1971

This Nottingham firm was famous for their bicycles long before they built a motorcycle and later took over the Sturmey-Archer firm to produce engines and gearboxes of that name. Their first motorcycle was built in 1901 with an imported Schwann engine mounted over the front wheel, which it drove by belt.

It was soon replaced by a better machine that had the 3hp engine set vertically ahead of the pedals. The frame was stronger than most, for in addition to the usual down, top and seat tubes, one ran from the headstock to the rear-wheel fork. The forks were rigid but the drive was by chain in two stages with a countershaft carrying a clutch. A two-speed gear was an option, as was belt drive, and the firm also listed a forecar with a 3.5hp water-cooled engine.

Raleigh also listed this forecar in 1904, using a water-cooled engine to keep the driver's feet warm. From 1906 to 1920, they left the market.

Their reputation was enhanced when G.P. Mills set a new time under fifty-one hours for the Land's End to John O' Groats ride, despite many stops. The engine gave no trouble at all and the ride was a remarkable feat on the roads of the time.

The downturn in trade that occurred around that time was reflected in a full-page advertisement in 1905 offering machines at a well-reduced price. Following this the firm left motorcycles after 1906 to concentrate on bicycles.

They returned in 1920 with an interesting and totally new model

The Raleigh Roma was really a Bianchi Orsetto from Italy, and was yet another import that they sold for a few years.

The 1928 Raleigh twin-port model with 498cc ohv engine offered good performance and full equipment with fittings and options.

which had a 698cc flat-twin sv engine fitted in line with the frame. This drove a three-speed Sturmey-Archer gearbox by chain, there was chain final-drive and the frame had pivoted-fork rear suspension controlled by leaf springs. A drum brake went at the rear, but the front remained a dummy rim.

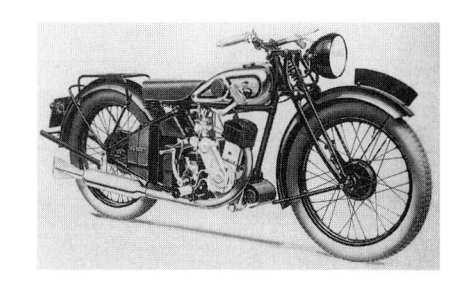

By 1932, the Raleigh range included this 297cc sv model with the inclined engine then in fashion.

The flat-twin was listed to 1923, but the year before that saw it joined by conventional singles of 348 and 399cc with two or three speeds and belt final-drive. These continued to 1924, with all-chain options for the singles, when the flat-twin was replaced by 798cc V-twin models. In that year they demonstrated their reliability with Hugh Gibson driving a combination round the British coast, while Marjorie Cottle rode a solo in the reverse direction. The next year, 1925, brought a 348cc ohv model.

In 1926 Marjorie undertook another long-distance ride and, for that, used a new lightweight with a 174cc engine that had its two-speed gearbox built in-unit with it. The same year also introduced a 249cc single, while all now had chain drive. A 495cc sv model was added for

1927, after when the 174cc single and the V-twin were dropped. This left three sizes of single, the two larger also in ohv form, for the rest of the decade. By 1929 the firm was selling Sturmey-Archer engines to several other makers and this practice continued on to 1933.

The 1930 range had sv models of 225, 248, 297 and 495cc plus the 348 and 495cc ohv machines. The two smallest were then dropped and the others had new, inclined engines for 1931, while 1932 brought a 598cc sv. At the end of 1933 the firm stopped motorcycle production, but continued with the bicycles and a three-wheeled car and van they had introduced in 1930. These were dropped in 1935, so it was bicycles only for many a year.

The name returned late in 1958 for a 49cc moped using a Sturmey-Archer two-stroke engine with V-belt drive to a countershaft. The engine was made by BSA and a version with a clutch was added the next year. At the end of 1960 they changed course and replaced their own moped by one built under licence from Motobécane and a copy of the French Mobylette. These came in a variety of forms and, during the decade, close to a dozen would come and go, all using the same basic engine and transmission. The one that varied was the Wisp, based on a small-wheeled bicycle format translated into moped form. Most had gone by the decade end but one did trickle on to 1971.

In addition to the mopeds, the firm listed the Roma scooter from 1961 but this was actually the 78cc Orsetto built by Bianchi in Italy with a change of badges. Typical of the type, it had arrived on a declining market, so was dropped after 1964 to leave the mopeds to carry the name into the 1970s. After that it was back to bicycles.

RAMBLER 1939–1962
This was the trade name used by the Norman company for some models when exported. Except for the tank badge they were the same machines, although some might have had minor alterations aside from the usual changes to lights and speedometer.

RANDALL 1912
A firm in Wanstead, London, who built a machine having rear suspension by means of semi-elliptic springs, surely one of the most awkward methods available for such a task. They fitted Saxon forks at the front end and used a 3hp JAP V-twin engine for power, this driving the rear wheel by belt.

RANSOME SIMS & JEFFERIES 1919
This firm concentrated on agricultural machinery and were located in the Norwich area of East Anglia. During 1919 they constructed a battery-powered sidecar outfit, the batteries being housed under the seat of a rudimentary sidecar body with the passenger sat atop. The motorcycle was of conventional outline, but a control box for the motor was fastened into the space normally taken by a fuel tank, the motor itself taking the place of the normal Otto-cycle engine. This outfit was registered for road use and proving trials conducted, but it seems unlikely that more than the prototype was built. The company also used the Orwell marque name for some of its products and could possibly have intended to market the outfit under this name had production proceeded.

RAY 1920
Adding gearboxes to old hub-geared machines and current single-speed lightweights was the stock in trade of the Ray Motor Company of Brick Street, London W1. But for a short time they also built complete machines with 269 and 331cc two-stroke engines, Burman or Roc two-speed gearboxes with chain-cum-belt transmission, Saxon spring forks and other proprietary fittings. The venture didn't last long and they soon returned to conversion work.

RAY 1922–1926
No connection with the London-built Ray, this Nottingham make came from W.H. Raven & Company, already well known for their pedal cycles, when they introduced a novel 198cc sv miniature, its engine in-unit with a two-speed gear and clutch. Final-drive by chain and a flywheel magneto were features from the outset, but buyers had to wait until 1924 for a kickstarter within the specification. A further miniature model called the T.S. Sports was added for 1925, still with the unit-construction theme, this having the 172cc Villiers-Jardine three-speed two-stroke unit. The 198cc machine then became known as the Ray Super Lightweight and it retained this style for 1926, when it continued alone to the end of production for the marque.

RAYBECK 1913
A lightweight powered by the Wall Auto Wheel. One also existed as an invalid carriage, with the driver seated between the two front wheels and the Auto Wheel fitted into the rear fork.

RAYNAL 1914 AND 1937–1950
This Birmingham name was first seen on a simple lightweight powered by a 269cc Villiers engine. Very basic, it had a two-speed Albion gearbox and chain-cum-belt transmission, but production soon ceased.

The name returned late in 1937 on a production version of the Jones autocycle. It was built at Handsworth, Birmingham by ABJ and had a 98cc Villiers Junior engine, open bicycle frame with the petroil tank between the frame tubes, rigid forks and no enclosure. A version with sprung

Raynal produced one of the first autocycles in 1937, using the Jones design as the basis, with the Villiers Junior 98cc two-stroke engine.

forks was added for 1939 and it was this alone that continued post-war to 1950.

RAYNER 1913
G.F. Rayner of Chancery Lane, London designed a model having a special frame and a 494cc flat-twin engine in which the crankshaft was set vertically. Above the crankcase sat a two-speed gearbox, its input shaft driven by worm and wheel at 3:1, final drive being by belt. Inside the engine the pistons were in line, so one had a double connecting-rod, the timing gear was on the underside along with an oil pump, and a large flywheel went outside the timing cover. An interesting design but no more was to be heard of it.

READY 1920–1922
Based in the Somerset seaside town of Weston-super-Mare, D. Read & Company introduced the marque with a model of conventional semi-sporting appearance, with 292cc sv JAP engine, Albion two-speed gearbox, chain-cum-belt transmission and Brampton Biflex forks. There was a single-speed option the next year and a Burman gearbox for the two speeder. Then, in 1922, they dropped the single-speed model but added a three-speed option and introduced a 348cc sv Blackburne version to the expanding range. These singles were supplemented with a flat-twin model powered by the 689cc sv Coventry-Victor engine in a duplex frame with duplicated downtubes from the steering head, making four tubes in all, for added strength. All Ready motorcycles had a patented silencer, consisting of truncated cones located in the ends of the exhaust pipes. Production had ceased by the end of 1922, although it is believed there was a connection subsequently with the Rebro marque.

REBRO 1923–1929
Lightweight two-strokes assembled from proprietary components comprised the Rebro range from its inception. Villiers engines in 147, 172

The Rebro was a typical lightweight of the time, with Villiers engines, and one that kept to belt final-drive rather late in the period.

and 247cc capacities with Albion two-speed or Sturmey-Archer three-speed gearboxes provided the power and drive. The marque was little advertised and held on to belt drive beyond its time, styling also had become dated by the time Read Brothers of Tunbridge Wells in Kent stopped production. It is thought that there was a connection through the Read family with the Ready marque.

RED ARNO 1914–1915
The name taken by the Gosford Street, Coventry firm of Arno in 1914, due to the red finish of its 3.5hp TT model. The name continued for 1915, when two models were listed, both with a Senspray carburettor and gear-driven magneto. The 3.5hp model had direct-belt drive but the 4.5hp one had a Sturmey-Archer hub gear, although it kept to the belt drive. The name was not listed after that year.

REDRUP 1920–1921
Charles Redrup came from Cardiff and had an aviation background that

The Redrup radial-three was an unusual engine, which was taken up by British Radial for their machine, although hardly the ideal motorcycle layout.

accounted for his interest in radial and rotary engines from as early as 1904. He set up in Leeds and, in 1912, built a three-cylinder engine that combined both types, for it was a radial in which both the crankcase and the crankshaft rotated, but in opposite directions. This was mounted in a motorcycle and both sections drove the rear wheel by shaft.

Post-war, he produced a design for a radial three that was, by comparison, quite prosaic. Displacing 309cc and rated at 2.75hp, it was specifically for installation in a motorcycle frame. His principal interest was the engine itself, but to prove his design he commissioned a small number of complete machines, one of which was entered and ridden by himself in the 1920 A-C.U. Six Days Trial. These were probably built by Beaumont Motors of Leeds, who also produced a few machines with this engine under their Beaumont brand name. However, during 1921, the rights to production of the Redrup engine were acquired by the British Radial Engine Company, makers of the British Radial motorcycle.

REFEREE 1904
Referee were the London agents for Ariel and, in 1904, offered their own make that was powered by a 2.25hp Ariel engine. They soon went back to being agents, so no more was heard of their model.

REGAL 1912–1915
Ernest Smith & Woodhouse of Birmingham used the Regal name with others, starting with the 4.25 Regal-Precision of 1912 which had two or three speeds. In 1913 they added other models using 2.75 and 3.5hp Precision engines, these having two or three speeds and belt or chain drive.

For 1914 the Regal-Green name appeared, the model fitted with the Green-Precision water-cooled engine, and having the three-speed gearbox and chain drive. There was also the Regal-Peco that used a 349cc two-stroke engine, three-speed

Sturmey-Archer hub gear or two-speed gearbox, and belt or chain-cum-belt drive. They continued for 1915, adding a 225cc two-stroke Peco model and a V-twin, before production ceased.

REGENT 1919–1920

This marque was the brainchild of a number of ex-Great War servicemen, who banded together with the intention of producing a motorcycle in large numbers. The basis of their design was the engine and frameset sold by Messrs Morton & Weaver of Coventry, which incorporated the 689cc sv Coventry-Victor flat-twin engine, lying in-line with the frame, the latter said to have a number of alterations making it exclusive to the Regent. Transmission was through a three-speed Sturmey-Archer gearbox and models suitable for solo or sidecar use were envisaged. It was announced that the London-based company would be building around 3,000 machines during 1920 alone, but despite much early publicity, it is extremely doubtful whether more than a handful were ever made.

The Regent of 1920 differed in using a Coventry-Victor flat-twin engine, while the wheel discs were a fashion of the time, but few were made.

REGINA 1906–1907 AND 1914–1916

Offered by the Magneto Motor Manufacturers of Lewisham, London, this was a basic model having a loop frame. The firm also imported the CIE models from Belgium but the venture was short lived and ceased in 1907.

The Regina returned in July 1914, based at a Derby address, the machine having a 292cc two-stroke engine, two-speed gearbox, chain-cum-belt drive and Druid forks. The engine was made by S. Barnett of Derby and a direct-belt drive model was also available. They continued with this one basic model for 1915, but added others for 1916, using 3.5 or 4.25hp Precision engines driving three-speed hub gears.

RELIANCE c.1902

A Southampton marque, most likely a small cycle dealer who bought an engine or two from a ship in the docks, bolted it into a heavy-duty cycle frame and tried his luck in this new market, but soon went back to the cycles.

REMUS c.1920–1922

A Birmingham assembler of light-weights who fitted the 211cc Radco two-stroke engine to a conventional model with belt final-drive.

REVERE 1915 AND 1919–1922

Choosing with some wisdom to adopt the then fairly new 269cc two-stroke Villiers engine for their entry into the motorcycle market, W.H. Whitehouse & Co. Ltd, of Friars Road, Coventry evidently didn't take an equally wise look at the state of world affairs when they launched in 1915. Not unexpectedly, the marque only lasted the one season before the Great War brought matters to a halt and the little bike with a two-speed countershaft gearbox and chain-cum-belt transmission was put to one side.

However, it reappeared towards the end of 1919 with Druid forks, an Albion gearbox, stirrup front brake and therefore much as before. By the spring of 1920 a two-speed Sparkbrook gearbox was being specified and a variant with single-speed direct-belt drive was listed for the first time. A two-speed Sturmey-Archer gearbox was the only change in 1921 and then it was back to the Sparkbrook for their final fling in 1922, with the single-speed model continuing to be available throughout this period.

Many were the claims for Edwardian machines, these for this 1904 Revolution not at all unusual.

REVOLUTION 1904–1906

A Birmingham firm, sometimes listed as the New Revolution, that offered a conventional model fitted with a 2.5hp NRCC engine hung beneath the frame downtube. Belt drive and braced forks completed the specification.

For 1905 they added a forecar, listed as the Revolette, using a Stevens water-cooled engine, two-speed gear and chain drive. The frame was built of channel steel and the engine mounted in its own cradle.

REX 1900–1921

The marque first appeared in November 1900 at the National show held in the Crystal Palace, London and was built by the Birmingham Motor Manufacturing & Supply Company. A forwards-sloping 247cc

The Rex for 1902, with central engine held in a steel cradle, direct-belt drive, strutted forks and a smart appearance with neat fittings.

Rex listed a Tricar by 1903, with one running in a 1,000 mile trial, and the next year saw the addition of storage space behind the fuel tank.

four-stroke engine was contained within the diamond of a safety-cycle frame with unsprung front forks, surface carburettor, battery ignition and direct-belt drive, all typical of its time. However, by 1902 the company had joined with the makers of the Allard motorcycle and production was moved to the latter's works in Earlsdon, Coventry. This brought about a redesign, with the engine now positioned vertically ahead of the bottom bracket and held within a flat steel cradle. Strutted forks were fitted and the complete machine had a smart appearance.

This is a 1904 solo Rex, with the silencer part of the right side of the cylinder, so that there was no conventional silencer.

It was changed for 1903, when the tank enclosure was extended to behind the cylinder. At the same time they adopted a 'beehive' silencer, incorporated in the right side of the cylinder, so there was no exhaust pipe or silencer of conventional form. That year they offered a forecar that had an attempt at air ducting to ensure adequate engine cooling and a Rex was entered for the Paris-Madrid race, to be ridden by Gaudry, but failed to start.

A combined tool and battery box was added for 1904, this fitting between the seat tube, chain stays and rear mudguard, while the engine was rated at 3.25hp that year. During the year, Harold Williamson used a Rex to set a new End-to-End record, retaining this to 1908. Tom Peck used a Rex to reduce the time in 1909, as did Arthur Moorhouse in the next year, when the Bentley brothers set a new figure for a sidecar outfit.

In 1906, Rex added a V-twin model to its range and retained the steel cradle to support the engine, while adding front forks working in line.

A 5hp V-twin joined the range in 1906, when a form of front suspension in which the wheel moved along the fork line as in telescopics and a conventional silencer were adopted. Expansion added other models, including a forecar, and in 1910 the engine cradle that dated back to 1902 went and leading-link front forks were fitted. New that year was the Rex Valveless 499cc two-stroke engine with magneto ignition that was later sold as the PMC.

The range of singles and V-twins was joined in 1912 by the Rex-JAP models, built in the Rex works but sold by the Premier Motor Co. of Birmingham. Over the next two years the Rex line shrank and by 1914 only V-twins with either name were made, all with a three-speed gearbox and all-chain drive, although a two-speed Roc gear and belt drive remained an option. A 2.75hp two-stroke and a shaft-drive version of a V-twin were listed for 1915 only, but for 1916 there were only the V-twins with three speeds and chain drive.

Production then ceased until 1920, when a three-model range appeared comprising two 4hp singles and an 8hp V-twin. All had three speeds and chain-cum-belt transmission. Late in

A 1927 Rex-Acme, from a firm that won three TT races in the 1920s and had a fine reputation throughout their life.

1921 Rex amalgamated with Acme and from then on the firm was known as Rex-Acme.

REX-ACME 1921–1933

After Rex and Acme amalgamated late in 1921, they commenced the new marque with a lightweight model in single- or two-speed forms with a 247cc two-stroke Morris engine. This was backed by a 292cc sv JAP four-stroke and 348 plus 549cc sv Blackburne models and a 1,000cc sv big-twin with choice of Blackburne or JAP engines. There was also the rare adoption of the locally made CAM engine of 350cc with a detachable head and unusually large finning. By late 1922 they took up the sleeve-valve Barr & Stroud engines in 348 and 499cc sizes, dropped the big twins, the CAM and Morris engines, and introduced a miniature with 170cc two-stroke engine that shared much in its make up with the similar Hobart and Wee MacGregor machines.

With JAP and Blackburne engines in the middleweight ranges, this took them through to 1924, when, after racing successes at the Belgium and Ulster Grand Prix, they introduced 250 and 350 ohv models with Black-

A neat 1929 Rex-Acme, with 348cc Blackburne sv engine whose magneto was driven by skew gears.

burne engines. Their racing exploits were to be guided by Wal Handley, one of the foremost riders and tuners of the day, who later became Works Manager at the Earlsdon plant and, in 1925, won both Junior and Ultra-Lightweight classes in the TT for them; the first occasion on which 'the double' had been achieved.

This simple lightweight came from the bottom end of the 1929 Rex-Acme range and was fitted with a 147cc Villiers engine.

Naturally, more sporting models followed in the wake of Handley's influence and the range began to expand to take in many options. In 1926 the miniature two-stroke gave way to a new four-stroke model, the Junior, which adopted the 173cc ohv AKD engine and an Albion three-speed gearbox, this continuing into the next year when the new two-port 348cc ohv Blackburne engine was added in a model that fitted Webb centre-spring forks and drum brakes fore and aft. This again was one of the results of Handley's work, with good placings in the TT and the capture of the world's one-hour record in covering 91.21 miles (145.94km) in the sixty minutes.

Handley won the Lightweight TT in 1927 and, for 1928, the 348cc Model TT8 was offered with a duplex cradle frame and specially tuned Blackburne engine based directly on the Handley racing machines. The everyday range was constantly updated too, so that the company kept abreast of trends, saddle-tank styling was embraced and for 1928 the Junior had its capacity reduced slightly to 170cc and a V-twin came back with the new 747cc sv engine from JAP. Otherwise, it was Blackburne or JAP single-cylinder power in sv or ohv forms, with Albion gearboxes on the miniatures and Burman for the remainder.

With the depression looming and Handley gone to fresh pastures, the marque then rather lost its way. The small four-stroke was replaced by a 147cc Villiers model in 1929, supported by similar 247 and 343cc Villiers offerings. Other humdrum lightweights with 197cc sv JAP and 295cc sv Blackburne engines crowded this section of the range, while further up the options and permutations continued apace, such that there were at least seventeen different models to choose from in that year. The company even revived a famous model name from pre-Great War Rex days, the Speed King, which now graced the best of the 348cc Blackburne-engined sports models.

This 1932 Rex-Acme was more in keeping with the image of the firm, with its 500cc JAP twin-port engine.

Then came the depression, but Rex-Acme still had their full list to offer buyers a fair choice using Villiers, Blackburne, JAP and Sturmey-Archer engines while, like many, they included a speedway model. A range was announced for 1931 with the addition of models with the Rudge Python engine, but before it could get underway production came to an end. However, the name was taken over by Mills-Fulford, who launched models with 346 and 500cc ohv JAP engines in May 1932. For 1933 they added two more, using the 249cc Villiers and 250cc ohv JAP engines, but the end came during that year.

REX-JAP 1912–1916
A range of singles and V-twins built by the Rex firm at their Coventry works

The Rex-JAP machines were built by the Rex firm, using JAP engines and using a trade outlet, but they failed to survive after the Great War.

using JAP engines in their existing frames, the result sold by the Premier Motor Co. of Birmingham. At first they had two speeds and belt drive; by 1914 there were only V-twin engines, but with three speeds and all-chain drive. They remained up to 1916, but were not revived post-war when the Coventry firm amalgamated to become Rex-Acme.

REYNOLDS 1931–1934
Albert Reynolds was a Scott dealer, based in Liverpool, who produced parts for the marque and in 1931 the factory began supplying him with models to his own specification. At first they were known as Aero Specials, from his initials, and both 497 and 598cc engines were listed along with Brampton forks, Velocette-type foot-change and twin headlamps.

By 1932 they were known as Reynolds Specials and, for 1933, only the larger engine was listed, to be joined by a model using a 249cc Villiers water-cooled engine in 1934. However, the best Scott days were past and Reynolds had to turn to other marques, although his ideas returned later as the AER.

REYNOLDS 1955–1956
A prototype moped built by Reynolds Tubes, who were much involved with the motorcycle industry. It was European in concept, with a two-speed German Victoria engine hung from a beam frame, front and rear suspension and a good line. Built to show what could be done, Reynolds had no intention of producing it themselves and no-one else took it up.

The Reynolds Runabout was one of many scooters that appeared after the Great War and, in their case, they made a good job of it until the fashion died.

REYNOLDS RUNABOUT 1919–1924

One of the post-Great War scooters that was built at first by the Jackson Car Manufacturing Company of Pangbourne in Berkshire and later by A.W. Wall of Tyseley, Birmingham, who also built the Liberty engine it used. It was better designed than most of that period and much on the lines of those to come some thirty years later. It had its 269cc two-stroke engine and two-speed Roc gear concealed by panels, a flat floor and an apron that carried the fuel tank behind it. The front forks were an Australian Flexifork design that used telescopic plungers with springs combined with a leaf spring for fore and aft movement. Wire 22in wheels were fitted and the transmission was by belt or chain, while two bucket seats were fitted on a wood platform mounted on a combination of coil and leaf springs to enhance the ride.

It was a design that deserved to do well, for it included details such as a lever to assist the use of the rear stand for parking. Unfortunately it suffered from the general collapse of the scooter market, for it was really too advanced for its day. The firm tried it with a JAP engine in place of the Wall but this did not help its sales.

REYRE-NEWSON 1921

S.C. Newson of Stamford Hill, London designed a single-cylinder ohv four-stroke engine of 63×80mm (249cc) in which the two vertically disposed valves were operated from a single-face cam. This was located at the top of a vertical shaft, bevel-driven from the crankshaft on the off-side. Fitted into neat lightweight cycle parts, this engine enjoyed some success in speed events, with the complete machine entered as the Reyre-Newson. It was, however, a short lived venture.

R&H 1923

This was a neat little miniature with 147cc Villiers two-stroke driving through a two-speed Albion gearbox with chain-cum-belt drive. Extreme simplicity was its keynote, though the sophistication of a clutch and kick-start could be obtained at extra cost. Hailstones & Ravenhall of Coventry, who switched their initials around to provide the marque name, didn't stay in the trade for long.

RIBBLE 1903

This name appeared on a machine ridden by W. Bottomley at the Southport Speed Trials held in October 1903. It was powered by a 400cc MMC engine, with direct-belt drive and was a typical primitive.

RICKMAN 1961–1976

Brothers Don and Derek Rickman were successful in scrambles from the start, but sought better machines to ride, the result being a Tribsa, combining the Triumph twin engine and BSA frame with Norton forks. They called the result Métisse, French for mongrel or crossbreed, the latter suggesting mating the best for a purpose. By 1961 they had developed the Métisse to have their own light and elegant frame, nickel plated, with glass-fibre tank, seat base, tail unit and air-filter panels.

At that point the brothers offered the design to the industry, who turned it down, despite the orders already flowing in. So the brothers became manufacturers, producing machines and kits that could take a choice of engines, although Triumph, BSA and Matchless were the more usual. The standards to which they were made were of the highest, so they were quickly in great demand and very successful in competition.

A Rickman fitted with the more usual Triumph twin engine, to give the owner one of the best café racer machines on the road.

A typical Rickman machine, in this case fitted with the Royal Enfield Interceptor engine and sold using both names.

Other projects came the Rickmans' way. One was the 250cc Bultaco Métisse scrambler, built to the same high standards, and in 1965 they had their first involvement with road racing. For this they were asked to build frames for an AJS 7R and a Matchless G50, which they did, and fitted them with disc brakes, working with Lockheed on that aspect.

In 1969 came the Street Métisse with a very sleek road-racing style and usually fitted with a Triumph-twin engine unit. By 1970 there was also a model with a Royal Enfield Interceptor engine and this led to a batch of machines sold in Britain as the Rickman Enfield.

In total contrast was a lightweight built for the USA and powered by a 125cc Zundapp engine unit. Later came a version with a 250cc Montesa engine and some of the smaller were sold to police forces, as well as larger ones with Triumph engines. A successful but short-lived period, it was followed by further versions of the Street Métisse designed to carry the larger Japanese engines. This led on into producing accessory lines such as fairings, top boxes and crash bars, while the original scrambles design was passed on.

Rickman motorcycle production came to an end around 1976, but their other products continued. As one market went down they transferred to another, so at one time they built BMX bicycles and later went into kit cars. Many of their accessories remain in production.

The Robin was unusual in having a diesel engine, which was installed in the cycle parts of the Indian-built Enfield to give low fuel consumption.

RIGO 1913–1914
A rare, pre-Great War marque powered by a 3.5hp engine.

A 1903 Riley Moto-Bi model, with the engine hung from the downtube; later models kept the name but had a vertical engine built by them.

RILEY 1899–1906
A Coventry firm, begun by William Riley, who was helped by four of his five sons. From 1890 they were involved with bicycles and in 1898 son Percy built a car in the works, with an engine of the De Dion type.

By 1899 the firm was producing tricycles and quadricycles using 2.25hp German Cudell or Belgian Minerva engines. The engine went behind the rear axle in either case and one or two front wheels were fitted according to type. Around 1900, the engines were changed to 2.75 or 3.5hp MMC but in 1901 came the first motorcycle.

The solo fitted a 1.5hp Minerva or 2.75hp MMC engine hung from the frame downtube, the machine a typical primitive. A forecar design was added to the range for 1902, while during 1903 a 3.5hp MMC engine was added to the options. The solos were advertised as the 'Moto-Bi' that levelled the hills.

Late in 1903, Riley began to fit their own engines, ending a dependence on others, and adopted the vertical mounting position while retaining the Moto-Bi name. Engines of 2.25, 3 and 3.5hp appeared, the last intended for forecar use and available with fan- or water-cooling. Forecars and sidecars were included in the range, the forecar revised during 1904 and joined by a further version for 1905, this last moving more to car practice.

A 6hp, 804cc V-twin was added for 1906, the whole machine of heavier build, but early in that year motorcycle production ceased to allow the firm to concentrate on tricars and later the motorcar.

RIP 1906–1907
A firm in Stratford, London, who listed 3.5, 4 and 6hp models fitted with leading-link front forks and pivoted-fork rear suspension. The engines had side valves and belt drive was employed on this short-lived marque.

ROADSTAR 1980
This was a venture to produce a road machine based on the CCM motocross engine unit. Three versions were proposed, the Roadstar in sports road trim, the Darkstar with extra bodywork, and the Customstar with chopper styling and rigid rear end. Engines were the 343, 499 or 580cc BSA unit singles with four-speed gearbox and the whole machine would be essentially built to order. The result had a nice line but was expensive, which could be why no more was heard of it.

ROAMER 1948 ON
Another name, like Rambler, used by Norman for its export models, this time in Australia in the early postwar years. Other than the tank transfer, the machines were the same product.

ROBIN 1987–DATE
Ernie Dorsett had a fancy for a diesel engine for his motorcycle, so he built a prototype and this led to Redbreast

Engineering lending him a Robin engine, first of 300cc, then one of 412cc. This produced a modest 8.5hp at 3,000rpm and was installed in a set of 1950s Matchless cycle parts. Such was the interest that, by 1993, the project went into modest production using the India Enfield imported by Bavanar Products as a basis; the resulting machine was termed the Enfield Robin.

The result was very sparing on fuel, with 150mpg (1.9ltr/100km) normal, but no great performer from the power output. However, it proved a fine machine for the byways and the cycle parts reflected this.

In 1997 the idea was taken further, to create the MZ Robin which used the same engine in an MZ frame. The big difference lay in the primary drive, for this was of the constant variable transmission (CVT) type using a V-belt and expanding pulleys. This was automatic in operation and suited the diesel engine better than a conventional gearbox.

The 1908 Roc Royal Military model had the same long wheelbase of the early Wall, but was just one of many bright ideas that Wall pursued.

ROC 1904–1914

A Guildford firm that moved to Aston Road, Birmingham in 1910, run by A.W. Wall and part financed by author Conan Doyle. Wall was a versatile designer who early on produced a free-engine clutch that went into the rear hub and a two-speed gear. Later came the Wall Auto Wheel.

For 1904, the Roc had a 3hp engine, the free-engine clutch and magneto ignition, and for 1905 the engine was fitted with an outside flywheel on each side.

A vertical twin-cylinder engine

For 1911, Wall came up with a completely new design on scooter lines, with front and rear suspension, two-stroke engine and shaft drive.

was tried in the 1905 Auto Cycle Cup event held in the Isle of Man, but did not race. It had a large flywheel between the cylinders, duplex downtubes to miss this, and was ridden by T.H. Tessier. It was listed for 1906 as of 792cc capacity, and had chain drive to a half-speed countershaft that carried the exhaust-valve cams. The inlets were automatic and the engine was mounted in a spring frame.

The 1908 model, the 4hp Royal Military, had a lengthy wheelbase and a live rear-axle with clutch and two-speed gear, all in the rear hub. This hub was offered as a conversion for other makes and proved popular. Engines for 1909 were a 4hp single and 5–6hp twin, while a new front fork using C-springs appeared.

They extended the range at the 1909 show, when the Wall Auto Wheel first appeared and the Roc range added a Tourist model with a 6hp 515cc four-cylinder engine, two-speed epicyclic gear, shaft drive and a pressed-steel frame. The same model was also listed with the 4hp single engine.

For 1911 they advertised two models under the A.W. Wall name, one a single with a two-stroke

In addition to the 1911 scooter design, Wall offered a variant with two rear wheels and a body to carry the rider and enclose the mechanics.

engine, shaft drive, worm gear, two-speeds, pressed-steel frame, C-spring front suspension and a well-sprung bucket seat. The second was a tricycle with twin rear wheels and a body that hid the engine and accommodated the rider. The engine for this had a rotary inlet-valve but single or twin four-strokes were options.

The 1912 model was a 5hp tricycle fitted with a Roc two-speed gear, while for 1914 they fitted Precision 2.75 and 4.25hp engines, the larger driving a four-speed gearbox. They also listed a 6hp model fitted with a three-speed gearbox and having chain drive.

ROCKSON 1920–1923

Built at Cradley Heath, Staffordshire by a well-established iron and steel firm, this make appeared in 1920 and benefited from the owners being enthusiasts who rode their machines in competition. They used the 269cc Villiers two-stroke engine and offered a variety of transmissions. By 1922 they had added 348 and 499cc Blackburne sv engines driving three-speed Burman gearboxes but, despite producing good and well-finished machines, they came to an end in 1923. It is reputed that production amounted to around 400 machines, with half exported to India.

RODGERS 1920–1922

Thomas Rodgers of St George's Parade, Wolverhampton assembled a few machines using bought-in parts during the hectic days of the early-1920s. Much as many others, he soon went back to motor engineering when the boom period was past.

ROE 1905–1926 AND 1957

A.V. Roe was an aircraft builder who disliked motorcycling without weather protection and, as early as 1905, he proposed a motorcycle having extra large mudguards. By 1913 he had a design for a vehicle in which the rider sat low, legs either side of the Douglas flat-twin engine. There were to be Druid forks, wheel steering, rear suspension, a 72in (183cm) wheelbase

A.V. Roe pictured with his Avro Mobile machine, its low seat position and a degree of weather protection among the features he pursued for years.

and outrigger wheels were fitted for stability when the machine was at a halt.

Little more was heard of this but, in 1922, he built a machine he called the Avro Mobile, which had low seating and was initially fully enclosed. He used a 349cc Barr & Stroud engine and three-speed Albion gearbox with all-chain drive. The frame was constructed from sheet steel formed into a channel section, and had front and rear suspension controlled by quarter-elliptic springs. Hub-centre steering was used, along with 12in disc wheels and drum brakes.

At first the machine had a completely closed body, as a bicar, but in due course this was revised to the manner of the scooter type of the 1950s. In this form there was a bonnet and screen at the front, and a seat and tail behind, with both made from aluminium sheet. The tail-panel lid hinged up to reveal a storage space, while the tools were carried inside the lid.

The machine was road tested in 1926, by when the designer had become Sir Alliott Verdon Roe, and in that year he introduced the Ro-Monocar. This used a 343cc Villiers engine driving a three-speed gearbox with shaft and worm to the rear wheel. Nearly full enclosure was again used and the result much as the Mobile. Later it was renamed the Saro Runabout to promote the new Saunders-Roe company.

Later still came the Arro model in similar form, but none of these really caught on. Much later, around 1957, came the Avle Bicar which used a Velocette 192cc LE engine, gearbox and rear axle in the same format, but again there was only one made. Years later, in the 1970s, from other minds, there was the Quasar in the same style and a few others, but the advantages seemed to count for little, as riders preferred the wind in their face.

ROLFE 1912–1913
First seen late in 1912 and built in Smethwick using a 6hp V-twin Precision engine, Rolfe three-speed gearbox, chain drive and Saxon forks. For 1913 this was joined by a single using a 3.5hp JAP engine, still with gearbox and all-chain drive. Their sidecar chassis was built entirely from straight tubing and had the wheel spindle supported on both sides. However, it was a short-lived marque.

ROMP & ROMPER 1913–1920
The company ssembled machines in a small way using the 3.5hp Precision engine in bought-in parts, no doubt built to order for local sale. Post-war the name appeared briefly as Romper, for a machine fitted with a 293cc Union two-stroke engine with direct-belt drive to the rear wheel. Saxon spring forks, Amac carburettor and a Runbaken magneto completed the essential elements of this simple machine, but even a maker's name or location were not divulged and before the end of the year it had gone.

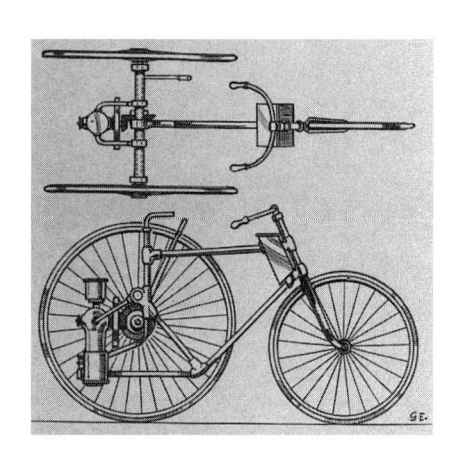

Built by J.D. Roots in 1892, this tricycle had a water-cooled two-stroke engine hung upside down and drove the rear axle by bevel gears.

ROOTS 1892
J.D. Roots built a tricycle in 1892, powered by a single-cylinder two-stroke engine operating on the Day cycle, utilizing crankcase compression. The engine was water-cooled, hung upside-down behind the rear axle and drove this by bevel gears. The cooling water was circulated through the frame tubes. Having a single front wheel, this design pre-dated the more famous De Dion-Bouton tricycle.

ROPER 1901–1905
These machines were built in Wolverhampton by one J. Roper, but details are sparse. No doubt it was a typical primitive using a proprietary engine such as a De Dion or Minerva. With the downturn in the trade in 1905 they turned to making motor fittings.

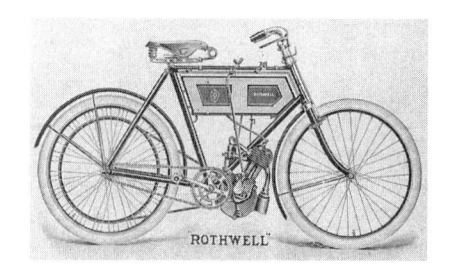

Some marques were short-lived and the Rothwell was one such, with its imported engine hung from a bicycle downtube with belt drive.

ROTHWELL 1903
A short-lived marque built by the Eclipse Machine Co. of Oldham, Lancashire, established back in 1872. The machine was a typical primitive, with its small engine hung inclined from the bicycle frame downtube, with belt drive and unbraced cycle forks. Truly a bicycle plus engine and tank, so with a brief life.

ROULETTE 1911–1914
Late in 1911 the Roulette Cycle Co. of Gosford Street, Coventry showed a motorcycle with a novel form of frame construction that they sought to licence to other firms. Invented by

This 1903 Rover was of neat design, including twin downtubes to give good support to the engine and braced forks to stiffen the steering.

F.T. Robb, the frame comprised duplex tubes that were bolted together, so that a light and rigid structure resulted with any tube easy to replace if damaged. For the prototype, a 2.5hp JAP engine and direct-belt drive were used.

For 1913 a larger 4.25hp model was added, but only the smaller ran on for the next year when it was joined by a lightweight with a 269cc Villiers two-stroke engine, two-speed gearbox, belt final-drive and Druid forks. Production ceased during the war and the make did not appear again afterwards, although the frame principle would appear once more at Francis-Barnett.

ROVER 1899, 1903–1906 AND 1910–1927

Best known for its cars and based in Coventry, this firm had its roots in the bicycle industry and first experimented with power in 1899. They built a tricycle in bath-chair form, with twin rear wheels between which went the driver and the De Dion engine. The passenger sat in front, just aft of the single small front-wheel. It

Rover listed this Tricar for 1904, using a water-cooled engine, chain drive and a steering wheel rather than the usual bars.

was exhibited at the Richmond show that year.

It was 1903 before they appeared again, this time with a well thought-out design of motorcycle, whose single 2.25hp engine had a mechanical inlet valve and spray carburettor. The frame had two downtubes, one to the crankcase and the other to its front to increase rigidity, while braced forks were fitted.

The engine was rated at 3hp for 1904 and also used for a forecar, when the rating was of 4hp. During the year the forecar had the option of a water-cooled engine, when its transmission became two-stage chain and included a clutch.

The frame was altered to a single

By 1912, the Rover single was well developed and continued along this path, complete with V-twin model, up to 1927.

downtube for 1905, when a 2.5hp lightweight was added, and the forecar remained in the list with wheel steering an option. The range was listed for 1906, but the firm then concentrated on cars for a while. However, during 1908–1909 they were supplying complete cycle sets to the British branch of MAG for the Motosacoche Motor Unit, so kept themselves involved with the trade.

They returned late in 1910, at the Meteor Works, Coventry, to offer a 3.5hp model designed by John E. Greenwood with rear-mounted Bosch magneto, B&B carburettor, belt drive from an adjustable pulley and Druid forks. Minor changes, including the option of Armstrong or Sturmey-Archer three-speed hub, kept them going right through the war, supplying private owners up to 1916, as well as the military.

In 1917 they added a 654cc JAP V-twin model for service use and this, plus the single, comprised the post-war range. Chain drive for all except the TT model came in 1921 and, in 1923 the twin was dropped and a neat lightweight with a 249cc engine appeared. This had ohv and drove a three-speed gearbox that was a unit enclosed by the crankcase, so was modern in looks. It continued alone for 1924 and was replaced by a 345cc version with a 60mph (96km/h) guarantee for the next year. This ran on to 1927, after which no more Rover motorcycles were made.

ROYAL AJAX 1904–1906

A typical primitive, built by the Silver Queen Cycle Co. of Gray's Inn Road, London, that fitted a 2.5hp engine upright in a cradle within the frame. Belt drive and rigid forks completed a basic machine that was most likely an Alldays & Onions model with a new tank transfer and detail changes. It was listed for 1906, but no later.

ROYAL BOSCOMBE 1901–1902

A cycle firm, based in the town of that name, that entered the powered market by hanging a 1.5hp engine from the downtube of a heavy-duty bicycle. A fuel tank, 28in wheels with 2in tyres, and belt final-drive completed the machine, but the make was short lived.

ROYAL CAVENDISH 1907

A most obscure make whose one claim to fame was to enter the first TT race in 1907. The rider was G. Horner, his machine one of seventeen in the singles class, and he ran out of fuel and retired before the compulsory half-distance refuelling break. Singles were required to better 90mpg (3.14ltr/100km)!

ROYAL CONSORT 1906

Royal Consort built an early vertical-twin using a 5hp Bercley engine, and singles fitted with 2hp Consort or 3.5hp Lloyd engines, but were a very short-lived make.

ROYAL DEFIANCE 1901–1904

From a works established in 1880 in the Clanamman Valley in southwest Wales, the Williams family built their first motorcycle in 1901. It was powered by a 2.75hp FN engine from Belgium installed in a cycle frame with braced forks. Soon after came machines with 2, 2.25 or 3.5hp Minerva engines, all similar in form and primitive, as they would have to be being built so far from the industrial centre.

ROYAL EAGLE 1901–1910

This name could be applied to Coventry-Eagle machines during the Edwardian era. This was then, and still is, a practice used by firms to suit the marketing needs to sell in some countries. This may be because their usual name might offend or clash with an existing one, giving rise to legal problems.

ROYAL ENFIELD 1898 & 1977–DATE

Located in Redditch, Worcestershire, this firm had its roots in needle making and thus precision engineering and mass production. In time this led to the manufacture of gun parts and later bicycles, so an involvement with powered transport was inevitable. It came in 1898 when they built a quadricycle and then a tricycle using De Dion engines. These were produced in some numbers over the next two years, the engines gaining in power and some, by 1901, having water cooling and a two-speed Enfield gear.

The firm entered the motorcycle field in 1901 with an early Werner design, where the 1.5hp Minerva engine sat in front of the headstock and drove the rear wheel by a crossed belt that must have worn badly. This model was built for 1902, but then replaced by a new design.

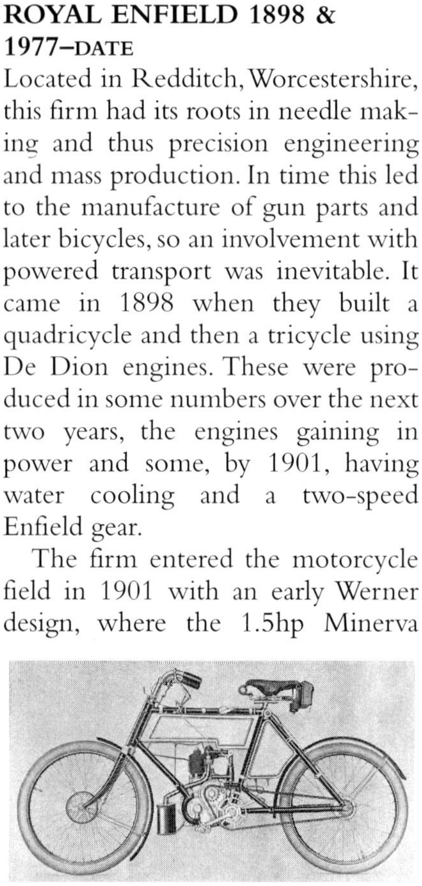

Two of the new 1903 models had Enfield engines mounted vertically in a loop frame. One, of 239cc, had the usual belt-drive but the other was radical, with a 2.25hp water-cooled engine that had the chain drive to the rear wheel taken from the camshaft, which ran at one-sixth engine speed with three cams on it to lift the exhaust valve in turn. In practice this machine was too expensive, while a third model with a Minerva engine hung from the downtube was soon dropped.

This left the simple single with 2.75 or 3.5hp engine and belt drive for 1904, along with a cheaper, air-cooled version of the chain-drive model, the latter with the two-speed gear for 1905. During this period the firm also built cars and, after 1905, concentrated on these and their bicycles, so dropped motorcycles.

They returned to powered two-wheelers late in 1909, with a model fitted with a 2.25hp, 297cc Motosacoche V-twin engine, belt drive and Druid forks. For 1911 it was joined by a 2.75hp model fitted with a 343cc Motosacoche V-twin engine, chain drive and the option of the two-speed gear. This was done by using twin primary chains of differing ratios with expander clutches to take up each in turn. An example of the model was fifth in the Junior TT that year, while other machines had some success at Brooklands.

There were three models for 1912: the 2.75hp V-twin, a 2.5hp ladies' single and a 6hp sidecar V-twin using a JAP engine. Chain drive, two speeds and Druid forks were common to all. That year also saw the Enfield Cush drive making its appearance, this being a shock absorber built into the rear hub which remained a feature of the make for many years. The twins were joined by a 3hp model for 1913, this having a 424cc Royal Enfield engine with overhead inlet-valves and a dry-sump lubrication system with a cylindrical glass oil-tank clipped to the saddle tube.

Little was changed for 1914, when a TT version of the 3hp twin was added to the line and the firm again entered the Junior TT. There, they had a mix of success and tragedy, for F.J. Walker led for two laps, punctured, but then pulled back to a fine third place only to crash at the finish, sustaining injuries from which he died.

During 1914 the firm added a 225cc two-stroke to their range, with a conventional engine, the two-speed gear, cush drive, and destined to have a long life as a simple, basic lightweight. Always it would have a large external flywheel. During the Great War years, the firm built the 6hp model for service sidecar use, some

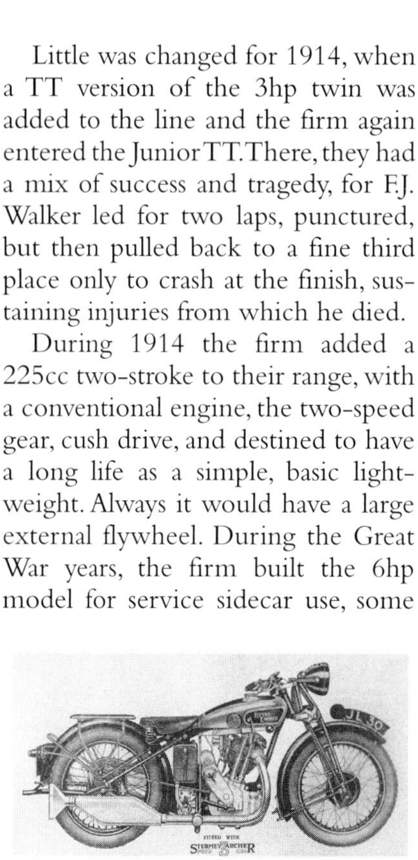

Motorcycles were dropped by Royal Enfield for a few years, but returned in 1910 with this neat V-twin, which kept the loop frame as before.

Typical 1929 Royal Enfield single, with 488cc overhead-valve engine fitted in a frame that was also used in the TT races.

By 1904 Royal Enfield had settled on this conventional design, with central engine but chain drive to the rear wheel as an option.

This is a typical 1930 Royal Enfield model, with fashionable 488cc ohv inclined engine, saddle tank and fittings of that era.

212 Royal Enfield

The Cycar was a radical Royal Enfield design introduced 1932, with a 148cc two-stroke engine and lots of enclosure to encourage daily use.

fitted out as an ambulance and others with a Maxim machine gun, but most of the effort was on general war materials.

During the war, Enfield experimented with a 675cc three-cylinder in-line two-stroke that had a bevel box to drive the two-speed gearbox and rear wheel by chain. Later came an 848cc in-line sv four built in-unit with a three-speed gearbox, but neither machine went into production.

This was how the Flying Flea Royal Enfield went to war, hung from a parachute and dropped to the troops who needed quick transport.

Civilian models returned in 1919 and the firm stuck to just two, the 6hp JAP V-twin with 8hp engine option for sidecar work and the 225cc two-stroke as basic transport. These two kept the firm going up to 1923 but, from 1921, the larger model was fitted with a 976cc V-twin Wolseley engine made by Vickers to an Enfield design.

The range was expanded late in 1923 by adding singles with 346cc sv and ohv JAP engines, but still only two speeds. Three speeds appeared, as an option at first, on the four-strokes in the next year, along with drum brakes, and some machines had a 346cc sv Enfield engine rather than the JAP. A similar ohv model came for 1925 and the next year saw them joined by a 488cc sv model with four speeds.

In 1928, their efforts in the TT races bore fruit, when Cecil Barrow was second in the Lightweight, and their road range adopted saddle tanks and centre-spring forks and was joined by a 225cc sv model. Most now had three speeds with four standard speeds for the 488cc single and sports big-twin, while 1929 brought a 488cc ohv twin-port model.

There were additions for the new decade, while most of the existing models ran on. Four of the new models had their lubrication oil carried in a chamber cast into the front of the crankcase, although the system was dry sump. Two of these models were of 346cc and two of 488cc, with each in sv and ohv form. A lighter 346cc sv machine had an inclined engine and a combined petrol and oil tank, this being joined by an ohv version later in the year. The 976cc V-twin continued to complete the range, still doing its sidecar-hauling job.

All the singles had inclined engines for 1931, but with some engine modifications, and were joined by one of 570cc and a 488cc four-valve single.

There was a radical new model for 1932, listed as the Cycar and fitted with a 148cc two-stroke engine. Its special feature was the sheet-steel frame that fully enclosed all the working parts to encourage everyday use. The next year brought the first use of the Bullet name for the more sporting models, while the V-twin was stretched to 1,140cc for export only.

Royal Enfield joined the twin-cylinder band wagon in 1949 with this model, listed simply as the '500 Twin', later to grow in size.

This range continued with minor changes until 1936, when a new series of singles, with vertical engines but retaining the oil sump in the crankcase, took over. They built up to cover all sizes and in standard and sports Bullet forms to keep a lengthy model list, still with its 225cc two-stroke and big twin. In this way the firm ran on to the war, when they had a newcomer in the 126cc RE two-stroke. This was copied from a 98cc DKW at the request of a Jewish-

First seen during the 1930s, this sturdy single served in the war and continued for some years after, in both 350 and 500cc capacities.

The sports Royal Enfield single was the Bullet, which was also listed in this trials form, as well as for road and scrambles use.

owned firm in Holland and it went on to serve during the war as the Flying Flea. The firm also built their 346cc models in both forms during the war, plus some smaller ones for training.

Post-war, they began by listing the RE and the 346 and 499cc ohv singles. These were all much as pre-war, aside from telescopic forks for the four-strokes, and this took them on to 1949. For that year they revived the Bullet name for a 346cc sports model that was listed in road, trials and scrambles forms, all with pivoted-fork rear suspension. The design was modified to move the oil tank to the back of the crankcase and to bolt the gearbox directly to it.

By 1951, the Royal Enfield 125cc model RE had a new style for the engine unit and foot change for the three-speed gearbox.

A second new model for 1949 was the 500 Twin, which had a 495cc ohv vertical-twin engine in the British format installed in the Bullet frame. In 1950 the RE gained telescopic forks and the next year saw its engine unit revised to improve its style and provide foot change. In 1953 it was joined by the 148cc Ensign, which also had rear suspension, and a 499cc Bullet appeared. To round out the range was the 693cc Meteor twin, much as the 500.

In 1954, the Bullets and twins had a styling cowl called a casquette, carrying twin pilot-lights fitted to the fork top, and a road-racing Bullet in both sizes was announced, although few were sold. There was also a 248cc single, with separate engine and gearbox, introduced in rigid and sprung frames; the first was soon dropped, the second sold as the Clipper. In 1955, Enfield arranged a link with Indian in the USA and, as a result, four models were sold there with the Indian badge on the tank. This link ran on to 1959, by when ten models were involved. A 346cc Clipper came in 1956, when the big twin became the Super Meteor.

A 248cc unit construction single with ohv appeared in 1957 as the Crusader and led on to a whole series of models over the years. It had telescopic forks and rear suspension, and was in the style of the times. A low-cost version was added for 1958 as the Clipper II, while there was also a 346cc Clipper with a Bullet-type engine and Crusader frame. A fairing became a factory option, resulting from a 1956 exercise with *The Motor Cycle* to build a full enclosure on a Bullet, the result called the Dreamliner. The option was simpler and known as the Airflow, soon offered for all models.

During 1958 the 500 Twin was replaced by the 496cc Meteor Minor and the larger twin joined by the Constellation, which had more power. In 1959 the Ensign was joined and then replaced by the 148cc Prince, which shared its engine and had better rear suspension, and a Crusader Sports model was added. New was a 346cc Works Replica Trials model in the format of the older Bullet.

The new decade brought a Meteor Minor Sports to the range that ran on to 1962, when it was joined by two

The Royal Enfield twin grew to 693cc for 1953 as the Meteor and used much of the original 500 Twin cycle parts as this model continued.

models, both Crusader based. One was the Super 5, the sports model with five speeds and leading-link front forks, the other the 250 Trials, which was not a success.

Models came and went in 1963, to leave the Clipper II, Crusader Sports, Super 5 and 250 Trials in that class, joined by the Continental, which had a fuel tank in the Italian style, match-

A 248cc unit-construction model was introduced by Royal Enfield in 1957 as the Crusader, with ohv and four speeds, later leading to a series.

This looks like the Royal Enfield Clipper with the 348cc engine, but is actually a Bullet with better engine, dualseat and long silencer with some style to it.

ing instruments and a flyscreen. There was also the 346cc New Bullet, a stretched Crusader, the 496cc Sports Twin, the Constellation, but only for sidecar use, and a larger 736cc twin, the Interceptor.

The Super 5, 250 Trials, Sports Twin and Constellation were dropped for 1964, but the option list was extended and the range joined by the Turbo Twin and its Sports variant. These used the 249cc Villiers twin two-stroke engine in the Crusader frame. In 1965 the 248cc Olympic joined them in yet another assembly of the Crusader series parts, but the major interest was in three other machines. One was the Continental GT, which was based on what young riders wanted and so was pure café racer with all the style then demanded. The other two were for competition: one was the Scrambler powered by a 247cc Villiers Starmaker engine, the other the GP5 road racer

Most Royal Enfield models were available in this Airflow form, this one on a Constellation twin and the result of the streamlining exercise.

with an Enfield engine based on an Alpha bottom-half.

However, times in the trade had become harder, so the 1966 range was much reduced and then the firm was taken over by Norton Villiers. In time the Interceptor was able to continue and, late in 1968, it was replaced by a Series II model that was much modified, with wet-sump lubrication and Norton forks and wheels. This took the model on to mid-1970, but early that year the Rickman Metisse had appeared, with the 736cc engine in the fine Rickman chassis. A further link joined Floyd Clymer in the USA with the Enfield engine and an Italian frame as the Indian Interceptor, but this project died with Clymer early in 1970. As a result Rickman built the engines into the Rickman Enfield sold in 1971.

The Crusader Sports was developed from the standard model with low handlebars for 1959 and proved popular with younger riders.

This ended the Royal Enfield story, but in 1977 the Enfield, in the form of a 346cc Bullet, reappeared in Britain for, in 1956, the firm had set up a subsidiary in Madras in India. Built under licence, the machine had stayed in a time warp with little change. It was imported on and off over the years, joined by a 499cc version and alternative forms in time, to run on to the present day.

ROYAL GEORGE 1901–1902

An early primitive built by Branson, Kent & Co. of Goswell Road, London, who later produced the BK marque. This one was based on a standard gents' bicycle and had its 1.25hp engine inclined and hung from the downtube. Direct-belt drive and rigid cycle forks completed the machine.

The Royal George had a fine name in a coronation year (actually Edward's), but was a simple primitive using stock cycle parts.

ROYAL MAIL 1902–1903

Three machines were shown by Chambers Engineering of Birmingham at the late-1902 Stanley show bearing this name. One used a Clement-Garrard engine mounted in a cross-framed cycle, while the second had a 2.75hp Kelecom engine and both had chain drive. For the third model a vertical 3.5hp engine with outside flywheel and spray carburettor was used, this machine having belt drive.

ROYAL ROEBUCK 1902–1903

Shown by J.F. James at the late-1902 National show, this make used a 2.25hp engine fitted vertically into a loop frame. It used an FN carburettor,

Clincher tyres and a front Crabbe brake. A second model had a 1.75hp Kelecom engine fitted behind the seat pillar and this location resulted in a longer wheelbase.

ROYAL RUBY 1911–1933

A Manchester-based firm that later moved to Altrincham in Cheshire and then to Bradshawgate in Bolton, Lancashire, and first offered their 3.5hp Cob model for 1911. This had an LMC engine, belt drive and sprung forks, but for the next year it used a 3.5hp JAP, Druid forks and either a Roc two-speed or Sturmey-Archer three-speed gear.

The Royal Ruby 1914 range included both singles and V-twins installed in typical cycle parts for that pre-Great War era, most models running on to 1916.

Royal Ruby added a two-stroke model to their 1914 range, using the Villiers engine, belt or chain drive, and sprung forks in a neat package.

More models were added for 1913, with a 2.5hp single and V-twins of 3.5, 6 and 8hp using JAP engines and mostly the Roc gear. A sidecar model was added for 1914 and this had the same high standard of finish as any of the motorcycles. During the year, a two-stroke model appeared, powered by a 269cc Villiers engine with belt drive or a chain-driven two-speed Albion gearbox and fitted with Druid forks. This line then continued up to 1916.

Post-war, the firm introduced a frame with pivoted-fork rear suspension that used leaf springs as the medium, as did the front forks, and they soon moved to fresh premises in Altrincham, Cheshire. There they also made their own 349cc sv engines and two-speed gearboxes to fit the cycle parts. However, they stayed with JAP for a big V-twin sidecar outfit, which had the 976cc sv engine, three speeds and all-chain drive. Rigid frame models were offered at option or in sports trim for 1921, when a larger single of 375cc with a three-speed gearbox became available.

The 1928 and 1929 Senior TT winner, Charlie Dodson, developed his expertise in tuning and riding as an apprentice at the Royal Ruby works at this time and the Altrincham factory was something of a model for the industry, hosting regular visits from overseas businessmen keen to learn of the best in British industrial practice.

The range continued into 1922 and Sturmey-Archer gearboxes were tried on some models, but the post-war recession caught the firm out and the business went into liquidation. Early in 1924 the name reappeared following acquisition of the goodwill and assets by Horrocks' Motor House of Bradshawgate, Bolton, Lancashire. They began with the 349cc sv model in its rigid frame form that kept the Ruby gearbox and cantilever front fork, and added a 292cc sv JAP version with a two-speed Albion gearbox.

These continued in 1925 with all-chain drive and were joined by a sports machine with the 349cc oil-cooled ohv Bradshaw engine and three-speed Moss gearbox, but this only lasted the one year. For 1927, only the 292cc JAP model continued, but a move to Villiers two-stroke power brought in a new 343cc model and both featured Albion three-speed gearboxes and chain drive.

There were 172 and 247cc Villiers models with the 343cc one for 1928, while the JAP models had 248 and 344cc ohv engines. The four-strokes went into redesigned frames with duplicated front downtubes, one behind the other, and saddle fuel-tanks but were discontinued for 1929. Thus, it was an all two-stroke range for the end of the 1920s, with Villiers engines in 172, 196, 247 and 343cc driving a Sturmey-Archer three-speed gearbox. Only the 247 and 343cc models continued for 1930, while for the next year there was just one, the 346cc Red Shadow. There were Club and Standard versions of this for 1932 while these were joined by three of 249cc for 1933, one with water cooling, but that was their final year.

Royal Ruby ceased production in 1933, this model with 346cc Villiers engine one of the last of the line.

ROYAL RYDAL 1903–1904

Little is known of this marque, which once built both pedal cycles and motor bicycles. Their adoption of the Minerva clip-on engine would have well suited the bicycle frames already under construction at their works, which were thought to have been in Coventry. Advertised features of pedal starting, single speed and direct drive, were all to be expected of this early date.

ROYAL SCOT 1921–1922

Donaldson & Kelso of Anniesland, Glasgow introduced the Royal Scot name specifically to employ the Barr & Stroud sleeve-valve engine, which was made in the same town. The partnership was soon turned into a company, as Knightswood Motors Ltd, and the machines had a ready market in their large home town although only for a brief time, possibly due to supply problems from the distant Midlands.

The 1903 Royal Sovereign differed from the general run of primitives in the form of its frame, but still stood too tall for ease of use on the road.

ROYAL SOVEREIGN 1903–1904

A short-lived make, built by the London Machinist's Co., High Street, Kingsland, London, that fitted a 2.25hp Minerva engine in an extended frame. This frame had members running either side of the crankcase on the crankshaft line, and curved down- and seat-tubes. Rigid forks and belt drive completed the primitive specification. For 1904 a 3hp forecar, also listed as a tricycle, was available.

ROYAL WELLINGTON 1901

One of the many firms, mainly cycle dealers, who bought a Minerva engine and hung it from the down-tube of a heavy-duty bicycle. With direct-belt drive and a bought-in set of fittings most were similar and as short-lived.

R&P 1902–1906

Robinson & Price of Liverpool built primitives using 2.25 and 2.75hp engines mounted vertically in the frame. Like the Bradbury, the crankcase was cast around the main frame tubes under Birch patents and the machines were well made. A forecar was added for 1904, but production would have been small.

RTS 1982–1990

Roger Taylor became involved in grass-track racing at an early age and, in time, moved from riding to tuning to manufacture. Based in Newent, Gloucestershire, he produced machines of all sizes, ranging from schoolboy class upwards, using a variety of engines. Full of clever details, reflecting his years of experience, there were variations in design, some to suit the age of the rider, others for the differing needs of grass and long tracks. There were also speedway frames without rear suspension, all of which kept Roger good and busy.

RTX 1991–2001

Manufacturers of low-cost, off-road machines designed for competitive fun at club level using components sourced from many countries and assembled in South Humberside. With an accent on quality and low maintenance needs, RTX found a ready market among both young and old riders who simply wanted to ride most weekends.

This is a typical low-cost off-road machine, as built by RTX in a couple of capacities for riders who compete at weekends or ride off-road.

The range used a common duplex frame with twin rear shocks or the more modern single shock to suit trials classifications. Engine units were 125 or 200cc two-strokes, these being assembled by the firm, and most models had drum brakes, although a front disc was also available. From these basic parts came trials models with either type of suspension or engine capacity, twin-shock motocross machines in both sizes and a 125cc enduro model. There were also smaller machines for children and a monkey bike.

RUDGE 1910–1940

The Rudge-Whitworth firm of Coventry was a combination of several bicycle firms that dated back to 1869 and the early days. They had a fine reputation and, in July 1910, *The 1911 Rudge's engine had an overhead inlet-valve and chain drive to the magneto and camshaft. It also had a typical frame, but strong forks.*

moved into the powered field with a prototype. This had a 3.5hp engine with overhead inlet-valve and chain drive to the camshaft and magneto. The frame was as others, but the forks introduced the Rudge features of a one-piece fork shackle and enclosed single-spring assembly they kept to the end of their days. Another useful feature was a rear stand that sprang up thanks to a tension spring.

The prototype had some engine development and, by October, it was revised with gear drive to the camshaft and magneto, plus a multiplate clutch built onto the end of the crankshaft along with an adjustable pulley. The detail design, fittings and finish reflected the firm's long experience of bicycles.

In July 1911 Rudge announced a variable gear in which both engine and rear-wheel pulley flanges were moved, thus enabling the ratio to vary without changing the belt tension. It appeared on the 1912 model, controlled by a single lever having twenty positions, and incorporating the free-engine clutch. This machine became the Rudge Multi, destined to continue for a decade, and other models were the TT and the tourist with just the clutch.

This Rudge Sports model of 1926 had a 499cc engine with four-valve cylinder-head, and rim brakes that hardly matched the engine power.

By 1928, Rudge were heavily involved with speedway racing and listed this machine specifically for it as the Dirt Track model.

Little needed to be changed for 1913, but there was one new model with a 5–6hp engine of 749cc thanks to a much longer stroke. It was intended for sidecar work and was available with the clutch or the Multi gear. It was 1913 when the firm came close to winning the Senior TT, for Ray Abbott finished just five seconds adrift of the first man. However, they improved on that in 1914, when Cyril Pullin brought his Rudge home first in the Senior, while the road machines continued much as they were. Early that year they did try mounting two 3.5hp engines side-by-side for sidecar work and later came a prototype V-twin.

Later they built a 999cc V-twin and from this came three listed for 1915, the Multwin with the variable gear and the others with either a three-speed hub gear or a four-speed Jardine gearbox. Motorcycle production then effectively ceased, as the firm turned to war work, with some machines used by the services.

Production started again in 1919, with the 499cc single in three forms, the 749cc single and then the V-twin. All used the Multi belt drive and ran on for 1920, with a three-speed Rudge gearbox and chain drive appearing on the twin towards the year end. The big single was dropped during 1921, to leave a 499cc TT and a Roadster Multi, and a Roadster and the 999cc V-twin with three speeds and chain drive. This continued to 1923, when a new four-speed gearbox was introduced, but the twin and the Multi era was coming to its close.

Trade at that time was poor so, for 1924, the Rudge engine was revised and the first result of this was a 346cc model with a four-valve cylinder head. This was later joined by one of 499cc and both had the valves in parallel pairs, or pent-roof form.

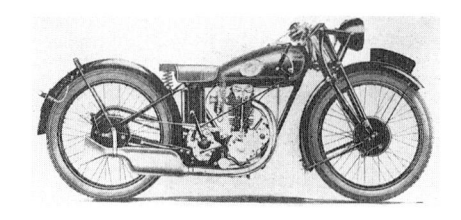

For the middle of the 1929 range, Rudge offered this 340cc single, with overhead valves among its features, along with the big drum-brakes.

The 1925 range comprised models of 346 and 499cc, the latter also built in Sports form, all with four speeds and with front and rear brakes coupled so that the foot pedal operated both. The smaller model was found to lack performance when compared with other marques so was dropped and only the 499cc machine in its two forms ran on for 1926. These were joined by the Special for 1927 and, in 1928, they adopted much-needed drum brakes. This need was especially marked if the machine was coupled to a sidecar and the outfit then asked to haul a new Rudge product, a caravan.

Saddle tanks also appeared for 1928, a year when Graham Walker came close to winning the Senior TT, retiring near the end when well in the lead. It also saw the introduction of the Speedway model for the new sport of dirt-track racing, in which the make would be successful in the early years.

For 1929, Rudge adopted fine drum-brakes of a good size for all models, including the smallest, which fitted a 246cc JAP engine.

In 1930, Rudge listed this 250cc model with the twin-port head, four speeds, a fine line, but still with hand change in their finest TT year.

After the TT, Walker went on to win the Ulster Grand Prix and from this came one of the most famous Rudge models in 1929, the Ulster. With it were listed the Special and Dirt Track models using the same engine, while a 339cc version was added to the list. At the bottom end came two models with JAP engines, one a 248cc sv and the other a 245cc ohv, both with four speeds.

For 1930 dry-sump lubrication was adopted for the Rudge engines, the option of a 300cc sv JAP engine was made available, and the firm had its best year ever at the TT. For this they developed a four-valve cylinder head in which the valves were radially disposed and controlled by no less than six rockers, two as normal and two pairs set across the head. The result exceeded all expectations, for the firm took the first three places in the Junior with Tyrell Smith the winner. Just as good and to complete the success was a one-two in the Senior with Wal Handley the victor.

Sadly, the economic slump made it hard for the firm to profit from this success, for the times meant few buyers for the more expensive sports models in 1931. Rudge introduced

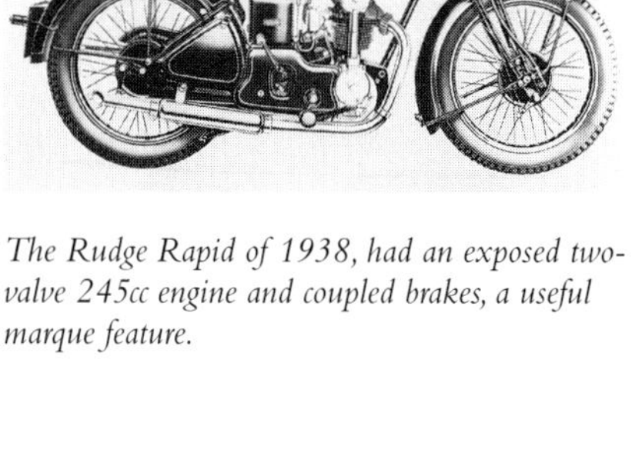

The Rudge Rapid of 1938, had an exposed two-valve 245cc engine and coupled brakes, a useful marque feature.

This long hand-lever was first seen on the Rudges in 1932; its purpose was to operate the centre stand and raise the machine, a 1937 500 Special.

350 and 500 TT Replica models, dropped the JAP engines and added a 248cc model of their own, but this had the costly four-valve radial head, so could hardly compete with the general run of models in that class. There were also two 348cc models with the radial valves, while the 499cc ones kept to the pent-roof. That year they also began to sell their engines to other firms in opposition to JAP and these were usually given the name of Python.

This situation did not stop them returning to the 1931 TT, where Graham Walker won the Lightweight, and they scored two seconds in 1932 and a third in the next year. The road machines had minor changes, including a lever-operated centre stand in 1932. For the next year both 499cc models had a revised cylinder head, this semi-radial where the inlets were parallel while the exhausts splayed out.

Only the 248 and 499cc models were listed for 1934, when the firm again had more success in the Lightweight TT with another one, two, three, led home by Jimmy Simpson. Once again this was unable to help them with their financial troubles and, for 1935, they added a two-valve 248cc model, but went into liquidation at the end of that year.

They were bought by EMI, who continued their production and, in 1937, the valve gear was finally enclosed. Production was moved to the EMI plant at Hayes, Middlesex and continued to 1939 but then ceased, as the factory space was needed for radar equipment. Early in 1940 an autocycle was announced and at first this was produced at Hayes, but later was made for them by Norman in Kent. During the war the name was sold to Raleigh, who used it post-war for a bicycle range, and many years later it appeared once more on a still-born project.

The Rudge Autocycle of 1940 was first built at Hayes and then by Norman, in the usual form with 98cc Villiers engine.

RUDGE 1981

The Rudge name resurfaced early in 1981 on a sports roadster, designed by Ron Gardner and Mike Cook and exhibited at a London show for comments and reactions. It used a 500cc twin-cam Weslake single engine with four valves fed by a Gardner carburettor. The monoshock frame was designed in conjunction with Tony Foale and carried the engine oil in its top tube. The gearbox was a five- or six-speed Quaife, the cast-alloy wheels and leading-link front forks from Foale, alternative forks were on test, and both wheels had disc brakes. It was enterprising using the old and well-known name, but nothing more was heard of the project.

RUDGE-WEDGE 1902–1904

A cycle firm, based in Mander Street, Wolverhampton, that began with 1.25 and 2.5hp models, the engine inclined along the downtube, but within the main frame. Belt drive and rigid forks completed a basic design.

In 1904 they produced a spring-frame model, where the handlebars, footrests and saddle were a single unit sprung relative to the main frame to insulate the rider. In this case the Minerva engine was hung from the downtube to leave room for the suspension parts. The front forks remained rigid and unbraced, with a link back to the handlebar stem for steering.

RUFFELLS 1919

An opportunist marque, launched in the London area in early 1919, during the rush for personal transport after the Great War. The Ruffells lightweight adopted the 269cc Villiers two-stroke engine, a two-speed Albion gearbox and Druid front forks. Footboards were specified on a touring version, with a sports model available at option.

RULEX 1904

This was built by the R.L. Motor Engineering Co. and seen at an early 1904 show. The machine was fitted with a 308cc engine and a two-speed gear was offered, but nothing more was to be heard of the make.

RUNBAKEN 1919
The Runbaken Magneto Co. Ltd, of Manchester was once a prominent supplier of magnetos and other electrical equipment to the motorcycle trade. In 1919 the head of the firm built a prototype scooter propelled by a 0.5hp electric motor in-unit with reduction gearing and chain final-drive. A huge 6 volt storage battery sat on the foot platform above the tubular open frame, but in its own cradle for easy removal when recharging. Miniature Druid side-spring front forks, 12in-diameter spoked wheels and twistgrip speed control were other features. Speeds of 9mph (14km/hr) and a cruising range of just 12 miles (19km) on a full charge obviously limited its future potential and it was not persevered with further.

RUNWELL 1913–1914
The Runwell was produced from works in Lawson Street, Birmingham, where the Perfect was also built, both marques also producing cycles. Both makes were much the same, although the Runwell specified a TDC 3.5hp engine with U.H. magneto and a different make of tyres, but otherwise took the same line with B&B carburettor, Albion free-engine clutch or an Armstrong three-speed hub, rims brakes and Saxon forks. Both were soon gone.

RUSHWORTH 1907
Based in Halifax, this firm offered a machine having a 3.5hp engine with ohv mounted well-forward in a frame that had a 60in (152cm) wheelbase. The forks were rigid and no further mention was made of this make.

RUSSELL 1911
Edgar Russell, a Derby man, designed and built an advanced 3.5hp single in 1911. It had ohv with each in a cage that screwed into the head, a B&B carburettor, Bosch magneto and stiffening ribs cast into the crankcase. It had a single speed and belt drive, and was used by the owner for a year or more although it did not go into production.

RUSSELL 1913
A small firm, so not seen in the buyers' lists or at the major London shows, who assembled bought-in parts. Capacities of 172 and 492cc were used in ohv form, so the engines could have come from Blackburne, Precision or JAP.

RW SCOUT 1920–1921
The product of a keen competition

Available for a couple of years in the early 1920s, the RW Scout was assembled from bought-in components and performed well.

rider from Billericay in Essex, this marque was assembled from components much as many others, but its designer gave it an attractive line and put it through its paces on the track. Reg Weatherell used the 318cc Dalm two-stroke engine with twin-port barrel, driving the rear wheel direct by belt, or via an Albion two-speed gearbox at option. A stripped racing version of the single speeder was listed, its pedigree ensured by Weatherell himself who rode regularly at Brooklands, a notable sixth place in the 350cc Class of the gruelling 500 Miles race in 1921 going into the record books. By that time a 269cc Villiers-engined model in two-speed form only had been added, but then the marque faded from the scene; unlike its promoter, who went on to create the Weatherell motorcycle

S

SALTLEY 1919–1925
A cycle company, who entered the motorcycle market with a 269cc Villiers-engined lightweight and a choice of single- or two-speed chain-cum-belt transmissions. For 1921 the latest Villiers Mk IV engine with flywheel magneto joined the earlier version and further models with Vulcanus and 545cc Blackburne engines were also added. These continued in 1925, when the range increased again through 292cc sv JAP and 348cc Blackburne models. This, however, proved to be the high point and, by 1925, the firm from Snow Hill, Birmingham had gone back to its origins and pedal power.

SAMSON 1910–1913
Reg Samson was fond of publicity, so his personal machine carried mark RS227. He built machines fitted with a 3.5hp Precision engine that went into a frame of his own design, fitted with Druid forks and employing belt drive. He continued with this for 1912 and, for 1913, offered an Albion two-speed gearbox while retaining the belt drive.

SANDOW EARLY 1920s
Built by a Cannock, Staffordshire garage owner in small numbers for a short while.

SANTLER 1897
Built by brothers Charles and Walter in Malvern, Worcestershire; general engineers who added bicycles and then generating sets to their business. In time these two were combined, with the engine mounted above the front wheel, which it drove by belt. They did not pursue this idea, but went on to build a car around 1899 and a three-wheeler in 1920, the Santler Rushabout that was much as the Morgan, also built in Malvern.

The Sapphire used a Triumph engine and Dot forks at first but, when supplies dried up, the firm had to give up building their excellent machines.

SAPPHIRE 1963–1966
Once the Triumph TR5 was no longer available, scrambler Roger Kyffin turned to the 5TA unit and squeezed this into a Dot frame. The result was fast, light and a winner, so the orders rolled into his Stockport, Cheshire premises.

The production machine used the Dot leading-link forks, but the frame had major alterations. Triumph would not supply complete engines, so these were bought as sets of spares and seventy-five machines were built before Meriden stepped in and stopped this. By then Roger was using his own frame with Ceriani forks; tried BSA, who refused to supply engines, and turned to Villiers. Using one of their engines he produced a trials model in a smaller format, but when Villiers went down he had to call it a day.

SARACEN 1967–1975
A trials machine built by Robin Goodfellow in Cirencester, Gloucestershire, that used a 125cc Sachs two-stroke engine unit with five-speed gearbox. This went into a very well-made frame fitted with high quality parts and the result was sold in kit form. It was successful but, although expensive, the firm still lost money on each one sold. In August 1971, at the liquidation auction, it was bought by David Brand, who was based at Watford, Hertfordshire and he added larger engines, although these turned out not too suitable for trials use. By then the Spanish marques were taking over and the Saracen came to an end.

SARCO-RELIANCE 1921–1922
Intended mainly for the overseas export trade, this marque began with a 262cc twin-port two-stroke engine and two-speed Burman gearbox in conventional cycle parts, which were strongly constructed and with good ground clearance. Sanders, Rehders & Co. Ltd, of London, were the promoters and, for 1922, they changed to a 269cc Villiers engine and Albion two-speed gearbox, at the same time adding a four-stroke model with the 292cc sv JAP single; it was, however, their final fling on the British market.

SATURN c.1925–1926
This firm was too small to appear in the 1926 Buyers Guide and had arrived well after the early post-war rush. They offered a conventional model powered by their own 346cc two-stroke engine, but sales were small.

SAUNDERS 1903
This gentleman was located at Croydon, Surrey and offered 3hp motorcycles via small advertisements in magazines. No doubt he was a cycle dealer, who used an imported engine in a heavy-duty bicycle frame with belt-drive transmission, promoted by a nice transfer on the fuel tank.

SAXEL 1923–1924
The Coventry-based accessories firm of Saxelby's was well known throughout the 1920s for components sold under the Saxessories brand name. In 1923 they began to market a range of motorcycles, choosing Saxel as their marque name and, at first, listing two models. One used a 349cc Barr & Stroud sleeve-valve engine and

three-speed gearbox with all-chain drive, the other was a lightweight and called the Saxel Junior, with the then newly introduced 147cc Villiers two-stroke engine, driving through an Albion two-speed gearbox.

Sales prospects must have seemed promising, because the next year the range proliferated. The Junior continued as before, but now with an option of a three-speed gear, to be joined by companions with 247 and 343cc Villiers two-strokes. These, too, had the option of three-speed, which was in fact common through the whole range, the standard fitment being a two-speed Sturmey-Archer. A 499cc version of the 349ccc B&S model was also added and then came a host of four-stroke sv models, 248 and 346cc powered by JAP, and 249, 348 and 545cc examples with Blackburne motors. This catch-all policy evidently failed to succeed and they were gone from the listings by the end of 1924.

SAXESSORIES 1923
For one brief season Saxelby's of Coventry listed one of their Saxel models under this marque name. In effect it was a cut-price version, which retained the 247cc Villiers engine but with belt final-drive. No doubt it shifted some old stock and was then dropped.

SAXON 1989–1990
A racing special with a frame built by Nigel Saxon and a 350cc Armstrong water-cooled tandem-twin disc-valve two-stroke engine driving a six-speed gearbox. The frame was a tubular spine and the suspension was rising-rate at both ends. The front end had telescopics, but the sliders were linked back to a spring unit in the frame so the legs were empty. At the rear was a further linkage for the rear fork. An enterprising design that worked well.

SCALE 1906–1920
Harry J. Scale started constructing motorcycles from premises in Alexandra Park, Manchester during 1906 and soon gained a reputation for quality and for his own riding abilities in competitive events. Belgian-built 6hp Antoine V-twin engines were used at first, then JAP motors from Tottenham. By 1910, he was entered in the TT races with a 3.5hp ohv JAP model, an outing which met with retirement, but his personal career tally of over 100 first-class awards showed that his products could normally be relied upon. After the Great War he recommenced production with a lightweight having the 348cc Precision two-stroke engine, but, shortly afterwards, Scale obtained outside finance through Messrs Robert & Hibbs, which permitted increased production from larger premises. The business was renamed as New Scale and continued thus until 1925.

Scamp produced a neat moped from the Isle of Wight, designed and built to be light and cheap, but it did not sell too well.

SCAMP 1968
This moped was produced in the Isle of Wight, with its 50cc engine attached to the left side of the rear wheel, which it drove via a centrifugal clutch and gear pair. Both wheels were of 12in diameter, with a drum brake for the front but a bicycle calliper for the rear. A simple tubular frame with cycle forks carried the wheels, there was no suspension and the cycle chain went on the right as usual. The model came complete with head and tail lights and was to be sold at a low price, but failed to find much of a market so was soon gone.

SCARLET 1915
This marque made the briefest of entries in the list, most likely to suit a war-time need – maybe a short contract for machines to go to the front in France. It used the 269cc Metro two-stroke engine and was of orthodox form.

SCITSU 1981
This machine was called the Manxman in 1980 and its claim to fame was that the frame was made from two plates of aluminium bolted together. Designed by Tony Dawson, who also produced the Astralite wheels in the same manner, it was successful in the road-racing 125cc class. Suggestions that it could be fitted with a number of Sachs engines from 125 to 250cc were made, but nothing came of this.

SCORPION 1963–1965
Based at Bishops Stortford, Hertfordshire, this firm introduced new thinking into its trials and scrambles models. It had a T-frame chassis constructed from sheet-steel box sections welded together. With a frame loop in square-section tube bolted in place it was easy to fit alternative engines, although they were the usual Villiers in most cases, the 197cc 9E or 246cc 32A for trials and the 36A or a Starmaker for scrambles.

The Scorpion, in trials or scramble form, was another product of a small firm with bright ideas, which fell victim to supply of major assemblies.

Late in 1964 a road-racing model was added and this differed in having a Scorpion designed and made engine, albeit very similar to the Villiers, Alpha and Royal Enfield units, and this was hung from a tubular spine frame. Only the show prototype was seen, and the make had gone soon after.

SCOTT 1901–1982

The Scott motorcycle was always as special as the founder of the firm, Alfred Angas Scott. A Yorkshireman, he built his first engine in 1901 and this set the pattern for most Scotts from then on, for it was a twin-cylinder two-stroke. He fitted it to his Premier bicycle in front of the headstock, from where it drove the front wheel by belt. This was revised for 1902, when the engine went behind the headstock with belt drive to a countershaft that drove the rear wheel by friction. This was soon replaced by a chain drive from the countershaft to the rear wheel.

The first Scott of 1901 had its twin-cylinder two-stroke engine fitted to the bicycle headstock, with belt drive to the front wheel but, for 1902, it changed to this rear-wheel drive.

Scott patented his engine design in 1904 as a twin-cylinder two-stroke, with a central flywheel, overhung crankshafts and access to the big ends via round crankcase doors. From this he developed a complete machine and when first seen in 1908 it had a 333cc 3hp engine, with air cooling for the cylinders but water cooling for their heads. The concept remained the same for many years and with it went a neat and simple two-speed gear. It worked by the use of two primary chains, one on each side of the central flywheel, that drove back to a countershaft carrying twin sprockets of differing sizes. Drum clutches selected either under the control of a rocking gear pedal and a further chain took the drive from the countershaft to the rear wheel. Yet another chain

By 1913, Scott had won a TT, with another to come, and had developed to this form, with the drum-shaped fuel tank, two speeds and a kickstart.

ran from the same shaft to drive the magneto at engine speed.

The engine and gear unit went into a triangulated frame with the cylinders inclined. The frame was of the open type, built up from straight tubes with duplex downtubes from the headstock to the engine cradle, two sets of chainstays and single top downtube and saddle tube to which the fuel tank was fixed. A further pair of tubes ran from the saddle to the rear wheel. The radiator sat on the lower downtubes in line with the engine and above the cylinder heads, and at the front went a form of telescopic fork with a single-spring unit fitted above the front wheel.

In 1908 Scott arranged for his design to be manufactured by the Jowett brothers, but only six machines were built before other arrangements were made and the Scott Engineering Company was formed with works in Bradford. During the year publicity was sought by Scott riding his machine in the Bradford hill climb late in July, where he won on formula. In mid-August he appeared at the important Newnham climb in Northamptonshire, where he won three classes on formula, with his machine attracting much attention

The Scott settled into this pattern for many years, with drum fuel-tank set behind the oil tank; this is a 1930 Sprint Special.

due to its type and ease of starting. These and other successes resulted in water-cooled two-strokes having their actual capacity increased by a factor of 1.32 when in competition. Thus the 1909 TT entries were listed at 585cc but the actual capacity was 443cc.

Scott front forks were of a telescopic form from early on, with the front wheel moving in a straight line in its support bushes.

The first production Scotts came in 1909 and these had a kickstarter added, while the engine was increased in capacity to 444cc. There were many detail improvements over the next year or two and, for 1911, the engine was enlarged again to 486cc and became fully water-cooled. The firm had run in the TT in the two preceding years and returned in 1911 with engines having a rotary valve to control the induction. This was gear and chain driven and located at the rear of the cylinders and across the frame. Sadly, it gave trouble in the race, the first over the Mountain Circuit, but one did set the fastest lap.

They returned for the 1912 TT with the 486cc engines, gear drive to the rotary valve, air cooling for the heads while retaining water for the

All part of the Scott mystique was the engine, with its central chain-drive continued on to magneto, transfer ports and easy access to the big ends.

cylinders, and twin plugs, one to fire the mixture and the other a spare already in place. It was Scott's year, for Frank Applebee won the Senior and set the fastest lap. They repeated this in 1913, when Tim Wood won, but only by five seconds in one of the closest of victories in TT history.

Meanwhile, the standard model for 1912 had the engine enlarged to 532cc and such was the demand for the Scott following its TT win that the firm had to look for larger premises. This resulted in a move to Saltaire, near Shipley and on the outskirts of Bradford. This location close to the Yorkshire Dales and Alfred Scott's detailed knowledge of the moors led to the Scott Trial, one of the toughest of motorcycle events. It was first held in 1914 for Scott machines only and for many years after as a combination of trial and scramble.

The two-speed Scott was further improved for 1913 and 1914 when they were in greater demand. For the 1914 TT, the works machines had a much revised engine with oscillating

By 1930 the Scott twin had added this form, with the fuel tank in a more conventional position but with no other major changes, only details.

valves and the two-speed gearbox built in-unit with it, but despite again setting the fastest lap they finished well down. Production of standard models continued in the first two years of the war and included sidecar outfits carrying a machine gun for the services.

This Scott demonstrates how each example of the marque could be as individual as its owner liked it, by changes, additions and deletions.

In 1930 Scott introduced a 299cc air-cooled single, but it had limited success amid a sea of Villiers models in those hard times.

Alfred Scott continued to develop new ideas and among them was a gun car that had three wheels in sidecar form. This led to the Scott Sociable, which really did look like a small car minus the left front wheel. Both driver and passenger sat within the body, which located on a triangulated tubular chassis that bolted together to carry the engine and gearbox. By this time he had little to do with the motorcycles and, in 1918, sold out to form a new company. It took time to bring the Sociable to the market and in little more than a year the Austin Seven came along to meet the needs of the family man.

Sadly, Alfred Scott died in August 1923, aged only forty-eight, as the result of a cold caught following potholing which turned to pneumonia.

The Flying Squirrel Scott of 1933 retained the usual water-cooling and had the angular fuel-tank in the more usual position.

Without his talent and remarkable innovative abilities, there was little to drive the firm forward.

Meanwhile, the existing motorcycles had returned post-war much as before and, for 1922, added a smaller version listed as the 489cc Squirrel, still with two speeds. The next year brought a three-speed version of the Standard 532cc model and 1924 a similar Squirrel. During this period the firm again ran in the TT, with a third in the 1922 Senior and fastest lap in the 1923 Sidecar when Harry Langman came close to winning. He was also second in the 1924 Senior but, after that, a third in 1928 was the best they could do.

The range was extended for 1925, when the engine stroke was lengthened a little. The smaller twin had a bore of the same size and a 499cc capacity, while the larger was of 597cc. They introduced the Super Squirrel name with the smaller in two-speed form only and the larger with two or three speeds. There was also a 489cc Super Squirrel with three speeds, while the 532 and 597cc engines were used by the two-speed Standard and three-speed Squirrel models.

A Flying Squirrel Scott from 1934, still just as individual as they always were, but no longer as light and easy to ride as in the past.

In 1934 Scott announced this model, with an in-line three-cylinder water-cooled engine that had style, but few were produced.

The Scott continued to be built in very limited numbers, virtually to order, as for this one in 1960, but the magic was no longer there.

The 532cc engine was dropped for 1926, but the Standard 489cc two-speeder ran on for two more years. Two-speed Flying Squirrels in both sizes appeared in 1926 and for the next two years most combinations of the two engine sizes and either gearbox were used in various ways and specifications. The Flying Squirrels differed from 1927 in having a more conventional fuel tank, three speeds and a more robust construction that put the weight up and moved away from the light and lithe style of the early models. As the decade neared its end the engines had their stroke lengthened again for TT Replica versions of the Flying Squirrel with the capacities 497 and 598cc. The older engines continued and a dirt-track model was added for a brief while.

In 1930 there was a Scott single with air cooling that was intended for the lower end of the market. They chose to make the 299cc engine rather than buy a Villiers, the machine was conventional in style, but had little success and was soon dropped.

By then the Scott twin had put on weight and become dated, for the essentials had progressed little from the early days. Something fresh was what was needed but there was no longer an Alfred to provide it, nor the capital to finance it, for the firm had fallen on hard times. Thus, what they had continued through the 1930s, with the two engine sizes in a whole series of models that gradually put on weight as the years passed by. Girder forks had replaced the original telescopics, plunger rear-suspension was a 1938 option, and by then there was only the Flying Squirrel left, but still in 497 and 598cc sizes.

The one bright moment came in 1934, when a water-cooled in-line three-cylinder model was announced. It was innovative and was shown at Olympia late that year, with a much improved line, some enclosure and a 986cc engine. While stylish, few were built and after three years it was no longer listed as available.

Then came the war and after it the firm continued with the 598cc model in its rigid 1939 form, soon with a change from girder to Dowty telescopic forks. However, demand for such a specialized and expensive machine was small, especially as it became seriously outpaced. With few sales, the firm went into voluntary liquidation and was sold to Aerco Jig & Tool in Birmingham, a firm owned by Matt Holder, who was a keen Scott man.

Holder did not get the Scott back into production until 1956, when both 497 and 598cc versions were listed. The engines were much as

Post-war the Scott had put on more weight, as well as the telescopic forks, so became too special and expensive for the majority of riders.

before, but the frame was rigid or in new pivoted-fork form. It ran on in this way in small numbers, the smaller model to special order and the rigid dropped in time. Holder also produced the Scott Swift, using an engine with flat-top pistons, and this became a stepping stone to the later Silk machines. During the 1960s a racing 345cc Scott twin made an appearance, but was of conventional form with air cooling. It did retain a central flywheel and was well designed, but it made no real impact.

The Scott continued to be available for many years, in effect being hand built to order. In the 1970s the Silk was derived from it, but the original remained available into the 1980s in ever smaller numbers. To the end it remained a special motorcycle.

SCOTT CYC-AUTO 1938–1958
The original Cyc-Auto was taken over by Scott in 1938, with the engines built at their Yorkshire works, although assembly of the machine remained in London, only moved to East Acton. The design continued with a 98cc two-stroke engine whose crankshaft was set along the machine axis to drive back to a worm and wheel, from which a chain drove the rear wheel.

Post-war, the two models continued little altered but, by 1953, manufacture had passed to Winsmith in Finchley, London. At the Earls Court show that year they showed a prototype motorcycle that used the existing engine with a two-speed gearbox and shaft final-drive. The loop frame had telescopic forks and plunger rear-suspension, but no more was seen of this development. The Scott Cyc-Auto name remained in use for the autocycle that ran on to 1958.

SCOUT 1906 AND 1913
Scott offered a basic 2.5hp single for the one year, it being nothing special, a typical primitive of the era with rigid forks and belt drive. It was claimed that they used their own engine, but it was more likely bought in. The name reappeared in 1913,

when it was used by Taylor & Hands of Coventry Road, Birmingham, and their 3.75hp model had a Precision engine, Druid forks and was one of a range of models.

SCRIVENER C.1900
An amateur design built by J. Scrivener of Yorkshire on early Werner lines. The 2.25hp De Dion engine was mounted above the front wheel, which it drove by a flat belt. The machine was mainly bicycle, the front fork being strengthened, but it served its owner for several years and shows that special building had very early beginnings.

Amateur J. Scrivener, shown with his machine designed and built by himself, but on the early Werner lines with the engine over the front wheel.

SEAL 1912–1924 AND 1930–1932
Built at Hulme, Manchester, this was an unusual machine that was classed as a three-wheeled Sociable and comprised a special form of motorcycle with sidecar. It differed in that the sidecar body was widened to carry both driver and passenger, while the mechanics stayed out in the wet.

A large V-twin JAP provided the power and drove a three-speed gearbox, both mounted in a frame built up from straight tubes clamped together. Front suspension was by a form of leading-link and the forks connected to a steering wheel in the sidecar. All told, a strange device, listed up to 1924.

In 1930 a commercial version appeared. This gave the driver a small

The Seal had odd front suspension and layout, with the driver seated in the sidecar along with the machine controls.

open-topped cabin on the machine to allow the whole of the sidecar to be used to carry goods. In this form it was known as the Progress, but during the year was amended.

The new form of the Seal with central front-wheel became the New Progress and, in 1932, was joined by a really odd carrier-version. This had the 680cc JAP V-twin engine mounted above the front wheel, which it drove by chain via a three-speed-and-reverse gearbox. This proved to be the final throw of an unconventional design.

SEELEY 1966–1979
Colin Seeley was the British Sidecar Champion for 1962 and 1963, and his outfits were as immaculate as his racing style. He used a Matchless G50 engine, later a BMW, to power his machines and, in 1966, his AMC connections enabled him to purchase all of the AMC race shop, including the rights. The Norton side he sold on to John Tickle, so that he could concentrate on the AMC models he was associated with and had experience of.

His first special had been built early in 1966 to carry a G50 engine and this was followed by others, at first with a duplex frame and later a tubular spine type. From this in 1971 came the Seeley Condor road version of

226 Seeley – SGS

Colin Seeley devised this Seeley Condor machine for the road, using a G50 engine mounted in a frame of his own design, finished superbly.

the G50, a real racer with lights in the café racer style. The frame was his Mark 3, finished in nickel plating with the engine hung from it and the whole machine immaculate.

However, by 1973, the day of the big single on track or road had passed, although it would return, so Seeley turned his attentions to the Yamsel, a machine he built using his own frame to house 250 and 350 racing Yamaha engines. These were most successful and many were built. There were also frames for the Norton Commando, and many one-offs and small batches for all manner of makes, including the Japanese and Italian. This continued throughout the 1970s before Colin turned to other fields, returning to motorcycling in 1993 as manager of the successful Norton Rotary racing team.

SERVICE 1906–1913
A sales firm based in High Holborn, London that offered machines carrying their own name. They were listed in 1906 with a small range of models of 3, 3.5 and 4hp, while for 1908 they were using 4hp single and 5hp V-twin Antoine engines. All were primitives, typical of the times.

By 1911 their machine was fitted with a 4hp JAP engine, with a Bosch magneto and B&B carburettor. Druid forks and belt drive completed the specification and the machine was probably bought in from Connaught. In 1912 a model fitted with an 8hp JAP V-twin engine and Roc two-speed hub was added, while for 1913 the range was a 3.5hp single fitted with an Armstrong three-speed gear. The firm also handled the WD marque and others.

SGM 1919
From the St. George's Motorcycle Co. of Birmingham, this early post-Great War machine used a 634cc Norton Big Four engine to drive a three-speed Sturmey-Archer gearbox with belt final-drive. These components went into a frame of lengthy wheelbase fitted with sprung forks.

Syd Gleave built a typical lightweight with JAP or Villiers engines. The model shown is the latter, and it was sold under his initials, SGS.

SGS 1927–1931
The Syd Gleave Special range was built in Macclesfield, Cheshire and appeared before Syd won the 1933 Lightweight TT on an Excelsior. The range used Villiers and JAP engines and, by 1930, had 196 and 247cc two-strokes, plus 245 and 346cc four-strokes, with nice lines and typical of the period. The frames were made at Macclesfield at first, but later by Diamond in Wolverhampton. However, times were hard for a small producer, so Syd sensibly stopped production during 1931.

This is a typical Seeley racing single, with AMC engine hung from the spine frame and all parts finished to the usual Seeley high standard.

SHACKLOCK c.1914

The firm of C.H. Shacklock in Wolverhampton was an early motor agent and repairer who no doubt served all types of motor vehicles. He also built a few motorcycles to his own design, most were conventional but including one with the V-twin engine set across the frame.

SHARRATT 1920–1931

Based in West Bromwich, John Sharratt was a cycle maker who first built a motorcycle in 1911 using a 4.25hp Precision engine. After the Great War he went into production by assembling machines from bought-in parts using JAP engines, including the 147cc Aza two-stroke when that appeared during 1923.

In time the range stretched from the 293cc single to the 996cc V-twin and included sporting models with ohv engines. After 1924 production was limited, but continued on for some years with Villiers and MAG engines sometimes used along with the JAP.

By the start of the new decade in 1930 they were down to three models, all with 346cc JAP engines, one sv and the other two ohv. Only the ohv ones continued for 1931, their final year, and after that the firm turned to car dealing with considerable success.

SHAW 1898–1905 AND 1920–1922

A pioneer design that squeezed the engine in behind the bottom bracket and in front of the rear wheel where it was clamped to the chainstays. A chain drove a countershaft mounted above and behind the crankcase and this drove the rear wheel by friction roller. In other forms the drive from the countershaft was by chain. In either case, simple footrests were fitted rather than pedals and engines were from Minerva or Kelecom.

Squeezing the engine in just ahead of the rear wheel was a feature of the Shaw, but meant an odd transmission to get the power to the wheel.

The firm was based at Chorlton-cum-Hardy, near Manchester and, in 1905, showed a tricycle that differed in that the two rear wheels had the passenger seat between them as usual but facing to the rear. This was claimed to improve the running over that of a forecar, while the machine had two speeds and the rider massive footboards.

After this, the name faded from sight but was revived much later when the firm imported a bicycle-attachment engine from the American Shaw firm of Galesburg, Kansas up to 1922.

SHEFFIELD-DUNELT 1931–1933

The name used by Dunford & Elliott, steel makers of Sheffield, for their range of motorcycles after they had transferred manufacture from Birmingham to Sheffield late in 1931. They used the revised name for 1932 and when they announced the 1933 range, but by late in that year had reverted to the plain Dunelt that the trade and public had never stopped using.

SHEFFIELD-HENDERSON 1920–1923

Henderson sidecars were well known, long before the company moved into motorcycle manufacture from the same premises on Fitzwilliam Street, in Sheffield. A 3hp two-stroke model with their own engine and two-speed chain-cum-belt transmission was their first offering, which also introduced their own peculiar design of front fork, with a C-spring linking the double tubed girder to the frame head. By late 1920, a 499cc sv Blackburne model had been added, this with a three-speed Sturmey-Archer gearbox and all-chain drive; it featured a vacuum-operated oiling system for the engine and was ideally suited to sidecar usage, for which the firm was well placed to build the necessary bodies. During 1921, local Sheffield speed ace Ernie Searle was trying out a new speed model of rakish outline and fitted with the 348cc ohv Blackburne engine. It was duly catalogued for the following year and sold together with a guaranteed 70mph(112km/h) top whack. There was a sporting sidecar outfit too, with a tuned 545cc sv Blackburne motor and streamlined sidecar, but despite this enterprise, the marque couldn't survive beyond 1923.

SILK 1975–1979

George Silk was a Scott enthusiast who prepared them for racing and then went on to build the Scott Silk Special for road use in 1972. This had a Scott engine, but much modified in the light of the racing experiences, mated to a Velocette gearbox and installed in a Spondon frame. The result worked well and some twenty were built.

From this activity came the Silk 700S, which was built at Darley Abbey in Derby and was in the tradition of the Scott marque, but brought up to date in the form of the original so it remained light and easy to handle. The 653cc Silk engine remained a water-cooled twin-cylinder two-stroke with the block inclined forward. Internally it was all new, with a full crankshaft supported on bearings either side of each pair of flywheels. The central flywheel disappeared and the crankcase was split horizontally, but the primary drive still came from the centre of the crankshaft.

The gearbox had Velocette-type internals and bolted to the back of the crankcase, the whole assembly slotted into a Spondon frame with forks and brakes from the same source. The result was light, smooth and economical. A production racing version was also listed for a couple of years, this having a tuned engine and race fairing.

Improvements were made as called for and ran to a Mk II form with vestigial cooling fins added to the cylinder block. A 326cc trials model was also built, which was air-cooled and essentially half of the twin, so was compact. Its four-speed gearbox had a choice of output ratios and the mechanics were suspended from a monocoque spine frame made from aluminium sheet.

The 700S was never a volume model, with around 135 built before production ceased in 1979. However, it was always special, as befitted a machine built by enthusiasts for motorcycles in general and the Scott in particular.

SILVA 1920
One of a number of simple scooter designs introduced in 1920 and which failed to last the year. The Silva incorporated the Auto-Wheel 117cc aiv engine and wheel unit in place of a normal front wheel. The fuel tank lay above the wheel, with unsprung and unbraced forks attending to steering and taking the full load of the device. Twin tubes ran downwards from the steering head to connect with a flat platform on which the plucky rider stood – there being no saddle. The Auto-Wheel had a single speed with chain drive and gear-driven CAV magneto. The machine was marketed by T & T Motors Ltd, of Conduit Street, London W1.

SILVER 1907–1909
Thomas Silver made the Quadrant name with his Land's End to John O' Groats record set in 1903 and four years later left that firm to build identical machines. These were advertised as 'An old friend under a new name', but in under a year the man and firm were reunited. However, 1909 brought another split and reconciliation, after which Quadant ran on without this pin-prick from their great rider.

SILVER PRINCE 1921–1924
An imposing brand name for an orthodox lightweight, which was introduced with Brampton forks, a 269cc Villiers engine and a choice of

Tom Silver made the Quadrant name with his exploits, and also built a few machine of his own in the same form.

single speed or two-speed Sturmey-Archer or Albion gearbox, and chain-cum-belt transmission. However, at the end of 1921, as if to emphasize the good quality of the standard product, a utility machine was added that fitted either the Villiers, as before, or a 292cc sv JAP engine to be sold under the Indian Prince model name. The marque slipped from the lists in 1923, but was back the next year with 147 or 247cc Villiers engines and the same transmission options.

SIMMS 1900–1903
Frederick R. Simms imported Daimler engines into Britain as early as 1891 and, in conjunction with Robert Bosch, developed the low-tension magneto in 1899. These two items show the breadth of his thinking and he was one of the major figures in the early days of transport. He built engines for use by others and in 1900 produced an odd tricycle known as the Motor Wheel. This differed from most, not just in having two wheels at the front and one astern, but in that the front were the driven wheels and the rear did the steering. The result was highly unstable but did run in the 1,000-mile trial of 1900.

Simms engines and his range of electrical equipment, plus other products, ran on for years but the tricycle production was limited.

SIMPLEX 1906–1908
This firm offered a spring frame in 1906, at a time when not all had sprung forks, and used a 6hp JAP V-twin engine with belt drive. This would have given the options of an adjustable pulley or hub gear as well as direct drive. For 1908, Fafnir singles or an Antoine V-twin were used, but production was limited.

SIMPLEX 1919–1922
This was the power unit of the Motoped lightweight, a strengthened bicycle fitted with a 104cc two-stroke engine. Made by Patrick Engineering of Birmingham, the unit was sold separately to be fitted to any suitable bicycle, gents' or ladies', above the rear wheel, which it drove by chain.

Fred Simms was involved with many projects and one was the production of engines for others. His Motor Wheel was not a success.

The Singer motor wheel installed, in this case, in place of the rear wheel of a stock safety bicycle, which retained most of its usual features.

SINGER 1901–1915
Another Coventry make that began with tricycles but became better known when they took up the Perks & Birch motor wheel in 1901. It went well in place of the front wheel of their tricycle with braced forks, or the rear wheel of a bicycle, the firm already producing these. A

It was just as easy to install the Singer motor wheel in place of the front wheel of a tricycle, although the result gave a shattering ride.

contemporary report describes the ride as shattering, as the wheel either bounced over every hump or thudded into the potholes.

One 1903 experiment was to fit a wheel at the rear of a Phoenix Trimo forecar, which indicated how versatile the design was. Later that year a ladies' model was offered, with an open frame and a motor wheel with spokes on one side only to improve access. The wheel fitted in place of the normal rear bicycle wheel and the drive was first taken forward by chain to a counter shaft in the bottom bracket and then back to the wheel by a second chain. A freewheel in the drive allowed the machine to coast down hills with a dead engine and, thus, no engine braking.

The forecar was quite established in Edwardian days, so the notion of using the Singer motor wheel in place of the rear was fine.

For 1904, Singer added a range of conventional models with an upright engine mounted in a cradle hung from the downtube, this passing the engine at cylinder level. Powers were 2 and 3hp, and belt or chain drive was listed, the belt running on the right side of the machine. Tricycles built for solo or tandem use were listed along with forecars, including the type that used the rear motor wheel.

During 1904 a tricar fitted with a V-twin engine appeared, with a two-speed gear, chain drive to the countershaft, but belt drive to the rear axle. One or both cylinders could be run, thus allowing the silent one to cool off, but all-chain drive and fan cooling was adopted for 1905, when the 3hp solo had the frame revised and gained magneto ignition.

Yet another variation in the use of the Singer motor wheel produced this Tri-voiturette, with hard ride at the front but better in the rear seat.

The make faded from sight around then, reappearing in 1910 with the 'Moto-Velo' lightweight model powered by a 1.25hp 211cc Dufaux engine mounted within the main frame. Sprung forks and belt drive, either direct or with a jockey pulley were used. In 1911, a 3.5hp 499cc model was added, with magneto ignition, a free-engine clutch in the rear hub and Druid forks. During the year a 2.5hp version was added, and later a 3.5hp sidecar model, this having unit construction of its two-speed gearbox within the crankcase. An

As well as the motor wheel, Singer produced this more conventional solo for 1904, with a spine frame layout not too unlike today's.

By 1912 the Singer was more conventional, with upright 3.5hp engine, various transmission options and sprung forks, but all with belt drive.

engine-shaft clutch drove a layshaft carrying two gears in mesh with the mainshaft, whose gears could be selected and that carried the belt pulley.

In 1912 the two-speed gear went on the 2.5hp model, with a three-speed hub gear an option for all. During the year, Singer built a 499cc racing engine, having a four-valve head which was water-cooled. Its chain-driven camshaft went at the front of the engine, the inlet port being at the left front of the head and the exhaust at the right rear. The magneto sat in front of the head, behind the twin radiators, and was chain driven from the camshaft. It was intended for G.E. Stanley, the main Singer rider, to race at Brooklands, but he kept to his successful and reliable sv model.

This is a Singer engine from later years, with side valves, neat drive up to the front-mounted magneto and direct gas flow in and out of the valves.

A 10hp cyclecar was built by the firm in August 1912, while the range continued with steady development for the next two years. Late in 1914, a model powered by a two-stroke engine built under Peco patents was added, with a two-speed gearbox, chain-cum-belt drive, Druid forks and footboards. This range was built for 1915 but then production ceased and, after the war, the firm concentrated on cars.

SIRRAH 1921–1925
Considered as a lower priced version of the Verus marque, both of which were built by Alfred Wiseman Ltd of Birmingham, the Sirrah began as a 292cc two-stroke Union-engined lightweight with two-speed Burman gearbox in solo or sidecar forms. The range then quickly grew to encompass models with 348, 545 and 697cc Blackburne, 292 and 976cc JAP, 349cc Bradshaw, 348cc Barr & Stroud, and 211 and 292cc two-stroke Wiseman engines, these always being mated with Burman gearboxes. Frame and forks sets were of conventional outline but, in late 1923, they adopted a new universal frame for all models, in which the tubing was manipulated to avoid all but a single joint, this being welded rather than brazed and lugged. Before production ended in 1925, the name had found its way onto a number of special purpose machines, such as an inspection trolley with wheels suitable for running on the railway lines of a South American country and a similar, but convertible device, for the Indian railways, which gave both road or rail running to choice.

SKOOTAMOTA 1919–1923
Introduced by the ABC firm and normally listed under that name, this scooter was often referred to by its model name alone and was later built and marketed by Gilbert Campling of Albermarle Street, Piccadilly, London. It had an open frame, no suspension, and wire wheels with a 124cc eoi engine carried over the rear one, the cylinder head pointing to the rear and the magneto clamped to the front of the crankcase. Late in 1920 it adopted ohv and continued in this form to 1923 with its single speed and chain drive to the rear wheel.

SL 1924
The initials stood for Sutton-Lewis and the model was of racy outline based around a 348cc twin-port ohv single-cylinder engine. This was unusual for its time in having two exhaust valves and but a single inlet. The engine was coupled to a close-ratio Sturmey-Archer gearbox and fitted into a low duplex frame, with Scott telescopic forks up-front. The prototype machine was built during 1924 by Davis Brothers of Rickmansworth in Hertfordshire and plans were laid for production to commence the following year. Sadly, nothing further emerged from the works.

SLADE-JAP 1921–1922
'Order at once to beat the rush' was the advice given by the makers of this marque upon its launch in mid 1921, but with nothing particular to distinguish its presence such advice was little more than hopeful bluster. A 292cc sv JAP engine, Albion two-speed gearbox, chain-cum-belt drive and conventional appearance made the Slade much like many another machine of its time. Their advertising copywriter tried again in 1922 with 'The last word in Lightweights' and 'last word' it nearly was, for the machine disappeared from the market soon afterwards.

SLANEY 1920
One of a number of similar introductions built up around the 689cc sv Coventry-Victor flat-twin engine and its accompanying frame set. It was demonstrated outside the Olympia show in November 1920 and was, in truth, the Bulldog motorcycle, first seen earlier the same year, now under a new name.

SLINGER 1901
Tricycles were common in the early

The extraordinary Slinger was built with two front wheels and the De Dion engine as one assembly, to pivot about the rest of the machine.

days, but this special had its three wheels in a line so remained a single-track motorcycle. Completed after six years of work by W. Slinger, an electrical engineer of Settle in Yorkshire, it had a normal frame and rear wheel, but a most unusual front end.

Where the forks normally went was what appeared to be a small motorcycle with two small wheels and a De Dion engine between them. The engine was water-cooled, with the radiator surrounding the cylinder and the system contrived by Slinger himself. A surface carburettor and coil ignition were from the period, and transmission was by chain down to a countershaft and then by a second chain to the rear small wheel.

Steering was via braced forks to the front assembly, with a further linkage to turn the forward wheel. Riding forward proved no problem, but wheeling the machine backwards was less easy, rather like reversing a car with a trailer attached.

SMITH 1904
An early machine built by J. Smith of Camberley, Surrey using a Fafnir engine in BSA cycle parts. This was a common practice for an established cycle dealer in those days, for Chater-Lea also supplied a range of frames or fittings to take Minerva engines as well as Fafnir and others.

SMITH & MILROY c.1901
Located in Orpington, Kent, this firm produced a few motorcycles in the primitive form, no doubt using an imported engine and bought-in frame fittings. Later, in the 1920s, they produced the Orpington car.

SMITH-SKAIFE 1913
Mr Skaife built a 567cc sleeve-valve engine in which two sleeves moved, the inlet inside the exhaust, within a cylinder bore adjacent to the main cylinder. It was built and installed in a machine and so could run on the road, where it was described as very quiet with a peculiar-sounding exhaust note.

SMS 1914
A machine made by S.M. Swingler of Aston Cross, Birmingham that had a 2.25hp two-stroke engine of unusual design. It combined the normal three ports with an automatic crankcase inlet that took the form of a metal disc acting as a reed valve under crankcase depression. The cover for the disc carried the carburettor, much as on the considerably later racing disc-valve engines of the post-Second World War period. The normal inlet port was simply a means by which extra air could be taken into the engine and was controlled by a slide.

Ignition was by a rear-mounted magneto that was gear driven and the intermediate gear of this train could be turned by a pedal to kick-start the engine. This gear also drove a clutch and, from this, the drive to the rear wheel was by fully enclosed chain. The frame was neat in design and fitted with Druid forks. Sadly, nothing more was heard of this interesting effort.

SOS 1927–1939
Variously said to mean Super Onslow Special or So Obviously Superior, this make was at first produced by Len Vale-Onslow at Hallow, near Worcester. Lacking a gas supply, he adopted electric welding for his frame while the rest of the industry continued with tubes brazed into heavy lugs for many a year.

Most SOS models fitted Villiers engines, but some with JAP appeared in their early days, finishing with 250 and 350cc ohv models in 1930. By then the 172, 196, 247 and 343cc Villiers units were all in use and the models well made and finished. Manufacture was transferred to Birmingham for 1932 and, for 1933, the first of the water-cooled models appeared. These were based on 148 and 172cc Villiers engines fitted with an SOS top-half plus a suitable radiator. Later that year a 249cc water-cooled model was added and, late in the year, control of the firm passed to Tommy Meeten.

A typical SOS larger model, as for 1931, was fitted with a 343cc air-cooled Villiers engine, the cycle parts common to most of the range.

For hard work over a long distance, SOS would use the water-cooled 249cc Villiers engine, such as for this 1934 Magnetic model C.

He expanded the range for 1934, giving the models names, and offered air- or water-cooled machines to various specifications, based on Villiers engines of 172, 249 and 346cc. During 1936, he opened Meetens Motor Mecca on the Kingston by-pass and continued to supply SOS models from there up to 1939. They were always well finished and at the quality end of their market, but were not built post-war.

SOUTHERN CROSS 1905
Chas Shaw of Manchester offered a tricycle with single front-wheel but having a fine wicker seat set between the rear ones. A special feature of this seat was that it could be reversed so the passenger faced to the rear, long before such techniques were used by cameramen filming the Tour de France. The Southern Cross had braced forks, spray carburettor for its single-cylinder engine and all-chain drive via a countershaft with free-engine position.

SOUTHEY 1905–1922
A small firm that produced frames for others as well as complete machines, the latter most likely for local owners and built to order. They would have followed the trends and used a variety of engines and transmissions as required.

Post-war, they were based at Berkhamsted, Hertfordshire and built lightweights with a sloping top-tube to the frame which required a wedge-shaped tank to suit. Druid forks were fitted and power came from a 269cc Villiers two-stroke engine driving a two- or three-speed Sturmey-Archer gearbox and chain-cum-belt transmission. Output was small and the maker advertised directly to the public to save on overheads, which permitted a reasonable selling price, but severely limited the market they could serve. There was also a model with a 346cc sv Blackburne engine and they were built up to 1922.

SOUTH HANTS 1903
This firm, of the Floating Bridge Works, Portsmouth, announced a new model for 1903, using an engine position aft of the rear wheel which

The strange 1903 South Hants from Portsmouth, had the Minerva engine hung out aft of the Humber bicycle which it drove by belt.

recalled the Pennington. The bicycle shown was an old Humber, the engine a 2.5hp Minerva and its position was claimed to remove all vibration from the rider while the actual vibration assisted in propelling the machine. On 1 April (!), the company manager sent the machine up a local hill and it was reported that it ran well, but nothing more was heard of the make.

SPA-JAP 1921–1923

The Spa Motor & Engineering Company occupied premises in the seaside town of Scarborough, on the North Yorkshire coast. They built a small number of conventional machines incorporating JAP sv engines of 248 and 292cc. Local rider A.O. Brett was very successful in A-C.U. Yorkshire Centre speed events on a specially prepared model, which doubtless aided sales to those who were able to witness his endeavours.

SPARK 1903–1904

A typical primitive built in small numbers by combining a 2hp engine with a heavy-duty bicycle frame and the necessary extra fittings. As brief a life as many others, and out of the business just before it slumped in 1905.

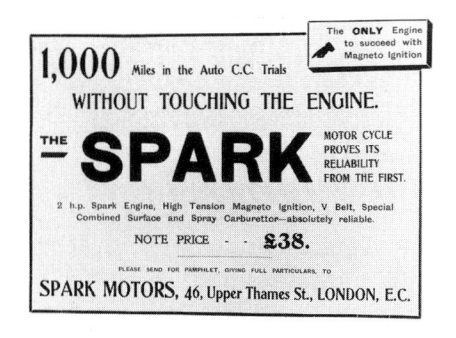

There is no picture of this machine, but it was a typical primitive that did run in the 1903 1,000-mile Trial, hence the many claims in this advertisement.

SPARK 1922–1923

Marque name used by the Sparkbrook Manufacturing Company for a utility model, using the 269cc Villiers two-stroke engine and direct-belt drive. A simple frame with pressed sheet-steel lugs was employed, together with Gosport front forks. The engine capacity became 247cc in 1923, after Villiers stopped making the older 269cc unit. It was very basic transport.

SPARKBROOK 1912–1924

A long-established cycle firm based in Coventry, Sparkbrook entered the powered field late in 1912, with a single sidecar model using a 6hp JAP V-twin engine, two-speed gearbox, chain-cum-belt drive and Druid forks. The sidecar had a coach-built body suspended on C-springs. They continued with this sidecar model up to 1915, adding an 8hp version for 1914, but did introduce a light solo for 1915. This had a 269cc Villiers two-stroke engine and two speeds, continuing alone for 1916.

They were back in business by 1919 with two models, each having the 269cc Villiers engine, one with direct-belt drive and the other with two speeds via their own countershaft gearbox with belt final-drive. These continued for 1921, when a two-speed Sturmey-Archer gearbox was an option and, during this year, a utility version of the direct-drive two-stroke was added but sold as the Spark. The range ran on for 1922, joined by a 346cc sv JAP model, and, for 1923, they changed to the new Villiers 247 and 343cc engines, kept the 346cc sv JAP and added another model with the 349cc sleeve-valve Barr & Stroud motor. All these models came with a choice of transmissions and speeds, together with complete sidecar combinations with the four-stroke engines. The JAP engine was replaced by a 349cc ohv Bradshaw for 1924 and this, with the others, brought the marque to its close.

SPARTAN 1920–1921

Previously sold under the Welland B trade name, the Spartan was of conventional outline and had 348cc sv Blackburne, 269cc Villiers or 349cc Broler two-stroke engines coupled to an Albion two-speed gearbox with belt final-drive. The marque was handled by Wallis & James of Nottingham.

SPARTON 1975–1982

This was the result of a link between Barton Engineering, who built racing two-stroke engines, and Spondon Engineering, who produced frames. The basis came from the work Barry Hart carried out tuning Suzuki triples and, for 1975, he went on to build a 500cc square-four engine modelled on the Suzuki RG500 in concept, but a good deal different in detail. From this came the Phoenix 500 and 750 fours that found fame as the Silver Dream Racer in the film that starred David Essex. Later, the firm was involved with CCM and Armstrong, so worked on their engines, but, in time, lost ground to the Japanese with their constant development and vast resources.

SPEED KING-JAP 1913–1914

This was the name given to a New Imperial Light Tourist model so that J.G. Graves of Sheffield could sell it as their own marque. Other than the tank transfer, it was the same machine with 293cc JAP sv engine driving an Albion two-speed gearbox with belt final-drive. The rigid frame had Druid forks and footboards, while Bowden brakes were fitted. Graves planned to sell the machine by mail order and offered interest-free credit, but the New Imperial was cheaper; and then came the war.

SPEEDWELL PRE-GREAT WAR

This firm was best known for its sidecars, which were produced in Alcester, Warwickshire, but did assemble some motorcycles.

SPIRC c.1902

Built by Messrs W.W. Crips of Sidcup Hill, these machines were typical primitives and produced along with the firm's bicycles. No doubt braced forks, Minerva engines were used and limited numbers were built.

SPONDON 1981–1985

This was a firm based in Derbyshire who built frames and rolling chassis for racing engines. Most were to take a Yamaha unit but anything could be accommodated and, in 1981, they offered a complete machine using the 250cc Rotax two-stroke engine. As with others that took this route, they found it hard to maintain an advantage when all used the same engine.

SPRINGFIELD 1921

A range that was possibly built by the Wolf company and was exported to Holland. They used the 269cc Villiers two-stroke and 346cc JAP sv engines driving a two-speed gearbox, plus a 600cc JAP with three speeds.

SPRINGWELL 1920

Seen only in prototype form, the Springwell took its name from the generous suspension provided by its designer and maker, E.J. Norton, who ran a welding and engineering business in Coventry. Pivoted-fork rear suspension was under the control of long leaf-springs and the motorcycle frame could be coupled to a matching sidecar chassis in which more leaf springs and coils were employed. Brampton Biflex forks, Burman gearbox and an unspecified V-twin engine were utilized. Norton patented the design and sought offers for the manufacturing rights, but that was as far as it went.

SPRITE 1964–1974

This firm came about like others, with owner Frank Hipkin riding in trials and scrambles on machines

Early version of a Sprite, built up from a scrambles frame kit and fitted with a unit-construction Triumph engine of 349 or 490cc.

A 1967 Sprite model, with narrow duplex frame and engine based on Villiers, but with Greeves and Alpha components to improve it.

A later ater Sprite with Villiers Starmaker engine fitted in the narrow frame, with leading-link front forks, although other options were available.

he built for himself, being successful, and then being asked to build for others. The first Sprite was made using parts that were to hand and suited, but production brought Sprite frames with duplex downtubes. The engine was a combination of Alpha and Greeves, much as other 246cc two-strokes of that era, and the machine was sold in kit form to reduce its cost. There was also a frame kit made to take the 500cc Triumph twin engine.

Both trials and scrambles models were available, the trials with a narrower frame, and, for 1965, leading-link forks were used, although others remained an option. Later came the 247cc Starmaker engine and, when the Villiers supply dried up, Sprite offered their own engine for scrambles which turned out to be a close copy of the Swedish Husqvarna unit. In 1969 this was joined by a trials model with a 125cc Sachs engine.

The firm ran on into the 1970s, when American Eagle, their US importers, collapsed and failed to pay for a major order. This brought Sprite motorcycles to an end, although the firm itself recovered.

SPUR 1915 AND 1919–1920

First advertised late in 1915 using a 3hp Dalm engine and two-speed Albion gearbox, this lightweight was from an existing range with a change of badge. Soon dropped under wartime regulations, it reappeared post-war using 269cc Villiers two-stroke and 292cc sv JAP engines. These went into lightweights with either single or two speeds, using an Albion gearbox and belt drive. Druid forks, Amac carburettor and EIC magneto were included in the specifications.

STAFFORD 1920–1921
Designed by T.G. John, and thus involved with the Alvis car, this scooter was built by Stafford Auto-Scooters of Coventry and sold as the Mobile Pup just after the Great War. It had a 142cc John ohv engine that sat on the left side of the front wheel with the flywheel on the right and connected by a long mainshaft through the wheel spindle. The fuel tank sat above the mudguard and the combination of this weight, offset to one side, and flimsy construction resulted in an unstable machine to ride. Wire wheels were used, the rear fully enclosed, and initially the rider stood, although a seat option came in time.

STAG 1912–1914
A firm reputed to be located in Sherwood Forest, Nottingham, who built machines fitted with Precision engines of various sizes. They also built Stag engines for others to use, no doubt combining Precision knowledge with their own ideas, and thus gained on both counts. Small, so not listed or seen at the London shows, and a war casualty.

STAN 1921–1922
Lightweights assembled from any readily available components were the products of the Stan Motor Company, of Westwood Heath near Coventry. Detailed specifications were not given, but a 2.75hp two-stroke in single-speed form was regularly advertised during the short period of manufacture.

STANGER 1919–1923
V-twin two-stroke engines were notoriously difficult to fuel and fire such that they performed reliably. However, Mr Stanger, whose experience with internal combustion engines stretched back to 1897, thought he had the problems under control when he introduced his 45-degree twin with three-port cylinders and separate crank chambers in 1919. Thanks to their arrangement, the cylinders gave equal firing intervals due to the offset of the crankpins. Rated at 5hp, it actually displaced 539cc and was originally intended to be available in engine-form only, for supply to established motorcycle producers. The P.V. marque in south-east London quickly announced a Stanger-engined model, but other interest proved to be slight. This prompted Stanger to build complete machines under his own name from premises in Tottenham, London and these were on the market in 1921, with a Sturmey-Archer three-speed chain-cum-belt transmission, Brampton forks, Senspray carburettor and a choice of rigid or sprung frames. This continued into 1923, when all-chain drive was standard, but it was their last season.

STANLEY 1902
A product of a bicycle firm, this short-lived motorcycle make added an engine to one of their bicycles. It is reputed that they used a friction drive to the rear wheel, rather than the usual belt, and that production was taken over by Singer.

STANLEY 1932
This was a machine built in Egham, Surrey and based on a stock tricycle. To this was fitted a 98cc Villiers engine that was hung just under the rear axle, with spur gears to drive the clutch and a differential. Intended to offer stability and assistance to the elderly, it failed to catch on.

STAR 1898–1905 AND 1912–1914
Another of the many early firms that began by building tricycles powered

Star were linked to the French Giffon company, hence the twin name used for some machines; this is a 1903 single of primitive form.

by De Dion engines. They were based in Stewart Street, Wolverhampton and, in 1902, they turned to motorcycles and formed a link with the French Griffon company, offering their 2hp import as the Star-Griffon. This machine was typical of the period, with vertical engine, belt drive, a bicycle frame and rigid forks, but was a temporary expedient.

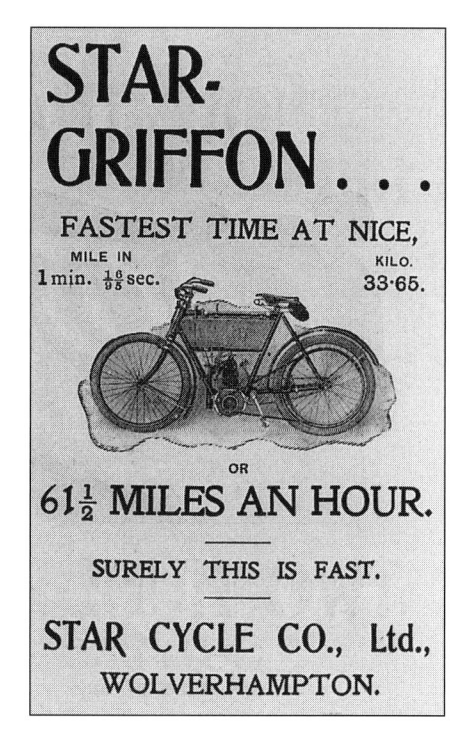

Something adrift in their calculations, as the Nice times for the Star-Griffon do not quite add up to the claimed speed.

For 1903 they had a 3hp machine and, a year later, this had a mechanically operated inlet-valve, braced forks and the option of a free-engine clutch and chain drive. For 1905 they listed 3 and 3.5hp solos, plus a 4hp water-cooled model available as a solo or a tricar with two speeds. They then left the motorcycle business, for they were also involved with cars as the Star Motor Co.

It was late-1912 when they returned to two wheels to show a 4.25hp single of distinctive design, the engine having a detachable cylinder head and an aluminium cover to enclose the valve gear. The carburettor was a multi-jet type made by the firm and the magneto was positioned behind the cylinder. A leather-faced cone-clutch went on the crankshaft to drive the three-speed gearbox via an enclosed chain, final drive also being by a chain in an oil-bath case, a shock absorber removing harshness from this. The rear brake was a drum in an era of dummy belt rims, there were sprung footboards and Saxon front forks.

Later, in 1913, came a similar machine fitted with a 6hp JAP V-twin engine, both models sturdy, well made but rather heavy. A sidecar was also offered but sales were slow, so, after 1914, the firm dropped two wheels to concentrate on four, producing other forms of transport that included cars, trucks, coaches and even a couple of aeroplanes.

STAR c.1919–1921

Another post-war hopeful who adopted the 269cc Villiers engine and proprietary parts to build a lightweight model. No doubt direct-belt drive or two speeds and chain-cum-belt were options, depending on supplies during the brief life.

Unusual for 1903, the Starley had two speeds, then used a worm and wheel to turn the drive, and finally a chain to the rear wheel.

STARLEY 1903

Inventor W. Starley of Coventry announced his machine in 1903, it differing from most in that the single-cylinder engine was mounted transversely to drive back through a two-speed gear and worm and wheel. The wheel was on a countershaft and drove the rear wheel by chain.

The Starley differed in having the vertical engine set transversely, which resulted in the frame layout with crossed downtubes.

Engine construction differed, in having the cylinder held down by a large ring, which screwed onto the crankcase top, and a one-piece overhung crankshaft, which turned the front flywheel by means of the crankpin, but without a fixing. The whole machine was really too complex for the times, so nothing further was heard of it.

STEELHOUSE 1911

Advertisements for this make appeared in 1911. It utilized a 3.75hp Precision engine, belt drive and Druid forks in conventional form. The machines were available from 123 Steelhouse Lane, Birmingham and were advertised as 'Fastest on the Road' – which seems rather unlikely and few seem to have believed the slogan.

STELLAR 1912–1913

First listed as the 'Stuart' and then as the 'Stella', this make was seen late in 1912, when it was handled by R.G. Nye & Co. of Hampstead Road, London, but made by Stuart Turner & Co. of Henley-on-Thames, Oxfordshire. Its chief feature was its 784cc water-cooled in-line-twin two-stroke engine, which drove back through a clutch to an all-indirect two-speed gearbox. This stepped the drive over for a shaft to run back to a worm at the rear wheel.

A Bosch magneto provided the sparks, an Amac carburettor the mixture and there was a kickstart pedal. The complete engine and gearbox unit was fitted between the downtube and saddle tube of the frame, which had sprung forks.

It was an interesting new design but too enterprising for the public, as no more was heard of it.

STEVENS 1897 AND 1934–38

The four Stevens brothers, who were to found AJS, built their first machine in 1897. It was powered by an American Mitchell engine mounted on the downtube of the bicycle-type frame, with the petrol tank hung from the cross-bar. The rear wheel was belt driven, but with a jockey pulley for tension and to reduce belt slip at the engine pulley.

Before they founded AJS motorcycles, the Stevens bothers built other machines, such as this 1903 forecar with water-cooled engine.

After building the one machine, they turned to building engines for Wearwell. In 1903, they built a solo with a 2.5hp engine in an open frame, suitable for their sisters to ride into town. There was also a forecar with a water-cooled engine. They then continued with engine production and later built the AJS motorcycles for many years.

After the company liquidator sold the AJS name to Matchless in 1931, the Stevens were left with their Wolverhampton factory and some machine tools and, in 1934, returned

After selling AJS to Matchless, the Stevens brothers restarted their Stevens models again, this 1936 500 typical of the line.

to motorcycle production. The first model had a 249cc overhead-valve engine, a Burman four-speed gearbox, duplex frame and Druid forks. The oil tank went in front of the crankcase and the valve gear was exposed.

It was joined by a 348cc version for 1935 and later that year came one of 495cc, the engine having hairpin valve-springs and the oil tank located under the saddle. For 1936, the two larger models had a megaphone-shaped silencer and the two smaller adopted the under-saddle oil tank location. Competition versions were available, 1937 saw the 250 with the megaphone silencer, but 1938 brought production to a final end and the brothers turned to other work.

STUART 1911–1912
Nye & Co. of London showed this make at the late-1911 Olympia show. It was built by Stuart Turner & Co. of Henley-on-Thames and featured a 2.5hp 299cc two-stroke engine, inside which turned full flywheels with aluminium plates to raise the primary compression.

The 1912 Stuart had a water-cooled in-line twin-cylinder engine driving a two-speed gearbox, plus shaft final-drive.

Crankcase pressure was used to force oil from its tank via a sight feed to the cylinder walls, a hand pump only being used to feed oil to the crankcase when thought expedient. A non-return valve was fitted in the inlet tract and the compression release connected to the exhaust pipe, so the design had some very modern ideas in it. Ignition was by chain-driven Bosch magneto, and Druid forks and belt drive were used.

Late in 1912 came another engine, this time a 784cc water-cooled in-line-twin two-stroke. It drove back through a clutch to an indirect two-speed gearbox that stepped the drive over for a shaft to run back to a worm at the rear wheel. Pressure lubrication was used along with Druid forks. It was first listed as the 'Stella', then as the 'Stellar', but nothing further came of this interesting enterprise.

SUDBROOK c.1919–1920
One more small firm based in Coventry that entered and left the industry in the heady post-war days. As with most, they used the 269cc Villiers engine and proprietary parts during their brief time.

SUMMERFIELD 1989–DATE
A large engineering firm located in Derbyshire and run by three brothers who, as classic racing enthusiasts, turned to producing spares for Manx Nortons in 1986. Three years later they and Bernie Allen gained permission to build complete machines and the results were most successful. Both 350 and 500cc models are produced, and engines sold separately, as well as all the individual parts.

SUN 1911–1961
The Sun Cycle & Fittings Co. of Aston Brook Street, Birmingham was run by the Parkes family, having been founded by James Parkes in Victorian times. The Sun name was first used in 1885 and was the final form of the company name adopted in 1907, when they were well established as bicycle makers.

For 1914 Sun added a model with a V-twin JAP engine to the range, while keeping the Precision singles and adding a two-stroke Sun Villiers.

Their first motorcycle came late in 1911, as the Sun Precision, with a 3.75hp engine from Precision, Amac or B&B carburettor, Bosch magneto, belt drive to a Sturmey-Archer three-speed hub gear and Druid forks. This model was joined by 2.5 and 4.25hp versions for 1913, plus one using a 3.5hp JAP engine that was soon dropped.

The 1921 Sun-Vitesse model had its developed two-stroke engine inclined in the frame with a two-speed gearbox and belt final-drive.

Late in 1913, the first Sun-Villiers model appeared but this was a four-stroke with overhead inlet-valve and of 2.75hp, with its two-speed gearbox built in-unit with it. It joined the line of Precision engines, but was soon replaced by the first Villiers two-stroke of 269cc. The Sun range also added V-twins, using a 4hp Precision or 5hp JAP engine in their well-finished motorcycles. This range took

Largest of the Sun four-stroke models in 1931 was this machine, with its 490cc JAP ohv engine.

This 1932 Tourist model with 147cc Villiers engine was part of Sun's 1932 range, all dropped after 1933, an autocycle marking their comeback in 1940.

them on into the war years and, in 1915, they used the Sun-Vitesse name for the two-stroke when fitted with their own 269cc engine.

After the war they developed their engine further, to add a disc valve in the side of the crankcase to control the induction. The engine was reduced slightly in size for their entry in the 250cc TT of 1921, but they had no great success.

The road model continued with their 269cc engine, inclined in the frame and driving a two-speed gearbox with belt final-drive. For 1922, the disc-valve two-stroke was listed as a road model and joined by one fitted with a JAP engine, while the next year brought models using 147cc Villiers and 348cc Blackburne engines, the latter alone in having all-chain drive.

It was Villiers engines of 147, 247 and 343cc for 1924, along with the Blackburne and, for 1925, the first became Sun-Villiers and added a 172cc model, and the second the Sun-Blackburne. This use of double names added the Sun-JAP of 300cc to the 1925 list, plus 346cc sv and ohv models for 1926. This habit persisted to the end of the decade but, before then, a 499cc sv Blackburne engine was added for 1927, but replaced by a 490cc sv JAP engine for the next year, when saddle tanks appeared. An ohv version came in 1929, by when the 147 and 343cc two-strokes had gone

Sun joined the enclosure theme, along with a Villiers twin-cylinder engine, with this 1957 Overlander model.

This is the Geni scooter prototype, as shown in 1957, polished but not yet painted. It had a 99cc Villiers engine and was later joined by the Sunwasp of 147cc.

but a Super Sports version of the 172 had been added.

In the 1930s, the marques became simply Sun again; Villiers and JAP engines continued in use, with the first ranging from 98 to 346cc and the second from 245 to 490cc. However, after 1933, motorcycle production ceased for a while, but the name reappeared in 1940 on an autocycle, powered by a 98cc Villiers engine and offered in three versions. It was one of these that returned to the market in 1946, their only model until 1949.

The autocycle was revised to use the 99cc Villiers 2F engine for 1949 and was joined by a motorcycle fitted with the similar two-speed 1F unit. For 1951 the autocycle went, but two new models appeared using 122 and 197cc Villiers engine units. A competition version was added for 1953 and the next year brought pivoted-fork rear suspension to the road models, plus the Cyclone, a road model fitted with the 224cc Villiers 1H engine. For 1957 the Overlander, with a 249cc Villiers 2T twin engine, took over and, at the bottom end of the scale, the Geni scooter with 15in wheels and 99cc engine was added. Two years later it was joined by the Sunwasp, a true scooter with a 174cc Villiers engine, but that year also saw the end of motorcycle production and the firm taken over.

This left the two scooters, but the smaller went after 1960 and the larger during the next year, to bring the marque to its close.

Competition riders were offered this 1955 trials Sun, with tuned Villiers 197cc engine, four speeds and leading-link front forks.

238 *Sunbeam*

The first of the Sunbeam motorcycles was followed in 1914 by this model, with gearbox lever and oil feed pump on the tank side.

SUNBEAM 1912–1965

The Sunbeam was advertised as the gentleman's motor bicycle and built by John Marston of Wolverhampton. It was one of the great British marques and noted for its high standards of workmanship and finish, which carried over from those held by Marston in his bicycle and other enterprises. These continued despite his age of seventy-six when he entered the motorcycle field, late in 1912.

The first Sunbeam was designed by Harry Stevens, of the AJS Stevens family, along conventional but up-to-date lines. It had a 2.75hp engine with rear-mounted gear-driven Bosch magneto and this drove a two-speed gearbox with clutch and kick-starter. Transmission was by chain, with both fully enclosed by the famous Sunbeam 'Little Oil Bath Chain Case'. Druid-pattern forks were used and the finish was to the normal Sunbeam high standard. It was prepared for production by John Greenwood, who would direct engineering policy at Sunbeamland from then until the 1930s.

A second model was added in June 1913 for sidecar work and this used a 6hp JAP V-twin engine, a three-speed gearbox, all-chain drive with the chain cases, and Druid forks. Later in the year a 3.5hp single joined the range and was based on the smaller model, but used the three-speed gearbox and had a cast-alloy primary chaincase.

A TT version of the 3.5hp model was listed for 1914 and, in that year, George Dance joined them, to become famous in the early 1920s for his many successes in sprints. They justified the TT model by entering the Senior and Howard Davies finished an equal second while the firm took the team prize. Then came the war, when the 2.75hp model was dropped; the 3.5hp ran on in limited numbers, as did the 6hp twin, although this had an Abingdon King Dick engine in place of the JAP for 1915. It changed again for 1916 to an 8hp MAG, with the sidecars often fitted with an ambulance body, and then to a similar JAP in 1917. There was also a 4hp model built for the French Army and this differed from all the others in having belt final-drive.

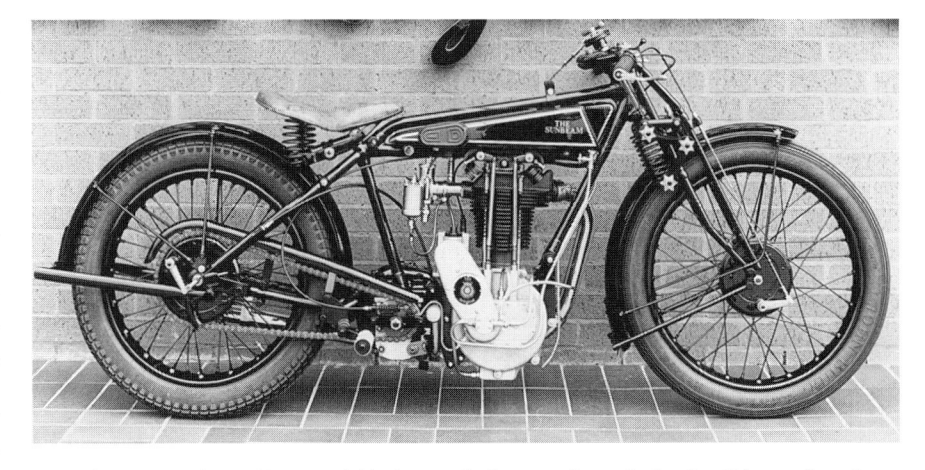

A Sunbeam Sprint from 1926, a model built specially for racing, hence the low handlebars and small, low-set fuel tank.

During the last year of the war tragedy struck the Marston family, for the eldest son died and, the day after the funeral, John Marston died, followed by his wife a few days later. This

Advertisement for the 1914 Sunbeam, with a change of gear lever, no oil pump, but still with the large gear in the magneto drive-chain.

Sunbeam did produce machines with sv engines, but were best known for the performance engines with ohv. The exhaust pipe is typical.

Sunbeam Model 9 line drawing, showing the machine as for 1930.

had a profound effect on the firm, for others controlled it as it entered a new and different decade as part of Nobel Industries.

The 1919 range was just the 3.5hp single and 8hp V-twin with JAP engine with only minor changes. George Dance began his domination of sprints and hill-climbs that year, using a much-lightened machine with his own ohv conversion. He rode to win and an offshoot was the George Dance knee grips, first seen in 1923 and highly popular with fast riders for many years.

In 1920 the firm returned to the TT with the aim to improve on 1914, and this they did. Dance led from the start until engine trouble stopped him, but then Tommy de la Hay moved up to win with Reg Brown third. The road models for that year had a leaf spring to control the front fork and, with several versions of the 3.5hp 499cc model, ran on for 1921.

Two new models arrived for 1922, one the Longstroke of 491cc which was based on the engine used in the French Grand Prix. The other was the Model 7 which combined the Longstroke bottom half with the 3.5hp bore to achieve its 599cc capacity; it would remain in production for a decade with the leaf-spring front fork, while the rest of the range reverted to the Druid pattern. Once again the firm ran in the Senior TT and among their riders was Alec Bennett, who had been fourth in 1921 and started favourite. In the event he confirmed this with an easy victory, his first TT win of five.

The smaller 246cc Sunbeam Little 90 model for 1933, was set up for racing with handlebars and footrests to suit, but based on the road model 14.

A 346cc model was added for 1923, along with a Light Solo version of the 499cc, and at the end of the year the V-twin was dropped. By then the firm realized that they needed ohv to remain competitive and the result was a major revision to the range. At the same time the practice of giving Model numbers was adopted.

Drive side of the 1933 Sunbeam model 8 of 346cc, with overhead valves, the finish just as good as always and the chains well-protected.

Thus, for 1924, the 346cc became Model 1 with full equipment and Model 2 in more sporting form. The 499cc was the Model 3 and became the Model 4 when fitted with the 599cc engine, while Model 6 was the 491cc Longstroke and Model 7 the 599cc variation. During the year the 346cc Model 8 and 493cc Model 9 joined the list; both had ohv engines, and were built in standard and sprint

Another sv Sunbeam, showing the exhaust pipe curled round to the left to leave space for the oil pump, and gear-change lever on the right.

The 1935 Sunbeam model 16 had a 248cc engine with high camshaft, and hairpin valve-springs driving a Burman gearbox with gear lever on the right.

forms listed as Models 10 and 11. All had an excellent cylinder-head design of hemispherical form with angled valves and the sprint machines had a sloping top-frame tube, a tapered fuel-tank and were not intended for road use. They were only listed for two years or so, for public road sprints were banned in 1926.

Drum brakes arrived for 1925 and, in that year, the firm built some ohc racing engines but these had no success. However, they did use hairpin valve-springs and these appeared on the ohv engine in 1926, among the few changes. It was much the same for the next year, other than for the 346cc Model 80 and 493cc Model 90 TT machines, which were for competition and took the place of the Sprint models.

During 1927, Nobel Industries became part of ICI and a reduced range was produced for that year and the next. They once again ran in the Senior TT and after the poor years came a success, when Charlie Dodson won in 1928 by an ample margin. He went on to repeat this in 1929, when Alec Bennett was second, but this was to be the last Sunbeam TT success.

Another of the late-1930 models, fitted with the Burman gearbox and right-side gear pedal, in this case with upswept exhaust pipe.

This was the largest of the four models with AMC-designed engines that came for 1939, with apparent plunger rear-suspension but, actually, pivoted fork.

There were saddle tanks for most of the range for 1929, although the old Model 7 continued with its flat tank. For the others there was a new frame and fitments, but the engines and Model numbers ran on with the 346cc 1, 2, 8 and 10, the 491cc 5 and 6, and the 493cc 9 and 90. There was also a speedway model in common with several other marques and just as short lived.

In addition to the Senior TT, Sunbeam riders had a number of successes in Europe in 1929, but it was an end of an era with the Depression about to take its toll. If it was to be hard for many firms, it was especially so for one producing a high-class product of exceptional finish. The whole range went forward for 1930, to be joined during the year by a revised Model 6, known as the Lion and soon fitted with Webb forks.

The range was down to four models for 1931, the Lion, 9 and 90, plus a new 344cc ohv Model 10. This had the sump cast into the crankcase, and the Webb forks, and was built in an effort to offer a Sunbeam at a lower price. The old flat-tank Model 7 remained available to special order but, during the year, a revised version appeared, again known as the Lion and with an updated version of the 599cc engine.

It was joined in 1932 by the 599cc ohv 9A model which was essentially a bored 9, and both had four-speed gearboxes. The list was extended for 1933, when the 8 and 80 returned with twin-port engines and there were three new models. For the first time the firm listed a machine under 350cc, the 246cc Model 14, which was the 8 with a reduced bore. With it came the Little 90, which was a racing version, despite the long stroke, and built in small numbers towards the year end. In a similar format came the 95, which was the 493cc machine to racing specification but also offered in trim for use on the road. In 1934 the Little 95 replaced the earlier machine and the 80 and 90 had gone,

This was how the new post-war Sunbeam was introduced, with its twin cylinders in-line, shaft drive and massive mudguards.

but the firm was in some trouble, for their sales were slow and costs high due to the standards they still built to.

The middle 1930s were still hard times when price was all, but most of the range continued, the 14 replaced by the 16 with a 248cc high-camshaft engine with hairpin valve-springs and a four-speed Burman gearbox. Unfortunately, it was not a good design, so a return was quickly made to the 14. The Model 95 was deleted in 1935 and in 1936 Burman boxes were standardized, except on the 598cc sv and 599cc ohv.

In this way the firm continued to 1937, when the business was sold to the AJS and Matchless companies to form AMC, where they learnt a good deal about quality finishes to good effect. AMC kept some of the range going to the end of the decade, but did introduce new engines for most in 1939, with rear suspension an option for the larger models in 1940.

During 1943, AMC sold Sunbeam to BSA and, in 1946, they announced a totally new model with the old name. It was designed by Erling Poppe, who had been one half of P&P in the 1920s, and had a 489cc in-line twin-cylinder engine with an overhead camshaft. This was built in-unit with the four-speed gearbox and the machine had shaft drive to an underslung worm, a duplex frame, telescopic forks with a single central spring, plunger rear-suspension and fat 16in tyres.

Highly innovative, it had some early problems due to vibration and a

Timing cover of the new high-camshaft Sunbeam engine for 1939, in 245, 348, 497 and 598cc capacities, but this engine was not to be too successful.

The BSA-Sunbeam scooter was listed with 175 or 250cc engine and also sold as the Triumph Tigress with just a change of colour and badges.

high wear rate of the worm and its wheel. To deal with this, the engine was rubber mounted into the frame, so this had additional members to strengthen it. The wear was dealt with by restricting the engine speed and power, although this reduced the performance to no more than a 75mph (120km/h) top speed, with poor acceleration due to the 400lb (182kg) weight. In addition, the handling was lively, it was an expensive model, and hardly the flagship grand tourer intended.

It went on sale in 1947 as the S7 and found a small following, but remained too slow, unusual and costly for most. An attempt to improve this was made in 1949, when the original was joined by the S8, which had narrower tyres, BSA forks and slimmer mudguards to lighten the appearance. The original concept continued as the S7 de luxe, with BSA fork legs in special yokes and other improvements, and from then on the two twins were built without change in ever smaller numbers up to 1956, although it took another two years to sell all the stock off.

The Sunbeam name then returned in 1959 on a scooter. This was a duplicate of that sold by Triumph as the Tigress, aside from colour and badges. Two versions were built, one with a 172cc two-stroke engine derived from the Bantam and the other a 249cc ohv twin with the option of electric starting. Other than the engine the two were the same, with a four-speed gearbox, based on that of the C15 and Cub, duplex-chain drive to the rear wheel and scooter-style chassis, wheels and body. There were few changes over the years and the scooters, really too late in the market, were dropped in 1965 to end the Sunbeam name on motorized two wheelers.

SUPERB FOUR 1920

Much press talk accompanied the launch of the four-cylinder Superb, which coincided with the Olympia Motor Cycle show in November 1920. It was heralded as the first British-built four since the demise of the Wilkinson TAC/TMC and promised a great deal. The in-line air-cooled engine, designed by W.F. Hooper, was in-unit with a three-speed gearbox and chain final-drive. Valve operation was by ohc, a vertical shaft running up the front of the well-finned light-alloy cylinder block to drive the camshaft, with all working parts fully enclosed and pressure lubricated. Capacity was 991cc and Zenith carburettor and Lucas Magdyno attended to mixture, ignition and lighting respectively. This handsome unit went into a purpose-built duplex frame and, although the specification was high throughout, it was said that costings indicated a realistic selling price would be achievable. However, either finance for production was not forthcoming or design problems were insuperable, because news of the Four stopped as quickly as it had begun.

SUPREMOCO 1921–1923

The Manchester-based Supreme Motor Company traded from premises on Lime Grove in the southern suburb of Longsight, but their output of complete machines was small. Between 1921 and 1923 they advertised a range of models with 269cc Villiers and 318cc Dalm two-stroke engines, plus 348 and 545cc sv Blackburne four-strokes. The simplest of these had direct-belt drive, then came two-speed Burman gearbox options, plus a three-speed from the same maker, but this only on the 545cc model; all, however, had belt final-drive. They also adopted the Vici carburettor in place of more regular fitments but, by 1923, their efforts were switched to a new type of spring front fork. This was made available to the trade under the H.T.S. brand name and it was with this that they sought future success.

SUTTON c.1905–1910

This marque was built by W. Jenkinson of Market Street, Long Sutton, Lincolnshire in a typical pattern for the period. Singles and V-twins were offered with belt drive, a choice of transmissions and braced forks. Most would have sold locally, as the main business was the repair of cars, motorcycles and bicycles.

SWALLOW 1903–1905

Built by a Mr Hodges at his garage in Park Lane, Tottenham, London, the name appeared on cars as well as motorcycles. The latter used Minerva and Fafnir engines with Chater-Lea frame and a two-speed gear where required. There was also a forecar using the Fafnir, but no doubt the normal garage business soon brought the venture to an end.

SWALLOW 1947–1951

Best known for its sidecars, this Walsall, Staffordshire firm introduced a simple scooter under the name of Gadabout to the British market in 1947. Crude in some ways, it also

Swallow were best known for their sidecars, but their panel-beating ability, plus a Villiers engine, resulted in the Gadabout scooter.

lacked performance, due to a combination of its weight and the pre-war 122cc Villiers 9D engine that propelled it. However, it offered transport and, in 1950, the engine was changed to the later 10D, while 1951 brought a version with the 197cc 6E unit and the name Major. By then the sleek Italian makes were appearing, so the angular Gadabout's days came to an end and the firm concentrated on sidecars and the Swallow Doretti sports car that was based on the Triumph TR2.

The Swan Electric Tricycle had the motor above the single front wheel and the batteries under the seat, which could carry two passengers.

SWAN 1909

The Swan Electric Traction Co. of London put an electric tricycle on the market during 1909, the patent for the drive system appearing in 1908 under the name of C. Lassen. The single front wheel had the motor mounted above it, the drive being by shaft to bevels. The wheel was supported by semi-elliptic springs attached to a strengthened mudguard and was steered by tiller. A two-seat body went over the battery storage and there was an option of a small van body in its place. A speed of around 15mph (24km/h) reflected the intended town use.

SWAN 1912–1913

Built by the Cygnus Engineering Co. of Frodsham, Warrington, which was founded by F.H. Thornton using finance from his father, the name later changed to Swan Motor Manufacturing. They offered an unusual machine for 1912, with an open frame built up from light alloy, braced by steel, and an inner alloy frame carrying the two-speed gearbox. The frame had a tubular

The 1912 Swan was built by Cygnus, with a built-up frame and front and rear suspension among its unusual features, but just a JAP engine.

rear-suspension fork, controlled by laminated springs, and Druid front forks. Power was by a 3.5hp JAP engine, whose crankcase was concealed in the frame to leave the top half exposed, while the oil tank went up behind the headstock. The chain-driven magneto went under the rider's seat, as did the petrol tank, while transmission was by chain. JAP V-twin and Precision engines were also used, but Thornton's father closed the firm on finding some employees purloining faulty parts for their own use. This brought production to a halt in 1913

SWIFT 1899–1915

This Coventry firm was closely associated with Ariel and also built cars from 1902. Their first tricycle was similar to the Ariel, in fitting the engine ahead of the rear axle, while the whole of the frame was boxed-in to enclose the carburettor and electrics, and the petrol and oil were carried in a cylindrical tank under the saddle. The driving gears were enclosed to enhance their life.

For 1904 they began to build a model under licence from Starley,

Associated with Ariel, the Swift tricycle followed the same line in 1899, so had the engine mounted ahead of the rear axle to improve stability.

The Swift copied the drive of the Starley with worm and wheel and also had a similar frame to clear the engine, but gave it more support.

copying the transverse engine built in-unit with a two-speed gearbox, and worm and wheel to turn the drive to suit the chain drive to the rear wheel.

The older models continued and, by 1910, were listed as the Swift-Ariel, fitting a 3.5hp engine to a rigid frame with Druid forks and a sprung saddle. For 1911, the engine was a White & Poppe for the two listed models, the Touring and TT. In 1913 they offered a Cyclecar fitted with a water-cooled vertical-twin engine, while the 3.5hp solo continued with the option of an Armstrong three-speed rear hub.

The range ran on for 1914 and into 1915, with an extra model fitted with a V-twin engine, but from then on the firm concentrated on cars up to 1931.

SWINDON 1981

This was an attempt to market a 250cc motocross model, with a rising-rate rear-suspension system on the lines then coming into fashion with the Japanese firms. Prototypes were built and raced but no more came of this venture.

SYMPLEX 1914–1915

This name was first noted in December 1914 and, no doubt, was one of the many that sought to offer basic transport to civilians and services alike in those early war-time days. The engine was a 318cc Dalm two-stroke and the model had two speeds or direct-belt drive. Brampton Bi-flex forks were used and the makers were based in Alma Street, Birmingham. As with so many of that time, it was short lived.

T

TAC 1909–1911
This stood for Touring Auto-Cycle, which was the name under which the Wilkinson four was first sold. It was a lengthy machine, with its in-line engine, clutch, three-speed gearbox and shaft drive. There was front and rear suspension, plus a bucket seat for rider comfort. For 1912 the name was changed to Touring Motor Cycle or TMC.

TAILWIND 1952
An enterprising cycle attachment built by Mr A. Latta of Berkhamsted, that placed its 49cc two-stroke engine above the bicycle front wheel, which it drove by friction roller. What made the unit unusual was not that the engine had a disc inlet-valve, but that there were two speeds. This was done by fitting a two-diameter drive roller and a means of shifting the complete assembly sideways to select the ratios. It worked well, but the moped era was close to hand, so it never reached production.

The clever Tailwind cycle attachment contrived to have two speeds for its 49cc disc-valve engine.

TALBOT 1903
Produced by the Talbot Cycle Co. of Wolverhampton, who fitted an imported 2hp engine in a heavy-duty bicycle frame, added other bought-in items and their existing transfer to introduce a new make.

TALBOT 1957–1960
A British moped built by bicycle dealer H.J. Talbot of Norwood, London, who used a 49cc Mini-Motor engine. This was hung under the open frame ahead of the pedals and drove a countershaft with clutch by V-belt with chain to the rear wheel. Pedalling gear with a two-speed Derailleur was provided, along with Webb girder forks, while braking was by stirrup at the front and drum at the rear.

The transmission was soon revised to drop the Derailleur gear and replace the countershaft with a two-speed Albion gearbox. Shields concealed the belt and chains to give the machine some style, but production was limited and, no doubt, ceased when the engine supply dried up.

TANDON 1948–1959
Indian-born Devdutt Tandon set this firm up to build cheap lightweights for home and export and the first model appeared in 1948. It was a crude device, with a 122cc Villiers 9D pre-war engine installed in a rigid tubular frame of bolted construction. There were telescopic forks but the angular tank and pillar-mounted saddle did little to enhance the style.

This model was built up to 1952, but was joined in 1950 by a much improved machine sold as the Supaglid, fitted with the later 122cc 10D engine and with pivoted-fork rear suspension controlled by a rubber cartridge. A version with a 197cc 6E engine and a competition model appeared in 1951, while later came machines using the 147cc 30C and 224cc 1H Villiers, and the 242 and 322cc British Anzani engines.

However, time and money ran out for the small firm and they were wound up late in 1955. Despite this, the name was back in 1956 with two road models using 8E and 1H engines and these were built up to 1959.

The first Tandon of 1948 used a crude frame of bolted tubes, a pre-war 122cc Villiers engine and lacked any style to speak of.

TATAM 1955–c.1968
Martin Tatam, known as Spud, was one of the first to build grass-track machines in the speedway style using JAP engines. For the grass he added a gearbox and brakes, but in other respects the speedway format was well suited to the grass circuits of the time.

TAVENER 1921
Ernest Tavener built this machine, when aged nineteen, to satisfy his interest in motorcycles and engineering. For comfort he adopted front and rear springing on a frame built up from straight tubes, triangulated for strength and stiffness. The front forks were also fabricated from tubes with short leading-links to carry the wheel, controlled by leaf springs with further links to them. At the rear went a pivoted fork made from sheet steel, with long leaf springs shackled to the rear end of the frame tubes that extended to the back number plate.

The Tavener was built in the 1920s and from the start incorporated the owner's ideas, being revised and later rebuilt as shown here.

Thorough offered quite a choice during its brief time on the market in 1903, with three engine sizes and other features.

The engine was a Swiss 1,000cc MAG V-twin and direct-belt drive with single speed and clutch were fine for the era. In 1926, Tavener decided to revise this to add a clutch and gearbox more in keeping with the increased traffic, but the machine was then left in a dismantled state. Some fifty-eight years later it was rebuilt by Colin Light using a three-speed Sturmey-Archer gearbox, so once again took to the road.

TAYLOR 1910–1911
A Birmingham firm who were wholesale agents for Peugeot engines. Late in 1910 they entered the motorcycle lists with models using 3.5hp single or 3.5, 5 or 7hp V-twin Peugeot engines. They had belt drive and sprung forks, but the firm soon returned to its wholesale agency.

TAYLOR GUE 1905
A name used by Johannes Gütgemann, later Goodman, and partner William Gue when in business in Birmingham in Victorian times. They made frames for Ormonde and took that business over late in 1904, which enabled them to offer their own machine the next year. It had a 2hp engine, belt drive and bicycle forks with girder forks an option. Sold as the Veloce, it led in time to the famous Velocette but this first venture soon failed.

TDC 1914–1915
T.D. Cross were well known for their transmission components for the bicycle trade – sprockets, freewheels and chains. They also made machines with 3.5hp own-brand and Precision four-stroke engines, plus, from 1915, a two-stroke with their own design engine, all sold under the TDC brand name. A two-speed countershaft gearbox with belt final-drive and Druid single-blade forks with a dropped top-tube frame on the two-stroke machine made for a conventional appearance, but with an attractive style.

TEAGLE 1952–1956
A clip-on engine made in Cornwall and derived from a garden power tool. It was a 50cc two-stroke that sat over the bicycle rear wheel with friction roller drive and was mainly made from light-alloy with one major casting. First seen late in 1952, it was 1954 before it reached the market, but was thus too late and soon overtaken by the moped.

TEE-BEE 1910–1911
A Glasgow machine, built by Templeton Bros, who fitted a 2.5hp JAP engine to a machine using an NSU two-speed gear, belt drive and sprung forks. Another make that was short lived.

TEJ 1922–1923
A lightweight machine built in the Stoney Stanton area of Leicestershire, most probably by a small cycle and motorcycle retailer. They adopted the 349cc two-stroke Broler engine, made in nearby Narborough, and would have enjoyed mainly local patronage.

TEMPLE-CROWSLEY 1906
This marque was listed in 1906 as offering two models. Their motorcycle had a V-twin engine and a spring frame, while the forecar was powered by a single. Not listed again and so soon gone.

THOMAS 1902–1904
A small producer, J.L. Thomas of Barnet, Hertfordshire exhibited three machines at the late-1902 Stanley show, one entirely of his own construction, including the engine.

Thorough also showed a forecar in 1903, which used a 3hp engine in the centre of a long frame based on a stretched solo one with its tank.

Claims rather than details were given, but the machine did have a form of leading-link front fork, known as the Celeripede, that had a coil spring to provide the suspension medium. An extra-long wheelbase, two-lever control and spray carburettor were also spoken of. Their own machine must have had problems, as, a year later at the same show, it was not in evidence and just two machines were on view. One had an inclined Minerva engine and the other a Kerry, made by Sarolea, but both retained the Celeripede front fork.

THOROUGH 1903
A small producer, based in Bethnal Green, London, who offered basic primitives with the choice of 1.75, 2 and 2.75hp engines. Trial trips were advertised, but not for long, as the firm was soon lost from the lists.

THREE SPIRES 1931–1932
First seen late in 1931, these machines were built by Coventry Bicycles who had produced motorcycles such as the Coventry-B&D and the Wee-McGregor in the early-1920s. The new offering was a lightweight, with a 147cc Villiers engine, two-speed

The short-lived Three Spires, which used the 147cc Villiers engine, was very basic to suit the times and was only on the market for two years.

Albion gearbox and a basic set of cycle parts. Its style was more late-1920s and it left the market before the end of 1932.

TICKLE 1969–1973
Spares for the Manx Norton became scarce once the firm stopped their production and, in 1966, AMC sold all their racing hardware to Colin Seeley. He concentrated on the AJS and Matchless models, so sold the Norton side on to John Tickle in 1969. John was already in the spares business and went on to produce both Manx spares and complete machines as the 350cc T3 and 500cc T5. They were as the existing Manx as far as the engine and gearbox were concerned, but had a high-level exhaust system and the frame was a Tickle design, although very similar to the featherbed. Both were built up to 1973, after which he sold out to another firm.

John Tickle acquired the Manx Norton spares, which led to this machine, built in 350 and 500cc sizes, with Tickle frame.

TILSTON 1919–1920
Probably few lightweights bearing this name were ever produced, as its maker's main business was in the manufacture and promotion of the Gosport spring fork incorporating the MacLean system. This resembled the rocking action fork used by Triumph for many years and, indeed, the Gosport fork was offered as a conversion for existing machines of this major marque. The Tilston had a two-stroke engine with belt drive and swinging-arm rear suspension, controlled by a MacLean spring unit sited under the saddle pan.

TINKLER 1927–1928
Almond Tinkler built his first motorcycle while still a teenager and opened a motorcycle business in Liverpool just after the Great War. He did some tuning work and ran in competitions, with a third place in the 1924 Sidecar TT to his credit. Two years later he took notice of the Guzzi single and from this came the idea of making a radical machine.

The conception of late-1926 was built for the 1927 TT by a super-human effort and the inevitable teething troubles of practice finally brought Tinkler to the point of total exhaustion, so the doctor forbade him to race.

This was hardly surprising, for the design was truly innovative and novel, but quite practical and a fine example of lateral thinking. What Tinkler did was to take the horizontal single Guzzi layout with its overhead camshaft, water cool it and turn it round so the crankcase was at the front, just aft of the radiator. The gearbox was then built in-unit with the cylinder head and alongside the camshaft, so the one drive to that was also the primary transmission. The magneto lay alongside the engine, skew-gear driven from the crankshaft, there was pressure lubrication throughout and the whole assembly was enclosed in an aluminium case with the petrol tank its cover. By using this layout the number of working parts was reduced and the complete box was housed in a duplex tubular frame with bottom-link forks.

After the TT practice, changes were made to the cooling system and the engine compression, following which the sole machine was extensively road tested during the autumn of 1927. Almond Tinkler and his brother then formed a company with premises in Langham Street, Liverpool, where they intended to start quantity production and a price of £75 was given by February 1928.

However, soon after that, the Tinklers joined forces with OEC, who took up the manufacture. They showed a machine fitted with this 490cc engine and their own duplex-steering forks at the late-1928 Olympia show. It had a good reception but neither firm had the finance to turn orders into machines, so nothing further came of this advanced but un-saleable ideal.

TMC 1912–1915
The name adopted by the Wilkinson four-cylinder, three-speed, shaft-drive luxury machine that had suspension for both wheels and a bucket seat for the rider. It was sold as the Touring Auto-Cycle, or TAC, at first but was best known by the company name.

TOBOGGAN TRICAR 1905
This machine had a variable gear and a reverse facility, but did not rely on conventional gears or clutches. Unfortunately, its makers, The Toboggan Tricar Company of Terminus Chambers, Holborn Viaduct, London EC, didn't elaborate further on their chosen method of operation. Two models were offered, a 4hp single and a 6hp twin, the frames were constructed around Chater-Lea fittings and the complete machines were assembled at works in Phipp Street, Finsbury, London N.

TONKIN 2003
The notion of building a road machine based on a racing one has attracted firms and individuals for many years. Steve Tonkin chose the Matchless G50 engine, a five-speed BSA-type Gold Star gearbox, belt primary drive and dry clutch for his Typhoon machine, which appeared in 2003. All went into a Titchmarsh Mk III Seeley replica frame with Ceriani front forks and drum brake, and conical rear hub. The whole machine had the style and line of the Seeley Condor, had the finest of detail fittings and, while not cheap, captured the classic image in the finest way.

TOOTH 1914
An experimental lightweight engine built by Mr Tooth of Humber Road,

Coventry and described in August 1914. It was of 50.5cc capacity and had a rotating sleeve to allow the mixture to enter and exit the cylinder, this sleeve driven by bevel gears at half engine-speed. The sleeve was in two sections, pegged for drive, and these revolved between the cylinder proper and a finned outer cylinder. Both had inlet and exhaust ports that were registered in turn with a single one in the top rotating sleeve.

This engine was mounted ahead of the bottom bracket of a bicycle and drove the rear wheel by a crossed round belt. It ran steadily, but could hardly have chosen a worse time for a radical design to appear on the market, so no more was heard of it.

As an alternative to the JAP engine Toreador also offered this model, with a 349cc Dorman-Bradshaw oil-cooled engine but no front brake.

TOREADOR 1925–1928
Having terminated his involvement with the Matador marque the previous year, Bert Houlding continued his talent for sporting motorcycle design with the Toreador range that appeared in 1925. A rakish 495c ohv MAG V-twin model came first, with Burman three-speed all-chain transmission and an exhaust system siamesed into a Mador silencer, which, together with patent adjustable handlebars of the same name, had already been pioneered by Houlding in his Matador days. JAP engines were standardized for 1926 – 346 and 344cc ohv and 490cc sv singles, plus a 490cc ohv model with a 90mph (144km/h) speed guarantee. All retained the Burman gearbox, as was the case the following season, when there was a three-model range. This comprised of a 349cc ohv oil-cooled Bradshaw model and just the 490 JAP, in either sv or ohv forms.

There were, however, supersports options on the Bradshaw and the ohv JAP, in which instance a two-port head became a part of the specification. The year 1928 brought a return of the 344 – in two-port racing trim – and 346cc ohv JAP models, and a new 498cc ohv JAP racing machine with the longstroke two-port JOR-type engine, but the marque folded after this and the works at Ribble Bank Mills, Preston, closed.

TORNADO 1924
Tornado sidecars, the products of Hudson & Matthews of Altrincham, Cheshire, were a popular brand through most of the 1920s. To demonstrate the capabilities of their sports models in speed competitions, H. Hudson built a racing big-twin under the Tornado name. Powered by an eight-valve Anzani 994cc V-twin engine, breathing through twin Amac carburettors and weighing under 300lb (136kg), this projectile was used successfully at sprint events over a three-year period. It remained, however, a one-off special and the company stayed with sidecar manufacture.

TORPEDO 1908–1915
F. Hopper & Co. of Barton-on-Humber, Yorkshire built the Torpedo, which was first seen at the late-1910 Olympia show, although a catalogue existed as early as 1908. Initially they intended to use a 4.25hp Fafnir engine, but changed to 2.5 and 3.5hp Precision engines, the machines with belt drive and Druid forks. In time came a 4.25hp model, hub gears and a 190cc lightweight, followed by a V-twin for 1914, this range continuing for the next year.

In addition to its complete machines the firm also sold motorcycle sets that were an assembly of frame, forks, tank, wheels, mudguards, pedals and handlebars. The trader could then add engine, transmission, tyres, saddle and minor details to have his own make of machine to offer. Various transfer outlines were available to suit the trader's name and style to complete the package.

TOWNEND 1901–1904
Typical primitive with a choice of engine powers mounted in a heavy-duty bicycle frame, to which was added suitable fittings and a new tank transfer. No doubt a cycle dealer who dropped the powered side as the downturn of 1905 came.

The 1902 Trafalgar Sociable Attachment was an early sidecar, at a time when forecars and trailers were more usual, and so was advanced for its year.

TRAFALGAR 1902–1908
Produced by G. Lyons & Co. of Baker Street, London, this machine featured a vertically mounted 2.75hp MMC engine. They also offered a 'Sociable Attachment', a wicker-work sidecar having a flexible attachment to the motorcycle. By 1904, the engine was rated at 3.25hp and, by 1908, Peugeot engines were fitted, either a 2.75hp single or 5hp V-twin.

TRAFFORD c.1919–1922
This was one of the many firms that turned to the 269cc Villiers engine to set up manufacture in the early post-war days that it was no wonder that supplies were hard to come by. The same applied to the proprietary parts, until the boom burst and the small firms then left the market, most returning to their previous garage life.

TREBLOC 1923–1924
A 67cc two-stroke auxiliary engine for attachment into the frame of a gents' safety cycle and sold either in complete ready-to-ride form or as a unit alone. The tiny engine was held in the frame centre by integral clamps on the crankcase, ignition was by magneto and drive by a sprocket on the crankshaft matching with another

on the pedalling bracket, from where the standard pushbike chain drove to the rear wheel. Weighing just 60lb (27kg), as a complete machine it was simple, unsprung and designed for short journeys, but failed to make enough of a mark, so the Trebloc Manufacturing Company of Bath in Somerset soon found it best to pursue other activities.

TRENT 1902–1905
A small firm that built primitives and was based in Shepherd's Bush, London. For 1904 they had both 2.75 and 3.5hp engines, mounted upright in a loop frame, and also a forecar that was fitted with a 3.75hp water-cooled engine driving a two-speed gear.

TRIPLE H 1922–1923
The three aitches involved in this marque were Messrs Hobbis Brothers & Horrell, who built a lightweight with a 247cc Morris two-stroke engine in their Northfield, Birmingham workshop. The machine also used a Moss two-speed gearbox with clutch and kickstarter and Maplestone centre-spring forks. A special cast silencer with detachable plate for ease of cleaning was its most noteworthy design feature.

TRIPLETTE 1923
Without the assistance of Horrell, the Hobbis Brothers alone – of the Triple H marque – were behind this short-lived venture. Another simple machine, powered by a 147cc Villiers two-stroke engine driving through an Albion two-speed gearbox in its most luxurious form, or with direct-belt drive otherwise. It was distinguished by very wide mudguards at the front, necessitating the fork blades to pass through slots cut into the top of the guard.

TRIPP 1922–1923
Advertised as 'The Motor Cycle for the Million', the Tripp miniature had an open frame and a two-stroke engine rated at 1.5hp. It was, in every respect, similar to the McKenzie machine, although no mention was made of any connection between the two marques. The company traded from premises in south-west London and, as part of their promotion, offered one year's insurance and free delivery to the buyer's home in the selling price of 23 guineas.

An early Triton from 1959, built by Eric Cheney in scrambles trim, with the usual pre-unit Triumph engine and Norton frame.

TRITON 1959–DATE
A generic name for the combination of the Triumph-twin engine and the Norton Featherbed frame. They were first built for road racing in the 1950s, when there were plenty of Manx Nortons about that had had the engine and gearbox removed for use in a 500cc racing car.

Later came others using the model 88 twin as the source and, later still, the model 50 and ES2 singles. The engine was the pre-unit twin in 499 or 649cc size at first; later, the larger unit construction unit was the most popular. Other forks and wheels were sometimes used and several dealers set up to build complete machines, usually in a café racer format with clip-ons, rear-sets, swept-back exhausts, new tank and racing seat.

This is a Dresda Triton from 1965, built by Dave Degens, who is best associated with the combination in its various forms.

The Triton was always individual, being built to what ideas the owner had. Some were better made than others and the best were to the highest standards. They are still being made.

TRIUMPH 1902–DATE
Perhaps the most famous of all British firms and the only major one that is still producing motorcycles, albeit under a different master and in a new home. Nothing new about that, for they had moved before and changed hands as well, but were founded by two Germans. While they were a firm to stick to the conventional in their early days, they were innovative at the right times and set the post-war trend in engines for many years.

The first Triumph was built in 1902 and featured a Minerva engine hung from the downtube of a bicycle and direct-belt drive.

Triumph was founded by Siegfried Bettmann in 1886 to make bicycles and the name was chosen to be easy to use in most European countries. Later he was joined by Mauritz Schulte and, although they parted in 1919 after a quarrel, it was they who played a major role in the British industry during the Edwardian period. Other firms might indulge in wild fancy but Schulte kept his sights on building simple, basic but reliable machines to a high quality. They soon earned their 'Trusty' nickname.

The firm was based in Coventry and produced their first motorcycle in 1902. Much as others, it had a Minerva engine hung from the bicycle frame downtube with belt drive, and other models followed on the same lines using British engines. In 1905 they turned to their own excel-

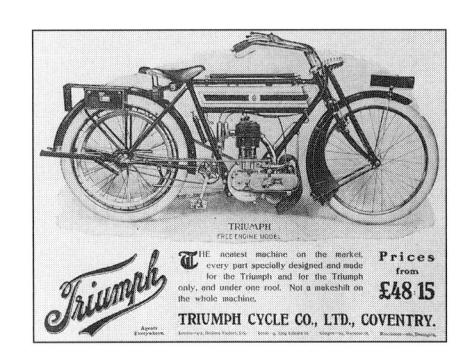

The 1912 Triumph kept to much the same engine and still used the rocking front-fork, which had appeared in 1906, the machine to become the model H with three speeds for 1915.

records on the John O' Groats to Land's End run, the last in 1911 at just over 30mph (48km/h).

Innovation came in the form of an experimental 600cc vertical-twin engine with horizontal crankcase joint, destined not to go into production. There was also the 225cc Junior model with two-stroke engine, two speeds and belt drive that was built from 1914 and known as the Junior. Then came the Great War and, in 1915, Triumph introduced their 550cc model H, which had a chain-driven three-speed Sturmey-Archer gearbox, but kept the belt final-drive.

lent 3hp engine mounted vertically in the frame and the next year brought their less desirable rocking front-fork. For the rest of the decade and on to 1914 they kept to the one model, with this steadily developed, enlarged to 3.5hp and then 4hp for 1914, to be listed with various transmissions. By then it was dated but well known, thanks to the publicity they gained by winning the 1908 TT and setting

The main Triumph single grew from the model H with three speeds, to this Ricardo model with four-valve cylinder-head in 1922.

Triumph singles proved popular with the AA in the late 1920s, when this photo was taken, the men and machines giving sterling service.

Some 30,000 went to the services and the type served them well.

After the war they kept on with the H and Junior, adding the all-chain-drive SD in 1920. Two years later came their famous 499cc Ricardo

In face of competition in 1926, Triumph brought in the model P at a rock-bottom selling figure, which proved an excellent move.

model, with four overhead-valves in the cylinder head, which soon became known as the 'Riccy'. It was to have some competition successes and remained listed up to 1927. In 1923 the Junior was enlarged to 249cc and joined by the model LS, which had a 346cc engine, gear primary-drive, unit construction of its three-speed gearbox and Druid forks with a drum front brake. In the same year they also began to produce cars.

An Edward Turner-designed 499cc Triumph Speed Twin, which first appeared in the 1938 line and set a trend to run through the industry post-war.

A further styling feature that was used to coax customers into the shops was engine enclosure, as seen on this 1932 model WA Triumph.

In the mid-1920s trade was slow, so Triumph combated this by introducing their 493cc model P, for 1925, to sell at a rock-bottom price – far below that of their rivals. They set up to produce 20,000 machines at 1,000 per week, so some minor, cost-cutting short-comings had to stay unchanged for a while. Not that there were too many; the second batch had them corrected and was joined by versions with some improvements for customers with a little more to spend.

Triumph singles of the late-1930s were a Val Page design and of a common pattern; this the model 3H with 350cc ohv engine.

By 1927 the range was up to eight models, including one of 278cc, which was the largest capacity they could achieve while keeping under a tax limit weight. There were fewer in 1928, when they were well stretched thanks to the introduction of the Super Seven car, but they were back to eight in 1929, when all but one was updated by the fitment of a saddle tank. This helped to improve the style and take it away from the vintage era for the next decade.

A 174cc two-stroke with two-speed gearbox built in-unit was added

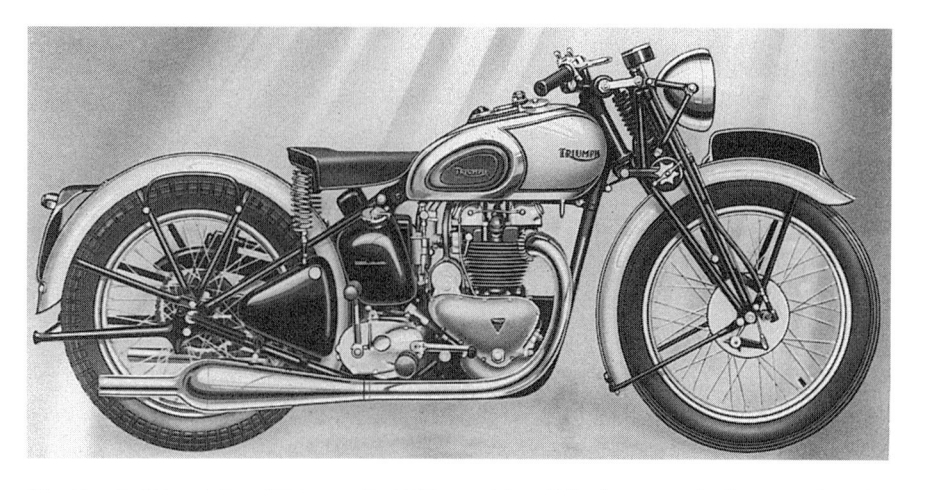

Matching the Triumph Speed Twin was the 1939 sports Tiger 100, where name, finish, perceived speed and megaphone-style silencers all played a part.

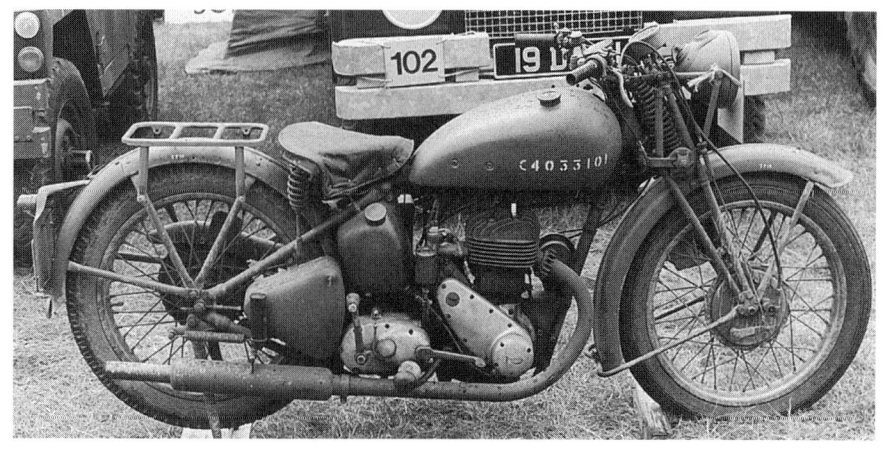

Typical sv single Triumph as used during the war by the services and, post-war, sold on for civilian use and now for rallies.

during 1930, in the search for buyers as the depression bit, and joined a six-model range of singles, all with upright engines and three speeds. The sv models were of 278cc, 498cc and 549cc, while ohv machines were of 348cc and 498cc. An inclined engine with dry-sump lubrication was the fashion for 1931, when a 249cc ohv single joined the range in this style that was adopted by two other models, and some machines had the right side enclosed by a panel.

This inclined trend continued for 1932, when all but one of the four-strokes were in this style and the two-stroke was reduced to 148cc to suit a tax classification. Competition versions of two models were added, these having high-level exhausts, and during the year, two further machines

As well as the Tiger 100 and Speed Twin models, Triumph also listed the 349cc 3T, with its smaller engine but using most of the same parts.

A war-time generator top-half formed the basis of the 500cc Triumph Grand Prix model, which performed well in private owners' hands.

appeared, listed as Silent Scouts. These were based on existing models, but had engine changes to reduce noise, and the option of enclosure.

For 1933, the two-stroke was replaced by a neat 148cc ohv single, for the firm continued to offer the first under its Gloria label. Of much more importance was the announcement in July of a machine with a 647cc vertical-twin engine that had been designed by Val Page, who had moved over from Ariel. Intended for sidecar work, the engine had a single gear-driven camshaft and its general layout would appear post-war in the BSA twin. The Triumph differed in having the oil carried in a compartment in the crankcase, a feature of the firm, and double helical gears for the primary transmission to the four-speed gearbox. The rest of the machine was conventional, but built on a scale to suit sidecar work, a Triumph chair with body that hid the chassis also being available. Work it certainly did, for the firm used it to take the Maudes Trophy that year.

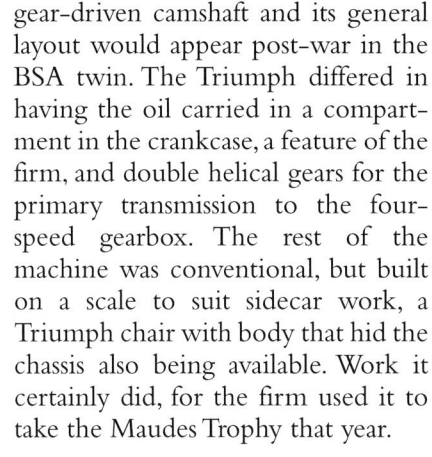

Triumph introduced this 650cc 6T Thunderbird model for 1950, to suit the US market, with nacelle, sprung-hub option and new tank style.

The twin headed up an even longer list for 1934, when a 175cc single was added, along with a series of machines with new vertical engines designed by Page. Not unlike the Ariel singles, they were simple, straightforward, easy to make and maintain, but not too exciting as regards style. Gear drive for the cams and magneto was used, because Triumph had the facilities for this, and models with 249, 343, 493 and 549cc all appeared, the first in ohv form only, the last in sv form only and the other two in both. During the year, a road-racing version of the 493cc model was added and the firm ran three in the TT that year, but all retired.

The range was slimmed down for 1935 to the new singles plus the twin, so the older models all went. It was much the same for 1936, but the firm was by then in financial trouble on the car side. This came to the knowledge of Jack Sangster, whose family had controlled Ariel for many years, and he was able to take over the Triumph motorcycle business. Once in control he moved Edward Turner from Ariel to Triumph with a brief to revitalize the business using any methods he saw fit. Turner was tough and ruthless, but able to command loyalty from his staff and with a great ability to perceive what the public would buy.

His first move at Triumph was typical of the man. He introduced sports versions of the existing three ohv singles, with polished cases, upswept exhaust systems and petrol tanks finished in chrome plating and silver sheen. These sparkled in the showrooms and Turner's final touch was to name them Tiger 70, 80 and 90 to suggest their top speeds, a brilliant move. For 1937 the largest sv single was enlarged to 598cc, the three Tigers became available in a competition form, the firm again won the Maudes Trophy and the finish and lines of all models were improved.

Late in 1937 came the machine that would set the trend for the industry

New in 1949 from Triumph was the Trophy TR5, which used the alloy engine and short frame to suit its purpose, and very popular it proved too.

The bottom end of the scale was catered for by the 150cc Terrier, which came in 1953 and displayed the line and style of the larger Triumph twins.

for decades ahead, the vertical-twin Speed Twin, or 5T, designed by Edward Turner. Brilliant in conception, its 499cc ohv engine with its gear-driven camshafts and magneto was simple to make and compact enough to fit into the existing cycle parts of the larger singles. It had a pleasant, even exhaust-note, was stylish and finished in amaranth red, while its lines were very close to those of a twin-port single. It was an immediate success and was joined by the expected Tiger 100 in 1939, this with megaphone silencers and the black-and-silver finish. The two twins were used for another successful attempt to win the Maudes Trophy but, by the time it was presented, few were interested, for there was a war on.

There was to have been a 350cc version of the twin for 1940, built in touring and sports forms, but the outbreak of war prevented this and the works turned to the production of singles for the services. However, the twin design was not wasted but became the basis of a machine intended to be the standard service model to be built by all firms. Using the existing design, prototypes were soon built and tested, so this plum seemed to lie in Triumph's hand.

Then came the blitz one night in November 1940 and the factory was in ruins. As a temporary measure, production was set up in Warwick while a new factory was built at Meriden,

Triumph introduced pivoted-fork rear-suspension in 1954 for the Tiger 100 and this new 649cc Tiger 110, which was based on the Thunderbird.

this opening in 1942. For the rest of the war it concentrated on 348cc singles, but did some work on a military sv twin, which led to the post-war TRW model sold mainly overseas. It was based on the Speed Twin engine, as was another wartime generator unit built for the RAF, this having a light-alloy top half.

Before the war ended Triumph had

For 1954 Triumph stretched the Terrier to the 199cc Cub, which was soon also listed in this T20C form for mild off-road use.

announced their new range, comprising four twins and a single, this last not to be built. They capitalized on their ten-year lead in the twin market and the final line-up consisted of the pre-war Speed Twin and Tiger 100, both now fitted with telescopic front forks. The only other model was the 349cc 3T, which was based on the 1940 prototype twin, but its sports version, the Tiger 85, never went into production.

These three gained some rear suspension in 1947 in the form of the famous Triumph sprung hub, and comprised the road range up to 1948. This gave limited and undamped

In 1959 the T120 Bonneville was launched and was to become one of the most popular models built by Triumph, this being one from 1962.

In 1957 Triumph brought in enclosure in a big way for a new model, with a 349cc unit-construction engine, the 3TA or Twenty-One.

wheel movement, but the whole assembly slotted straight into the existing frame. The wartime generator gave a bonus late in 1946, when its alloy top-half was allied to a Tiger 100 and gave Ernie Lyons a famous victory in the Manx GP of that year. This led to David Whitworth campaigning a tuned Triumph in 1947 and from this came the Grand Prix model for 1948, a pure road-racing model. It was competitive, fast but fragile.

Partial enclosure went onto the Tiger Cub for some years, with the skirt lines as used by some of the twins, all keeping it in the family.

With the instrument panel no longer set in the tank, a neat parcel grid took its place and proved to be a firm favourite. There was also a new model, the TR5 Trophy for the off-road rider, which used the Speed Twin engine fitted with the alloy top-half in a shorter frame with sports mudguards. The two exhaust pipes curled round to join and run along the machine waist in fine style, while the machine performed well on the road and in trials.

A larger engine had been the cry from the USA for some time and Triumph obliged in 1950 with the 649cc Thunderbird or 6T. It was launched in September 1949 by running three of them round the Montlhéry track for 500 miles (800km) at a running average exceeding 90mph (144km/h) and it introduced a new tank-style with four horizontal styling bars on each side, the same theme decorating the firm's stand at the 1949 Earls Court show. The engine was based on the existing twin, but the gearbox was uprated and the new version used by all models.

A die-cast alloy top-half replaced the older form on the TR5 for 1951 and this also went onto the T100, which was listed with the option of a race kit that year. It was the last year for the 3T, but the kit was listed for three years and, in 1953, there was also a T100c model which was the basic machine plus the race kit, but with full road equipment. It was only listed for the one year but a longer lasting model, first seen that year, was the 149cc Terrier single, listed as the T15.

The machine had the cylinder inclined and the engine built in-unit with its four-speed gearbox. It went into a simple frame with plunger rear-suspension, telescopic fork and a nacelle, so had the looks and lines of the larger twins. In 1954 it was joined by the 199cc Cub or T20 model and, while the Terrier had a short life, the Cub would run on for many years.

Among the twins, the Thunderbird had adopted an SU carburettor for 1952 and the Speed Twin an alternator the next year, with this reaching the 6T in 1954. That year saw other changes, with the Tiger 100 having a pivoted-fork frame and being joined by a larger 649cc version, the Tiger 110, both machines fitted with a dualseat and an 8in front brake. The new frame was used by the touring twins for 1955 and also by the TR5, which was tuned as well but lost some of its charm in the process. It was joined by a 649cc version, the TR6, for 1956 and this machine had a light-alloy cylinder head that was also used for the T110.

This Triumph Tigress scooter was a match to the BSA-Sunbeam machines, other than for colour and badges, both built in two sizes.

By 1949 it was time to move forward and the first result was the appearance of the Triumph nacelle, which cleaned up the front end of the machine by carrying the instruments and headlamp in one unit that blended into the top of the forks and helped to conceal the control cables.

A sports version of the 3TA appeared in 1963 as the Tiger 90, with the skirt enclosure, which was not used for long.

The T120 Bonneville, with unit construction and its usual twin-carburettors, was to become one of the most popular of all Triumphs.

During 1956, American Johnny Allen attacked the world motorcycle speed record and set a figure of 214.5mph (343.2km/h) using a 649cc Triumph engine in a streamlined shell, running on the Bonneville salt flats in Utah. The FIM rejected the claim on spurious grounds relating to the timing gear and Triumph took legal action on this, but to no avail. This followed runs of 193mph (309km/h) in 1955, also rejected, and others in 1958. Finally, in 1962 Bill Johnson ran at 224.57mph (359.31km/h) and had the figure accepted, so Triumph officially held the absolute world record. A twin-engined machine took the figure on to 245mph (392km/h) in 1966, again not recognized, which showed just how good Allen's machine had been.

The Tiger 100 model with twin carburettors was listed as the T100T and as the Daytona, the latter thanks to the US links to that circuit.

Top of the Triumph range in 1969 was the T150 Trident, with three-cylinder engine, the model also built as the BSA Rocket.

There were more changes in 1957, when the Cub went into a pivoted-fork frame and was joined by a competition version, the T20C. All models had a new tank badge and were joined by the 349cc model Twenty-One, so called to celebrate twenty-one years of Triumph Engineering

This Triumph 247cc single was a BSA clone, using the C25 with colour and badge changes in the main, and was built for off-road use.

254 Triumph

Part of the last-ditch efforts of the BSA-Triumph group was a series of machines badged and painted to suit either marque, this one of 247cc.

trend that led away from enclosure to out-and-out sports machines and the café racer.

The second new model was the 5TA, which replaced the old Speed Twin but took over its name, the TR5 also leaving the range. It was just as the 3TA, but with a larger 490cc engine, and kept the amaranth-red finish of the past. The other two models were scooters that mirrored those built as BSA-Sunbeam models. Thus they shared body and much of the mechanics, but had the same choice of 172cc two-stroke or 249cc twin cylinder four-stroke engines. For Triumph they were called the Tigress and finished in shell blue, but had little success in the marketplace. There was a change for the Cub that year, when it was fitted with partial rear enclosure, more a skirt than a bathtub, but in the style of the firm, and during the year the T20S replaced the T20C.

At the start of the new decade the old T100 was replaced by the T100A since the 1936 take over, and that the engine fell into the 21 cubic-inch class in the USA. Elsewhere it was just the 3TA and was a typical Meriden design, but with the four-speed gearbox built in-unit with the engine. Frame, forks, tank, parcel grid and nacelle were all as expected, but where the model differed was in its rear enclosure, which combined a fine line with good weather protection, a trend that Turner thought would flourish. The shape of the enclosure was such that it was soon known as the 'bathtub', thanks to a line akin to the old-fashioned hip-bath.

Four new models appeared in 1959 and by far the most important was the Bonneville T120, for this would become one of the great motorcycles of all time. Based on the Tiger 110, it had the twin-carburettor conversion fitted to its tuned engine and was named to commemorate the world record runs. For the rest it was as the T110, complete with the nacelle for that first year only. It was also in the

The Triumph T150 triple was modified for 1971 and joined by this styled Hurricane version with three pipes on one side in 1973, but used the BSA engine.

in a very different format, for it was based on the 5TA, kept the full enclosure and was finished in black despite being the sports model. In the same year, the 650s all went into a new frame with duplex downtubes, both the 6T and T110 adopting the bathtub. The sports singles changed again for 1961, when the T20T and T20S/L appeared, the latter soon recoded as the T20S/S. The TR6 took a new form for 1961, when it dropped the off-road line and became, effectively, a single-carburettor Bonneville, while the T110 went at the end of the year.

The rather boring T100A was replaced by the T100SS for 1962 and this was fitted with a skirt rather than a bathtub, a siamesed exhaust system, no nacelle and finished in brighter colours to enhance its style. The T20S/S was joined by the T20S/H and the competition versions became the TR20 for trials and TS20 for scrambles. The one new model was the Tina scooter, which had a 100cc two-stroke engine and automatic transmission, but limited appeal.

There was a major change for the big twins for 1963, as they turned to unit construction of engine and gearbox, although the basis of the design remained as it was. The three models stayed in the same format, with the Bonneville the sports machine, the TR6 more the sports tourer and the 6T, now with a skirt in place of the bathtub, the tourer. There was also a new sports 350, listed as the Tiger 90, based on the 3TA and in the style of the T100SS.

This set the firm well on its course for the decade, as the line of models

This 1981 T140ES was a late twin-cylinder Triumph model, which had a 744cc engine and many improvements, but suffered from company ailments.

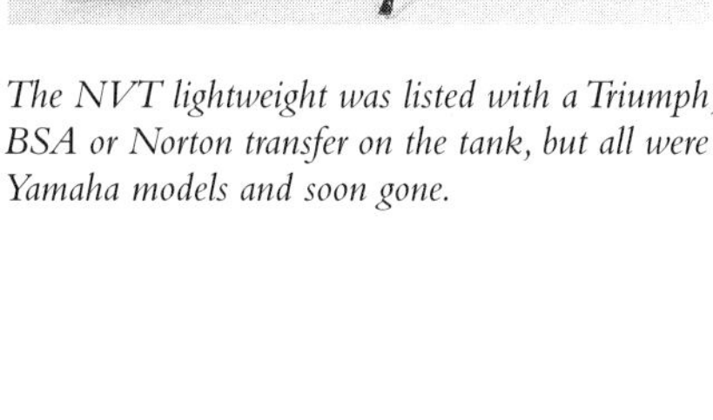

stayed much as it was for some years. There were special versions of the TR6 and T120 for the USA, mainly altered to suit off-road use, variants of the Cub for the same market, the end of the Tigress scooters after 1965, when the Tina became the T10, and the disappearance of the skirts, in time. The Tiger 100 became listed in versions for off-road use in the same way as the 650s and, by 1967, the Thunderbird had been dropped. In that year the single became the Bantam Cub using various BSA parts, and then the Super Cub, its production ceasing after 1969.

A year earlier, for 1968, there was a new Triumph single sold as the TR25W Trophy, but this was really a BSA B25 Starfire with a change of badges and modifications for trail use. Of far more importance was the announcement during the year of the three-cylinder Trident, along with the similar BSA Rocket Three. Although both had a 740cc engine built in-unit with a four-speed gearbox, the Triumph had its cylinders vertical and a line more clearly linked to the familiar one of the twins. The cycle parts were much as for the Bonneville

and the result an impressive and successful machine, but it did not reach the public until 1969 and, by then, had to compete head-on with the new Honda CB750 four. In this it was helped by a successful racing programme.

The range then ran on for 1970 with a major revamp announced at the end of the year, when Triumph and BSA staged a massive launch of their 1971 ranges which included many new models and much common to both marques, with considerable use of common parts such as forks and wheels. Only the Tiger 100 models continued much as they were and this was to be most fortunate. The 650s were given a new frame which carried the engine oil within its tubes and this proved to have too high a seat, so had to be modified. There were two new 247cc unit singles based on the TR25W, but with oil-carrying frames and the same slimline forks and conical hubs that most of the range now had. The machines were the T25SS street scrambler and T25T Trail Blazer models. The Trident ran on with the new forks and wheels, and there was also a

The NVT lightweight was listed with a Triumph, BSA or Norton transfer on the tank, but all were Yamaha models and soon gone.

New firm, new models, new factory, but the old Triumph name; launched by John Bloor in 1990 and still going from strength to strength despite a major fire and other setbacks. Now challenging the opposition, on all counts.

349cc dohc twin shown that was never to go into production. All this was far too much for the production department to cope with at once and the firm was also embroiled in the financial troubles of the BSA group.

By 1972 the singles had been dropped and the seat-height troubles of the 650s solved to some extent, aided by the good news that a five-speed gearbox was available for them and the Trident. The next year saw the off-road version of the Tiger 100 replaced by the Trophy Trail, also listed as the Adventurer but, by 1974, all the 490cc models had been dropped. In 1973 a custom version of the triple was seen, as the X75 Hurricane; its main feature was to have all three exhaust systems on one side and a tank cover that ran back to also form the seat base. It used the BSA engine and frame, plus extended forks for its stylish image. Also new that year was a disc front brake and the first of the larger twins with 744cc engines, as the T140 Bonneville and TR7 Tiger.

Then came the Meriden sit-in, brought about by the problems of the industry, the collapse of the parent BSA company and some political events. It lasted until 1975, when a worker's co-operative was set up at Meriden to build the big twins, while production of the Trident was moved to the BSA Small Heath works under the auspices of NVT. That year the Trident was revised to use the BSA inclined engine with Triumph covers, kept the Triumph frame, and added electric start, rear disc brake and left gear-change to be listed as the T160. As this it ran on to 1976, after which production ceased.

Meanwhile, production of the 650s had effectively come to an end and, from the middle of 1975, only the larger models were built, fitted with a rear disc-brake and left gear-change to suit the USA. The new set-up tried very hard to make a success of the venture, producing a variety of machines using the one engine and gearbox unit. There were two basic models through this period and, for 1976, they were the TR7V Tiger and T140V Bonneville.

In 1977 they were joined by the Silver Jubilee model, in UK and US forms, to celebrate the twenty-five years of the Queen's reign and, for 1978, the Bonneville became the T140E, with changes to allow it to comply with the emission rules in the USA. The next year, 1979, brought the T140D Special with cast-alloy wheels, and electric start appeared on the Bonneville the year after, when the model became the T140ES. There was also the Executive Bonneville that year and this came fitted with a fairing, panniers and top box in its own special colour.

More variants appeared in 1981, with the TR7T Tiger Trail in an off-road format, the TR65 Thunderbird which had the engine size reduced to 649cc and was built as an economy model, and the Royal, to mark the wedding of Prince Charles to Lady Di, again in UK and US forms. Late in the year there came a 649cc version of the Tiger Trail and 1982 brought the TSS, with an eight-valve engine, and the TSX in custom style. Two more models followed in the year, this time with 599cc engines and listed as the Thunderbird 600 and Daytona 600 with different styles.

Sadly all this effort came to nothing, for the firm just ran out of money and had to call in the liquidator, so production came to a halt at the end of the year. However, this was by no means the end of Triumph. The manufacturing rights were bought by John Bloor, who licensed Racing Spares to produce the Bonneville for five years. Run by Les Harris, they built the one model from 1985 to 1988. Meanwhile, Bloor set his team to work to design a completely new range and build a new factory at Hinckley where it would be produced. There was no publicity at all during this stage, so even speculation dried up for want of any facts.

It was not until September 1990 that the new machines were unveiled at the Cologne show and they totalled six in all. They shared a modular design centred on a common bore-size, and thus common pistons and valve gear. Both triples and fours were available, each in two sizes thanks to changes in stroke. All had a common theme with dohc and four-valve heads, liquid cooling, gear primary-drive to the gearbox and chain final-drive. All shared a common frame, forks, wheels and much else, with the individual style achieved by varying the tank, seat and fairing.

The new models sold well and, before long, were joined by others, while the less popular ones were dropped. By 1993 the marque was once more well established and added a trail model. Within the next two years there was also a retro and then a cruiser. In 1997 they added the T595; this broke new ground with a larger engine and new frame. Then came the T509, with a bold, street-fighter style to show how up-to-date the firm was, and how ready to match the rest of the world in its machines.

There was no doubt that John Bloor had revived Triumph and returned it to the important place it had held in the past. In this he carried forward the reputation that had been established at Coventry and Meriden.

However, in 2002, as plans were laid to increase the production area to improve output, a major factory fire occurred that could have been a real set-back to the company. Nothing daunted, they set to and, before the end of the year, in a bare six months, the assembly lines were up and running once again and even improved as planned, to boot. New models continued to flow from the firm, so Triumph were truly back in business as they had been for a century, despite the various traumas along the way.

Trobike were one of many small firms to build mini-bikes for use in the paddock at race meetings or on big estates. It used a Clinton engine.

TROBIKE 1960–1965

This was a mini-bike built at the Trojan works in Croydon, Surrey and sold in kit form. Intended for use in factories, on airfields, at race circuits and mainly large private areas, they could be used for short trips on the road. It had a 94cc Clinton two-stroke engine with an automatic clutch to take the drive to the rear wheel. This was mounted in a simple frame without suspension, other than the fat 5in tyres. The type was quite popular in the USA but less so in Britain, where the Trobike had a short life.

The Trump usually fitted a JAP engine in its early days, this solo has a 4hp single placed vertically in the low frame and with belt final-drive.

TRUMP 1907–1923

Frank A. McNab was the director and main force behind this firm and had many successes with the machines at Brooklands from 1909 on, using a 3.5hp single at first. As early as May that year, he won the 500cc one-hour race to set a new record of over 48 miles (77km). First based in Liphook, in 1912 they moved to the works in Lombard Street, Birmingham, but they also had the Foxdale Works at Byfleet, Surrey, convenient to the track.

They used JAP engines in the main, so were sometimes listed as the Trump-JAP, and, by 1910, their 3.5hp model was offered in two forms, along with a 6hp V-twin. These ran on in the style of the era on Druid forks with belt drive for the next year or so. For 1913 the range was extended to add 3.25 and 8hp V-twins, but, for 1914, it was just a 4hp single and 6hp V-twin.

During 1914 they added the Trump-Peco, fitted with the 349cc two-stroke engine of that name, an Albion two-speed gearbox and belt final-drive; single and three-speed versions were also available. A 208cc version was added to the 1915 list, which included several sizes of V-twin.

After the Great War, it was mid-1921 before they returned, as Trump Motors Ltd of Byfleet, Surrey, with McNab involved in design and track-work, but control of the firm lay with Col R.N. Stewart, a prominent figure in motor record-breaking activities at the time. Not surprisingly, a 976cc JAP V-twin sports model was the first offering, soon to be joined by a 548cc sv JAP single with Sturmey-Archer gearbox and close ratios an option. By 1922 the range comprised 292, 346 and 490cc sv singles, plus 747 and 976cc sv V-twins, all of JAP manufacture. This was slimmed down for the next year to the 346cc sv single, in standard or sports trim, and the two sizes of V-twin, plus another with a 994cc ohv Anzani engine. This was the swan song, as McNab had retired early in 1923 due to ill-health and the marque itself succumbed soon after.

TURNER 1946

This was an eccentricity seen in Brussels in April 1946 labelled the Turner Byvan. It was powered by a 126cc Royal Enfield wartime Flying Flea engine unit with its three-speed gearbox, of which there must have been a good few lying around in the immediate post-war period. This was mounted on top of the pressed-steel front forks and drove the wheel by chain. The rest of the machine was simply a large box, which had the forks fitted to it, provided a mounting for a wheel at the rear and a seat for the rider on top. This made it a large parcel carrier, but it was just too radical and no more was heard of it.

TURNER SPECIAL 1927

The twenties witnessed numerous attempts by would-be engine designers to get their ideas translated from paper into metal, but few of them were to succeed. A 1925 attempt at a 348cc single cylinder ohc design with gear drive to the camshaft, by Mr. Edward Turner of Rye Hill Park, London, was one such failure, but two years later the same designer partially succeeded with an alternative design in an identical capacity.

This time a vertical shaft replaced the gears, carrying both cams at its upper end and positioned horizontally. These were contacted by short pushrods, which applied pressure to the outer end of each rocker, the other rocker-end bearing upon the valve stem, the valves being inclined at 80 degrees. Lubrication was assured by means of a Best & Lloyd mechanical pump, and ball or roller bearings were used on the crankshaft. An unusual two-port exhaust arrangement led the gases away through open pipes. This engine was then shown fitted into an experimental machine, in which a loop frame supported the motor at three points. Webb front forks and 7in-diameter brakes from the same maker, together with a twistgrip-controlled Amac carburettor, three-speed Sturmey-Archer gearbox and a nickel-plated petrol tank of saddle type were the main features. A separate 6-pint (3.3ltr) oil tank on the saddle downtube completed the purposeful air of the Turner Special.

In this form the machine was included in the major 1927 *Buyers Guide* during February of that year and priced at £75, however it is doubtful if further examples were made or sold. Mr Turner, though, wasn't out of the news for long, for within a couple more years his name would be closely associated with Ariel and the revolutionary Square Four. This was followed later by his even more important Speed Twin parallel-twin design for Triumph and the rest, of course, is, as they say, history!

TUSROKE 1919
Built by a company in Luton, Bedfordshire, whose main interest was in manufacturing and supplying their two-stroke engine for use in portable generating sets. The 350cc engine fitted into a frame with curved front downtube, but was otherwise of conventional appearance. Druid front forks and either direct-belt drive or a two-speed Albion gearbox with chain-cum-belt transmission could be specified.

TYLER 1913
The Tyler Apparatus Co. of Gerrard Street, London, began by offering their lightweights with a choice of Precision two-stroke or four-stroke engines, both in a form of unit construction with their two-speed gearbox. Under this name they had limited sales but on changing to the Metro engine were more successful as Metro-Tyler.

U

UNECAR 1909–1912
Made by W.W. Bannister of Maidstone, Kent, this was a tricycle having a motorcycle front end coupled to two rear wheels that had the seat mounted between them. A 3.5hp engine and two-speed gear were used, the engine mounted on the right of the driver's footwell, and transmission was by belt. For 1911 a 4.25hp Fafnir engine was fitted and this continued for 1912, their last year.

UNIBUS 1920–1922
Built by Gloucester Aircraft, this scooter was designed by Harold Boultbee and the result was one of the best of that period. Unlike most, it had enclosure in the modern style and a flat floor behind the apron, the body sitting on a channel-section frame with leaf-spring suspension for both 16in pressed-steel split-rim wheels.

The 269cc two-stroke engine sat just behind the headstock, with the crankshaft on the machine axis. The magneto went in front and a clutch and two-speed gearbox behind, this then driving a shaft running back to an underslung worm at the rear wheel. The worm wheel housing incorporated two sets of brake shoes in the rear hub.

The Unibus was an advanced design but too expensive for its market, so soon gone.

The Unibus scooter of 1920 had a modern style, shaft drive, front and rear suspension, pressed-steel wheels and 269cc engine at the front.

• V •

VAL 1914
A small Birmingham firm who offered a 3.5hp single-cylinder model with fixed-belt drive just before the Great War. Really a sidecar firm, their solo probably used a stock JAP engine and its dated specification meant that it did not survive for long.

VASCO 1921–1923
Built by C.E. Taylor at premises in Kingston, Surrey and ridden successfully by him in several long-distance reliability trials, the Vasco marque nevertheless had but a small impact on the British market. The machine was constructed along established lines and had a 349cc single-cylinder Broler two-stroke engine with the then usual choice of single-speed, plain two-speed, two-speed with clutch and kickstart, or three-speed transmissions. All had belt final-drive and a complete sidecar combination was also listed in the three-speed form.

VAUXHALL 1921–1922
This was the product of the famous car firm who sought something to build just after the Great War. They called in Major Halford of Ricardo to design them a prestige machine, one to be better than the norm of the time. He did just this and a pilot batch of six was laid down, although only two were completed.

The design was one of the most advanced of its day, for it had a four-cylinder air-cooled engine set along the frame and drove a car-type three-speed gearbox with shaft final-drive to a worm rear-axle. The 945cc engine had an equal bore and stroke, fully enclosed ohv, timing gear to camshaft and ignition system at the front, and wet-sump lubrication.

The engine unit went into a duplex cradle frame with leading-link front forks in the American style. On each side went cast-alloy footboards, with that on the left the silencer and the other a toolbox. A saddle tank, complete with the Vauxhall flutes as on their car bonnets, was fitted and had the gear lever working in a gate at its rear, behind a housing for the speedometer and electric switch.

It was a great design, being smooth, quiet, flexible and capable of 80mph (128km/h). It would also have been expensive to produce and times were not right for such a machine, so it never went into production. One still exists.

VELOCETTE 1905–1971 AND 1998
This firm was always run by the Goodman family, who came from Germany in the nineteenth century and changed their name from Gütgemann, at first to Taylor. They were innovators and always sought the best solution to their problems, utilizing good materials and sound engineering practices. The result was a quality product, sometimes really a little too good for their customers to afford.

They traded initially as Taylor Gue and their first motorcycle came in 1905 with a 2hp engine and belt drive, and was sold as the Veloce. Unsuccessful, it was soon dropped and it was 1910 when their next model appeared. This had a 2.5hp engine with overhead inlet- and side exhaust-valves, mechanical lubrica-

The first Velocette of 1905, with 2hp engine and belt drive, was sold as a Veloce by Taylor Gue after two name changes for firm and family.

The 1912 Veloce engine unit had the two speeds built into the crankcase with pedal control, overhead inlet-valve and mechanical lubrication.

tion, outside flywheel and an overhung crankshaft. It drove a two-speed gearbox built in-unit in the front of the crankcase with belt final-drive. This sophisticated unit went into a rigid frame with Druid forks.

As an alternative to this advanced model, there was a 3.5hp machine of conventional construction, with this also listed in Colonial form. A ladies' version of the 2.5hp, with an open frame, was offered in 1912 and continued up to 1916, with the engine enlarged in 1914, when the other models were dropped. The engine was further increased in size to 3.5hp for one machine that was run in the 1913 TT, but with little success.

In 1913 the firm changed direction and produced the first in a long series of two-strokes that would run for many years. Rated at 2.25hp and of 220cc, it kept the overhung crankshaft and had a lubrication system that carried the oil in a chamber in the crankcase and fed it to the big end. This was a major improvement on the usual petroil mixture. The engine went into a rigid frame fitted with

This was the final form of the early Velocette two-stroke models with overhung crankshaft, the model USS of 1929, soon to be replaced.

Druid forks and was set over to the right to keep the final drive tucked well in to reduce the transmission loads on the main bearing. Either direct-belt drive or a two-speed gearbox and all-chain drive was offered, but neither had a clutch. Because the machines were lightweights they were listed as Velocette models rather than Veloce and thus was born one of motorcycling's most famous names.

In 1924, the 348cc model K, for Kamshaft, made its debut and its success soon led to this KTT racing model of the early 1930s, the first of a long line.

The first two-stroke was soon joined by others, with a ladies' version appearing in 1914, before war brought production to a halt. Postwar, in 1919, the model was back with a drum rear-brake but otherwise little changed. It was soon joined by others that had a new frame, Brampton forks, a revised lubrication system and a circular door on the crankcase for access to the big end. By 1921 there were three speeds, but still no clutch, and a front drum-brake. They returned to the TT once more and took a third in the 1921 and 1922 lightweight races.

It was in 1922 that the famous Velocette clutch made its first appearance. It was a brilliant design that fitted into the small space that existed between the inboard primary and outboard final drives, this being essential to avoid having to either move the engine across the frame, alter the gearbox or increase the main-bearing loads. It would remain a legend and mystery to owners to the firm's last days and beyond. That year also saw the first of the Sports models that had a larger 249cc engine, a capacity that would remain for the rest of the decade.

The Velocette two-stroke was much modified for the 1930s as the 249cc GTP, with pump lubrication from the start and throttle regulated from 1932.

Variations continued to be offered, with two or three speeds, economy and colonial models, and a steady improvement of frame, forks, brakes and fittings. By 1927 there was just the model U that took over from the rest, with many engine improvements, three speeds, Webb forks, larger brakes and a saddle tank. There were also sports and economy versions and this took the two-stroke Velocette to 1929, but before then there had come a much more interesting model.

Back in 1924 the firm had run an advanced two-stroke in the TT, but its temperamental behaviour persuaded

Drive side view of the Velocette KTS model for 1934, showing the final-drive outboard of the clutch and the forward drive to the dynamo.

In 1933 a new Velocette line was born with overhead valves, the 248cc MOV, in a form to expand to 499cc and run to the end of the firm.

them to change to a four-stroke, and an advanced one at that, to ensure plenty of power for then and the future. They therefore settled on an overhead-camshaft design and the result was a classic.

The new machine was the model K and its engine was of 348cc with the camshaft driven by shaft and bevels. The crankcase was extremely narrow, with the main bearings tucked right under the walls of the cylinder, so in the best place to carry the loads placed upon them. This arrangement was dictated by the need to retain the existing chain lines and

Leading Velocette rider Ted Mellor won the 350 and 500cc classes of the 1937 French Grand Prix on his Velocettes.

would remain a feature of the Velocette single. The magneto was chain driven and went behind the cylinder, the gearbox had three speeds and the cycle side was well made and conventional. There were Druid forks at first, with Webb from 1928, and big drum-brakes. The first machines went out under the Veloce label, but this

The fabulous Mk VIII KTT Velocette won races before and after the war. The outboard clutch is clearly to be seen, also the rear units.

was quickly changed to Velocette under demand from the dealers and thanks to the high regard for the two-strokes.

The firm entered the 1925 Junior TT without success and then developed the engine using a stroboscope that allowed them to watch it operating at speed but in slow motion. The troubles and their remedies were thus brought to light and, in 1926, they had Alec Bennett in the TT and he won by over ten minutes. He won again in 1928, while Freddie Hicks took the win in 1929 to make it three wins in four years. The first success brought such a demand for Velocettes that they had to move to larger premises at Hall Green, Birmingham in 1927. Twice second in those events was Harold Willis, who played a large part in Velocette fortunes as an innovative engineer with a dry sense of humour, who would dub machines and their parts with evocative names. Double knocker for twin-cam engines was one such, while a piston was a cork and a horse a hay-motor.

The model K was soon joined by the sports KSS, which had a tuned engine, narrow mudguards and a larger fuel tank. In 1927 there came the KS which combined the style of the KSS with the cheaper K engine to cut the price, and the KT for touring, which was the K model fitted with leg shields and footboards. There were also the KE and KES economy models for 1928 only.

During 1928 Willis ran a machine with rear suspension in the TT, this

Velocette innovation brought the Roarer, with twin cylinders and geared crankshafts, one driving the supercharger and other the transmission.

Close up of a 1949 Mk VIII engine showing camshaft drive, magneto drive, oil drains from cambox and other details.

Post-war Velocette innovation produced the 150cc LE, with water-cooled flat-twin engine, shaft drive, some enclosure and many other features.

Pre-war, the MOV had been stretched to the 349cc MAC and then the 495cc MSS, this example being the 1951 MAC with rigid frame.

known as Spring-Heeled Jack, but of more lasting importance was his design of a positive-stop, foot-change mechanism for the gearbox. Now universal, it introduced a great time saver in racing, as well as a good safety measure as the riders kept their hand on the bars. Late in the year the new gear-change went on sale on a new model, the racing KTT that was, in essence, the TT winner with some changes. In this way the private owner could now buy a machine with a real chance of finishing well in any eligible event.

A new two-stroke was introduced for the new decade as the 249cc GTP. This differed from the past, in having a two-bearing crankshaft and coil ignition, but kept the pump lubrication with this amended to be regulated by throttle control from 1932, in the manner of engines some thirty years later. The cycle side was conventional, with Webb forks and three speeds at first with four speeds and foot-change to come later. In this way it was built through the decade, with a brief post-war appearance.

In 1930 the KTP joined the other camshaft models with coil ignition and twin exhausts, but was not popular with enthusiasts for the marque. The next year brought improvements

The 1954 MSS Velocette, with rear suspension and humped dualseat, made a fine touring machine.

for the KTT, a supercharged engine and a 350cc sv prototype, which lacked performance so never reached production. In 1932 the KTS became the touring model, with larger mudguards and different wheel sizes from the similar KSS sports version.

A new Velocette design appeared in 1933, when the firm introduced the MOV with ohv. It was intended to fill the gap between the GTP models and the expensive K-series, while offering a good performance and build standard. The engine followed many of the principles of the camshaft type, with the narrow and tall crankcase giving good support to the cylinder. The capacity was 248cc, the bore and stroke being close to identical, and the valves were opened by a camshaft mounted high in the timing chest and driven by a helical gear-train that continued on to the rear-mounted magneto. The dynamo was belt driven and clamped to the front of the crankcase.

It was a classic design and one that the firm would run to the end of their days. The engine drove a four-speed gearbox and went into a frame based on that intended for the 350cc sv engine. It was most successful and was joined by the 349cc MAC in 1934, the extra capacity coming from an extended stroke. In this form it was just as popular as the MOV and also much less expensive than the K-models.

The next stretch came in 1935, when the MAC engine was bored out to 495cc and the result listed as the MSS, all three with the same line and much the same specification, but the MSS had heavier frame, forks and cycle parts. In 1936 the KSS and KTS were altered to Mk II form, with an alloy cylinder-head with fully enclosed valve gear, which went into the MSS frame set.

The four-speed gearbox of the Valiant went into the LE for 1958, when it took Mk III form with the 192cc engine, kickstart and the two-level seat.

By 1959, most of the big singles could be equipped with side covers to shroud the mechanics – and save the cost of polishing them!

Progressive KTT development had led to the adoption of Mk numbers and, by early 1938, it became the Mk VII and had a massive alloy-head with the valve gear fully enclosed. Late that year this was replaced by the Mk VIII, which finally gave the model pivoted-fork rear suspension, controlled by Dowty Oleomatic units that used air as the spring and oil for damping. It was based on the machine that had won the 1938 Junior TT and also won in 1939, in both cases ridden by Stanley Woods.

In 1939 the firm showed just how innovative it could be, with two twins, one for racing and the other for the road. In both cases the cylinders sat side by side in normal vertical-twin fashion, but each had its own crankshaft set along the frame. These were geared together, one side driving back to the four-speed gearbox and thence by shaft to the rear wheel. On the racer the other crankshaft drove a supercharger, for this machine was to take on the blown multis from Europe, and on the road model it drove the generator.

The racing twin was called the Roarer and had cylinder heads based on the KTT, rear-facing exhausts and rear suspension. It practised in the 1939 TT but was never raced. The road machine was the model O and featured rear suspension with units whose angle could be varied to suit the load carried, thanks to slots in arc-form for the top mounting. Only the prototype was made, but the suspension principle was used post-war.

During the war the firm built some machines based on the MAC, these being the MDD for the French and the MAF, which mainly went to the RAF. Post-war they continued where they had left off, with the three M-series models, a batch of GTP machines and the KSS. In 1947 some Mk VIII KTT racing machines were produced, while for 1948 the road models turned to Dowty Oleomatic forks in place of the Webb girders. By the end of that year only the MAC and KTT remained in the list, for they were to be joined by a completely new and different Velocette model.

This was the famous LE, which was small, smooth and ultra-quiet, aimed at the mass market and meant to be easy and clean to ride. Thus, it aimed at the 'Everybody' market so often expected to produce real volume sales, but it was to take the scooterette to achieve this. For all that, the LE was a brilliant attempt by a relatively small firm which came very close to succeeding.

The machine had a 149cc flat-twin engine with side valves and water

The Valiant joined the Velocette range in 1957, and was based on the later 192cc LE but with air cooling, ohv and four speeds.

The Venom and smaller Viper were Velocette's sports machines from 1956, this being the Venom Clubman of 1960, a highly desirable machine.

cooling. This drove back to a three-speed gearbox with hand change and a car-type gate, and thence on by shaft to the rear wheel. Starting was by a hand lever and the whole assembly hung from a steel pressing that included the massive rear mudguard. Telescopic forks went at the front and rear suspension was by pivoted fork, controlled by units with adjustment of their angle as on the model O. Wire wheels with drum brakes were used to give motorcycle handling and control. There were built in legshields and footboards, but the result was rather expensive and angular in line, so unable to really compete with the chic scooters that were soon to arrive from Italy.

Not that the firm lacked publicity, for they won the Junior TT in 1947, 1948 and 1949, along with the first 350cc world title, when Freddie Frith won all five races, Bob Foster taking the 1950 crown on his Velocette. In 1951 the LE was enlarged to 192cc and the MAC changed to an alloy head and barrel. By 1953 it was listed with rear suspension as well as in rigid form and in the next year was joined by a new version of the MSS in the spring frame. For 1955 the MSS was offered additionally as the 500 Scrambler with tuned engine and cycle parts to suit, with a similar Endurance model for the USA appearing for the next year.

The major Velocette news for 1956 was the launch of two sports models, based on the existing MSS and listed as the 349cc Viper and 499cc Venom. Both took the well-developed ohv engine and kept the good four-speed gearbox and special Velocette clutch. Frame construction continued to be by the older tube-and-lug method but was of the best quality, as were the forks, rear suspension and wheels. Along with the two new models came a 350 Scrambler, and all three off-road machines would continue on to the late-1960s, the Scramblers with a revised frame for 1959.

Another ill-advised venture was the 1964 Vogue, which clothed LE mechanics with glass-fibre and style, but brought few sales.

Before then, in 1957, there came the Valiant, which was based on the LE but amended to make it a sports model. To this end it kept the flat-twin engine, but changed to ohv and air cooling, and mated this with a four-speed gearbox with foot change, while the shaft drive was kept, these mechanics fitting into a tubular frame with rear fork and fixed rear units. It was sophisticated but expensive, and the size went against it, for buyers either chose a cheaper 200 or opted for a 250 of similar price but better performance. Unfortunately it was not possible to open the engine out to 250cc and the firm did not choose to revive the MOV by using a short-stroke MAC engine.

For 1958 the LE was given the four speeds and foot change plus kick starter of the Valiant and in this form was taken up by many police forces around the country, for it could cover a beat so quickly and quietly. The traditional policeman's tall helmet was adapted for protection and the term 'Noddy Bike' was soon commonly in use. The next year brought the Valiant Veeline, which came with a dolphin fairing as standard, while the Viper and Venom were fitted with glass-fibre side panels to shield the lower part of the engine and the gearbox. For those who wished, these could be left off, as they were anyway on the Clubman version.

This was really the start of the time when the firm would produce its two sports singles in a variety of guises, but all essentially much the same. Thus there was the basic Viper and Venom, the Clubman, the Veeline with fairing, the Clubman Veeline and the Special, which was an economy job. Built at different times, some would run to the end of the 1960s while others had a shorter life or were replaced by newer versions. All were promoted by one remarkably standard Venom that was taken to Montlhéry early in 1961, where a team of riders broke the world 24-hour record at just over 100mph (160km/h). While the outright figure was increased later that year, the 500cc record remains with Velocette.

It was also in 1961 that the firm introduced their last really new model and, to the disgust of enthusiasts, it was the Viceroy scooter. It used a 247cc two-stroke flat-twin engine with reed valves, shaft drive and four-speed gearbox. Built as Velocette thought a scooter should be, it was a massive machine and came at a time when the market was shrinking, so sales were poor. A further venture into ideals came in 1964 in the form of the Vogue, which was, in essence, a LE engine unit in a new frame, with a glass-fibre body with twin headlights, screen, legshields and optional panniers. It was stylish but had little impact on the market.

Velocette fans were much better pleased when the firm reverted to

The 1961 Viceroy scooter was one of Velocette's worst mistakes, for it was just too massive to compete with Italian scooters.

The last Velocette was perhaps the best of all; the Thruxton single, which was based on the Venom but had all the desirable parts added.

their true nature in 1965 with the Thruxton single, which was based on the Venom but had various high-performance parts incorporated into it. It became the epitome of the sports British single with its lithe lines and ability to cover ground quickly.

However, times were poor for Velocette, as sales of the LE faded, they lost money on the Viceroy and Vogue, and the market for sports singles with all their funny ways shrank with buyers turning more to multis with their easy starting. Some ground was recovered in 1969, when Floyd Clymer arranged for Italjet to build the Indian Velocette. This took the 499cc engine and fitted it into an Italian duplex frame with wheels, forks and brakes from the same country. It was lighter and worked well, but when Clymer died in 1970 so did the project, although some machines were built.

By late in 1970 the firm was close to the end and, early in the next year, went into liquidation. True to their principles, all debts were settled by the Goodman family, but it was a sad end for such an enterprising firm. Their singles are now amongst the best regarded in classic circles.

The rights to the name and trademark passed to Matt Holder and then on to his son David, so that spares continued to be available. Then Simon Goodman, a direct relative of the family who had been making engine spares for some years, was given permission by David to use the Velocette name on a complete machine.

The result was seen at the 1998 Classic Bike show at Stafford and was a 500cc road model using a revised form of the Thruxton engine, in the marque image. A street-scrambler version was also planned.

VELOSOLEX 1948–1957
A French design, always sold as a complete machine, although of the cycle-attachment type. The 45cc two-stroke engine sat above the front wheel, which it drove by friction roller, and the bicycle had an open frame based on a single curved tube. Built in vast numbers in its homeland, it was also made by Solex in North London for some years until the moped took over.

The Velosolex was a French design that was sold in massive numbers all over Europe, including by a firm in North London. It was always mounted over the front wheel.

VENUS 1920–1922
This firm differed a little from most of those that set up in the early post-war days to produce lightweight motorcycles. While they kept to the norm of fitting a two-stroke engine, they chose the 318cc Dalm rather than the more common Villiers. In other respects they followed the usual format during their brief life.

VERUS 1919–1926
The de luxe marque of the Alfred Wiseman company, whose standard brand went under the Sirrah name. Lightweights with 211 and 269cc Verus two-stroke engines began the line in 1919, the smaller with a single speed, the other with a Burman two-speed gearbox and chain-cum-belt. These were retained for 1920 and joined by two Blackburne four-strokes, a 348 and 499cc sv with two- and three-speed Burman boxes respectively. It was the same again in 1921, when trials were conducted with V-twin Blackburne-engined sidecar outfits, and into 1922, when the very simple lightweight and the 499cc Blackburne models went, but the 348 four-stroke was given the option of a three-speed gear and all-chain drive. Only the four-strokes lasted to 1923, with extra models being introduced with 248 and 348cc ohv Blackburne and 248 and 346cc JAP motors. This range was carried through to 1924, when the universal Wiseman tubular-frame with but a single welded joint appeared on both Verus and Sirrah ranges and, for the 348cc ohv Blackburne sports model, there was a high-level exhaust pipe running along the offside of the machine – certainly setting a vogue, to be followed by many others in the years ahead. A smaller 292cc sv JAP machine came for 1925 only and, into its last season, 1926, the range was reduced to just two, a 348cc sv Blackburne and 344cc ohv JAP. Both had three-speeds and the Burman boxes, which had been the almost exclusive choice throughout the period of production.

VICTA 1912–1913
An assembler of bought-in parts much as many in those years, in this case using the 3.5hp Precision engine. Possibly built to order with a variety of transmission options ranging from direct-belt drive to three-speed hub gear.

VICTORIA 1902–1928
A Scottish firm, based in Dennistoun, Glasgow, who made their own frames to carry the bought-in engines and other components. Their machines were typical of the time but of excellent quality, gradually improving technically over the years.

266 Victoria – Vincent-HRD

This is a very early Victoria machine, with its engine mounted high inside the frame, to drive the rear wheel by belt over a tension pulley.

They added a lightweight, two-stroke model at the late-1908 Stanley show, this having a 143cc engine, a Ruthardt magneto and the option of a drop frame to provide a ladies' model. Conventional lines continued and, by 1912, they were using Precision engines along with an Armstrong three-speed rear hub. To these were added a Precision V-twin, Villiers two-stroke and a 2hp lightweight for 1914, and this carried them to 1915.

This marque was built in Glasgow along conventional lines up to the start of the Great War; in this case, a 1913 Victoria using a Precision engine and direct-belt drive is shown.

Post-war, they offered a small range using 147 and 247cc Villiers engines plus a choice of transmissions, but augmented this in 1924 with four-stroke models using JAP power. This consolidated to 147, 247 and 343cc Villiers, plus 293 and 596cc JAP by 1925, by when they all had three speeds but only three had all-chain drive. This line ran on little altered up to 1928.

VILLIERS-STRAND 1914
As with the Governor-Villiers, this was an assembled model built in Britain specifically for the empire market but, in this case, Australia rather than New Zealand. Yet another lightweight using the 269cc Villiers two-stroke engine and belt drive.

VIN c.1912
A rare make that had a 573cc ohv single engine, a two-speed Jardine gearbox and all-chain drive. The petrol tank followed the line of the drop-frame top-tube, so had a distinct kink in it. Braced forks were in the Druid form, but with their one spring located inside the steering column. Possibly a London marque.

VINCENT-HRD 1928–1955
When Philip Vincent bought HRD in 1928 he already had firm ideas regarding motorcycle construction and had built his first machine. As with all that would carry his name, it had pivoted-fork rear suspension controlled by springs under the seat. Thanks to family money, he was in a position to buy an existing business and, as a fan of Howard Davies and his machines, the choice was easy.

The young company managed to attend the late-1928 Olympia show and all the models had rear suspension, the design in the form it would keep, to disguise it and give the looks of a rigid frame. This was done to combat the real prejudice against rear springing at that time. Engines were a

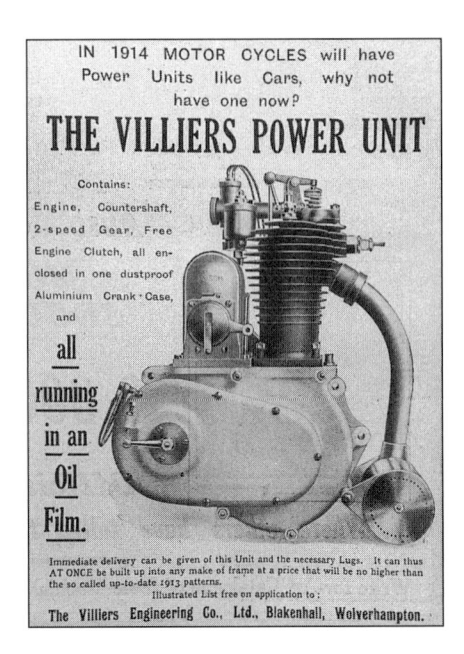

Not the 269cc two-stroke Villiers engine, but their first motorcycle engine, which was built as a unit and so was just right for Villiers-Strand.

variety of 346 and 490cc ohv, and 490 and 596cc sv JAP units driving a three-speed Burman gearbox, but no orders were taken at the show.

Gradually the message spread that the Vincent-HRD machines worked well, despite their spring frame, and sales were made in small numbers, slowly increasing. JAP engines continued to power them but were mainly replaced by the Rudge Python in 1932.

Late in 1931 Phil Irving joined the firm and set about redesigning the

From the start, the Vincent-HRD had rear suspension in a form that would continue right through the range. Early models used the JAP engine.

By the 1930s Vincent had cleaned up the rear suspension lines, but was still using the 490cc JAP engines, this machine from 1935.

plenty of torque but not much power. The Rapide was quite different, for it had the power and proved very fast indeed. In fact, the power was too much for the transmission and clutch slip was the usual result of too much sustained heavy use.

Motorcycle production ceased late in 1939, as the firm turned to war work, and the two Phils began to plan for the future. Their aim was to produce a grand tourer, well able to cruise at 80mph (128km/h) on the pool petrol then available, a top speed around 110mph (176km/h), fine acceleration and effortless to ride.

A close-up of the engine unit of the 998cc V-twin Vincent-HRD of pre-war days reveals a lot of external pipes, which gave it the 'plumber's nightmare' name.

The basis was the pre-war Rapide engine, which kept the 998cc capacity and the valve-gear concept, but was otherwise new. It was lighter, compact and had the four-speed

By removing the rear cylinder and adding a strut and separate gearbox, the 499cc Comet single was created, with almost all the rest unchanged.

gearbox built in-unit with it. The valve gear was fully enclosed, the magneto went in front of the crankcase, a triplex chain drove the gearbox and the clutch had a servo action to enable it to transmit the power while remaining light in action.

The engine was only part of the new design, for the team found it impossible to fit it into a frame with a downtube without extending the wheelbase. From this came the solution of using the engine as a stressed member, with the cylinder heads attached to a beam above it. This beam doubled as the oil tank and joined the headstock to the top end of the rear suspension. The rear fork triangle attached to the rear of the engine structure and its upper tubes carried the rear mounting of the dual-seat that thus moved with the suspension to some extent. At the front went Brampton girders and both wheels had twin brake-drums.

frame into the format it would keep pre-war. A lightweight with a Villiers engine was listed but not produced for 1933, and then revised to water-cooling and fitted into a model with extensive enclosure for the next year. By then the larger models were fitted with Vincent's Duo-brakes with two drums on each hub, but all this was simply setting the scene for the great days to come for the firm.

In 1934 Phil Vincent decided to design and make his own engines in order to be independent of outside suppliers. The result incorporated his ideas with Phil Irving's considerable engineering experience and practical outlook, and they designed a 499cc high-camshaft ohv single with short pushrods that worked in splayed-out tubes up to the rockers that ran across the head. In the head, each valve had a two-piece guide and a groove for the rocker end that worked between the guides, while the hairpin valve-springs went above the rocker and were fully exposed. For the rest, the engine was simple and robust with a deep crankcase and rigid construction.

The engine was built in three states of tune and the machines they fitted into were the Meteor, Comet and racing TT models with the spring frame and Duo-brakes. They made a real impact on the scene and, in 1937, were joined by the famous Rapide, with its 998cc V-twin engine that used two Meteor top-halves on a common crankcase. The result was a remarkably compact engine unit and this resulted in a reasonable wheelbase at a time when the big V-twin engine had become identified with the sidecar as a workhorse with

By 1934, Vincent was determined to build his own engine and this was the early result, with high camshaft and rigid, robust construction.

The Vincent Rapide was much cleaned up for the post-war years and came back as the Model B, with girder forks and then the Girdraulics as shown here.

The new Rapide was the Series B model, the pre-war being A, and the first was completed in May 1946 with production starting later that year. It was advertised as 'the world's fastest standard motorcycle – this is a fact, not a slogan', and road-test reports of 112mph (179km/h) supported this, while the machine proved to be the high-speed tourer Phil Vincent wanted. Early in 1948 the Rapide was joined by the faster Black Shadow, with improved engine and well able to top 120mph (192km/h). One of its most visible features was a large, 150mph (240km/h) speedometer mounted on top of the forks.

In 1949 the firm's name became Vincent without the HRD and the two twins were joined by Series C versions that had new Girdraulic forks. These were of the girder type, as the two Phils thought little of telescopics, with forged alloy blades, immense strength and the ability to be revised easily to give sidecar trail in place of solo. A third V-twin was added as the Black Lightning and was to racing specification, while the single re-appeared as a Series B Meteor and a Series C Comet. For this Phil Irving replaced the rear cylinder of the twin with an alloy member and used a Burman gearbox.

In 1950 they were joined by the racing Grey Flash single, campaigned with much success by John Surtees. The twin was better known for sprinting and George Brown won many of these, as well as setting world records on his specials. There were also road-racing successes, including the Clubmans' TT.

The Series C models continued much as they were to 1954, but the firm found it ever harder to build machines to their high standards at an affordable price. To help with the finance they began to sell the Firefly 48cc two-stroke clip-on engine in 1953, taking this over from Miller electrical. In 1954 they augmented this with a deal to sell NSU machines; while the Quickly moped was a success, the other models proved to be too expensive for their market.

Last of the mighty Vincents was the Model D with its full fairing, to give a grand tourer, which was what the firm always aimed to build.

In 1955 Vincent launched their Series D range, which had full enclosure, fairing and screen using glass-fibre mouldings. This took the grand tourer concept on further, but achieving the high standard of surface finish they sought on the moulding proved difficult. As a stop-gap, some machines were built without the enclosure, but in a revised form that lacked the lithe lines of earlier models. By then the company was in financial trouble and this brought motorcycle production to an end late in 1955.

VINCO 1903–1905

This make was built in Elton, near Peterborough in Cambridgeshire by

The Vincent Firefly was never mentioned in club circles, and this 50cc engine that clipped to a standard bicycle did little for the firm.

W.R. Heighton Ltd, using a Minerva 2.75hp engine hung from the downtube. One such was used by B.C. Holmes in an End-to-End attempt in 1903, but he fell near Warrington and had to give up when well inside record time. A 3.5hp model was added for 1904, plus a forecar powered by a 4hp Rex engine that was also sold as a Heighton.

VINDEC 1902–1929

This was a marque name used by Brown Brothers of Great Eastern Street, London, who were suppliers of parts and fittings as well as the Brown motorcycle. The Vindec name was not advertised or used much until late in 1914, when it appeared on a 225cc two-stroke model that had a two-speed gearbox and chain-cum-belt transmission. At the same time they listed a 4hp V-twin, with an overhead inlet-valve, Bosch magneto and various transmission options. The two-stroke was still listed for 1916, when the V-twin had a 6hp JAP engine driving a three-speed Sturmey-Archer gearbox.

Post-war, they listed a 225cc two-stroke single and then added a 976cc sv JAP V-twin for 1920. These continued through to 1922, but the two-stroke was replaced for 1923 by a 292cc sv JAP model, attractively finished in art grey. As Brown Brothers were trade wholesalers rather than producers, it is probable that most Vindec machines were bought-in designs from established manufacturers, finished and badged for sale under the Vindec name. By way of example, the models from this era can be seen to bear a strong family resemblance to those of the Rex-Acme factory.

In 1924 the big twin went and a 170cc two-stroke joined the JAP single for the one season. The twin returned for 1925 only, along with the 292cc sv model, which, for 1926, was enlarged to 300cc, and another lightweight two-stroke, this one of 147cc, was tried. Again, this lasted but a single season, and so it was the 300cc sv JAP machine that carried them through into 1929 and their final year.

VINDEC SPECIAL (VS) 1903–1914

These machines were sold by the South London Trading Co. of Wilson Street, Finsbury, London, but were actually made by Allright of Cologne in Germany. Built in the British style, the early machine was a typical primitive with a Belgian 2.75hp FN engine, belt drive and unbraced forks, but had contracting-band brakes on both wheels.

A 1904 Vindec Special sold by a firm in London, but actually made by Allright of Cologne in Germany using a FN engine from Belgium.

This model was soon joined by a 3.5hp single and a 5hp V-twin with a 45-degree Peugeot engine. Front suspension using Truffault leading-link forks was an option for all, while, for 1906, magneto ignition was fitted as standard. That year also brought a two-speed rear hub with chain drive from the crankshaft.

The marque was promoted in competition and was present at the first TT in 1907, when Billy Wells was second in the twin class. Early in 1908 a private match race at Brooklands, the first two-wheeled event on the track, saw Oscar Bickford second, using his Vindec Special with its Peugeot V-twin engine.

For 1909 the range comprised 3.5hp singles and V-twins of 5 and 7hp, and advertised as the Vindec Motor Cycle Co., still at the same address. By late in the year the name was changed to V.S. Cycle & Motor Co. in Great Portland Street, London, to avoid confusion with the Vindec name used by Brown Brothers.

The 1910 range continued with the European engines, the 3.5hp single from Peugeot or FN, and the 5 and 7hp V-twins from FN. All retained the Truffault front forks, but many of the fittings were British. Only the twins were offered for 1911 and there were changes for 1912, when the agent became Martin Geiger, still in Great Portland Street, and the engines became 6 or 8hp JAP V-twins. The Peugeot engines, in 3.5hp single and 7hp V-twin forms, returned to join the JAP ones for the next year, but their business was declining and ceased in 1914.

VIPER 1919–1921

Located in the carpet manufacturing town of Kidderminster, the Viper Motor Co. Ltd produced a single model with the 292cc sv JAP engine, two-speed Albion gearbox and chain-cum-belt transmission, CAV magneto and Amac carburettor. Thus it mirrored others of its type and, once local demand had been met, doubtless found it impossible to compete with the larger makers, when needing to find sales further afield.

VISCOUNT 1960

Way back in 1953, a 998cc Vincent V-twin engine unit was shoe-horned into a Norton Featherbed frame out in Australia and the Norvin was born. Once it was known to be possible others followed, but in small numbers, especially after the Vincent went out of production.

A brief revival from a dealer in 1960 brought the Viscount, which was traditional in the use of the wide-line frame, Norton forks and a Manx

By 1913 the firm name had changed to VS to avoid confusion. This was part of their range with a V-twin JAP engine and Truffault front forks.

Joining the big Vincent engine and the Norton Featherbed frame resulted in a number of specials, but the Viscount was aimed to sell.

front hub. It worked well but demand was low, so the project short lived.

VIVID 1904
Whether this marque name referred to the fierce acceleration of the machines, or to the imagination of the constructor, isn't recorded. However, a few were made under the name by W. Elderly of 177, New North Road, Clerkenwell in London.

VOYAGER 1989–1990
Royce Creasey was a good friend of Malcolm Newell of Quasar fame and an advocate of feet-first motorcycles. His work in this field led to the construction of the first Voyager and this was exhibited at the Essen show in 1987.

In this form it continued the theme of placing the rider low down between the wheels and with considerable enclosure. The engine was a four-cylinder 848cc Reliant, the gearbox and shaft drive from a Moto Guzzi, and the steering by centre-hub Difazio. Two years later the finalized machine was launched at the NEC near Birmingham, still with the same mechanics but with a Bob Tait centre-hub front suspension. It was the body that set the machine apart, for it offered real weather protection, plenty of luggage accommodation, excellent crash protection, and the ability to cover ground fast and easily.

Manufacture was to be by Speak & Co. at Powys in Wales under licence and hopes ran high. Road tests indicated a machine that might be different, but was an impressive grand tourer that worked well. Sadly, only two were built and, despite the interest at the show, none were sold.

VULCAN c.1922–1924
This small firm hailed from Welshpool, Montgomeryshire, where they built typical lightweights. These used 269cc Villiers and 292cc JAP sv engines with belt drive, but were soon gone from the scene, by when they had moved to Stafford Street, Birmingham.

The Voyager was built in the feet-forward style, developed from the Quasar by Royce Creasey, and was much admired but did not sell.

WABO 1957

A Dutch-made scooter that was fitted with Villiers engines when sold in Britain. Those used were the 99cc two-speed 4F and the 147cc three-speed 30C, while the scooter lacked the flat floor behind the apron common to the type and had 16in wire-wheels. It was only listed for the one year.

Made in Holland with a 99 or 147cc Villiers engine, this Wabo scooter was only sold in Britain for one year.

WADDINGTON 1902–1906

Built in Middlesbrough, Yorkshire, this make used Minerva single-cylinder engines for its solos and Fafnir or Peugeot V-twins for their forecars. Typical of the period, with direct-belt drive plus options of an engine-shaft clutch or two-speed gear.

WADDON 1981–1982

Early in 1981, Waddon Performance Products of Croydon, Surrey staged a spectacular launch of their racing machines at a London show. Said to be for their own Grand Prix racer, the frame was to accommodate a range of engines and was the result of considerable development. However, the press and public were sceptical, for the frame was similar to the existing Foale and much that was shown was not practical.

It was wonderful public relations and it did lead to Dr Joe Ehrlich becoming involved in developing the 250cc Rotax tandem-twin two-stroke engine for Waddon. With his experience, the machine was soon on the pace and a Waddon won the 1982 Junior TT race for 250cc machines. By 1983 the machine had become an EMC.

The Waddon, as it was when first seen on show in 1981, but it still needed some chassis developments due to the rush in exhibiting – as usual!

WAG 1923–1925

This rare make was built at Woods Garage in Rea Street, Birmingham by two brothers of that name and had a 494cc 60-degree V-twin two-stroke engine without crankcase compression. It managed this by blanking off the crankcase mouth to create a chamber beneath the piston and utilizing a mechanical system, akin to a steam engine, to achieve the sealing and movements needed. The engine drove a three-speed gearbox, but production was very limited.

A team of three was entered in the 1924 Scottish Six Days Trial and two managed to finish, which was quite an achievement. There were other occasional appearances in competition as well, but it was too unconventional to attract many buyers.

The Waddon chassis depended on the engine unit for its rigidity but, in many respects, was in a form common to race machines at that time.

WAKEFIELD 1902

A primitive built using a heavy-duty bicycle to which was fitted a small Minerva or MMC engine with direct-belt drive to the rear wheel. No doubt a cycle dealer, who soon went back to bicycles only.

WALKER 1908

A curious vehicle built by Walker & Co. of Lutterworth, Leicestershire and, in effect, a motorcycle with a sidecar, the wheel of which was about midway along the machine and thus much further forward than usual. Both front and sidecar wheels steered, while both driver and passenger sat, side-by-side, in the sidecar body that was enlarged to suit. Power came from a 6hp V-twin engine and the drive was by belt from a variable engine-pulley.

Built in 1903, by A.W. Wall to his own design, with twin tanks under the top tube held in place by the lower tubes bolted in place.

WALL 1903–1904

This machine was built by A.W. Wall of Guildford from his own design. In this the frame was extended and lowered, a bolted-in tube running below the top tube to support the tanks, which were grooved to fit to both. A 2.75hp engine with magneto ignition was fitted and the drive pulley incorporated a clutch. Both seat and handlebars were set well back in the style of a pacing machine and, in 1904, the make became the Roc. Wall was also

Hub-centre steering, well-inclined Blackburne engine, all-chain drive and front suspension were all Wallis features that showed his flair.

involved with the Auto Wheel and numerous other ideas and designs in the formative years of the industry.

WALLACE 1904–1906
Based in Kingston-on-Thames, Surrey, one Wallace Batchelor built forecars using a 4hp water-cooled White & Poppe engine in a well-made design. The transmission was by chain drive to the rear wheel and included a clutch, while the machine was fitted with footboards to improve rider comfort.

Timing side of the 1926 Wallis, which had added a drum front-brake by mid-year, so it now stopped, as well as going and handling well.

WALLIS 1925–1929
George Wallis had an inventive mind that came up with ideas, the engineering to build them, and the business sense to make them pay. One of his more revolutionary motorcycles first appeared in 1925 and had hub-centre steering. For this he used a chassis with a pivoted-fork at the front to carry the hub assembly, with leaf springs to provide the suspension. To achieve a low riding position and centre of gravity, the Blackburne ohv engine was inclined around 45 degrees in the prototype. The transmission was all-chain and the whole machine sat low and handled well.

This good handling prompted Wallis to enter the 1926 Junior and Senior TT races, for which the machines had JAP engines and drum brakes front and rear. In the first, Syd Crabtree finished sixteenth but non-started in the Senior. The Wallis was shown at Olympia that year and listed for 1927 with a variety of engines from a 249cc sv to a twin-port of 490cc, but the project collapsed.

Wallis then became involved with the early days of speedway and started to build machines on the lines of the Harley-Davidson Peashooter model. These made their debut in 1929, one the Wallis-Blackburne, with that make of engine, and the other more successful with a 344cc JAP. In 1930, the latter adopted the new JAP speedway engine and they were taken up by Comerfords, the big dealers at Thames Ditton, Surrey, while George Wallis moved on to other ideas.

Years later, these included the banking three-wheeler that BSA revised wrongly into the Ariel 3 and, later still, became the Honda Stream, which worked better although it lacked some of the design's salient points.

WALWIN 1968–1972
A small production trials machine range that used a variety of engines, including BSA and Ossa. Typical of the period, with duplex frame and conventional cycle parts, some of these machines were fitted with a trials sidecar. Drum brakes, alloy mudguards, pivoted-fork rear suspension and telescopic front-forks all made for an attractive machine.

WARD 1915–1916
A firm that had its brief moment during the Great War when it produced a lightweight powered by a 293cc two-stroke engine. No doubt an assembler, they turned to war work when civilian sales were halted late in 1916.

WARDILL 1927–1928
One of several two-stroke engine designs that have attempted to adopt a separate pumping cylinder, instead of relying upon crankcase compression to perform that function. In the Wardill engine, a pumping cylinder was formed around and concentric with the working cylinder, the pumping piston having an annular form, with the working piston and its cylinder passing through the centre. The working piston fastened to a connecting rod driven from the crankshaft, as in standard practice, but the pumping piston was supported by two rods, each eccentrically mounted from the mainshafts either side of the big-end throw. This was both neat and compact, and the engine proved to have a good performance under racing conditions. Wardill & Sons of Mitcham, Surrey had a complete machine on sale by 1927, the engine displaced 347cc and drove by chain through a three-speed Albion gearbox. Only the engine was unconventional, but the public were still wary and therefore kept away.

WARLAND-BLACKBURNE 1923
Built by the Bordesley Engineering Company, who were also makers of the Connaught, to sell at a popular price, the Warland used a 348cc sv Blackburne engine with three speeds and all-chain drive. Druid side-spring forks, BTH magneto and an Amac carburettor were all standard industry fittings and available in quantity, thus helping in the quest for a low retail selling price.

WARRIOR 1923–1924
Promoted from offices in London and premises in Newport Pagnell, Northamptonshire, the Warrior fitted Villiers engines in either 247 or 343cc capacities, coupled to three speeds from Burman or Moss, with all-chain or chain-cum-belt options. A complete sidecar outfit was available, surprisingly with the 247cc engine.

WARWICK c.1908–1910
This was a veteran produced by badge engineering a Roc motorcycle for

the Premier Motor Company of Aston Road, Birmingham. This was a large retail firm, who took the Roc that was built by A.W. Wall in Birmingham, added their own tank transfer and fitted Rex sprung front forks in place of the Roc rigid ones. They retained the lengthy wheelbase and two-speed hub and clutch.

WASP 1964–DATE

Based near Salisbury, Wiltshire, this is another firm that grew from requests for replicas of a successful competition machine, in this case built for sidecar scrambles and grass-track events. Founded by Robin Rhind-Tutt, the early machines used Norton twin engines and were sold either complete or in kit form. At first they used trailing-link forks but later changed to leading-link.

They were most successful, winning the 1971 European Championship and many more, so by the mid-1970s Wasp was a full-time business. They dominated the sport for some years, using many other engines as well as the Norton, although the big, rugged twin with its massive torque suited the type of going the outfits raced on. Other products came along over the years, always with three wheels and made to a high quality standard.

Typical Wasp outfit set up to do its job to its very best, in this case powered by a Norton Atlas engine, which suited it so well.

WASSELL 1970–1975

A major supplier of motorcycle accessories, this firm, based at Lichfield, Staffordshire, produced a range of trials, scrambles and enduro models from 1970. Many of the parts came straight from their shelves, but the frames were special and, at first,

Wassell built some off-road models, using parts they sold in general plus their own frame and, in this case, a Bantam engine.

accommodated the 172cc BSA Bantam engine unit. When the supply of these dried up they switched to the 125cc Sachs unit with its six-speed gearbox, while the other components were all of high quality. In their major export market in the USA they were sold as the Penton, but eventually became too expensive due to an adverse exchange rate, so production ceased.

WATNEY 1922

These machines were built by Watts Ltd of Lydney, Gloucestershire around 1922, with 296cc Villiers two-stroke engines, and 292cc JAP and 348cc Blackburne four-stroke engines. The carburettor was an Amac or B&B. Burman gearboxes were fitted, with two-speeds for all plus the choice of three for the four-strokes, with belt final-drive. The frame was designed so that all its tubes were straight and Brampton Bi-flex forks were used, while the main brake operated on the rear wheel belt-rim.

The Watsonian outfit exhibited at the National Motorcycle Museum, showing the big JAP engine and other details.

WATSONIAN 1950

A prototype machine was built by this sidecar firm, using a 996cc V-twin JAP engine and four-speed Burman gearbox, installed in a plunger frame with Dunlop telescopic forks. Massive 9in drum brakes ensured the outfit could stop and the whole machine was well thought out and built. Unfortunately, the market for such a machine was being filled by the new 650cc vertical twins and JAP had little interest in the project, so only the one machine was built.

WAVERLEY 1910–1912

Built by F.M. Lee in Liverpool, Waverley listed a 3.5hp single plus 6 and 8hp V-twins for 1910, all with JAP engines, a variable gear, belt drive and sprung forks. They also offered an open-frame model, first built for a lady in Cheshire. These models continued for 1911 and, during 1912, a Waverley fitted with an American overhead-valve engine in its Chater-Lea frame won an Irish race. However, little more was heard of the make.

WAVERLEY 1921–1923

This name appeared in March 1921 as a new marque based in Lichfield Road, Birmingham. They listed a trio of 269cc two-strokes with Pero engines, and the choice of direct-belt drive or an Albion two-speed gearbox and chain-cum-belt drive, with push- or kick-starting. The engines were mounted high in the frame to suit the needs of overseas markets. They also listed a model with a 348cc sv Blackburne engine and Burman two-speed gearbox. For 1922 it was just one two-stroke, the 348cc model and one of 499cc with three speeds; these three ran on for their final 1923 year.

WD 1911–1913

Produced by Wartnaby & Draper in Coventry late in 1911, this machine differed from others in having a pressure lubrication system with a gear pump submerged in the oil in the sump. Both main bearings, the big end and the gudgeon pin were force fed in an era when most still relied on a hand pump, sight bowl and drip feed. Other engine details were a separate cylinder head, both it and the barrel being held by three long bolts, and a front-mounted magneto. The machine had belt drive and Druid forks and continued in this form to 1913.

The 1903 Wearwell solo, with inclined Stevens engine mounted high in the frame, with belt drive to the rear wheel.

WEARWELL 1901–1904

Based in Pountney Street, Wolverhampton, this firm had a long life, but mainly with the name of Wolf. They produced cycle components, built bicycles and dabbled with cars at the turn of the century, while their first motorcycle came in 1901. It was a real primitive based on a heavy-duty bicycle fitted with a 2.5hp Stevens engine mounted inclined above the downtube and with direct-belt drive.

The machine sold well and, in 1903, was joined by the Wearwell Motette forecar, which had its two front wheels and wicker passenger-seat fitted in place of the motorcycle front wheel. At the late-1903 Crystal Palace show, the 2.5hp model was joined by a 3.25hp machine with the engine vertical within the frame. The machine was of sturdier construction,

The addition of the forecar to the Wearwell solo produced this Motette model, which later took the Wolf name.

with braced forks but still with belt drive.

The Motette was revised to this layout, but its 3.5hp Stevens engine was water-cooled and drove a Bowden rear hub that incorporated a clutch by chain. By the end of the year the machines had begun to adopt the Wolf name and, from then on, used that one right through to 1940, except for a brief period when they were known as Wulfruna, another company branch name.

WEATHERELL 1922–1923

After his involvement with the RW Scout, sporting rider/agent Reg Weatherell turned his talents and name to this marque. Located in Kilburn, North London, his machines were Blackburne-powered, with 248 or 348cc singles in sv or ohv forms plus the big sv 697cc V-twin. The twin had a duplex frame and a very low riding position, making it suitable for racing purposes with an alternative engine in place. Island entries were, indeed, made for the 1923 TT races, when Weatherells finished twentieth and twenty-third in the Junior, but the marque soon floundered.

The Welbike was built for the army to parachute into battle using this container. It did the job, and post-war became the Corgi.

WEAVER 1923–1925

This marque was named after its designer, who was the works manager at the Alfred Wiseman company, builders of Verus and Sirrah machines. The first model, known as the Cyclette, was just that, an open-framed commuter machine with the marque's own 150cc ohv engine, single-speed and chain final-drive. For 1924, this was continued and joined by a true lightweight motorcycle, known as the Colonial model,

Close up of the Villiers engine that drove the Welbike, also the pressurized fuel tank and folded handlebars, saddle and footrests.

with a 130cc version of the same engine, two-speed Burman gearbox, all-chain drive and 24in-diameter road wheels. Later the same year, 147cc Villiers or Aza two-stroke engine options were offered on this machine. Only the motorcycle continued into 1925, which, with the Wiseman business itself coming to a close, proved to be the final one.

WEE MACGREGOR 1922–1924

An ultra-lightweight, as its name might suggest, being a sub-marque of Coventry Bicycles, builders of the Coventry B&D and other badged products. The first examples had 170cc two-stroke Hobart engines and either plain two-speed or two-speed with clutch, kickstart transmissions and belt final-drive. Later the engine capacity was increased to 205cc and an open-framed ladies' model could be obtained.

WELBIKE 1942–1945

The wartime machine built by Excelsior, from which the post-war Corgi was developed, the Welbike was designed to be dropped by parachute in a container no larger than 15in (38cm) diameter. Meant for rapid troop dispersal, it had to be a fold-up design and had a 98cc Villiers engine, single speed and no suspension other than its 12in wire-wheels. For use the seat was pulled up, the bars and rests unfolded and the machine push-started into action.

WELLAN 1904

Built by J.T. Andrews of Spalding in Lincolnshire, this was a two-seat tricycle, whose single front wheel was chain-driven from a 3hp engine mounted above it. Driver and passenger sat side-by-side over the back axle.

WELLAND B 1919–1920
A lightweight two-stroke that utilized the 348cc Broler engine. By late 1920, it was renamed the Spartan and continued in production for a while under its new name.

The 1903 Weller was a typical primitive, but the engine fins were loose washers clamped onto the plain cylinder.

WELLER 1902–1904
A firm based in West Norwood, London that built both cars and motorcycles. The latter had a bicycle-type frame, the 1.75 or 2.25hp engine being mounted vertically to the right of the downtube, its drive belt to the rear wheel on the left of the tube. The cylinder fins were loose washers, dropped over the plain diameter and held by the long studs that secured the head. All controls were handlebar mounted and included a twisting-handle throttle, while the rear brake was an internal-expanding drum with cam operation.

In 1903 they advertised a 50-mile trial-run for any would-be buyer, but soon turned to cars.

WENLOCK 1912–1913
An assembled machine made in small numbers by Wenlock Motors Ltd of Hull. Precision and Arno four-stroke engines with Armstrong three-speed hub gears were mainly used, but at least one machine had the 269cc two-stroke Villiers engine. Saxon spring forks, Eisemann or Bosch magnetos and Brown & Barlow carburettors were amongst the other fittings typical of the time. Difficulties with delivery of bought-in components hampered production and it is thought only about a dozen machines were constructed before the firm closed down.

WERNER 1897–1908
Although Werner is a French marque it is included, as it was the Werner brothers who moved the engine from an unstable position above the front wheel, which it drove by belt, to a centre-frame location. This established the position of the main weight in the best place and later suited the transmission layout in its various forms. In Edwardian years they were the first, or one of the first, to build a vertical-twin engine, so their influence was widespread.

Werner were the firm that gave the industry the engine move to the centre of the frame and set the pattern.

WERRY 1927
A one-off machine built up as a test bed for an unusual flat-twin two-stroke engine set along the frame. It was based on the uniflow principle, where the two pistons faced one another in a common cylinder with a crankshaft and crankcase for each at the outer cylinder ends. The cranks were linked so as to rotate in unison and the Werry did this by each driving a primary chain to a special clutch with two sprockets, one chain much longer than the other. The capacity was given as 248cc and the rear crankshaft drove up to a Lucas magneto, while the front one drove a Pilgrim oil pump.

The engine was designed by W.C. Werry, an Australian, and built by Beardmore of Glasgow. It and a Sturmey-Archer gearbox were fitted into Chater-Lea cycle parts and, in this form, was reputed to have attacked one of the 250cc world records at Brooklands, but crashed at some 90mph (145km/h). Many years later it was rebuilt, as an interesting example of innovative thinking, although not unique.

WESLAKE C.1972–DATE
This firm, based at Rye in Sussex, was best known for their engines and their work on cylinder heads for cars. However, in the early-1970s, they combined with John Caffrey to build the Weslake Vendetta. The engine was a 492cc eight-valve vertical twin and drove a five-speed gearbox. The frame was duplex tubular and rode on wire wheels with a disc front brake and conical rear hub.

Later came larger versions of the engine but, in most cases, with limited chassis involvement for Weslake. They also built 500cc singles running on dope for grass-track use and, by the 1980s, these had a five-valve head. This exercise then led to a 998cc ohc ten-valve V-twin design, on the lines of an earlier eight-valve engine. Some of the Weslake singles were used for speedway and long-track events but, for the most, the firm kept to engines rather than machines.

Late in the 1990s they offered the Wexton Sprint road model, with their 498cc dohc single engine mounted in a Norton featherbed frame with a Norton or Quaife gearbox. The style was café racer to customer specification and production limited.

WESTFIELD 1903–1904
Made by the Rising Sun Motor

Works in London, this machine appeared in 1903, fitted with a 2.75hp engine designed to clamp to lugs on the frame. Both valves and the sparking plug were at the front of the engine and this, plus ample fins, showed an understanding of the need for good cooling.

For the rest, the model was a typical primitive with pedals, belt drive and braced forks. By 1904 they listed a forecar, this fitted with a 3.5hp engine and much as many others.

WESTLAKE 1905–1906
Anthony Westlake of London built a 7hp machine fitted with an 816cc V-twin engine for the International Cup race. It weighed in at 112lb (50.8kg), pulled a high gear and was claimed to be good for 70mph (112km/h), but was not selected for the Cup team. Westlake offered to build 4hp touring versions of the machine, but it is doubtful if there were any takers.

WESTOVIAN 1914–1916
Machines built by R.V. Heath of South Shields, who used Precision engines of 2.5 to 4.5hp for basic models fitted with belt drive, hub gears and Druid forks. For 1915 there was also a model powered by a TDC engine, while, for 1916, this machine continued but with only one other using a Precision engine. The rest turned to JAP single and V-twin engines for this final season.

W&G 1927–1928
Announced in July 1927 by Wright & Gasking of Rea Street, Birmingham, this marque fitted a 494cc vertical-twin two-stroke engine with the cylinders inclined forward a little. There were four small internal flywheels, one large external flywheel on the right, plain bearings at centre and each crankshaft end, and high primary and secondary compression ratios. A single rear-mounted B&B carburettor supplied the mixture, which was fired by a chain-driven Bosch magneto mounted immediately aft of the crankcase. This put it just above an aluminium expansion chamber with internal baffles into which the two exhaust pipes ran, with twin exit pipes and silencers. Lubrication was from an oil tank via a needle valve to the mains.

The engine drove a three-speed Sturmey-Archer gearbox and went into a conventional frame with Druid forks and drum brakes. A flat petrol tank was fitted at first, but this was soon replaced by a saddle tank. The machine was said to perform quickly and quietly, but it did not sell well, while the magneto could have proved troublesome due to its proximity to the exhaust heat. Whatever the reason, it was soon gone.

WHEATCROFT 1924
This name saw the return of New Era of Liverpool to the market with two models. The lightweight used the 318cc Dalm two-stroke engine, while the other had the 545cc sv Blackburne single. Cycle parts of each were to suit, but the enterprise was short lived.

WHIPPET 1903–1905
The Whippet Motor & Cycle Co. showed two machines at the late-1903 Crystal Palace show, fitted with a two-speed gear. This comprised two chain wheels of different diameters fitted to the rear hub and a device to shift the drive chain from one to the other, just as on a bicycle. One machine was a solo fitted with an FN engine, the other a forecar powered by a 3.25hp Aster engine.

One of the many scooters that appeared after the Great War, the Whippet was no more successful than the rest.

WHIPPET 1920–1921
A neat 150cc ohv engine with magneto ignition and drip-feed lubrication distinguished the Whippet scooter and thus separated it from most of its two-stroke-engined contemporaries. Chains took a single-speed drive through a countershaft and then to the rear wheel, both wheels being shod with 18in tyres. Multiple tubes formed the frame, with a flat foot-platform, simple bicycle saddle above the engine and cylindrical fuel tank behind. It was soundly engineered by W.G.C. Hayward & Company of Twickenham in Middlesex and came in three forms, including a sports version with racing saddle and wide handlebars, but it couldn't survive the collapse that followed the post-Great War boom.

WHIPPET 1957–1959
One of the models produced by Dunkley of Hounslow, London was the Whippet 60 Scooterette, which had a 61cc ohv engine and two-speed gearbox. The unit went into a spine frame with front and rear suspension. Later it was joined by a 64cc model with a pressed-steel spine frame which became the Whippet Sports. Although part of the Dunkley range, they were also known as Whippet models, but both disappeared with the rest of the Dunkley range in 1959.

WHIRLWIND 1901–1903
An early proprietary engine built by the Dorman Engineering Co. of Northampton and then Stafford, who later built the oil-cooled Bradshaw engines. In the early days they produced a few primitive machines in the form of that period, with the engine hung from the downtube or within the frame. They had belt drive and were of basic construction.

WHITE c.1990–DATE
A former Norton-Villiers engineer, Norman White is based in Hampshire and built up his business producing special parts for Norton twins and Commandos, as well as carrying out specialist work on these models. In

time, this led to producing complete machines of these types, which were effectively Norton twin specials built to the customer's specification.

WHITE & POPPE 1902–1914

This firm was best known for the engines it supplied other companies, one of these being Ariel, who later built their own engine in the same style, with the valves to one side of the head but spaced much further apart than usual. By late-1904, they had a 5hp vertical-twin engine that had the pistons at 180 degrees and could be water cooled for tricycle work instead of the usual air cooling.

As well as engines, the firm also built some motorcycles, but must have found this unpopular with their engine customers, so production was limited. In 1921, they listed a small two-stroke engine but, by then, were making car engines for, among others, William Morris.

A short-lived primitive, Whitley built their own engines and produced both solos and forecars for their brief life.

WHITLEY 1902–1905

This Coventry firm built its own engines, which hung from the downtube of their motorcycle and forecar, the latter fitted with air scoops to aid engine cooling. A primitive design with belt drive and braced forks.

WHITWOOD 1934–1936

Built by OEC, this was another attempt to produce a car on two wheels and no more successful than the rest. It was announced during 1934 and was fully enclosed, so from the side looked like a small saloon car with a short bonnet, or a vast sidecar. In fact, it carried two people in tan-

Another attempt to build a car on two wheels in the 1930s, in this case by OEC who would try anything, using much from their stores.

dem and had a stabilizing wheel on each side.

Under the body was a tubular frame, much as that of the OEC Atlanta, with the OEC duplex steering system but controlled by a steering wheel. The engine and gearbox went under the seats and the engine ranged from a 150cc Villiers to a 750cc V-twin JAP. It was much revised for 1936, when the smallest engine became a 250cc JAP, but there were few takers and the idea was dropped.

WHITWORTH 1924

Sold under the trading name of Frank Whitworth Ltd, a large retail dealer in Birmingham, this was a 147cc two-stroke Villiers lightweight, with Albion two-speed gearbox and belt drive. It was built elsewhere, probably at the Arab factory, to be sold cheaply without a middleman's trade cut. Selling price was set at just £27.

WIGAN-BARLOW 1921–1922

Although a 348cc Barr & Stroud sleeve-valve-engined model was contemplated, it is unlikely that other than the 292cc sv JAP-engined machine shown on announcement of the marque in 1921 was ever made. Maplestone forks and an Albion gearbox were specified by Wigan-Barlow Motors of Stoke, Coventry, who had but a brief stay in the motorcycle trade.

WILBEE 1902–1906

A typical primitive, but better made than many others thanks to the use of BSA frame parts and the Minerva engine, although belt final-drive and transmission options were the same as many others. It became another victim of the downturn in trade of 1905.

WILKIN 1920–1921

Designed by G.W. Wilkin, who was already an established motorcycle retailer in Sheffield, Yorkshire when the machine bearing his name appeared in 1920. It was of conventional outline and sound in construction with either a 348 or 499cc sv Blackburne engine connected with three-speed Sturmey-Archer gearboxes and fully enclosed all-chain transmission. A lighter model was also offered and this had the 269cc Villiers two-stroke with two-speed gear from either Albion or Burman. In an ambitious attempt to establish the marque, Wilkin set out from Liverpool in September 1920 to ride around the coast of Great Britain on a sidecar outfit, accompanied by an Auto-Cycle Union observer in the sidecar. In thirty-two days, 3,315 miles (5,334km) were covered before the ride was completed, with only a fractured rear fork stay and broken exhaust pipe to report. The product was thus proven and the objective attained, yet the fickle public still didn't buy in big enough numbers.

WILKINSON 1909–1915

A luxury machine built in Acton, London by a firm then famous for swords and bayonets, later for razor blades. The motorcycle was lengthy, having an in-line four-cylinder engine, clutch, three-speed gearbox and shaft-drive to a worm at the rear wheel. Engine capacity was 678cc, the crankcase cast-iron and split

The 1910 Wilkinson, with its four-cylinder engine and many special features that made it the Touring Auto Cycle or TAC.

By 1912, the Wilkinson had a larger water-cooled engine while retaining most of its features, but bevels replaced the worm rear drive.

horizontally, the drive from clutch to gearbox by spring steel to absorb shocks and starting by hand lever.

The long frame began with leading-link forks from Chater-Lea, but these were quickly changed to a Wilkinson design. At the rear, the wheel was supported by four quarter-elliptic springs. The oil tank went just behind the headstock but the petrol tank was placed on the rear mudguard behind the rider, who was provided with a bucket seat. It was listed as the touring auto-cycle or TAC.

The forerunner of the Wilkinson was a similar design, built for military use and fitted with a lightweight quick-firing Wilkinson gun, the engine in that instance a transverse V-twin.

Late in 1909, the TAC began to appear fitted with a steering wheel and was so advertised in 1910. For 1911 the engine size became 550cc for one model that had mechanical inlet-valves, while handlebars returned. The capacity went up to 848cc for 1912, when the engine was water-cooled and had the Bosch magneto mounted on top of the gearbox and thus under the seat. Bevel drive replaced the worm at the rear axle, and Druid forks the leading links, while the name changed to the Touring Motor Cycle or TMC.

In 1913 the TMC was only sold as a sidecar outfit, while a brief link with Wooler was reported. This went in 1914, when both solo and sidecar versions were offered, while, during the year, manufacture was taken over by the Ogston Motor Co. of Acton and many detail improvements were made. The Wilkinson was still listed in 1915, as of 848cc when using the bevel drive, and of 1087cc with the worm drive, both still fitting the three-speed gearbox.

WILKINSON 1939–1962

This was a special built by Frank Wilkinson, who designed and constructed the whole machine at his home in Nottingham just before the war. What made it special were the mechanics, for the engine was a 592cc V4 with overhead camshafts mounted transversely, which drove a home-made three-speed gearbox bolted to it, with a bevel box to turn the drive to suit the rear chain. Obviously, Frank not only had considerable skills in making things, but he also had access to some useful workshop machinery.

The first layout was not the success hoped for, so, in the 1940s, the machine was modified to mount the engine along a military Ariel W/NG frame to drive an Albion four-speed gearbox by chain. The camshafts continued to be driven by vertical shafts, with bevel gears at the bottom and skew at the top, with hairpin valve-springs later changed to coils. Ignition was by a BTH magneto from an aircraft, adapted to suit the V4, and there was a carburettor on each side of the vee.

The Wilkinson-Antoine was built in London using a Belgian engine with flat-belt drive to the rear wheel, the belt pulley also serving as the brake drum.

Frank continued to modify the machine right up to his death in 1962, after which it languished for many years before being found and restored to a running condition. With twin open-megaphone exhausts it sounded fine.

WILKINSON-ANTOINE 1903–1905

Built by the Cadogan Garage in Chelsea, London, using Belgian Antoine engines of 2.25 or 2.75hp fitted into a loop frame. Shown at the Crystal Palace show late in 1903, the machine had flat-belt drive to the rear wheel, the rear pulley also acting as a brake drum.

WILLIAMS 1976–1998

One Triumph Trident won the Production TT five times from 1971

The Wilkinson was a special built by one man, with a V4 engine having overhead camshafts and many other special features.

and was known as 'Slippery Sam'. By 1975 it belonged to Les Williams, who had been the race shop manager, and, in time, he set up in business for himself to produce replicas of Sam.

This led on to his own model, sold as the Legend, and based on the last of the triples, the T160V. They were built to the customers' requirement and most were in a sporting style, not a café racer, but with short, flat handlebars and set-back footrests to encourage fast and easy riding. As the supply of triple engines began to dry up, he repeated the exercise using the 744cc twin engine unit and the result was known as the Buccaneer.

Williams was based at Kenilworth in Warwickshire but, when he retired, he part exchanged the business for the seventeenth-century home of Trevor Gleadall, an early Buccaneer customer. In time the business moved to Warwick, to mainly deal in spares and major work on the triples, but in 1994 the final Williams creation appeared as the Renegade. Built to suit Trevor, it used the triple engine but retained the sixties style, with drum brakes and other features. One more was built in 1998. The machines were always called by their model names rather than as Williams, despite their origins.

Timing side of the 1913 Williamson, with its flat-twin water-cooled engine, actually made for them by the Douglas firm.

WILLIAMSON 1912–1920

This marque was based at Earlsdon, Coventry and made its debut in 1912, when it offered power with silence and no vibration, thanks to its 8hp flat-twin water-cooled engine. This was actually made for them by the Douglas firm in Bristol and was part of their stationary engine range, so had a starting handle in the manner of

Drive side of the 1914 Williamson twin, which also used a gearbox made by Douglas, but postwar saw them turn to a JAP V-twin.

a car. Typical of the Douglas, it had side valves, a gear-driven magneto and was installed low down in a long frame to drive a two-speed Douglas gearbox with all-chain drive.

For 1913 an air-cooled version was added, but did not sell as well, for it lacked the charm of the quieter machine and its ability to avoid overheating. However, it did continue as an option. Most sold were water-cooled and bought for sidecar use, for which they were best suited. They continued on to 1916 but, post-war, returned in late 1919 with the air-cooled flat-twin and a new model, having the 771cc sv JAP V-twin engine and three-speed Sturmey-Archer gearbox with all-chain drive. By early 1920 only the V-twin remained, this being sold with sidecar as a complete combination. It was their last fling.

WILLOW 1920

Utilizing a complete Auto-Wheel as its rear wheel, the designer of the Willow scooter added two simple tubes to support a bicycle saddle and two more to support the steering head, before connecting everything together with a stout wooden footboard. The chosen wood was ash, which was claimed to give greater flexibility than a metallic frame, and the rider's comfort was therefore greatly enhanced. This was fortunate, as the machine was otherwise devoid of springing. A single handlebar-lever gave control over the 117cc aiv four-stroke engine, which was supplied with fuel from a tubular tank above the wheel, as in standard Auto-wheel practice. Makers were the Willow Autocycle Company of Victoria, London.

WILTON 1910–1912

A London firm that used a 1.5hp Motosacoche or 2.5hp JAP engine, belt drive and sprung forks for its early models. For 1911 the engine became the JAP or a 3.5hp Norton single, or a 5hp Norton V-twin. It was another short-lived make.

WIN 1910–1914

First listed late in 1910, using a 3.5hp Precision engine, B&B carburettor, belt drive and Druid forks, the machine was built by Wincycle Trading Co. of Great Saffron Hill, London. They continued for 1912 and added 2.5 and 4.25hp models for 1913, still using Precision engines. Their final year saw the range reduce to 3.75 and 4.25hp Precision-powered machines.

The 1911 Win used a Precision engine and other common components of the period during its short life, which was cut off by the Great War.

WINCO 1920–1922

One of the many who entered the boom time of the market just after the Great War, using proprietary components, no doubt assembled in a cycle shop or a back-street garage. Few such firms lasted for long in those times without real capital and the boom went bust in a few years. The bright dealers had moved on early, as here.

WINDRUSH c.1910

Built by Henry Preece, a cycle maker of Coventry, to special order, so only a dozen or so were completed. A 500cc JAP sv engine provided the motive power and the whole specification would have been agreed with the customer, but belt drive and a three-speed Sturmey-Archer rear hub were usual. One feature well before its time was that the fuel tank covered the frame top-tube, in a style used by a few other firms, although the result was not a true saddle tank.

WINN 1966
A battery-powered small-wheeled motorcycle with full enclosure of the working parts, the Winn City Bike was intended to provide pollution-free transport around built up areas. Range between battery charges was given as 10–20 miles (16–32km) with a 30mph (48km/h) top speed, and an overnight recharge from the mains was said to cost just 2p. The bodywork was moulded from glass-fibre, a twistgrip controlled motor speed and drum brakes were applied by handlebar levers. Promoted by inventor Russell Winn, it was built by High Speed Motors of Witney, Oxfordshire.

WINSTER-JAP C.1927
An assembly job that used a sv JAP engine in a typical set of bought-in components in the style of the late 1920s. No doubt it went down in the depression.

WIRRAL 1902–C.1906
The Edwardian decade had its boom and bust times, just as the 1920s. Early sales fell off around 1905 and the Wirral, most likely a primitive, would have soon gone to the wall as did so many.

WITALL 1920
Two quite differing models launched this marque, both were lightweights and both two-stroke powered, but one was of sporting outline, the other more with touring in mind. The sporting Model A had a sloping top-tube to its frame and a 269cc TDC engine with Roc two-speed gearbox, TT handlebars and Saxon forks. Touring Model B kept the forks and Roc transmission, but its frame had a horizontal top-tube dropped at the saddle end and the engine became a 269cc Arden. The Witall Garage of New Cross, London offered sixteen days delivery in April 1920, a time when machines of any kind were difficult to acquire, but seemingly few gave them a try for they were soon gone from the scene.

WIZARD 1914
The marque name used by Fowler & Bingham, or FB, of Coventry Road, Hay Mills, Birmingham for their model fitted with the 269cc Villiers engine, Albion two-speed gearbox or fixed gear, belt drive and Druid forks. In this form it was only listed for a few months, but did appear post-war as the FB, up to around 1922.

WIZARD 1921–1922
Built in the Rhondda Valley near Cardiff, South Wales by the Wizard Motor Company, this make first appeared in July 1921 as a lightweight model, having a 269cc two-stroke engine designed by A.W. Wall with the gearbox linked to the engine in a steel-plate cradle to form a unit. This then located in a bolted-up, four-tube frame with duplex top and bottom tubes running from the steering head to the rear-wheel spindle. The straight-blade front forks had enclosed coil springs and the whole machine was of simple construction with belt final-drive, but the make was short-lived.

The 1904 Wolf Motette was made by the Wearwell firm; in this example it used a Stevens engine mounted with vertical cylinder.

A Wolf for 1910, with V-twin engine and direct drive but the firm always offered many options, which kept them in business for forty years.

Another 1910 Wolf, in this case with a small engine mounted high in the frame, much as the early Wearwell had used.

WOLF 1903–1940
The Wolf name began to be used by Wearwell of Wolverhampton in 1903 and took over for all their models, along with the Wulfruna name that was used occasionally. They were a firm on the fringe of the industry and went through some hard times, but kept going longer than most. They also made bicycles and this helped them when in difficulties.

By 1912 the Wulfruna name was being used by the firm for three singles, all fitted with first Stevens and then Arno engines.

Wolf was first used for the Wearwell Motette forecar late in 1903, when it was revised to use a 3.5hp water-cooled Stevens engine with chain drive to a Bowden rear-hub with clutch. From this modest start came a good range of singles and V-twins, using Stevens engines ranging from 2.5 to 5hp. These went into solos, forecars and even a three-wheeled car built for a couple of years. At the bottom end, the essentials of the first Wearwell continued in the Wolf Featherweight, with its 1.5hp Stevens engine mounted inclined high-up in the frame with belt drive over a jockey pulley. All models had many options and improved through the Edwardian era in line with most other makes.

During 1911 the Wulfruna name began to be used by the firm, with the range down to three singles, all still using Stevens engines, and, for 1912, there was a V-twin fitted with a 4hp Moto-Rêve engine. During that year they were advertised as using Arno engines and Thornton two-speed gears, but, late in 1913, the tanks again carried the Wolf name, while the machines were using JAP as well as Arno engines, an Illston for the 2.5hp model, and a variety of transmissions, many with chain drive.

The range, using Villiers, TDC, JAP and Abingdon engines, ran on to 1916 and continued post-war in reduced form, with just a 269cc Villiers two-stroke model, soon to be joined by 292cc sv JAP, and 348 plus 545cc sv Blackburne-engined machines. Eventually a wide range was tried, with changes coming each season through the early- to mid-1920s, mostly with chain-cum-belt transmissions, though they had introduced all-chain drive and three speeds on some models by 1924. Ohv sports models were another innovation, with Blackburne engines. Then a 172cc Villiers sports arrived by 1925, to stay in the range through to 1927, when it was accompanied only by two variants with 147cc Villiers engines, all the four-strokes having gone, and by 1928 production had ceased. However, it began again in 1931 with two models, again using Villiers engines, of 147 and 196cc. From this they expanded their range, to add 98, 122, 148 and 249cc engines at various times, always using Villiers power, and built lightweight models through the decade, right up to 1940.

Later, simple Wolf, utilizing two-stroke power and basic front forks. Cheap, but able to offer the transport needed at the right price.

By 1937 the lightweight Wolf had a 122cc Villiers engine, but came with twin exhaust-pipes and silencers plus legshields, so continued its work.

WOOLER 1911–1926 AND 1945–1956

Few machines of this make were actually made but nearly all were special, unusual and the novelty of their day. John Wooler had his own ideas for a motorcycle, far removed from the conventional of the time, so made sporadic but interesting forays onto the scene. His models were always news.

The first Wooler made its debut, uncompleted, at the late-1911 Olympia show on Nye's stand and had features that would remain with the make for many years. The engine was a 2.75hp two-stroke with horizontal cylinder, but differed from the rest in having a double-ended piston coupled to external connecting-rods by an extended gudgeon pin. An external pipe transferred the compressed mixture from rear to front chamber, where it was fired by a magneto mounted on the crankcase.

This unusual engine was mounted in a simple frame, with belt drive via a variable pulley to the rear wheel. Both wheels had plunger suspension, in an age of girders and rigid, and the fuel tank was shaped to a bullet head, tapering back to a point with the forward part around the headstock.

This novel design was back at Olympia in the next year as the Wilkinson-Wooler T.M.C. with the same 345cc engine, but, by late-1913, it was again the Wooler, with works at Harrow. By then the engine had pump lubrication, but the machine remained as before.

A 1931 Wolf Minor, which was fitted with a 147cc Villiers engine to offer a cheap lightweight for the ride to work in those tough times.

For 1913 Wilkinson-Wooler formed the combination with the curious Wooler engine, the TMC name and the odd plunger suspension.

Front end of a Wooler with the horizontal engine, to show the plunger suspension unit used front and rear.

Post-war, the two-stroke was listed briefly, along with a new 345cc flat-twin four-stroke engine with ioe valves and conventional build. It still went in the same type of frame, having plunger suspension front and rear, while the petrol tank continued in the same form. Entered in the TT, this was painted yellow and earned the nickname of the 'Flying Banana', but had no success.

It was this twin that then went ahead into 1920, retaining the variable pulley drive, but, late in 1921, this form of transmission was replaced by a three-speed all-chain drive and, shortly after, there was a break in production whilst the business received a much needed injection of fresh finance. The company was bought by William Dederich, a successful railway contractor, and, as the Dederich-Wooler Engineering Company, both belt- and chain-drive versions were offered, the touch of John Wooler remaining as he became Chief Designer and Engineer. In 1924, the ioe 345cc model was joined by one having full ohv arrangements and this system was also used by a new 499cc flat-twin, added the following year. Business problems continued, however, and production moved from the Alperton, Middlesex works to Twickenham, where Grigg Engineering undertook manufacture for a time. In 1926 the twins were swept away and a conventional looking 511cc vertical single with a form of overhead camshaft, three-speed Sturmey-Archer gearbox, rigid frame and girder forks was tried. After this the Wooler name dropped out of sight for a while.

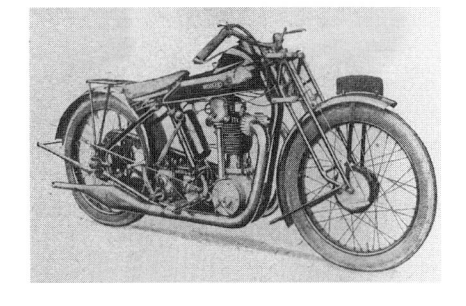

The name returned with a vengeance in 1945, when their new machine was announced. It was to have a transverse-four beam engine, the cylinders one above the other on each side, the pistons connected to the beam and this to the crankshaft set below the cylinder level. Capacity was 500cc, there was ohv, a direct drive back to a four-speed gearbox and shaft final-drive. There was also talk of a variable gear and the whole unit went into a duplex frame, having twin plunger boxes on each side for front and rear suspension. The petrol tank once again ran round the headstock and carried the headlamp in its nose.

It was all too wonderful to really work, especially in those austere days, so, after the 1948 Earls Court show, it was late-1952 before there was more news. This brought a completely new 500cc engine, still a flat-four, but of conventional overhead-valve form with the original gearbox and shaft drive. The cycle side remained much as before until 1956, when a new

This Wooler dates from 1926, when the firm fitted an ohc engine into a duplex frame with twin-tube forks.

In 1920, the Wooler had a flat-twin four-stroke engine, the special fuel tank and still the plunger suspension.

The first post-Second World War Wooler had a transverse-four beam engine among its many special features, but years of work just saw it replaced by a more conventional design.

frame with telescopic front and pivoted-fork rear suspension appeared. This proved to be the final form for the Wooler, but it never did make it into production.

WRAY-PRECISION 1912
A sidecar outfit built for one George Wray, which used a 4.5hp Precision engine to drive a Bowden countershaft gear. Druid forks were fitted to this one-off.

WREN 1924
The coming and going of the Wren is bathed in some mystery, for it was, in truth, the Clement ultra-lightweight machine under a different name. Following its announcement, the Clement company took immediate offence and redoubled their own efforts to continue marketing the product under its existing name and no more was heard of the newcomer. Possibly the Jennen Engineering Company of High Holborn, London, who advertised the Wren, had erroneously thought they had an agreement with Clement, when evidently they hadn't.

WRIGHT c.1913
A rare, pre-Great War make that used Blumfield engines and gained some publicity thanks to the efforts of Hilary Greatwich of Stourport.

The final Wooler form appeared around 1956, with flat-four engine, shaft drive, the expected unusual fuel tank and its more conventional suspension.

During that year he won his class at ten hill climbs, using a 5hp twin engine for power, no doubt in cycle parts typical of the time and with belt final-drive.

WULFRUNA 1911–1913
One of the names used by Wearwell, whose machines first used this and Wolf in their early years. Wulfruna models had a short production life for just three years before the firm went back to using the Wolf name, but the company went under the name for many years.

WYNNE c.1919
One of the many hopefuls who entered the market at the end of the war, when there was a real boom in the demand for transport. This one was a scooter, again exploiting a short-lived boom of that time, and chose a 269cc two-stroke engine for its power. Built by J.W. Oates, it differed from most machines in having both front and rear suspension, but was no doubt underfunded and suffered supply problems. It went as quickly as it came.

X

XL 1921–1924
Initially, 499cc Blackburne or 490cc JAP sv engines were used by the Excel Company of Woking in Surrey. These went into frames with a duplex tubular subframe running in a straight line from the front downtube to the rear spindle, thus surrounding the engine itself. All frame lugs were fashioned from pressed steel and this material was also used in the construction of the front forks, rear stand and carrier. All-chain drive through a three-speed Sturmey-Archer gearbox was well shielded and the mudguarding, too, was extensive, making for a worthwhile touring motorcycle. Later, a larger 597cc sv JAP single or a 496cc sv V-twin of the same make could be specified.

XL-ALL 1902–1906
Built by the Eclipse Motor & Cycle Co. of John Bright Street, Birmingham, these machines had 2 or 4hp, 90-degree V-twin engines mounted in a loop frame. They were claimed to be the most powerful road machines, and to both pull a trailer and push a forecar at the same time. 'Any speed from 4 to 50mph' and 'passes everything on the road' were other claims. To this end, either cylinder of the engine could be used alone, thus allowing the other to cool when not required, or both together to make good the claims!

Extravagant claims were made for the XL-All, with its twin-cylinder engine that could be run on one or two pots with power to spare.

Y

YELVERTON UNION 1921

W.G. Battershill was a carpenter, no doubt based in the town of Yelverton in Devon, so it was natural to him to construct the frame and forks of his motorcycle in wood – ¾in square-section ash in point of fact. Naturally, this meant straight members; they were laid out in a duplex form, with the forks in the style of girders, controlled by a tension spring and using bicycle hubs as link pivots. The engine was a 292cc Union two-stroke, with the EIC magneto mounted in-line with the crankshaft on the right and a large flywheel on the left. Transmission was by direct-belt drive and the builder used the machine for thirty-five years before it went to another owner.

YOUNG 1904–1908

E.G. Young of Nottingham was a small producer, who offered a forecar powered by a 3.5hp fan-cooled Minerva engine. The fan was belt driven, but there had been an aim to use the exhaust gas to drive it.

Their name cropped up again early in 1905, when they showed a ladies' Bentinck motorcycle whose engine was inclined and mounted below the downtube of the open frame. It had braced forks and a degree of protection for the clothing of the rider.

Another model, built in 1908, was a lightweight that had a 2.5hp V-twin engine mounted low down in a Chater-Lea frame, so it appears that Young was an occasional constructor who built machines to order only.

YOUNG 1919–1923

This firm offered a clip-on with a two-stroke engine to fit over the rear wheel of a standard bicycle, which it drove by chain. At first a 269cc Mohawk engine was used but, for 1921, this changed to a 131cc engine made by Waltham Engineering of North London. This had the cylinder, in aluminium with a cast-iron liner, mounted horizontally with the head to the rear. The ML magneto was chain driven and the mixture supplied by a WEC carburettor, the whole engine unit carried in an aluminium cradle. Lubrication was by petroil, with the fuel carried in a cylindrical tank mounted above the frame top-tube. Transmission was by chain to a counter-shaft carrying a clutch and then by a further chain on the left down to the rear hub. The firm also offered a simple attachment to provide springing for the front forks and the unit remained in production to 1923.

The Yelverton was a one-off that had both frame and forks made from ash wood to carry a 292cc Union engine with direct-belt drive.

◆ Z ◆

The post-war Zenith V-twin with 747cc JAP engine, which was listed up to 1950 but seldom seen at shows, in dealers or on the road.

ZENITH 1905–1950

This firm began in North London with one of the strangest of machines, which was called the Bicar and said to be 'a revolution in motorcycles'. The design was first seen early in 1905 at the Crystal Palace show, where it was called the Tooley Bi-car, after its inventor, and was shown by Bitton & Harley of Great Yarmouth. By July that year, it had been improved and become the Zenith.

The Bicar had a novel frame, with its main tube running from the rear wheel spindle along the machine, round the front wheel and back again. Below this, on each side, ran a second tube to carry the weight of rider and engine, with this hung from joints to eliminate vibration. Hub centre steering was used, so there were no front forks in the normal sense, the handlebars being connected to the wheel axle by stays. The engine was a 3hp Fafnir, with a free-engine clutch and belt drive to the rear wheel, which had a drum brake. They also offered the Tricar with a 5hp engine and two speeds, both of which were soon options for the Bicar.

The firm was run by Freddie W. Barnes and, in 1907, he patented his Gradua Gear system, which combined a variable engine pulley with movement of the rear wheel to maintain the correct belt-tension. This used a system of rods connected to a single handle, so the gear could be altered while on the move. So useful was this to be in hill climbs that some clubs prohibited the Zenith machines from their events and the firm profited from this with their 'barred' trademark.

Before this came about, the original Bicar was revised to become the more conventional Zenette. This had the looks of the period, but retained the concept of carrying the engine in a frame sprung to that of the rider. Braced front forks were used along with the Gradua Gear and the engine was a 3.5hp Fafnir. Late in 1908 it was joined by a rigid model that had sprung forks and improved hill-climbing ability, thanks to its lower weight.

At the end of the year the firm moved to Church Street, Weybridge, Surrey, close to Brooklands where Barnes set the first record for the Test Hill early in 1909. With the move the machines were sold as Zeniths and from then on the firm became much more successful.

For 1910 the Gradua Gear mechanism was improved and tidied up, as

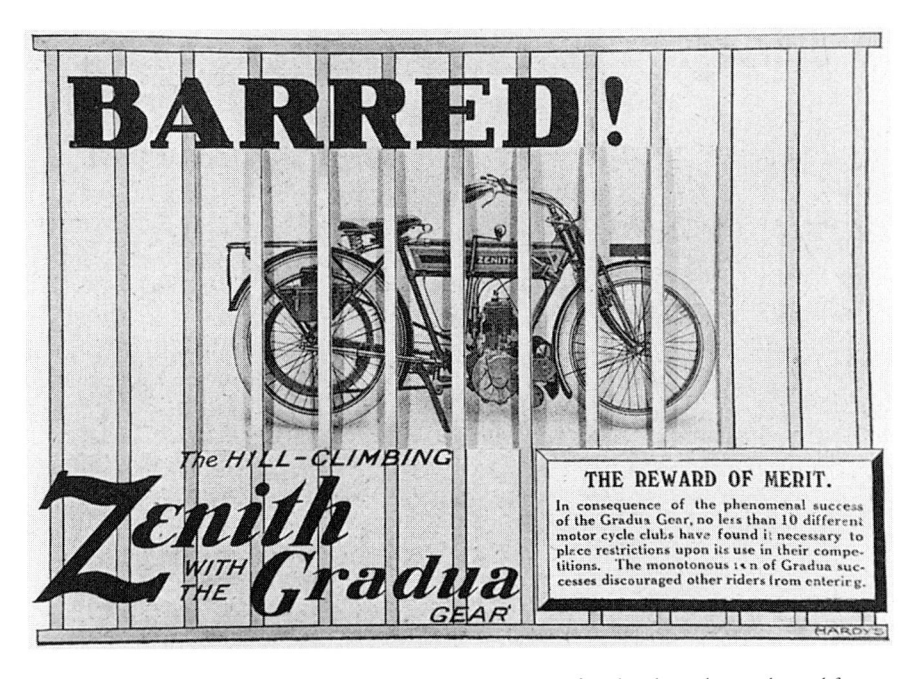

The Gradua Gear system was so successful in competition events of its day that it became banned from some, hence this 1911 advertisement.

was the whole machine, which took on the typical style of the time complete with Druid forks. The Zenette continued to be offered for that year, but the 1911 range was the Zenith Gradua with 3.5hp single or 6hp V-twin JAP engines. During 1911 the 'barred' advertisement was used as a promotion of the easy manner in which the Gradua Gear disposed of hills and, for 1912, there were many detail improvements.

The 1913 range added three racing models with JAP ohv engines, 2.75 and 3.5hp singles and an 8hp V-twin, plus a road model with a 4hp water-cooled Green engine. This was all interim, for the 1914 models were much revised, with a chain-driven countershaft, complete with clutch and kick-starter, mounted in front of the crankcase. The countershaft carried a large pulley to drive the rear wheel by a lengthy belt, while retaining the Gradua Gear and rear wheel movement. The engines continued to come from JAP, but all were twins of 3.5, 6 or 8hp.

During 1914, the firm moved to Hampton Court, Middlesex and continued with their twins until war stopped production. They started up again in 1919 with the 6 and 8hp models, still with the countershaft and Gradua Gear, but, by November 1919, these were joined by a 346cc flat-twin, still with the same transmission.

By 1932, Zenith was owned by Writer's in London and among their range was this model with 490cc JAP ohv engine.

Minor changes only were made for the 1929 Zenith Club model with the 346cc ohv engine.

In 1921 a model fitted with a 494cc oil-cooled Bradshaw flat-twin engine was introduced and was soon listed with the choice of the Gradua Gear or a three-speed Sturmey-Archer gearbox and all-chain drive. For 1922 most models had this option and in 1923 came the introduction of several singles, all of conventional form. There was also a special built for an enthusiast, which used a Barr & Stroud V-twin sleeve-valve engine.

For 1924 it was all chain drive, the Gradua Gear having run its course, and the firm now offered a range of singles and V-twins that increased annually and were typical of the decade. One that year used an ohv single-cylinder Bradshaw engine, while 348cc Blackburne, 490cc JAP singles and 680 and 980cc V-twin JAP engines of this type followed by 1926. A 175cc sv lightweight was added for 1927 only and replaced the next year by one using a 172cc Villiers two-stroke.

The firm had not forgotten its sporting history and, in 1928, O.M. Baldwin set the motorcycle world speed record at over 124mph (198km/h). Two years later Joe Wright used a Zenith, and not the publicized OEC, to take the figure to over 150mph (240km/h).

However, this did not sell many machines in 1930, after which the firm was taken over by Writer's, a large south London dealer. They listed a reduced range, all with JAP engines, for 1931 but soon expanded this, using Blackburne engines as well for a few years. This carried them on through the decade in a conventional, perhaps slightly old-fashioned, format, up to the war. Post-war, only one model was ever listed and this used

Part of the 1934 Zenith range was this model with inclined 245cc JAP engine, typical of the line, although old-fashioned in style.

The early Zenith model of 1905 was known as the Tooley Bi-car and had an unusual frame with hub-centre steering among its features.

the 747cc sv JAP V-twin engine in the pre-war format with Druid girder forks. In time these were changed for Dowty Oleomatic telescopics, but production ceased in 1950.

ZEPHYR 1917–1922

Although first announced late in 1917, this motorized pedal cycle did not reach the market until after the war. It was also sold under the Aerolite name by its manufacturers, the Small Engines Company of Coventry Road, Birmingham. Ready to ride, it weighed just 70lbs (32kg) and was, therefore, ideally suited to those unable to haul about a heavy motorcycle, which evidently included the fairer sex, for whom an open-framed version was made available.